AZORES

T0283583

DAVID SAYERS
UPDATED BY TIM BURFORD

FOREWORD BY BEN FOGLE

www.bradtguides.com

Bradt Guides Ltd, UK
The Globe Pequot Press Inc, USA

Bradt GUIDES
TRAVEL TAKEN SERIOUSLY

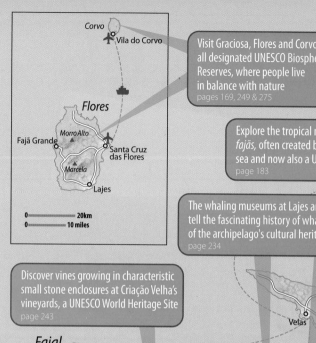

Visit Graciosa, Flores and Corvo, all designated UNESCO Biosphere Reserves, where people live in balance with nature
pages 169, 249 & 275

Explore the tropical microclimate of São Jorge's *fajãs*, often created by lava flowing into the sea and now also a UNESCO Biosphere Reserve
page 183

The whaling museums at Lajes and São Roque tell the fascinating history of whaling as part of the archipelago's cultural heritage
page 234

Discover vines growing in characteristic small stone enclosures at Criação Velha's vineyards, a UNESCO World Heritage Site
page 243

Visit the Volcano Interpretative Centre of Capelinhos, site of the 1957 eruption and now a world-acclaimed visitor centre
page 212

Lajes, Horta and Ponta Delgada – world-class hotspots for whale watching
page 97

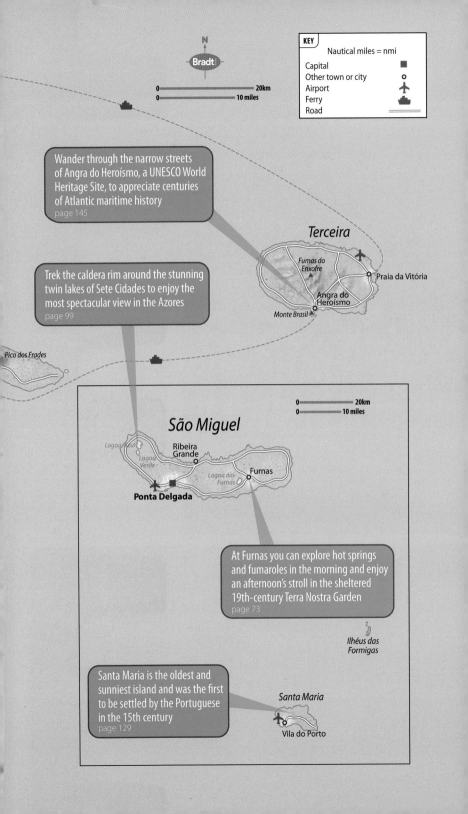

N

Bradt

KEY

Nautical miles = nmi

Capital
Other town or city
Airport
Ferry
Road

0 ————— 20km
0 ————— 10 miles

Wander through the narrow streets of Angra do Heroísmo, a UNESCO World Heritage Site, to appreciate centuries of Atlantic maritime history
page 145

Trek the caldera rim around the stunning twin lakes of Sete Cidades to enjoy the most spectacular view in the Azores
page 99

Terceira

Fumas do Enxofre
Praia da Vitória
Angra do Heroísmo
Monte Brasil

Pico dos Frades

São Miguel

0 ————— 20km
0 ————— 10 miles

Lagoa Azul
Lagoa Verde
Ribeira Grande
Lagoa das Furnas
Furnas
Ponta Delgada

At Furnas you can explore hot springs and fumaroles in the morning and enjoy an afternoon's stroll in the sheltered 19th-century Terra Nostra Garden
page 73

Ilhéus das Formigas

Santa Maria is the oldest and sunniest island and was the first to be settled by the Portuguese in the 15th century
page 129

Santa Maria
Vila do Porto

AZORES
DON'T MISS...

SMALL-SCALE CHARM
Little shrines or *impérios* like this one on Terceira act as the hub of the island's exuberant religious festivals PAGE 28
(AT/S)

CLIMBING PICO
The ascent of Portugal's highest mountain, on the island of Pico, is hard work but not technically difficult, and rewarded with breathtaking views PAGE 237
(MB/S)

AWE-INSPIRING VIEWS
The coastal path on the west of
Flores reveals a rocky shoreline
PAGE 260
(HD/S)

**TRANQUILLITY AND
TIMELESSNESS**
Farmers still use ponies – pictured
here in Sete Cidades on São
Miguel – to bring the milk churns
down from the higher fields
PAGE 38
(SS)

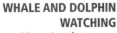

**WHALE AND DOLPHIN
WATCHING**
Some 25 species of cetaceans
have been sighted off the Azores,
making the archipelago one of the
world's viewing hotspots
PAGES 11 & 62
(VA)

AZORES
IN COLOUR

above
(RG/S)

Pico's wines were once sent to the Russian Tsar; still producing good wines today, the unusual vineyards are a UNESCO World Heritage Site PAGE 225

left
(VA)

The sometimes isolated *fajãs* of São Jorge island create striking landscapes, with tiny settlements PAGE 183

below
(SD/S)

Remote Corvo island may be tiny, but its landscape is truly dramatic PAGE 275

On São Miguel, many roads laid down in the beginning of the last century were landscaped with plane trees, hydrangeas, azaleas and roses PAGE 107

above
(HD/S)

Beautiful Flores is renowned for its jaw-dropping waterfalls; pictured, Poço da Ribeira do Ferreiro PAGE 267

right
(LH/S)

The Flemish style of the Moinho do Frade windmill on Pico gives a clue as to the origin of some early immigrants PAGE 234

below
(EV/S)

AUTHOR

David Sayers is a horticulturist who studied at Kew Gardens and overseas, and has spent a lifetime exploring the world for plants. Abandoning gardening after 20 years and graduating in social sciences, he worked in social policy and corporate planning, at the same time leading occasional adventure/botanical holidays to the Himalayas for Thomas Cook and others. In 1982, he formed a company specialising in botanical and garden travel and for 26 years arranged

and led tours worldwide, pioneering many new destinations with his wife Hedvika Fraser. In 1984 he led the first ever tour group to climb Pico and to visit São Jorge, Flores and Corvo. He now writes on botanical travel.

UPDATER

Tim Burford studied languages at Oxford University. In 1991, after five years as a publisher, he began writing guidebooks for Bradt, starting with a hiking guide to Romania. Since then, he's worked across east-central Europe (notably Georgia, Ukraine, Transylvania and Bratislava for Bradt), as well as in Central and South America and Alaska. He also leads hiking groups in the Alps and elsewhere.

ILLUSTRATOR

Hedvika Fraser (1943–2018) Born in Prague, she was a science editor and technical translator, and came to the UK in the 1960s. From childhood she was an outstanding gardener ingrained with traditional skills; self-sufficiency in fruit and vegetables was second nature, while growing orchids and then peonies were her special interests. A talented artist, she painted these in watercolour, and contributed line drawings for publications, including for this guide.

CONTRIBUTOR

Murray Stewart is an award-winning travel writer who has written and updated several guidebooks for Bradt over the last decade. He has twice updated Bradt's *North Cyprus* guide and their *Cape Verde* guide, and also two previous editions of this *Azores* guide. He also wrote the very first edition of *The Basque Country and Navarre*, published in 2016 and winner of the British Guild of Travel Writers' Award for Best Guidebook in that year. With Angela Bird, he co-wrote the first edition of Bradt's *Vendée* guide, published in 2018. Prior to 2009, he enjoyed a career in corporate restructuring and received a House of Commons commendation for saving a Norfolk pea-processing factory. He has walked four routes of the Camino de Santiago pilgrims' route, including the 1,600km from Le Puy en Velay to Santiago de Compostela, raising thousands of pounds for charity in the process. Murray lives in Amersham, Buckinghamshire.

Eighth edition published November 2024. First published 2001
Bradt Guides Ltd
31a High Street, Chesham, Buckinghamshire, HP5 1BW, England
www.bradtguides.com
Print edition published in the USA by The Globe Pequot Press Inc,
PO Box 480, Guilford, Connecticut 06437-0480

Text copyright © Bradt Guides Ltd, 2024
Maps copyright © Bradt Guides Ltd, 2024; includes map data © OpenStreetMap contributors
Photographs copyright © Individual photographers, 2024 (see below)
Project Manager: Susannah Lord
Copy editor: Gina Rathbone
Cover research: Pepi Bluck, Perfect Picture

ISBN: 9781804691731

British Library Cataloguing in Publication Data
A catalogue record for this book is available from the British Library

Photographs AWL Images: Mauricio Abreu (MA/AWL); Carina Costa (CC); Dreamstime.
com: Agami Photo Agency (APA/D), Ayla Harbich (AH/D), Eyewave (E/D), Geza Farkas
(GF/D), Henner Damke (HD/D), Henrimartin (HM/D), Jaime Debrum (JD/D), Nadezda
Slobodinskaya (NS/D), Olena Buyskykh (OB/D), Paulo Rocha (PR/D), Rechitan Sorin (RS/D),
Richard Higgins (RH/D), Rui Vale De Sousa (RVDS/D), rybarmarekk (R/D), Sérgio Nogueira
(SN/D), Stefano Neri (SN/D), Vidalgophoto (V/D); Gerby Michielsen (GM); Shutterstock.com:
AMA (AMA/S), Anibal Trejo (AT/S), DaLiu (DL/S), Eric Valenne geostory (EV/S), Henner
Damke (HD/S), Loredana Habermann (LH/S), Marcel Bakker (MB/S), Rafal Gadomski
(RG/S), Samuel Domingues (SD/S), trabantos (T/S); SuperStock (SS); Visit Azores (VA)
Front cover Waterfalls at Poço da Ribeira do Ferreiro, on Flores Island; in the foreground the
giant leaves of the inhame (*Colocasia antiquorum*) (MA/AWL)
Back cover, clockwise from top left Summer flowers, Flores (RS/D), ancient stone windmill,
Corvo (PR/D), Cavalhadas de São Pedro parade, Ribera Grande, São Miguel (V/D), detail of
tea plantation at Gorreana tea estate, São Miguel (R/D)
Title page, clockwise from top left Terceira island view (VA), Chapel of Nossa Senhora da Paz,
São Miguel (E/D), Monteiro's storm petrel (*Oceanodroma monteiroi*) (APA/D)
Part openers Page 71: Ponta do Arnel, São Miguel (DL/S); page 143: mountain biking, Terceira (VA);
page 247: azalea flower (NS/D)

Maps David McCutcheon FBCart.S. FRGS
Typeset by Ian Spick, Bradt Guides and Dataworks, India
Production managed by Gutenberg Press Ltd; printed in Malta
Digital conversion by www.dataworks.co.in

Paper used for this product comes from sustainably managed forests, and recycled and
controlled sources.

Foreword

By Ben Fogle

For me the Azores represents a bite-sized piece of a national identity. The islands offer a taste of Portugal wrapped up in their own unique Atlantic geography and geology. The island archipelago has been described as like heaven and hell: defined both by a lush green environment and by the fiery belly of the earth.

It's a heady mix that can overwhelm the senses. Birds, plants, whales and dolphins, combined with Portuguese architecture, are akin to heaven; sulphurous water bubbling up from deep underground, thick volcanic ash and pumice that blanket vast swathes of land, and black lava flows, frozen like fossils that dip into the turgid Atlantic Ocean, are all reminiscent of hell.

It is truly astonishing to think that these islands emerged from the ocean relatively recently in geological terms and that all the flora and fauna are immigrants, migrating halfway across the Atlantic, borne on the ocean current or the wind.

The Azores is a hauntingly beautiful chain of nine islands spread over more than 600km of ocean, midway between Lisbon and New York. In some ways the Azores is to Portugal what the Outer Hebrides is to Scotland – a remote archipelago many kilometres offshore – but there the similarities end. Where the Hebrides are flat, sandy isles, the Azores islands are rugged and volcanic, dominated by their geology and influenced by the warm Gulf Stream that has created an ecosystem unlike anywhere else.

The Azores High is responsible for the unique ecology of this archipelago. This area of high pressure is semi-permanent and ensures the islands are more tropical than you might expect. It combines with the warm ocean currents of the Gulf Stream, creating a subtropical climate.

Ponta da Ferraria must rate as one of the greatest places in the world for a saltwater swim. A natural swimming pool formed by lava lies next to the ocean but is heated by a bubbling spring that pumps water into the pool at 61°C. Indeed, the water in the pool is too hot to swim in at low tide and is only cool enough when it mixes with crashing Atlantic waves that tumble in at high tide, bringing the temperature down to a comfortable 28°C. It is the perfect combination of exhilaration and relaxation.

One of the most memorable experiences for me was my first visit to Terra Nostra Garden on São Miguel, the main island. In 1770, Thomas Hickling built a summer house on a small hill overlooking a thermal-spring swimming pool. Twelve hectares of rich gardens were planted in the ensuing years, and now there are more than 2,500 trees, abundant ferns, a formal flower garden, a garden devoted to cycads and another to camellias. The garden thrives in the subtropical climate and it is simply breathtaking.

This is in Furnas, where boiling pools and steaming vents offer a portal to Middle Earth. For decades, if not centuries, families have come here to cook the famous *cozido nas caldeiras* in huge pots buried in the volcanic sand; prized cooking spots are passed down from generation to generation. Holes about a metre deep have been dug into the hot earth into which a container is lowered. Filled with different meats, sausage, vegetables, kale, potato and cabbage, the pot is left to cook gently for 7 hours. The long, slow simmer ensures that meat becomes tender and flavours meld. This simple form of cooking is, in my eyes, symbolic of how the land and the geology have shaped the unique culture and heritage of these islands.

Volcanic activity has, of course, cast, moulded and created these unique islands, and Faial is an example of how the Azores has been changed by the power of the earth. The western tip of the island exemplifies this, its entire landscape formed by the great eruption in 1957–58. Walking on this moon-like terrain is like stepping on to another planet. On the face of it, it is a bleak, soulless place, but it takes on a gritty beauty that overcomes most visitors.

Perhaps one of the most iconic activities in the Azores is to climb the tallest peak, Pico mountain, at 2,351m. The 5km journey begins at Cabeço das Cabras, at 1,231m. The difficulty of the ascent varies according to the weather, but the views from the summit are well worth the 6-hour round trip. No matter how many mountains you have climbed, there is something utterly mesmerising about looking out over thousands of kilometres of ocean and cloud below.

Most people associate the Azores with whales. Indeed, the ocean around the islands offers one of the best habitats in the world for marine mammals and more than 20 species have been identified off the coast. For many years, until the 1980s, sperm whales were hunted commercially in the Azores from small boats with hand-held harpoons. Fortunately, today whale hunting has been replaced by whale watching. Short-finned pilot whales and sperm whales are the most common in the Azores and can be seen all year round.

Early one morning on my last trip I headed out to sea in a fast rigid inflatable boat. Dressed in wet-weather gear to protect me from the ocean spray, I travelled out deep into the Atlantic Ocean. The boat leapt from wave to wave, directed from the same observation huts used by the hunters of previous decades. The difference was that I was armed with a camera rather than a harpoon gun.

There can be few sights as moving as that of a breaching sperm whale. These marine mammals can measure up to 20m and are surprisingly elusive considering their size. Persevere, however, and you will be rewarded with an experience that will, quite literally, take your breath away.

Whale watching, swimming, bathing in hot springs, eating volcano-cooked food, mountain biking, kayaking, walking, birdwatching, visiting tea plantations, island hopping…the list of eco-friendly activities available on the Azores is endless. In an era when more and more people are looking for something different from their holiday, the islands of the Azores really are at the forefront of the 'natural' travel movement.

Acknowledgements

This guide to the Azores began its life in the archipelago's earlier days of tourism, and has evolved through eight editions as the islands have themselves adapted to welcoming visitors. Now it is over 23 years old and in adulthood its future will be in the hands of younger travellers, most capably led by Murray Stewart and Tim Burford who have undertaken recent editions. As one who has spent much of his life globetrotting, it is perhaps surprising these tiny islands so far away came to play such a large part in my life from my first visit in 1983. I feel very fortunate to have had the challenge of surveying unmarked walking trails and finding the most interesting botanical locations, putting together programmes very different from the then tourist norm, and then leading tours to all the islands, but also to have been entrusted with the daunting responsibility of assisting with the restoration of some of the Azores' heritage gardens.

As one edition changed to the next, so have the many kind islanders who gave unstintingly of their support and advice. Of those whose contributions continue to sustain the life of this guide, most significant is the Melo Agency in Ponta Delgada and Senhor Albano Cymbron, the doyen of Azores tourism. To him I am indebted for guidance, insights and contributions about Azorean life and history, and for his long-sustained practical support. As time went on Catarina, his daughter and successor at Melo, generously assumed this vital role. Also to both go my thanks for invaluable introductions to kind and hospitable people throughout the islands who helped me in so many different ways.

For invaluable textual contributions to this guide and for their time and interest I am most grateful to Dr Isabel Soares de Albergaria from São Miguel who contributed the pages on art and architecture and thus revealed treasures that might otherwise have remained hidden; to Monique Cymbron from São Miguel for her Azorean kitchen; to Luis Silva for delving into the history of the Azorean cow; and to geologist Pedro Freire of Geo-fun in Ponta Delgada who generously gave his knowledge and time to steer me through the lava flows of volcanic history. Significantly, to my late wife Hedvika for her illustrations and indulgent support at home during my many and often extended visits to the islands. Finally, and central to the whole project, the superb team at Bradt Travel Guides.

David Sayers

DEDICATION

In memory of Hedvika, plantswoman and fearless traveller

UPDATERS' ACKNOWLEDGEMENTS

MURRAY STEWART To many, many Azorean islanders, I am greatly indebted for unstinting assistance in my second update of this book.

First of all, however, a big thank you to David Sayers for providing such a wealth of knowledge and expertise in the first five editions of this guidebook to the Azorean archipelago. His sterling work is reflected in the fact that much of the text regarding geology, botany and history again remains blissfully untouched in this eighth edition.

For effortlessly pulling together a complex logistical schedule and supporting me in my research, I would like to thank Ian Coates and Jake Cardigan at Archipelago Choice in the UK. On the islands themselves, many people have unflinchingly assisted in putting together this new edition – too many to mention. Nevertheless, on São Miguel, let me express my particular gratitude to Carina Costa and Gerby Michielsen; on Graciosa, to Marta Quadros; Elisabetse Alves on São Jorge; Guilherme Santos on Flores; and Ioannis Rousseaux, Laurinda Sousa and Miguel Henrique on Santa Maria. Thanks also to the various tourist offices across all the islands and the hotels and guesthouses that so kindly supported me.

At Bradt, many thanks to Adrian Phillips and Rachel Fielding for the opportunity and to Heather Haynes for editorial expertise.

And of course, a huge thanks to my dear friend Sara Lister for her support throughout the process.

TIM BURFORD I am also very grateful to the many very helpful people I met in the Azores, especially those who provided me with accommodation. Many thanks to David Sayers and Murray Stewart for all their hard work on previous editions, leaving me a fairly simple task in producing this latest edition, and to all those at Bradt who have helped bring it all to fruition. Above all, many thanks to Ian Coates and his staff at Archipelago Choice for helping to plan my trip and booking travel and accommodation so efficiently.

Contents

LIST OF MAPS

For me the Azores were an immediate *coup de foudre*. The scenery is very beautiful, I could never tire of walking the hills, there is an interesting flora, the geology is fascinating, the natives are extra friendly, and there is blissful peace. I was spending months each year in distant countries where travel is hard work, and to suddenly find all the natural attractions with the wonderful bonus of good coffee, excellent wines, a comfortable bed and an easy flight seemed a paradise. It still does, even after 35 years. The long-established Azorean travel agent Albano Cymbron and I pioneered a series of walks (and even marked the routes with blobs of red paint), and in 1991, wrote and jointly published a modest guide to six of the islands. We sold 2,000 copies.

A year later I was invited to advise on the restoration of the Terra Nostra Garden in Furnas, one of the great gems of Azorean heritage. This developed into a major project, and from there came two more garden restorations, this time for the Ponta Delgada Municipality. Friendships have matured over the years, and the islands remain as lovely as ever – what more could one wish for? Now three entire islands have been recognised by UNESCO as Biosphere Reserves for their balance between humans, nature and sustainable development. Someone else must have fallen in love with the Azores!

I hope this guide will help you discover some of the hidden delights of this little-known cluster of islands, and that you will have a memorable holiday. And maybe go back again!

KEY TO SYMBOLS

══════	Expressway	†	Church/cathedral
═════	Main road	⛺	Campsite
─────	Other road	❀	Garden etc
======	Track/4x4	⚑	Golf course
··········	Featured footpath	※	Viewpoint
··········	Other footpath	♛	Lighthouse
⇒╞═╡⇐	Tunnel	⋀⋀	Beach
-------	Ferry route	⚓	Swimming
🚢	Passenger ferry	✈	Birdwatching
✈✈	Airport (international/domestic)	⌒	Cave/grotto
🚕	Taxis	○	Hot springs
⛽	Filling station/garage	∬	Waterfall
ℹ	Tourist information	♧	Woodland
⚱	Museum/art gallery	▲	Summit (height in metres)
🏛	Important/historic building	⌣	Fortifications/city walls
🏰	Castle/fortification	☼	Volcanic crater
⊠	Post office	🏃	Stadium
✚	Hospital/clinic etc	▭▭▭	Runway
✛	Health centre/pharmacy	▦	Protected area/reserve
		▨	Urban park
		▧	Market

Introduction

by David Sayers

It is perhaps strange to think there is a cluster of nine small islands, completely isolated but thriving, lying between Lisbon and New York and surrounded by the great Atlantic Ocean.

Very much part of Europe and members of the European Union, they have many of the accoutrements of modern life: the latest fashion trainers, cars, second homes, and the very latest communications technology connecting home computers with the internet.

Yet few people are aware of the existence of the Azores and many of those who are hold an image of dry, sun-baked volcanic islands like Lanzarote in the Canaries. And they almost always assume they belong to Spain.

The Azores are Europe's best-kept secret: verdant, tranquil, diverse, exquisitely beautiful, always welcoming. Further south and close to the African coast lies Madeira, Portugal's more familiar Atlantic island; sunnier and with less rain and cloud but considerably more developed for tourism, and famous for its well-promoted flowers and gardens. It was going to Madeira that aroused my curiosity about those other far-off islands; a flight from Funchal took me to Ponta Delgada, and back to an ambience that possibly could have been found in Madeira half a century ago. One needs to take the Azores at their own speed. Fight it, and you will be frustrated; relax along with it and you will return a different person. Old-world courtesy prevails, a reminder of the many tiny niceties of life that have been sacrificed to the exigencies of faster lifestyles.

Since they were settled in the 15th century, each island has developed at a different speed, depending upon the quality of its harbour, terrain, crops, and its distance from the others. Today this is reflected in their diversity, each island offering the visitor its own individual character that makes the Azores such a varied entity.

All the islands are green, the flowers are mostly sophisticated and subtle, the gardens are steeped in history and, like the flowers, are more cerebral than flamboyant. While some main towns have their roads and traffic, just a short distance away men ride horses to their pastures and pony carts filled with milk churns clatter over cobbles. Flashing neon lights are rare, streets are narrow, shops modest and in keeping with the streetscape, coffee bars are numerous while nightclubs are few. The islands reflect their turbulent geological past and offer rural landscapes enhanced by rocky or precipitous coasts surrounded by an often travel-brochure-blue sea. Religious and secular festivals riot through the calendar and touch the lives of every island and islander. There are sailing regattas, golf tournaments, big-game fishing tournaments, cycle races, car rallies and other events that come as rather a surprise and largely leave the non-enthusiasts in happy oblivion. There is so much to explore, so much to experience; these islands should be savoured like a rare wine.

AUTHOR'S FAVOURITES Finding genuinely characterful accommodation or that unmissable off-the-beaten-track café can be difficult, so the author has chosen a few of his favourite places throughout the country to point you in the right direction. These 'author's favourites' are marked with a ✳.

PRICE CODES Throughout this guide we have used price codes to indicate the cost of those places to stay listed in the guide. For a key to these price codes, see page 52 for accommodation and page 54 for restaurants.

MAPS

Keys and symbols Maps include alphabetical keys covering the locations of those places to stay, eat or drink that are featured in the book. Note that regional maps may not show all hotels and restaurants in the area: other establishments may be located in towns shown on the map.

On occasion, hotels or restaurants that are not listed in the guide (but which might serve as alternative options if required or serve as useful landmarks to aid navigation) are also included on the maps; these are marked with accommodation (🏠) or restaurant (✖) symbols.

Grids and grid references Several maps use gridlines to allow easy location of sites. Map grid references are listed in square brackets after the name of the place or site of interest in the text, with page number followed by grid number, eg: [80 C3].

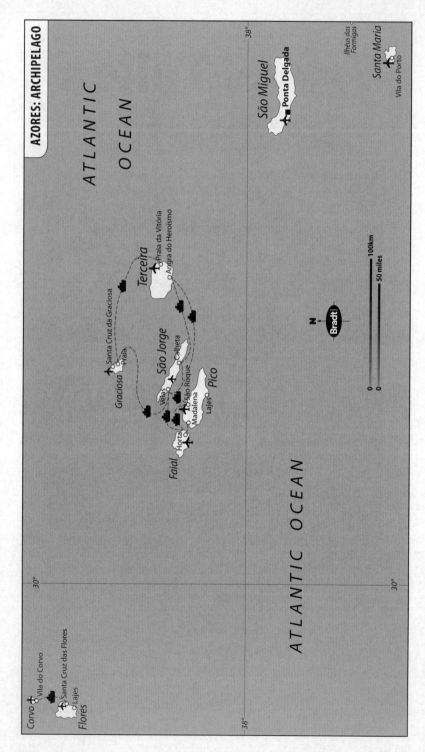

AZORES: ARCHIPELAGO

ATLANTIC OCEAN

ATLANTIC OCEAN

Corvo
Vila do Corvo

Flores
Santa Cruz das Flores
Lajes

30°

38°

Graciosa
Santa Cruz da Graciosa
Praia

São Jorge
Velas
Calheta

Terceira
Praia da Vitória
Angra do Heroísmo

São Roque
Pico
Madalena
Lajes

Faial
Horta

São Miguel
Ponta Delgada

Ilhéus das
Formigas

Santa Maria
Vila do Porto

38°

30°

N
Bradt

0   50 miles
0   100km

Part One

GENERAL INFORMATION

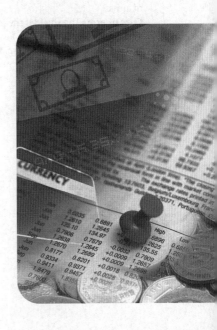

AZORES ARCHIPELAGO AT A GLANCE

Islands São Miguel, Santa Maria, Terceira, Graciosa, São Jorge, Faial, Pico, Flores, Corvo

Location In the Atlantic Ocean, approximately 1,500km from Lisbon and 3,900km from the east coast of North America

Size Nine islands varying in size from 17km^2 (Corvo) to 746km^2 (São Miguel), spread across some 600km of ocean

Climate Temperate, maritime climate with agreeable temperatures ranging from 13–14°C in January/February to 22–23°C in July/August. Rain throughout the year; light cloud common.

Status Autonomous region of Portugal

Population 237,000 (census 2021)

Economy Major earners are beef, dairy products, fishing and tourism

Language Portuguese

Religion Roman Catholic

Currency Euro

Rate of exchange £1 = €1.17, US$1 = €0.90 (August 2024)

Time GMT –1; 4 hours later than US Eastern Standard Time, and 1 hour earlier than mainland Portugal

Electricity 220 volts

International telephone code +351

Flag Blue-and-white block colour. At the centre is a goshawk, with nine golden stars, one for each island. In the left corner is the national coat of arms.

Coat of arms The shield is silver with a red border, and includes a goshawk and nine golden stars.

National anthem *Hino da Região Autónoma dos Açores* (Anthem to Autonomy)

Motto *Antes morrer livres que em paz sujeitos* ('Better to die free than live enslaved')

Public holidays See page 58.

1

Background Information

GEOGRAPHY AND CLIMATE

LOCATION The nine islands of the Azores – the westernmost point of Europe – are spread over some 600km of ocean and are located roughly 1,500km or 2 hours' flying time from Lisbon and about 3,900km or 5 hours from the east coast of North America. Running along a southeast to northwest axis, they lie on either side of the line of latitude that links Lisbon with New York, and are between latitudes 36–39°N and longitudes 25–31°W. The islands separate conveniently into three groups: the Eastern Group of São Miguel and Santa Maria; the Central Group of Terceira, Graciosa, São Jorge, Pico and Faial; and the Western Group of Flores and Corvo. The islands closest to each other are Pico and Faial at just 6km apart. In area, they range from Corvo at 17km² to São Miguel at 746km². Highest altitudes vary from 412m on Graciosa to 2,351m on Pico.

CLIMATE For small islands the weather, especially when in the middle of a large ocean, is all-important. For the busy city worker, as everywhere, the weather impacts little on a daily basis, and for the visitor rain is but a passing nuisance. However, for Azorean farmers even a relatively short dry period causes problems because the volcanic soils are very quick-draining, while a rough sea means fishermen cannot go out, there is no income for them, and no fresh fish for the villages.

The Azores have a mild and equable climate, surrounded as they are by a huge expanse of sea and influenced by the warm Gulf Stream. This means that the temperature is pleasant at any time of year. The average winter temperature is 13°C, only sometimes dropping to around 4°C at night; frosts occur only above 1,000m. In summer, the average temperature is 23°C, with a maximum of 27°C.

Rain can and does fall in every month, but it is seldom persistent; and one can drive from rain through a world of rainbows into sunshine. If it is raining in the morning, do not despair – there could be clear skies and sunshine by lunchtime. Of course, the reverse is often true! The annual rainfall increases westwards and ranges from 730mm on Santa Maria to 1,600mm in Santa Cruz on Flores. Average humidity is around 80–85%, but can go up to 100%. Flowers love it! June to August is the driest period. Many days are still or with a gentle breeze. However, winds can occasionally be strong and this is especially noticeable on exposed mountains. A winter gale can also bring an invigorating chill, but the scudding clouds and turbulent seas can be inspiring for the visitor. Snow can sometimes be seen on Pico's summit, even in April.

For swimmers, the sea temperatures also vary relatively little and you will often see people bathing off the beaches throughout the winter, when the lowest sea temperatures are 15–16°C in February and March. The highest are in August and September, with an average of around 22–24°C, and are still a welcoming 21°C even in October.

Average minimum temperatures in °C

Jan	Feb	Mar	Apr	May	Jun	Jul	Aug	Sep	Oct	Nov	Dec
11	10	11	11	13	15	16	17	17	15	13	12

Average maximum temperatures in °C

Jan	Feb	Mar	Apr	May	Jun	Jul	Aug	Sep	Oct	Nov	Dec
16	16	16	17	19	21	23	25	24	21	18	17

Average sea temperature in °C

Jan	Feb	Mar	Apr	May	Jun	Jul	Aug	Sep	Oct	Nov	Dec
16	16	16	16	17	19	22	23	23	21	19	18

Source: w weather2travel.com

NATURAL HISTORY AND CONSERVATION

It was not until the middle of the 19th century that the first studies of the flora, fauna and oceanographics took place, when the Azores were frequently visited by scientists. In 1841 and 1845, the British warship HMS *Styx,* commanded by Captain Vidal, undertook hydrographic studies of the Azores, drawing up the first map where the islands appear correctly surveyed and with their positions correctly given. HMS *Beagle* stopped in Terceira and São Miguel on its return from voyaging round the world, enabling Charles Darwin to make shore excursions. In 1850, HMS *Rattlesnake*, on the way home from a four-year voyage surveying the Coral Sea and the New Guinea coast, sailed into Horta for six days' recuperation. It had taken almost nine weeks to travel from the Falkland Islands, their last landfall, and the islands' plentiful supplies were much needed for the health of the crew and passengers. The ship's assistant surgeon and naturalist was Thomas Huxley, who later famously defended Darwin and his theory of evolution; during their week in port, he made an ascent of Pico. Prince Albert I of Monaco (1848–1922) stayed several times on the islands making oceanographic studies, then a new scientific discipline, and exploring the caldera on Graciosa. There are references to these studies in the Oceanographic Museum in Monaco.

Many of the remaining patches of native vegetation are now in protected zones and you might see notices to this effect. The vegetation of the islands, particularly on Pico, Terceira and São Miguel, is interesting not only because it represents communities that were once widespread in parts of Europe millions of years ago, but also because very few aspects of its ecology and biology have been studied and the opportunities for simple observation and research are considerable. There is a desire to know what is happening in among the evergreens. Many stretches of coastal cliff are protected zones, mostly for seabirds; again you might see the signs. The marine environment is similarly protected.

You may be curious about the yellow plastic traps that you may see around the islands. These are pheromone traps for the rather colourful iridescent copper and green Japanese beetle, a very serious pest about 15mm long and 10mm wide. Not a problem in its native Japan, where there are natural predators, it was accidentally introduced into the USA in the early 1900s and in the 1970s arrived in the Azores, presumably from a military aircraft landing at Lajes on Terceira. The larval stage is mostly spent in lawns and pastureland feeding on roots, and the adult eats the foliage of many plants including vines, roses, oak and fruit trees.

GEOLOGY The archipelago is formed from the upper sections of volcanoes. In the mid-Atlantic, tectonic plates are pulling apart on the ocean bed. The gap between them is filled by molten volcanic material that rises from the earth's mantle and continuously forms new oceanic crust. This extrusion wells up and forms an enormous underwater mountain chain or mid-ocean ridge, and the sea floor spreads. The **Mid-Atlantic Ridge** runs from the Arctic to the Antarctic, meeting on its way the Indian Ocean Ridge off the southern tip of Africa. Along its length lie Iceland, the largest landmass created from oceanic crust, the Azores, Ascension, Saint Helena and Tristan da Cunha islands. Mid-ocean ridges occur beneath all our major oceans, and only in exceptional cases are there so many eruptions that they build up to appear above sea level and form islands. Much more frequent activity occurs under the ocean's surface on the seabed than is seen on the surface of the islands. Seamounts constantly rise and fall, and new lava pressure ridges are formed.

In the Azores, giant linear ridges have been created, conspicuously Pico and São Jorge, and these are among the largest such volcanic ridges actively forming anywhere on our planet. With the ocean floor roughly between 1,000m and 3,000m below sea level, it is fun to try to imagine the landscape that would confront the traveller if the Atlantic Ocean could be emptied.

The situation is more complicated because, near the Azores, three plates meet in a T-shaped junction. The North American, African and Eurasian plates meet at a point between the Western and Central groups of islands, between Flores and Faial. Flores and Corvo are on the North American plate. The Mid-Atlantic Ridge forms two legs of the 'T' and the other islands are alongside a spreading centre called the **Terceira Rift**, formed about 36 million years ago. It is not certain on which plates, African or Eurasian, the remaining islands belong or whether some might be on an Azorean microplate.

The seismic tremors felt in the islands are mostly caused by magma flowing up through the cracks left in the earth's crust as the plates separate. At times these

A DICTIONARY OF AZOREAN TERRAIN

For newcomers to the Azores, translation of a few key words that regularly appear on maps may help to understand the geography. Here are the most common:

caldeira – caldera (volcanic crater)
canada – path, trail
fajã – piece of flat coastal land (created by lava flow or landslip)
furna – cave, grotto
gruta – cave, grotto
lomba – ridge (of mountain)
miradouro – viewpoint
pico – summit of mountain
praia – beach
quinta – manor house, farm, estate
ribeira – small river, stream
serra – mountain range

Of the few things generally known about the Azores, the 'Azores High' probably tops the list. This is an area of high pressure or anticyclone that is semi-permanent.

Very simply, warm moist air rises over the tropics leading to low pressure there; this warm moist air then moves north towards the subtropical latitudes and cools. It then descends, increasing the pressure over the subtropical latitudes, at the same time becoming drier and resulting in largely clear skies. This tropical/subtropical circulation varies little in position; in summer it is more northerly, in winter and spring more southerly, usually lying to the south or southwest of the archipelago. This high-pressure belt is part of the global circulatory system and is called the Hadley cell. In the north Atlantic it is often centred close to the Azores, hence the 'Azores High'. The reason it is centred there is because the Azores lie roughly midway between the influence of the African and American continents. Landmasses distort the process and strong summer heating at these latitudes can cause, for example, low pressure in the northern summer over southeast Asia and India and bring monsoon rains. Surface layers of the ocean do not heat up in the same way as the land does, and therefore allow the high-pressure belt to persist.

Sometimes the 'Azores High' extends northeast towards the British Isles, especially when they have a good summer. In winter it can sometimes recede southwards, if the jet stream is also further south. Occasionally it disappears altogether to be replaced by low pressure, while often, at the same time, high pressure dominates northern Europe, giving cold weather in winter and hot, often eventually thundery, weather in summer.

In the Azores the weather is influenced by the strength and location of this high, particularly in summer. A strong high gives pleasant, warm weather with

tremors, measuring less than 5.0 on the Richter scale, will occur with surprising frequency. Six of the islands have been subject to **eruptions and earthquakes** within recent history, but the remaining three, Santa Maria, Flores and Corvo, are now considered inactive.

Of the central and eastern islands, Santa Maria was the first to rise above the sea some 5 million years ago but changes in sea level and tectonic activity caused it to submerge. It was at this time that the island acquired its marine fossils, the only ones in the Azores. A million years later, the Formigas islets and part of São Miguel rose above the sea and Santa Maria reappeared. The oldest part of São Miguel is around Pico da Vara in the east; at the far western end, Sete Cidades began around 290,000 years ago, at the same time that Água de Pau started out from the ocean bed. Thus São Miguel was once two islands, only becoming united when the Picos region north of what is now Ponta Delgada began a long series of eruptions starting 50,000 years ago. Terceira, Graciosa, São Jorge and Faial are all younger than a million years, Pico being the youngest at a mere 300,000 years or less. The two western isles, Flores and Corvo, lie on the western flanks of the Mid-Atlantic Ridge; the oldest rocks on Flores date to around 2.5 million years and are below sea level; the youngest are about 3,000 years old.

In 1811, about a mile off the coast of São Miguel, opposite Ferraria, a new island appeared. One hundred metres tall and about 1.5km long, it took about a month to create. The British frigate HMS *Sabrina* was in the area and her commanding officer, Captain Tillard, landed on the still-steaming island, planted a Union Jack, named the island '**Sabrina**' and claimed it as British territory! Unfortunately for his little wind. A weak high gives weather that is changeable and wet, and you can tell when a depression is coming by a sudden drop in the barometer and a southerly wind, veering from southwest to northwest. A low approaches with steadily lowering and thickening cloud. The wind increases, bringing heavier cloud and rain showers, and then often torrential rain, by which time all sight of any nearby island has vanished. Then comes a break, the wind changes direction, and blue skies return. Finally, it all calms down, and the high reasserts itself. This drama might sometimes be over within a few hours and, if you are on land with a good vantage point, it can be fun to watch the rain squalls skating across the ocean. Winds come from the west, travelling eastwards, and this is reflected in the higher rainfall of the Western Group. In early summer, winds are mainly from the southwest and by July and August are predominantly northeasterly, gentle and with frequent calms. By September they return to the southwest and become gradually stronger. Occasionally bad storms hit the islands, but mostly they follow a narrow path. As you drive round the islands from time to time you will see cryptomeria trees snapped off like broken toothpicks.

Another major climatic influence on the Azores is the ocean currents, especially those originating from the Gulf Stream. This is a movement of warm water of equatorial and tropical origin into the colder northern waters of the Atlantic. West of the Azores, the Gulf Stream splits into two main branches: the North Atlantic Current that passes north of the islands, and the Azores Current passing to the south. This Gulf Stream gives the Azores their warm temperate climate. A further complication is the North Atlantic Oscillation (NAO), a northern equivalent of El Niño, which concerns atmospheric circulation.

credibility, when the next surveyors arrived, there was no trace of the island; in just four months the sea had washed it away and all that remains now is a bank 40m below sea level. Most recently, in 1957, an eruption began just off the west coast of Faial that added a further 2km² of land to that island (page 221).

More information about the volcanoes and how the islands were formed is given in the chapters on the individual islands. See also **w** azoresgeopark.com, the website of the Azores Geopark Association, a non-profit association established in 2010 and based in Horta, with wide objectives concerning the environment, socio-economic, cultural and sustainable balanced development of the Azores. A geopark is a defined area with an exceptional geological heritage that is a base promoting the population's wellbeing at the same time as respecting the environment. There is a wide network of geosites on the nine islands and surrounding sea floor representing the geodiversity of the archipelago, and the website lists the principal sites on all the islands.

COLONISATION Oceanic islands such as the Azores differ from continental islands in that they are usually basaltic volcanoes, distant from the mainland and surrounded by vast oceans. They have to gain their flora and fauna by invasion, unlike continental islands that are close to geologically diverse landmasses to which they were once attached. The flora and fauna of an oceanic island is therefore distinct because it is made up of those organisms that can cross oceans. This barrier filters out many potential colonists so that the Azores lack certain groups, such as mammals (excluding bats), that are important on the mainland.

1

Not only has half the Atlantic Ocean to be crossed to reach the Azores from the nearest land, but landfall on arrival is extremely tough on a new, raw, volcanic island presenting hardened flows of lava or desert-like ash. How tough a challenge it is to colonise new ash deposits can be seen at Capelinhos on Faial. This area was engulfed and enlarged by an eruption in 1957. When you stand by the remains of the old lighthouse and the wind drives sharp volcanic sand into your face with stinging force, look at the few plants that are establishing. There is the giant reed *Arundo donax*, planted and artificially aided by humans, and the human-sponsored evening primrose *Oenothera biennis*. Left entirely to nature, colonisation takes a long time.

Winds and sea brought life to the Azores. Ocean currents transported marine organisms and shoreline animals to scavenge and survive upon what the sea washed ashore, along with others such as land crabs that have a marine larval stage. Travelling on prevailing winds and also the jet stream came spores of ferns, algae, fungi, lichens and mosses, seeds and microscopic animals, even spiders and other insects. All lightweight and adapted to wind dispersal, they landed in the Azores, even falling to earth in raindrops. Ground-nesting seabirds deposited their guano, providing further food for scavenging invertebrates and micro-organisms, while rain slowly washed out minerals from the lava, all helping to create a very fertile soil. Currents, prevailing winds and distance from landmasses all influence which organisms will become established on an island, and where they, or their ancestors, came from. Land birds that have wandered or been blown off course by storms will bring seeds, either in their stomachs or attached to their bodies. For the early colonists, survival would have been a harsh process, but it needed only some to succeed.

Slowly these first organisms changed the bare habitat by contributing organic matter to form soil. By retaining moisture, and modifying light, temperature and exposure, they enabled later arrivals to establish, thus slowly creating a more hospitable environment which in turn would allow further colonists to establish. They had to be adaptable, able to adjust to climatic variations and different food sources, and to survive both competition from other species and many other challenges in a new habitat. Variation in some species may have allowed them to adapt better to the conditions, thus leading over time to new species and subspecies. Today, there are 60 endemic plant species in the Azores, unique to the islands and found nowhere else in the world.

The Azores, along with the other archipelagos of Madeira, the Savage Islands, the Canaries and Cape Verde, comprise the region known as Macaronesia. The most characteristic vegetation is the dense evergreen forest, or **laurisilva**. It is a representative relic of the evergreen forests that grew in late Tertiary times (around 2.75 million years ago) in what is now southern Europe and northwest Africa. Possibly because of the Azores' oceanic climate, these forests escaped the extremes of climatic changes and thus survived while elsewhere they became extinct.

Colonisation and evolution never cease. New plants will arrive (page 11) and others will be eliminated by changing circumstances. Islands are living laboratories where the processes of dispersal, immigration, establishment, adaptation and extinction can all be studied. These are just some of the reasons why areas need to be protected from human depredation so that they may be there for future generations of students and provide an account of the changes going on around us.

THE VEGETATION The dense evergreen forest that once covered much of the islands has long been cleared for agriculture and settlement. Visually, the quite extensive plantations of the exotic conifer *Cryptomeria japonica* now add considerably to the aesthetics of the Azorean landscape since tree cover is now considerably less than it was within the lifetime of elderly islanders. Planted to reduce erosion and water loss, provide shelter for cattle and produce timber, these plantations are nonetheless controversial. Emigration has left many previously cultivated areas abandoned, to be invaded by a mix of native *Myrica faya*, *Erica azorica* and introduced and subsequently naturalised *Pittosporum undulatum* and, encouragingly, some other **native species** such as the endemic *Picconia azorica*. There is a tremendous battle raging, because *Myrica faya* is light-demanding, and must fight with the pittosporum for survival.

The native vegetation remains in a number of isolated areas. Evergreen forest is found as remnant forest or as individual species surviving in hedgerows above the 500m contour. The quite different coastal region of steep cliffs, lava flows, agricultural land and seashore have their own mix of native, endemic and introduced exotic species.

The Azores archipelago has a total of 850 or more **plant species**, most of which have been introduced by humans. Of the total, some 300 are native, and of these possibly 60 species are endemic, found nowhere else in the world. Of the 11 species of native trees, eight are endemic to the Azores, and two others are found elsewhere only in Madeira. Dominant species of the forest include holly (*Ilex perado* ssp. *azorica*), juniper (*Juniperus brevifolia*), tree heather (*Erica azorica*) and laurel (*Laurus azorica*). Growing in the mountains at altitudes where the hillsides are often embraced by cloud, such vegetation is called **cloudforest**; often the trunks and branches are adorned with epiphytic ferns, while bryophytes (mosses and liverworts) can be exuberant, sometimes even thriving on the leaves as epiphylls.

The largest area remaining of undisturbed forest is on Terceira, on the Caldeira de Santa Bárbara and a small area between Juncal, Pico Alto and Serra do Labaçal, not the easiest to access. The forests of the Caldeira de Santa Bárbara, at over 800m, are often cloud covered and are largely dominated by juniper (*Juniperus brevifolia*), although all of the Azorean tree species can be found in gullies and other places. Areas of natural grassland are to be seen inside the caldera, and endemic grasses such as fescue (*Festuca jubata*) and soft-grass *Holcus rigidus* are to be found growing with endemic herbaceous species such as *Tolpis azorica*. However, the caldera is a reserved area and to visit one should contact Os Montanheiros (the Mountaineers Society) in Angra do Heroísmo (page 156) and book a local guide as there are no trails and the weather can suddenly close in within 20 minutes.

São Miguel's only remaining area of natural forest can at least be easily seen! At the eastern end of the island, it covers about 600ha on Pico da Vara. Pico island has the most accessible of all native forest, although little remains and that's in small patches, often where the ground is badly tumbled with small lava boulders and has therefore escaped the predations of farmer and cattle. There are patches of *Viburnum treleasei*, *Euphorbia stygiana*, *Ilex perado*, *Vaccinium cylindraceum*, *Frangula azorica*, *Hedera helix* ssp. *canariensis*, *Juniperus brevifolia* and its green-branched parasite *Arceuthobium azoricum* and occasionally, in the loose gravel at the edge of the asphalt road, *Thymus caespititius*.

The coastal flora has been badly disturbed by numerous developments and in places by the escape and spread of garden ornamentals such as the several members of the succulent *Aizoaceae*. However, while some of the species are endangered, none is on the verge of extinction and all are to be found, often in places where one least expects them, and in the most inhospitable sites. All the islands have suitable habitats. Characteristic species include the endemic grass *Festuca petraea* and the

Once given little attention as a birdwatching destination, the Azores are now seen as an excellent choice for the observation of avian species. For keen birdwatchers, the starting point in the archipelago are two of Europe's rarest birds, the Azorean bullfinch (*Pyrrhula murina*), endemic to a small area of São Miguel island (pages 69 and 120), and Monteiro's storm petrel (*Oceanodroma monteiroi*), which breeds only on two tiny islets lying off the coast of Graciosa. May and the end of August/beginning of September are the best times to join a pelagic tour to search for this elusive storm petrel, with opportunities to sight other seabirds like the Macaronesian shearwater (*Puffinus baroli*), band-rumped storm petrel (*Oceanodroma castro*), Bulwer's petrel (*Bulweria bulwerii*), Zino's petrel (*Pterodroma madeira*), and Fea's petrel (*Pterodroma feae*). Pelagic tours can also be organised on São Miguel (page 95).

Other species that are well worth a trip to the archipelago to see are the Atlantic canary (*Serinus canaria*), an exclusively Macaronesian species, as well as several subspecies such as the common chaffinch (*Fringilla coelebs moreletti*), three different subspecies of goldcrest, the Azores woodpigeon (*Columba palumbus azorica*), and the common buzzard (*Buteo buteo rothschildi*).

Currently, the Azores hold the world's largest colony of Cory's shearwater (*Calonectris diomedea borealis*), a somewhat enigmatic bird whose strange call can often be heard at nightfall, when it returns to land to feed its chicks. Here also is one of the largest colonies of roseate tern (*Sterna dougallii*) worldwide. Altogether, the archipelago has over 30 bird species that nest here, and due to the islands' central position in the Atlantic you may also observe a large number of migratory birds coming from America and Eurasia. The total number of species recorded in the Azorean islands is over 400, including a few which are extremely rare and some which have been newly sighted in the western Palearctic.

Rare 'vagrants' from both the Americas and Eurasia, often blown in on Atlantic storms, can be seen all year and on all islands but the chances of seeing American birds are higher in the Western island group during October. The most popular island for American vagrants is Corvo and October is a tough month to find a hotel bed as the limited stock is eagerly taken up by avian fanatics flocking from many parts of Europe to see the winged visitors. The tiny size of the island makes it easy to compile a good list of vagrants. On neighbouring Flores, there's plenty for birders to see, but they have to work harder for it.

Hotspots for birdwatchers on other islands are Fajã dos Cubres on São Jorge, Cabo da Praia and Paul da Praia on Terceira, Pico island's Lajes do Pico, and the lakes of Sete Cidades and the northwestern tip of Mosteiros on São Miguel. The small ponds around Santa Maria's airport can also bring rewards. To increase your chances and save time, a local specialised wildlife guide can steer you towards the avian highlights that might coincide with your visit.

rush *Juncus acutus*. Widely located but found in small concentrations by the coast is one of the most handsome of all Azorean endemics, the perennial, slightly shrubby *Azorina vidalii*. (See also page 288 for an aid to identifying plants you are likely to see.)

Two bullies Amid all the excitement of introducing new plants into the show gardens of São Miguel came two very gardenworthy species which have more than outlived their mid 19th-century patrons. From the middle altitudes of the Himalayas came the **Kahili ginger** (*Hedychium gardnerianum*) a handsome plant about 1.5m tall with beautiful, sweetly scented, terminal spikes of orange-yellow spidery flowers. Away from its native habitat it found itself in the Azores in a permanently moist climate, with nothing to limit its growth. It has become a superbly aggressive invader: it can adapt to various Azorean habitats; it is a strongly competitive plant; cut it down and it can quickly recover; it produces abundant efficiently dispersed seeds; can easily reproduce vegetatively; and once established it dominates the site for many years. As a consequence, it has smothered areas of native vegetation, prevents the re-establishment of desirable species and has invaded large areas of cryptomeria forest – a real pest, and very difficult to eradicate. The second garden delight is **Gunnera tinctoria**, one of the 'giant rhubarbs' from South America. You will see this plant invading parts of the Furnas Valley and especially the pastures high above; also Lake Fogo, a protected area for flora, and Sete Cidades. Deeply rooted and with a strong constitution, it covers hectares of pastures; the occasional container-load taken to Holland for sale to garden centres makes little impact.

WHALES AND OTHER CETACEANS Cetaceans, from the Greek meaning 'sea monster', are members of the order Cetaceae, commonly known as whales and dolphins. Altogether there are a little over 80 species worldwide, and some 27 species have been sighted off the Azores: the islands are now recognised as being one of the world's best whale-watching destinations. Cetaceans are mammals, have lungs and nostrils (blowholes), suckle their young and have front flippers evolved from forelegs. Within the Cetaceae are two subgroups: toothed whales and baleen whales. The former have teeth and a single blowhole while the latter have, instead of teeth, a horny baleen or plate descending from the upper jaw and paired blowholes. This difference is important when feeding; the toothed whales eat larger fish and squid and the baleen whales use their comb-like plates to filter very small fish and the shrimp-like krill. Many of these filter-feeding whales undertake long migrations because they need warm waters for the growth and development of their young, but they also need the food resources that concentrate in colder waters.

The mid-Atlantic location of the steep-sided volcanic islands of the Azores causes great upswellings of coldwater currents from the ocean depths which meet the warm waters of the Gulf Stream, producing nutrient-rich waters. The species most readily identified with the Azores is the sperm whale or cachalote (*Physeter macrocephalus*), the largest of all toothed whales. Other toothed whales frequently seen during the main season are Cuvier's beaked whale (*Ziphius caviostris*), northern bottlenose whale (*Hyperodon ampullatus*), short-finned pilot whale (*Globicephala macrorhynchus*) and Sowerby's beaked whale (*Mesoplodon bidens*).

Dolphins seen regularly are common Atlantic (*Delphinus delphis*), bottlenose (*Tursiops truncates*), Risso's (*Grampus griseus*), Atlantic spotted (*Stenella frontalis*) and striped (*Stenella coeruleoalba*). Since 2001, observations of baleen or great whales have increased during early April to late June. Species include fin (*Balaenoptera physalus*), sei (*Balaenoptera borealis*), humpback (*Megeptera novaeangliae*) and the blue whale (*Balaenoptera musculus*), thought to be the largest animal ever to have lived on earth.

CONSERVATION The Azores Regional Government has committed to a policy focused on the environment and national heritage – sites of high botanical, fauna, ecological, landscape and geological interest – and the surrounding marine environment. The Azores have one of the richest marine ecosystems in the world, including some eight hydrothermal vents of the Mid-Atlantic Ridge.

Designating areas to be protected began in 1972 with the Faial caldera and, two years later, Lagoa do Fogo on São Miguel. In the next decades there followed forest nature reserves with a wider remit, and the first marine reserves. Today, visitors see on-site noticeboards declaring protected areas, often followed by a run of acronyms.

The European Union's Natura 2000 network of sites (w ec.europa.eu/environment/nature/natura2000/index_en.htm) is a European-wide partnership at the heart of which are two directives. The 1979 Birds Directive seeks the establishment of Special Protection Areas (SPAs) for birds, aiming to protect and manage areas important for rare and vulnerable species because they use them for breeding, feeding, wintering or migration; the 1992 Habitats Directive requires Special Areas of Conservation (SACs) to be designated to provide increased protection and management for rare and vulnerable animals, plants and habitats. These Natura 2000 sites now cover about 20% of the European territory and, as their website says, most European citizens will not live far from a Natura 2000 site. There are further acronyms, including Site of Community Importance (SCI), which contributes to the maintenance or restoration of a natural habitat or species or biological diversity, and also contributes significantly to Natura 2000. The rich geological and volcanic heritage is recognised

WHALING IN THE AZORES

Although organised commercial whaling was first carried out by the Basques in the Bay of Biscay, as early as the 10th century, whaling reached the Azores only in the 18th century and thus its history is short. For the Basques, the hunt was for the northern right whale (*Eubaleana glacialis*) and they pursued it to near-extinction, first in the Bay of Biscay, then much later across the Atlantic on the eastern seaboard of Newfoundland.

In the Azores, only the resident sperm whales (*Physeter macrocephalus*) were hunted, starting around 1765 when American colonists arrived in the archipelago. At 20m the sperm whale is the largest of the toothed whales, and their odourless oil fuelled lamps and made candle wax. Later it provided watch oil, lubricants for delicate instruments, cosmetics, textiles (preventing fibres from unravelling when twisted into threads), soap, jute, varnish, explosives and paint, and went into margarine until the 1960s, when it was replaced with vegetable oils. Despite the attacks of privateers and pirates, the Americans found the Azorean waters to be profitable, recruiting locals as crew and exploiting their expert seamanship.

By the 1800s, American whalers were regularly calling at Horta for victuals and water, and also to trans-ship barrels of oil. This golden age of American whaling, when New Bedford in Massachusetts was known as 'the city that lit the world', continued until the 1850s, but by then whale oil was becoming unaffordable and was being replaced by kerosene, a product of the embryonic petroleum industry. Additionally, whaling ships were destroyed by Confederacy ships in the American Civil War, and the golden age was drawing to a close.

But in the Azores, the demise of ship-based whaling encouraged the growth of shore-based whaling in Faial. In Pico, whaling provided welcome compensation for the simultaneous collapse of its wine industry and the island established several whaling companies, then obtained concessions from other islands to whale. By 1908, there were whaleboats in Terceira, Graciosa and Faial. Flores and São Miguel by selected locations under Regional Natural Monuments (RNMs). Most recently, to better administer and manage the protected areas the regional government established three management units: Island Nature Parks, on all nine islands; Marine Parks; and Local Protected Areas, created by local municipalities to safeguard local parks, gardens, lookouts and the Recreational Forest Reserves.

At the same time the OSPAR Convention for the Protection of the Marine Environment of the northeast Atlantic (w ospar.org) is creating in conjunction with Natura 2000 a network of Marine Protected Areas (MPAs) that are both ecologically coherent and well managed. The northeast Atlantic has been divided into five regions. In the wider Atlantic region six MPAs have been established, four in collaboration with Portugal, covering a total area of $285,000km^2$, protecting a series of seamounts and sections of the Mid-Atlantic Ridge and hosting a range of vulnerable deep-sea habitats and species. This is of special significance for the Azores since their maritime area is greater than their terrestrial. Member states are expected to pay for the management of their sites, but there are various community funds that can assist.

The presence of on-site wardens, rangers, professional naturalists and voluntary workers is still in its infancy throughout the Azores. Exceptions are the Capelinhos eruption site of 1958, the base supervising access to Pico mountain, lava caves on São Miguel, Terceira, Pico and Graciosa, the whaling centres of Lajes on Pico and Horta on Faial, Santa Cruz on Flores, and the Priolo Environmental Centre on São Miguel.

began whaling a couple of decades after Pico, the latter with its whale station and tryworks at Capelas, which benefited from the greater number of whales that passed its shores than those of the Central and Western groups. Corvo, with its dangerous coastline, caught few whales and these were mostly taken to Flores for processing (working-up). There was also whaling at Santa Maria, but it lapsed in the 20th century, only to be revived just before World War II, with the highest catch per boat of all the islands, while São Jorge became as active as Faial during the first 40 years of the 20th century.

The whaling industry suffered market vicissitudes beyond the control of the islanders. New substitute products, prices and, in the late 1940s, the big Antarctic sperm whale catches, impacted upon Azorean sales, but the two world wars and the Korean War saw high demand. In 1935, 99 sperm whales were taken, and in 1969, the catch was 263. In terms of overall totals, the Azorean catches made little impact: annual worldwide catches in the 1930s exceeded 40,000 whales, and some species were driven almost to extinction. The Washington Convention of 1946 was an attempt to regulate whaling and as the century continued the numbers allowed to be caught were reduced substantially. Economics, declining stocks, falling prices and the ready availability of substitutes caused nations to abandon whaling. By 1954, Azorean whaling was seen as a relic industry. The factory on São Miguel closed in 1972, bringing whaling to an end in the Eastern Group of islands. The International Whaling Commission in 1982 agreed zero commercial quotas, but Norway, Japan and Iceland continue (while Iceland aims to cease whaling from 2024). Whale hunting in the Azores became a very minor affair, and had ceased altogether by the mid 1980s. I remember standing on the quay at Lajes on Pico watching in the shallows a huge jawbone slowly being grazed by sea creatures; it must have belonged to one of the very last whales to be caught.

1

Whether through whale hunting or whale watching, these largest of sea creatures have impacted across the Azorean archipelago and its economy for over 250 years, and continue to do so today.

In the heyday of ship-based whaling, carried out by visiting American whalers, the Azoreans, so long accustomed to seafaring from childhood, excelled in jobs as lookouts, oarsmen and harpooners in the small boats lowered from ships to hunt and kill the whales. A hard life, often with poor food and conditions, low pay, and increasingly long voyages, nevertheless offered an escape from compulsory military service. For some, it provided a new life in New England and the chance to send money home to dependants in the islands.

Portugal itself never established a deep-sea industry. Attempts to fit out whale ships in the Azores failed due to the lack of capital available in the islands and the increasing success of shore-based whaling.

Shore-based whaling relied on onshore lookouts spotting passing whales. On sighting a blow, a rocket was fired from the *vigia* (lookout tower) to let the whalemen know to launch their boats, and a white flag was raised. If a kill was made, the flag was flown at half-mast to warn the tryworks to get ready for processing. The boats would sail or row out, and in later years were towed out by motor launch, guided by large sheets laid out on the cliffs or by radio telephone. Once the whale felt the harpoon it fled or dived, rapidly taking out line; friction could set it on fire, so water was poured over it. Sails and mast had to be lowered, and the crew had to avoid the running line to avoid the loss of a leg or worse. Once several hundred feet of line had been taken out and the pace began to slacken, the line would be fixed to the loggerhead, a post at the back of the boat. With the line fixed, the whale would feel the drag and take off again to tow the whalers at around 25–30km/h, often called the 'Nantucket sleigh ride', which was another dangerous period because the boat could capsize. When the whale tired, rope was taken in, but let out if the whale surged again. Since a whale in one breath can exchange 85–90% of air, an objective was to break the animal's breathing pattern to prevent it from diving deeply. Eventually the whale tired sufficiently for the boat to close, when lances were used for the kill.

The most important modern innovation was the gradual introduction from 1909 of motorised tow boats or *gasolinas*, enabling several boats to be rapidly

The islands of Corvo, Flores and Graciosa are recognised by UNESCO as Biosphere Reserves; these are protected areas intended to demonstrate an equilibrium between man and nature, conservation and sustainable development. More recently, in 2016, the *fãjas* (page 185) of São Jorge island were also given UNESCO Biosphere Reserve status. With the islands' increasing emphasis on renewable sources of energy, conservation strategies and environmental management, it is hoped that the Azores could in time become a model for future sustainability.

HISTORY

DISCOVERY It was long thought that the islands were pristine until the Portuguese began to settle them in the mid 15th century; however, scientists have found that forests were cleared by burning in about the 9th century, and there are traces of sheep towed to the whale regardless of unfavourable winds; this greatly extended their range. The engine noise would have scared off the whales, so the last mile was covered by sail, oars and finally paddling to within harpooning range. Tow boats enabled longer chases and offered rescue in case of a whaleboat being smashed by the whale; they also allowed the towing of dead whales back to shore, a backbreaking task when done by the whaling boat under oars. Although harpoon guns and exploding lances were used to hunt whales from ships, the Azorean whalemen used the hand harpoon and lance. Similarly, processing or *saving* of the dead whale changed little; first the whale was *cut in*, meaning the blubber was cut up or *flensed* with the animal either beached or tied alongside a jetty, using cutting-spades, ropes and at most a hand capstan. With the blubber and spermaceti removed, these were then *tried out*, by being placed into try-pots or iron cauldrons to melt and reduce over a basalt oven to make sperm oil and 'head oil'. The carcass, with its meat and bone, was simply towed back out to sea and abandoned. It was not until 1934 that sufficient capital became available to invest in modern processing equipment using powered winches and pressure cookers, so that the whole animal could be utilised. Just after World War II radio-telephones were first used for communication between the lookouts and the motor tow boats, purchased from the US military, who sold off the stock very cheaply.

Nowadays, many examples of the old *vigia* can still be spotted all around the islands, some restored, most of them redundant. But not all, as the many companies engaged in whale watching still spot their 'prey' from a few of these coastal towers, communicating with the boat captains by radio. As well as enjoying the wonders of whale watching, visitors to the Azores can choose to visit one or more museums dedicated to the era of whalehunting, to learn about the rigours of a life at sea and the intricacies of catching and processing whales.

The annual whalemen's festival, Festa dos Baleeiros, continues to be held on the first Sunday in August in the tiny church on Monte da Guia, above Porto Pim in Horta. In Lajes do Pico there is also a whalers' festival, and still some of the old whaling villages beautifully maintain old *canoas* (whaling boats) and sometimes even commission new ones, now used for sailing races and offering opportunities for visitors to take to sea and experience the sensations of past days.

and cattle droppings from the same period. What's more, the mitochondrial DNA of mice on the islands indicates a northern European origin, so it is presumed that the Vikings were here for a time. The islands were certainly known to exist, for in the *Medici Atlas* of 1351 the seven islands of the Central and Eastern groups are shown; slightly later maps show all nine islands, and give some of them similar names to their present ones. Less than a century later the Portuguese 'Age of Discoveries' began and Portuguese explorers made the first recorded landfalls on Madeira (c1419), the Azores (c1427), Cape Verde (1456–60), Saint Helena and Ascension (1501–02) and Tristan da Cunha (c1506). Bartolomeu Dias rounded the Cape of Good Hope in 1488 and thus opened access to the Indian Ocean, and Pedro Álvares Cabral landed in Brazil in 1500, to say nothing of the numerous inland expeditions in Africa and elsewhere. It is not known for certain who discovered the islands for the Portuguese, nor the exact dates; numerous stories abound from which to take your choice. One

From their initial settlement in the 15th century, the Azores have played a pivotal role in the history of the Atlantic. On Terceira, the Bay of Angra (Angra meaning 'Anchorage') provided protection and was soon defended, later by the great fortress of São Filipe and smaller São Sebastião. By the early 1500s, it was an obligatory port of call for the fleets serving Africa and the East and West Indies and for 300 years was a link between Europe and the New World.

When Spain overran Portugal, the 'Reprisal Pirates' of England sought to capture their treasure ships, and to protect them the Spanish in 1555 formed the first convoy system, with merchant ships defended by armed escorts.

Powerful nations must have long coveted the Azores for their strategic location. However, one enthusiast in the early 1800s proposed that Britain should acquire the archipelago, not only for use as a base between Africa and America and as a staging post in the transportation of troops to the Cape of Good Hope and the East Indies, but also because at the time the British Empire had no colony that produced wine (!), and because São Miguel and Terceira would make excellent penal colonies, with transportation costs much less than the long voyage to Australia.

In November 1914, Portugal declared war on Germany, co-operating closely with the Allies and giving them access to the ports in Horta and Ponta Delgada for anti-submarine warfare and for repairs and refuelling convoys – convoys being a repeat of the Spanish strategy centuries earlier. In World War II, agreement to the use of the facilities in the Azores came much later as President Salazar was very reluctant to give Nazi Germany cause to invade mainland Portugal. Churchill famously called upon the Treaty of Eternal Friendship of 1373, or Treaty of Windsor; this was between England's King Edward III and King Dom João I of Portugal and had been further sealed a year later when João married Philippa of Lancaster, daughter of John of Gaunt. Reinforced from time to time through the following centuries, the treaty is still in force today after more than 600 years, and is the oldest alliance between any two countries. Negotiations were time-consuming, but eventually Britain was allowed by August 1943 to develop

is that a caravel came upon them by chance when sailing homewards from the west coast of Africa using the trade winds. Another is that the Infante Dom Henrique (Prince Henry 'the Navigator') ordered one Gonçalo Velho Cabral to sail westwards to find the islands he thought must exist. Cabral found only the Formigas ('Ants') rocks and went back home, getting a low mark from the Sagres Management School. Sent back the following year, and sailing 24km further southwest from the Formigas, a much better prospect came into view. Since it was 15 August, the Feast of the Assumption of the Virgin Mary, he called the first island he reached Santa Maria and was later appointed governor. São Miguel was supposedly discovered when an escaped slave clambered up a hill and saw a much larger island in the distance; this was settled around 1444. By chance some unknown mariners spotted a third island, and with a stroke of originality called it Terceira, 'Third Island'. Another version is that Prince Henry sent out caravels, date unknown, to find the islands and they discovered five, later named Santa Maria, São Miguel, Terceira, Faial and Pico. Most popular accounts give the Portuguese explorer Diogo de Silves the credit for finding the first island, Santa Maria, in 1427. In 1439, Alfonso V sanctioned Henry to settle seven islands, so they must have been discovered before that year. Flores and Corvo were certainly added last.

an airstrip at Lajes on Terceira. Known as *aerovacas*, these simple airstrips were on several of the islands and regularly grazed by cattle. This time the farmers on Terceira were not only losing pasture, but to greater consternation there was also an *aguardente* (firewater) factory in the middle of the site. Marsden matting, an interlocking perforated metal sheet, was used initially to make a 1.8km runway. Soon afterwards, the United States military were also allowed to use Lajes and they later made it a permanent airfield for heavy transports as the eventual liberation of Europe drew closer. A second airbase was needed and the US was given permission to construct one on Santa Maria, under cover of Pan American Airways, so that it would seem Portugal was building it for post-war communications. Work began in late 1944 and three runways were built in an A shape. Access to the Azores proved vital to the Allies in protecting the Atlantic convoys from German U-boats. There was a north Atlantic route which had protection from bases in Newfoundland and Iceland, and a southern route, but these left the mid-Atlantic as an undefended black hole; significantly, it was also the shortest crossing, saving time and vital fuel. Enemy U-boats prowled the seas around the Azores and Allied shipping losses were appalling. With the Lajes base, and the cracking of the Enigma codes, the odds were turned, U-boats were sunk and shipping losses dramatically dropped, and eventually the wolf packs were called off. Had Hitler built more U-boats as his admirals wanted, and invaded the Azores, how different might the outcome have been.

By 1947, all military operations had been transferred to Lajes, leaving Santa Maria as an important stop for commercial transatlantic flights until the 1970s, when newer aircraft could cross non stop. The only airstrip in the Azores long enough, it even hosted visits from Concorde for a while. In 1948–49, Lajes was used in the Berlin airlift to counter the Soviet blockade, and this experience influenced the decision to negotiate long-term use by the American military for a base. It also continues as a Portuguese airbase. Portugal was one of the founding members of NATO, and in Ponta Delgada there is a NATO naval fuel depot and terminal.

SETTLEMENT Colonisation of the islands was undertaken in a typically medieval way. King Afonso V granted them to his nephew, the Infante Dom Henrique (Henry the Navigator) as Master of the Military Order of Christ, successor to the crusading Templars. It was this Order of Christ that financially supported the discoveries of the 15th century and for reward was given the new lands to explore and populate. The Infante in turn delegated control over administration, defence, justice and land grants to the Captain Donatário (donatory or lord proprietor, the Portuguese equivalent of a colonial governor), together with the revenue from certain taxes, and the monopoly control over mills, salt and the ovens for baking bread. The king retained oversight of customs, control of selected taxes and of the death penalty.

The usual practice was followed when discovering islands; cattle, goats and pigs were landed to provide future food, and also very likely to begin the tremendous task of penetrating the dense vegetation. The first islands to be populated were Santa Maria and São Miguel, followed by Terceira in about 1450. Settlers came from mainland Portugal, particularly the Algarve and Alentejo, and from Madeira. Portugal's population was only 1.5 million, so Henry encouraged **immigration from Flanders**, and in 1466 Flemings, under the Captain Donatário Josse Van der Huertere, settled on Faial and Pico, and a few years later, led by Willem Van der

Luis Silva

In the 15th century, when the islands were settled by the Portuguese, one of the first things that was done was to introduce domestic animals. Of these the cow was extremely important because she not only provided milk and meat but was also a hardworking animal around the farm, for ploughing, carting, etc. Some of the distinct cattle breeds that were imported from Portugal include Alentejana, Mirandesa, Minhota and Algarvia. There is also historical suggestion that some cows were imported from Flanders but there is no information on specific breeds. Importation would have continued until the numbers reached a reproductive level that was self-sustaining, and then probably stopped. The following five centuries of cross-breeding between the original breeds imported from Portugal and Flanders evolved into a distinct breed known today as Ramo Grande, which dominated on most of the islands. Then, in the 1950s, Friesians were imported from England and later on from the USA and soon after that an artificial insemination programme was set up on Terceira and São Miguel. By the 1980s, there were quite a few importations of dairy heifers (Holsteins) and beef breeds (Limousin, Charolais and Fleckview) from Germany, England, Holland, France and Canada. A small number of Jersey heifers have since been added, plus Jersey embryo transfers. Consequently, and in a very short time, the Ramo Grande breed became almost extinct.

Fortunately, in the area of Ramo Grande on Terceira, a group of farmers continued to maintain small herds of these animals. Today there is increasing interest in the conservation of this Azorean genetic heritage, and in its potential for producing beef; its specific characteristics have been defined and all individuals are now registered. At present, the genetic line in the Azores is mostly Holsteins for dairy and Limousin and Charolais for beef, although the University of the Azores, through its Agricultural Sciences Department, concluded that Jerseys would be the most suitable dairy breed for the region. Hopefully, the Azorean Ramo Grande will survive the effects of globalisation and someday might even contribute its distinctive characters to future breeding.

Hagen, on Flores; for a time, these islands became known in northern Europe as the Flemish Islands because so many settled there, refugees from the Burgundian takeover of the Low Countries.

The first settlers faced an enormous task and probably used fire to begin to clear the vegetation, though cattle also played their part. On some of the islands this would have revealed a very stony soil, and especially on Pico it must have been heartbreaking. Huge neatly piled stacks of stones metres square and 2m tall remain testimony to this tenacity and determination, as do the numerous stone walls; their creation had nothing to do with marking territorial boundaries. With such an inhospitable coastline, wherever it was possible to land must have dictated the location of those first settlements. Looking at them today, some still appear daunting, often at the foot of steep cliffs or ravines. Farming slowly spread across the islands as the vegetation was cleared and by the next century there was a surplus of production for export: wheat for the Portuguese garrison in North Africa, sugar and woad for dyeing to Flanders. Each island grew more of the crops that best suited its climate and terrain. However, by the end of the 17th century, the peasants were eating the introduced American corn (maize) and yams, so freeing the wheat crop for export for townspeople and cash export.

During the middle of the 16th century, vessels returning from India using the westerly trade winds passed through the Azores, but it was at the beginning of

WOAD, PASTEL AND ORCHIL

For me, and I suspect for many, the name woad brings to mind school lessons telling of Boadicea and her warriors painted blue doing battle with the Roman invaders. Knowledge of the dye goes back to the Ancients, and the Greeks and Romans used it medicinally – it is a good astringent. In the cabbage family, *Isatis tinctoria* (*pastel* in Portuguese) is a greyish, medium-tall biennial herb native to eastern Europe and western Asia; cultivated in Europe since the 10th century, it may now be found naturalised as a relict of former cultivation. First the leaves and stems were washed and dried, then ground in a mill; the powder thus obtained was again wetted and again sun-dried. The resultant concentrated black and granular extract was then formed into cakes and large balls. By the 13th century, French Languedoc became a main area of woad cultivation, centred on Toulouse, making the city very wealthy. It was from here the plant was introduced into the Azores at the end of the 15th century, where it was grown for almost 200 years, but only 100 of these were economically important. Woad's success was linked to the fortunes of the European textile industry, and the Azores enjoyed a mutually profitable trade with the English textile towns, especially Exeter, and more than a dozen English merchants lived in Ponta Delgada. At its peak, it is thought that woad was grown on more than 30% of São Miguel's arable land. Unfortunately, the dye constituent indigotin in woad is the same as in a dye plant in the pea family, *Indigofera*, or indigo, and being chemically inert they can both dye the same textiles; indigo also is much less vulnerable to fading, and was thus ideal for military uniforms. Limited supplies had come from India, but when the Portuguese discovered the sea route to India, imports rose. The woad lobby was considerable, and in England indigo dye was prohibited for over 100 years, until 1685. Because it was so valuable, the French began its cultivation on their Caribbean islands; the climate was ideal, and the crop demanded slaves. Britain followed in Jamaica and South Carolina, and by the middle of the 17th century, cheap imports and heavy taxes imposed by Lisbon had killed the Azorean pastel trade, and the resident English merchants slowly dwindled.

Orchil or archil, *urzela* in Portuguese, is the source of a dye prepared from certain lichens of several genera. The Cape Verde Islands were a major producer, using it to dye their cotton trade cloth, but the discovery of abundant supplies in the early 19th century in Angola and Mozambique killed their market. In the Azores the lichen *Roccella tinctoria* is found on maritime rocks and when processed with stale urine (or ammonia) and dried it was sold in powder form, later known as cudbear, or as a paste, which gives a purple-red colour. Lichen dyes change colour in reaction to acids or bases – red to acid and blue to alkaline – and are used in litmus paper, while Orcein from *Roccella tinctoria* is used to make a purple stain for studying chromosomes. Never as significant in the Azores as pastel, its export was short-lived; indeed, one commentator claimed the revenue went as pin money to the queen!

the Portuguese colonisation of Brazil and the discovery of America when the islands began their great development, mainly in the sheltered anchorage of Angra on Terceira. It became a principal port for exporting Azorean produce, and significantly an assembly port for ships returning from Brazil laden with valuable cargoes. Here they would form convoys for the journey to Lisbon, protected by warships against the marauding pirates.

In 1580, Spanish Castile annexed Portugal and the Azores supported Dom António, Prior of Crato and next in line to the throne, who, with French help, held out on Terceira, becoming the last Portuguese resistance to Castilian power. The Spaniards defeated the French fleet off São Miguel in July 1582 and the following year overran the islands. In 1591, the Spanish were attacked by the English, giving rise to Tennyson's famous poem *The Revenge* (page 251). Portugal had been allied to England since 1386 (now the world's longest-lived alliance), while England and Spain were at war on largely religious grounds. Piracy and privateering were also rife, especially when Spain held the Azores, and the Azorean genome is 81.3% European, 7.5% Middle Eastern/Jewish, and 11.3% sub-Saharan African, doubtless due to the influence of the Barbary pirates. Liberated in 1640, the islands became an important staging post for British trade and for British naval strategy, until the opening of the Suez Canal over 200 years later.

Although so distant from the Portuguese mainland, the Azores nevertheless have often played an important part in Portuguese history. They contributed to the conquest, defence and supply of the Portuguese strongholds on the north African coast, caravels stopped in the Azores on their return from India, they supported the ships sailing to the Americas, and they strongly resisted Spanish domination between 1580 and 1640. Two centuries later the islands featured in the Liberals' struggle with the Absolutists (page 21); two presidents in the First Republic came from the Azores and, most recently, the islands provided important bases for the Allies in the two world wars (page 16), and in the Gulf War.

GOVERNMENT AND POLITICS   with Albano Cymbron

Initially, except for a period during the Spanish occupation, the Azores had no central government, and it was not until 1766 that a governor and captain-general for the whole group were appointed by the **Marquis of Pombal**. He was very much a man of the 18th-century Enlightenment, and had lived for several years in the main capitals of Europe, so was well aware how backward Portugal had become. He became Prime Minister of Portugal in 1750 and implemented economic and educational reforms, abolished slavery, revised the tax system and introduced commercial regulation. He implemented a new administrative system throughout the kingdom, creating districts or provinces. The Azores became a single province, governed by the captain-general (*capitão-general*), with Angra on Terceira becoming the archipelago's capital – doing away with the semi-feudal privileges of the various donatories and the islands losing their autonomous captaincies. While this may have been logical in Lisbon, it went against the vigorous individualism of the islands and greatly displeased the people of São Miguel, for theirs was the largest and richest island and they were accustomed to resolving their problems directly with the central government. Under the new arrangement, each island was totally independent of the others, and for approximately 60 years this regime prevailed; it was a time of struggle and indiscipline between the governor in Terceira and the other islands, mainly São Miguel.

In 1807, Napoleon's forces invaded Portugal; Napoleon wanted to stop **Anglo-Portuguese trade** and demanded Portugal close its ports, but the Portuguese refused to comply, so beginning the **Peninsular War**. The Portuguese royal family, their court and important citizens fled to Brazil and made Rio de Janeiro the capital of Portugal, leaving Portugal to a military junta with orders not to resist. In 1808, British and Portuguese troops under Sir Arthur Wellesley (the later Duke of Wellington) gained control over Lisbon and a treaty allowed the French to withdraw. The French invaded twice more but were eventually driven out of Portugal in 1810 and out of Spain in 1814, presaging Napoleon's final defeat. The Azores played a valiant part in the Peninsular War, but it would take many long years for Portugal to recover from the ravages of the war.

Liberal ideas resulting from the French Revolution spread to Portugal with the French invasion and found fertile ground in a country that was in a deplorable state, its king and government in Brazil, and in their absence Lisbon ruled by the English Marshal Beresford and British commercial interests. The economy was in crisis, previously being dependent on a trade monopoly with Brazil, but now, with the king residing there, this commerce had been opened to all friendly countries with the English benefiting most. Lisbon felt it was a colony of Brazil.

A **Liberal revolution** quickly spread from its beginnings in Porto, demanding the return of the royal court, a constitutional monarchy and that Brazil revert to its old status of colony trading exclusively with Portugal. Beresford was replaced by a junta and, in 1821, a Constituent Assembly was elected in Lisbon, the same year as the publication of the first Liberal constitution. A few months later the king, João VI, returned to Lisbon, leaving his son, Dom Pedro, Regent of Brazil. In September, the assembly voted to abolish the Kingdom of Brazil and so bring it under direct control of Lisbon; the following year Brazil declared its independence, and Dom Pedro became its first emperor.

Under the new constitution, adopted in 1822, deputies were elected by the people (landowners and merchants) and the king had no powers, not even to dissolve parliament. This was strongly opposed by João VI's queen, Carlota-Joaquina, who, together with her younger son Dom Miguel, prompted a countrywide insurgency against it in the name of Absolutism and a call for the king to abdicate. It was a very troubled time, as is common with any change of regime, with revolts against revolts with either the Traditionalists (Absolutists) or the Liberals in power. João VI died in 1826 and eventually, in 1828, Dom Miguel was declared king absolute, totally against the constitution only recently accepted by the crown. Liberals opposed to the Absolutist regime withdrew to Terceira, which remained loyal to the Liberal cause.

Meanwhile, in Brazil, following a political crisis Dom Pedro abdicated in favour of his son, Pedro II, in 1831, and crossed to Europe to oppose his brother Dom Miguel. Going first to England where there were many exiled Portuguese Liberals, he moved in 1832 to Terceira, which he used as his base for the coming invasion of Portugal, and formed an interim **government-in-exile**. In July, he led an army including French and English troops, and took Porto in the north, with the Duke of Terceira capturing Lisbon. Final victory came in 1834.

Reforms followed, and a new administration for the Azores was created by making the islands a province of Portugal, with Angra the capital and a governor appointed by Lisbon. Again, São Miguel strongly opposed the dominance of Terceira and this was eventually resolved by first creating two districts, and then three. São Miguel and Santa Maria came under Ponta Delgada District, while Angra administered the islands of Terceira, Graciosa and São Jorge. Horta District presided over Faial, Pico, Flores and Corvo. Each district was independent of the others and managed its affairs directly with the central government in Lisbon. So began the process of territorial division which later led to the creation of further autonomous districts that lasted until 1974. Interestingly, it was resentment over taxes that first prompted the idea that the islands should have autonomy. This first occurred in 1869 with the **'Dízimo' tax** that obliged people to pay 10% of their earnings to the Church. Later came a tax on the alcohol produced in the Azores, introduced to protect the same industry on the mainland.

Prime Minister, and later President, Salazar led the authoritarian right-wing government which controlled Portugal from 1932 to 1974. He established public order which was previously lacking, and the political and financial stability for economic growth. A basic education was provided for everyone, and a substantial investment made in infrastructure. Many of the often very attractive schools in the Azores date from this period. His dictatorship followed a strict Catholic social doctrine opposed to class struggle and economic dominance, with a secret police to counter opposition. On his death a leftish military coup slowly changed the regime to a democracy leading to free elections and in 1976, the first constitutional government.

In 1976, the Azores became an autonomous region with its own Executive or Regional Government answering to the Legislative Assembly. The region elects five deputies to the national parliament in Lisbon, and two MEPs to the European Parliament. The Legislative Assembly has 51 deputies elected every four years and meets in Horta. The President of the Azores, whose official residence is in Ponta Delgada, is the leader of the party with the greatest number of elected deputies. There are nine regional secretaries, each in charge of a department, eg: Finance and Planning, Tourism and Environment. The secretariats, or ministries, are based in Ponta Delgada, Angra do Heroísmo and Horta. Each island is divided into district councils, from six on São Miguel to just one on each of the smallest islands, which are in turn divided into *freguesias*, or parishes. The islands have responsibility for their economy, education and health, while the army, police and judiciary are controlled directly by the national government in Lisbon. The Portuguese government is represented by the Minister of the Republic, resident in Angra do Heroísmo, Terceira.

ECONOMY

During the 30 years before the 2008 economic crisis in Europe, island infrastructure was given priority, and new airports, harbours and telecommunication systems were completed. The Azores, or at least Ponta Delgada, have changed hugely in the past few years with new industrial/commercial estates on the outskirts and many new shops in the town. Everywhere in the islands one frequently saw (and still sees) the European Union flag on a hoarding announcing funds for some new development, from new port facilities to a tiny family enterprise for rural tourism. While some of the road building may be questioned, such as the asphalting of many of the minor farm tracks throughout the islands that once were easy and enjoyable walking trails, the airfields, new port facilities for cruise liners and tourism are clearly paying economic dividends. But the economic crisis brought austerity, with substantial increases in taxation and cuts in government budgets. Portugal was quick to try to reduce its budget deficit, and to meet the conditions of its EU bail out, and the economy has recovered. The Azores, while affected, have fared better than the mainland and Madeira due to lower debts and a strong family structure, although there were many job losses in the construction industry. Apart from the public sector, the greatest contribution to GDP has been and remains the export of cattle and dairy products. Then there are minor crops of pineapples, potatoes, wine, tobacco and tea; all labour-intensive. Tourism has long been gaining in importance, and 2019 was a record year,

ISLAND SIZE AND APPROXIMATE POPULATION (LATEST AVAILABLE OFFICIAL FIGURES, CENSUS 2021)

	Length (km)	Breadth (km)	Surface area (km²)	Population
São Miguel	65	14	746	133,300
Pico	42	15	447	13,900
Terceira	29	17.5	382	53,200
São Jorge	56	8	246	8,400
Faial	21	14	173	14,300
Flores	17	12.5	143	3,400
Santa Maria	17	9.5	97	5,400
Graciosa	12.5	8.5	61	4,100
Corvo	6.5	4	17	430

with a total of 972,000 visitors, before Covid-19 put tourism on hold. Although proportionately small, Azorean fishing is also artisanal, providing a relatively high number of jobs per tonne of fish landed. Given their different characters, it is not surprising economic activities have different relevance for individual islands. Dairy and beef are more relevant for Graciosa and São Jorge, fishing is more important to Faial and Pico, tourism for São Miguel, Pico, Faial and Flores, and other exports on the more diversified São Miguel. Transfer payments from central government are important to Corvo because of its small size, to Terceira for its military airbase, and to Santa Maria, which hosts the air traffic control of the mid-Atlantic.

ENERGY The Azores have been dependent upon imported oil to generate electricity but are now increasingly seeking and exploiting energy from geothermal, wind and solar sources. The first hydro-electric plant was built on São Miguel in 1899 and ran until 1950.

In 1975, the Institute of Geosciences of the Azores was founded and in the following year began drilling wells down to 1,500m on São Miguel. The first pilot geothermal plant generating 3MW opened in 1980 and its success led to the exploration of the Ribeira Grande field. Now some 44% of São Miguel's electricity is from geothermal sources, and Terceira also has a 4MW geothermal plant.

Nine separate islands in the archipelago mean nine isolated energy grids, each with specific characteristics and possible solutions for renewable energy. Flores generates almost 50% from renewables (33% hydro), São Miguel 55% (mostly geothermal), and Terceira 8.5% from wind, the island's Serra do Cume wind farm setting in 2010 a then world record for generation. On Graciosa, a combination of wind and solar power was introduced in 2019, with short-term power fluctuations balanced by lithium batteries, to produce carbon-free electricity for the island.

São Jorge gets 15% of its energy from wind. Tiny Corvo has fitted solar panels to most of its houses and combined with heat pumps, this has reduced imports of liquefied petroleum gas. Overall, 40% of the Azores' power is from renewable sources, with 60% from imported fossil fuels.

PEOPLE

The total population of the Azores is around 237,000 (2021 census), a decrease of 4.2% over the preceding decade. Movement within the islands varies, with some islands or towns losing populations while others increase.

For centuries emigration has played a major part in the life of the islands. Overpopulation and economic hardship have been the underlying causes. Since the early days there were numerous attempts to find crops that could be exported to give a cash income to the islands. Many succeeded, only to be dashed by changing world markets, war in Europe or America, or pest and disease, leaving thriving communities destitute. Other natural disasters like earthquakes and eruptions drove islanders away after their homes and fields had been destroyed, even as recently as the 1980s. As a result there are large populations of Azoreans in Canada, the US, Brazil and elsewhere, still preserving their culture and heritage and returning regularly to the archipelago, particularly at festival times. Mass emigration largely ceased with the entry of Portugal to the EEC. Attracted by the peace and beauty of the islands, and the relative lack of stress, a small number of Europeans from France, Italy, Germany, mainland Portugal and elsewhere have settled in the Azores, creating small businesses mainly in the tourism sector.

EMIGRATION Emigration has deeply impacted upon the psychology and economics of the Azores over the centuries and is integral to the culture of the islands.

Following the decline in commerce with India, exploration of Brazil was encouraged, and sugar plantations were established in the northeast. In 1746, King João V announced a package of incentives to promote settlement in the south: land, tools, seeds, two cows and a mare. As a result, some 6,000 Azorean peasant farmers and fishermen settled in Brazil over a period of six years, mainly in the state of Santa Catarina.

Throughout Azorean history, poverty and lack of opportunity have been the main driving forces underlying the need to emigrate. Fundamental to this was overpopulation, eased by a wave of emigration, the population then only to increase again. By the 19th century, the land was the only source of income for the islanders, but land tenure did not offer opportunities for individuals to better themselves, and landowners were conservative and not open to innovation, so crop yields were low.

For a young man living in a close-knit community on a small island in a vast sea, with no big-city experience or that of a faster way of life, and speaking only Portuguese, emigration must have been a daunting prospect.

Around 1800, the Portuguese government introduced compulsory military conscription for 14-year-olds. Pay was poor, advantages few, and this, coupled with the trap of peasant land tenure, spurred many to emigrate. At the same time American ships, including whalers, increasingly visited the Azores and many young males escaped by joining the crew and eventually landing, often years later, in America's east-coast whaling ports. Then disease and pests struck the grape vines, and later came the collapse of the orange crop, disasters that led to huge further exoduses from the archipelago.

Between 1878 and 1888, 17 ships carried 11,057 immigrants from the Azores and Madeira halfway round the world, including rounding Cape Horn, to Hawaii for work in the cane fields. Unlike to other destinations, this was the only mass emigration and contact was lost with the Azores. Only in the 1980s was the connection resumed by the Azorean regional authorities, although the community had kept alive their Portuguese names and traditions such as the Holy Ghost celebrations.

Bermuda, another warm-temperate archipelago with geological origins linked to the Mid-Atlantic Ridge, was from the second half of the 19th century a popular destination for Azoreans, especially from São Miguel, peaking in the 1960s and 1970s. Most worked in tourism or gardening, but permanent residence was never permitted, and a contract of employment was essential to obtaining a visa.

With Brazil less inviting after gaining its independence, America offered better jobs and opportunities, and many Azoreans had already settled there from the whaling ships. By 1920, there were over 100,000 Azoreans in the United States, those from São Miguel having settled mostly on the east coast and Rhode Island, while people from the Central Group of islands made for California.

Immigration then virtually ceased due to new US immigration laws, until 1957, when Capelinhos volcano erupted on Faial, destroying villages and farmland. Thanks in part to then-senator JF Kennedy, the US passed refugee laws for Azoreans, and Canada also opened its doors. The emigrants were not only refugees from the volcano, but many were also economic migrants since the Azorean population was at its highest ever, at around 350,000 (110,000 more than it is today).

Repeatedly through history, some Azorean migrants have returned to their home island, with material goods and money to build a new house or maybe refurbish an old family holding. Both hardy and hardworking, the Azoreans' work reputation has a long pedigree and their labour has always been welcomed. But the generations that have been born abroad, while recognising their ancestral links with the islands, often visit now as American tourists along with their American culture, sadly a price that perhaps has to be paid. On the other hand, some are returning permanently, preferring to raise their young children in the Azores. The quality of life in the islands, where few are wealthy, but rich in a traditional way, where there is little crime and the landscape beautiful, is ironically now attracting foreign nationals seeking tranquil retirement.

LANGUAGE

Portuguese is both the national and native language, but there are strong regional dialects and vocabulary that often mother-tongue Portuguese-speakers from the mainland find difficult to understand. Natives of each island can be quickly recognised by fellow Azoreans, and even from which part of an island they come. Try learning some Portuguese before you travel; it is a gesture that will be welcomed, though English is widely and willingly spoken on the bigger islands, especially by the young. It is mostly in smaller cafés that it is useful to speak Portuguese, and in villages to ask the way. Some taxi drivers are fluent in English; many know enough to get by, but many others speak only Portuguese. In the towns very many people speak English, it is a standard subject in school, and there are numerous Azoreans who have worked abroad and even more who spend time online and watch Hollywood films. There are English-language television channels as well: CNN, BBC World and Sky News. Some French is spoken in Faial and Flores. Worldwide, Portuguese is the third-most widely spoken European language. (See page 283 for a list of useful phrases.)

RELIGION

The Azores have been Roman Catholic from their first settlement. The rare Protestant churches were built much later, for example in Ponta Delgada on São Miguel in the 19th century, primarily in response to the mainly English merchants who came to live on the islands to manage the orange trade. Although very much a minority, there was also a strong Jewish presence from the early days, with some Jews originating from North Africa. The Catholic parish priests were very influential, and the religious orders, especially the Franciscans, built many convents and churches and organised the first schools. In modern times it is the older parishioners who mostly make up church congregations, although young people still make up the numbers on festival days and religion is noticeably stronger here than in many European mainland regions. In particular, the cult of the Holy Ghost (page 34) is very important here.

CULTURE

ARCHITECTURE AND ART *with thanks to Dr Isabel Soares de Albergaria*
Secular architecture Architecture in the Azores is derived from that of continental Portugal, sharing the simplicity of form common to the Mediterranean. It does, however, have its own characteristics. The most obvious are the easy integration of the buildings in the landscape and the structure of the settlements, in which streets tend to converge in small irregular squares where the most imposing buildings stand, the church and town hall. In past times, most houses were modest in size and appearance and had distinctive features: they were built of stone, with a characteristic contrast between whitewash and black basalt.

Vernacular architecture, less affected by variations in style and the dictates of fashion, perhaps best reflects the Azoreans' relationship with their island environment. Their isolation, the simple agrarian way of life and the use of naturally available materials have led to very simple, almost rudimentary, designs for both houses and utilitarian buildings such as barns, cowsheds and mills. These, together with the small shrines and chapels, have, through the centuries, gradually developed their own style and form, leading to regional styles.

WINDMILLS – MOINHOS DOS AÇORES

From the writings of early travellers to the Azores, it appears that at least until the end of the 16th century only watermills, *moinhos de água*, were present in the islands, and that the windmills were a later innovation. Long-disused watermills are still abundant, now often hidden beneath the vigorous growth of ginger lilies that also like the humid stream beds. The mills were built either over streams or below specially constructed dams, or were even seasonal, relying upon the heavier winter rains to drive them.

Like so many aspects of the archipelago, individual islands developed their own style of windmill (except for Flores, which has more than enough water power), and there were at least eight different versions, of which four are still extant. Moving with the times, and tapping into tourist fashion, some windmills have now been restored and adapted to provide holiday accommodation.

SÃO MIGUEL TYPE These are similar to the so-called 'Dutch' type and are found mainly on São Miguel, Santa Maria and Graciosa, with small differences between those on each island. They have a conical stone-built base with a wooden semi-ovoid rotating roof, and have four cloth-covered sails.

FAIAL TYPE This has a truncated cone-shaped stone base with a substantial timber upper structure called a *casota*, or 'little house'. Access is by a staircase which also acts as a central tail to the casota. Originally it should have had a long mast

As you go around the different islands variations emerge: Santa Maria has white houses with coloured bars marking the shapes and windows and Algarve-style prismatic chimneys, while on Pico, houses are black with no plaster on the walls and balconies running along the upper floors are accessed via outside staircases. On Terceira a long house is common, with its row of windows and doors with the kitchen at one end indicated by the presence of the broad chimneys called *de mãos postas* ('with joined hands'). On São Miguel low window–door–window-style houses are more frequent, similar to those in the Alentejo or, in some areas, houses with their gable end directly on the street. Variations can also be seen in the generally very simple decorative elements, focused around the windows and doors: mouldings of curved lines; the *aventais* (aprons) of the windows outlined in black; the characteristic staircase eye-windows decorated with geometric motifs, possibly Arabic in influence; or the windows with wrought-iron balconies, with a more cultivated influence. Another very common element, especially in the islands of the Central Group, is the bands of basalt that cut vertically and horizontally across the façades, as a form of proof against earthquakes.

Religious architecture

On approaching any Azorean village from the sea, the most prominent feature is always the more or less imposing façade of a church. The most notable in this respect is the view of Horta on Faial, with the façades of the parish church, the Convent of São Francisco and the Carmelite monastery dominating the group of houses and 'gazing out to sea'. Hills near the villages are

with a pointed tip and eight crossed poles tied by guides and wire fasteners for triangular cloth sails, without bars. Today it is almost always of the square type, or is even replaced by rotors of two or four vanes. This type of windmill is to be seen on Faial and Pico.

SÃO JORGE TYPE São Jorge has two types of windmill: the mechanical mill now most commonly seen is a modified form of an earlier mill. This earlier version had four triangular sails made of cloth without lattice work. The later, adapted version has a stone-built conical base upon which is a narrow vertical mill providing an elevated support for the rotor of either two or four blades. This small mill can either rotate or be fixed, in which case only the dome rotates. The narrow tail leads either from the body of the mill or its dome, reaching to the ground.

CORVO TYPE Corvo's distinctive type has a low stone base and a squat conical tower, almost always rendered and whitewashed. The tower is built well inside the edges of the base so there is a wide ledge all round. The mast is long and pointed, leans upwards at a low angle and has eight sail poles with guides and fasteners for triangular cloth sails. Internal access is through a door in the tower reached by an external stone stairway rising from the ledge.

often topped by little pilgrimage chapels; of the many scattered through the islands perhaps the most striking is the group of chapels and pilgrimage houses of Nossa Senhora da Ajuda above the small town of Santa Cruz da Graciosa, among which is also what is perhaps the best example of a fortified church with huge buttresses, decorative battlements and ribbed vaults inside.

In addition to the various types of chapel, you'll also see one of the most peculiar and unique aspects of the archipelago's heritage: the *impérios* (small shrines) of the Holy Spirit. Linked to age-old beliefs, the impérios are fundamental to the ritual practices of this extraordinary cult which exists in the Azores since the times of their earliest settlement but on the mainland disappeared long ago. Here again variations can be seen between the various islands, but the most famous are those on Terceira, immediately recognisable for their festive appearance, bright colours and designs, and triangular pediment.

In spite of limited resources, religious art in the Azores always had the benefit of fine talents and this enabled the islands to keep up with the artistic developments of mainland Portugal. The initial period, until the mid 16th century, was characterised by Gothic-Manueline architecture, and is represented by almost all the surviving early parish churches of the main towns; for example those of São Sebastião in Ponta Delgada and of São Sebastião on Terceira. Then followed a long period of Portuguese classicism, known as *estilo chão* (plain architecture) because of its bare, austere and purely functional style exemplified by the Cathedral of Angra and the parish church of Santa Cruz on Graciosa. The majority of monastic buildings in the Azores belong to this group, in spite of decorative alterations during the Baroque period, of which fine examples include Nossa Senhora da Graça in Ponta Delgada and São Boaventura in Santa Cruz on Flores.

The religious way of life, with its ritual of offerings, processions and pilgrimages, had its origins in the mendicant orders established in the early Middle Ages in continental Europe. Monks came to the Azores during the early phase of settlement (15th century), the Franciscans being the most prominent; their monasteries soon sprang up in every town and city. Later on the Jesuits joined them. Soon after receiving papal approval, in 1540, the Company of Jesus promoted the building of great and elaborate colleges for the whole Portuguese Empire, including the islands. By royal initiative, the Colégio da Ascenção in Angra (the present Palácio dos Capitães-Generais) was founded in 1570, then the Colégio de Ponta Delgada, dedicated to All Saints (1591) and only much later, in 1680, the Colégio de São Francisco Xavier in Horta (today the seat of the parish church, municipal hall, treasury and museum). The present churches of Angra and Ponta Delgada are not, however, the original ones, there being various reconstructions and additions in later years.

Baroque architecture is well represented in the islands, particularly on São Miguel. It was dominant throughout the 18th and early 19th centuries, and is characterised by exuberant sculptural and decorative forms. Monastery churches entirely rebuilt or substantially altered (for example, the Monastery dos Frades in Lagoa, São Miguel; Santo André, c1744; Esperança, 1740–86, and Conceição (Carmo), c1754, all in Ponta Delgada; São Gonçalo, Angra, 1730–50) use black basalt in capricious curves, highly indented mouldings, twisted columns, garlands and medallions, which form the new decorative language. The reconstruction of the Parish Church of São Pedro de Ponta Delgada (1737–42) was developed on an octagonal plan, original for the period, and the idea was repeated in the Parish Church of Fajã de Baixo. The Church of Santo Espírito, on the island of Santa Maria (18th century), is another example of originality, this time with the application of a dense and compact decoration, which is reminiscent of South American Baroque. Private chapels were often associated with the construction of Baroque manor houses such as Santa Catarina in Ponta Delgada; also typical of the 18th century were extravagant Baroque *misericórdias*, institutions for the poor offering medical care, food and other charitable benefits.

Military architecture Because of their strategic location between Europe and the New World the Azores were important for shipping, especially the returning treasure ships, but the islands were constantly threatened by corsairs. During the reigns of Dom João III and Dom Sebastião in the mid 16th century, a series of fortifications were begun 3km apart around the coast, with São Miguel, Terceira and Flores the most fortified. Construction was inspired by Renaissance technology and supervised by Italian military engineers; examples are São Brás in Ponta Delgada and Santa Cruz in Horta. In Angra on Terceira the castle of São Filipe, later renamed São João Baptista, was built during Philippine sovereignty (1580–1640), again as part of a general defence plan; construction was supervised by the Portuguese military engineer João de Vilhena and the Italian fortification specialist Tiburzio Spanochi, and was only completed after the Restoration. Practically impregnable, the castle benefited from the natural situation of Monte Brasil and included, on the landward side of the isthmus, a defensive platform with bulwarks and powerful curtain walls with deep moats. By this device the forces loyal to the Spanish crown were able to resist for long months after the King of Portugal took power.

Surprisingly few vestiges of this vast military effort are left to us. This is probably due to two factors. First, the quality of the constructions varied since often, with an attack imminent, the work was organised by the town hall and executed by the population using the materials and technology immediately to hand. Second, advances in warfare made many buildings obsolete, so that they were abandoned and left to the mercy of the elements and vandalism. Only more recently has the historical and architectural value of this heritage been recognised and efforts are slowly being made to save it from total ruin.

PAINTING AND DECORATIVE ARTS Most paintings, carvings, glazed tiles, furniture and gold artefacts in the Azores come from studios abroad following commissions made in a religious context. Only in a few cases are the artist or school, those who commissioned the item and the iconographic association known to us. On the whole, however, the quality of the work is comparable to the rest of Portugal, with the obvious exception of the royal court.

As with the architecture, genuinely Gothic artefacts are extremely rare. One of them is the triptych of the Virgin Mary in the Anjos chapel (on Santa Maria), a portable altarpiece that according to tradition belonged to Christopher Columbus, on which Gothic designs can be distinguished. Another example is the murals of the Church of São Sebastião on Terceira.

Later 16th-century **Flemish art** is much more visible in the archipelago, both in works imported from the workshops of Antwerp, Brussels and Mechelen, and in the works of local artists who succumbed to a veritable passion for the Flemish style. There were strong trade and cultural links with this northern European region in the 15th and 16th centuries, due to Flemish settlement and the significant trade in woad and urzela, two dye plants used in the textile industry.

Imported Flemish art includes numerous small sculptures such as the *Virgin and Child* (Horta Museum), *St Sebastian tied to a dry tree trunk* (Ponta Delgada Museum), or the larger sculpture *Our Lady of the Miracles* in the Church of Vila

1

do Corvo, all from Mechelen. More elaborate and emotionally charged is the *Crucifixion and Saint Mary Magdalen* (Horta Museum), a delicate work that must have come from the hands of a Brussels artist around 1520. Another theatrical composition is the *Christ Being Taken Down from the Cross*, probably also from the 15th century, in the church of Altares on Terceira. A moving group presents the scene of *Our Lady, St John and the Holy Women*, with Roman soldiers and citizens; at the bottom you can see skulls, the bones of Adam and some souls from purgatory. Probably also of Flemish influence, but from the first half of the 17th century, is the magnificent sculpture of *Our Lady of the Tears* (Church of São Pedro, Ponta Delgada), a powerfully modelled work of great expressiveness.

Among paintings, the triptych of *Saint Andrew* (Church of Nossa Senhora da Estrela, Ribeira Grande, on São Miguel), which came from the chapel of the same name, is a 16th-century work whose Flemish affiliation is obvious in the drawing and sculptural appearance of the figures, the warm colours and delicate play of light on the background landscape, made in perspective. Although more archaic, the Flemish influence is visible also in the magnificent triptych of the *Adoration of the Magi* (Angra Museum) and in the painting of *Saint Ursula and the Eleven Thousand Virgins*, commissioned by the Jesuits of Angra perhaps in the late 16th century, in which a Mannerist style is already evident.

Purely Portuguese painting also achieved very high standards in the 16th century. Some exceptionally good works of this period can be seen in the Azores, including the polyptych in the Church of Santa Cruz da Graciosa depicting scenes from the Passion of Christ and the Legend of the True Cross, and showing all the late-Renaissance pathos that characterises this work. In the recently renovated Carlos Machado Museum in Ponta Delgada, there are two paintings from the Coimbra studio of Manuel Vicente and Vicente Gil, with Gothic-style features, as well as the polyptych of the *Holy Martyrs of Lisbon*, by an anonymous artist but from a major Lisbon studio, closer to the Italian Renaissance style.

The **Counter-Reformation** movement, the setting up of the Inquisition in Portugal (1547) and Catholic orthodoxy dictated by the Council of Trent (1545–63) dealt a serious blow to artistic expression; painting became increasingly conventional. Altarpieces developed a tendency for compositional repetition and the command of anatomical detail became somewhat precarious. In spite of that there were still some worthwhile works of art, linked to the Italian or Spanish school. These include *Our Lady with Angel Musicians*, commissioned by Ponta Delgada's Jesuits from Vasco Pereira for the Church of Ponta Delgada (now in the Carlos Machado Museum) and produced in Seville in 1604, and a set of Mannerist paintings by Francisco Álvares in the sacristy of the Church of São Pedro (Ponta Delgada). Outstanding is the group of eight anonymous paintings of the infancy of Christ, for the Church of São Gonçalo in Angra; it is already linked to the early Baroque and shows a clear Italian influence. Simultaneously with the imposition of artistic conventionality ran the taste for luxury and ostentation in religious rituals; this led to churches being covered in gilded carvings, panels of glazed tiles and altars adorned with gold, silver and marble.

Sailing ships arriving from the **Orient** brought new riches: marble figurines of the Good Shepherd in the meditative pose of the Buddha or Virgins in Glory with oriental features and a hieratic pose, of which a collection can be seen in the Carlos Machado Museum. Others include Indo–Portuguese counters with inlays of marble and mother-of-pearl (examples in Angra Museum and the Palácio de Sant'Ana in Ponta Delgada) and bookcases designed to hold the plainsong books (Ponta Delgada parish church, Angra Cathedral). In the same way Chinese porcelain –

pots, vases, plates and platters – was brought by the Companhia das Índias from the 17th to the 19th centuries, as were Hindu tapestries which greatly influenced the designs of glazed tiles. Worthy of special mention in the context of Hindu–Portuguese art originating from the Malabar coast (Goa) and Sri Lanka are the two paintings in the Church of Santa Cruz da Graciosa, depicting Saints Francisco Xavier and Inácio de Loyola in long robes with golden adornments, brought in during the 17th century.

Portuguese art makes great use of **glazed tiles** (*azulejos*) that bring colour and brightness to architectural space and can be used to depict natural scenes, tell stories in narrative sequences or extend architectural patterns by illusion. There was no local production in the Azores, so these are the product of commissions from the mainland where they have been made for centuries. After the phase of Hispano–Arabic glazed tiles, some 16th-century examples of which are in various Azorean chapels (the most complete comes from Seville and is now in the Museu Municipal (formerly Casa da Cultura) at Ribeira Grande), Portuguese azulejo-making expanded, patterns diversified and new techniques developed. There are polychrome altar fronts with a symmetrical composition and plant motifs, directly inspired by oriental textiles, which were once in shrines and chapels. Good examples are to be seen in the Carlos Machado Museum; the sets are full of peacocks, vases of flowers and friezes of exotic animals. There is also the pediment of the private chapel of the Chaves, now in the Palácio de Sant'Ana in Ponta Delgada; another is from the chapel of Anjos, on the island of Santa Maria, dating from 1679. Equally abundant are the wall coverings with blue, white and yellow glazed tiles, called *padronagem de tapete*; they repeat stylised plant motifs, applied inside decorative borders. A fine example of these is the 17th- and 18th-century glazed tiles that completely line the beautiful chapel of the Monastery of Caloura (São Miguel). Entirely Mannerist are the tiles from the sacristy of the Church of São José de Ponta Delgada, Church of São Roque (São Miguel), chapel of the Almas of the Church of São Francisco de Vila do Porto (Santa Maria), and Church of Conceição de Angra (Terceira).

In the **Baroque** period glazed tiles reached their zenith in terms of figurative, narrative compositions in blue and white. There are many examples. Among the finest are the panels in the lower choir of the Church of Esperança (Ponta Delgada) by António de Oliveira Bernardes, dated 1712 and relating scenes from the Passion

WOMEN IN BLACK

1

On São Jorge, the island of black lava rocks, many women were always seen in black. Religious custom required any widow to dress in black for the rest of her life. Apart from black clothes, she had to wear a black-fringed square shawl and have her head covered by a triangular woollen scarf. After a loss of a parent, black was obligatory for two or three years; the loss of a brother meant black clothes for a year.

Many women therefore spent most of their life in black. The rule was less strict for the men: mourning was expressed by a simple black band on the upper arm, except for Sundays when they all took out their black suits; this was usually the suit made for the wedding and used until the last journey to the cemetery. In the last 20 years, young people have adopted the colour black as a fashion statement, and under American influence, the widows are changing slowly to wearing grey and even some colours, but in the countryside the traditional black persists.

of Christ; and the tiling of the main chapel in the Church of São José (Ponta Delgada) and in the Church of São Francisco in Horta: both illustrate the life of St Francis of Assisi and date from the same period. Also in Horta and worthy of special mention is the set from the parish church (former church of the Jesuit monastery) with scenes relating the life of Saint Inácio de Loyola. In Angra the glazed tiles which line the Church of São Roque (c1725) are worth seeing; in Livramento there is a fine picture depicting the Sermon of St Anthony to the Fishes; and the chapel of the Santíssimo Sacramento in the Church of Nossa Senhora do Monte do Carmo, with an excellent allegorical composition on the Eucharist, is one of the finest works in the archipelago, made in Lisbon around 1740.

The **Rococo** period is represented in the Azores by some top-quality pieces. The return of polychromy, the spread of borders, bands, garlands, shells and other forms of decorative framing of great linear elegance, make the aesthetics of this Baroque period easily identifiable. The little Church of Santa Bárbara das Manadas on the island of São Jorge has one of the finest sets of polychrome glazed tiles with *rocaille* (shell) motifs, as well as locally made carvings and paintings, which make this church a precious example of the alliance between cultivated and naïve art. Other examples of Rococo glazed tiles are in São Pedro de Alcântara at Lajes do Pico and in the Church of Santa Cruz da Graciosa. In the Piedade chapel in the Church of São José (Ponta Delgada), the Rococo glazed tiles are combined with mouldings consisting of gilded carvings on white backgrounds.

Azorean Baroque is not expressed just in richly decorated glazed tiles; the entire church interior is usually full of gilded carvings, paintings and painted wood. The history of **woodcarving** also goes back a long way but again it peaked in the Baroque period, especially during the reign of King John (Dom João V), when many shipments of gold came from Brazil, enabling the carvings to be gilded. The Renaissance retables (carved and sometimes painted panels behind the altar) are replaced by Baroque-style ornamentation with twisted columns, fluttering angels, birds pecking at grapes and drawn-back curtains. Examples can be found in almost every church; particularly rich are those in the Church of São Gonçalo, Angra; in the main chapel of the Church of Esperança, Ponta Delgada, covering the whole vault; in the Parish Church of Horta; and the most imposing of all the Azorean retables, the one in the main chapel of the Church of the Jesuits in Ponta Delgada, already in transition to Rococo style.

The range of **devotional sculptures** is impressive, if not always of great quality. In addition to the gallery of Catholic saints and tutelary figures, the Virgin in Glory is a favourite theme; Horta parish church contains one of the most spectacular examples. Other subjects include the Holy Family, the cycle of Christ's Passion, including *pietàs*, and nativities such as in the churches in Vila Franca do Campo (on São Miguel) and Angústias in Horta.

Throughout this period in which religious art dominated, gold work was associated with liturgical ritual. A vast range of ornaments and precious objects, including chalices, salvers, monstrances, incense boats, censers, chandeliers, candlesticks, crucifixes, processional crosses, etc, today fill the church treasuries and are still used in worship. Only a few genuinely old pieces have survived the centuries of constant plundering by pirates, for whom churches and monasteries were a particularly rewarding target. The processional cross of the Church das Altares on Terceira is a late Gothic rarity, Flemish-made; also unique is the altar front in wrought silver in the Chapel of the Sacramento in Angra Cathedral (17th century), probably Spanish in origin. Much more common, yet having enormous symbolic significance for the Azoreans, are the Crowns of the Holy Spirit in wrought silver, some dating back to the 17th century. In material riches and artistic value, however, nothing surpasses the treasury of Senhor Santo Cristo (Santuário da Esperança, Ponta Delgada). Consisting essentially of five pieces (*Glory, Crown, Sceptre, Cords* and *Reliquary*) that accompany the figure of Ecce Homo, originally designed and made in the 18th century during the reign of João V, it was later enriched with new gifts from the faithful. The *Glory* stands out, a fabulous piece weighing 4.85kg; it is made of gold-plated platinum and contains 6,842 precious stones, among them four extremely rare topazes from Brazil. Made in Lisbon by the finest goldsmiths of João V, the *Glory* presents a complete lesson in theology, containing the symbols of the Trinity, Redemption and the Passion of Christ, all executed with wonderful precision and detail.

Gradually moving away from the religious context, the 19th and 20th centuries began to place art in the service of a bourgeois public with secular ideas. The initially timid decorative schemes that the Azorean nobility used in their manor houses and town houses (an unusual example dating from the 1940s is the glazed tile panels alluding to the loss of independence and restoration of Portugal in the Palácio Bettencourt in Angra) gradually expanded and diversified. The new urban and Liberal bourgeoisie, grown rich on the orange trade, contracted artists to paint their portraits and indulged in luxurious furniture, porcelain and textiles bought in England or France. Ambitious artists went to Paris to receive a proper academic training; notably Marciano Henriques da Silva (1831–73) and Duarte Maia (1867–1922), the first a romantic, the second a naturalist, both with work in the Carlos Machado Museum, Ponta Delgada.

The **20th century** began with a new generation of artists who gathered in Paris, the city of light, along with many others seeking inspiration from the artistic avant-garde. Two Azoreans stand out: **Domingos Rebelo** (1891–1975) and **Ernesto Canto da Maia** (1890–1981). Rebelo, a painter, caricaturist and ceramicist, followed a path that diverged from the vanguard, focusing all his attention on local reality, on the landscapes, appearances and attitudes of the simple and common people that he perceived as the most authentic aspect of this landscape, and capturing them with the detail of an ethnographer. His most famous work, *Os Emigrantes (The Emigrants)*, portrays with contained feeling the drama experienced by thousands of Azoreans obliged to leave the islands in search of a better future. His paintings may be seen in the Palácio da Conceição, Museu Carlos Machado, Viseu, Caldas da Rainha, The Gulbenkian Foundation for Modern Art and Arte Contemporânea in Lisbon, and in countless private collections.

Sculptor Canto da Maia embraced Parisian life with enthusiasm, showing in his synthetic and graphic style traces of the symbolism and stylised decorativeness of the 1920s and 1930s. Even so, his work reflects the deeper quest of a probing mind, meditating upon the themes of life, death and love. Examples of his works can be found in the Núcleo de Santa Bárbara in Ponta Delgada (page 87), The Gulbenkian Foundation, Musée des Années 30 in Boulogne, and the Musée Jeu de Paume in Paris, as well as in various public spaces.

In 1901, Carlos and Amélia, the Portuguese royal couple, officially visited the Azores. Their temporary residence was to be the Palácio de Sant'Ana in Ponta Delgada, and the occasion was a perfect excuse for the most complete decorative renovation that had ever been carried out in a non-religious context. From 1915 to the late 1930s, painters, sculptors, decorators and carvers, both Azorean and from the continent, worked at Sant'Ana. Worth examining are the enormous paintings in the vestibule by Ernesto Condeixa, referring to the royal visit; the frieze in the former armoury; a bas-relief in gilded plaster of Paris by Canto da Maia; and the dining room lined with magnificent carved panelling and furniture entirely made

The Festival of the Holy Ghost differs a little from island to island and from village to village and São Jorge celebrates the festival in its own way. Every village that has a church also has a small shrine called an *império*. The festival extends beyond its religious role; it is also a good excuse to have a great time.

The old traditions can still be enjoyed in the village of Rosais; they are centred on the *Carro das bandeiras* – an oxcart carrying a boat constructed from bamboo canes and green leaves and decorated on all sides with paper flowers, with colourful flags waving from long canes on the top. The carts are not just decorative, they have an important role: to bring to the império wine, sweet bread, cheese and lupin seeds. The lupin seeds have to be soaked in seawater for three tides, after which they are boiled. The festive food is then served free to all visitors during the Saturday. Usually there are two carts and much rivalry exists between them. The ornaments with which the horns of the oxen are decorated are kept strictly secret until the festive day and can never be repeated.

Independent of the religious festival is Mordomia, in which anyone in the village can participate, after joining one of many local groups. Donations of corn and other products are made, usually the previous year, and sold, and the proceeds are used to help with the preparation of the festival. The remaining expenses are divided between the members of individual organising groups. Mordomias are organised by most villages on São Jorge, so don't be surprised if you see cars stopped in the middle of the street to be offered some wine and sweet bread. These celebrations take place on the Saturday before the Festival of the Holy Ghost.

The organiser of the religious festival is called the *imperador* and is usually someone who has undertaken the work voluntarily. These types of festivals are increasingly expensive to organise because in some villages, like Beira and Topo, there is a tradition to invite anyone who passes through to eat for free. In the past people did not have cars to get about and only local people came for the

by local artists. There are also extensive glazed-tile pictures made by the painter Jorge Colaço.

In the second half of the 20th century, particularly in the last two decades, Azorean arts blossomed. Art exhibitions and galleries of fine arts were supported and new art programmes initiated. Throughout its history, Azorean art has mirrored movements in Europe, and developed its own style affected by local conditions and materials. In the 21st century, the internet adds to the external influences, while artists and photographers pursue contemporary Azorean themes and concerns.

FESTIVALS These are many, both religious and secular, which take place on all the islands, mostly during the summer months. They are listed in each island's chapter; some festivals are common to all the islands, while others are island-specific. Some dates are fixed, others change each year, and you should check with the tourist information office. Visitors during the summer months will be very unlucky not to chance upon one during their stay; they are often joyful occasions and the kindness and generosity given to strangers make for happy memories.

The most important festival celebrated throughout the archipelago is that of the **Holy Ghost (Espírito Santo)**, held on the seventh Sunday after Easter. It can also be repeated on the following Sunday if enough people have made promises to make the festival, and if emigrants come back to visit in the summer it can again meal. Now the feast can attract many people from the entire island and it can be crowded. The village of Manadas has its festivities at lunchtime on the Thursday before the Holy Ghost day. Food is served on long tables, sometimes outside in the street. There is a special Holy Spirit soup, wine, *alcatra* sweet bread and sweet rice for dessert.

In Rosais you can also see the *foliões*: two or three men, one or two playing drums and another singing, in front of the império and walking up and down the square. The singing is improvised, sometimes repeated; it can be about God and the kindness of the Holy Ghost, or it can praise the organisation. The musicians are accompanied by the *cavaleiro*, a young man with two helpers. The cavaleiro carries a flag and the helpers bring two huge loaves of bread, called the castles, usually quite hard because they are so big (100cm × 50cm). On Sunday afternoon after the mass and the procession, the foliões and the cavaleiro perform a traditional dance with the bread, to the accompaniment of the drums and the singing. After that there is a merry game for all. The cavaleiro comes out of the império with a cake or dolls made of sweet bread in his hands, and attempts a dance, to be accosted suddenly by someone trying to steal the cake and run away with it. The helpers must then run behind and try to touch the thief with a rod. If they succeed, the thief has to return the cake; if he escapes, the cake is his. The more people that take part, the more fun there is to be had.

In Norte Grande, each evening of that week a big dog-whelk shell is blown to call everyone to the imperador's house. The sound carries round the entire village. The imperador then invites the guests to sing the rosary at his house, where he keeps an altar made especially for this event. It is decorated with candles and flowers and at the top is the crown of the Holy Ghost. The rosary is sung in a way unique to this event. After the rosary, the imperador offers sweets and drinks to all comers.

be celebrated. Of 13th-century medieval origin imported from the mainland, it is one of the most traditional festivals, although each island and each village has its own variation. On the chosen day, offerings of bread, meat and wine are distributed among the needy, followed by a procession through the town or village. You may notice small, pretty shrines called impérios in most of the villages at road junctions or on prominent corners. These are a source of great pride and they form the centrepoint of the **Espírito Santo Festival**. This festival is under the direction of a local group of men, a brotherhood, who undertake the care of the impérios and the giving of food to the poor, an important feature of Espírito Santo. Above the doors of most impérios you will find symbols: the crown, the sceptre, the dove and a red banner. The symbols are also to be found on the silver crowns which are worn by the imperador, the member of the brotherhood in charge of that day's festivities. Several imperadores may be crowned in each village during the festival season and each has the honour of guarding the crown and sceptre on a throne in his home until the next procession. Some of these precious village crowns and sceptres are many hundreds of years old. Fireworks signal the end of the opening church service and the start of a procession from the church to the império led by the crowned imperador. Music is provided by the local brass marching band, or *filarmonica*. These bands are a major part of village life in the Azores, where there are more such groups than in all of Portugal. After the procession, a beef-based broth, called *sopa do Espírito Santo*, is served along with another Azorean food with a strong tradition: *massa sovada*, a slightly sweet bread made in homes by groups of women taking turns during hours of hand-kneading. This festival, brought by the first settlers to the islands in the early 1400s, is seldom seen in Europe today, but is celebrated by communities of Azorean ancestry around the world, especially in the USA, including Hawaii, and in Canada.

Other festivals are for saints' days or for vows made long ago to God. The most colourful is the **Festival of Corpus Christi** in June, and the preparation is as interesting as the procession. Early in the morning many baskets of various small colourful flowers and finely chopped soft branch tips of the conifer *Cryptomeria japonica* are brought in and laid out in geometrical patterns upon the roadway using wooden templates, the colours all kept in separate shapes. The flowers and petals are frequently sprayed with water to keep them fresh and to stop the wind from disturbing the patterns or blowing them away. Sometimes dyed woodshavings are also used. Summer flowers in baskets and pots adorn balconies, and bright bedcovers hanging from windows add further colour. The procession is led by the priest under a pallium escorted by his followers and many small children dressed as angels. Much less formal is the June **Festival of São João**, marked with picnics at the many barbecue sites throughout the islands. The secular festivals get bigger every year and are celebrated by music, dance, arts, local culture, food stalls and sporting events. Music includes not only folk, but also pop groups from the mainland and Brazil, something not always viewed with enthusiasm by everyone.

Tourada à corda (bullfights on a rope)

In the Portuguese version of bullfighting, the bulls are not killed and the only blood spilt is that of overconfident humans. Terceira is especially noted for its *tourada à corda*, but other islands also participate.

The organisers have introduced regulations and planned a classification system for the bulls. No more than four bulls are allowed at any one event. Each must be at least three years old, and can appear only once for no more than 30 minutes. Cloaks and similar items are allowed, but anything that could cause injury to the bulls is banned. Action can only take place during daylight, and in the late afternoon/early evening. In practice, they mostly start around 18.00, between 1 May and 15 October, almost daily during July and August, with some 50 runs in the latter month.

The bull is at the end of a long rope that is held by several men to try to keep him under some control. The fun comes in approaching the bull as close as one dares and then outmanoeuvring him while keeping clear of his horns. One year, the bull really got up speed and chased five boys the length of the quay. Having nowhere else to go, they leapt off the end into the harbour and the bull had so much momentum he could not stop and went in on top of them to a tremendous cheer from the crowd and creating a huge tidal wave. The bull appeared to rather enjoy it, a nice cooling swim to the slipway at the end of a warm afternoon! Terceira and Graciosa both have bullrings, but here the bull is let loose without a rope.

These events have become very popular, with over 200 meetings each year. Dating back to the 16th century, in the past it was not only an entertainment but also an excuse for people from different villages to meet, both socially and for business. Animals could be bought and sold, goods traded or exchanged, youths could demonstrate to the girls their dash and courage with the bulls, there would be refreshment stalls and it was all huge fun. It still is.

2

Practical Information

These mid-Atlantic islands are nothing if not green. This means the weather is variable, and while at any time there can be a week or more of continuous glorious sunshine and blue skies, it can also be fickle.

You will be welcomed everywhere and find that English is widely spoken in the main towns, but when you enter a café away from the main centres or seek directions out in the country you might have fun trying to communicate. You should also be very safe, for there is little crime or street violence in the Azores. Although drugs and alcohol are problems locally, they are no more so than elsewhere in western Europe.

Ferry services and domestic flights keep reasonably well to the timetables except for understandable delays through bad weather – in the case of aircraft this can just be wind or fog affecting certain airports. Communications are excellent, the islands and their public facilities are very clean, and standards are high.

The cost of many items is greater than in mainland Portugal but compared with northern Europe or the United States prices are still reasonable, and the well-informed budget traveller can certainly get by comfortably. In winter it begins to get dark about 18.30, in summer about 21.00, and the time is Greenwich Mean Time –1.

WHEN TO VISIT

There are small variations between the individual islands, with Santa Maria seen as the sunniest, while the western islands of Corvo and Flores are the wettest. July to September are the warmest months and should have the most stable weather. November to January are the wettest. April and September tend to be the most changeable, but all the old patterns are changing, like everywhere else in the world. Every month is a delight in the Azores and even in January it can be possible to enjoy the walker's lunch ritual of local cheese, fresh bread and a bottle of wine, sitting in a field in bright sunshine without jackets or jerseys.

The time to go depends upon what you want to do. If it is to do with the sea – inter-island ferry travel, whale watching, sailing or fishing – then you need to go between mid-April and early October. People swim throughout the year, but the popular times for the beaches are again the summer months and into October. Remember that the Azores are not beach destinations, however. Regarding flowers, there will always be something of interest but May to September is the recommended time for native species, and to see the beautiful and spectacular hedgerows at their best you should consider June and July. For walking, the whole year is good, but the rain in winter is usually colder than in summer. In winter you will also have to take extra care in the mountains. In summer there are more accommodation and eating places open, and the latter keep longer opening hours. During the high season of

July and August hotels are usually fully booked and the casual traveller may have difficulty in getting accommodation. Some accommodation establishments close for a short period of repose between November and January, so advanced booking is advisable. In high summer – July and August – it is almost impossible to rent a car on arrival and advance reservation is essential; similarly for bicycles. Increasingly this is becoming the case in June and September, as the growing visitor numbers cause a lengthening of the busy season. In addition, many Azoreans who emigrated to North America return to see relatives, particularly at festival times, while second and third generations come to discover their roots. March and April, still officially low season, are beautiful months because spring is usually early in the Azores and by now nature is wide awake; autumn is a much longer season than in northern Europe, and October and November have lovely warm days while the golden hues of falling leaves prevail into December. And December is the Christmas festival season, when every town is festooned with lights and decorations in a very Azorean way that is so charming and largely devoid of commercialism.

HIGHLIGHTS

The greatest attraction for many is the tranquillity and the lack of pollution: the quiet rural scenes of small houses, the pastures, the grazing cows on a stage of lush green grass and the backdrop of a deep blue sea, farmers on horseback with milk churns hanging from their saddles, the little pony cart clattering along the cobbles with more milk churns, and cattle dogs perched on top. The scenery is the true star of the Azores: ever-changing, from sea to coast and often spectacular cliffs, to pastures or stony vineyards, up into forests and hills of often conical shape until culminating in a volcano's caldera and other heights lost in cloud. Blue hydrangeas and the Azores may have become a cliché but to see an island seeming as if a fisherman's net with extra-large holes had been thrown over it creating a pattern of blue lines and enclosures remains, all the same, a remarkably lovely sight.

Even the largest towns, including relatively busy Ponta Delgada, have an irresistible allure that urges the visitor to explore them. Many ordinary street buildings have an elegant simplicity with lovely adornments of wrought-iron balconies or perhaps some ornamented basalt carving while grander places may show a more ornate Manueline influence. Small retailers are modest and sometimes do not even bother to advertise their presence while often the stock is held in dark recesses so that it is difficult even to decipher what it is they are selling. Frustrating? No – simply refreshing. The narrow cobbled backstreets have constricted pavements while bigger thoroughfares have grander ones; whatever their size they are made of small cubes of black basalt and imported white granite that is used to make designs appropriate to the place: caravels, whaling boats, whales, fish, figures dressed in the no-longer-worn capote or cloak, windmills, sheaves of corn – there is no end to the pavior's enterprise. For the foot-weary there are pleasant street cafés to enjoy a drink while watching island life pass by, or many a quiet church for deeper contemplation.

The larger islands are perfect for exploring by car, and endless hours can be spent discovering rural roads or following up those that do not appear on maps. There are so many tempting places to park your vehicle and just lean on a fence post and enjoy a view or listen to the birds. Should you tire of rural scenery, then comes the satisfying contrast of dropping down to the coast and into a little village; maybe at its centre is the main church, a tiny public garden with its bandstand, and a café, or perhaps you have chanced upon a fishing village with a harbour and nearby natural swimming pools for an ocean swim and a fish restaurant to follow.

Whale watching has become tremendously popular since it first began on Pico years ago and still uses the old expertise of the lookouts in hilltop towers to spy the cetaceans. It is a truly world-class cetacean hotspot and a single 3-hour trip might reveal two or three whale species and almost certainly some playful dolphins. Numerous enterprises now offer the experience. Diving affords a range of unique opportunities, from wrecks to sea cliffs and extraordinary underwater lava formations, and several companies on many islands offer their services. Many small fishing boats can be seen in the harbours, and if you feel tempted there are fishermen registered to take you out to fish for your supper. At the other end of the spectrum, the Azores are renowned internationally for sport- or big-game fishing, especially for blue marlin, and many world-record catches have been made, although of course these are for putting back in the sea and not for eating.

Going hand in hand with the tranquillity and clean environment are walking and cycling, the finest ways to acquire a real feel for the islands. Several companies offer organised cycling tours, and it is often possible to borrow or hire bicycles from hotels or guesthouses. There are short and long walks, in the mountains, along the coast, sometimes on narrow trails, at other times on seldom-used farm roads. The views are always changing, and relics of the past are everywhere, from wheel-worn donkey paths hidden beneath the summer's flush of vegetation to abandoned farmhouses and crumbling watermills. Hiking routes have been waymarked and documented and are kept reasonably well up to date. Some published walks are short and many are linear rather than circular; the narrative descriptions can be vague and maps weak, but the waymarking itself is good and the whole trails programme is under constant review. Winter storms cause landslides, and vegetation is so lush that in a very few weeks freshly cleared paths are concealed.

For all walks it is best to check with a tourist information office or travel agent that the walk is clear before setting out; also make use of the official trails website (w trails.visitazores.com). One gets the impression that some routes are devised by office-based bureaucrats, and not by a practical ranger or forester on the ground. However, if you are prepared to risk some possible frustration and the need to fall back upon your own sense of direction, you will enjoy many a memorable walk. For those who prefer, guides are available, as listed in the individual island chapters or through the local travel agencies (page 41). A couple of hours' walking with a guide gives you a wonderful opportunity to download information, face-to-face, about the Azores.

The golf course at Furnas (page 95) on São Miguel must be one of the world's most intimate and exquisitely beautiful courses, given its mountain setting with sheltering forests and numerous elegant tree ferns. It is little known, but for any golfer who values the environment and surroundings in which he or she plays, this course cannot fail to impress. However, it is not without hidden challenges, for its luxuriant vegetation reflects its relationship with the clouds, and it can be quite entertaining to drive off into a white mist that has suddenly descended and might well instantly clear to give advantage to your opponent. There are two other equally green courses to play, both at much lower altitudes, at Batalha (also on São Miguel) and on Terceira (pages 95 and 156 respectively), as well as a pitch and putt on Faial.

PLANNING AN ITINERARY: WHICH ISLANDS?

The pace of the Azores is slow, and slowly is how one should discover them. There are nine islands and if you were to attempt to see them all in one visit to the archipelago you would need several weeks to do them justice. Should you try to visit too many islands in a short period you will end up spending a disproportionate amount of time waiting in airports or for ferries. If you have just a week, then you might be well advised to concentrate on the largest and most diverse island, São Miguel, which is also the aviation hub and therefore the most accessible for foreign visitors. If you have more time, maybe combine São Miguel with Faial and Pico, with perhaps Terceira as well for your first visit (these islands will easily take up two weeks) and then see other islands on return visits. Different islands suit different means of touring. Plan your trip carefully and consider hiring a car for just *some* rather than *all* of your stay on each island.

If you like to hire a car and take your time exploring then São Miguel, Santa Maria, Terceira, Pico, São Jorge and Flores would make the best choices.

If you prefer to tour with someone else driving, then much of São Miguel can be accessed by bus. Graciosa is small; there are buses, but distances are so short and taxi fares are reasonable. Terceira largely means the city of Angra, for which you do not need a car, and adjacent Monte Brasil can also be explored on foot. A half-day taxi tour would provide a glimpse of other Terceira highlights, although using buses, which is cheaper, will still allow you to see a fair number of sights. Faial offers Horta and nearby attractions, and a half-day taxi tour will take in the island's main features. Pico can be visited by ferry in a day from Horta, with a half-day tour seeing the western sector, but do stay a night or two there, especially if you intend to conquer the summit of the volcano.

For walkers, São Jorge, São Miguel, Faial and Flores are all excellent, and there is Pico if you want to climb Portugal's highest mountain. In truth, there are now walks on every island. For cycling, São Miguel and Santa Maria are the most developed, with activity companies to guide you, though bikes are easy to rent on Pico too. São Miguel is best for gardens and Pico has the most accessible native flora. Birdwatchers should give priority to São Miguel, São Jorge, Pico and especially Flores and Corvo in the autumn, although the old quarry at Praia on Terceira is also excellent for rare waders at this time, and the airport area of Santa Maria attracts many species as well.

TOUR OPERATORS

In terms of foreign visitors, the Azores are most popular with the Germans, after which come visitors from the USA, the Spanish, French and Dutch and then the British. British numbers 'bounced' after the introduction of budget flights in 2014, and have now levelled off somewhat; visitors from the USA can take advantage of increased direct flights and numbers have soared accordingly. Of course, there is a very heavy Portuguese tourist traffic from the mainland, making up around 55% of the total visitors. For years it has been mostly small companies that have offered this destination to foreigners, but now bigger tour operators are also doing so. Tour operators sell the Azores for their tranquillity, landscapes and authentic way of life. Earlier, the average high-street travel agent knew little about the Azores, and the poor inbound agents in the islands found themselves at the receiving end of irate complaints from clients who had just arrived to realise that there was no constantly blazing sun and endless sandy beaches; this is changing, but still some visitors arrive ill-informed. For those who wish to travel out of the main season or go to different islands from those offered in the standard package, some operators will be able to create a bespoke tour. There are over 20 UK tour operators offering the Azores, including those listed here.

There is an ever-increasing number of **travel agents** based in the Azores, offering the usual services of car hire, hotel reservations, airport transfers, etc. Those listed below offer certain other activities.

INTERNATIONAL TOUR OPERATORS
UK
Archipelago Choice 1b Museum Sq, Keswick, Cumbria CA12 5DZ; ☎01768 721020; e info@ azoreschoice.com; w azoreschoice.com, archipelagochoice.com. Well-established UK operator, offering tailor-made holidays & with a great reputation on the islands.

Biosphere Expeditions The Henderson Centre, Ivy Lane, Norwich NR5 8BF; ☎0870 446 0801; e uk@biosphere-expeditions.org; w biosphere-expeditions.org. Hands-on conservation projects collecting useful data on whales, dolphins & turtles.

Explore Nelson Hse, 55 Victoria Rd, Farnborough, Hampshire GU14 7PA; ☎01252 240 504; e sales@ explore.co.uk; w explore.co.uk. Spring/summer island-hopping tours.

Naturetrek Mingledown Barn, Wolf's Lane, Chawton GU34 3HJ; ☎01962 733051; e info@ naturetrek.co.uk; w naturetrek.co.uk. Whale- & dolphin-watching holidays.

Ramble Worldwide Lemsford Mill, Lemsford, Welwyn Garden City, Hertfordshire AL8 7TR; ☎01707 537 227; e info@rambleworldwide.co.uk; w rambleworldwide.co.uk. Walking holidays, usually covering 4 islands.

Regent Holidays 6th Fl, Beacon Tower, Colston St, Bristol BS1 4XE; ☎01174 536 455; e regent@ regentholidays.co.uk; w regent-holidays.co.uk. A well-established tour operator which includes the archipelago among its worldwide holiday destinations.

Saga Holidays The Saga Bldg, Enbrook Park, Folkestone, Kent CT20 3SE; ☎0800 9885 886; e european.reservations@saga.co.uk; w holiday. saga.co.uk. Island hopping & cruises for the over 50s.

Sunvil Sunvil Hse, Upper Sq, Old Isleworth, Middlesex TW7 7BJ; ☎020 8568 4499; e discovery@sunvil.co.uk; w sunvil.co.uk. One of the leading promoters of responsible tourism, offering the Azores since 1990.

TravelLocal w travellocal.com. A UK-based website where you can book direct with selected local travel companies, allowing you to communicate with a ground operator without having to go through a 3rd-party travel operator or agent. Your booking with the local company has full financial protection, but note that travel to the destination is not included. Member of ABTA, ASTA.

Wexas Travel 45–9 Brompton Rd, London SW3 1DE; ☎020 8125 4260; e europe@wexas.com; w wexas.com. Tailor-made holidays.

Canada
ElderTreks 23 Clinton St, Toronto, ON, M6J 2N9; ☎1 800 741 7956; w eldertreks.com. Specialising in small group tours for the over 50s.

Out Adventures 945 Pape Av, 3rd floor, Toronto, ON, M4K 3V4; ☎from Canada/USA toll-free 1 866 360 1152; from other countries 1 416 531 8795; e info@out-adventures.com; w outadventures. com. LGBTQIA+ friendly group tours.

Netherlands
Girassol Vakanties Gildestraat 1, 1704 AG Heerhugowaard; ☎+31 20 428 0555; e info@tyleintravel.nl; w girassolvakanties.nl, styleintravel.nl

SNP Natuurreizen Molukkenstraat 7, Nijmegen; ☎+31 24 3 27 7000; e info@snp.nl; w snp.nl

USA
Archipelago Choice See left. ☎+1 800 490 0446; e info@azoreschoice.com; w azoreschoice.com, archipelagochoice.com

Biosphere Expeditions (see UK, above; also France, Germany, Ireland) 2801 Ocean Park Bd #1008, Santa Monica, CA 90405; e northamerica@biosphere-expeditions.org; w biosphere-expeditions.org

Journeys International 2531 Jackson Av #341, Ann Arbor, MI 48103; ☎+1 800 255 8735; e info@journeysinternational.com; w journeysinternational.com

Tour Azores 176 Columbia St, Fall River, MA 02721; ☎+1 888 678 9093; e eduard.demelo@ tourazores.com; w tourazores.com

LOCAL TRAVEL AGENTS
Melo Agência de Viagens Rua de Sta Luzia 7–11, Ponta Delgada, São Miguel; ☎296 205 385; e info@melotravel.com; w melotravel.com.

Well-established company with nearly 50 years' experience. Tailor-made holidays are a speciality, as are self-guided programmes for nature lovers. They also pioneered cycling holidays & offer an 8-day package. Daily whale-watching departures are offered in season from São Miguel, Faial & Pico, & a 7-night package on Pico. Again, for individual travellers, 3-, 4- & 5-island tours are available. **Teles Agência de Viagens** Rua da Sé 138, Angra do Heroísmo, Terceira; ☎ 295 213 236; e tta.

angra@telestravel.com; w telestravel.com. Offers a variety of packages from 2 to 10 nights to various islands, an 8-night golf package to Terceira & São Miguel, a week whale watching on Pico, & various anti-stress, recuperation & revitalisation health programmes at the Hotel do Caracol on Terceira. **Whale Watch Azores** c/o Norberto Diver, Marina da Horta, Horta, Faial; ☎ 292 293 891; e info@ whalewatchazores.com; w whalewatchazores. com. Week-long cetacean-watching tours.

TOURIST INFORMATION

The **Azores Tourism Authority** has information offices on all the islands (contact details are given in each island chapter). They publish informative brochures on each island, as well as maps and other publications. Lists of approved hotels, *residenciais* and rural accommodation are all available via its comprehensive website (w visitazores.com). The site also features all sorts of activities and their operators, and details of island walking trails with downloadable maps and guides. To keep right up to date with opening times for the archipelago's numerous natural parks and interpretation centres, the English-language website w parquesnaturais. azores.gov.pt is a useful resource.

Confusingly, as well as the tourist offices, there are also a string of tourist kiosks labelled *Quiosque*, often within spitting distance of the official offices. Why? Politics. Either version of tourist office will have maps and basic information, though the quiosques earn some of their revenues from commissions on selling tours, and during the research for this update, some of the quiosque staff were not able to speak English.

RED TAPE

As the Azores are part of Portugal – a full member of the European Union – nationals of other EU countries do not require a visa. Holders of British, American and 58 other non-EU passports may enter without a visa for up to 90 days in any 180-day period; however, from mid-2025 they will require an ETIAS online pre-authorisation. All others require a visa for the Schengen area.

Should you need **consular assistance** during your stay, a regularly updated list of contact information for those consulates represented in the Azores can be found at w embassypages.com/city/pontadelgada. Largely these responsibilities are undertaken by private individuals in an honorary capacity without official premises. They can issue emergency passports and contact relatives.

GETTING THERE AND AWAY

BY AIR From the UK there are direct flights with **Azores Airlines**, formerly SATA Internacional (w azoresairlines.pt), from Gatwick to Ponta Delgada (São Miguel) every Saturday between April and October, with a flying time of around 4 hours. **Ryanair** (w ryanair.com) currently offers once-weekly, year-round flights on a Tuesday direct from London Stansted to Ponta Delgada. **TAP Air Portugal** (w flytap. com), a Star Alliance member, has departures throughout the year from Heathrow and Gatwick, changing planes in Lisbon, and then onward to Ponta Delgada or less

The standard way of getting to the Azorean islands from the UK is increasingly to book a direct flight from London to your chosen island with Azores Airlines, which will involve a plane-change or stopover in Ponta Delgada. If booking with a budget airline from London, you will have to book a separate inter-island flight with Azores Airlines from Ponta Delgada to your chosen island. However, it *could* be more economical to do things a bit differently. If you are flying to Ponta Delgada, Faial, Pico or Santa Maria **from either Lisbon or Porto**, then Azores Airlines includes a free onward flight to any other island from any of those four 'gateways'. Even if you arrive in the Azores on another airline from Lisbon or Porto, Azores Airlines will provide you with an onward flight to your chosen island, at no extra cost. However, a stipulation is that you cannot stay more than 24 hours in the 'gateway' on your way through, and this is strictly enforced. For foreign visitors, this is how you work it:

• Either on the Azores Airlines website or via their call centre, first check the timing and availability of seats on your intended onward flight from the 'gateway' to your chosen Azorean island.
• If seats are available, then book your flight from your starting destination (London, Amsterdam, Paris, etc) to Lisbon/Porto. Also book your flight from Lisbon/Porto to the 'gateway'.
• Contact Azores Airlines immediately, telling them what flight you want from your 'gateway' to your chosen island, and that you have a flight already booked from Lisbon/Porto to the 'gateway'. You'll have to prove it, and ensure that you have less than 24 hours in Ponta Delgada, but your onward inter-island flight should be provided free.

Why would you bother with all this? Well, going via mainland Portugal *might* work out cheaper than flying directly into Ponta Delgada from your home, and then buying a flight from there to your chosen Azorean island. Also, flights from London, etc, do not service the Azores daily, so might not suit your schedule. For your journey back, the same restriction applies: no more than 24 hours in the Azorean gateway on your way through! You should also consider simply booking an Azores Airlines ticket from your starting point (eg: London) to your final Azorean destination, as this is cheaper than separately booking two flights (eg: starting point to Ponta Delgada, then Ponta Delgada to final destination).

frequently from Lisbon to Horta (on Faial), Lajes (Terceira), Santa Maria and Pico. The second leg of these routings is often operated by Azores Airlines. You could also break your journey and spend some nights in Lisbon or Porto, using TAP's stopover programme – see the airline website for details. Flights take just over 2 hours from the UK to Lisbon and another 2 hours from Lisbon to the Azores.

From the rest of Europe, there are direct flights from Gran Canaria to the Azores and connections through mainland Portugal from Frankfurt, Munich, Amsterdam, Copenhagen and Paris; from Portugal there are direct flights from Faro, Lisbon, Porto and Funchal (Madeira).

From the USA and Canada there are direct Azores Airlines flights throughout the year from Boston, Providence and Toronto to Ponta Delgada, and now a weekly flight from Boston to Terceira. Delta Airlines fly directly once a week from New York JFK. Flights generally increase in summer, and there are indirect code-share flights to/from other US and Canadian cities.

BY SEA

By cruise ship Increasing numbers of cruise ships are calling in at the Azores, particularly at Horta and Ponta Delgada, and this is now a very important part of Azorean tourism. Ponta Delgada receives the most cruise visitors and with a single ship carrying up to 5,000 passengers, the impact on the town's cafés and restaurants can be instantly overwhelming. Small-ship cruises also operate, visiting all nine islands and using onboard Zodiac craft for some excursions. It was in 1867 that the first scheduled cruise ship put in at Horta, steaming from New York on a five-month cruise to the Mediterranean.

Ponta Delgada (São Miguel) The largest town in the Azores has a bespoke terminal complex – *Portas do Mar* or 'Gateways of the Sea', opened in 2008. From the pier into town is just a 200m walk. A separate tourist information office is located on the pier, and around the promenade are shops, a bank and pharmacy, bars and restaurants. Various onshore tours are available, going to some of the places described in the São Miguel chapter, and there are plenty of guides touting for business from the cruise-ship passengers as they disembark. Depending on what shore-time you have available, a trip to Sete Cidades or even Furnas is possible.

Horta (Faial) The cruise-ship quay is about a 1km walk along the harbourfront. Bus excursions usually take in Capelinhos, site of the last Azorean volcano eruption, and its excellent new visitor centre.

Praia da Vitória (Terceira) Cruise ships dock 4km from the town (usually covered by bus excursions). Tourist information is available in town, and excursions to Angra do Heroísmo and other highlights start from the quay.

By yacht Facilities are concentrated in the principal ports, the most popular of which for transatlantic yachts is Horta on Faial. Opened in 1986, and having held the European Blue Flag since 1987, it can take 300 vessels and claims to be the world's fourth-most-visited ocean marina. Second-most popular is Ponta Delgada on São Miguel, with a modern marina taking 470 yachts, followed by Praia da Vitória on Terceira. All three provide fuel, water, waste handling and repair services. Small marinas have also opened in recent years at Velas on São Jorge, Madalena on Pico, Lajes on Flores, Vila do Porto on Santa Maria and Vila Franca do Campo on São Miguel. The website w noonsite.com/Countries/Azores gives the latest information on facilities, immigration, etc, and anchorages on the other islands.

HEALTH *with Dr Daniel Campion*

PREPARATIONS All EEA nationals visiting the Azores are entitled to the reciprocal arrangements covering medical care and expenses but will need the appropriate documentation. Dental treatment will mostly have to be paid for. British nationals should have their Global Health Insurance Card (GHIC), obtainable by phone (℄ 0845 606 2030), online (w services.nhsbsa.nhs.uk/cra/start), or from the post office and some travel clinics. You should in any case have additional private travel insurance. Pregnant women, travellers with pre-existing illnesses and those travelling with children should identify health-care facilities prior to departure. However, larger hotels and tour company representatives are usually able to provide addresses for local services. The Foreign, Commonwealth and Development Office (w gov.uk/fcdo) can provide details of the nearest relevant embassy or consulate for emergencies.

It is wise to be up to date with routine vaccinations in your home country, including MMR and diphtheria, tetanus and polio. Occasionally hepatitis A and hepatitis B vaccines may also be recommended; these will depend more on lifestyle and/or occupation.

Travel clinics and health information A full list of current travel clinic websites worldwide is available on w istm.org. For other journey preparation information, consult w travelhealthpro.org.uk (UK) or w wwwnc.cdc.gov/travel (USA). All advice found online should be used in conjunction with expert advice received prior to or during travel.

MEDICAL PROBLEMS
Insect- and tick-borne infections
A few cases of leishmaniasis from sandflies and West Nile fever from mosquitoes have been reported from the Azores. There are no vaccines against these diseases, so use a good insect repellent on exposed skin, ideally containing the active ingredients DEET 50% or Icaridin 20%. Compared with mainland Europe, human tick-borne infections are rarely reported in the Azores, but check yourself for ticks after hikes in grassy or forested areas (see below for advice on removing ticks).

Rabies Rabies is not considered a risk in the Azores in terrestrial animals, but all bites from animals should be assessed carefully. Rabies vaccine is only recommended for travellers involved in activities that could bring them into direct contact with bats. These travellers include wildlife professionals, researchers, veterinary surgeons, or adventure travellers visiting caves or other areas where bats are commonly found.

Drinking water Tap water in the hotels is generally safe to drink; on some islands it tastes better than some bottled waters. If you have to drink from a

> ### TICK REMOVAL
>
> Ticks should ideally be removed complete, and as soon as possible, to reduce the chance of infection. You can use special tick tweezers, which can be bought in good travel shops; or failing this, with your fingernails, grasp the tick as close to your body as possible, and pull it away steadily and firmly at right angles to your skin without jerking or twisting. Applying irritants (eg: Olbas oil) or lit cigarettes is to be discouraged as a means of removal since they can cause the ticks to regurgitate and therefore increase the risk of disease. Once the tick is removed, if possible douse the wound with alcohol (any spirit will do), soap and water, or iodine. If you are travelling with small children, remember to check their heads, and particularly behind the ears, for ticks. Spreading redness around the bite and/or fever and/or aching joints after a tick bite imply that you have an infection that requires antibiotic treatment. In this case seek medical advice.

potentially unsafe source, you should boil and/or filter the water, or treat it with chlorine tablets. Mineral water is widely sold by the bottle, imported mostly from the mainland, but also sourced locally, and is inexpensive.

HEALTH CARE The hospitals on São Miguel, Terceira and Faial are modern and equivalent to normal European standards. Emergency medical cases have to be flown here from the other islands, where there are limited services. Health centres (*centros médicos*) provide non-hospital treatment.

Pharmacies are widespread, but you should always take a sufficient supply of prescription drugs to more than last the length of your holiday. The pharmacies in larger towns will have a rota for out-of-business-hours opening; if you need anything, ask at your hotel or a police station to see which one is open.

SAFETY

The Azores are considered to be one of the safest places in the world and crime is, on the whole, limited to minor thievery. However, you should sensibly take the same precautions as you would at home. A few beggars operate in Ponta Delgada, but are not aggressive; they seem to be non-existent in other towns.

With the usual common-sense approach, **women** travelling to the Azores on their own should not expect any difficulties or unwanted attention from local males. Foreign females residing in the archipelago report that it is a safe and unthreatening place to live.

The emergency number across the Azores is \112.

TRAVELLING WITH A DISABILITY

The Azores are not geared towards travellers with mobility problems, since narrow cobbled streets and a lack of ramped kerbs don't create a wheelchair-friendly environment. However, latest developments do recognise the difficulties, and some hotels have facilities and adapted rooms. Some beaches are specifically signposted as having ramped access for disabled visitors. Enquiries should be made when booking. Airports have wheelchairs for use on site. New museums are adapted, with some offering information in Braille. Visitors with disabilities requiring assistance or seeking tours or activities adapted to their needs could contact São Miguel-based Cresacor – Azores for All (m 919 538 214; e turismoinclusivo@cresacor.pt; w azoresforall.com), a company that can arrange holidays, help with adapted tours and provide equipment.

The UK's **gov.uk** website (w gov.uk/government/publications/disabled-travellers/disability-and-travel-abroad) has a downloadable guide giving general advice and practical information for travellers with a disability (and their companions) preparing for overseas travel. The **Society for Accessible Travel and Hospitality** (w sath.org) also provides some general information.

Specialist UK-based tour operators that offer trips to the Azores include: **Disabled Holidays** (w disabledholidays.com) and **Disabled Access Holidays** (w disabledaccessholidays.com).

LGBTQIA+ TRAVELLERS

Despite the Azorean culture being a relatively conservative one, and one in which the Church is still strong compared with many parts of the European mainland, it is also very tolerant. As a result, it would be highly unusual for LGBTQIA+ visitors to experience any discrimination; bars are generally relaxed places in which everyone is welcome. Hotels are also tolerant. As in many places, intense displays of public affection – by visitors of any sexual orientation – are found distasteful by some locals. By way of legal background, any discrimination on grounds of sexual orientation is contrary to the Portuguese constitution; same-sex marriage has been recognised since 2010, and the first Azorean Pride festival took place in Ponta Delgada in 2012.

TRAVELLING WITH KIDS

With so many different things to see and do, the Azores are a perfect family destination for those with children who enjoy the outdoors and an active downtime. Swimming has to be approached with caution, but the novelties of bathing in natural rock pools or carefully crafted manmade alternatives will surely excite most youngsters. Biking and hiking are abundantly available, and the more adventurous still can try kayaking, canyoning and coasteering. The islands will also suit inquisitive youngsters, with educational opportunities provided by the volcanic landscapes, geothermal activities, whale watching and nature at its finest.

WHAT TO TAKE

The clothes you take will need to cope with the ever-changing weather so always remember you are in the mid-Atlantic! In summer, the temperatures are generally very comfortable and at sea level it is doubtful if you will need a jersey. In winter, there will also be days when you will not need a jersey, but then for many days at sea level there will be times when you are very pleased to have one, as well as a windproof jacket. At all times you will need to be prepared for weather changes, so waterproofs are recommended, although in summer you may find them too warm and prefer to have an umbrella. It can also be very humid. If travelling in winter, early spring or late autumn, some warm nightclothes or thermal underwear are a good idea, as some accommodation does not have heating.

Many of the streets are cobbled, so wear sensible shoes; you will be handicapped in high heels or fashion shoes. Generally, townspeople dress smartly casual, and cotton items are popular. If heading up into the hills you should always take a windproof and waterproof jacket. Always ensure you have sufficient warm clothing if you are going into the mountains, or if you are making any ferry journeys and like to stay on deck. At lower altitudes many find waterproofs too warm and a poncho style may be more comfortable. Walkers will need to bring their own equipment, including their favoured walking shoes or boots, as outdoor shops are few and far between. Always take water with you. You might find a whistle useful to keep in touch with straying companions should the clouds descend and kill visibility. A mobile phone can be a huge asset.

Hotel laundry services are very good, but for same-day service a 50% surcharge is usually levied, and beware of weekends and public holidays. Finding a self-service laundry is virtually impossible, though service washes can be sourced in Ponta Delgada, Horta and Madalena – tourist offices will advise of their location. They charge by weight, usually around €4/kg, which works out quite expensive. Increasingly, hairdryers are provided in hotel bedrooms, but this should certainly not be relied upon, and in the cheaper hotels there is not always a shaver socket. The electricity supply is 220V, the standard in western Europe, and the plugs are the usual continental European two-pin.

Budget travellers should take a towel as those provided in cheaper accommodation are often thin and very small, and hostels don't usually provide any; a universal basin plug can be useful.

Photographers using a digital SLR camera could usefully take a standard UV filter to minimise glare off the sea – and protect the lens at the same time. In winter the light is wonderfully clear and sharp and there are some dramatic results to be had.

MONEY AND BUDGETING

MONEY Portugal is a member of the European Monetary Union and the currency is the euro. Most banks in the main centres have plentiful multilingual ATMs and this is certainly the fastest way to obtain cash. Acquiring a pre-paid currency card in advance is a good way of avoiding transaction charges while abroad, though some ATMs do now charge even for these. Credit cards, especially Visa, are accepted in hotels and some shops but not in all rural accommodation, restaurants or the smaller cafés/bars, nor in some petrol stations. American Express cards are not always accepted. Contactless payment is increasingly normal and some petrol stations are automated for 24-hour operation.

Banks are generally open between 08.30 and 14.30 Monday to Friday, but are closed on Saturday, Sunday and public holidays.

BUDGETING Many overseas visitors come to the Azores on a pre-purchased package bought from a travel agent, so the main costs are paid upfront. From the UK, prices start at around £500 for a seven-night stay in São Miguel on a bed-and-breakfast basis including flights. Specialist cycling, walking, whale and dolphin watching, and fly-drive tours are also available.

The Azores are also reachable by budget airlines, making it in theory a cheap-flight destination if you book at the right time. Having arrived, you will find a wide range of accommodation, from one- to five-star hotels and apartment hotels, to small residencias and camping sites. There are also youth hostels, open to all ages. The most visited islands, São Miguel, Terceira, Faial and Pico, are a bit more expensive than the others. Using ferries to travel between the islands is cheaper and more fun than flying (though see page 43), but you do need to be prepared for changes in the timetables and these can be complicated. Using buses will be considerably cheaper than taxis, but they can be logistically challenging, as their schedules are geared mainly to local people going to and from work, and children going to school.

Hiring general guides can be expensive if you are on your own and in the busy summer months they are often already occupied with pre-booked clients, cruise-ship passengers and tour groups. If you need a guide, then you can pre-book, using the contact details in the individual island chapters that follow. An alternative is to contact the local travel agencies (page 41), who may be able to assemble individual clients to make a small tour group, thus cutting costs.

ADMISSION CHARGES

Although there is the odd exception, admission to museums throughout the Azores is very modest or sometimes even free, usually around €2, with discounts for students, seniors, adolescents and teachers. Children under 7 or so are nearly always free. It's worth asking about family tickets, too. Some museums are free on Sundays.

Litre of milk (UHT)	€0.77
Litre of petrol/diesel	€1.50/1.35
Bottle of mineral water	€0.60 (1½ litres)
Cup of coffee	€0.80
0.5 litre of beer	€2.70
Postcard	€0.40

Without any really top-end restaurants, price differences between establishments are often not significant. Those that are a bit more expensive are indicated in this book. Eating in smaller bars/cafés will be cheaper than the tourist restaurants and hotels, and lunches can be either a cheap and filling *prato do dia* (dish of the day) in a modest restaurant, sometimes a buffet or even a delicious picnic with island products from the local supermarket or market. In fact, restaurant portions are so generous that taking a light picnic for one meal is often preferable.

A budget traveller can expect to spend around €65 per day in the high season. This roughly breaks down into: accommodation (based on camping or dorm bed in a youth hostel) €20; supermarket lunch/prato do dia €8 per person; dinner including wine €20 per person; bus fares, occasional taxi, museum entrance, coffee, say a daily average of €17 per person. Any inter-island travel or car hire is excluded from this estimate.

For the traveller who likes more comfort and privacy, and who enjoys spending time over dinner, then allow around €100 per day, to include: €45 per person for accommodation (based on sharing with a partner/friend); a light lunch with wine €10 per person; dinner €25 per person; bus fares, occasional taxi, museum entrance, coffee, etc, a daily average of €20 per person, excluding inter-island travel or any car hire.

Beyond that, you can spend more by staying in a four- or five-star hotel and hiring cars or private guides, though spending a lot of money on eating out is difficult.

If you are travelling off-season, you can expect costs to be a bit less than those detailed above.

TIPPING In the Azores it is not normal to leave a 10% tip, and you would rarely leave any more than that. A small tip, one or two euros, can be left on the table but it does depend on the category of the restaurant. If you do wish to give a tip, consider a euro to hotel porters, but tipping taxi drivers or guides is not a common or 'must-do' thing.

GETTING AROUND

INTER-ISLAND TRAVEL Most visitors coming by air from Europe or North America arrive in Ponta Delgada on São Miguel or Lajes on Terceira, much less often in Horta on Faial.

By air Azores Airlines (also still known as SATA) is the only inter-island airline and its website (w azoresairlines.pt) contains all the information you require to plan your trip.

Flights are inevitably subject to the weather, and can be delayed or cancelled. When this happens, it is bad luck and you simply have to be philosophical about it and make sure there is a good book to hand.

Getting between the islands is not always straightforward, especially in winter, but more flights are being introduced every year, and independent travellers should spend time studying the Azores Airlines website. Most non-stop flights between each island take about 30 minutes, except São Miguel to Flores, which takes 75 minutes. For travellers with an international Azores Airlines ticket, the airline offers some advanced purchase reductions; again, see the website and page 43 for further information.

Not all flights are non-stop: some will stop at one or two islands en route, and others will involve a layover of a few hours and a change of plane; not all flights operate every day, with islands such as Graciosa and particularly tiny Corvo being served less than daily.

Azores Airlines operates modern Airbus jets to the Portuguese mainland and beyond, and Dash-8 turboprops between the islands, perfectly adapted for short hops and shorter runways. Careful planning is required, but the airline is generally reliable. One-way flight prices are from €39 for the 10-minute hop between Flores and Corvo, to around €90 for longer inter-island trips.

By ferry

Taking a boat is great fun if you have the time; there are always seabirds to look out for, and if you are lucky you may see dolphins or maybe even a whale. Tickets can be purchased at the ferry terminals a few days in advance, or via travel agents. On smaller islands, you can buy the tickets at the RIAC (Citizens' Support Office) – see individual island chapters. There are discounts for those under 13 and over 64, and disabled passengers. With a credit card you can also reserve online at w atlanticoline.pt and print off your ticket or save it to your phone.

Not all services operate year-round; some are summer-only and some see an increased schedule in the warmer months.

Between Flores and Corvo, there is a year-round passenger service (45mins, €10), although this only operates on Tuesday and Saturday in winter, subject to weather conditions.

Throughout the year there are several sailings daily between Horta (Faial) and Madalena (Pico), a 30-minute crossing, costing €3.80. The 'triangular' service from Horta to Velas (São Jorge) (around 2hrs, €15.50) stops at Pico (Madalena or São Roque) in at least one direction. On some days, especially in summer (Jun–Sep) this operates twice daily, making possible day excursions to São Jorge from Faial or Pico, and vice versa.

Also in summer, there's a sailing on Monday and Friday from Horta, San Roque and Velas to Graciosa (2hrs 35mins from Velas, €29.50) and Praia da Vitória (Terceira) (6hrs 25mins from Velas, €29.50). This service leaves Horta at 07.00 and returns at 01.20, so plan carefully.

Again in summer, there's a sailing on Tuesday and Saturday from Horta and Madalena to Calheta (São Jorge) and Angra do Heroísmo (Terceira), 5 hours from Madalena (€29.50).

For up-to-date details of all current ferry services, a route map, prices and reservations, always check the website w atlanticoline.pt, which has an English-language option.

By car

As in mainland Portugal, driving is on the right. The Azorean pace of life is relaxed and generally this is reflected in a fairly modest average driving speed. Azoreans are respectful and patient, certainly not crazy drivers, and the best advice for visitors is to show similar patience, too. If a local wants to stop his pick-up truck in the middle of the road to chat to his neighbour…well, so be it. Very refreshing is that pedestrian crossings are universally respected by drivers, so make sure that, as a driver, you do the same. At the few crossroads without signs, vehicles approaching from the right have priority. Seat belts have to be worn at all times, including the rear passengers, though on some islands the rule is ignored.

The main roads are good, including a few new expressways, but the small country roads can be pot-holed and narrow. One thing to be very careful about when driving in fog or low cloud and poor visibility is the Azorean black-and-white cow wandering on the road, either singly or in a scattered herd; in such conditions they are superbly camouflaged! Vehicles are often parked on the main road, however narrow it may be, so careful driving is required. Many of the minor roads are not signposted. Diversions for roadworks are signposted, but if the sign disappears after a few days it is seldom replaced because by then it is assumed everyone knows the way!

Vehicle rental A full driving licence and passport are required to rent a car. Those aged under 25 years should check minimum requirements for hiring a car at the time of making a booking. They may have to pay a premium. Normally there is no upper age limit but again this should be checked at the time of booking. In peak summer season there is a shortage of hire cars, and reservations should be made well in advance. A daily rate for a small car in high season would be around €55, dropping in low season to €30.

There are many car-hire companies in the Azores, and some are very small. Companies are usually flexible, allowing an airport pick-up and a ferry terminal drop-off, for example. Two well-established firms with their main offices in Ponta Delgada and coverage across most of the islands are Autatlantis (✆ 296 205 340 for reservations; e info@autatlantis.com; w autatlantis.com) and Ilha Verde (✆ 296 304 891 – reservations; e reserve@ilhaverde.com; w ilhaverde.com).

A few other companies are detailed in the relevant island chapters. Prices can differ between islands. Rates do not include any extra insurances, such as CDW (collision damage waiver). Diesel cars, where available, cost substantially more; nearly all cars are equipped with a manual gearbox, something that may shock visitors from North America. It should be noted that many car-hire companies do not allow their vehicles to be taken on unsurfaced roads or on board the ferries, or charge a fee for doing so. Do check when making your booking.

Several islands have **motor scooter** hire, but this is not for the faint-hearted or inexperienced. However, it is a cheap way to get around, costing from around €25 per day. A full driving licence is again required and helmets are supplied and must be worn. **Bicycles** are also available, and some companies renting these are detailed in the individual island chapters. Otherwise, check with the tourist office.

By bus Some islands are better served than others. On São Miguel you can see a lot of the island by public bus. You can make a circuit on the islands of Faial and Pico, and some trips by bus on Terceira, and São Jorge. Tiny Corvo has no buses, and services are not very frequent on the other three islands. For details see the *Getting around* section for the individual island. Timetables can be found online and at tourist offices.

ACCOMMODATION

This varies hugely, from the comfort of large conventional hotels and apartment hotels, to simple family hotels, smart guesthouses/B&Bs, delightful old manor houses with character, converted forts, youth hostels and camping. There is a

HOTEL PRICE CODES

Based on a double/twin room per night, for two guests, breakfast included:

€€€€€	over €200
€€€€	€140–199
€€€	€90–139
€€	€60–89
€	under €60

five-star hotel on Terceira, plus a handful on São Miguel. In addition to serviced accommodation, there are also self-catering apartments and cottages to rent. Apart from the self-catering options, breakfast is usually included in the price quoted.

Some of the larger hotels were built several decades ago and need refreshing, but increased visitor numbers have brought welcome investment, especially around Ponta Delgada on São Miguel. Angra on Terceira and Horta on Faial have also seen a substantial increase in the number of new places to stay, and there is new accommodation on the other islands too.

All this building has greatly eased the acute shortage of beds in the peak season, but of course it creates a surplus in the winter months – another reason to come off-season, when deals can be done! One word of caution: the Azorean weather means constant painting and maintenance for accommodation owners, and sometimes they will close suddenly in winter when the weather allows for a bit of decoration: booking in advance will ensure you get a bed.

Hotels are graded according to the price of a double or twin room in high season. Low-season rates can fall by up to 50%. The highest season is generally July and August, but prices in May/June/September will be somewhat higher than in midwinter. Single-room rates are generally only a little below the double-room rate. Many hotels offer special deals; check their websites for the latest offers. For off-season visitors, note that some establishments may close for some or all of the winter.

For self-catering, check the website w casasacorianas.com, which lists dozens of quality-checked rural houses rentable usually by the week or longer, though sometimes by the night. The site has photographs and details of all the houses, many with online reservation available. You'll also see AL (Alojamento Local) signs on houses, usually beautifully restored – search online or ask at tourist offices to track down booking details.

All islands have official campsites, most with very basic amenities and nominal charges, and some are very attractive, though sometimes lacking in shade or shelter. Details are given under the respective islands. The sites are very popular with the local people – it's just nice to get away from home for a couple of days or so, read a book, go fishing, find a good restaurant or eat outside at the barbecues provided. They are also very popular with teenagers in the school holidays, but don't expect on-site restaurants, waterslides or kids' clubs!

For youth hostels, which can currently be found on São Miguel, Santa Maria, Pico and São Jorge, see the website w azoresyouthhostels.com, which includes an online booking facility. You don't have to be a youth or a member, and most have a limited number of private rooms as well as dormitory accommodation. The latter costs less than €20 per night. There are also some excellent independent hostels on São Miguel, Graciosa and Pico.

EATING Eating out in the Azores can be a very variable experience. The true positive is the quality of the meat and the fish, which is first-class. Usually, these dishes are simply prepared, and a rich accompanying sauce would be a rare find. Sometimes you can strike it lucky in the more expensive eateries and be given a sophisticated and well-presented dish, depending on who is cooking that night. Many Azoreans admit that there is often a focus on quantity rather than sophistication and you will surely never be underfed here. Most islands have one or two stand-out restaurants (though not really 'top-end' by European or North American standards), raising the level or doing something a bit inventive or different, and these are highlighted by this guidebook. Azoreans have fairly conservative tastes, which results in the appearance of boiled potatoes or chips with many meals. Often, meals will be served with potatoes *and* rice, plus a huge basket of bread to accompany it: for many, far too much carbohydrate. Vegetarians will have to look hard for variety, though Ponta Delgada has two excellent meat-free restaurants and more and more restaurants and larger hotels usually have some vegetarian options, too. Failing that, they may be able to improvise a *pasta vegetariana*. One peculiarity is that many of the places calling themselves 'snack-bars' are in fact almost indistinguishable from many middle-of-the-road restaurants; *café-pizzarias* are also available.

Sadly it cannot truthfully be claimed that the islands are a gastronomic delight, but this is changing, albeit slowly. The lower- and mid-priced restaurants often seem to share the same menu so that after a week you are hunting for novelties. To find these is easier in Angra, Ponta Delgada and Horta, where there are more restaurants to choose from. With such a good growing climate there should be a wonderful range of vegetables on offer but it seems most townspeople prefer simply to buy from the supermarket rather than grow much for themselves, and the supermarkets are not very adventurous. This is then reflected in the restaurants, which is no excuse, however, for serving tinned diced mixed vegetables. Salads are mostly lettuce, some tomato, sliced onion, maybe grated carrot and if you are lucky, some cucumber, rarely all together; dressing is usually left to you, from bottles of olive oil and vinegar. Hotels often offer more variety, and can be very good, but even the best can include some of the routine ingredients cooked unimaginatively.

Portions are generally huge, sometimes overpoweringly so, especially meat. Fish, including seafood, is usually excellent, best eaten plain grilled or else as a local

Practical Information **EATING AND DRINKING**

2

EATING OUT

Generally, most restaurants open for both lunch and dinner and the usual hours are noon–15.00 and 19.00–23.00. Depending on the town or island, they are often closed all day either on Sunday (especially Ponta Delgada) or Monday, but there is always somewhere open.

Prices range from €6 to €15 per main dish for lunch and €10 to €20 for dinner and it is rare that you will pay any more than this. Desserts are around €2–3. A bowl of soup is usually a bargain €2, sometimes less. Some places have special lunchtime offers for around €7, including coffee. There are some restaurants that offer buffet meals only which often include a selection of regional dishes for €7 to €12 per person, excluding dessert and drinks.

Many large hotels offer a buffet meal from around €22 per person, usually excluding drinks, plus an à-la-carte menu.

Based on the cost of a main course per person:

€€€€	over €20
€€€	€14–19.99
€€	€10–13.99
€	under €10

version of *bouillabaisse*; the *alcatra* on Terceira is an excellent example, though often this is made with meat instead. *Bacalhau* (dried cod), the traditional village dishes and Azorean sausages can be very good indeed, as can the spicy *chouriço* (smoked sausage) and the black blood sausage, *morcelas*, with pineapple, but not too often in the same week!

Mercifully, Azorean cheeses are good and quality mainland Portuguese wines have been unsung for far too long, leaving the diner feeling very content with the world. Some chocolate desserts can be gorgeous, and there are various kinds of tasty *queijada* pastries on most islands.

DRINKING
Wine The settlers in the Azores had their priorities well ordered because wine has been produced since the very early days. On Pico, grape varieties brought by the first settlers from mainland Portugal failed to acclimatise. The more successful Verdelho grape was imported around 1500, possibly from Sicily, or maybe from Madeira, or perhaps by a Jesuit from Italy.

Vines were first planted on a large scale in the 16th century by the Catholic orders of Franciscans and Carmelites and by Jesuits in the following century. On Pico the vines were brought to Silveira, but the land here was too good for grapes and needed for essential foods such as wheat. Instead they went to the geologically youngest area of the island where the ground was very poor and stony, around the west coast. It is so heavily lava-strewn that it was only with great labour and difficulty that sufficient stones were cleared, using them to make what became the characteristic walls of the currais or corrals, the small enclosures that provide such wonderful shelter from salty winds and at the same time extra heat. Surplus stone was neatly stacked into rectangular piles called *richeiros*. Now, almost half a millennium later, much of this western edge of the island is protected by UNESCO because of its history. Other interesting features of this extraordinary memorial to the energy and persistence of the islanders include the *descansadouros*, the resting places for those carrying full baskets of grapes; made of stone, they are in two levels, one for those carrying on their heads and one for those carrying baskets on their shoulders. Because of the rocky terrain, transport of the barrels was difficult, and to get them to the waiting ships, wooden boards were laid over rocks that had previously been cut and roughly levelled. You might see old stone slipways or *rola-pipas* used to get the barrels into the sea, where they were then towed out to the waiting ship.

At the height of production, some 30,000 barrels or 15 million litres were produced annually. Among the countries it was exported to were Britain and famously to the Russian tsars, apparently by a German trading family. Quite how this wine was produced is not known as few written records were kept. However, Edward Boid, visiting in 1832, wrote that the merchants in Horta took the Pico wine and mixed it with wine from São Jorge and added brandy. It was then heated to between 110°F and 130°F and stored for four to six months, during which time any evaporation from the casks was topped up with more wine and brandy. It seems that different blends were produced for different markets. The best Pico wine was said to be 'so good it should be drunk in the middle of a prayer'.

When disease struck in the mid 1800s the first vines were replaced with the hardy Isabella grape whose strong aroma gave rise to the *vinho de cheiro* – fragrant wine. This is widely made throughout the islands for village consumption, and many a walker has staggered onward under the influence of spontaneous hospitality.

Just over 20 years or so ago, small-scale experiments were conducted with new continental varieties, and some old stone enclosures replaced by long, straight rows supported by wires that always looked impressively immaculate in their level fields of cinders. However, it is the traditional method with its long history that is the remarkable showpiece and has in recent decades been rejuvenated in a number of ways, firstly by recognising various areas of vine growing and production – the Zonas Vitivinícolas – and secondly by the establishment of a Regional Commission based in Madalena to guarantee quality and production methods, and certification. Named quality wines produced in a demarcated area are designated VLQPRD (*vinhos licorosos de qualidade produzidos em região determinada*), which covers *vinhos licorosos* or fortified sweetened wines recommended as an *aperitivo*, and includes the white table wine Pedras Brancas from Graciosa, now happily much reduced in price from a few years ago. The VLQPRD include the Brum wine from Biscoitos on Terceira and Pico's Lajido. Also from Pico is a more versatile red wine from Verdelho and Arinto grapes called Czar. Finally, there are the certified Azores Regional Wines (Vinho Regional Açores): the whites Viosinho and Gouveio, Frei Gigante, Terras de Lava and Maresia from Pico, Moledo from Terceira and the red from Pico, simply labelled Cabernet Sauvignon and Merlot.

On Pico the Cooperativa Vitivinicola da Ilha do Pico now has some 250 small growers. Wine production is far from conventional, not just because of the lava habitat but also because complications affecting acidity, sugar content, maturation and other aspects are created by the extremes of cold air falling from Pico mountain and the sun on the rocks and the salt in the air.

Terceira's first true vineyard was planted more than 400 years ago. A certain Pero Anes do Canto was in charge of the Portuguese navy and owned land at Biscoitos, and it was he who introduced a Verdelho grape from Sicily. Production took off and records for 1693 show that taverns in Angra sold over 1,000 barrels of 500 litres each of Verdelho wine. It seems the same quantity was also sold to the island's eight

THE UNWANTED COVER CHARGE

An aspect of Azorean restaurant dining that can cause confusion is the 'unwanted cover charge'. Having ordered your meal, or perhaps even before doing so, your waiter may present you with a basket of bread, sometimes accompanied by a plate of cheese or even some olives. Tuck in if you feel like it, but don't be surprised when it's added to your bill as 'couvert', as it invariably will be. Some visitors may think that there has been an attempt to dupe them, but the bringing of these items is simply an Azorean custom. If you don't want them, simply tell the waiter politely that this is the case and he will remove them, without complaint and without charge.

The Azorean kitchen has more or less maintained the flavours of the Portuguese kitchen from the time of the Discoveries. There does not seem to be any influence from the early Breton or Flemish population. History tells us that they kept their language only for a generation and the same seems to be true of their food. One reason may be that the Portuguese have always kept in touch with their continental homeland while other settlers perhaps did not.

The Azorean staple is soup. In the old times the main meal of poor rural inhabitants was often simply a thick vegetable soup with chouriço and bread. People are now better off but soup is still served twice a day, the thicker the better. There is a variety of vegetable soups, notably *caldo verde*, a potato soup with finely shredded cabbage leaves cooked in it. Chicken broth is also popular and sometimes fish soup. Until the 1950s, the rural social structure was very archaic and the limited economic possibilities of the population meant that fish was the basic component of daily meals, meat being a luxury served only on festive days, when tradition required three dishes of chicken, pork and beef, some boiled, others roasted.

Interestingly, on the island of São Miguel all dishes are flavoured with hot pepper (*pimenta*) in different forms: powdered, salted or as a paste.

Cod is one of the main raw materials on the islands. According to Portuguese tradition, there are 365 different recipes for cod, one for each day of the year. Even at formal dinners, it is usual to prepare a codfish dish. There is *bacalhau à Brás* (fried potatoes, small pieces of boiled cod mixed with scrambled eggs), *bacalhau com natas* (fried potatoes, small pieces of codfish, olive oil-based béchamel sauce and cream on top), or *bacalhau na chapa* (a thick piece of codfish baked in the oven with olive oil, onion, garlic and red pepper).

There is a large variety of local fish. Small fish, *chicharros*, were regarded in former times as food of the poor since they were very cheap and eaten fried almost daily for lunch, on their own, with a garlic and lemon or a hot pepper sauce, or with parsley, olive oil and onions (green sauce). A few years ago, the price rose astronomically – no-one could explain why the fish almost completely disappeared, only to return. Many medium-sized fish appear on restaurant menus, fried, grilled, steamed, sometimes filleted. They include *abrotea*, white hake, and *cherne*, 'wreck fish'. These are considered the best of the white fish. They are huge, so they appear mostly filleted. In summer one can find fresh tuna, which is sliced as steaks and served fried. Swordfish (*espadarte*) is also a dark-fleshed fish that is usually served fried.

As for seafood (*marisqueira*), octopus cooked in the regional wine, *vinho de cheiro*, is very popular, as is barbecued European squid. *Cracas* (a type of barnacle) are typical of the Azores but increasingly rare, now found only in restaurants specialising in seafood. They are eaten as an appetiser, the tiny morsels retrieved with a special hooked tool from the shell. *Lapas* (limpets) are another shellfish eaten in various ways, most commonly baked with garlic and lemon juice. Rice with lapas is also popular, or *lapas de molho Afonso* with a spicy sauce. There is *cavaco*, an endemic kind of crab, and *lagosta* (spiny lobster), and shrimps that are mostly imported.

For meat, pork, beef and chicken are all on the menu. Typical dishes are *cozido à portuguesa* – pork, beef and chicken mixed mostly with cabbage or kale, root

convents! This may have been a translation error, but wine was certainly exported to the Portuguese colonies. Subsequent introduction of the Baco variety helped make the vineyards more resistant to disease.

vegetables and potatoes, all cooked together. Many restaurants serve this dish once a week as the dish of the day. In Furnas (São Miguel), *cozido* is a speciality, cooked slowly in volcanic heat in the ground and called *cozido nas caldeiras* (page 117). Terceira has *alcatra*, a special meat dish cooked in wine and spices.

A meal in an Azorean restaurant is often preceded by cheese, bread and pepper sauce, shown on the menu as *couvert* (page 55). A local cheese is usually given: on Faial and Pico the cheese will be *São João do Pico*; on São Jorge it is *São Jorge*, a strong sharp-flavoured cheese, considered the best in the Azores. On Terceira the *Castelinhos* cheese and on São Miguel the *Agua Retorta* cheese or a fresh white cheese with the ever-present *massa de pimenta* are served. The standard Gouda-like cheese, found sliced on every breakfast buffet, is known as *flamengo* or Flemish.

The most typical appetiser on Faial, Pico and São Jorge is *morcela* or blood sausage with yams, a tropical vegetable cultivated on all the islands, while on São Miguel blood sausage comes with fresh pineapple.

Religious festivals have their own special dishes. During the Holy Spirit festival, a meat broth with bread is cooked in the islands of the Central Group. During the carnival, *malassados*, a rich dough, like that for doughnuts, is deep-fried and sugared. *Massa sovado*, a sweet bread somewhere between bread and cake, is baked year-round.

Formerly, village people ate only home-baked bread, because corn was widely cultivated to feed both humans and animals. Corn bread is greyish and moist and tends to mould rather quickly. Typical local restaurants often serve both corn and wheat bread. White Azorean bread tends to be too dry; the so-called home-baked bread, a big round loaf, is better.

There is a great variety of locally grown fruit in the Azores and many fruits were introduced following the disease that attacked orange trees in the last century. Pineapples were cultivated but it was soon found that the climate was not warm enough for outdoor growing, so greenhouses were built to obtain a reasonable crop. The Azores are now the only place in the world where pineapples are grown commercially in greenhouses. Economically they cannot compete with pineapples imported from Africa and South America and are heavily subsidised. They are generally sweet and juicy but can be acidic in winter. Again, the Azorean climate is a little too cool for bananas, which are generally smaller and sometimes brownish, but compensate by being sweet.

Other tropical fruits such as avocados, guavas, mangoes, papayas, annonas, *maracujá* (passion fruit) and *diospyros* (persimmon) are also grown. Citrus fruits including oranges, mandarins, clementines and lemons are still grown in quantity. While bananas and pineapples are ripening all the year round, the others are mostly winter fruit starting in October and available until May or June. Typical summer fruits such as apples, pears, plums and peaches do not grow too well in the islands. A lack of a definite cold period means poor flowering; thus cherries do not crop at all, although insects are abundant in summer, since insecticides are not generally used. Only in the higher altitudes such as the Furnas Valley can one get a reasonable crop.

Legislation ensures urban development is limited in the Biscoitos region to protect the vine-growing area. In 1993, the Biscoitos Society of Verdelho Wines was founded with the objective of promoting the Verdelho wines of Biscoitos as well as all of

In the Azores coffee comes in different strengths and sizes, but all bar one are made from the same amount of coffee, just different levels of dilution.

Café normal A strong, small cup
Café duplo Two strong small cups in one small cup
Café curto Strong coffee with a little water in a small cup
Café carioca A larger but weaker coffee, again served in a small cup
Café chávena cheia Strong coffee with plenty of water served in a small cup
Café chávena grande Strong coffee with more water served in a larger cup
Café chávena grande com leite Strong coffee with milk served in a larger cup
Café garoto Strong coffee with milk served in a small cup
Café galão The nearest to caffé latte and served in a tall glass
Café galão escuro A stronger version (*escuro* meaning 'dark')
Café galão claro A weaker version (*claro* meaning 'light')

the quality wines of the Azores. Members wear a blue cape with a gold trim, blue representing the colour of the Azorean flag and gold the colour of the Verdelho. In addition to the arms of the Azores, the society's coat of arms includes a *tambolhadeira*, a drinking cup resembling the traditional clay *taladeira* used in Terceira to taste the new wine, a ritual that takes place on St Martin's Day (11 November). The Brum family wine museum at Biscoitos is open to visitors (page 153).

Graciosa quietly produces wine from its one remaining winery, the Adega Cooperativa da Ilha Graciosa, which started in 1960 with an initial production of 200,000 litres of dry white wine. By the 1980s, this had languished and production ceased for a time, but now with government support the situation is reversed, and its white table wine Pedras Brancas has certified status.

Several liqueur wines are also made, especially São Miguel's well-known *Maracujá* (passion fruit) liqueur. This, mixed half and half with aguardente – fire and passion – is a great ending to a feast of traditional Azorean dishes. Others are made from fruits such as Japanese plum (*Eriobotrya japonica*, the loquat), figs and blackberries. This last, called *Amora*, is less sweet than the others, and if not imbibed in moderation has the kick of an island donkey.

Beer Beer-drinkers can try the Especial lager, a pleasant if unexceptional drink on a hot day; it's been produced since 1893 by Melo Abreu in Ponta Delgada, who also make Munich, a malty dark beer. Many locals prefer the imports from the Portuguese mainland, mainly Super Bock and Sagres. The first Azorean craft beers (ask for *cerveja artesanal*) are now appearing, from breweries such as Korisca and Atlantic on São Miguel, Brianda on Terceira and A Nossa on Santa Maria, but distribution is very limited.

When ordering beer, you can choose a *fino* (very small, in a straight glass), *tulipa* (small, in a tulip-shaped glass) or *caneca* (half litre). Prices are very reasonable when compared with elsewhere in Europe.

PUBLIC HOLIDAYS AND FESTIVALS

The main public holidays are 1 January; 25 April (marking the Revolution of 1974); Good Friday and Easter Sunday; 1 May (Labour Day); 24 May (Autonomy

Day); end of May/beginning June, second Thursday after Whitsun (Corpus Christi); 10 June (National Day of Portugal); 15 August (Feast of the Assumption); 5 October (Proclamation of the Republic); 1 November (All Saints' Day); 1 December (Restoration of Independence); 8 December (Feast of the Immaculate Conception); and 25 December (Christmas Day). There are also municipal holidays, each municipality taking them on different dates so that there are some 18 of these during the summer, but they should not significantly affect the visitor.

New Year's Eve is celebrated throughout the islands and in Ponta Delgada there are fireworks and brass bands, and sometimes a rock band. More modest celebrations are also held in Angra do Heroísmo, Horta and smaller towns.

Carnival is another islands-wide celebration, marked in Ponta Delgada by a grand ball and a masked ball during the third week of February. Visitors are welcome, but tickets need to be pre-booked. On the last day of this five-day festival the carnival ends with a water battle at the marina.

Portugal's second-largest religious festival takes place in Ponta Delgada on the fifth Sunday after Easter, the **Festas de Santo Cristo dos Milagres** (Christ of the Miracles). There are many festivals in August throughout the islands and two of the most important are the **Sea Week** with music and sailing regattas based on Horta between the first and second Sundays in August, and **Whaler's Week** on Pico during the last week of that month. The **Angra Jazz Festival** (w angrajazz.com) is held every year in early October when performers come from both Europe and America to play for several days. Ticket prices are very reasonable.

There are festivals throughout the year, and the principal ones are detailed in the chapters for the individual islands. You can also use the useful calendar on the w visitazores.com website.

SHOPPING

In addition to handicrafts, cheeses from the islands are always a popular purchase. Homemade jams are as good as or better than grandmother's, while tea from the two tea estates on São Miguel is a very original gift and easiest of all to carry home. Somewhat heavier are one or two fresh pineapples in a presentation box, and island wine, aperitivos, liqueurs and aguardentes. For food gifts try the supermarkets; at the airports on São Miguel and Faial there is at least one shop selling Azorean products, and new outlets are appearing all the time. Also, check out the main markets in Ponta Delgada and Horta. Azorean tea can also be purchased directly from the estates (page 123). Note that some shops close from 13.00 on Saturday until Monday morning.

HANDICRAFTS – ARTESANATO There are many items common to all or most of the islands, with their own variations, while some handicrafts are specific to one island or village. All use natural raw materials; you cannot fail to see charming folk figures made from maize husks, basketry, ceramics, various items from cut basalt, embroidery, delicate flowers made from fish scales or fig pith, simple rugs made from maize or rags, and superb woven bedspreads made on São Jorge. Look for products bearing the *Cores* label, which guarantees their Azorean origin. There are also models of whales and items to do with whaling, and some scrimshaw (products made from whale teeth; page 60). Shops do offer whalebone items, but please be aware it is illegal to take these products out of Portugal and their purchase encourages this trade. Several shops now sell items made from environmentally friendly alternative materials. Something new is very attractive local jewellery made from basalt, such as earrings, brooches and necklaces, but only a few jewellers stock them.

ARTS AND ENTERTAINMENT

Entertainment is very modest, but the number of places to go out in the evening is increasing, although their names are not emblazoned across the night sky and they are still relatively few in number. In larger towns on summer evenings there will often be rock, jazz and folk bands playing in the public squares or by the harbour. There's a handful of pubs, again scattered widely. A lively nightlife thrives, but is much more private than commercial and has a quite different meaning from that in the big city. There can be evening dress balls and other social events associated with the many organisations that thrive in the islands, of which the casual visitor remains unaware. As you travel around the islands you will see many barbecue sites at *miradouros* and in sylvan roadside glades. In summer these are busy after office hours when family and friends meet for an alfresco supper and evening together. At weekends and holidays they will again all be occupied, as will the woodland picnic sites laid out in so many lovely places by the forestry service. Summer is for outdoor living, and is also when the festivals and folklore gatherings mostly take place. Very noticeably over the past few years, cafés and bars have put out tables and chairs on the pavements, especially around the new marinas, quaysides and pedestrianised squares, so that now friends and families stay out late quietly enjoying a beer, bottle of wine or coffee. On a balmy summer evening the visitor can enjoy a promenade around the main harbours with their pretty lights reflecting on the water, sit in a garden square and nibble a snack from a street stall, or watch the world go by from a pavement café.

During your stay in Ponta Delgada, check whether there is anything on at the restored **Teatro Micaelense** (**w** teatromicaelense.pt); this offers a wide range of cultural events throughout the year, from ballet, musicals, *fado*, jazz and chamber recitals to fully staged operas, the programmes often linked with the Coliseums in Lisbon and Oporto. In Horta, on Faial, the *teatro* near the main square has also been restored and offers a mix of Hollywood and art cinema together with occasional orchestral and jazz music.

SPORTS AND ACTIVITIES

WALKING Walking in the mid-Atlantic is a most wonderful experience. Whether you are high in the mountains, following a coastal walk, or merely strolling along a country lane, there is a purity in the air, an exhilaration in the light, and ever-changing cloud patterns. In places trails lie dark and dank between 2m-tall embankments, with hedges of cryptomeria, pittosporum and endemic shrubs, while the banks themselves are moss-covered or draped with soft green curtains of selaginella, a primitive fern ally. At other times when high up in the mountains the scene is more akin to moorland, with low-growing grasses, rushes and mossy flushes in the wetter areas, and elsewhere a knee-high scrub of heather, and often a view of the distant sea. Perhaps best of all is to file along a narrow path contouring a steep sea cliff, when the views are spectacular, very special and pure Azores. However, gentler walks along farm roads through patchworks of pastures with the sight of healthy, contented cows out to grass all year, and past farm buildings with ever-changing rural scenes, are equally satisfying in their different way. A survey of visitors from the UK a few years ago showed that 80% came principally for walking, though this may have diminished with the arrival of budget flights and the increased popularity of other land- and sea-based activities.

Buried beneath the vigorous alien vegetation of the islands lie many old cobbled trails, used long ago to travel between the villages by donkey, ox-cart and horse. Before the advent of roads these trails were the economic and social lifelines for the villages, for the fishermen bringing basketloads of fish, for the workers walking to their fields, to the vineyards, their fruit and orange orchards, and for religious pilgrimages. The history and stories they could tell are as lost to the visitor as the dustiest archive in the deepest cellar. Maybe one day local historians will make all this tangible and readily accessible, but meanwhile all we have are brief glimpses of this earlier age. If old trails happen to lead to pastures or to vineyards then their weathered surfaces can still be seen, perhaps for just a few metres, maybe for 100m or more. They are there for the observant traveller to find, and then to let the imagination fill in the stories. Certainly if these hidden paths could be rediscovered they would make wonderful walks and stories for our time. And if time and tide have in part destroyed them, then maybe new routes could be found to link them.

Walks are being lost, but 'new' ones are being spruced up, waymarked and presented to visitors. For years unsurfaced farm tracks were given asphalt surfaces with the help of EU funding; great for the farmer, but bad news for the walking tourist. Seismic tremors and flash floods cause human tragedies, and also send favourite walks permanently into memory, their imprint on the landscape forever destroyed by nature. Whether the pioneering efforts and appeals over the years have influenced the authorities one does not know, but recently waymarking and maintenance of walking routes has at last been taken seriously and there are now over 80 official walks covering all the islands: 30 on São Miguel, 13 on Pico, 12 on Terceira, 10 on Faial and between two and nine on each of the others. This is tremendous news, and hopefully they will now go from strength to strength. These trails vary in length from 2km to 78km. Some are circular; others follow some of the old inter-village paths. Unfortunately cows like to use the marker poles as scratching posts and, pushed sideways, they do not always point in the right direction, while walls with paint marks get knocked down, so one still needs to keep a good sense of direction! There are descriptive brochures for each trail available from the local tourist offices, and all can be downloaded from the website w trails. visitazores.com. The texts are perhaps not as detailed as they should be, the maps are a bit sketchy and how one accesses the walks or gets home afterwards is often frustratingly vague.

While all the islands now have attractive walks, the best are on São Jorge, São Miguel and Flores, and new trails on Pico and Faial are rightly proving very popular. Pico also offers the ascent of Pico mountain, the highest in Portugal, and Santa Maria has a new round-island circuit with a supporting accommodation network. Some of the circular walks are described in the relevant island chapters.

Remember always to take sensible kit – layers for warmth, a waterproof/ windproof outer jacket, and sun protection. Always take adequate water and, for walks where the route takes you across lava or the few arid areas, take double the normal quantity. A most useful item to have with you is a mobile phone to call a taxi at the end of a walk – and the number of a taxi firm!

CYCLING Next to walking, this is the finest way to get to know the islands, following quiet rural lanes and passing through pretty villages for frequent pit-stops. Some tour operators in the UK and travel agencies in the Azores offer fully supported eight-day packages with two-centred accommodation and daily transfers for around £850 excluding flights, while UK and other tour operators offer all-inclusive cycling holidays. São Miguel has the best choice of companies offering bike hire or guided cycle tours, while Santa Maria has the best infrastructure.

WHALE AND DOLPHIN WATCHING Whale and dolphin watching has become a major focus of ecotourism and the increase in its popularity is phenomenal; it's the fastest-growing tourist activity worldwide. Beginning as a commercial enterprise in 1955 on the southern California coast, it is claimed whale watching is now organised in about 120 countries with 15 million participants – 2017 figures. For some economies, it has become an industry in its own right; divide the cash generated by the number of whales viewed, and each whale must be worth a small fortune. Certainly they are more valuable than if they were hunted and killed. Another important plus is that in many places commercial whale watching has become a recognised tool for education, and is supporting research by the observations and recordings made during whale-watching trips and other inputs. All the more extraordinary that, with government subsidy, Norway and Japan continue to hunt and kill around 1,500 whales commercially each year…and at the same time offer whale-watching trips.

It is essential that these 'subjects' of our recreational curiosity are viewed with the respect they deserve. In the Azores, whale and dolphin watching has become a much-advertised and popular activity and there are now many operators offering whale-watching trips; some have more than one boat. This brings into question what effect this has on the cetaceans; they are sensitive animals surviving in a very tough environment doing the things we do, finding food, rearing young and socialising. They have highly sensitive hearing and are distressed when their communication is interfered with, when speedboats tear around them, gunning their engines. Bothering them by too close a contact and in other ways can alter their migration patterns, separate groups and interfere with their reproduction. What the stress thresholds are is not known and more research is needed, so given our ignorance the best policy is: don't do it unless you know it is harmless. Swimming with cetaceans is controversial and is banned in several countries.

WHALE- AND DOLPHIN-WATCHING ETIQUETTE

Legislation has been passed in the Azores to regulate the increasing demand for whale and dolphin watching but supervising behaviour out at sea and out of sight is not easy. You, 'the client whale watcher', can do this by reporting back any malpractice you encounter or posting it on the ubiquitous review sites. The new economic significance of whale watching and the widening concern and support from those who participate is likely to do more than anything else to help protect these animals on the world stage and change political opinions.

- Cetaceans should not be chased.
- Boats should approach carefully by maintaining direction parallel and slightly to the rear of the cetaceans, keeping an open field of 180° to the front of them.
- When approaching, boats should avoid changes in direction, keep to slow speeds of under 10 knots and when 400m from the area reduce to 4 knots.
- A maximum of only two boats are permitted inside a radius of 400m around an individual whale or group of whales.
- It is prohibited to approach cetaceans closer than 50m; when they are resting they may not be approached at all.
- Only one boat at a time is permitted to approach to the minimum distance of 50m from the whales, and the engine should always be kept on low revs.
- Boats should not come between animals in groups thereby separating them, especially the young.
- Whales with small calves should not be approached closer than 100m.
- Movements of all boats must always be on the same side, parallel to and a little to the rear of the animals.
- The maximum time to be spent in the area observing is 30 minutes near the animal.
- After observation, boats must depart from the area to the rear of the animals, and maintain a slow speed within 400m of them.
- No swimming is allowed with whales.
- Skippers must explain to clients the dangers of swimming with dolphins and that they do this at their own risk (there is no insurance available).
- When swimming with dolphins, one extra crew member, apart from the skipper, must be allocated for surveillance of swimmers at all times and be equipped for swimming.
- Only two swimmers with dolphins should be allowed in the water at the same time and they should be equipped with snorkels; they must remain quietly on the surface and not touch the dolphins.
- Swimming time with dolphins is limited to 15 minutes maximum.
- The boat's motor must be in neutral at all times when swimmers are in the water.

A 2011 estimate revealed that some 48,000 people went whale watching in the Azores that year, supporting 53 boats and 195 jobs. Although no more recent figures are available, it seems that that figure will have increased substantially –

12.5% of visitors to the Azores say that whale watching is a priority. It is pleasing to note that the Azorean government has passed regulations controlling the number of boats allowed, passenger safety, and visitor behaviour when near the animals. The regulations also aim to encourage the companies involved to work more closely together, reduce competition and limit the number of boats around any one pod. This was validated in 2023 when the Azores became a designated Whale Heritage Area, one of ten so far worldwide (also including Madeira).

If you are going to visit them, there is an accepted etiquette to follow (page 63). Rather than book a trip at random, study the notes about what you should know before you go out to sea, and how your boat crew should handle the situation. When you have absorbed these, check out the operators, ask the right questions, and when you find one that suits you, go ahead. Check whether they have an experienced biologist on board at all times; ask how many people they take as a maximum, if there is shade from the sun, a lavatory, and if drinking water is supplied. You can also ask if you are contributing to scientific research by choosing their boat.

For those who do not like the idea of venturing into the mid-Atlantic in a small rigid inflatable boat and enduring 3 hours' banging into the waves as you speed along, there are now larger, more comfortable vessels that have cabins and decks where you can move around. You are no less likely to see whales and dolphins this way and your view from the raised decks of these vessels is much better. Seeing whales and dolphins out at sea is a memorable and special experience; to really get the most out of your boat trip, do your homework first and read up about the creatures; only then should you intrude upon them and with a clearer conscience.

Because of the weather, the main season is from April to October, although cetaceans may be seen throughout the year and you may find there are opportunities in winter. Winter trips are more prone to cancellations, caused by rough seas or bad weather. With 28 species now recorded in Azorean waters out of a total of some 83 species of whales, dolphins and porpoises, the Azores are one of the world's top places to observe them. In 2009, the first northern right whale for 110 years was recorded in the Azores, five miles south of Faial. The islands most geared up for organised excursions are Pico, Faial and São Miguel.

Typically there are two departures each day, around 09.00 and 14.00, each lasting about 3 hours. At 30 minutes before departure there is usually a pre-trip briefing. The cost varies, but is generally around €50–65 per person. A seven-night whale-watching programme, staying on Pico or Faial, costs from around £700 excluding flights. Typically this would be: arrive and briefing on day one; further briefing and talks on the history of whaling, etc, and afternoon whale-watching boat trip on day two; then days three to six morning boat trip with afternoons free for optional land-based activities or at leisure; and final day flexible, allowing for any replacement boat trips if earlier bad weather caused cancellations. Several tour operators offer whale-watching packages including international flights and various extras on São Miguel, Faial and Pico.

Should you like more information, then Whale and Dolphin Conservation (WDC), the world's most active charity dedicated to the conservation and welfare of all whales, dolphins and porpoises, has an excellent website (w uk.whales.org).

SWIMMING The steep rocky coasts mean that swimming opportunities are mostly focused on small beaches, little bays and a combination of natural and manmade rock pools. The more popular locations often have changing facilities, toilets, showers and sometimes lifeguards, while amenities are improving rapidly all the time. In 2023, the coveted European Blue Flags, signifying beaches or swimming areas that meet stringent standards, were awarded to 44 sites in the Azores. The number varies from year to year, but most are on São Miguel and Terceira. Few of the natural swimming places are really suitable for non-swimmers. There are various adverse conditions and dangerous currents unknown to the visitor and swimming should be enjoyed only in clearly designated areas. Please be very aware of the coded flags flying according to prevailing conditions on designated swimming beaches:

Green	Safe to swim
Yellow	Be careful, no swimming
Red	Danger, keep out of the water
Chequered	Beach temporarily without a lifeguard

Many larger hotels and even rural accommodations have conventional swimming pools and recent investment has created attractive public pools near some of the main population centres, while local municipalities have created simpler facilities, often modifying rocky sea-washed locations – many with natural built-in wave machines! Seldom, however, is shade provided from the sun around any of the sites. But the sheer diversity of opportunities to swim is remarkable, from the sea and rock pools, formal and indoor pools, volcanic lakes, to a naturally warm geothermal pool.

DIVING For a long time few people thought of the Azores as a diving destination, but this has changed, with operators in most of the islands taking advantage of a unique underwater environment and excellent marine life. The seabed, being of volcanic origin, offers large areas of lava and various volcanic debris, tunnels, arches, vertical cliffs, small caves and rock needles, while the Gulf Stream brings together both Atlantic and tropical fish. Large schools may often be seen – barracuda, mackerel, trigger fish – and very large stingrays as well as occasional giant mantas, curious octopuses and a diversity of other marine organisms. Giant whale sharks have also been spotted. With a visibility range of up to 20m, the great joy of diving off the Azores is that you never know what you are going to see.

Because the weather is unpredictable, dives usually take place in the mornings when the sea is most likely to be at its calmest. June to November are the best months, but diving can be enjoyed in any month.

There are now specialist companies listed on all the islands except Corvo, offering shore dives with easy access to the water, and boat dives. Experienced divers are catered for as well as the less experienced, and instruction is available for beginners and refreshers. Night diving is also offered. Single dives start from around €45 and ten dives from €330 plus hire of dive gear. For those who prefer to snorkel, both instruction and tours are available with most of the diving companies.

COASTAL FISHING Open-boat fishing with a guide is available out of Faial, São Miguel, and from other islands offering bottom-fishing, jigging, trolling live bait and sea fly fishing. Species include mackerel, barracuda, bonito, scabbard fish, sea bream and more, depending on the depth. The cost is around €250 for a maximum of three persons for a half day's (4–5 hours') boat hire.

SPORT OR GAME FISHING The Azores marine environment attracts large fish including 'granders', a fishing term for blue marlin weighing 450g or more, and many world records have been achieved in these waters. The season usually runs from early July to mid-October when the water temperature is above 20°C and

2

the weather is generally warm and calm. Apart from the Atlantic blue marlin, various tuna species, several different sharks and numerous white marlin, there are also small game fish. With an instructor and skipper, prices are around in excess of €1,000 per day for a group of up to four, with São Miguel and Horta on Faial being the principal centres. Some operators are listed in the individual island chapters.

CAR RALLIES Several rallies are held annually in the islands and those wishing to attend should make sure they have their hotel accommodation booked well in advance. Anyone coming to the Azores for a quiet holiday should plan their itinerary accordingly! Dates vary each year and should be checked with your tour operator or the Azores Directorate of Tourism, or look at w tac.com.pt. Some of the major ones are:

São Miguel	Azores Airlines Rallye. See w azoresrallye.com for dates.
Santa Maria	First or second weekend of August, usually one week before the big religious festivities of 15 August: Rali de Santa Maria
Terceira	Early April: Além Mar Rali (Beyond the Sea Rally)
	Between August and October: Rali Ilha Lilás
Graciosa	November: Rali Ilha Graciosa
Faial	April: Rali Além Mar Ilha Azul; w caf-faial.com
Pico	October: Rali Ilha do Pico Além Mar

SAILING Skippered boat charter is available on São Miguel. With a minimum of four people, maximum six, prices are around €85 per person with a minimum charge of €450 for a full day sailing along the south coast of São Miguel; to Santa Maria for the weekend €1,500. Other trips are possible, too: for further information, see the website w boataround.com.

Inclusive sailing holidays from the UK, including international flights, sailing between and around São Miguel and Terceira with an option to extend to Santa Maria, start from around £1,300; sailing around the three central islands of Faial, Pico and São Jorge costs from around £1,100.

These notes are made for the land visitor: sailors have their own cruising guides! Apparently the first American pleasure yacht to cross the Atlantic called in at Horta on its way to the Mediterranean in 1867, and in 1895 Joshua Slocum put into Horta while making the first single-handed circumnavigation of the world. Since then small boat arrivals have increased and with the construction of marinas and onshore facilities (page 44) the number of yachts now visiting Horta is around 1,400 annually. Many are doing the milk-run, bringing boats over from Bermuda or the West Indies to the Mediterranean or similar for the summer, allowing their owners who do not like real sailing to fly across later. The Azores are also a major focus for several famous international races, and there are also local yachting events. The calendar is something like this:

Last Saturday in April	Competitors windsurf from Velas to Cais do Pico, then cycle via the coast road to Madalena and then kayak to Horta.
First week in July	Faial yacht club organises a race for cruising yachts from Horta to Velas on São Jorge and back, including an overnight party in Velas.
End of July	Atlantis Cup: a big date in the calendar; the route varies from year to year, ending in Horta.

Beginning first Sunday in August	Semana do Mar or Sea Week, with events connected with the sea as well as other cultural events. In Horta.
Every four years	The famous Azores and Back race organised by the Royal Cornwall Yacht Club every four years since 1975, binding Falmouth with Ponta Delgada. For further details, see w azab. co.uk. Next due in 2027.
Every four years	The Défi Atlantique from Guadeloupe to La Rochelle via Horta with at least two crew; next due in 2027.
Every two years	Race from Les Sables to Horta and back is organised by Société Nautique.
Further events	Include the Yachting World ARC Europe rally from the Canaries to the West Indies; Canaries–Bermuda–Horta–Ponta Delgada to either Plymouth or the Algarve; Rotterdam–Horta and back by Dutch Sports Planning International; rally by the Ocean Cruising Club of England.

GARDENS Portuguese gardeners took their inspiration from the Romans and Moors, as well as the Italians and French, and later the romantic English style of the 19th century, and made their own landscape style. Combined with the unchanging skills and methods of Azorean gardeners, the historic gardens in the Azores offer a special charm. Around the mid 1850s there was a veritable outbreak of garden development and of these, one garden on Terceira and five gardens on São Miguel are now open to visitors (and don't miss the wonderful Botanic Garden on Faial). The owners of three gardens in Ponta Delgada vied with each other to have the latest introductions and the rarest plants, importing plants from famous nurseries in Belgium, France and England, and from mainland Portugal and Brazil. Architects and gardeners were invited from overseas to superintend the landscaping, including David Mocatta from Britain, who studied under Sir John Soane and designed several of the stations for the London to Brighton railway; Peter Wallace, a gardener to the Duke of Devonshire at Chatsworth who later died in Ceylon; Jean-Pierre Barillet-Deschamps, a leading French horticulturist who worked with Haussmann and transformed Paris, creating the Jardin du Luxembourg and Parc Monceau among many others; Georges Aumont, designer of the Barbieux Park in Lille; and Francisco (François) Gabriel, who came from the famous Makoy nursery in Liège and introduced many plants from Parisian and Belgian nurseries to the Terceira Garden (page 154).

RECREATIONAL FOREST RESERVES These areas have been designated for public recreation and are found on all islands except Corvo. They're dominated by *Cryptomeria japonica* forest, often along with oaks, chestnut and other non-native species, as well as camellias or azaleas, but more recently native species have been introduced as part of a broader educational and conservation programme. These mature habitats offer peaceful places for a relaxed and tranquil walk or a picnic, and often a loo. Those listed in this guide have special merit for the overseas visitor. They are generally open 08.00–19.00 Monday–Friday and 10.00–20.00 Saturday and Sunday in summer, 08.00–16.00 Monday–Friday in winter.

OTHER ACTIVITIES These include kayaking, canyoning, coasteering and other physical pursuits. Specialist companies are listed in the relevant island chapters. If you want to design an action-packed holiday involving these activities before you leave home – advisable in high season – then one of the tour operators listed on page 41 should be able to help.

Canyoning This is walking in streams, rappelling down waterfalls and generally getting wet in a diversity of geological settings. Because this is usually the only way to experience some of these places, there is often undisturbed native vegetation and rare plants plus birds as a bonus. Barely heard of just a few years ago, this activity has now burgeoned and has an enthusiastic local following as well as organised expeditions for visitors. There are at least 50 secure (bolted) routes, of various difficulty levels and three islands are especially good; on São Miguel the challenges are less steep, Flores has the greatest diversity, and São Jorge offers the hardest routes as most are accessible only by boat.

Horseriding There are programmes available throughout the year for both beginners and experienced riders, with excellent centres on São Miguel, Faial and Pico. Contact details are given in the relevant island chapters.

Kayaking and canoeing This is largely done on the caldera lakes of Sete Cidades and Furnas on São Miguel, and on the open sea exploring small islets, visiting caves and watching seabirds off the islands of Terceira and Flores. On Flores there is a spectacular coastline and waterfalls to enjoy and, by contrast, Terceira offers the bay of Praia and the southeast coast with its many sandy shallow bays and is emerging as one of the best locations. Organised trips are either half day or full day, with experienced guides.

MEDIA AND COMMUNICATIONS

POST Postal services are efficient and reliable. Expect cards and letters to take around three to five days to Europe, a little longer to North America from Ponta Delgada or Lajes on Terceira. Add a day or two from the other islands. You can recognise a post office by the sign *correio*, or *ctt*, and they open Monday to Friday only, though they often have stamp dispensers outside. There are two levels of service, and outside post offices you will see two postboxes, one for ordinary mail and one for express blue mail, which costs three times as much.

The ordinary rates for mailing abroad are: up to 20g, Europe €1.20; to rest of the world €1.30.

TELEPHONE The telephone service is excellent. The international code for the Azores (Portugal) is 351. The islands also have codes: 296 for São Miguel and Santa Maria; 295 for Terceira, São Jorge and Graciosa; 292 for Faial, Pico, Flores and Corvo. You need to dial the whole nine-figure number no matter where you are.

The number of public telephones is diminishing, but they still are more prevalent than in other Western countries. PT (Portugal Telecom) chargecards can be bought in many shops, kiosks and post offices, and many phones also accept debit or credit cards. You can select foreign-language options on the instruction screen.

Mobile reception is generally very good in the Azores, though the mountains do create blank spots. Cheap prepaid SIM cards can be bought on arrival, and e-SIM cards (bought online) can provide plenty of data for as little as €5.

NEWSPAPERS AND BROADCASTING The main daily newspapers are *Açoreano Oriental, Diário dos Açores* and the *Correio dos Açores,* all in Portuguese. Some cafés have copies available for their clients to read.

Portuguese state-owned RTP (Rádio e Televisão de Portugal) provides local radio and television in the Azores. Most medium and large hotels have at least one English-speaking television news service, usually CNN, BBC World or Sky News, and sometimes all three.

INTERNET It was once said that Portugal had the best internet coverage in Europe. Whether this is (or ever was) true is difficult to prove, but certainly all Azorean towns of any size have free municipal Wi-Fi, as do all the island airports and many of the marinas. Additionally, nearly all accommodations now provide this service and you never have to look hard to find a café with free Wi-Fi. On the other hand, internet cafés are now almost non-existent. The larger hotels offer internet services, or if you are stuck then it's worth trying the local library.

CULTURAL ETIQUETTE

Through the ages the Azoreans have had plenty of contact with the outside world, from pirates to tourists, and from their own travels for work abroad, family members in mainland Portugal, business, higher education and so on. For all this, the communities remain tight-knit, especially in rural areas. It is also a country with strong Catholic traditions. Simple courtesy and respect remain refreshingly important and the visitor will find these greatly contribute to first impressions. Boorish behaviour is not appreciated and will not go unremarked. Neither will topless sunbathing, or changing on the beach – use the cabins provided.

If you are taking **photographs** of people, then do ask first; your smile will in most cases be returned and permission granted.

TRAVELLING POSITIVELY

If you have enjoyed your visit and the islands' hospitality, you may have the feeling you would like to say thank you, and give something back.

The **Portuguese Society for the Study of Birds (Sociedade Portuguesa para o Estudo das Aves)** (SPEA; Rua Antonio Alves de Oliveira No 1 R/C, Nordeste, São Miguel; ✆ 296 488 455; m 912 895 679; e acores@spea.pt; w spea.pt) is a not-for-profit organisation promoting the study and conservation of birds in Portugal. They are very active in the Azores and need all the support and help they can get since there is much to do to protect and regenerate wildlife habitats in the islands.

Early farmers killed the once locally abundant endemic Azorean bullfinch or *priolo, Pyrrhula murina,* to save their crops, especially oranges, from its attacks. However, from the 1920s, forest clearance and general habitat destruction, together with the invasion of alien plant species supplanting its food plants plus probable predation by rats and feral cats, made this small bird increasingly rare. It is now confined to about 6km² of native forest on Pico da Vara and Serra da Tronqueira in the east of São Miguel. Long thought to be down to between only 200 and 300 individuals, in 2008 the first full census was made and the estimate revised to 775 individuals. Under the 2009 IUCN Red List, the priolo was officially categorised as 'Critically Endangered', because of its small population and limited distribution.

The area where it survives is designated a Special Protection Area under the EU Wild Birds Directive and is included in the São Miguel Natural Island Park. Since

2003, SPEA, along with governmental agencies and municipalities, have undertaken conservation work in the priolo's main distribution area; they have recovered its habitat, the Azores laurel forest or laurisilva, by controlling invasive plant species and planting native species to increase its desperately needed food supplies. This is a long-term commitment. This work allowed the priolo's population to increase to the present-day estimate of between 650 and 2,000, allowing it to be downgraded from 'Critically Endangered', first to 'Endangered' and now to 'Vulnerable' by the IUCN. SPEA's work has also contributed to sustainable development of the territory by restoring peatland areas in the Planalto dos Graminhais and promoting sustainable tourism in the territory. In 2012, the 'Lands of Priolo' (Nordeste and Povoação municipalities) were awarded the European Charter of Sustainable Tourism.

The society's first ever visitor/interpretative centre is located within the protected area, in the Cancela do Cinzeiro Forest Recreational Reserve. The **Priolo Environmental Centre** (m 918 536 123; e centropriolo@spea.pt; ⊕ May–Sep 10.00–18.00 Tue–Sun, mid-Feb–Apr & Oct–mid-Nov noon–17.00 Sat–Sun, other times available by appointment only) offers information about the flora and fauna of the Serra da Tronqueira and Pico da Vara and especially about the priolo, with temporary exhibitions, a nearby small garden of native plant species, and facilities for its education programme for schools and the local population. In addition, there is a shop with merchandising.

Visitors are made very welcome, and the centre may be reached by an unsurfaced road off the main Povoação to Nordeste road, either just beyond Povoação, or from above the village of Lomba da Pedreira, or from Nordeste (10mins). You can find more information about the centre and its activities at the website w en. centropriolo.com. Membership is available to families or individuals. Members receive the society's magazine three times a year and news of regular field trips (free to members).

Your financial donation and/or your participation in voluntary work (educational activities, fieldwork activities, professional or academic visits) are fundamental for the success of the project and for the conservation of the priolo and its habitat.

Part Two

EASTERN GROUP

ATLANTIC

OCEAN

Ponta da
Bretanha

Mosteiros

Ponta do
Ferraria

Termas da
Ferraria

Lagoa
Azul

Sete
Cidades

Lagoa Verde

Vista
do Rei

Feteiras

Santa Bárbara
Remédios

Bretanha

Miradouro de
Santo António
Santo António

Capelas

Relva

Lagoa do
Canário

Poços de São
Vicente Ferreira

Fenais
da Luz

Golf course

Pinhal
da Paz

EN4-1A

Ponta
Delgada

São Roque

Livramento

Lagoa

Ribeira
Grande

Caldeira Velha
(hot waterfall
& picnic site)

Miradouro da
Santa Iria

Caldeiras

Chã da
Macela

Lagoa do
Fogo

Ribeira
Chã

Lombadas

Lagoa do
Congro

Água de
Alto

Água de Pau

Caloura

Praia

Vila Franca
do Campo

Ilhéu de Vila

Franca do Campo

Ponta do
Cintrão

Baía de
Santa
Iria

Porto
Formoso

Porto
Maia

Fenais da Ajuda

São Brás

Sorreana

Monte Escuro

Lagoa das
Furnas

Furnas

Golf
course

Lomba da Maia

Ribeira dos Caldeirões

Achadinha

Achada

Miradouro Salto
do Cavalo

Serra da Tronqueira

Pico da Vara
1,103m

Pico Bartolomeu
845m

Povoação

Ribeira Quente

Ponta Garça

Santo António
de Nordeste

Lomba da
Fazenda

Algarvia

Ribeira do
Guilherme

Nordeste

Priolo
Environmental
Centre

Concelho do Cinzeiro

Miradoura da
Ponta do Sossego

Ponta do
Arnel

Foz da
Ribeira

Lomba da
Pedreira

Ponta da
Madrugada

Água Retorta

Faial da Terra

N

0 ─── 10km
0 ─── 5 miles

3

São Miguel

With photographs of the lakes of Sete Cidades featuring across travel brochures and Instagram, São Miguel has become the best-known island of the archipelago; it is also the biggest in terms of area and population, has the greatest diversity of interests, the best choice of accommodation and restaurants, and the most operators of outdoor activities. In short, it is the best developed for visitors. It also has the largest town in the Azores, Ponta Delgada, with the busiest harbour and airport. Although all the islands are green, São Miguel is known as the *Ilha Verde*, the 'Green Island', after the highly productive central area that has very good soil. There is an area of true mountain wilderness with endemic plants around its highest point, Pico da Vara (1,103m), and a varied coastline with small black-sand bays and precipitous sea cliffs. Ponta Delgada is large only by Azorean standards and charms its visitors with its gentle Portuguese architecture, pedestrianised streets, cafés, shops and long esplanade that wraps itself around the ferry terminal, marinas, commercial port area and fishing harbour.

Becoming ever more cosmopolitan than the other islands, São Miguel has emerged as the focus for the archipelago. Yet, in spite of new marinas, hotels, boutique hostels and restaurants, a second golf course, out-of-town supermarkets and so on, considerable rural charm is still to be found: even on the western edges of Ponta Delgada, cows graze peacefully in fields up-close to adjacent industrial units.

Most famous of the island's attractions are the two lakes of Sete Cidades, one blue, the other green, steeped in mythology and nestled in the caldera that dominates the western topography. Ribeira Grande, midway along the north coast, has a charming town centre that you can pass through to reach almost the only tea estates in Europe, at Gorreana and Porto Formoso. In the southeast, the small spa of Furnas, which physically has changed little over the years, is a must. Here, bubbling hot springs and fumaroles, together with the smell of sulphur, remind you that you are on a volcano in spite of the verdant surroundings; in fact you are in the centre of another large crater. Twenty-two mineral waters, all with different tastes, spout out of the ground; some have elaborate manmade ornamental surrounds, while others just flow from between the native heather bushes. The 12ha garden of Furnas's Terra Nostra Garden Hotel, mostly dating from well over 150 years ago but with beginnings in the late 18th century, with its naturally heated swimming pool and meandering walks beneath some 2,000 trees, provides contact with the genteel life of earlier times. In the far northeast is Nordeste, a region little visited by tourists, with a spectacularly beautiful coast which can be enjoyed from several splendid viewpoints and picnic sites. Vila Franca do Campo in the middle of the south coast was São Miguel's first capital, and is still a thriving and pretty town; the town square and the nearby harbour should be seen before taking a coffee and trying the local *queijadas* or Vila Franca cake.

If you have a full week to spend exploring São Miguel, you will depart still leaving unseen places for your next visit. If you have the time and are entering and leaving the Azores through Ponta Delgada, it is a good idea to spend the first two or three nights of your holiday in Furnas, and then the last two or maybe three nights in Ponta Delgada itself. This way you can get a real feel for the island and its diversity, and Furnas is an ideal 'inland resort' to begin to relax, unwind and get into a holiday mood. São Miguel has changed, and is changing, faster than the other islands. But for the moment, its charms are still plentiful.

BACKGROUND

GEOLOGY Now the biggest island of the Azorean archipelago, São Miguel was at one time two islands as evidenced by the two large volcanic massifs, one at each end, and the low central area that linked them following further eruptions. About 4 million years ago, the first island appeared, from an eruption on the seabed 2,000m below sea level. Erosion has given us today a broad upland of thick basaltic flows, probably originating as a shield volcano (one gently sloping and built of lava from many closely spaced vents and fissures) with frequent eruptions, with Pico da Vara the highest point. Towards the edge of this upland the stratovolcano (a steep-sided cone of layered lava flows and other volcanic products) of Povoação developed about 3 million years ago, and the caldera is thought to have occurred

THE ORANGE TRADE

Even today there is evidence of the great orange-growing industry that dominated several of the islands in the 19th century; look in the numerous small gardens with their tall enclosing walls or hedges of banksias and pittosporum. Grand townhouses also reflect the wealth this crop generated, and the development of the rural estates was historically significant.

Far less known are the implications all these oranges had for transportation between the Azores and England, the major export customer. Citrus was a luxury fruit, available in season from November to May only, and its peak of desirability for the Victorians was Christmas, when oranges and lemons were the fruit to have displayed on the table. And most of these came from the Azores.

'Buy my fresh St Michael's' was a common streetseller's cry, although it is doubtful that, like today, many customers would have known where 'St Michael's' was. Oranges were grown in the Azores already by the 16th century, brought in from Lisbon, having been introduced by Portugal's Indian viceroys. From 1600 to 1800, the citrus trade steadily increased, with most of Britain's oranges coming from Valencia and lemons from Sicily, but it was the ending of the Napoleonic Wars that accelerated exports from the Azores so that by the mid 1800s, several hundred ships and several thousand seamen were employed in the trade. The topsail schooner was the favoured ship, one that could travel fast, for oranges are a quickly perishable cargo. There was no need for larger ships; the boxes of oranges could not be stacked high otherwise those at the bottom would have spoilt. Also, should a large consignment have arrived in one ship, the quantity would have swamped the market and reduced the price. In 1854, 60 million oranges and 15 million lemons were exported to London alone, using at least 70 vessels.

At first, English merchants came out to the Azores at the start of the season to supervise purchase and loading, but by the mid 19th century many, along with in two stages about 820,000 and 700,000 years ago, though the southern wall is lost.

Approximately 1 million years ago, a stratovolcano from the sea added more land. About 18,000 years ago its caldera collapsed, and later – some 13,500 years ago – further collapsed to form an inner caldera; it may be that there was a third, even later, collapse. There were three lakes. A series of explosive eruptions followed, with the largest throwing out a huge volume of pumice from a vent in a flat area which today gives us one of the most loved places of the entire archipelago – Furnas. In 1630, a violent eruption lasting just a few days sent a pyroclastic flow, a fiery avalanche of hot gases, rocks, pumice and ash down the gorge to Ribeira Quente into the sea to form a small delta, and distributed pumice and ash over a wide area. Two of the lakes disappeared and the surviving lake was probably dammed, resulting in Lake Furnas now being almost 100m above Furnas village. It is thought the average interval between eruptions over the past almost 3,000 years is just 362 years.

Around 290,000 years ago, two stratovolcanoes began to form on the ocean floor, one to form the separate Sete Cidades volcano to the west, and Água de Pau volcano to add to the already extant island to the east. Água de Pau, more or less in the middle of São Miguel, is known for its much-visited Lagoa do Fogo ('Lake of Fire'), 250m below the caldera rim. With more than 200,000 years of eruptive history, its most vigorous period of growth was between 100,000 and 40,000 years

their families, lived permanently on São Miguel in their large houses. Each fruit was picked as it turned from green to yellow and was wrapped in a dry sheathing leaf of the maize cob. Loading was done with small boats from the shore taking the boxes out to the waiting ships in the open roadsteads. Speed was vital, for should bad weather suddenly blow in, the vessel would have to stand out to sea only part-loaded, and several days might pass before loading could be completed. Typically a crew of not more than six under a master ran the ship, and it was tough sailing during winter in the north Atlantic. The average sailing time was 10–14 days, but it could sometimes be done in seven days. An added anxiety for the voyage home was to inspect the boxes daily for rotten fruit, since a clean cargo meant a bonus for the master. Today such an event would have been spun to equal the fame of the tea clippers, but there was a race each year to deliver the first oranges of the season. It is recorded that the first ship home sold all its cargo within 6 hours at three guineas a box (£3.15 in decimal money but worth over £100 at current values). When others arrived, 47 ships within 40 hours, the price fell to 4/6d (22½p).

These schooners flourished until about 1860; steam ships were already transporting lemons from Sicily by the early 1850s, but there was no harbour suitable for the ships, a real problem in bad weather if they had to stand off burning coal, with no bunkering facilities onshore. Once harbour construction began in Ponta Delgada in the 1860s, the schooners' days were numbered, with an ever-decreasing number being chartered up until about 1870. The Coccus hesperidum pest struck the orange trees from the 1840s and harvests plummeted, but supplies from other places, including California and Florida, gradually became available, from orchards established with parent trees taken from the Azores.

ago, with the caldera enclosing a lake formed some 15,000 years ago. It has a history of violent eruptions followed by long periods of dormancy. Plinian eruptions, explosions of gas, steam and ash followed by pyroclastic flows, occurred over the following millennia. The most recent happened in 1563, over a period of six days, burying crops and houses in ash and lapilli, small volcanic stones, together with further destruction from the associated earthquakes. Four days after this eruption began, another started to the northwest in Pico Queimado, of Hawaiian type, with lava fountains and scoria or cinders, which flowed down to engulf the village of Ribeira Seca, just west of Ribeira Grande. There you can see the fountain and the surrounding lava.

Sete Cidades volcano is now 14km across at sea level; the caldera is 620m deep, with an average diameter of 5.3km. The early eruptions of dark basalt were slowly followed by pale-grey trachyte, then violent explosions left abundant layers of pumice. The caldera collapsed about 36,000 years ago and remained largely quiet until eruptions again began in the caldera around 5,000 years ago, creating a number of broad cones including those containing the crater lakes of Lagoa Rasa and Lagoa de Santiago; these craters, together with other sites within Sete Cidades, later erupted again, as did numerous satellite vents on the outer lower slopes. The last eruption on Sete Cidades was in 1439, with 19th-century eruptions out to sea northwest from the Ponta da Ferraria. At Ferraria you can see an example of a littoral cone, a secondary cone caused by steam trapped under lava which has flowed into the sea.

The middle region, the Região dos Picos or Complexo dos Picos, which united the two islands by joining Sete Cidades to Água de Pau, began to form about 50,000 years ago. In contrast with the stratovolcano and the collapsed calderas of São Miguel's two extremities, volcanism here is fissural, and produced about 250 cinder cones and domes, and ash-covered lava flows that are now cultivated. These fissures, or cracks so deep they allow magma to reach the surface, are in places close enough that some of the cinder cones are joined together while smaller, separate cones are as high as 200m. These cones lie in a broad band parallel with the south coast and some 5km inland, and are a most conspicuous landscape feature when seen from the sea or from an aeroplane coming in to land at Ponta Delgada airport. The dominant cone, distinguished by its double hump, erupted about 4,400 years ago. During the past 3,000 years, more than 18 eruptions have occurred. This bridging fissure zone, and the volcanoes of Sete Cidades, Fogo and Furnas, are all potentially active zones, and only the very far eastern end of the island is considered inactive.

HISTORY After visits by the Vikings, São Miguel's first settlers came from the Estremadura, Alentejo and Algarve provinces of Portugal, and there were also Madeirans, Jews, Moors and French. The first capital was Vila Franca do Campo, but in 1522 a severe earthquake and mudslide that killed over half of the 5,000 inhabitants and was so destructive that the island's principal port, Ponta Delgada, which was also sited on a more geologically stable area, took precedence and became the capital in 1546. Already there were some wealthy merchants, trading with mainland Portugal, Madeira, the Canaries, Flanders and elsewhere; some 25 English merchant ships are recorded as having visited in one year. Early crops included wheat, woad and sugarcane, and there were also dairy products. The port area was fortified during the 16th and 17th centuries against the frequent attacks by pirates and corsairs. Terceira was the key island in maritime trade and journeys, but with the restoration of Portuguese independence in 1640 São Miguel became the commercial centre, although there were many economic difficulties. During the 18th and early 19th centuries, the island prospered, much of the time through the development of the new export crop, oranges, and many substantial homes and churches were built. In 1831–32, resistance to the Absolutist regime was organised from the island and it was from Ponta Delgada that the Liberal expedition with some 3,500 Azorean troops sailed to northern Portugal.

Around 1860, oranges began to lose their share of the British market, partly to cheaper sources of supply from mainland Portugal and Spain, and partly because the orange trees succumbed to disease. This eventually caused an economic crisis and resulted in emigration to the Americas. New crops such as tea, pineapples, chicory, sugar beet and tobacco were then introduced, together with livestock and, later, the development of fishing. Work began in 1861 to improve the port in Ponta Delgada which stimulated industrial development, but it was after World War II, in 1947, that it was greatly expanded. The basalt city gateway was removed to its present position in the nearby square (page 91), and the new Avenida do Infante Dom Henrique and its colonnaded buildings along the seafront transformed the town's appearance: truly a piece of excellent town planning much enjoyed today by townspeople and visitors alike.

GETTING THERE AND AWAY

For information on getting to and from São Miguel island, see pages 42 and 49. By any international measure, São Miguel's John Paul II Airport (w ana.pt) is small; by Azorean standards, it's large. It has all the facilities and it acts as the main hub for the archipelago. There is no longer an airport bus service, leaving those without a rental car with a longish walk or taxis as the only options to get into town. A taxi costs €8–13 to downtown Ponta Delgada, depending on time of day and amount of luggage, and around €45 to Furnas; prices for other destinations are listed on w taxispdl.com.

There is a tourist information kiosk at the airport (⊕ Apr–Sep 06.00–00.30 daily, Oct–Mar 06.00–midnight daily), post office, ATMs, bank branch, money exchange (⊕ 07.00–noon & 14.00–17.00 Mon–Sat), cafeteria, free Wi-Fi, several car-hire companies (including names such as Hertz, Thrifty, Europcar and Sixt), and airline offices for Azores Airlines/SATA and Ryanair. Note that TAP airline enquiries are handled by Azores Airlines.

Airport information ☎296 205 400; w ana.pt

Azores Airlines [81 H6] Av Infante Dom Henrique 55; ☎296 209 720, 296 205 414; ⊕ 09.00–18.00 daily

GETTING AROUND

BY CAR/TAXI Usually starting in Ponta Delgada, island tours by taxi generally fall into two separate programmes. One covers Sete Cidades in the west, often a half-day tour, while the second is a full day going to Ribeira Grande and the tea estates on the north coast, followed by Furnas and Vila Franca on the south coast, combined with some viewpoints on the cliffs or mountains, depending upon the route taken. Another option is to take a guided tour, guaranteeing some insights into what you are seeing (see page 78 for tour guide details). Visitors with a rented car could divide their tour into three sectors, depending on available time: the western part including Sete Cidades and the northern coast to Capelas; the central area of Ribeira Grande, Lagoa do Fogo and Vila Franca; and the eastern part embracing

Nordeste, Povoação and Furnas. Alternatively, do the western section in a day, then spend two or three days exploring the east and centre with an overnight stay in Furnas or elsewhere. Taxis (✆ 296 382 000, 296 302 530) can be found either outside the Turismo [81 G7] or on nearby Praça Gonçalo Velho Cabral. Call m 938 346 759 for a wheelchair-adaptable cab. Prices for island tours by taxi are displayed at the above two locations and at w taxispdl.com.

Starting from the airport, there's a bypass road around Ponta Delgada, linking to the SCUT (ie: toll-free) expressways that head east (largely as dual carriageway) to Vila Franca do Campo, Ribeira Grande and Nordeste.

BY BUS São Miguel has a good bus service, with services running along both the north and south coasts. With an early start in Ponta Delgada, it is possible to enjoy a full day in Nordeste, Furnas, Povoação, Ribeira Grande, Sete Cidades and Capelas. The timetable changes little from year to year, but to be safe and to use the buses most effectively, get a current timetable from the tourist office. Out of hours, there are also bus timetable posters displayed just west of the main Ponta Delgada tourist office [81 G7]. The websites w smigueltransportes.com and w autoviacaomicaelense. pt contain useful bus information, but seem to be operationally temperamental. The bus schedules may not always be very convenient for tourists – they are set up to suit workers, students and schoolchildren – but they work well in combination with taxis, perhaps taking a bus for the outward journey and a taxi for the return.

All buses from Ponta Delgada leave from many stops along the esplanade – Avenida Infante Dom Henrique – including from stops by the tourist office. Bus stops for Capelas and Sete Cidades are on the north side; the others are on the south (harbour) side nearer the fort.

TOURIST INFORMATION

Being the most visited island, São Miguel is best set up in terms of tourist information services. As well as offices at the airport and Ponta Delgada, there are others dotted around the island and their details are given throughout the chapter. Most staff manning the offices are multilingual. The following two companies offer island tours:

Azores Private Tours m 914 616 240, 962 758 186; e rm@vivazores.com; w azoresprivatetours. com. A reliable & reputable guide, speaking perfect English, Rui Medeiros has both a saloon car (max 3 passengers) & a van (max 6 passengers), but the tour is always private. €230/150 full/half day (car); €320/220 full/half day (6-seater).

Harmony Trail Azores m 910 591 678; e harmonytrailazores@gmail.com; w harmonytrailazores.com. Hiking, biking & guided tours, by a personable & knowledgeable young Azorean-Canadian.

PONTA DELGADA

With a population of around 35,000 – and double that in its wider parish – this is the largest town in the Azores, serving as an administrative capital and commercial and transport hub. It's also home to a university, established as recently as 1975. Natives of other islands view Ponta Delgada and São Miguel with ambivalence, perhaps envious of how the availability of budget and other direct flights has swiftly accelerated its number of visitors, yet at the same time worried at how this influx has changed the town and island.

The laziest and fastest way – ideal, perhaps, for cruise-ship day trippers – to get to know Ponta Delgada is to take the Lagarta Trolley (a road train; see below), but in a town this pretty, following the walking trail (page 91) allows for a more leisurely and deeper appreciation of its charms.

The fairly nondescript, utilitarian apartment blocks that characterise the outskirts of town should not diminish the appreciation of Ponta Delgada's attractive core. No visitor, surely, can fail to be smitten by the patterned cobbles of the old town's narrow streets and pavements, the shuttered or balconied houses – alternately with peeling paintwork or adorned with new, bold colours – and the well-manicured gardens, often dedicated to poets or Azorean luminaries, that manifest themselves on a stroll around the compact centre. A few funky murals add a dose of alternative ambience to this easy-on-the-eye, delightful town.

Ponta Delgada is also the main centre for São Miguel's whale-watching operations and other sea-based activities (see page 97 for operators), though Vila Franca do Campo is an alternative choice (page 98).

GETTING AROUND For most visitors to Ponta Delgada, walking around the compact centre will be both the most convenient and most rewarding way to savour the joys of the town. For anyone who doesn't fancy it, there is a frequent service of half-sized buses (the PDLs) which tootle around the narrow streets, with four lines servicing most places of interest in and near the centre. These run from 07.30 to 19.30 and the routes are marked on the bus stops, with a single ride costing just €0.50.

Bikes can be rented from the **Azores Bike Shop** [81 E4] (Rua do Mercado 17; **m** 915 142 938, 968 392 143; **e** azoresbikeshop@gmail.com; **w** azoresbikeshop.com/en; ⏲ 10.00–13.30 & 14.30–18.00 Mon–Fri, 09.00–13.00 Sat), opposite the market. The car rental company **Autatlantis** [80 D4] (↘ 296 281 248; **w** autatlantis.com) also rents out e-bikes at their office near the cruise terminal. See also page 51 and individual towns.

Town tour by road train The Lagarta ticket office and stop [80 D5] (↘ 296 629 446; **e** info@lagarta.pt; **w** lagarta. pt; ⏲ ticket office: 09.00–17.00) are at the western end of Avenida Infante Dom Henrique, almost opposite the Forte de São Brás. Year-round, three different themed circuits are offered at different times: historical, beach or gardens. In winter, the schedule reduces, sometimes only running in good weather or when a cruise ship is ready to discharge its hordes. A taped commentary is given in English, and

PONTA DELGADA

For listings, see from page 82

Where to stay

Where to eat and drink

PONTA DELGADA

↗ Furnas, Ribeira Grande, Nordeste

A   B   C   D

Hospital

← Airport, Sete Cidades, Mosteiros, Gruta do Carvão

RUA ARCANJO LAR

AVENIDA DOM MANUEL I

RUA DA ARQUINHA

Jardim Botânico José do Canto

Cemetery

Jardim do Palacio de Sant'Ana

Parque Atlanticó

RUA DA JUVENTUDE

RUA DO PAIOL

RUA JOSÉ DO

RUA DE SANTANNA

RUA DE SÃO JOAQUIM

RUA MANUEL AUGUSTO AMARAL

RUA CASTELO BRANCO

AVENIDA ANTERO DE QUENTAL

RUA ANTÓNIO BORGES

Jardim António Borges

13

14

Igreja do Colégio

Núcleo de Arte Sacra

RUA DR GUILHER

RUA DA VITÓRIA

Antero de Quental

28

25

Autatlantis

RUA DR ARISTEDES DA MOTA

6

RUA CARVALHO ARAUJO

Canada

RUA DOUTOR FILIPE DA CUNHA ALVARES CABRAL

RUA DIREITA DE SANTA CATARINA

RUA DOS CAPAS

RUA DE SÃO MIGUEL

RUA CORONEL SILVA LEAL

RUA MACHADO DOS SANTOS

RUA DA VILA NOVA

Largo Mártires da Pátria

RUA PINTOR DOMINGOS REBELO

RUA DE SANTA CATARINA

RUA JOÃO DO REGO

Nossa Senhora da Conceição

Centro Municipal de Cultura

Airport

RUA DE LISBOA

1

Jardim Padre Senas Freitas

19

9

RUA DA CRUZ

Coliseu Micaelense

Sweden

i

RUA JOÃO FRANCISCO CABRAL

Convento da Nossa Senhora da Esperança

RUA DR GIL MONT ALVERNE

Praça Vasco da Gama

AV ALBERTO I PRINCIPE DE MONACO

USA

São José

Praça 5 Outubro

Lagarta Miniature Train ticket office

Bus stops

Cais da Sardinha

RUA JOÃO DO REGO

RUA JOSÉ BENSAUDE

RUA D'ALGERIA

10

Forte São Brás (Museu Mifitar)

RUA DOUTOR TEÓFILO DE BRAGA

RUA ENG ABEL FERIN COUTINHO

A   B   C   D

80

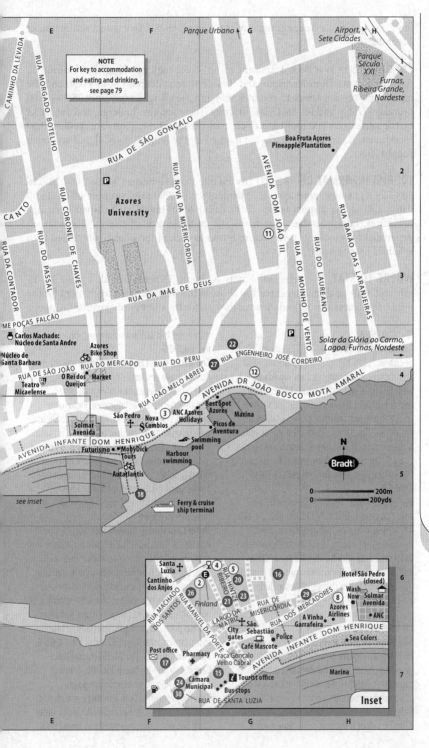

E   F   *Parque Urbano*   G   *Airport,*   H
Sete Cidades

NOTE
For key to accommodation
and eating and drinking,
see page 79

Parque
Século
XXI   1

Furnas,
Ribeira Grande,
Nordeste

CAMINHO DA LEVADA

RUA MORGADO BOTELHO

RUA DE SÃO GONÇALO

RUA NOVA DA MISERICÓRDIA

AVENIDA DOM JOÃO III

Boa Fruta Açores
Pineapple Plantation

RUA BARÃO DAS LARANJEIRAS

2

CANTO

RUA CORONEL DE CHAVES

RUA DO PASSAL

Azores
University

P

RUA DO MOINHO DE VENTO

RUA DO LAUREANO

RUA DA CONTADOR

RUA DA MÃE DE DEUS

3

ME POÇAS FALCÃO

♿ Carlos Machado:
Núcleo de Santa André

Núcleo de
Santa Bárbara

Azores
Bike Shop
🚲

RUA DE SÃO JOÃO

RUA DO MERCADO

RUA DO PERU

22

27 RUA ENGENHEIRO JOSÉ CORDEIRO

P

Solar da Glória ao Carmo,
Lagoa, Furnas, Nordeste
→

Teatro
Micaelense 🎭

O Rei dos
Queijos

Market

RUA JOÃO MELO ABREU

12

4

AVENIDA DR JOÃO BOSCO MOTA AMARAL

7

Best Spot
Azores

Marina

Solmar
Avenida

São Pedro
✝

Nova
S Cambios

3 ANC Azores
Holidays

Picos de
Aventura

Futurismo ● MobyDick
Tours
🚲

AVENIDA INFANTE DOM HENRIQUE

🏊 Swimming
pool

Harbour
swimming

N

5

Autatlantis

18

Ferry & cruise
ship terminal

see inset

Bradt

0   200m
0   200yds

Inset

Santa ✝
Luzia

🚩 ④

4 ⑤

Hotel São Pedro
(closed)

6

Cantinho
dos Anjos

E

②

RUA TINTE RIBEIRO

20

16

Wash
Now

Solmar
Avenida

26

Finland

21

23

RUA DE
MISERICÓRDIA

29

RUA DOS MERCADORES

8

Azores
Airlines

● ANC

RUA MACHADO DOS SANTOS

RUA MANUEL DA PORTE

LARGO DA
MATRIZ

✝ São
Sebastião

City
gates

A Vinha
Garrafeira

AVENIDA INFANTE DOM HENRIQUE

Café Mascote

● Police

Sea Colors

Post office
✉
17

Pharmacy
➕

Praça Gonçalo
Velho Cabral

Marina

15

🛈 Tourist office

7

24

Câmara
Municipal

● Bus stops

30

RUA DE SANTA LUZIA

E   F   G   H

fares are generally (depending on the route) €8/6/4/free adult/senior/under 12/under 2.

Parking There is a decent amount of on-street parking along the seafront on Avenida Infante Dom Henrique and its side streets. An hour costs €0.80 and the maximum stay is 6 hours 15 minutes (€5), but the charges apply only 08.00–19.00 Monday–Friday and 08.00–13.00 Saturday. There are also underground car parks on the same street and multi-storey car parks around town. Costs are around €3.50 for 4 hours. A few free car parks are marked on the map [80 B4/C4], but are much sought after.

TOURIST INFORMATION [81 G7] (Av Infante Dom Henrique; ✆ 296 308 610, 296 308 625; e pt.smg@azores.gov.pt; ⊕ winter 09.00–17.00 daily, summer 09.00–19.00 daily; also at the airport 06.30–20.30 daily) Multilingual staff dispense various brochures, bus timetables and maps, all available free of charge. The tourism department also sells its own picture books to each of the islands, illustrated with splendid photographs.

WHERE TO STAY The principal hotels in Ponta Delgada are all within 10–15 minutes' walk of the town centre, but those in the west are more convenient for the public buses and airport and those in the east for the marina and swimming pools.

In the west

Azoris Royal Garden [80 B5] (193 rooms) Rua de Lisboa; ✆ 296 307 300; e centralderservas@ azorishotels; w azorishotels.com/royalgarden. A well-designed, oriental-themed, 1970s building with lots of light & feeling of space, built round an attractive enclosed inner garden planted with bamboos & cloud trees. Good-sized indoor, outdoor & children's pools (all heated), tennis court (extra charge), sauna, Turkish bath, jacuzzi & gymnasium, free off-street parking. Copious buffet b/fast. **€€€€€**

Hotel Vila Nova [80 C6] (102 rooms) Rua João Francisco Cabral 1; ✆ 296 301 600; m 963 447 496; e vilanova@mystoryhotels.com; w mystoryhotels.com. A comfortable, modern hotel suited for both holiday & business use. Buffet restaurant, gymnasium, outdoor heated pool, parking (extra charge). Rates include b/fast. **€€€**

In the centre

São Miguel Park Hotel [80 C3] (163 rooms) Rua Manuel Augusto Amaral; ✆ 296 306 000; e smph@bhc.pt; w bensaudehotels.com/en/ saomiguelparkhotel. A modern block a bit short of atmosphere but with a good view over Ponta Delgada. Some rooms have balconies, all have AC & sat TV. Indoor & outdoor pools, fitness room,

restaurant, bar, children's playroom. Buffet b/fast inc. **€€€€€**

Comercial Guest House [81 F6] (8 rooms) Rua Machado dos Santos 73; m 919 294 000; e residencialacomercial@gmail.com; w comercialazoresboutique.com. Right in the centre, this is a small, pleasantly renovated house, with wooden floors, outdoor terrace & communal lounge area. Rooms are not the biggest, there's no parking of its own, but all rooms have bathroom. B/fast (not inc) can be had at the restaurant down below. Good value, but do phone in advance, as there's no permanent English-speaking receptionist. **€€€€**

Hotel Casa Hintze Ribeiro [81 G6] (22 rooms) Rua Hintze Ribeiro 64; ✆ 296 304 340; e reservas@ casahintzeribeiro.com; w casahintzeribeiro. com. Ultra-chic & dripping with style, a welcome addition to the town's accommodation choices. Innovative touches, some rooms with balconies, all with s/c option (extra charge). Adults' & children's rooftop pools, sunloungers, spa (sauna, steam room, jacuzzi), small gym. B/fast not inc. **€€€€**

Hotel do Colégio [80 D4] (55 rooms) Rua Carvalho Araújo 39; ✆ 296 306 600; e info@ hoteldocolegio.pt; w hoteldocolegio.pt. Tastefully converted from a former convent, this is conveniently located in a quiet & narrow street. Good bar, restaurant, courtyard swimming pool,

Turkish bath, sauna. Renovated in 2017, rooms now have AC, cable TV. B/fast inc. €€€€

Hotel Neat Avenida [81 H7] (120 rooms) Rua Dr José Bruno Tavares Carreiro; 📞296 209 660; e neathotelavenida@bensaude. pt; w neathotelavenida.com. Very central, a complete remodelling of a former hotel which lay abandoned for years. Rooms are spacious, with AC, sat TV. Buffet b/fast is available, though not included. Sauna & small gym on site. €€€€

Hotel Talisman [80 C5] (53 rooms) Rua Marquês da Praia Monforte 40; 📞296 308 500; w hoteltalisman.com. A charming hotel, an 18th-century house stylishly converted in 1992 in Art Deco-style by a French architect, & later enlarged & refurbished with small rooftop pool, gym & lift. Right in town on a pedestrianised street, a quite delightful place to stay. Try to get a room with a balcony, preferably overlooking the garden. €€€€

Hotel Alcides [81 G6] (15 rooms) Rua Hintze Ribeiro 61–67; 📞296 282 677; e geral@alcides.pt; w alcides.pt. A very good-value 2-star hotel with friendly staff, fine b/fast & decent rooms with TV & AC. Central, but no parking. Excellent restaurant next door (page 84). €€

Pousada da Juventude (Youth Hostel) [80 C3] Rua São Francisco Xavier; 📞296 629 431; e bookings@azoresyouthhostels.com; w azoresyouthhostels.com. Fairly central, with easy access to shops & transport. A former nunnery with modern rooms behind, it has 90 beds in shared rooms & 2 family rooms with bathroom. There are also twins with private bath. €

In the east

Grand Hotel Açores Atlântico [81 F4] (140 rooms) Av Dom Infante Henrique 113; 📞296 302 200; e ghaa@bhc.pt; w bensaudehotels.com/ grandhotelacoresatlantico. Upgraded in 2018, this is now a true 5-star, with high standards of service and sustainability in this elegant waterfront establishment. Part of the Bensaude group, nautical touches in the décor pay homage to its shipping interests. Std rooms have bath or shower, suites have both. Live music is offered every night. Smart pool & small gym. €€€€€

Hotel Marina Atlântico [81 F4] (184 rooms) Av João Bosco Mota Amaral 1; 📞296 307 900; e hma@bhc.pt; w bensaudehotels.com/ hotelmarinaatlantico. Next to the Grand Hotel

Açores Atlântico (which is part of the same group, but more expensive), this is a smart hotel with external detailing influenced by the adjacent marina. If you want a sea view, specify when booking. A pedestrian bridge across the main road gives easy access to the marina & public swimming pools, & it's a 10min promenade into the centre of town. Outdoor pool, health club, sauna, jacuzzi, Turkish bath & reading room. Parking is extra, but free if you book through the website. B/fast inc. €€€€€

Lince [81 G3] (154 rooms) Av Dom João III 29; 📞296 630 000; e info.tla@thelincehotels.com; w thelincehotels.com/azores. A striking modern high-rise towards the pineapple plantation, with spa, gym, indoor pool, excellent restaurant (plus a lounge bar with pizza & *petiscos*) and impeccable service. €€€€€

Octant Hotel [81 G4] (118 rooms, 5 suites) Av Doutor João Bosco Mota Amaral 4; 📞296 249 900; e reservations-pontadelgada@octanthotels.com; w pontadelgada.octanthotels.com. Opened in 2016, this 5-star boasts spacious, modern rooms which all overlook the sea, with sat TV. There's a spacious restaurant, lobby bar, spa & gym, while up on the roof you'll find a pool, sunbathing area & the whale-watching bar: if you can't spot a cetacean, they'll lend you binoculars. Still no luck? Try a cocktail – they create a new one each month. Next door, but under separate management, is one of the Azores' 2 casinos. Restaurant has a daily-changing lunch menu, good value (2 courses for €18) for a 5-star hotel. €€€€€

Around Ponta Delgada

Quinta da Abelheira [72 B4] (14 rooms) Caminho Abelheira de Baixo 17, Fajã de Baixo; 📞296 383 903; e info@azoreanbliss.com; w quintadaabelheira.com. On the eastern side of Ponta Delgada & just a 10min drive to the centre, yet very quiet. A lovely old manor house, traditionally furnished, some rooms within the house, others in a modern annexe. Games room & swimming pool. Relaxing garden, decorated with tiled panels from 1932 & illustrated quotes from Azorean poets. Dinner provided with 24hrs' notice. No facilities for children, free bike hire. 2-night min stay. €€€€€

Solar Branco Eco Estate & Boutique Hotel [72 C3] (4 rooms, 4 cottages) Estrada José Francisco, Livramento; 📱919 076 779;

e hello@solarbranco.com; w solarbranco.com. This British-owned hotel is known for its 1,000-bottle Gin Library and the daily free Gin O'Clock. No TV, no meals other than a good b/fast. Not easy to find, just west of the EN7-2A; 2-night min. €€€€€

Solar da Glória ao Carmo [72 C4] (3 rooms, 2 apartments) Rua da Glória ao Carmo 5, Livramento; ☎ 296 629 847; e info@

gloriaaocarmo.com; w gloriaaocarmo.com. A few km east of town, a rather austere, 300-year-old building conceals a beautifully restored interior with period furniture, plus modern s/c apartments. The suite is sumptuous, if your budget can stretch. Heating, no AC or TV in rooms, but a roof terrace & a truly excellent b/fast. Family-run. Evening meals available on request. Free parking on street. €€€€€

✗ **WHERE TO EAT AND DRINK** São Miguel now has many, many restaurants, and you can even find Chinese, Japanese, Mexican or Italian cuisine in Ponta Delgada if you need a change from the local fare. In town, you can easily encounter cheap eats (lunchtime main courses from around €6) in the backstreets, though price largely reflects the quality. Popular, though verging on fast food, are the relatively new places along the promenade next to Ponta Delgada's marina, near the ferry terminal. The restaurants listed below are recommended, though of course the scene changes all the time.

Anfiteatro Restaurant & Lounge [81 F5] Pavilão do Mar; ☎ 296 206 150; ⏰ noon–14.30 & 19.00–22.30 Mon–Fri, noon–15.00 & 19.00–22.30 Sat–Sun. With a lounge & a fine-dining restaurant to choose from, this establishment also trains culinary students & tries hard to do something different. It is hidden beneath the can't-miss amphitheatre on the waterfront. The lounge/café/bar on the ground floor serves a wide choice of cocktails & gins, salads, sandwiches, etc – not much of a nod to Azorean traditions, but a pleasant change; the dining room on the 1st floor is focused on tasting menus. Upstairs is not cheap: somewhere for a special occasion, perhaps. €€€€

A Reserva [81 G7] Travessa do Aterro 1; m 910 543 159; e reserva@antunesida.com; ⏰ summer 18.00–22.30 Mon–Sat, winter 19.00–22.00 Mon–Thu. Nothing Azorean about this highly rated place: food & wines are all from the Portuguese mainland. Tapas are heavily orientated towards sausage, tinned fish & a variety of tasty cheeses. You can 'mix & match' & order as many as you want. Wine list is huge, with bottles starting around €8. Not expensive, but order wisely, as your bill can quickly spiral upwards. €€€

A Tasca [81 G6] Rua do Aljube 18; ☎ 296 288 880; ⏰ 11.30–midnight Mon–Sat. Firmly established as one of the town's top tables, justifiably popular with visitors, but with an excellent ambience. Check out the daily changing dishes, or order

from an extensive & inexpensive menu. Not many vegetarian options, but there's a good wine list. €€€

Michel [81 G4] Rua Eng. José Cordeiro Antiga da Calheta 55; ☎ 296 700 385; w michelrestaurant.com; ⏰ 12.30–14.30 & 19.00–21.30 Mon–Fri, 19.00–21.30 Sat. A stylish little place on the east side of town, serving classic French & Portuguese dishes, with some vegetarian options. Excellent service. €€€

Adega Regional [81 F7] Rua do Melo 70; ☎ 296 284 740; ⏰ noon–15.00 & 18.30–22.00 Tue–Sun, closed last Sun of the month. Well-priced regional specialities, without any fancy touches but with a good choice of fish dishes. €€

Alcides [81 G6] Rua Hintze Ribeiro 61–77; ☎ 296 281 290, 296 282 677; w alcides.pt/restaurant; ⏰ noon–15.00 & 19.00–22.00 daily. Has a well-deserved reputation for its steak, renowned by locals as possibly the island's finest. Also fish, grilled meat & a vegetarian dish. Part of the hotel next door, but with the feel of a separate establishment. €€

Focaccia [80 C5] Largo 2 de Março 69; ☎ 296 282 196; m 961 132 446; w focacciaazores.pt; ⏰ noon–15.00 & 18.00–22.00 Thu–Tue. Probably the best pizza in town, from a wood-fired oven of course, plus authentic pasta & other Italian treats (inc the wine list). €€

INTZ48 [81 G6] Rua Hintze Ribeira 48; ☎ 296 707 655; w intz48.business.site; ⏰ 09.00–15.00 Mon & Wed–Sat. A chic establishment, boasting

3rd-wave coffee (roasted & ground on site) & the best brunches in town. Vegetarian options & pizza. Tempting homemade gelato & ice lollies, great for a hot day. €€

Osteria Casa Nostra [81 G6] Rua Hintze Ribeiro 22; m 934 335 552; fi casanostrapdl; ⊕ 18.30–22.30 Sun–Tue & Thu–Fri, 19.00–22.30 Sat. A classy Italian restaurant – try the gnocchi, or go for the full tasting menu. Good service, although sometimes the courses come almost too fast. €€

Restaurante Nacional [81 F7] Rua Açoreana Oriental 18; \296 629 949; ⊕ noon–15.00 & 18.30–22.00 Mon–Fri, 18.30–22.00 Sat. Established in 1947 & some of the smart, friendly waiters have been here nearly as long! Traditional fare, served in a quaint, semi-formal dining room. Portions are generous, prices reasonable. €€

Restaurante Rotas da Ilha Verde [80 D4] Rua Pedro Homem 49; \296 628 560; e reservasrotasilha@gmail.com; w rotasdailhaverde.com; ⊕ noon–15.00 & 19.00–22.00 Tue–Fri, 19.00–23.00 Sat. A rare vegetarian restaurant, with a creative & extensive range, all excellent quality. Cheap pratos do dia. Vegans also catered for, gluten-free options available on request. Specials might include pear soup or aubergine strudel. Small & usually packed, so booking advisable. €€

Santo Seitan [81 F6] Rua Machado dos Santos 75; m 925 348 233; ⊕ 18.30–22.00 Mon, noon–15.00 & 18.30–22.00 Tue–Sat. A new vegetarian restaurant (perhaps a bit pricey; also doing take-aways & deliveries) where almost every dish can be made vegan. Seitan is a major component, of course, with tofu & vegan cheese. €€

Taberna Açor [81 H7] Rua dos Mercadores 41; \296 629 084; ⊕ 10.00–23.00 Tue–Thu, 10.00–02.00 Fri, noon–02.00 Sat, noon–22.00 Sun. With a tempting selection of tapas-style dishes, you can graze at your own pace & eat as much as you like. You can also wise-up on your knowledge of Azorean cheeses here. It's a pub-style place with an energetic young team of servers, but no reservations. €€

Louvre Micaelense [81 G6] Rua Antonio Jose Almeida 8; \938 346 886; ⊕ 11.00–midnight daily. A lively café-bistro with appealing brunch, vegetarian & cocktail options. The interior dates from its time as a haberdasher's shop, & there's seating on the traffic-free street too. €

Sardinha ('Mané Cigano's') [81 G4] Rua Engenheiro Jose Cordeiro 1; \296 285 765; fi mane.cigano; ⊕ noon–15.00 Mon–Fri, bar 09.00–20.00 Mon–Sat. Cheap lunchtime eats, with *chicharros* (horse mackerel) the speciality. Served in a cramped dining room, at tables shared with locals. Octogenarian Mané still cooks, & his family serve the tables. It's rough & ready, you won't be encouraged to linger, but Mané's is a Ponta Delgada institution – & it's cheap. €

Suplexio [80 D4] Rua Pedro Homem 68; w suplexio.com; ⊕ noon–15.00 & 19.00–22.00 Tue–Thu, noon–15.00 & 19.00–23.00 Fri, 13.00–16.00 & 18.30–22.00 Sat. They don't take reservations, hence no phone number. If you're homesick for a burger, this is the place. Good quality & variety – vegetarian options, too – you can wash it all down with one or several of the bottled craft beers on offer. The fries are excellent as well. Attentive & knowledgeable staff. €

Varandas da Avenida [81 F7] Rua de Santa Luzia 28 (crnr Praça Vasco da Gama); \296 284 156; ⊕ 07.00–20.00 Mon–Fri, 07.00–19.00 Sat. With a great selection of pastries & an early opening, this is a good, unpretentious b/fast location. Popular with locals heading to work, José & crew will even do you bacon & eggs, if you ask. Lunchtime prato do dia is good value & there is a well-priced menu of snacks. Outside tables, too. €

ENTERTAINMENT AND NIGHTLIFE Although Ponta Delgada is by far the most important and busiest town in the Azores, nightlife here remains mostly quiet and traditional. One popular late-night bar is the nautically themed **Cantinho dos Anjos** [81 G6] (Rua Hintze Ribeiro 83; ⊕ 08.00–02.00 Mon–Sat, 16.00–02.00 Sun). Many simply enjoy an evening promenade by the harbour after a good dinner, though in summer things can get quite lively, with popular music events in the city's squares and by the marina. **Teatro Micaelense** [81 E4] (w teatromicaelense. pt) offers a wide range of cultural events throughout the year, from ballet, musicals, fado, jazz and chamber recitals to fully staged operas, the programmes often linked with the Coliseums in Lisbon and Porto. **Coliseu Micaelense** [80 C5] (Rua de

Lisboa; ✆ 296 209 500; e geral@coliseumicaelense.pt; w coliseumicaelense.pt; tickets ⊕ 14.00–18.00 Tue–Fri or until start of performance) has a similar variety of performances as the Teatro. The Coliseu is a beautiful, old-world venue with 76 numbered, private boxes which will transport you straight back to 1917, the year of its opening. Fully restored in 2002, it's worth poking your head into the auditorium to admire the architecture and period décor. Temporary exhibitions are sometimes held upstairs, usually with a small admission charge. It's also home to Lava Jazz (m 917 350 418; e lavajazzbar@atalhosdelava.com; w lavajazz.com), a lounge bar that's open Tuesday to Saturday, with live music Friday and Saturday.

SHOPPING Pottering around the quaint streets of Ponta Delgada will bring you in contact with a few souvenir shops, especially around the Praça Gonçalo Velho Cabral [81 G7]. As well as the slightly tired commercial centre of **Solmar Avenida** [81 H6], which does contain a good bookshop, the **Livraria Solmar** (✆ 296 629 720; w livrariasolmar.blogspot.com; ⊕ 10.00–20.00 Mon–Sat, 10.00–18.00 Sun), there is another (and much bigger) mall – the **Parque Atlanticó** [80 C2]– at the north edge of town. It has no Azorean character – nor *any* character – but could help you pass a wet afternoon if you like to browse in shops.

A Vinha Garrafeira [81 H6] Av Infante Dom Henrique 49; ✆ 296 205 358; w avinhagarrafeira. pt; ⊕ 13.30–17.30 Mon, 10.00–14.00 & 15.00–19.00 Tue–Sat. A wine shop on the main promenade, a century-old business with a good selection of Azorean wines & liquors. Very popular with cruise-ship escapees. Magma is a renowned brand of white wine from Terceira, & from Pico, Frei Gigante is also reputable, while the Tinto Atlanticó is a good-option red from the same island. Atlantis is semi-sweet & fortified. Excellent mainland wines are also sold here.

O Rei dos Queijos [81 E4] Rua do Mercado; m 914 298 641; w oreidosqueijos.pt; ⊕ 08.00–18.30 Mon–Fri, 08.00–14.00 Sat. By the market, this is the place for artisanal cheeses from the Azores & across Portugal & Europe, also cured meats, wines, & other gourmet products, including Gorreana teas.

OTHER PRACTICALITIES
Hospital [80 B1] Av Dom Manuel I; ✆ 296 203 000. Northwest of the town centre.
Laundry Wash Now [81 H6], unit 004, Solmar Avenida Center; ✆ 296 283 427; ⊕ 10.00–17.00 Mon–Sat. Not self-service, nor very cheap, but cheaper than your hotel's service. Occasionally also opens on Sun in summer.

Money exchange Nova Cambios [81 F5], Av Dom Infante Henrique 111; w novacambios.com; ⊕ 09.00–18.00 Mon–Fri, 10.00–14.00 Sat
Police [81 G7] ✆ 296 205 500
Post office [81 F7] Praça Vasco da Gama; ⊕ 08.30–18.00 Mon–Sat

WHAT TO SEE AND DO For individual **activity** listings, see page 94.

Museums Ponta Delgada's main museum, the Museu Carlos Machado (named after its founder in 1876), consists of three nucléos or sections – the main one recently underwent a decade-long restoration. Around the island, smaller museums can also be found, most charmingly staged, often in picturesque settings.

Museu Carlos Machado: Nucléo de Santo André (Santo André section) [81 E4] (Rua Dr Guilherme Poças; ✆ 296 202 930; ⊕ Apr–Sep 10.00–18.00 Tue–Sun, Oct–Mar 09.30–17.30 Tue–Sun; €2/1/free adults/under 25s & seniors/under 15s, free Sun. Audio guides also available: €2. Note you can visit this museum & the two described opposite – on the same day – for a combined price of €5) This important museum occupies the former convent of Santo André, founded in 1567 and named after the first patron saint of Ponta Delgada. Built for the Clarissite nuns, it has undergone several structural changes and its present appearance dates from the first half of the 19th century. An imposing building in itself, exhibits start with a useful historical timeline that gives context to the islands' place in the world. The convent's Baroque chapel is hugely impressive, particularly the upper choir, and the arrangements to isolate the nuns from visitors from the outside world are astonishing. There are a number of rooms upstairs dedicated to natural history, with an astonishing range of stuffed creatures. If you are interested in the latter, you could get metaphorically lost in here; if not, you get literally lost. Nearly all the information signs are translated into English; note that there are some steep stone steps, but also lifts to make it more accessible. Ethnographic sections are promised in the future.

Museu Carlos Machado: Núcleo de Santa Bárbara (Santa Barbara Centre) [80 D4] (Rua Dr Carlos Machado, adjacent to the main Santo André section; \ 296 202 930; w museucarlosmachado.azores.gov.pt; ⊕ Apr–Sep 10.00–18.00 Tue–Sun, Oct–Mar 09.30–17.30 Tue–Sun; prices as per the Santo André section, opposite) Mainly temporary exhibitions, plus a display of sculptures by Ernesto Canto da Maia (1890–1981), one of the Azores' greatest artists, revered also in mainland Portugal. A visit to the adjoining church is included. English-speaking staff will help with information.

Museu Carlos Machado: Núcleo de Arte Sacra (Museum of Sacred Art) [80 D3] (By the Antero de Quental memorial garden, Largo do Colegio; ⊕ Apr–Sep 10.00–13.00 & 14.00–18.00 Tue–Sun, Oct–Mar 09.30–13.00 & 14.00–17.30 Tue–Sun; prices as per the Santo André section, opposite) The church has the two most important examples of 18th-century Portuguese art: the magnificent carved cedar-wood altarpiece is the greatest wooden monument in Portugal, begun after 1737 and left partially gilded in 1760 when the Jesuits were banished; the tiled panels are 5m high and depict Eucharistic allegories framed by Baroque ornamentation. For these two works alone it is well worth visiting, but there's also a fine *Coronation of the Virgin* by Vasco Pereira Lusitano (1604) and temporary exhibitions which focus on aspects of island culture. Audio guides are available in English, for €2 extra, but only cover the old Jesuit church. The public library next door also puts on temporary exhibitions, as does the **Centro Municipal de Cultura** on Largo Mártires da Pátria (\ 296 306 510; e geral.cmc@mpdelgada.pt; ⊕ 09.00–17.00 Mon–Fri, 14.00–17.00 Sat; free).

Museu Militar dos Açores [80 C6] (Forte de São Brás, at the western end of the harbour; \ 296 308 633; ⊕ 10.00–18.00 daily (last tickets sold at 17.00); €3/1/ free adult/under 17s & seniors/under 13s) Housed in the ancient fort, the Military Museum of the Azores has displays of uniforms and weapons going back 200 years, military communications, field equipment and medical services. Two rooms have recently been handed over to former combatants, who have created exhibitions dedicated to Portugal's colonial wars of the 20th century. Opened in 2006, the museum affords fascinating access to the fort itself which makes it well worth the visit; enjoy the view from the walls along the waterfront towards town, as well as the World War II guns used to defend the harbour. You'll come down and leave via a covered area full of vehicles and artillery. The fort was built in the late 16th century to defend the port and still serves as a regional command centre for the

Portuguese military. Limited information is available in English, but the exhibits are nevertheless mainly visual.

Gardens During the middle years of the 19th century, at least three great gardens were developed in Ponta Delgada, and their owners vied with each other to have the latest introductions and the rarest plants. They are all within walking distance of the town centre.

Jardim António Borges [80 B3] (entrance from Av Antero de Quental or Rua António Borges; ✆ 296 304 400; ⊕ May–Sep 09.00–20.00 Mon–Fri, 09.00–21.00 Sat–Sun, Oct–Apr 09.00–18.00 daily; admission free) Begun in 1858 by the affluent landowner António Borges, this 3ha garden remains by far the most ornate, or rather the most fanciful, of the gardens. Managed by the municipality since 1957, there remain a great fern ravine with its romantic bridge, as well as

---

FESTIVALS ON SÃO MIGUEL

One of the most important festivals is that of **Senhor Santo Cristo dos Milagres** (literally Lord Holy Christ of Miracles), to whom intense devotion was given during the 17th century when the island was racked by frequent earthquakes and tremors, and whose celebration has strengthened through the centuries. In Ponta Delgada, the Convento da Nossa Senhora da Esperança (page 93) and nearby Praça 5 Outubro [80 C5/6] (Square of 5 October) are illuminated and the street decorated with flowers, and at the end of the week, on the fifth Sunday after Easter, a large procession passes round the town with the crown of golden thorns at the front. Behind come men in religious robes, some barefoot, some carrying large, very heavy candles to declare their thanks for a blessing received during a period of affliction. These are followed by youth organisations with their brightly coloured banners, children, some dressed as angels, priests, then the figure of Senhor Santo Cristo dos Milagres carried under a dossel of velvet and gold decorated with 18th-century woven flowers. Temporary bars are set up around and about.

A much less conspicuous celebration, but one that perhaps makes a greater impression upon the visitor by its gravity and simplicity, is that of the **Lenten pilgrims**. During the seven weeks of Lent, groups of men led by a 'master' walk right round the island (*romarios*) and pray at the churches and chapels dedicated to Our Lady. As they walk they say the Ave Maria; you can ask them to say one for you, but in return you must say as many yourself as there are men walking in the group. Flyers are issued, warning of their presence on the roads!

Of great significance in the religious calendar is the **Holy Ghost Festival** that climaxes on the seventh Sunday after Easter. It arose in medieval Germany when an Imperial Brotherhood was set up to help people in times of calamity; it spread widely in Christian Europe including Portugal. On São Miguel its importance grew after the tragic earthquake that virtually destroyed Vila Franca do Campo in 1522. The **Procession of Bom Jesus da Pedra** is one of the oldest religious festivals and attracts many emigrants from around the world.

Cantar às Estrelas, Sing to the Stars, is celebrated by singing to Our Lady of the Stars at night in the streets in thanks for the star that guided the Three Kings to Bethlehem.

In May is the festival of **São Miguel Arcanjo,** which has been celebrated for more than 400 years. Its secular content involves a procession of different professional small lakes and watercourses. Boating and garden parties here must have been huge fun in bygone days. Most of the original planting has long gone but a great buttress-rooted *Ficus macrophylla*, and a huge *Albizia* are worth seeing. Although kept clean, the garden has seen better times – it's now a popular hangout for schoolchildren.

Jardim Botânico José do Canto [80 D2] (Rua José do Canto; ✆ 296 650 310; w josedocanto.com; ⊕ Apr–Sep 09.00–19.00, Oct–Mar 09.00–17.00, daily; €5/2.50/free adult/under 12s/under 8s) José do Canto was probably the most knowledgeable gardener of his time and, from the mid 1800s, began to build a plant collection that over the next 50 years would total several thousand species. Not only did he compile lists of the species he wanted to acquire, he even kept a long list of the plants he did not want to grow! This garden of more than 5ha was considered one of the finest private botanical gardens in Europe. Much of the

groups – fishermen, potters, shoemakers, barbers and farmers, etc. The **Festival of São João** on 24 June is also Vila Franca's municipal holiday; celebrations continue for a week with marching bands, dances, bonfires and barbecues.

Cantar às Estrelas Ribeira Grande; beginning of February.
Festa de São José Ponta Delgada; procession third week of March.
Easter March/April.
Festa Sr dos Enfermos Furnas; weekend after Easter. The streets are covered with azaleas and other flowers for the procession.
Festa de São Pedro Gonçalves – Festa do Irró Vila Franca; end of April. The fishermen process down to the harbour.
Festa do Sr Santo Cristo dos Milagres Ponta Delgada; fifth Sunday after Easter.
Festa da Flor Ribeira Grande; May. Flower festival.
Festas do Espírito Santo May to September; intermittent.
Festas de São João da Vila Vila Franca; middle of June. With popular singing groups and food stalls, dancing, bonfires and barbecues.
Império da Trindade Ponta Delgada; third week of June. Ending of the Holy Ghost Festival.
Festa do Corpo de Deus Povoação; last week of June.
Cavalhadas de São Pedro Ribeira Grande; last week of June. Horsemen pay tribute to St Peter in traditional song asking protection for the island's governor.
Semana do Chicharro Ribeira Quente; middle of July. Fishing festival.
Festa de N Sra de Lourdes Capelas; end of July.
Festa de Santana Furnas; end of July.
Festa de São Nicolau Sete Cidades; middle of August.
Festa de N Sra dos Anjos Água de Pau/Fajã de Baixo; middle of August.
Festa de N Sra da Conceição Mosteiros; third week of August.
Semana da Cultura Povoação; last week of August. Handicrafts & other activities.
Festa de Bom Jesus da Pedra Vila Franca; last week of August. One of the oldest religious festivals, attracting many emigrants from around the world.
Festival de Bandas Povoação; first week of October. Road show.
Dia das Montras Ponta Delgada; second week of December. Shop windows are dressed for Christmas and prizes awarded for the best.

design and planting was supervised by English gardeners. The garden, next door to the Sant'Ana Palace (see below), remains in private ownership. Without doubt the finest specimen trees in the Azores are to be found here, in maturity a noble memorial to the man who worked so hard to introduce them. Look especially for Australian Moreton Bay figs (*Ficus macrophylla*), honeymyrtle (*Melaleuca decora*) and Kauri pine (*Agathis robusta*), *Araucaria columnaris* from New Caledonia, the Japanese Kusamaki tree (*Podocarpus macrophyllus*), and Chinese camphorwood (*Cinnamomum camphora*). If you follow the cobbles to the top of the hill, you won't get much of a view, but you will meet a magnificent 160-year-old rubber tree.

Jardim do Palacio de Sant'Ana (The Presidential Palace Garden) [80 C2] (Rua Jacome Correia; ☏ 296 301 100; ⊕ (garden only) Apr–Sep 10.00–17.00 Tue–Sun; €2, max 30 visitors at any time, guided tours can be booked) Now the office of the President of the Autonomous Region of the Azores, it has (unsurprisingly) one of the best maintained gardens in the Azores. The house was once a family home of the Correia family, who commissioned the English architect David Mocatta to build it in 1846. With three wings, it is in a Neoclassical style with sculpture and statuary on the front elevation. Inside, in the main entrance and stairway, there are paintings by the Lisbon artist Ernesto Ferreira Condeixa commemorating the royal visit of King Don Carlos and Queen Dona Amélia in 1901. In the first-floor dining room an *azulejo* (tile) panel depicts the 1831 Liberal victory over the Absolutists at Ladeira da Velha, on the north coast east of Ribeira Grande. The 7.5ha garden is principally attributed to the work of two gardeners: Peter Wallace from Chatsworth for the general design; and, later, the Belgian François Gabriel who notably introduced many camellia cultivars. With the original layout little changed, it is a good example of 19th-century Victorian garden design. There are a number of mature trees, an attempt at a garden of native Azorean plants, and an impressive long *allée* of box trees. For the sharp-eyed, there are interesting shrubs to discover.

Parque Urbano (Ponta Delgada City Park) [81 G1] (North of the city's historic centre, off the road to Capelas, the Caminho da Lavada, entrance near the park's clubhouse; ⊕ 08.00–22.00; admission free) This public park of 18ha was begun in 2007 and completed in 2011 with the construction of a clubhouse with bar and restaurant next to a golf driving range. Soil contouring has been added, to reduce traffic noise from the busy radial road and create a sense of privacy. The defining pathways and their secondary paths, the traditional stone walls creating enclosed walkways like the rural *canadas* separating farm fields, the long pergola of granite pillars, expansive grass areas with groups of endemic and indigenous plants, others of ornamental shrubs, and of course many trees promise a most inviting future.

Boa Fruta Açores Pineapple Plantation [81 H2] (Rua das Laranjeiras; m 964 087 745; w boafruta.pt; ⊕ Apr–Sep 09.00–20.00, Oct–Mar 09.00–18.00) Admission is free to see the greenhouses, and for a tasting of pineapple liqueur and delicious pineapple boiled sweets in the café. There are pineapple fruits for sale, loose and in presentation boxes, plus various handicrafts. This was first planted as an orange farm in the 19th century; with the demise of the orange trade towards the end of the century, the farm adapted and went over to pineapple production under glass, and remarkably set out at the same time to be a tourist attraction. There is a belvedere which was used as a lookout for the arrival of the orange boats.

Gruta do Carvão [80 A1] (Rua do Paim; ☎ 296 284 155; m 961 397 080; w grutadocarvao.com; ⊕ guided tours 10.30, 11.30, 14.30, 15.30, 16.30 daily; €9/7/free adult/7–14s, students & over 65s/0–6) Just across the Ponta Delgada bypass, you can go down into a lava tube cave that extended almost all the way under the town to the sea. Visits are by guided tours (about 45min, reservations recommended), with guides who are keen to explain the details of the cave's formation in an eruption about 2,000 years ago. One recent development is the discovery of bacteria in the cave that may produce new antibiotics.

Walking trail around town The town trail detailed below should take about 2 hours, excluding any time spent in cafés or museums. It begins at the tourist information office on the main promenade [81 G7], Avenida Infante Dom Henrique.

With your back to the office door, turn left and left again around the corner into the square, the **Praça Gonçalo Velho Cabral**, where you will find the three ornate and distinctive arches of the original (1783) **gates to the city** [81 G7], once part of the old harbour wall. The modern statue commemorates the man after whom the square is named, believed to be the discoverer of the islands of São Miguel and Santa Maria.

Ponta Delgada had become important as a trading port, and in the 18th and early 19th centuries it was especially significant for the export of oranges. On several houses you will see square attic-like structures on the roof; here a servant would be stationed to watch for and give early warning of the approach of an orange schooner. This gave the grower or merchant valuable extra hours to harvest the fruit as it had to be picked fresh to travel well. Ships had to anchor offshore and lighters (barges) conveyed passengers and cargo from shore to ship. The harbour in those days was very small, and in fact was situated in the very square in which you are now standing. The bank on the east side and the adjacent buildings all have many

---

PINEAPPLES

Pineapples were introduced as a replacement crop for oranges around 1850 and became so successful that after ten years they were being exported to northern Europe, including England where they featured in royal banquets. The Azores are not warm enough for their outdoor cultivation, and there were some 3,000 glasshouses producing yearly about 2,000 tonnes of fruit. The main growing area is in Fajã de Baixo on the edge of Ponta Delgada, also in Lagoa and Vila Franca do Campo. It takes two years to produce a ripe fruit with an average weight of 1.5–2kg. Earlier, heather, ferns and moss were taken from the mountains and made into a thick growing bed but nowadays, to protect the mountain vegetation, leafy branches of pittosporum and other shrubs are used. As these decay they give off heat, and in a closed or carefully ventilated glasshouse this is sufficient for the plants to thrive. Old stems are used for propagation, which take six months to produce young plants. These are planted out to grow on for another 12 months, at which stage ivy and other vegetation is burned in old oil drums to create a dense smoke. This triggers the plants to flower all at the same time, and in six months they are ready for harvesting. Without 'smoking', flowering would occur intermittently and it would take much longer before the crop could be cleared and the cycle begun again.

internal arches which once fronted the sea. Land reclamation work pushed the sea back, allowing a new main promenade road and other buildings to be built in 1947.

Cross the square diagonally to the **Church of São Sebastião** [81 G6], with a fine Manueline portal. Built to fulfil a vow made during the plague of 1523–31, it was greatly added to in the 18th century in the Baroque style, and the interior was decorated with ornate woodcarving. The exotic timbers used, especially jacaranda, reflect imports from the Brazilian colonies. (Some additional information about the church, in English, is given by a panel by the entrance.)

Standing with your back to the church, you are now facing the back of a run of buildings that once fronted on to the sea. The city gates originally joined on to these. On your left, facing the side of the church, is a tiny entrance to the **Café Mascote** [81 G7] (previously known as the Café Chesterfield); go into the old part, No 66, and see the arched roof while sipping a coffee. This was once part of the original colonnade at the harbour's edge. Tiled murals in the café give a good indication of how things looked in times gone by.

Leaving the café, turn right and then right again down a small side street. At the end on the left is the police station, formerly the customs house. Take the little turning on the right about halfway along to go to the rear of the Café Mascote. Again you will see some arches in the outside wall, part of the colonnade at the edge of the harbour, also with decorative tiling.

Retrace your steps towards the city gates and turn right, to see the **Câmara Municipal** [81 F7] or town hall beyond the Praça do Municipio. Originally it was the residence of one of the town's wealthy families and was converted only at the beginning of the 20th century. The bell tower dates from 1724 and houses the oldest bell (16th century) in the Azores. Look in at the ground-floor entrance between the steps; here there is often a temporary exhibition of local interest. The statue in front of the building is of São Miguel Arcanjo (the Archangel Michael), patron of the island.

Continue past the town hall taking the road on your left, **Rua de Santa Luzia** [81 F7]. At the end, on the left, the large, handsome building is the old post office. Cross the square, the **Praça Vasco da Gama** [80 D5], diagonally and continue westwards along the main promenade towards the **Forte São Brás** [80 C6] at the end of the present-day harbour. This was built in the 16th century to defend the village against corsairs and privateers, including some from England. Enlarged in the 19th century, it is now the army headquarters and military museum (page 87). Behind you is a pleasing homogeneity of architecture along the waterfront. Try to ignore the one blemish, the intrusive tower block at the far eastern end of town.

Well before reaching the fort, opposite the Praça Vasco da Gama square, note the floating deck at the harbour edge with its café tables; this is the **Cais da Sardinha** [80 D5], and was where sardines were once landed. Continue along the *avenida*, past the present-day customs house, and see a white corner building with a circular tower, the local naval headquarters. In the harbour opposite, there may be activity around the colourful chunky fishing boats, landing their catch.

Opposite the fort is the wide square of **Praça 5 Outubro** (aka the Campo de São Francisco) [80 C5], which is the traditional site for festivals. Dwarfing the many pollarded trees around the square is a massive tree (*Metrosiderus tomentosa*), an Australasian import over 140 years old. On the west side, the square is overlooked by the fine, green-washed, former Franciscan monastery, now a fancy hotel. Immediately to the north is the **Igreja São José** [80 C6], the major church of the old village and parish of São José, which took 60 years to build in the 16th century. It has an 18th-century façade and inside a fine ceiling and much 18th-century decorative art.

On the northern side of the square, parallel with the seafront, is the **Convento da Nossa Senhora da Esperança** (Our Lady of Hope) [80 C5], completed in 1541 and occupied by the nuns of the Order of St Francis. The chapel is decorated with magnificent 18th-century tiles and gilding and is associated with the worship of the Christ of the Miracles. The *Ecce Homo* statue was brought to the Azores in the 16th century. The sculptor is unknown, but it came from Paris to the convent that was then in Caloura. To protect the statue against frequent pirate attacks, the nuns left the coastal convent and took it with them to the newly built Nossa Senhora da Esperança. Some 150 years later a young girl called Teresa da Anunciada (1658–1738), from a rich family in Ribeira Grande, devoted herself to the nunnery and especially to the worship of this image. News of her devotion and fame of the miracles granted carried to all the islands and even as far as mainland Portugal. Subsequent emigration spread the worship of the Christ of the Miracles, and now pilgrims come from Azorean communities overseas to join the annual festival, the second-biggest religious festival in the whole of Portugal. The image may be seen from closer up, between 17.30 and 18.30 every evening, when a nun opens the internal gates (around the corner on Avda Roberto Ivens) to allow visitors in. There is also a splendid ceiling and Baroque ornamentation. On the fifth Sunday after Easter, the Santo Cristo Festival, the image is taken on procession through the city, passing along the narrow roads carpeted with fresh flowers in geometrical designs.

In the garden in front of the chapel, there is a statue to Madre Teresa da Anunciada. Behind, at the first seat, is where the poet and political activist Antero de Quental shot himself in 1891, aged 49.

Returning eastwards from the square by the convent, the cobbled, semi-pedestrianised road is officially signed as Rua Dr Gil Mont' Alverne but has always been called the central road or **Rua Direita**, although today it is not so central. Rua Direita becomes Rua Marques da Praia e Monfort, where even now traditional shops can still be found. On the right, opposite the Hotel Talisman, is the former house of the Marquis de Praia, now a government building, with a square observation tower on the roof. Next to the hotel, note the attractive garden, the **Jardim Padre Senas Freitas** [80 C5], named after a priest, writer, orator and polemicist. It was the Marquis's father, the 1st Viscount of Praia, Duarte Borges da Câmara Medeiros, who, in 1848, purchased the land in Furnas and began the great expansion of the renowned Terra Nostra Garden (page 114). Continue in the same direction, then take the next road on the left, up **Rua Comandante Jaime de Sousa**. Shortly you will come to **Largo Mártires da Pátria** (Martyrs' Square) [80 D5], at the far side of which is a secondary school, originally the grand home of the wealthy 'Fonte Bela', so nicknamed because of his many water installations on the island. He was one of the first and most important of the orange growers and the largest landowner. The blue-and-white building on the left, to the west, is the old government or **Parliament House** of the autonomous region. Note the church of Nossa Senhora da Conceição [80 C5] with its ornate Manueline façade.

Take the **Travessa de Conceição** and then turn left into the Rua Machado dos Santos. A small chapel at the top of a short flight of basalt steps is the **Chapel of Santa Luzia** [81 F6], dated 1584. Luzia was the daughter of a rich family and was losing her sight; she promised that if she could keep her sight she would build a chapel to her name-saint in gratitude.

Turn left into the **Rua Carvalho Araújo**; your attention is immediately grabbed by the splendidly ornate early 17th-century Baroque **Igreja do Colégio** [80 D3], which dominates the far end of the street. Built by the Jesuits, the church remained open for worship following their expulsion, but after a tenuous period in the early 19th century was used for storage and then abandoned. The regional government bought it and began renovations in 1993, and in 2004 it opened as a museum, housing the Carlos Machado Museum's collection of sacred art (**Núcleo de Arte Sacra**; page 87). By the early 18th century in Ponta Delgada there were three male religious communities (Franciscans, Augustinians and Jesuits), four nunneries, three sanctuaries for lay females and 28 churches. There were over 650 people in religious orders plus others totalling about 1,200 – one in eight adults of the Ponta Delgada population, with probably about a third of the population benefiting economically from the religious foundations. Enjoy the many wrought-iron balconies as you walk up this street. Next to the convent is the memorial garden to the São Miguel-born poet Antero de Quental (1842–91), with its elegant Art-Deco sculpture, *Emotion and Reason*.

From the convent go eastwards along Rua Dr Aristides da Mota and Rua Dr Guilherme Pocas and keep going until the narrow road opens out and you see a large building to the right surrounded by a tall, whitewashed wall enclosing a garden. This is the main Santo André section of the **Carlos Machado Museum** (page 86), thankfully now reopened after a decade of disuse; here, turn right and follow the wall round to the entrance. If you have time, do make a visit; meanwhile the **Núcleo de Santa Bárbara** (page 87) is just across the road.

Take the Rua Santa Barbara downhill and turn left on to the Rua de São João to soon reach the tall **Teatro Micaelense** [81 E4]. Ugly from the rear, elegantly modern from the front, this was the site of a fortress, destroyed by fire in the early 1900s. The theatre was opened in 1917, and is modelled on the Coliseum in Lisbon. It has been restored and seats 1,500. If you want to visit the **market** (the Mercado de Graça) [81 E4], selling fresh fruit, vegetables, flowers, meat, fish, cheese and some handicrafts, continue along on to the Rua Mercado for about 100m and you'll find it on the right-hand side. On Saturday mornings and festival times, it generates a certain buzz. (Next door is an excellent cheese shop – page 86.) There are also public lavatories, and a snack bar.

Afterwards, retrace your steps to the theatre. Walk down the hill and turn left into the **Rua da Misericórdia** and you will come to a **library** on your left with red gates at the top of the steps. Take the right fork along past the now closed **Hotel São Pedro** [81 H6]; this was once the residence of Thomas Hickling, built 1799–1812, in Georgian style. Hickling was the wealthy Bostonian who built a summer house at Furnas and began what later became the Terra Nostra Park (page 114). Opposite on elevated ground is a church, the main **Church of the Parish of São Pedro** [81 F4], rebuilt in the 1760s and 1770s. Climb the steps for a good view out over the ferry terminal, the marina and out to sea. Ponta Delgada has over the years absorbed the surrounding villages and today has three parishes, two of which we have now met, and the central parish of São Sebastião.

From here walk down to the seafront and continue right along the promenade to return to the tourist office.

SPORTS AND ACTIVITIES

Operators for most, though not all, outdoor activities are based in Ponta Delgada, and will transport their clients to the venue for the chosen activity. Note that while some operators offer a whole multitude of activities on their websites, often in reality they have a few 'core' activities which they carry out themselves while subcontracting the others out. Thus, your whale-watching company might offer canyoning, but is unlikely to actually run the activity themselves. Wherever possible, we list here the companies that actually *do*, rather than simply outsource, the activity.

On the north coast, **swimming** can be dangerous as there are many currents and hazards; you will see local people swimming, but they know where the dangers are. Use only obviously developed swimming areas. All beaches are black sand.

Whale and dolphin watching remains one of the most popular Azorean adventures. There are now several well-established operators on São Miguel, mostly in Ponta Delgada but with one in Vila Franca do Campo. In Ponta Delgada, many operators have kiosks along the main promenade, but if these are closed, there are offices in the Portas do Mar complex, below the promenade. Lifejackets are provided. Off the south coast of São Miguel was once a profitable area for hunting whales and now, some three generations or so since the last whales were killed, they are again swimming past the former killing shores. For details on whale-watching etiquette, see page 63.

BIRDWATCHING
Gerby Birding m 967 958 566; e info@ gerbybirding.com; w gerbybirding.com. Dutchman Gerby (Page 10) speaks excellent English, German & Portuguese, an expert birder who was also instrumental in documenting many of the walks on the Azores Tourist Board website. Passionate, personable & knowledgeable, he regularly receives birders from many countries. From €75 pp.

CANYONING, COASTEERING AND CLIMBING
Azorean Active Blueberry m 914 822 682; e info@azoreanactiveblueberry.com; w azoreanactiveblueberry.com. An experienced canyoning operator who has also pioneered 'coasteering' on the island, giving you the chance to get wet in salt water as well as fresh. Climbing adventures also offered. Full & half-day trips available. Prices from €60–95, including pick-up, drop-off, equipment (inc boots) & insurance.
Azores Adventure Islands m 925 480 350; e info@azoresadventureislands.com; w azoresadventureislands.com. Enthusiastic & highly rated, will adapt programmes to suit clients. Prices from €65 pp, including equipment & insurance; pick-ups €15 extra.

CYCLING
ANC Azores Holidays [81 F4] Dr João Bosco Mota Amaral (in front of the Marina Atlanticó hotel); \ 296 249 382; m 967 309 909; e anc. azoresholidays@gmail.com; w azoresholidays. pt. Cheap bike hire (inc electric options), scooters,

quad bikes & buggies. Also guided 4x4 tours on the west side of São Miguel island.
Azores Adventure Islands See left. Respected operator will take you on mountain bike tours, with an option of electric bikes, gauging your ability & adapting as you go. Also, straightforward bike hire is available.
Harmony Trail Azores Page 78.

DIVING
The diving operators more or less all set up shop by the marina, just east of the Portas do Mar in Porta Delgada, below the promenade. Most of these companies will take snorkellers, as well as offering try-dives, single dives, full-day excursions & courses.

Best Spot Azores m 963 469 932, 912 108 658; e bestspotazores@gmail.com; w bestspotazores. com. A PADI 5-star centre, with a good reputation. A single dive comes in at €55, while a day's gear rental costs about €35. Try-dives & PADI courses also available.

FISHING
Oceantur Sportfishing Azores Marina de Ponta Delgada; m 915 744 048, 917 415 369; e geral@azores-sportfishing.com; w azores-sportfishing.com. Never a cheap activity, prices for tuna or marlin trips start at €600 for a half day. Trips include equipment & insurance.

GOLF
There are 2 courses on São Miguel: Batalha at Fenais da Luz just a few kilometres north of Ponta

Delgada, the other off the main road northwest of Furnas. Under the same ownership, various 3- & 5-day packages are available, allowing visitors to play both courses with a worthwhile discount. There is a strict dress code. Shirts must have a collar & sleeves; jeans & tracksuits cannot be worn on the course or in clubhouse facilities. Soft spikes are mandatory, & note that there is no golf-shoe hire available.

Prices
Green fee inc trolley 18/9 holes €66/58
Green fee inc buggy 18/9 holes €94/66
Set of clubs (18/9 holes) €40/25
Driving range (50 balls) €6

Tee times
16 Oct–15 Mar ⊕ 08.00–18.00 (Furnas 09.00–18.00); 18 holes until 14.00, 9 holes until 16.00
16 Mar–15 Oct ⊕ 08.00–20.00 (Furnas 09.00–19.00); 18 holes until 15.00, 9 holes until 17.00

Courses
Golfe da Batalha [72 C3] Rua do Bom Jesus, Aflitos, Fenais da Luz; ↝296 498 559 (clubhouse); e reservas@ilhasdevalor.pt; w azoresgolfislands. com. Designed by Cameron Powell Associates & built in 1996 with long fairways, large flowing greens & sinuously contoured bunkers, the course is a combination of links & woodland course with views over the sea. With 27 holes, golfers can mix up the 3 nines for variety. To play, there is a required maximum handicap: men 28; ladies 36, though they will allow higher handicap players with advance notice. The clubhouse has a restaurant with a stunning view, open to non-players.
Golfe das Furnas [72 E3] Achada das Furnas; ↝296 584 651 (course); e reservas@ilhasdevalor. pt; w azoresgolfislands.com. Designed by MacKenzie Ross (who also built the Estoril course near Lisbon & restored the Scottish Turnberry courses) & built in 1939 with 9 holes, it was extended in 1990 by Cameron Powell Associates to the full 18-hole course, par 72, & 6,232m long. Required maximum handicap: men 28; ladies 36. It is an intimate course set in a glorious landscape with always verdant grass, forest & tree ferns. At 500m altitude, clouds & mist can often swirl around the course & present a different kind of

challenge to the golfer. About 10mins' drive from Furnas or 45mins from Ponta Delgada. Restaurant on site.

HORSERIDING
Quinta da Terça Rua Padre Domingos Silva 221, Livramento (just east of Ponta Delgada); ↝296 642 134; m 968 122 398; e reservation@ quintadaterca.com; w quintadaterca.com. With 40 horses, this excellent establishment based in a 17th-century estate provides a wide variety of full & half-day excursions, plus week-long courses, as well as beginners' courses. They also offer packages with accommodation & excellent food; half-day trips cost €60–95.

SURFING
Azores Surf Center Praia de Santa Bárbara, just west of Ribeira Grande; m 915 970 726; e info@ azoressurfcenter.com; w azoressurfcenter.com. Surfing is still fairly rare on the islands, due to the lack of sandy beaches, but you can learn from scratch or perfect your skills with Josephine or Ricardo, fully qualified instructors on the north coast. They surf all year, but if the sea is too rough, then it's time to decamp across to the south coast for gentler waters – ideal for beginners. Prices, starting at €40 per lesson (in a group), include wet suit, board & insurance. English spoken. Will hire equipment to experienced surfers, too, & can arrange accommodation in a surf-house.

SWIMMING
The beaches & pools below are listed in an anticlockwise order, starting from Ponta Delgada.

Ponta Delgada [72 B4] At the eastern end of the harbour promenade, join the locals for a harbour swim. Use of changing rooms & showers attract a nominal charge, & sunbeds can be hired (€2). It's not scenic…but this is what the locals do! Immediately up above (⊕ Jun–Sep 10.00–19.00; €2.50), there's a complex of manmade pools, including a 50m pool, with full services, sunbeds and an adjacent café. There's no towel hire at either facility.
São Roque [72 C4] The 2 beaches, Milicias/Areal Grande & Areal Pequeno, have supporting facilities. Very popular, being only a short distance east of Ponta Delgada.

Lagoa [72 C4] Originally this was a long, popular 150m stretch of irregular coastline, but the old complex was virtually destroyed during the winter storms of 1997. A new complex has been built with greater protection against storm damage with 2 pools, both heated to 24°C in winter. The largest is a 4-lane, 25m pool; the 2nd is for children. There is also an ocean swimming area surrounded on 3 sides by lava – swimming is subject to tides & strength of the sea. Sunbathing area, diving boards & slides complete the picture, together with a snack bar.

Caloura [72 D4] Fishing cove, natural & artificial pool, no beach, though there are also 2 small stretches of sand just west of the Caloura Hotel.

Água de Alto [72 D4] A long stretch of sand between 2 promontories, by the Pestana Bahia Praia Hotel (where there's a bar); there's a wheelchair ramp to the beach.

Vila Franca do Campo [72 D4] The Ilhéu de Vila Franca do Campo is an offshore collapsed crater with a naturally protected swimming area, including a shallow place for children. It is also good for scuba-diving & snorkelling. From Jun to Oct, hourly boats take visitors out & back (€8) to let them enjoy this protected nature area: numbers are limited to 400/day, & queues form for the ticket office which opens at 09.30. In high season the tickets are sometimes all sold by 10.00. You can buy in advance (m 911 927 039; e bilheteira@cnvfc.net; w cnvfc.net, in English). This islet is also a venue for cliff-diving championships, held in Jul each year.

Ribeira Quente [72 F4] A fishing village, at the western end of which, beneath steep cliffs, is the Praia do Fogo. All facilities are on offer, including showers, café & car park up above, & in summer there are several open-air restaurants. An extremely popular area.

Foz da Ribeira [72 G3] Just a mile north of Nordeste, across a footbridge from the car park, with picnic area, WCs & changing facilities.

Ribeira Grande [72 D3] Municipal swimming pools are now available east of the bridge on the new esplanade.

Praia de Santa Bárbara [72 D3] Just west of Ribeira Grande, facilities include good parking, toilets with showers, cafés & a restaurant with sea view. Sea can be rough, care is required. Excellent surfing; beach used for competitions.

Poços de São Vicente Ferreira [72 B3] At the former whaling factory just east of Capelas, there are pools both inside & outside a breakwater, with ramps for disabled access.

WHALE AND DOLPHIN WATCHING
Ponta Delgada
Futurismo [81 F5] Marina Pêro de Teive, Loja 24–26, Portas do Mar; ☏ 296 628 522, 967 805 101; e reservations@futurismo.pt; w futurismo. pt. The biggest operator, with 10 boats of varying sizes, including RIBs & catamarans. Also the longest established, with over 30 years' experience. Each boat is accompanied by a marine biologist. English spoken. Shop & information centre on site. €65/100 (half/full day whale watching).

MobyDick-Tours [81 F5] Marina Portas do Mar; ☏ 296 583 643; m 919 942 831; w mobydick-tours.com. A new and very sustainability-oriented operator, using a former inter-island ferry. €50/30 adult/child (half day whale watching).

Picos de Aventura [81 G5] Marina Pêro de Teive; m 912 525 356; e reservas@ picosdeaventura.com; w picosdeaventura.com. A big & very experienced operator, operating 4 boats from Ponta Delgada. €65/95 (half/full day whale watching).

Sea Colors Marina Portas do Mar; m 918 529 795, 963 766 073; e seacolorsazores@gmail.com; w seacolorsazores.com; ⊕ Mar–Nov. At the other end of the scale from the big operators, this is a husband & wife owned & run firm, with their RIB taking a max of 12 passengers. They carry out research during their trips & data gathered by them on cetaceans is shared with the university, so your patronage helps to support this work. With a passionate concern for the mammals, they do not specifically sell trips that include swimming with dolphins, believing that some firms that do so then feel obliged to put people in the water even if the dolphins are not 'in the mood' to be swum with. If the mood's right, swimming is possible & no extra charge is made. A marine biologist accompanies each trip. €65/45 adult/child.

Mosteiros
Terra do Pico Rua do Porto 32; ☏ 296 915 264; w terradopico.com. On the island's northwest coast, once a major whale-hunting area and now

a great place for watching marine wildlife. Whale watching from €50, also coastal jaunts €20–25.

Vila Franca do Campo
Terra Azul Marina de Vila Franca do Campo 4; ℡296 581 361; **m** 913 453 030; **e** info@ azoreswhalewatch.com; **w** azoreswhalewatch. com. Operates all year round, with 2 trips daily in low season, & an extra 1 in summer. Owner Miguel's passion for wildlife, environment and community is infectious. A biologist or naturalist accompanies the boat & speaks English. Swimming with dolphins is another possibility, Oct–Apr. Miguel has also invested in the restoration of an old-style whaling boat – don't forget to admire it! €72/54 adult/child (whale watching), €89 (swimming with dolphins). Slightly cheaper in winter.

EXPLORING NATURE The most famous rarity of São Miguel is the much-promoted Azorean bullfinch – the priolo – found only in the native shrubbery of the **Serra da Tronqueira Nature Reserve** [72 F3].

There are now thought to be upwards of 1,000 individuals and they may be seen best from along the unsurfaced road between Povoação and Nordeste. Gardeners will have some sympathy for the early farmers who shot the species almost out of existence to protect their crops from its infamous depredations. (Indeed, a 'bounty' was offered by the authorities for each dead bullfinch!) Here one may also find the Azorean wood pigeon. This mountainous area with its deep ravines and watercourses is densely covered with laurisilva or Macaronesian evergreen forest and the endemic species include holly, juniper, laurel, Portugal laurel and bilberry, together with ferns. Make a point of visiting the Priolo Centre and its easy walking trail (pages 70 and 120).

Lagoa do Fogo Nature Reserve [72 D3] provides the most accessible site for endemic plants and even if not tempted by the path descending to the lake through this vegetation, exploration around the viewpoint can be rewarding enough. Juniper, laurel, frangula and erica shelter native hypericum and euphorbia, and a patient search will reveal several more endemics. You cannot fail to hear and see the Atlantic yellow-legged gulls.

Sete Cidades [72 A2] (see opposite) and its varied sheltered habitats of fields and gardens can be productive for birds, while the lake offers respite for migrant species and in autumn occasional American vagrants.

The varied habitats around the village of **Mosteiros** [72 A2] are often rewarding, with migrating passerines in the cultivated areas and, on the lava beach, turnstones, whimbrels, little egret, roseate terns, and less often, sandpipers. **Caloura** [72 D4] is good for the common and roseate terns which breed here.

For birdwatching excursions, see page 95.

Recreational forest reserves
Pinhal da Paz [72 C3] (Rua de Cima, Caminho da Adutora; ☉ Oct–Mar 08.00–16.00 Mon–Fri, 10.00–17.00 Sat, Sun & hols, Apr–Sep 08.00–19.00 Mon–Fri, 10.00–20.00 Sat, Sun & hols; free) Midway between Ponta Delgada and Fenais da Luz in the north: from Ponta Delgada take the EN4–1a towards Capelas, turn right at Carreira village and follow the signs. This is a 49ha woodland garden developed on poor land of rocky outcrops and volcanic residues, once used for grazing goats and sheep. In the mid 1900s it was planted by the grandson of plantsman José do Canto with ornamental trees and flowering shrubs including camellias and

> **⚷HIKING**
>
> For further details of organised and guided walking and hiking options on São Miguel island, see page 78.

azaleas. Secured by the Regional Government over 30 years ago, it has recently been replanted and small themed gardens added, along with a forest study centre. Quite a few native species occur naturally throughout the reserve. So close to the city, it is a perfect place to spend easy hours walking in delightful woodland, especially in the less frequented northern areas, or to take a picnic. There's a viewpoint and children's play area.

Woodlands of Canário [72 B2] On the way to Sete Cidades, and a walk of 15 minutes to the Miradouro do Canário, one of the finest views in all the Azores (see below).

Chã da Macela [72 D3] (⊕ Oct–Mar 08.00–16.00 Mon–Fri, 10.00–17.00 Sat–Sun & hols, Apr–Sep 08.00–19.00 Mon–Fri, 10.00–20.00 Sat, Sun & hols; free) Along the road from Lagoa to Lagoa do Fogo, turn off at Remédios, and follow signs via Cinco Caminhos. The 28ha range from 350m to 550m and at the reserve's highest point is the Macela miradouro from where on a clear day one gets a fine view of the island. As well as cryptomerias, there is a fair mix of trees, and away from the play area and other amenities, the reserve has large areas of relative wilderness along with fine scenery.

Cancelo do Cinzeiro [72 G3] From the R1–1, take the signposted forest road to Pico Bartolomeu from Lomba da Pedreira. In 10ha at around 550m altitude there are forests and meadows, plus children's and picnic areas and playing fields. Significantly there are pockets of natural native laurel forest and a collection of endemics, along with a resident population of Azores wood pigeons and a breeding population of little shearwaters.

WALKS ON SÃO MIGUEL

São Miguel's steep increase in visitor numbers in recent years has thankfully been accompanied by the development of new, waymarked walks, though in high season these can still be busy. Right from the early years of walking holidays in the Azores, the walks around Sete Cidades and Furnas Lake have been true highlights. The last decade has seen an increasing number of companies and individual guides offering their services – see Harmony Trail Azores (page 78). For those who prefer to walk without a guide, four walks are described below. In addition to those detailed, another recommended walk is the Faial da Terra–Salto do Prego trail, detailed on the tourist board website (medium difficulty, 4.7km, 2hrs). This is an excellent, waymarked circular route via the Salto do Prego waterfall and the small, restored settlement of Sanguinho.

The Azores Tourism Authority's website (w visitazores.com) now details no fewer than 30 waymarked trails for São Miguel. Detailed maps and information can be found at either end of the trail; these can also be downloaded and printed. Always check a trail's status with the tourist office before setting out.

SELF-GUIDED WALKS
Sete Cidades (Mata do Canário) (Time: about 4½hrs; distance: about 12km; see map, page 100) There are numerous choices when it comes to exploring this area for there are several roads going down into the caldera and to the village of Sete Cidades, and there are various roads leading from the caldera rim down to villages along the coast. You will doubtless find various published descriptions of these.

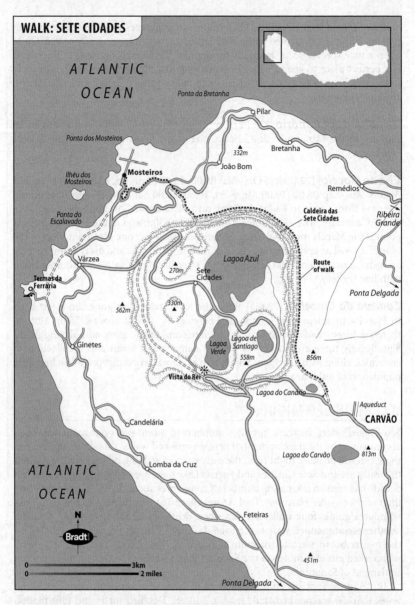

ATLANTIC
OCEAN

Ponta da Bretanha

● Pilar

Ponta dos Mosteiros

▲ 332m

Bretanha

João Bom

Ilhéu dos
Mosteiros

● Mosteiros

Remédios ◎

Ponta do
Escalavado

**Caldeira das
Sete Cidades**

Ribeira
Grande

Várzea ◎

Lagoa Azul

**Route
of walk**

Termas da
Ferraria

▲ 270m

Sete
Cidades

Ponta Delgada →

▲ 330m

▲ 562m

Ginetes ◎

Lagoa
Verde

Lagoa de
Santiago
558m

▲ 856m

Vista do Rei

Lagoa do Canário

‖ Aqueduct

CARVÃO

Candelária ◎

Lagoa do Carvão

▲ 813m

ATLANTIC
OCEAN

N

Bradt

Lomba da Cruz ◎

Feteiras ◎

▲ 451m

0   3km
0   2 miles

Ponta Delgada ↘

The walk described here, known as Mata do Canário, is best, since, in one route, you have the most magnificent caldera views which constantly change as you progress along the rim, and the end of the day offers the contrast of approaching the sea with fine views of Mosteiros and the chance to see what living on a fajã is like. Even on a national holiday, at most you will meet a farmer or two attending their cows and maybe another walker. (Note that there have been problems with tourist vehicles driving along the southern caldera rim, which rather spoils the peace and quiet of anyone walking between Carvão and the Vista do Rei viewpoint. At the northern rim, traffic has been restricted and it is hoped that similar measures will soon be taken in respect of the southern rim. This walk hopefully avoids the traffic problems.)

Footpath conditions are easy, more or less level, with some steep pitches at both the start and finish.

If the weather is very windy it can be very unpleasant, and if there is low cloud, do wait for another day since you will miss all the wonderful views. Half the fun is identifying all the landmarks.

If driving and intending to finish in Sete Cidades, you are advised to park in the centre, but before doing so arrange for a taxi to take you from there to the area known as Carvão. (There is only one taxi driver based in Sete Cidades, an English-speaker by the name of Vitor Cordeiro, ⟍ 962 373 353. By doing this, you can complete the walk, finishing back at your own vehicle.) An alternative option is to drive/take a taxi from Ponta Delgada, go past the Miradouro de Carvão, past the sign on your left to Lagoas dos Empadadas and then take the second asphalted turning on your right. This soon curves round in front of a rather beautiful stone aqueduct, the 'Moro do Carvão', built in about 1830, and then into cryptomeria forest. Stop at the first unsurfaced farm track on your left – it is on a bend in the road. The problem with leaving your car here is that, once you reach Sete Cidades – or Mosteiros, depending which route you take – you are going to have to find a cab to take you back to your car, or back to Ponta Delgada: difficult to arrange in advance if you don't know when you'll finish your walk.

You begin the walk here, slowly ascending through the forest and upon emerging come to a cement road making a very steep ascent up to the caldera, finishing by a building. You may be lucky and have an enthusiastic taxi driver prepared to risk damaging his car; mine had never been there before and insisted on driving all the way to the top where there is a level turning area. He ran to the caldera edge and was dumbstruck by the stupendous view; it is so much more dramatic than from the usual viewing place at Vista do Rei. On a clear day with no wind this has to be the finest view in all the Azores.

From here you simply follow the farm road going anticlockwise around the eastern caldera rim; it soon forks and you bear round to the left. Continue ignoring all roads and tracks leading off from the main road around the caldera. In about 2 hours you reach a miradouro with some picnic tables and a road descending off on your right.

Continue on round the caldera and in about another 30 minutes you see the Ilhéu dos Mosteiros just off the coast; you are more or less above a tunnel that takes the overflow from the blue lake out of the caldera above Mosteiros. The track descends a little to come to a junction by a large smooth face of grey tuff with names carved into it. Two roads go down on your right, one either side of the bluff; take the second of these. The road you were following continues on round the caldera, or you can descend to your left, on the road, to Sete Cidades, if this is where you left your vehicle.

Those going to Mosteiros should descend, at times between high walls of tuff and, lower down, reeds, to reach an asphalt road after 20 minutes. Cross this and continue down on the track and within 2 minutes come to a T-junction at the main road. Turn left and right, down off the road, and take the fork to the left of a fountain bearing the sign 'Rua Direita Pico de Mafra'. Follow this steeply down to the houses and continue to a miradouro giving a splendid view over Mosteiros, its white houses contrasting with the black lava and blue sea. To go down to Mosteiros, take the small concrete road going steeply down on the right, about 50m below the Espírito Santo chapel. From Mosteiros you can get a bus back to Ponta Delgada, or phone for a taxi (m 968 435 022 or 962 408 325), if you haven't arranged one in advance.

ATLANTIC OCEAN

EN 1-1A

Start of walk
P

Shop
João Bom

Pico do Mafra
▲ 320m

Mosteiros

RUA DA CASA VELHA

N

Bradt

0 ___ 400m
0 ___ 400yds

EN 1-1A

Ponta Delgada

Bretanha Coastal Walk (Atalho dos Vermelhos) (Time: about 2½hrs; distance:

about 4.5km; see map, above) Easy, as long as you have a head for heights. Not suitable during or shortly after heavy rain. This is a pleasant partially coastal walk which affords good views along the spectacular cliffs near Mosteiros. Drinks are available at the shop in João Bom, where you begin and end your walk.

To reach the start point, look out for the car park next to a picnic area, at the side of the main regional road that passes above João Bom. Park here (or take the bus to the same place) and descend for 80m on Rua do Argentina into the village to reach a junction at the mini market (Mini Mercado Pavão). Turn left to follow the waymarking and pass the chapel on your left before turning right into Rua de Relvinha.

Continue down this road, heading for the sea. The tarmac runs out after a couple of hundred metres, but you continue down this track, lined with bamboo, fern and false tobacco plants, with pasture lands on either side for around 700m. (Occasionally, farmers may put string across the road to deter straying cattle: simply duck underneath and continue.)

Look out for a gate on your left with waymarking at which you turn sharp left to cross a narrow pasture. Head for a gap visible on the other side, go through the gap and follow the path which descends on steps through a small forest. The ocean is soon visible.

Descend down a steep path and cross a stream, before climbing again to follow the clifftop path around and pass some white water reservoirs which perch on a ledge. After the last of these you climb on a wide path, leaving the ocean behind you. The path turns up to the left on a wide ash and grass path.

After a steep climb, the path flattens and you head towards the volcanic, wooded cone of Mafra. Eventually the path takes you around this, leaving it to your left (ignore a turn-off to your left). After a few hundred metres, you reach a crossroads at the end of the Rua de Pedra Queimada and turn left down the Rua da Casa Velha. Follow this unsurfaced track to a three-way junction at which you continue straight ahead, downhill. The road continues, then starts to climb and turns into tarmac and returns you into João Bom village where you began.

Rota da Água/Janela do Inferno (Time: about 2hrs 45mins; distance: about 7km; see map, below) This easy to moderate circular walk includes four tunnels and some narrow bridges. A torch is advisable, though a mobile phone with flashlight will suffice. Not to be attempted during rain or after heavy rainfall. It is well waymarked. The middle section is beautiful: with lush vegetation, a beautiful waterfall and deep ravines, it has the air of a real 'lost world' and once you exit it back into pastureland, you may scarcely believe that such scenery exists in such a location.

To reach the start, take the main road east out of Ponta Delgada, then turn north on to the ER–6, heading for Lagoa da Fogo. After a couple of kilometres, turn right to Remedios and stop at a triangular junction on the edge of the village, where there is a car park, toilets, information panels for the walk and the **Casa da Água** (✆296 912 088; e casadaagua@lagoa-acores.pt; ⏰ 09.00–12.30 & 13.30–17.00 daily), which gives information on hiking and also on nearby bolted climbing routes. It starts unpromisingly with a trek up the hill on the tarmac road. Note away to your left the volcanic cones which form the 'middle section' of the island. After around 700m, follow the waymarking off to the right, leaving the tarmac to head downhill on concrete. Note the aqueduct on your right. Soon, follow a dirt track off to your right heading back towards the coast.

After a few hundred metres, turn left down a path with fields on either side. Follow this path, sometimes muddy, downhill until it opens into a pasture, at the end of which you enter a 50m-long, narrow tunnel. Continue for a few hundred metres to reach some abandoned buildings before turning sharp right down some stone steps and cross a stream. The water pipes here once fed the Lagoa alcohol factory, but now simply supply the coastal towns with their water.

Ignore a path off to your right. With steep drop-offs to your right, follow the path until you reach a bridge with handrails. Cross and immediately at the end of the bridge follow the signs to your left for Janela do Inferno, the 'Window of Hell'.

WALK: ROTA DA ÁGUA TO JANELA DO INFERNO

After 200m you reach a beautiful vertical rockface with a waterfall gushing from a high-up cave. The pool below is a favourite residence of newts.

Retrace your steps to the bridge and enter the very short and narrow tunnel which takes you to the other side. The path descends gently, then more steeply to reach another bridge (slippery after rain). Cross the bridge and ascend to then turn right through a further tunnel, where a torch or flashlight would be useful. Cross a stream (or stream-bed, in dry weather), then another, then a third and in a few hundred metres look out for tunnel number four. This is the longest one, around 100m in length and down to around 1.4m in height in places (mind your head!).

After exiting the tunnel, you reach a wooden gate which you pass through to pick up the waymarking to your left. Follow the path across pasture land, heading for two large grassy mounds. Before reaching them, turn left at a crossroads following the waymarking and continue down the path towards the coast. Eventually you reach a wide, unsurfaced road (Caminho do Norte) where you should turn right and return to the car park after about a kilometre.

Around Lagoa das Furnas
The walks to Furnas lake can easily be varied according to the time you have and how far you want to walk. Don't forget to allow time to visit the Furnas Monitoring and Research Centre (page 117). See also the map opposite.

Option A (Time: about 2hrs; distance: about 5km) The easiest option is to take a taxi from Furnas to the chapel of Nossa Senhora das Vitórias at the far side of the lake, then walk back along the east side of the lake beside the main road and then downhill to Furnas, reversing the descriptions given below under option B.

Options B, C and D The following walks begin at the petrol station near the Teatro das Furnas, just a short distance from the Terra Nostra Garden Hotel. At the garage the main road bears round to the left and a cement road, Canada do Ferreiro, leads off very steeply up the hill. Take this cement road towards the south; it's a former farm track with virtually no traffic and the scenery remains as lovely as ever. When it bears strongly round to the left, turn on to a good track on your right going steeply up into the shade of a belt of trees towards the top of the ridge. From here the track very quickly goes down the other side to the lake. You will smell sulphur and may notice steam coming from fissures in the banks. Now you have a choice of how long a walk you want to make; approximate times are given from the petrol station.

Option B (Time: about 3½hrs; distance: about 11km) To walk around the lake, turn right and pass the cooking area of the famous **Furnas cozido** (available in all the town's restaurants) and simply continue along this track, first along a small stream, following more or less the edge of the lake. You will have noticed an old house by the water on the far side, and a chapel. These once belonged to the family of José do Canto, who created here yet another fine garden. There are many fine old camellias, some magnolias and a fern gully, and the garden is now fully accessible to the public (page 117). Passing the Monitoring and Research Centre, garden and church, the road continues to join the main south coast road from Ponta Delgada, which has been left in its original cobbled state here. Turn left on to the path alongside this road to complete your circuit of the lake, pass the entrance to the *caldeiras*, and about half a kilometre after the road has left the lake

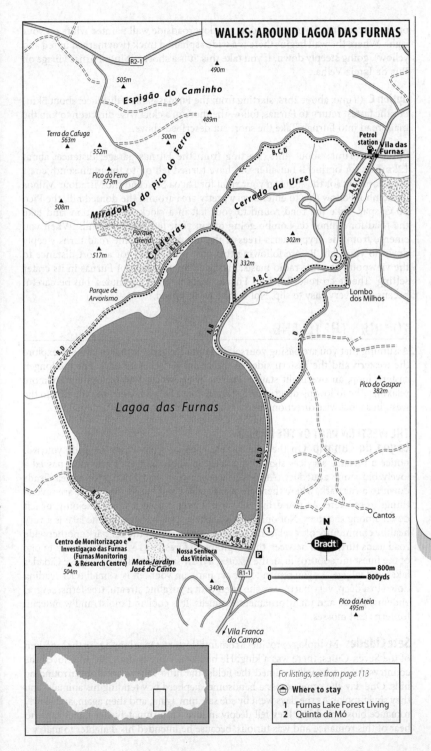

R2-1

505m

490m

Espigão do Caminho

489m

Terra da Cafuga
563m

552m

500m

Petrol
station

B, C, D

Vila das
Furnas

Pico do Ferro
573m

Cerrado da Urze

A, B, C, D

508m

Miradouro do Pico do Ferro

Parque
Grená

Caldeiras

B, D

302m

2

517m

332m

A, B, C

Parque de
Arvorismo

Lombo
dos Milhos

B, D

A, B

Pico do Gaspar
382m

Lagoa das Furnas

D

A, B, D

A, D

Cantos

Centro de Monitorizaçao e
Investigaçao das Furnas
(Furnas Monitoring
& Research Centre)
504m

N

Mata-Jardim
José do Canto

A, B, D

1

Nossa Senhora
das Vitórias

P

R1-1

Bradt

0   800m
0   800yds

3

340m

Pico da Areia
495m

Vila Franca
do Campo

For listings, see from page 113

⌂ **Where to stay**

1 Furnas Lake Forest Living
2 Quinta da Mó

São Miguel WALKS ON SÃO MIGUEL

on its descent into Furnas you come to a low roadside wall painted white on your right. Where the wall begins there is a wide asphalted track (waymarked in red and yellow), going steeply down. If you take this, it is a short cut into Furnas village on Rua da Igreja Velha.

Option C (Time: about 2hrs, starting from the Furnas garage; distance: about 5km) For the fastest return to Furnas, follow the shore in a clockwise direction to join the main road into Furnas. Take the short cut described above.

Option D (Time: about 4hrs, starting from the Furnas garage; distance: about 12km) As for option B but after you have turned left on to the main south coast road, look out for the signs on your right for Lagoa Seca and the Miradour Milhos da Lombo. Follow this to enter a very pretty area around the domed hill, the Pico do Gaspar. Take the road round to your left in a clockwise direction, and take the road for Milhos da Lombo going off on your left, steeply uphill. When you emerge from the cryptomeria trees at the top of the hill, the road turns steeply down to your left. Before following this, just walk ahead for a short distance to the viewpoint at some radio masts, giving an appreciation of Furnas in its crater setting. The steep road down to Furnas takes about 15 minutes, but be careful because it is very easy to slip. Not for the weak-kneed.

TOURING THE ISLAND

Assuming that you are basing yourself in Ponta Delgada, it makes sense to explore the western and the eastern sides of the island on separate days. For the longer, eastern loop, an overnight stay in Furnas or elsewhere will make the tour more relaxing. The following descriptions start in Ponta Delgada and take you first to the west, in a clockwise direction, then to the east in an anticlockwise direction.

THE WESTERN PART OF THE ISLAND
Lagoa do Canário On the way to Sete Cidades from Ponta Delgada you will notice a forestry services sign to this lake on your right after you have passed a lovely old stone aqueduct. An unsurfaced narrow road lined with azaleas leads down to a car park, where there are picnic tables and barbecues. There are several things to see here. As you drove in you will have passed a small lake on your left down among the trees. Not only is this a lovely spot, but around the lake is a very healthy community of royal fern, *Osmunda regalis*. From the car park another wide road leads further on between the cryptomeria forest; it is a 15-minute walk to one of the finest miradouros in all the Azores, a truly stunning view of the Sete Cidades lakes and village. As you return to the car park, on your left is a small track leading down to a deep, very narrow ravine filled with a gurgling stream, tree ferns, several endemic plants and many ornamental azaleas. It is cool and moist, and wonderful for ferns and mosses.

Sete Cidades Mythology provides a romantic history. Once long ago in the kingdom of the Seven Cities, there was a king. He had a very pretty daughter who loved the countryside and happily roamed the fields, the little valleys and the surrounding hills. One day she came across a handsome shepherd boy tending his animals, and they shyly spoke. As the days went by she saw him again, and then again, and slowly romance blossomed and they fell deeply in love. Unfortunately, her father came to hear of this romance and was furious, because he intended his daughter to marry a neighbouring prince who was heir to a large kingdom. He forbade his daughter ever to see her shepherd boy again, but she pleaded so well that he agreed they could meet for one last time. At the final parting, they both cried so much two lakes were formed, one blue from the princess's eyes, the other green from those of the shepherd boy, and although they were parted forever, their tears have remained united.

Inevitably you will stop at the main viewpoint, the **Vista do Rei**, named from King Carlos's visit in 1901, where you can see both lakes of tears. The one-way road to the car park loops around a brutalist hotel that opened in 1989 and was abandoned barely 18 months later; it seems tourists were unwilling to stay in such a remote, cloudy location.

The raffish traveller Thomas Ashe, describing his travels on São Miguel in 1813, wrote that the banks were planted with hemp or flax, which was cured in the lakes. There were only half a dozen houses in the valley where the hemp growers lived, and manufacturing was done in Bretanha and neighbouring villages; some 50,000 yards was used domestically and more for export. The surrounding hillsides with their trees in little groves and bowers and the long winding valleys 'made them pre-eminently beautiful, and particularly favourable for romantic leisure and tender passions'. See page 99 for a self-guided walk around Sete Cidades. By the lake in the village of Sete Cidades is the **Complexo Ambiental** (Environment Complex; ⊕ Apr–Oct 09.00–12.30 & 13.30–17.00 daily, Nov–Mar 09.00–12.30 & 13.30–17.00 Mon–Fri); it's not worth a detour but there's information on the protected area and the staff are keen to answer questions. Next to it is the Green Love café (❉296 915 214; e green-love@sapo.pt; ⊕ 09.30–18.00 Mon–Thu, 09.30–19.00 Fri & Sun, 09.30–20.00 Sat), a pleasant stopover for a snack, although it can get overwhelmed at busy times.

The northwest coast along to Capelas
Out beyond the airport the whole of this coastline is very pretty, and there are some especially lovely stretches of road running beneath tall, elegant plane trees with grass banks solid with blue agapanthus and topped with blue hydrangeas. At **Ponta da Ferraria** [72 A2] you can view the fajã from the road at the top of the cliff. In the rocky parts by the sea there are the **Termas da Ferraria** [72 A2] (signposted, page 108), thermally heated natural pools. The level track leading from the sea was used by horse-drawn carts to carry water to the bath house, used by patrons who could not afford to travel to Furnas. If the wind is up, the crash of Atlantic Ocean on volcanic rock here, and the height to which the spray is projected, is truly humbling. There is a restaurant, too. **Bretanha** [72 B2] is a pretty area originally settled by Bretons; there's a spectacular cliff walk starting in João Bom (page 102), and a restored windmill near the Pico Vermelho viewpoint. After passing through **Remédios** and **Santa Bárbara** [72 B2] you'll come to the **Miradouro Santo António viewpoint**, overlooking small fields, the village and church of Santo António and the sea beyond. Finally you come to the large village of **Capelas** [72 B3], which was an important whaling centre with a factory (active 1945–74) just to the east for processing the animals. Don't forget the quirky **Museu M J Melo** (page 108), before you complete the loop back to Ponta Delgada.

 Where to stay

Whalesbay Hotel Apartamentos [72 B3] (15 apartments) Canada do Terreiro, S Vicente Ferreira, Capelas; ❉300 509 810; e info@whalesbayhotel. com; w whalesbayhotel.com. A compact, gated complex with very modern, very high-end seafront apartments on the north coast. Sleeping up to 6 guests, there are full s/c facilities, as well as AC, sat TV & balcony. On-site gym, jacuzzi, sauna, steam room; outside heated year-round pool & putting green. Playroom & garden area for children. Located 20mins from the airport. No b/fast, but a baker calls daily. Units available for those with lesser mobility. €€€€€

Quinta N Senhora de Lourdes [72 B3] (2 apartments, 1 room) Rua da Igreja 132, S Vicente Ferreira, Capelas; \296 919 626; m 914 954 509; e qnsl@yahoo.com; w quintanslourdes.com. On the left, just before Capelas as you approach on the main road from the east. Look for the pink building on the corner. Quirky place, set in a pleasant garden which adjoins a house built by a priest. Some interesting artefacts, including whaling harpoons. 2 of the units (1 of which is a family apartment) are s/c. Wine cellar (they make their own), snooker table, sun terrace. Gym, small pool & children's pool, bar & communal lounge. Usually a 2-night min stay. €€

What to see and do

Termas da Ferraria (thermal pools) [72 A2] (Rua Ilha Sabrina, Ginetes, at Ponta da Ferraria; \ 296 295 669; e reservas@termasferraria.com; w termasdaferraria.com; ⊕ 11.00–19.00 Tue–Sun, closed 1st 3 weeks in Jan; €6/3 adult/under 12s. Spa costs from €20; note that under 6s are not allowed in any of the pools or spa.) These are thermally heated natural pools. The old bath house is where a doctor would visit twice a week, descending by donkey along a little trail where the road now winds down. Now, it houses a plush spa downstairs, with sauna, jacuzzi and so forth, and you can indulge yourself for a few hours. If the tide is right, the seawater mixes with hot thermal outflow to produce a hot ocean bath! There's a bar, as well as a restaurant (⊕ noon–15.00 Tue–Sun & 19.00–22.00 Fri & Sat).

Oficina-Museu M J Melo (museum) (Rua do Loural 56, Capelas; \ 296 989 497; e oficinamuseu@gmail.com; ◆ oficinamuseu; ⊕ 10.00–noon & 14.00–16.00 Mon–Fri, 14.00–17.00 Sat; €3/free adults/under 10s. Guided tours may be available – ask on arrival.) Signposted from Capelas town centre (by the Santander bank), this is a most remarkable and extensive display of recreated bygone retail and artisan shops in the style of a street, all the work of a retired Capelas schoolteacher. From the modest entrance door, you would never guess what's about to be revealed. Not only has Senhor Melo made the museum, he has also financed it, without any grant-aid. It is located in part of his house, and he may well be there to greet you himself. Well worth visiting, as it will surely rekindle some childhood memories. Recordings of traditional Azorean music are available from the gift shop. Recommended.

THE EASTERN PART OF THE ISLAND: THE SOUTH COAST FROM PONTA DELGADA TO FURNAS
Once you're heading east out of Ponta Delgada, particularly if you divert where possible from the dual carriageway, you'll realise how sophisticated the island's biggest town can seem when set against the gentle rural life outside its municipal boundaries. While you may well be heading directly for Furnas with its unique setting and ambience, it is far more pleasant to take your time, potter along and visit some of the towns on the way and perhaps include an overnight stay or two. Completing an anticlockwise loop, visiting Furnas, Nordeste and Ribeira Grande and ending at the Lagõa do Fogo, would best be done over two or three days, taking in the sights and places described in the *From Furnas to the east and north coasts* section (page 118). Alternatively, you could make a series of day trips from Ponta Delgada.

From the road just east of Ponta Delgada, you can see the high stone walls which once protected the orange trees. On a hilltop there is also one of the remaining 'orange towers', once used to spy the approaching ships coming from England to trade. The places on the following pages are listed from west to east, starting in Ponta Delgada.

Lagoa [72 C4] Lagoa was the centre of São Miguel's pottery industry, which began in the 19th century. Crockery, pots, vases and other items in traditional designs and colours are made here and visitors are welcome to tour the factory, showrooms and museum of Cerâmica Vieira, founded in 1862 (see below). The old town's harbour was once busy with exports of woad and wheat.

✗ *Where to eat and drink* Next to the Vulcanological Observatory, Aroma das Ilhas (Av Vulcanológica; ☎ 296 916 419; m 967 616 884; e geral@aromadasilhas. com; f aromasdasilhas; ⏰ noon–15.00 Mon, noon–15.00 & 19.30–23.00 Wed–Sat, 12.30–16.00 Sun; €€) serves up excellent meals by catering students, including steak, seafood, and a creative menu of the day that's posted daily on Facebook.

What to see and do
Observatório Vulcanológico e Geotérmico dos Açores (Volcanoes House) (Av Vulcanológico 95; ☎ 296 965 376; e casadosvulcoes@gmail.com; w ovga. centrosciencia.azores.gov.pt; ⏰ 14.30, 15.30 & 16.30 Mon–Fri (by guided visit only, with English-speakers); €2.50/free adult/under 10s) On the west side of Lagoa, signposted right as you enter the town from Ponta Delgada, the half-hour tour explains the geological and volcanological history of São Miguel and the other islands, and finishes with the founder's collection of minerals and fossils from around the world, including dinosaur eggs from China; there are also temporary exhibitions.

Expolab (Av da Ciencia; ☎ 296 960 520; w expolab.centrosciencia.azores.gov.pt; ⏰ 10.00–17.00 Tue–Fri, 14.00–18.00 Sat; €2/1/free adult/seniors & students/under 6s) A fairly modest science teaching centre, with a few interactive displays for children, at whom it is largely aimed. They can also carry out their own laboratory experiments(!) with some instructions in English, or play with robots. There are also exhibitions on insects, forests, marine life and temporary displays.

Cerâmica Viera (Rua das Alminhas 10; ☎ 296 912 116; ⏰ 08.00–17.00 Mon–Fri, 09.00–12.45 Sat; admission free) A chance to buy some of the distinctive pottery from one of the island's last remaining manufacturers. Poking around the factory, you will come across workers finishing the pieces by hand. A family business founded in 1862, it is now in its fifth generation. There's a display of their products and some tools; it could be a greatly improved experience with guided tours, so perhaps it's more of a retail experience than anything else.

Caloura [72 D4] Caloura is a pretty village with a tiny fishing cove and a natural swimming pool at the end of the breakwater, surrounded by old vineyards, each with its own stone wall. In the past few years substantial new homes have been built and it is obviously a very desirable place to live; for the property-curious, it is interesting to see how a severe, stony landscape can be transformed. Seek out the **Castelo Centro Cultural** (Canada do Castelo, Caloura; ☎ 296 913 300; m 919 231 675; w cccaloura.com; ⏰ 10.30–12.30 & 13.30–17.30 Mon–Sat, closed Jan; €2/0.50/ free adult/student/under 12s), an art gallery with a private collection featuring Portuguese artists, including Azoreans Canto da Maia and Domingos Rebelo. The centre also has a 10-minute video (in English) introducing the islands and you

3

should wander outside into the surrounding garden, full of fruit trees sheltered by high stone walls.

By the harbour is an excellent fish restaurant and café, the **Bar Caloura** (Rua da Caloura 20; \ 296 913 283; ⊕ noon–21.30 daily), with a great terrace; reservations are advisable in summer; a tourist information office in the harbour should be open daily in high season (⊕ 09.00–12.30 & 13.30–17.00), and is closed on Mondays in low season. There is also a charming little convent with a beautiful tiled façade, dating from the 16th century, now privately owned.

In the adjacent village of **Água de Pau**, do visit the **Casa do Pescador** (Rua dos Ferreiros 26, Água de Pau; ⊕ 15.00–19.00 Mon–Fri, though opening times can be inconsistent), a small museum created by and dedicated to the local fishermen. In the centre of the village, the **Mercearia** museum (Rua da Praça da Republica 1; ⊕ 09.30–13.00 & 14.00–17.30 Mon–Fri; free) preserves a shop and tavern downstairs (with a bottle of aguardente on the bar), with living quarters upstairs, although there's not a lot of information. If you rejoin the highway by Água de Pau, note the tobacco-drying sheds with metal roofs. Tobacco grown on the islands is nowadays used in making cigars.

🏠 ## Where to stay

Caloura Hotel [72 D4] (80 rooms & suites) Rua do Jubileu 27, Água de Pau; \ 296 960 900; e info@calourahotel.com; w calourahotel.com. An oceanfront resort 17km from Ponta Delgada offering double rooms including junior suites for 4 people, most with private terrace; panoramic restaurant, bar, swimming pool, fitness room, sauna, scuba-diving base & tennis. The location is stunning, & you can walk the narrow roads round to Caloura's pretty harbour with its fishing boats & simple swimming facilities. Formerly an area of tiny vineyards, these have largely been removed in favour of pasture & housing. A sheltered sun trap, it is ideal for a winter holiday. AC, cable TV, b/fast inc. €€€€€

Quinta do Mar (6 rooms) Rua da Portela 43, Caloura; \ 296 913 990; m 917 716 669; e nick. heathcote@mail.telepac.pt; w quintadomar-caloura.com. An exquisite boutique hotel in a former winery, with striking modern extensions, swimming pool & gardens, also s/c cottage. €€€€

What to see and do nearby

Ribeira Chã museums (\ 296 913 770; ⊕ Oct–Mar 09.30–13.00 & 14.00–17.30 Mon–Fri, Apr–Sep 10.00–13.30 & 14.30–18.00 Mon–Fri; visit the religious art museum first, to get access to the others – if you're lucky, there may be someone who speaks English; €2 adults, €5 for all 3 museums) The charming hilltop village of Ribeira Chã [72 D4] between Lagoa and Vila Franca has three small museums of interest. To the right of the modern church, a small museum displays exhibits related to the various **religious festivals** held in the village, including the Cavalhadas de São Pedro, a horseback procession held on 29 June. Exhibited also is a replication of the way the imperador displays the crown and sceptre as part of the Espírito Santo Festival (page 34). The museum was the idea and initiative of a long-serving parish priest whose statue is outside the church, and includes many photographs and items such as wedding dresses and old school textbooks donated by the parishioners, and the priest's own collection of coins.

At Rua da Boavista 2, the **Casa Museu Maria dos Anjos Melo** was the home of a lady (1909–92) who as a child emigrated to the US and returned when 17 years old and taught English in the village, marrying a local stonemason. She bequeathed her house to the parish on her death and the priest had the idea of making it a museum. The house has not been changed, and reveals the very simple way of living once typical of the Azores.

A short downhill walk takes you to the **agricultural museum and ethnographic garden,** another excellent local initiative. Cultivated in the garden are yams, woad, oranges, flax and other early crops together with traditional medicinal herbs and endemic species. In the farm building is a series of model nativities cleverly made by schoolchildren from corn cob husks, pine cones, tiles or wire wool. There are gourds once used as swimming aids, wine barrel cleaners, and a nice section on Dragon's Blood (from the dragoeira tree, not a fire-breathing monster!); it was grown in Flores for export as a dye to Germany, and it seems Azoreans diluted it with aguardente and egg yolk for treating back pain, and the girls used the pure sap to paint their nails. Another interesting exhibit is the manufacture of pastel balls for export to Flanders, the *goma e rezinhas*, a mix of pastel and beeswax; during the 16th and 17th centuries, Ribeira Chã had 700 people working on pastel. Another small storeroom has wine-making equipment. In the grounds are several wooden buildings with fitted artefacts: a typical bar, shop, shoemaker, barber, a weaving shed, carpenter's shop, and homemade toys, among others.

Vila Franca do Campo

[72 D4] Located on a fertile plain or 'campo', Vila Franca was once a duty-free zone whose residents were exempt from paying taxes, hence its name. It was also the island's first capital. There is good swimming here (page 97), a marina on the east side of town, a health centre and Clube Naval. The bus terminal is on Rua 24 de Junho, just east of the centre. There is a harbour with small fishing boats and there are fish restaurants – try the **Casa de Praia** (Praia da Vinha d'Areia; ✆ 296 539 162; ⊕ noon–22.00, meals noon–15.00 & 19.00–22.00 Tue–Sun; €15) – and the famous local cakes called *Queijadas da Vila*, which you can see being made and munch with a coffee at **do Morgado** (Rua do Pinedo 18; ⊕ 09.00–18.00 Mon–Fri, 09.00–19.00 Sat–Sun). Don't forget the museum (page 112), also on this side of town. Among many buildings of historical architectural merit is the **Matriz**, the Church of São Miguel Arcanjo or the Archangel Michael. Completed in 1537, it has an impressive façade built completely of basalt, with a carving of Christ on the Cross. Across the road, the church of Bom Jesus da Pedra, also built in the 16th century, is just as striking. On the western edge of the town by a pretty little public garden is the old church and convent of São Francisco, dating from 1525; it is now a hotel (see below). On the way into town you will pass the tourist office.

Just off the beach is the **Ilhéu de Vila Franca do Campo**, the remains of a volcano where the sea has breached the crater wall creating a protected swimming area. Extremely popular with local people, it is accessed by a regular boat service between June and September (page 97). The island is also a nature reserve, so there is a daily quota of visitors.

If you have time, it is well worth driving up to the **Chapel of Nossa Senhora da Paz**, which can be seen high on the hillside behind the town. From here there is a splendid panorama of Vila Franca and its surrounding pineapple glasshouses, and of the green landscape spreading down to and along the coast.

🏠 *Where to stay*

Hotel Convent São Francisco (12 rooms) Av da Liberdade; ✆ 296 583 532; m 962 651 593; e manuela.m.guerrero@sapo.pt; w conventosaofrancisco.net. On the west side of town, this is a restored convent, built after the 1522 earthquake, with an air of serenity befitting its former purpose. All heavy stone, polished wood & impressive furniture in large rooms. There is a communal lounge with TV & an outdoor pool. Buffet b/fast served, but no other meals. Some rooms have views to the sea. Next door is a well-kept garden, accessible at any time. €€€€

Apartamentos Francisco Martins Rua Dr Augusto Simas 11; ✆ 296 583 000; m 969 049 193; e reservas@fmartinstravel.com; w fmartinsapartment.com. This friendly and efficient travel agency has various comfortable rooms and apartments available in the town centre. €€€

Quinta dos Curubás [72 E4] (5 houses) Estrada Regional 1, Ribeira Seca; m 961 739 880, 962 515 189; e geral@quintadoscurubas.com; w quintadoscurubas.com. Just east of Vila Franca, s/c timber chalets, set in a large garden on a hillside overlooking Vila Franca & its bay. Very comfortable, with all eco credentials & mod-cons, plus a popular colony of resident ducks. Free use of 3 bicycles & BBQ equipment, free access to the produce from the owner's vegetable garden, & a welcome pack of basic foodstuffs included. Special deals for 7-night stays. Some chalets have connecting doors, ideal for families. B/fast available, but at extra cost. €€€

 Where to eat and drink

Mercado da Vila Rua Vasco da Silveira; ✆ 296 102 057; w mercadodavila.pt; ⏱ noon–23.00 Wed–Mon. In the former fish market (built in 1903), 4 friends came together to create 4 restaurants in one – Azorean, Asian, Italian & desserts. None of them actually cooks here now, but it's a classy operation & the best food & drink for miles around. €€€

What to see and do Note that the town's little marina offers whale-watching trips, an alternative to the operators in Ponta Delgada (page 98).

Museu Municipal de Vila Franca do Campo (Rua Visconde Botelho; ✆ 296 539 282; ⏱ 09.00–12.30 & 14.00–17.30 Tue–Fri, 14.00–17.00 Sat & Sun; admission free) An excellent museum in the renovated house of an orange merchant, built in about 1854 with a distinctive square lookout. Exhibits cover archaeology (ie: what was here before the 1522 earthquake), ceramics and guitar-making, the Senhor Santo Cristo dos Milagres festivities, and the development of the port from the 15th century (when there was one annual visit by a supply ship) to 1861, when the modern port of Ponta Delgada took over. Original wall and ceiling paintings survive in the Noble Hall, and you can end by going up to the lookout tower. Some captions are in English, and laminated sheets are available for other displays.

Furnas Furnas enjoys a hint of the ambience you might find in an English spa town, with boisterous geothermal activity adding a tinge of exoticism. If you approach from the north, get an aerial perspective by taking the turning off to your right, signposted **Pico do Ferro**. This is a fine viewpoint over the Furnas lake and valley, helping you to get your bearings once you're finally down below. There is also a circular walk starting from here, as well as a shorter one down to the lake. Along with the view of Sete Cidades, this village in its huge caldera is among the best-known images of the Azores, certainly of São Miguel. Two places from this area appear in all the brochures: the **hot springs** with their bubbling, and burping mud and clouds of steam, and the beautiful **Terra Nostra Garden**. Popular as a spa in the 19th century, Furnas attracted patients from as far away as England. The spa building, which dates from the mid 19th century, has now been turned into a plush hotel. The municipal garden in front of what is now the Octant Hotel (page 114) was laid out in 1940. The bus terminal is on Avenida Victor Manuel Rodrigues; the Posto de Turismo (Rua Dr Frederico Moniz Pereira; ✆ 296 584 525; e pt.f.smk@ azores.gov.pt; ⏱ 09.00–16.00 daily) is helpful.

The largest, noisiest and perhaps most fearful of the many fumaroles (outlets for sulphurous steam) in the Jardim da Courela is named *Pêro Botelho*, a 16th-century nickname for the devil. Around the caldeiras area some 22 different mineral waters

FURNAS TOWN

N

Observatório Microbiano dos Açores (Microbe Observatory of the Azores)

RUA DE SANTANA

Beatriz do Canto Park

Lagoa das Furnas

RUA PADRE JOSÉ JACINTO BOTELHO

AV DR MANUEL DE ARRIAGA

Terra Nostra Garden

RUA DAS CALDEIRAS

For listings, see from page 113

Where to stay
1 Hotel Vale Verde
2 Octant Hotel Furnas
3 Parque de Campismo das Queimadas
4 Terra Nostra Garden

Where to eat and drink
5 3 Bicas
   A Terra (see 2)
6 Café Rosa Quental
7 Caldeiras e Vulcões
8 Summer Breeze
   Terra Nostra Garden (see 4)
9 Tony's

emerge from the ground, the best tasting from fountains, the lesser ones out of simple plumbers' pipes.

There are several large summer homes built by grandees in the 19th century, some with once-lovely gardens. Terra Nostra Garden (page 114) has a long history; it belongs to the Terra Nostra Garden Hotel but is open during the day to non-residents, for whom there is an entrance charge (page 116). Another most charming 19th-century garden is the **Beatriz do Canto Park** (page 116) on the Rua de Santana; originally called Myrtle Park, from the Ribeira das Murtas stream that flowed nearby, it was created as a public park to further beautify Furnas. North of town, golfers will find a peaceful haven to perfect their swing (page 96), while those who like a good – but flat – walk should take a stroll around the lake (page 104).

 Where to stay *Map, above, unless otherwise stated*
A constant stream of visitors ensures there is a high level of accommodation in this charming town, and fairly high prices, too.

Furnas Lake Forest Living [map, page 105]
(10 timber chalets sleeping 2+2 or 4+2) Estrada Regional do Sul, Lagoa das Furnas; ✆292 584 107; m 912 525 656; e reservas@furnaslake.com; w furnaslake.com. At the southern end of Furnas lake, a comfortable, well-fitted s/c option on a quiet, spacious site with a pool, surrounded by mountains. Friendly staff. Chalets feature TV & AC, some with a wood-burning stove. Canoe & cycle rental. Special packages offered; lower prices if you stay more than 1 night. Meals with advance notice; b/fast extra. €€€€€

THE TERRA NOSTRA GARDEN

In 1776, the noted orange farmer Thomas Hickling built a simple summer house on the high mound overlooking what is now the thermal swimming pool at Furnas. It was surrounded by trees which would have sheltered fashionable summer parties and music; of those trees, I believe the old pollarded English oak by the pool, supported by steel props, is the only one that remains, and is therefore probably the oldest tree in the garden, though its days are numbered. Hickling died in 1834, and it was not until 1848 that the Visconde da Praia purchased the property and built the present house on the mound. The Viscondessa was a keen gardener, and over the years they enlarged the estate and laid out the garden in a grand style with water, dark groves of trees and parterres of flowers. After the Visconde's death in 1872, his son enhanced the house and laid out the garden more or less as it is today with its serpentine canal and grottoes, and walks. New tree species were introduced from around the world so many of these now-mature trees are at most 140 years old.

The Terra Nostra Garden Hotel (see opposite) opened in 1935, and soon after, its owner Vasco Bensaúde, who was a very keen gardener, purchased the now-neglected garden; the family's company still owns it today. With a Scottish head gardener, John McInroy, and a veritable army of workmen, he totally refurbished the house and restored the garden within two years. World War II came and ended the fashionable life of Furnas based on the hotel, casino, spa and gardens, and the place continued to slumber for years afterwards until tourism once more asserted itself.

In 1990, restoration began once again, this time with English gardeners (led by David Sayers), and a team of tree surgeons climbed the equivalent of Mount Everest from sea level working on the 2,500 trees while local engineers refurbished the canals. Many new trees were planted, a garden of Azorean native species begun and, significantly, a collection of Malesian rhododendrons was planted. This is the only garden in Europe that can grow, out of doors without protection, these tender rhododendrons native to tropical mountains; they flower intermittently all year and come in spectacular colours and some are perfumed. The head gardener, Fernando Costa, together with his daughter Carina and a team of around a dozen workers, continue with new developments. In recent times these have included fern and cycad gardens, a formal flower garden, an ever-expanding collection of camellias – which in 2024 numbered around 800 different cultivars – a bromeliad outdoor garden and a new collection of aquatic plants, which includes the wonderful and giant *Victoria cruziana* water lily. Finally, there is a new area exclusively dedicated to the endemic and native flora of the Azores.

Octant Hotel Furnas (54 rooms) Av Dr Manuel de Arriaga; \ 296 249 200; e reservations-furnas@octanthotels.com; w furnas. octanthotels.com. Just outside the centre, on the east side of town, this is a design-led experience. Indoor & outdoor thermal pools, Turkish bath & full spa menu. Restaurant, bar, gift shop, & an ultra-chic designer interior. Excellent off-season rates. €€€€€

Quinta da Mó [map, page 105] (3 separate 1-bed houses & restored watermill with 3 beds) Rua das Águas Quentes 66; m 917 800 281; e reservas@quintadamo.com; w quintadamo. com. Secluded accommodation with full catering facilities & bicycles within a luxuriant & very different garden crossed by a briskly flowing stream in Furnas village. Can sleep up to 6 people. Outdoor jacuzzi. Min stay of 4 nights. €€€€€

above
(OB/D)

Ponta Delgada's attractive central square, Praça Gonçalo Velho Cabral, occupies the site of its original tiny port PAGE 91

left
(SN/D)

The Misericórdia church, overlooking the harbour of Angra do Heroísmo, is built on the site of the first hospital in the Azores PAGE 159

below
(T/S)

Horta is an important stopover for many yachts crossing the Atlantic PAGE 215

Well-ordered and quiet, Santa Cruz town is the main settlement on Graciosa island PAGE 180

above (SN/D)

A bright, neat farmhouse in typical Azores style, on Santa Maria island PAGE 129

right (VA)

São Mateus on Terceira is one of the most important fishing harbours on the islands PAGE 162

below (MB/S)

above left
(AH/D)
Involved patterns of carefully laid flowers, chopped conifers and coloured wood shavings are used in many Azorean religious festivals as seen here at Ribeira Grande, São Miguel PAGE 36

above right
(VA)
The *viola da terra* or Azorean guitar has double strings and, more importantly, two heart-shaped openings

left
(VA)
Cozido nas caldeiras is a delicious stew, prepared using vegetables and several different meats and gently cooked in volcanic steam for about 7 hours PAGE 117

below
(RVDS/D)
Visitors are welcome at Europe's first commercial tea plantations, located on the main Azorean island, São Miguel PAGE 123

Each island has its own form of *queijada* or small cake – these on Graciosa are similar to treacle tarts PAGE 174
above left (VA)

Bread is traditionally distributed to the poor during the festival of Espírito Santo PAGE 34
above right (JD/D)

For a different swimming experience, try the iron-rich warm-water pool at Terra Nostra Garden PAGE 116
right (VA)

Religious festivals take place in many villages and towns across the islands, like Cavalhadas de São Pedro in Ribeira Grande on São Miguel PAGE 89
below (V/D)

top
(both CC)

The Azores' diverse plant life consists of rare endemics such as *Viburnum treleasei* (left) and invasives such as *Hedychium gardnerianum* (right) PAGES 9 AND 11

above
(RH/D)

On São Miguel, Terra Nostra is one of the archipelago's finest gardens PAGE 114

below
(VA)

Rather than a single dominant caldera, there are seven volcanic lakes in the centre of the island of Flores; pictured, Lagoa Comprida PAGE 271

Endemic to the Azores, Monteiro's storm petrel (*Oceanodroma monteiroi*) breeds on only a few rocky islets off Graciosa PAGE 176

above
(APA/D)

The rare priolo, or Azorean bullfinch (*Pyrrhula murina*), can be found only in one small part of São Miguel island PAGE 69

above right
(GM)

Steep sea cliffs are important nesting sites for Cory's shearwater (*Calonectris diomedea borealis*) PAGE 10

right
(H/D)

The sperm whale (*Physeter macrocephalus*) is the largest of all toothed whales: males can measure up to 20m PAGE 11

below
(SS)

left
(GF/D)

The bubbling hot springs and mud pools of Furnas draw many visitors to taste some of the 22 different mineral waters PAGE 116

below
(HD/D)

Capelinhos on Faial was the site of the 1957–58 eruption and now hosts a widely acclaimed visitor centre PAGE 212

bottom
(AMA/S)

The famous crater lakes on the west of São Miguel are timeless and glorious to explore PAGE 106

Terra Nostra Garden Hotel (86 rooms) Rua Padre José Jacinto Botelho 5; 296 549 090; **e** tngh@bhc.pt; **w** bensaudehotels.com/en/terranostragardenhotel. This elegant hotel dates back to the 1930s & has a very strong period atmosphere. There is a newer wing with large balconied rooms looking into the garden. Most rooms in the original part of the hotel overlook the road with a view across it to the handsome former casino & its little formal garden. The hotel was completely refurbished in 2012–13, but the Art Deco styling has been retained. Features include a restaurant, bar, comfortable residents' lounge, children's play area, indoor pool, spa, gym, jacuzzi, massages (extra charge) & outdoor thermally heated pool. In 2022 Botania Hall, on the site of Hickling's mansion, was opened as a luxury villa. Residents have free access to the famous gardens at all times. €€€€€

Hotel Vale Verde (10 rooms) Rua das Caldeiras 3; 296 549 010; **e** geral@hotelvaleverde.com; **w** hotelvaleverde.com. Right in the centre, 200m from the tourist office, a no-frills, pleasant, family-owned & managed hotel with polished floors, spacious rooms & foreign-channel TV. Most have balconies. Downstairs bar & (in summer) a restaurant. Buffet b/fast inc. Staff are helpful. Great value. €€€

Camping
Parque de Campismo das Queimadas 296 584 307; **e** parquecampismovaledasfurnas@gmail.com; all year. In a lovely position overlooking the fumaroles, a large but rather confused site with hideously built facilities, tennis court, children's play area, restaurant/snack bar & large, surfaced car park. €

✗ Where to eat and drink *Map, page 113*

If you want to try a *cozido nas caldeiras* (page 117), then advance booking is advisable – after all, it takes a few hours to cook! The large flat soft rolls (like English muffins) called *bolos lêvedos* are made in Furnas and are delicious, especially when filled with cheese and ham and toasted; the best place to sample them is **Café Rosa Quental** (Rua Botelho 26; 296 588 040; **w** boloslevedos.pt/en; 08.00–19.00 daily; €).

A Terra Av Dr Manuel de Arriaga; 296 249 200; **w** furnas.octanthotels.com/en/a-terra-furnas. The conservatory of the Octant Hotel Furnas is a lovely setting for some of the best food on the island, although service can drag. €€€€
Terra Nostra Garden Hotel Restaurant 298 549 090. Probably the town's top choice, a formal-ish setting inside the posh hotel. Their cozido is lighter on the stomach than other places, though their vegetarian version lacks any punch. Otherwise, good quality & the plush setting is reflected in the slightly higher price. Service is efficient but friendly. €€€€
Caldeiras e Vulcões Rua das Caldeiras 36; 296 584 312; **e** caldeiras.e.vulcoes@ sapo.pt; noon–15.00 & 18.30–21.30 Wed–Mon in winter, daily in summer. Furnas is not blessed with gastronomic diversity, though this place, above the Caldeiras bar, is making efforts to provide something different in its stylish dining room.

Yes, you can get your cozido here, but the chicken breast with honey & mustard sauce provides a lighter experience. Vegetarian & children's options, too. Recommended by many locals. €€€
Summer Breeze Rua das Caldeiras 18; 296 588 204; noon–15.30 & 18.00–21.30 Tue–Sun. Ideal for something less than a full meal, at prices that are a step down from elsewhere in town. Simple fare, almost fast food, no fancy frills. Craft beers available. €€
Tony's Rua Largo Teatro 5; 296 584 290; **w** restaurantetonys.pt; noon–15.30 & 18.00–21.15 daily. A good mid-range option with huge portions that's popular with walkers refuelling after a day's exercise; decent vegetarian options including cozido. €€
3 Bicas Rua Padre José Jacinto Botelho 19; 296 584 222; 3bicaspub; 10.00–23.00 Fri–Wed. A lively pub, serving affordable pizzas & burgers, with a good range of drinks. €

What to see and do After visiting the gardens and fumaroles of Furnas, you can head out of town to walk around the **Lagoa das Furnas** (page 104) or visit its sights. Canoes are available for rent at the caldeiras (page 116). On the return journey to

Furnas, take the sign marked Lagoa Seca and head up to the viewpoint (Lombo dos Milhos) for a view over the town and the crater in which it sits. A steep descent takes you back to Furnas.

In Furnas town

Terra Nostra Garden (w parqueterranostra.com; ⊕ 10.30–16.30 daily (closed 25 Dec); admission €10/5/free adult/3–10/0–2) Admission to these beautiful gardens (page 114) is for the whole day, and includes use of the outdoor thermal pools and jacuzzi – a real bargain. Visitors have to be out of the pool by 17.00, to give hotel guests exclusivity, but are free to linger in the gardens a bit longer.

Beatriz do Canto Park (Rua dos Moinhos 23; ⊕ Aug 09.00–18.00 daily) Once known as Myrtle Park because it lies on the banks of the Ribeira das Murtas that flows through the village, this was funded by a group of property owners from Ponta Delgada who spent their summers in the valley. The English gardener George Brown dammed the stream to make a lake, and created lawns and walkways. Completed around 1862, it was also intended to include five summer residences for the members of the partnership, but this collapsed and only Ernesto do Canto built his chalet. Designed by the French architect A Hugé in 1866, it is a most charming building with ornate embellishments and balconies, its pink-washed walls fitting enticingly into the mature garden. Privately owned, it has been a long tradition to open the garden during August, but it is closed the rest of the year.

Poça da Dona Beija (Thermal Pools) (Lomba das Barracas; ⟍ 296 584 256; w pocadonabeija.com; ⊕ 08.30–23.00 daily; €8/5 adults/under 7s. Towel hire €2.) With changing rooms, showers, towel hire and even a shop selling swimming costumes, this group of five smallish thermal pools is all geared up to let you take a hot dip. *Very* hot, actually, with average temperatures of 39°C. Very popular; in high season you should book online. Café and parking on site.

Recinto das Caldeiras (Hot Springs Area) At the extreme east end of town, in the Jardim de Courela, you can wander, free of charge and unhindered, around this area of hot springs and pools as they bubble menacingly below you. A pleasant garden has been crafted in among the sulphurous fumaroles. Keep your balance, and keep hold of small children!

Observatório Microbiano dos Açores (Microbe Observatory of the Azores) (Antigo Chalé de Misturas; ⟍ 296 584 765; m 910 544 269; w omic.pt; ⊕ Jul & Aug 10.00–17.00 Mon–Fri, 14.30–18.00 Sat, Sep–Jun 10.00–17.00 Mon–Fri; guided tours 11.00 & 15.00 Mon–Fri, 16.00 Sat–Sun; €1/0.75/0.50 adult/seniors/under 18s, with guided tour €2/1.50/1) An observatory in a heritage building promoting the importance of microbial life on earth, with an emphasis on the microbial diversity in the Azores thermal springs. Exhibits explain what micro-organisms look like, where they live and what size they are, whether there is life inside the fumaroles and many other related topics and visitor activities. Adds a fascinating dimension to fumarole watching.

Around Furnas lake

Caldeiras (⊕ 06.00–20.00; entry to car park €3/free adult/under 12s, €3 extra if you bring your own food to have it cooked underground) Down by the north side of the Furnas lake, south of town, amid an area of geothermal activity, are the caldeiras, where for generations people have come to cook the famous cozido nas caldeiras. Holes are made about 1m deep in the hot earth into which a container is lowered filled with different meats, sausage and some vegetables, mostly kale, cabbage and potatoes. It is all left to cook gently for 6 or 7 hours. You can see the mounds of earth marking where the cooking is happening, with the restaurant names on signs showing whose is whose. If you bring your own food, assistance is on hand. Cooked slowly, and so evenly, all the flavours and delicious juices are retained, although those with timid appetites can find it a little daunting. Up to 1,000 visitors per day make their way here in high summer, to marvel at this traditional cooking method and walk the wooden walkway among the bubbling hot pools. A colony of ducks and a few stray cats add to a rather strange scene. Toilets and picnic tables on site.

Canoes and pedalos are available for rent here, and just to the south is the **Parque Grená** (**w** parquegrena.pt; ⊕ Oct–Mar 09.30–17.30, Apr–Sep 09.30–18.00; €10 over-5s), a new wildlife park in 18ha of forest that was a holiday home and then a hotel from the mid 19th century. There are 5km of trails, through the forest and to a waterfall. Also in the forest just to the south, the **Parque de Arvorismo** (Azores Treetop Park; **m** 911 712 462; **w** azorestreetop.com; ⊕ 10.30–17.30 Sat & Sun) is a ropes course that's popular with families.

If you fancy a walk around to the lake's southern side, there are other attractions to see. If arriving by car, continue south of the caldeiras area to find the car park on your left at the lake's southeastern corner. Modest parking charges apply in summer. Cross the road, go through the barrier, and follow the lakeside path for about 10 minutes to find the church, garden and finally the interpretation centre, all detailed below. On the way, look out on the tree trunks for a few 'bat-boxes', helping to preserve the only endemic Azorean mammal, the Azorean bat (*Nyctalus azoreum*).

Capella Nossa Senhora das Vitórias (Chapel) (Ask at the garden ticket office for a guided visit) This pseudo-Gothic chapel dedicated to Our Lady of Victories was built by José do Canto, one of the Azores' great gardeners, who vowed in 1854 to build a chapel if his wife recovered from illness. She did recover, and the chapel was built during the 1870s, but she died shortly after it was inaugurated in 1886. It is a family vault and do Canto and his wife are now buried there.

Mata-Jardim José do Canto (Jose do Canto Garden) (\ 296 285 295; **w** matajosedocanto.com; ⊕ winter 10.00–17.00, summer 10.00–18.00; €3/1.25/ free adults/juniors & seniors/children under 12, includes entrance to the church; a €5 combined ticket gives admission to the Centro de Monitorização, too – see below) Now open to the public, you can stroll around the 10ha garden, created in the 1860s, discover the waterfall and the 'Valley of Ferns', and enjoy the 1,000 or so camellias, which are in bloom from December to March. The ticket office, on your left opposite one of the lakeside houses, sells local handicrafts, and an information leaflet/map in English is included in the ticket price.

Centro de Monitorização e Investigaçao das Furnas (Furnas Monitoring and Research Centre) (\ 296 584 436; **w** siaram.azores.gov.pt/centros-interpretacao/ mi-furnas/texto.html; ⊕ Nov–Mar 09.00–17.00 Tue–Sat, Apr–Oct 09.00–18.00 daily; €3/1/free adult/seniors & juniors/under 14s; guided tours available at 11.00, 13.00 & 15.00 Tue–Sun, lasting 30mins; combined tickets with Mata-Jardim possible – see above) Next stop on your lakeside walk is this newish centre, 10 minutes' walk in from the main road. This very modern building was designed by the Portuguese architects Aires Mateus and Associates; inspired by the landscape, it uses building

AN ACCOUNT OF THE WARM BATHS

At the end of December 1839, Joseph and Henry Bullar spent a winter in the Azores and later published in London a detailed account of their travels. Here is their description of a thermal bath at Furnas, or the 'Baden-Baden of St Michael' as they named it.

After looking at the calderas, we took our bath, and it was certainly never my good fortune before to bathe in an invigorating warm bath. It produced a feeling of strength instead of lassitude, and the skin seemed not alone to have been cleansed and rendered most agreeably smooth, but to have been actually renewed.

While bathing, our man cooked eggs for us in one of the small boiling springs, and we afterwards went to the iron-spring for a draught [of mineral water]. This flows from a stone spout into a hollow stone basin, and trickles down a bank into a stream below: it has a strong but not disagreeable iron flavour, effervesces slightly, and is extremely grateful and refreshing. The bath and the spring seemed the two things best suited to the outside and inside of man, on first rising from his bed; natural luxuries when in health, natural remedies when sick – luxuries without after-pain, remedies without misery in taking them – both which evils seem to be inseparable from the luxuries and the remedies of our own invention. Most invalids feel that before-breakfast existence is burdensome; but this bath and draught of liquid iron were as breakfast in producing serenity and happiness, and were more of a breakfast in giving warmth and briskness, and a feeling of health, as of the flowing of younger blood through the veins...

materials traditional to the island and blends in harmoniously. Owing to the extensive conversion of woodland to pasture for cows and the subsequent fertilisers applied, the nitrogen run-off into the lake has caused eutrophication, an algae and phytoplankton bloom causing the death of animal life from oxygen starvation. The research centre is monitoring the various actions taken to recover the quality of the lake, by the removal of grazing animals, converting old pastures to productive legumes, establishing native flora on watersheds and other projects. Much is being learned about the life histories and requirements of individual plant species from the process of propagation and establishment of new native forest (*laurisilva*), and trials are still underway to select from the native blueberry (*Vaccinium cylindraceum*) one that produces improved fruit for possible commercial use. There is a café and a small gift shop.

THE EASTERN PART OF THE ISLAND: FROM FURNAS TO THE EAST AND NORTH COASTS Leaving eastwards from Furnas, you could take a diversion directly south down a phenomenally lush valley to the coast at Ribeira Quente, a busy fishing port with a car park by its beach, its size indicating its summer popularity. Swimming is a possibility here (page 97). You will then have to come back to rejoin the road to continue east, as there is no connecting coast road from Ribeira Quente (although there is a hiking trail). From Furnas to Povoação, you will be confronted with a landscape of green, cows grazing peacefully while seemingly oblivious to the improbably steep inclines, villages clinging to narrow ridges above deep-cut *ribeiras* as they plunge down to the sea. Beyond Povoação, the road is prone to winter washouts and landslips, so it's wise to check before setting out that the route is open. Assuming that all is well, you can take the signposted gravel track up to the left to the Serra da Tronqueira, or continue along the tarmac coastal route.

The gravel track runs for around 17km, and can be badly affected by heavy rain at any time of the year. However, should it have been recently graded and in good condition it is a wonderful drive on a clear day. If the clouds are low, however, you will not see anything, so do not waste your time.

If you choose the coastal road, at Água Retorta [72 G3], a signpost informs you that you are 2,500km from London, 4,500km from Toronto and 7,500km from Rio do Janeiro. 'Coastal' is possibly a misleading adjective, as the steep cliffs prevent you from getting very near the sea at all, though the route is still positively exhilarating.

Between Água Retorta and Nordeste there are several viewpoints along the road, with toilets and manicured gardens, but really nothing much else by way of facilities until you reach Nordeste itself. The coast between Faial da Terra and Ponta do Arnel is a Special Protected Area; it is an important nesting site for shearwater and common tern, and there are some endemic plants and invertebrates. The coast both north and south of Nordeste is dramatic, with many waterfalls and watermills, and a succession of fine viewpoints.

Ribeira Quente [72 F4] The valley which you take to approach the village from the Furnas–Povoação road is particularly verdant and on the way you will pass through two tunnels where there is a waterfall. The town has a long, well-developed seafront, protected by sea defences, and a beach reachable by following the 'Zona Balnear' signs where swimming is possible (page 97). Maybe one of the locals will tell you where the thermal area is; here, at low tide, the sea is very warm. At the east end of the promenade is the busy fishing harbour. Between beach and harbour are several restaurants, popular in summer for their seafood. The village is divided naturally by the watercourse bringing its fresh load down the ribeira to discharge into the ocean; tiny, colourful houses line the banks. In the eastern side of town, a large area is set aside for disentangling and mending the fishing nets.

Povoação [72 F4] This was the first settlement on São Miguel, and now has a pretty little town square and old streets leading down to the harbour, where a sculpture pays homage to the early arrivers. The harbour is big and bolstered against the waves, yet there is virtually no fishing fleet here, compared with Ribeira Quente. Just west of the harbour, the church of **Nossa Senhora do Rosário**, built in the late 15th century but restored in the 19th century and again recently, is thought to have been the first building of worship on the island. Don't forget to visit the Wheat Museum, a couple of kilometres out of town (see below).

🏠 ***Where to stay***
Hotel do Mar (36 rooms) Rua Gonçalo Velho; 📞296 550 010; w hoteldomar.com. A modern development overlooking the harbour with a lighthouse-style tower, this has AC rooms with & without sea views, outdoor pool & restaurant. €€€€
Quinta Atlantis [72 F3] (5 rooms) Lomba do Botão 87; 📞296 559 172; m 916 256 055; e info@ quintaatlantis.com; w quintaatlantis.com. Built

in 1910 high on a ridge, a few km inland from Povoação, Atlantis has tasteful themed rooms, some with shared, some with private bath. Free Wi-Fi, communal TV, lots of books, DVDs available. Prices include b/fast, which focuses on local products. Would suit those who (genuinely) want to get away from it all. Owners will send detailed directions when you book – you may need them! Usually a 3-night min stay is required. €€€

What to see and do
Museu do Trigo (Wheat Museum) (By the Ribeira dos Bispos, between the ridges of Lomba do Loução & Lomba do Alcaide; 📞 296 550 200; m 967 932 096;

There are several miradouros and picnic sites along this road, and they are constantly being improved and added to. The Nordeste Municipality has always taken a great pride in these, and deservedly so. You should take advantage of them, to absorb the sheer isolation of this region, and to slow your journey.

Ponta da Madrugada is a favourite stop, with toilets, a pleasant garden area, picnic tables and barbecue facilities ideal for family lunches. Good views up and down the coast.

Ponta do Sossego, the 'Place of Quietude', is a beautifully gardened belvedere offering splendid views of the steep coastline to the south. The garden is on different levels, with delightful paths amid flowering hydrangeas, hibiscus, azaleas, camellias, palms and summer annuals. Toilets, picnic tables and barbecue facilities.

Ponta do Arnel, just south of Nordeste, provides a dramatic view down to the lighthouse, the first modern one to be built in the Azores, in 1876.

Vista dos Barcos, just south of Arnel, gives fine views of the lighthouse from the other side.

w cm-povoacao.pt; ⊕ 11.00–17.00 Mon–Fri, 11.00–16.00 Sat & Sun; admission free) Signposted left off the main road as you leave Povoação on the Nordeste road, this splendid watermill has been skilfully restored in a glorious setting of pastures and hedgerows. Ask the staff and they will open the sluice and set the mill-wheel in motion. It is a triumph of restoration and capture of a past culture, and highly recommended. Although the wall panels are in Portuguese only, translations are promised for the future and staff give explanations in English. Visitors are offered a taste of a local liquor, and there are Azorean handicrafts for sale. If you're heading towards Nordeste, staff will advise you of a short cut, avoiding a retracing of your steps.

Diversion to the Pico Bartolomeu
Turning off the coast road at Pedreira, you can cut inland to visit the Parque Florestal and Centro Ambiental do Priolo (Priolo Environmental Centre) and continue up the road to the heights of the Pico Bartolomeu mountain. The return journey is 16km. Note that this is a dead-end: whatever some maps might tell you, there's no road down the other side of the Pico! If there's low cloud, it's not worth going beyond the Priolo Centre, and if heavy rain is forecast, it is inadvisable. First along this route is the **Parque Florestal Cancela do Cinzeiro** (⊕ May–Sep 08.00–midnight Mon–Fri, guides on duty 08.00–15.30, 10.00–midnight Sat–Sun, guides 10.00–17.00; Oct–Apr 08.00–21.30 Mon–Fri, guides 08.00–15.30, 10.00–21.30 Sat–Sun, no guides; free), with play area and a collection of endemic plants, then a few metres further up the road is the **Priolo Environmental Centre** [72 G3] (m 918 536 123; w en.centropriolo.com; ⊕ May–Sep 10.00–18.00 Tue–Sun, 15 Feb–30 Apr & 1 Oct–15 Nov noon–17.00 w/ends & hols), where you can learn about the priolo (Azorean bullfinch), endemic to this part of São Miguel. Once critically endangered, its population has been revitalised by the careful work of conservationists (page 69). At the entry to the park, you can take a sharp left and continue upwards towards the Pico Bartolomeu. After a few kilometres of climb, you take a right (signposted), first passing the Miradouro da

Tronqueira then crossing along a ridge with drop-offs on both sides before the final ascent to the radio masts of the Pico (847m). The views are great, both inland and along the coast.

Nordeste [72 G3] Nordeste is so far from the rest of the island and had such poor roads, that boats were the preferred means of travel until the end of the 19th century. It has always been a charming, sleepy little place that few tourists ever reached, but now this princess has been kissed by progress and is slowly awakening, with restaurants and other small developments, and a fast road connecting it to Ponta Delgada. The town centre is dominated by the 18th-century church, by the left side of which is a small **museum** (see below). The town square is neat, with a central bandstand. There is a **tourist information office** nearby (\ 296 480 066; ⊕ Mar–Sep 09.30–17.30 Mon–Fri, 10.00–15.15 Sat, Sun & hols, Oct–Feb 09.00–17.00 Mon–Fri), and a couple of inexpensive but unexceptional restaurants in the area behind the church. Buses run to/from a large shelter in the main car park, with timetables and WCs.

On the northeast side of town, you can turn right off the roundabout to access the town's saltwater swimming pool (*Piscina da Boca da Ribeira*), separated from the raging ocean by a sturdy wall.

Where to stay nearby

Lince [81 G3] (24 rooms, 4 apartments) Rua dos Clerigos 1; \ 296 101 390; e centralreservas@ thelincehotels.com; w thelincehotels.com/ nordeste. An excellent addition to the area's accommodation options, this modern low-rise block, in simple gardens on the western edge of the town, has indoor & outdoor swimming pools, gym, spa & bike rental. All rooms have views east over the town to the sea; the restaurant is very affordable, with good vegetarian choices. €€€€
Quinta das Queimadas [72 G3] (2 apartments, 1 room) Pedreira; \ 296 488 578; e queimadas@ sapo.pt; w quintadasqueimadas.be. Open all year, a quirky rural option south of Nordeste, signposted off the road to the Priolo reserve. Frenchman Pierre has been here for 20 years, his own piece of

wilderness. He keeps pigeons & 2 horses, which have gone a bit wild since his daughter went back to France. B/fast inc, other meals by arrangement. Apartments have kitchen corner, wood-burning stove – valuable in winter – and own BBQ. Good value & prices reduce for longer stays. €€€

Camping

Parque de Campismo da Feira [72 G2] Boca da Ribeira; \ 296 488 353; m 919 060 141; e parquecampismonordeste@gmail.com; ⊕ all year. Off the main EN1 road just north of Nordeste, tucked away at the bottom of a river valley, this pretty campsite is beneath trees by a stream with many watermills. Showers & WCs. Semi-natural swimming pool near the sea. €

Where to eat and drink nearby

Restaurant Cardoso Estrada Regional 19, Lomba da Fazenda; \ 296 486 138; ⊕ noon–15.00 daily, café open all day. A little north of Nordeste, on the east side of Lomba da Fazenda (just west of the church), a good-quality, well-

established restaurant offering daily dishes at favourable prices. Fish are a combination of fresh & frozen, meat portions are generous. English-speaking owner. €€€

What to see and do

Museu Etnográfico do Nordeste (Rua Dona Maria do Rosário, Nordeste; \ 296 480 065; ⊕ 08.30–12.30 & 13.30–16.30 Tue–Fri; free admission) Down behind the church, this features displays of local cultural traditions and skills with old ceramics from Lagoa and Vila Franca, early clothes, weaving and other items pertaining to the area, all housed in an interesting old building, recently refurbished.

Ribeira do Guilherme [72 G2] Just after leaving Nordeste, look out for the signpost on your left to the Ribeira do Guilherme picnic site, from where a trail leads upstream past a lime kiln. Below the road bridge is the Quinta do Moinho botanic garden (⊕ 08.00–15.30 Mon–Fri), laid out parallel with a stream feeding a watermill.

Santo António de Nordeste To see the local handicrafts, including weaving, pop into the Centro Cultural, on the main road just west of the church.

Algarvia [72 F2] The next village to the west, Algarvia has a viewpoint with a beautifully restored whale lookout post (*Miradouro Vigia das Baleias*) with toilets, a big car park, children's play area, picnic shelters, barbecue facilities and garden.

Ribeira dos Caldeirões [72 F2] (Signposted between Achada & Achadinha; ⊕ park open at all times, shop 10.00–18.00 daily, summer until 19.00) Taking the old road rather than the expressway west from Achada, you'll come to this delightful valley with its lovely tree ferns, working watermill, and in February the heavenly scent of all the pittosporum trees in flower. In 1986, severe floods destroyed most of Nordeste's watermills, of which there were once over 100. Three have been acquired by the municipality as features of the natural park area of Ribeira dos Caldeirões and to preserve the area's heritage and connect with a past traditional way of life. One mill has been restored as a working museum, and there is a visitor centre (\296 488 320; ⊕ 10.00–17.00 Mon–Fri), café and one of the most well-stocked gift shops on the island. Opposite are two waterfalls, very pretty, though the waters are artificially diverted to ensure your holiday photos look their very best! The park is manicured and not at all wild, but with its excellent café, picnic area and toilets, it makes an ideal family-friendly stopover.

Achadinha [72 F2] About 1km west of Achadinha (before Salga) a turning leads north to the **Miradouro Salto do Farinha**, from where there's a good view of the waterfall of the same name. After heavy rain the 40m waterfall flows briskly and becomes a twin fall. You can walk down the path to the valley bottom and to the sea, with a picnic area, toilets and a saltwater bathing pool. On the west side of Salga, trails lead down into another valley, with waterfalls and a preserved watermill; another signposted road leads to the **Miradouro do Rocha**, with a tiny car park as well as a play area and picnic shelters. If you walk a short distance down the concrete road to the sea you'll have a good view of the Cascada do Homem.

Fenais da Ajuda [72 E2] If you have time, drive down to the village and past the main church until you come to a much simpler, smaller, church, which was the first one to be built in the village in the early 19th century. Behind is a cemetery, at the far end of which is a splendid view along the coast to Maia and Ponta do Cintrão in the middle distance, and way beyond to the Ponta da Bretanha at the northwest tip of the island.

Maia [72 E3] This is a small fishing village where the large pink building houses a theatre, meeting hall and other community facilities. There is also a tobacco museum here.

 Where to stay nearby

Herdade Nossa Senhora das Graças [72 E3] (4 rooms & 2 apartments) Estaleiro, Lomba da   Maia (east of Maia); m 961 127 350; e reservas@ nsgracas.com; w nsgracas.com; ⊕ closed Oct–Feb.

A true agrotourism place, your neighbours are the turkeys, cows & goats. The 1920s house is situated in peaceful farmland far off the beaten track, with the s/c apartments in a separate building. You need a car to get here, but Lomba da Maia, the nearest village with supermarket & restaurant, is 2km away, about 30mins' walk along a farm road. Visitors are given a warm welcome & hospitality standards are high, with splendid evening meals (by arrangement) with authentic Azorean flavours. English & German spoken. €€€

What to see and do

Museu do Tabaco (Estrada Regional de S Pedro, Maia; \ 296 442 905; w ribeiragrande. pt/geo/museu-do-tabaco; ⊕ 09.00–noon & 13.00–17.00 Mon–Fri, 09.30–noon & 12.30–16.00 Sat; arrive at least 45mins before closing; €2.50/1/free adults/seniors & 14–18s/under 14s) Especially on São Miguel, until relatively recently one would see large open-sided drying sheds laden with tobacco leaves. Now much rarer, the Azores still produces cigarettes, Coroa and Robusto Estrela cigars and the smaller and thinner Pérolas curubas. The museum documents the Azores' tobacco industry.

Gorreana tea estate (Plantações de Chá Gorreana, on the north side of the EN1, Gorreana; \ 296 442 349; w gorreana.pt/en; ⊕ 08.00–18.00 Mon–Fri, 09.00–18.00 Sat & Sun; there is a shop & free green or black tea is available in flasks. Admission free, guided tours free if staff are available; buggy tour through the plantation €10 pp, book in advance) The first records of tea growing in the archipelago date from the late 18th century, although it is thought to have been known before then because of the Portuguese ships passing through on their return from Asia. It was the demise of the growing and export of oranges that stimulated the development of new crops, such as pineapples and tea. Seeds from China were planted on the Gorreana estate in 1874 and the first harvest was in 1883. It proved so popular that further varieties were brought from India, but Gorreana is now one of the last two estates on São Miguel; 37ha remain, producing over 40 tonnes of tea annually.

Lupins were planted around the shrubs to fix nitrogen in the soil. Fungicides, pesticides and herbicides are not needed, and tea plants have thrived so well in the Azores that an especially aromatic variety has developed. The leaves, or rather the young shoot tips, are harvested between April and September by a simple machine operated by three or four men that straddles the rows of bushes; previously they were hand-plucked by women and girls. The leaves are then processed in the usual way in old but beautifully engineered British machines, and finally sorted and packed by hand. The distinctive packets are exported to the other islands, continental Portugal, Germany and Azorean communities in North America. In Germany an association has been formed – the Friends of Azorean Tea – and cuttings for propagation have been sent to Tregothnan Estate in Cornwall for their plantation. You'll exit through the shop, where you can buy tea and other souvenirs, and the excellent café (⊕ noon–16.30 daily), which offers a soup of the day, pasta, salad, craft beers and of course tea and cakes. Charming staff speak excellent English, and there is a short, subtitled video. Although the estate is open all year, you can see the factory actually processing the tea between April and September (Mon–Fri).

Chá Porto Formoso (tea estate) (On the north side of the EN1; \ 296 442 342; e chaportoformoso.com; ⊕ Nov–Apr 09.00–17.00 Mon–Sat, May–Oct 09.00–18.00 Mon–Sat; admission free) A small tea estate just west of the more feted Gorreana (look out for the big black kettle), it has a visitor centre and shows an interesting video of tea production. It also has a charming tea room, shop, panoramic gardens and lovely view to admire while you choose from their four different brews. Founded in the 1920s and relaunched in 2001, since 2018 their tea has been officially certified as organic. The visit and tea-tasting is free of charge. If you happen to visit on the first Saturday of May, you will find that a big party is taking place, with dozens of locals dressed in traditional costumes, picking the tea by hand. Everyone is welcome – and it's free!

Porto Formoso

Porto Formoso [72 D3] has a fishing fleet and a beach by the port; continuing west takes you to Praia dos Moinhos, with a beach and a watermill converted into a restaurant, **O Moinho** (Rua dos Moinhos 18; ℓ 296 442 110; w moinhoterracecafe.com; ⊕ noon–19.00 Tue–Sun; €). It's simple and pleasant... but do try the one listed below, first.

✖ Where to eat and drink

* **Cantinho do Cais** Rua do Ramal, São Brás; ℓ 296 442 631; ⊕ noon–22.00 Thu–Tue. Well worth a diversion, but only if you like seafood. The owner/chef Jorge is a master, & his *molho de peixe* (fish stew, always made with fresh fish) is divine. The fish of the day (usually half-a-dozen choices) is also always fresh; other fish on the menu will be frozen. All served efficiently in a couple of formal dining rooms. Sublime desserts. Menu in English, advanced booking advisable. €€

Miradouro de Santa Iria

Right on the main road just east of Ribeirinha, this is one of the loveliest viewpoints along the north coast. In summer on a balmy night you can stand here for ages listening to the cry of Cory's shearwaters as they swoop around the cliff below you and, at the same time, become intoxicated by the perfume of the Himalayan ginger lilies. If you have just arrived in the Azores and are transferring to your hotel in Furnas, always ask your driver to stop here; the pressures of the big city fall away and after just 5 minutes of these scents and sounds you already feel at peace and rejuvenated.

Diversion inland to Caldeiras and Lombadas Valley

Just east of Ribeira Grande, follow the signs for Caldeiras [72 D3], a 5km drive inland to reach this tiny village of large old houses where there is a hot spring and a thermal pond (no bathing, though). It must have been delightfully romantic in its heyday; the **Restaurante Caldeiras** (ℓ 296 474 307; ⊕ 10.00–22.00 Tue–Sun; €€) offers typical Azorean dishes, with buffets on Sundays. Above the restaurant is an area set aside for the underground cooking of cozido (page 117), though it seems a bit manufactured compared with the lakeside activities of Furnas. A loop walk called the *Salto de Cabrito* is well waymarked and leads west to a waterfall and hydro-electric power station (open from 1902 to 1972) just off the Lago de Fogo road; you'll have to step out on to the rocks to see the second, upper waterfall. The road continues to **Lombadas** [72 D3], through wild country along a narrow, mainly cobbled road, slippery when wet. At the head of the valley are the remains of buildings where a mineral water spring used to provide most of the bottled mineral water on the island, coming from a length of domestic garden hose whose further end disappeared somewhere under the heather on the adjacent hillside. A landslide several years ago wrecked the operation, but hopefully one day Lombadas water will again go into bottles. From here you must either return towards Ribeira Grande or take the mountain road over the Cumeira Massif to the south coast.

Ribeira Grande

The fast-flowing stream that now runs along the side of the very nice-looking town square and past the pretty former town hall attracted early settlers to build watermills here. In 1507, Ribeira Grande [72 D3] received its town charter. During the second half of the 17th century, the French government boosted economic development, but then religious intolerance made many skilled workers emigrate. With the arrival of French workers, linen and wool weaving brought great prosperity to Ribeira Grande in the 18th and early 19th centuries. Today it is expanding with light industrial development, but still manages to keep much of its old charm tucked away. Visit the main church of **Nossa Senhora da Estrela** (1507) to see the sacristy and its paintings of the Flemish School. The Misericórdia church, the **Church of Espírito Santo**, in the main square, has one of the best Baroque façades in the Azores; unusually it has two doors. There are a few museums to visit and you should certainly drive or walk to the sea, for a grand promenade has been constructed with swimming pool and esplanade. To the west of town is the island's best surfing beach, Praia de Santa Bárbara (page 97). Ribeira Grande has a slightly rough-edged feel to it, compared with Ponta Delgada, but has several points of interest and a couple of good restaurants and guesthouses. There is also a **tourist office** (Rua Luis da Camões; ⊕ 09.00– 17.00 Mon–Fri), with English-speaking staff, at the bus station, just west of the centre.

🏠 Where to stay

Verde Mar & Spa (152 rooms) Rua Dr José Nunes da Ponte; 📞296 247 710; m 912 246 202; e reservas@verdemarhotel.com; w verdemarhotel.com. Just west of the town centre, this is the best hotel in the area, a long low block with spacious AC rooms, a large outdoor pool, wellness centre & a good restaurant. €€€€€

A Casa de Cascata (5 rooms) Largo Gaspar Fructuoso 33; m 919 797 183; e ascasasdaribeiragrande@hotmail.com; w ascasasdaribeiragrande.com. Very light & spacious, this beautifully renovated house is now an excellent guesthouse, with rooms overlooking the square, or towards the sea. Guests have use of an enclosed courtyard, there's a kitchen (no b/fast provided, but there's a café/restaurant across the pretty square) & communal TV lounge. Not all rooms have private bathroom, some have balcony. A pleasant & good-value choice; 2-night min stay in high season. €€

Costa Norte (5 rooms) Rua de Santa Luzia 1; m 914 575 361; e guesthouse@costanorteazores@gmail.com; w costanorteazores.com. A bit more ramshackle than the Cascata down the road, this cosy place is popular with surfers. Bike hire, kitchen, terrace, b/fast inc 2-night min stay. €

Camping

Parque de Campismo Rural Quinta das Laranjeiras [72 C3] Canada Roda do Pico 30, Rabo de Peixe; m 962 823 766; w azorescamp. com; ⊕ May–Sep. An attractive comfortable site; tents & mobile homes can be rented. €

🍴 Where to eat and drink

Quinta dos Sabores [72 C3] Rua Caminho da Selada 10, Rabo de Peixe (signed off the EN3–1A, south of Rabo da Peixe); m 917 003 020; w quintadossabores3.wixsite.com. A different kind of experience, this 'farm-to-table' restaurant truly delights with the quality of ingredients, innovation, ambience & personal touch of the family owners. A bit out of (any) town, advance booking is required. They will also discuss the menu with you, in advance. Expect an excellent 5-course feast, but portions are suitably restrained. Vegetables are sourced from their organic farm. No à la carte, just a very good set meal. €€€€

Alabote Restaurant Largo East Providence 68, Ribeira Grande; 📞296 473 516; w alabote.net; ⊕ noon–17.00 & 19.00–22.00 Thu–Tue. Plenty of fish & meat on the menu, plus children's menu & a very limited veggie option in this highly rated modern restaurant by the sea. €€€

Botequim Açoriano EN1-1A, Rabo de Peixe; 📞296 708 401; f botequimacoriano; ⊕ noon–15.00 & 18.00–22.00 Tue–Sun, winter closed Sun, Jan closed for 2 weeks. In the attractive fishing village of Rabo de Peixe, this is a local restaurant but is dedicated to maintaining the highest standards of traditional Azorean cuisine, especially fish and seafood. €€€

Restaurante da Associaçao Agrícola Recinto da Feira, Campo de Santana; ✆296 490 001; w restauranteaasm.com/pt; ⊕ noon–23.00 daily for dining, 08.00–midnight for bar/ coffee service, closed Jan. A few kilometres west of Ribeira Grande (not in the town, as wrongly shown on some internet maps), take the 'Santana' turn-off to the south. If the name conjures up a vision of burly farmers discussing the price of milk, forget it. Having shaken off its rustic roots, this is now a huge modern unit, specialising in beef – & a lot of it. Even the waiters admit they are well beaten by the 400g steak which tops the bill. Don't ask for vegetarian, though fish dishes are available. Book in advance at w/ends or hols. €€€

Monte Verde Rua da Areia 39; ✆296 472 975; w restaurantemonteverde.com.pt; ⊕ noon– 15.00 & 19.00–22.00 Tue–Sun. Near the sea in an unpromising part of town, a very promising restaurant. Fresh fish every day, served simply. Excellent fish soup, too. Justly popular. €€

What to see and do

Museu de Emigração Açoriana (On the south side of Rua do Estrela, the main road west out of Ribeira Grande; ✆ 296 470 770; w ribeiragrande.pt/geo/museu-da-emigracao-a-oriana; ⊕ 09.00–17.00 Mon–Fri; €2/1/free adult/senior/under 6) Opened in 2005 and refreshed in 2016, this museum was the result of requests by emigrants to document the movements from the islands over the years, which it does with some interesting photos, artefacts and personal stories from emigrants. It's clear that the extreme rural poverty here was on a level with that in 19th-century Ireland. The excellent information panels are in Portuguese and English. Next to the market, this building was the fish market, and the large car park opposite, behind the wall, used to be the cattle market.

Museu Municipal (Formerly Casa de Cultura) (Rua São Vicente Ferreira 10, Ribeira Grande; ✆ 296 470 736; w ribeiragrande.pt/geo/museu-municipal-da-ribeira-grande; ⊕ 09.00–17.00 Mon–Fri; €2/1/free adults/seniors & children/under 6s) With some excellent working models depicting town life in times gone by and a 1920s nativity scene, a visit to this handsome old manor house is recommended, providing a good insight into life as it was in the past. Replicas of an old barber's, a pharmacy and a milliner's shop. Also contains a tiny chapel and a display of old tiles. Almost no English-language information.

Casa do Arcano (Museum) (Rua João d'Horta, Matriz, Ribeira Grande; ✆ 296 470 763; w ribeiragrande.pt/geo/museu-casa-do-arcano; ⊕ 09.00–17.00 Mon–Fri; €3/€1.50/free adult/over 65s/under 6s; you can ask for a guided tour, in English, at no extra charge) On the road off to the left of the Chapel of Santa Luzia, the focus of this relatively new museum is an extraordinary assemblage of models made from rice flour, clay, glass, shells, cork and wire. With no fewer than 3,972 figures and models such as the Temple of Solomon, the Palace of Ahasuerus and the House of Caiaphas, it was an aid for teaching the catechism. Margarida Isabel Narcisa (Madre Margarida do Apocalipse) was the daughter of a wealthy family, and entered a Clarissan convent in 1800. In 1832, the king closed all the convents, so she moved into this house with her sister and began the now-revered construction devoted to São João, only ceasing to add to it a year or two before her death in 1858. For years it remained hidden in the Mother Church, but is now on show in the restored house. Texts are in Portuguese, but a video with English subtitles explains more.

Museo Vivo do Franciscano (Rua São Francisco; ✆296 470 730; w ribeiragrande. pt/geo/museu-vivo-do-franciscanismo; ⊕ 09.00–17.00 Mon–Fri; €2/1/free adult/ over 65/under 6) A museum of Franciscanism might not seem very interesting, but this is mainly concerned with the Terceiros or Third Order of Penitence (following the Franciscan friars and nuns), lay men (mostly) who work in their communities and organise festivals, above all the Senhor Santo Cristo dos Milagres procession five weeks after Easter. In the church of Nossa Senhora da Conceição, built in 1592–1613 and rebuilt in 1748–73, you'll see an introductory video with English subtitles, then the cloisters and 18th-century altars, and the elaborately bedecked figures carried in the procession.

Arquipélago (Contemporary Arts Centre) (Rua Adolfo Coutinho de Medeiros; \ 296 470 130; w arquipelagocentrodeartes.azores.gov.pt; ⊕ 10.00–18.00 Tue–Sun; €3/1.50/free adult/under 25s & seniors/under 14s, free to all on Sun) A fairly new creation, in a former tobacco and medicinal alcohol factory, with a full programme showcasing both visual and performing arts. For students of architecture, the prize-winning restoration of the building will be of interest; for the casual visitor, it is perhaps worth ensuring that there *is* an exhibition taking place to coincide with your visit.

Cerâmica Micaelense (Rua do Rosário 42; \ 296 472 600; ⊕ 09.00–18.00 Mon–Fri) On the road east out of town is a ceramic workshop making excellent tiles. Numerous original and ambitious designs are displayed in their showrooms and around the workshops, and they will make any design to your order: pictures of your garden, your house, figurative, abstract. More of a shopping trip than a factory tour, though you can watch the tiles being hand-painted.

Diversion inland to Caldeira Velha and Lagoa da Fogo
Caldeira Velha [72 D3] (Estrada Regional da Lagoa do Fogo; \ 296 704 649; ⊕ Nov–Mar 09.00–17.00 daily, Apr & Oct 09.00–18.30 daily, May–Sep 09.00–20.30 daily; admission for 2hrs €3/1/free adult/under 14s/under 7s, or €10/5/free if you want to bathe) On your way up to these now fully developed hot baths, you will pass the geothermal installations in the hillsides behind Ribeira Grande. The complex of silver-painted structures is part of the energy supply to the island. Caldeira Velha itself has been turned into what some will see as a little oasis, though its transformation from a rather random place into a slicker operation may dismay others. There is now an interpretation centre, giving out information about subjects such as volcanoes (including the island's previous eruptions, something to ponder as you bathe), biodiversity, etc. There is a small warm-water waterfall which runs into a small artificial pool; there are plenty of iron deposits and sulphurous smells, and it is a popular place to bathe. There are changing facilities and lavatories, and picnic tables beneath the trees. The car park is 300m down the hill; outside the main entrance is a gift shop and – usually – a food van.

Lagoa do Fogo [72 D4] Just 5 minutes' drive past the Caldeira Velha and you reach the viewpoint over the Lagoa do Fogo – 'Lake of Fire'. This deep caldera contains a lake whose waters display a fascinating range of colours when the light catches them right. Wheeling and arcing over the waters there will be some of the colony of yellow-legged gulls (*Larus michahellis atlantis*). Common terns (*Sterna arundo*) frequent the area between March and September. The caldera walls are steep, but there is a path to the bottom; it is a protected area and several endemic plant species can be seen here. On a day when there are clouds and a strong wind blowing it is good fun to stand at the viewpoint near the edge of the crater and watch the clouds pour in and then get sucked up out again. There is an information panel at the viewpoint car park, from where you can see both the south and north coastlines of the island. The road continues southwards, in a surprisingly long series of switchbacks, to Remédios and Lagoa. Since 2023, between 09.00 and 17.00 daily from mid-June until September the road from the Caldeira Velha to Remédios is only open to a shuttle bus, costing €5.

4

Santa Maria

Santa Maria sees itself as the sun island. Its claim that, being a little further south and east than the other islands, it receives more sunshine and enjoys higher sea temperatures is indeed borne out by statistics. Sheep graze the flatlands around the airport, an area with virtually no trees, but this scenery changes rapidly on the approach to the central peak of Pico Alto, the island's highest point at 590m. Here again is the typically lush Azorean green forest with cryptomeria trees and pittosporum, mixed in places with native shrubs. Then comes the eastern half and its idyllic, picturesque, tranquil, verdant landscapes of woodland and pastures. These may be sprinkled with glimmering white traditional houses that are scattered, either in little clusters or in small villages. In places there are no buildings at all, or perhaps just a time-weathered basalt shelter tucked away in a corner of a field. There are dramatic coastlines, proud headlands and sheltered bays, and a novelty for the Azores: white sand. This island supplies the potters on the other islands with their clay, and deposits at Santana and Figueral produce the lime to whitewash all the archipelago's houses.

Serious hikers can now spend a few days doing the Santa Maria circular walk (page 138). For drivers, to hire a car and meander along almost empty winding roads through such glorious countryside, stopping for views and parking the car at the end of a farm road and just exploring to the sound of birdsong, makes for a wonderful three or four days' holiday. High sea cliffs provide precipitous views and you can drop down to the coast at Maia or São Lourenço for sea swimming in manmade pools with their own natural wave machine. Between exploring the varied environments you have the white sandy beach at Praia Formosa (though it disappears in the winter waves), and the sea pools at Anjos in which to relax. Other places of interest include the little chapel at Anjos associated with Columbus's first landfall on his return from the Americas and the quite remarkable stone terraced vineyards at Maia and São Lourenço, extraordinary work of such great skill and energy you are left wondering at the effort humankind is prepared to make to produce wine! And then there's the amazing red soils and almost desert landscape of Barreiro da Faneca, not forgetting that, in keeping with its status as the oldest Azore, this is the only island in the archipelago where you can find fossils.

BACKGROUND

GEOLOGY Santa Maria has not suffered any earthquakes or eruptions during historical times, nor does it have any fumaroles or hot springs; its original volcanic structures are partially eroded or completely destroyed, yet the island nevertheless has features unique in the archipelago.

Being volcanic in origin, like all the other islands, it offers its own interesting volcanic landscapes. It is the only island where several major outcrops of pillow

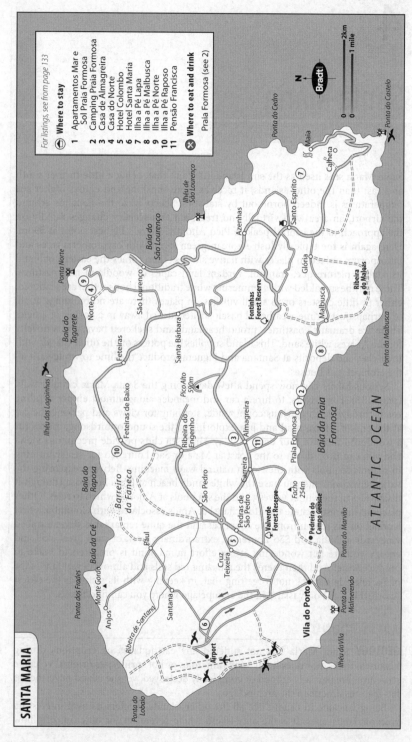

SANTA MARIA

For listings, see from page 133

Where to stay

1. Apartamentos Mar e
   Sol Praia Formosa
2. Camping Praia Formosa
3. Casa de Almagreira
4. Casa do Norte
5. Hotel Colombo
6. Hotel Santa Maria
7. Ilha a Pé Lapa
8. Ilha a Pé Malbusca
9. Ilha a Pé Norte
10. Ilha a Pé Raposo
11. Pensão Francisca

Where to eat and drink

Praia Formosa (see 2)

lavas can be seen, sometimes in well-preserved layered sequences. Pillow lava is hot fluid magma that erupts underwater, rather like toothpaste coming out of a tube, and then rapidly cools upon contact with the water, forming heaps of pillow- or cushion-like structures up to 1m across. Finally, it has many outcrops of sedimentary rocks including limestones, conglomerates and sandstones, often with abundant and diversified fossil content. Known for its sunnier climate, its beaches are also more like those typically associated with seaside resorts rather than the black gritty volcanic beaches largely found elsewhere in the archipelago. Their light colour is due to the erosion of carbonated rocks, ie: sedimentary limestone.

Santa Maria, the oldest island of the Azores, emerged from the sea around 8 million years ago, having been built up from basaltic eruptions from about 2,000m below current sea levels. That some lava flows include layers of sandstones and limestones indicates that at some point the island subsided below the sea level. Erosion has exposed these marine sediments intercalated with volcanic outputs. The oldest basalts are around Vila do Porto – appropriately, as this town was the first settlement in the Azores. Following closely are the lavas from Pico Alto, one of a series of peaks that together define a north–south alignment separating a quite distinct flat area in the west, which is very dry and poor in vegetation, from a younger hilly area to the east that is very much greener with higher rainfall.

Outcrops of fossil-bearing marine sediments can be seen on the north coast and cliffs of Baía da Cré and Baía do Raposa, just east of Anjos, and most notably along the south coast between Vila do Porto and Baía da Praia Formosa. The Barreiro da Faneca or Red Desert, east of Anjos and Monte Gordo, reminds one of the vast red landscapes of central Australia. It is an arid area of Pliocene (5.2 million to 1.64 million years ago) sediments composed of clay minerals on top of a lava flow from the Pico Alto complex. The soils and vegetation, however, developed in a cover of very thin pyroclasts (small fragmentic rocks and ash) coming from the most recent explosive eruptions. The resultant altered clay is red owing to the oxidation of the volcanic products through the alternating warm and humid and contrasting dry periods of the Pliocene. Wind erosion has levelled the areas where there is no vegetation cover. The Ribeira do Maloas, in the south between Malbusca and Ponta da Malbusca, is an old elevated beach, where nodules of manganese typical of an ocean floor can be found. In parts, it resembles a high-level version of Northern Ireland's Giants' Causeway. Nodule minerals derive from the interaction of hot, upwelling, metal-bearing solutions at a plate boundary with organic sediments and grow very slowly; a centimetre can take well over a million years.

HISTORY Santa Maria is generally considered the first island of the archipelago to be discovered by the Portuguese, sometime between 1427 and 1432, and is so named because it was sighted on the Feast of the Assumption of the Virgin Mary. It was also subsequently the first island to be settled. The initial settlement was made in 1439 by people mainly from the Algarve and Alentejo on the Portuguese mainland, at Praia do Lobos, just west of what is now Anjos, near the cape of Ponta do Lobaio on the northwest coast. However, between 1460 and 1474, Vila do Porto became the principal administration centre of the island, being less exposed to attacks from Spain. Woad and urzela were exported for dyeing, then in the 16th century, land in the west was developed for wheat. Santa Maria became a commercial satellite of São Miguel and sent wheat, orchil, pottery clay and cheese to the larger island. Needless to say, during the 16th and 17th centuries, French, Turkish, English and Moorish pirates attacked and destroyed the settlements many times. By the 19th century, demand for Santa Maria's exports had dwindled and emigration increased.

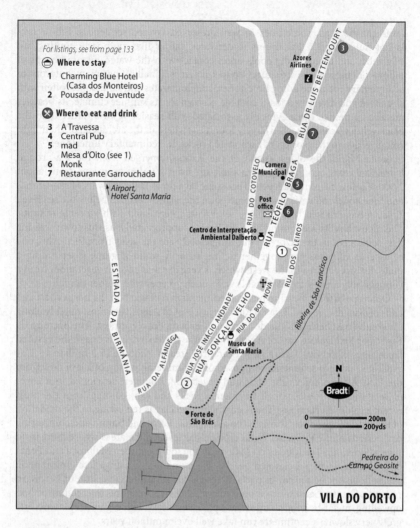

For listings, see from page 133

⊕ **Where to stay**
1 Charming Blue Hotel
  (Casa dos Monteiros)
2 Pousada de Juventude

⊗ **Where to eat and drink**
3 A Travessa
4 Central Pub
5 mad
  Mesa d'Oito (see 1)
6 Monk
7 Restaurante Garrouchada

Airport,
Hotel Santa Maria

Azores
Airlines

Camera
Municipal

Post
office

Centro de Interpretação
Ambiental Dalberto

Museu de
Santa Maria

Forte de
São Brás

Pedreira do
Campo Geosite

VILA DO PORTO

0 ——— 200m
0 ——— 200yds

It was the American wartime airbase built in 1944 that brought real change to Santa Maria, and although military aviation activity moved to Terceira, Santa Maria later became a stopping point for transatlantic flights; between 1977 and 1983, Air France's Concordes from Paris to Caracas refuelled here. Currently it hosts an air-traffic-control centre for flights between Europe and Central/South America (with 130 staff based here); nearby is a European Space Agency base which tracks rocket launches from French Guiana and monitors the Galileo satellites. The population has dropped considerably over the decades owing to emigration: in the 1960s, it had around 14,000 inhabitants; now it is down to some 5,400.

GETTING THERE AND AWAY

For getting to Santa Maria, see pages 42 and 49. The airport's former status as an airbase has bestowed it with a long runway. The terminal building is modern, with a tourist information office, a few car-hire options (Autatlantis ✆ 296 886 530 & Ilha Verde ✆ 296 886 528; m 917 369 160), a cafeteria (once famed as the Concorde Restaurant), ATM and free Wi-Fi. There is currently no ferry between São Miguel and Santa Maria, but it might restart.

There are about nine buses into Vila do Porto every day – see w transportesdesantamaria.com for full details. It's a leisurely triangular route which can take up to 35 minutes. Taking a taxi from the airport to town will cost you only a few euros.

Airport ✆ 296 820 180

Azores Airlines Rua Dr Luís Bettencourt 92, Vila do Porto; ✆ 296 820 701; ⊕ 09.00-16.30 Mon-Fri, & at the airport

GETTING AROUND

There is a limited bus service on weekdays and Saturday mornings (with none for the rest of the weekend) linking some of the villages, mainly bringing people into Vila do Porto in the mornings and returning them late afternoon. Full details are online (w transportesdesantamaria.com), and times are posted on the bus stops, too. Be sure to stick your hand out for the bus, as drivers do not expect tourists as passengers, so if you are alone at a bus stop they could simply drive past without stopping. For touring, you can use a taxi (✆ 296 882 199), which wait at the town hall in Vila do Porto, but this is an island best explored with an organised tour or self-drive car, on foot or by bicycle. This is the best of the Azores for cycling, with a good cycleway from the airport to town and route signs elsewhere, a cycle hub with maps and tools at the Valverde forest reserve, and stands with tools in other villages; mountain bikers will find a good set of trails down from the summit of Pico Alto.

ISLAND TOURS

Smatur m 926 468 668; e smatur.37@gmail.com; w smatur.pt. A young dynamic company offering guided walking, mountain-bike & jeep tours. A company with an in-depth knowledge of the unique island geology. English spoken.

BICYCLE HIRE

Paraiso Radical Rua do Cotovelo (Mercado Municipal), Vila do Porto; m 962 588 940, 962 587 537; w paraisoradical.pt; ⊕ 09.00-12.30 Mon-Fri, 09.00-noon Sat. Offers a variety of bikes, scooters & kayaks for hire.

TOURIST INFORMATION

The tourist office is on the main drag in Vila do Porto (Rua Dr Luís Bettencourt 88b; ✆ 296 883 124; ⊕ summer 09.00-18.00 Mon-Fri, 09.00-13.00 Sat, winter 09.00-12.30 & 13.00-17.00 Mon-Fri). In addition, there is a desk at the airport (✆ 296 886 335; ⊕ 07.00-14.00 Mon-Fri).

 ## WHERE TO STAY *Map, page 130, unless otherwise stated*

There are just two hotels in the town centre (one a fairly new boutique option) plus two large conventional hotels outside town. Having a car increases your choices, as there is also some rural accommodation. Given the lack of hosted accommodation on the island, renting a house by the week is also an option. Out of season, shorter stays might be possible at the houses to rent listed on page 134.

HOTELS AND GUESTHOUSES

✳ **Charming Blue Hotel (Casa dos Monteiros)** [map, page 132] (15 rooms) Rua Teófilo Braga 31, Vila do Porto; ☎296 882 083; e info@charmingblue.com; w charmingblue.com. Santa Maria's boutique hotel arrived in 2016, central to town & exuding class in an island with few choices. Rooms are spacious, furnished in contemporary style, with AC & TV (international channels), some with balcony. Outside is a pool & there's a spa with sauna & jacuzzi; there are bikes for hire & a dive centre on site offering dive packages including accommodation. A smart restaurant (Mesa d'Oito; see opposite) is a notch or 2 up in quality from the standard island fare. Recommended as the island's best choice.€€€€

Hotel Colombo (87 rooms) Rua Cruz Teixera, Vila do Porto; ☎296 820 200; e santamaria@colombo-hotel.com; w colombo-hotel.com. Ostensibly a 4-star establishment, it suffers from under-investment & in reality struggles to reach such a lofty standard. North of town – not really walkable – facilities including a restaurant, bar/coffee shop, pool, and gym, plus in theory Turkish bath, jacuzzi, massage & children's room with inflatables, PlayStation, table tennis, etc . . . but frequently some of these are out of service (likewise the lifts). Rooms enjoy AC & TV with international channels. €€€

Hotel Santa Maria (50 rooms) Rua da Horta, Vila do Porto; ☎296 820 660; e reservas@hotel-santamaria.pt; w hotel-santamaria.pt. Built on the site of the old wartime officers' mess near the airport, the rooms are all on ground-floor level, each a short walk to the pool & with access to a large garden & the tennis courts (extra cost). The bedroom floors are tiled which seems cold & uninviting in winter, but could be an advantage in summer as this part of Santa Maria can be hot. Rooms have AC/heating & TV with international channels. Facilities include a restaurant & bar. €€€

Pensão Francisca (3 rooms, 1 apartment) Brejo de Baixo, Almagreira; ☎296 884 033; m 963 128 111; e pensaofrancisca@azorean-spirit.com; w azorean-spirit.com. A few km northeast of Vila do Porto, this secluded Austrian/Swiss-owned, eco-conscious B&B serves renowned b/fasts (not inc if renting apartment) combining local, organic products & Swiss muesli. Rooms have heating, private bath. €€€

Ilha a Pé (4 shelters: Malbusca, Lapa, Norte & Raposo); ☎964 474 768, 915 815 659; e info@ilhaape.com; w ilhaape.com; ⊕ Apr–Oct. Comprising 4 barns that have been ecologically converted into shelters & strategically placed to allow hikers to complete the 78km round-island walk (page 138). Each sleeps up to 6 people & is equipped with electricity, composting toilet, hot shower, crockery/cutlery & BBQ. At extra cost, the company will bring in evening meals &/or b/fast. Linen rental, luggage transfer, etc are also available. Accommodation may be shared with other hikers or can be booked exclusively. Booking a night in all 4 costs €160 pp. €

HOUSES AND APARTMENTS TO RENT

Casa de Almagreira Canada do Outeiro, Almagreira; m 912 650 006; e azores@nada.pt; w intoazores.com. A larger house in the island's centre, sleeping up to 6 adults, plus 2 children. Plenty of outdoor space, BBQ & a peaceful setting. 3-night min stay. €€€€€

Casa do Norte Lugar do Norte, Santa Barbara; m 910 649 407; e info@norteazores.com; w norteazores.com. A beautiful small house, in splendid isolation with an attractive garden. Ideal romantic hideaway. €€€

Apartamentos Mar e Sol Praia Formosa; ☎296 884 499; m 926 610 722, 963 921 806; e geral@apartamentosmaresol.com; w apartamentosmaresol.com. A smart block of beachfront apartments, sleeping up to 5 persons. Kitchenette, TV. Restaurant nearby. Open all year, low season rates are very cheap. €€–€€€

YOUTH HOSTEL

Pousada de Juventude [map, page 132] Rua Frei Gonçalo Velho, Vila do Porto; ☎296 883 592; e bookings@azoresyouthhostels.com; w azoresyouthhostels.com; ⊕ closed last 2 weeks of Dec. Modern building just 800m from the port, with outdoor pool, TV room & table football. Dorm beds are €18, doubles are more. €

CAMPING

Camping Praia Formosa Open in summer only, near the sea; all facilities available; restaurant (see opposite) nearby in village. €

✕ WHERE TO EAT AND DRINK

VILA DO PORTO *Map, page 132*

✳ **Mesa d'Oito** Charming Blue Hotel (see opposite); **m** 964 303 531; ⏰ 18.00–23.00 Tue–Sun, closed Jan. A hotel restaurant, but without feeling like one. Very smart modern interior, elegant surroundings for a short but varied menu. Some vegetarian & Italian specialities, created by an enthusiastic chef, but still at reasonable prices & with a good wine list. €€€

Central Pub Rua Dr Luís Bettencourt 20; ☎296 882 513; ⏰ 17.00–02.00 Mon–Sat, 17.00–midnight Sun. Something like the American idea of a pub, with its stained-glass lampshades & Boston pizza, this also serves up some Italian dishes, as well as the usual fare & some decent grilled squid. Occasional live music at the w/ends, patio & good atmosphere. €€

Restaurante Garrouchada Rua Dr Luís Bettencourt 25; ☎296 883 038; ⏰ kitchen 09.00–22.00 Mon–Sat. Usual variety of large snacks, *bifana* (pork sandwich), burgers, etc, plus omelettes & fish/meat dishes. €€

A Travessa Rua Dr Luís Bettencourt 97; ☎296 882 213; ⏰ 07.30–22.00 Mon–Fri, 08.30–23.00 Sat, 11.00–22.00 Sun. A good café-snack bar, serving b/fasts, lunch buffet, fish, burgers, pitas & crêpes. The owner also runs the A Nossa brewery (**w** anossacerveja.pt), producing bottled IPAs, brown & melon beers, Bavarian lager & a dark Vienna lager. €

mad Rua Teófilo Braga 109; **m** 915 964 903; ⏰ noon–14.30 Wed–Fri, also Tue in summer. An excellent veggie-friendly restaurant that can be forgiven its limited opening hours as Ricardo is a one-man band, cooking, serving & changing the vinyl LPs. Weekly menus posted at facebook.com/mad.restaurante. €

Monk Rua Teófilo Braga 73; **m** 964 212 105; **e** neonjoyride@gmail.com; **w** monk.pt; ⏰ 09.00–16.00 Mon–Fri. Run by a very friendly US/Latvian couple, this is a vegan & organic café

(serving b/fast, snacks, lunches & a dish of day) & surf shop. In summer they may stay open till 17.00 & do Sat brunch, but they'd rather catch that wave. Surfboard rental €25/day including wetsuit (wetsuit alone €10). €

ALMAGREIRA

Snack Bar A Moagem ☎296 884 133; ⏰ noon–15.00 & 19.00–22.00 daily. A cheap daily dish makes this a good lunchtime stop, just north of the main road. More varied menu available, too, & opens as a bar from early to late. €

ANJOS

Bar dos Anjos Anjos waterfront; **m** 296 886 734; ⏰ summer 10.00–midnight daily, winter 11.00–22.00 Tue–Sun. Serving fresh fish, plus a few island specialities such as *caldo de nabos* (turnip soup). Good sunsets. €€

Bar do Blues near Anjos church; ☎296 886 801; **m** 966 272 024; ⏰ 16.00–23.00 Tue–Sun. Home to the blues festival in July, this serves decent snacks & is also a lovely spot for a sunset drink. €

PRAIA FORMOSA

Praia Formosa [map, page 130] Lugar da Praia; ☎296 884 154; ⏰ noon–15.00 & 18.30–22.00 daily. Set a little back from the beach, efficiently churning out hearty Azorean favourites in generous portions at decent prices. Not much finesse, but good value. €

SÃO LOURENÇO

Ponta Negra ☎296 098 148; ⏰ 11.30–23.00 Tue–Sun. Genial hosts, seaside location on the bay, good food, generous portions & reasonable prices. An island favourite; vegetarians catered for. €€

Snack Bar O Ilhéu ☎296 886 093; ⏰ Apr–Oct until 04.00 daily. In a great seaside location, with generous portions. €

OTHER PRACTICALITIES

Free Wi-Fi can be found in most cafés around town, plus in the marina area.

Hospital (Centro de Saude) Av Santa Maria; ☎296 820 100. With 24hr A&E, though serious cases will be airlifted to São Miguel.

Police Rua Jose Leandres Chaves; ☎296 820 112
Post office Rua Teofilo Braga 38; ⏰ 09.00–12.30 & 14.00–18.00 Mon–Fri

WHAT TO SEE AND DO

MUSEUMS

Museu de Santa Maria – Núcleo de Vila do Porto (Rua Frei Gonçalo Velho, Vila do Porto; ↘ 296 884 844; w museu-santamaria.azores.gov.pt; ⊕ Oct–Mar 09.30–17.30 Tue–Sun, Apr–Sep 10.00–18.00 Tue–Sun; €1/0.50/free adult/under 25s & seniors/under 15s) Opened in 2018, this is a welcome addition, documenting the island's geological and more recent history – including the airport's impact; modern underground galleries house temporary shows.

Dalberto Pombo Environmental Interpretation Centre (Rua Teófilo Braga 10–14, Vila do Porto; ↘ 296 206 790; ⊕ 09.00–12.30 & 13.30–17.00 Mon–Fri; €5/2/free adult/under 15s & seniors/under 7s; family ticket €10) Founded on the collections of Dalberto Pombo, a pioneer in the study of Santa Maria's biological and geological diversity, there are bilingual exhibits on butterflies, insects and birds. A linked building is the Casa dos Fósseis (House of Fossils), where captions are only in Portuguese, but interactive screens provide English information.

Museu de Santa Maria – Núcleo de Santo Espírito (Rua do Museu, Santo Espírito; ↘ 296 884 844; ⊕ Apr–Sep 10.00–17.30 Tue–Sun & hols, Oct–Mar 09.30–17.00 Tue–Sun; €1/0.50/free adult/under 25s & seniors/under 15s) The Ethnographic Museum, hidden behind the church in Santo Espírito, is well worth seeing. Exhibits include early Santa Maria pottery, period household items, costumes and ethnographic items. There are also occasional temporary exhibitions. Most information is now in English as well as Portuguese. This can be combined with a visit to the nearby craft co-operative, Cooperativa de Artesanato de Santa Maria, for some of their delicious handmade biscuits (page 141).

RECREATIONAL FOREST RESERVES

Fontinhas Forest Reserve (Santo Espírito) In the centre of the island on the western slope of Pico Alto, this is particularly noted for its tall trees which provide a cool ambience amid beautiful rural scenery. There are pleasant walks between the trees, tree ferns, azaleas and camellias; barbecue facilities and picnic shelters.

Valverde Forest Reserve A well-used and much-developed park at the edge of Vila do Porto, its 4ha are dominated by eucalyptus and cupressus trees. There is a deer enclosure and a cycling hub with tools and maps. A belvedere offers a view of Vila do Porto and the immediate countryside.

SPORTS AND ACTIVITIES Of all the islands, Santa Maria is the best set up for **cycling**, with a hub at the Valverde forest park, DIY repair stations in several villages, well-marked routes and a set of downhill MTB trails from the top of Pico Alto. See page 133 for rentals.

Conditions dictate that June to September provide the best **scuba** opportunities, with warmer, calmer seas and gentler winds. Manta rays are the biggest attraction, clustering around the Ambrósio and Dollabarat seamounts 5km offshore, with blue, hammerhead and whale sharks also in the area.

Diving is mainly by boat, rather than from the shore. Dive companies are based at the port, but are best contacted in advance. Single dives cost from around €50, but generally the operators need a minimum of four to six people.

Festas de Santo António Santo Espírito; second or third week of June.
Festas de São João Vila do Porto; last week of June.
Maia Folk world music; first week of July.
Blues Festival Anjos; second week of July.
Festa do Sagrado Coração de Jesus Santa Bárbara; first week of August.
Festa de Nossa Senhora da Assunção Vila do Porto; middle of August.
Festival Maré de Agosto Praia Formosa; third week of August.
Festa das Vindimas São Lourenço; first week of September. Grape harvest.
Festa de Nossa Senhora da Anunciação Vila do Porto; third week of September.

Santa Maria is not exactly a **surfing** destination, but if you have a free day, the Monk café and surf shop (page 135) will rent you gear and point you to the breaks that might be working. Praia Formosa has something for everyone, while Anjos and São Lourenço are not for beginners.

Activity tours

Bootlá m 963 874 547; e info@bootla.pt; w bootla.pt. Offering a full range of day/half-day activities, including jeep tours, bike hire, hiking, canyoning & coasteering.
Smatur m 926 468 668; e smatur.37@gmail. com; w smatur.pt. A young, dynamic company offering guided walks, mountain-bike & jeep tours, & they also hire bikes out to visitors who prefer to go it alone. They have contacts with local birding experts, too.

Diving

Mantamaria Dive Center m 917 287 286, 918 685 447; e info@mantamaria.com; w mantamaria.com. Well-respected & long-established operation. Snorkelling & boat trips also available.

Swimming

Praia Formosa This white-sand beach is very popular in summer, but the sands are often invisible beneath the waves in other seasons. There is an area marked off for surfing, & changing facilities with showers, plus seasonal snack bars & ice creams. At the west end, there is a ruined fort with an information panel detailing Santa Maria's system of defensive forts.
Anjos 2 pools, sunbathing areas, changing rooms & showers; disabled access to the water.
Maia Facilities include a sea swimming pool with changing rooms, showers & a café. **O Grota** (m 927 296 708) is the village's open-all-year restaurant while **Flor da Maia** (⊕ summer only) at the furthest end of the bay is the café.
São Lourenço In addition to a sea swimming pool with changing rooms & showers, & a snack bar & restaurant, there are also small white beaches between the rocks, popular in summer.

WALKS ON SANTA MARIA

There are now six official trails, including one long-distance option, the Grande Rota, which forms a circuit of the entire island. Summaries are given here; maps and route guides can be downloaded from the w visitazores.com website.

PICO ALTO (Medium difficulty, 6.2km, 2hrs) A super circular walk, enjoying views from the highest point of the island, on forest paths.

SANTO ESPÍRITO–MAIA (Easy, 4km, 2hrs) Beginning in Santo Espírito, the route takes you on a descent through woodland, pastures and vineyards passing several village artefacts and finally down to the sea near the bathing zone. You can extend the walk by continuing along the bay to the Ponta do Castelo.

ENTRE A SERRA E O MAR ('Between the mountains and the sea'; medium difficulty, 9.7km, 2½hrs) A circular walk starting from the parish church in Santa Bárbara past typical houses, rural landscapes and good views.

TRILHO DO COSTA SUL (From Vila do Porto to the beach of Praia Formosa; medium difficulty, 7km, 3hrs) Waymarked, and fairly straightforward, it follows well-used tracks and offers close-ups of fossils and terrific views from cliffs high above the sea.

TRILHO DA COSTA NORTE (Northern coastal walk; medium difficulty, 9km, 4hrs) A linear walk from Bananeiras to Anjos, along the northern coast.

SANTA MARIA CIRCULAR (Medium difficulty, 78km, 30hrs' walking, to be spread over 4 or 5 days) The first long-distance 'round-island' trail, the Grande Rota, ideally should begin and end in Vila do Porto. Plan carefully, remembering that wild camping is prohibited. A mini network of shelters – Ilha a Pé – makes this much more doable (page 134).

TOURING THE ISLAND

As you travel around the island note the different house chimneys, especially the square-like ones topped with tall slender round chimney pots. Some of the parishes have their house windows and doors trimmed in the 'village colour': Santo Espírito, green; Santa Bárbara, blue; Almagreira, red; São Pedro, yellow; and Vila do Porto, tile coloured.

VILA DO PORTO Originally known simply as Porto, it became Vila do Porto in the 16th century when it was given its charter, the first town in the Azores to have this status. What is left of the old town runs downhill from the attractive Matriz church to the fort overlooking the harbour, now a modern port. The façades of the old grand houses give an idea of what it must have been like, together with the tiny cottages in the streets behind. All these are protected but sadly many owners of the large houses left for Lisbon in the 1950s and their houses became very run down. They are now being redeveloped. As you walk down from town towards the port (along Rua Teófilo Braga), look out on your left for the Gothic windows of the 15th-century building that supposedly belonged to Governor João Soares de Sousa. Nearby houses have interestingly carved lintels and other details. The **Fort of São Brás** was built in the 17th century and of course provides a good view out to sea; with nine cannons still in place it is a fertile place in which to imagine early events. A stroll down to the fort after dinner is a pleasant ending to the day. In summer the cooling evening contrasts with the still-warm stones and makes a different but parallel smell to rain on sun-scorched earth. If you have time, take the old cobbled walkway down to the port and continue right round to the end of the *mole* (breakwater), where there is a splendid view of the fort.

The modern part of the town, which starts roughly around the beginning of the Rua Teófilo Braga, is a linear development which looks as if it will go on growing longer. All the usual small shops are here including several small-scale supermarkets and a market. The **Câmara Municipal** is a grand building that was the first Franciscan monastery to be founded, in 1607, in the islands by the monks who came with the settlers; it grew wealthy, was looted, then rebuilt from 1725, then finally converted into the town hall. This is a history repeated throughout the islands, other uses being as hospitals and youth hostels. During working hours you can step inside to see the cloister.

At the northern end of the town is the Valverde **forestry park** (page 136) with a children's play area, picnic tables and washrooms beneath pine trees.

THE PEDREIRA DO CAMPO GEOSITE
The coastal path east from Vila do Porto (you'll have to ford a stream then follow a field track) reaches a rather surreal wooden structure after about 30 minutes. This is a boardwalk and viewing platform at the Pedreira do Campo Geosite gravel pit, famous among geologists for its mix of pillow lavas and sedimentary rocks, with fossils of molluscs, corals, annelids and echinoderms.

Continuing east, just before reaching Praia Formosa the coastal path drops down to Prainha, a secret beach with no road access where marine fossils can be found on a sea-carved abrasion platform about 4m above current sea level.

AROUND THE AIRPORT
The area around the airport is limestone country and was once the most productive wheat-growing area. Now the airport takes a large share of the land, while beyond the boundary remains of the wartime airfield linger in the form of old Nissen huts and concrete slabs. There is also the tracking station, and much new housing (and a cinema) greatly in need of tree planting to soften it. The old officers' mess was the only hotel on Santa Maria until only a few decades ago; it burned down some years ago, but was then rebuilt. Now the farmland is down to cattle that are thought by the locals to be better eating than those on the higher pastures, and Romney Marsh sheep, farmed for wool, and originally imported from England. If you leave the airport road and take the minor road to Santana you pass through this utterly different countryside; in the height of summer when all is brown and the sun blazes down it can seem quite hostile, but from October/ November to May it is green. From Santana the road continues to join the main road down to Anjos, but before it does you pass through an area of acacia forest which shows a splendid example of wind pruning.

SÃO PEDRO
This small village near Vila do Porto is noted for its *mata-mouras*, literally 'moor killers'. These are pits in the ground once used to hide grain and other desirables from pillaging pirates.

ANJOS
Once a tiny fishing village, Anjos then became a centre for tuna; now the factory is closed. The little bay has now been very nicely developed for swimming. The island of São Miguel, 44 nautical miles away, can sometimes be seen on the horizon. On the roadside above is a picnic site with barbecue facilities.

The village is historically very significant as the first landfall of Christopher Columbus on his return from the Americas. A modern statue commemorates the quincentenary of this event in 1993. The **Chapel of Nossa Senhora dos Anjos** is possibly the first place of worship built in the Azores, having been built in 1460–74 and rebuilt in the 17th century and again restored at the end of the 20th century. The small chapel has a triptych, now restored, representing the Holy Family, St Cosmas and St Damian which, according to tradition, is from Gonçalo Velho's caravel. The iron rod displayed on the pulpit was a weapon used by pirates. On the outside wall is built a porch dedicated to the Holy Ghost; bread is distributed from here on the feast day.

4

Almost opposite the church is the **Associação Escravos da Cadeinha** (Association of the Slaves of Cadeinha; **w** escravosdacadeinha.com), founded in the 17th century by ransomed prisoners of the Barbary pirates and revived in 2001 as a local cultural organisation (there's an amphitheatre at the rear). They run the Bar do Blues (page 135) and the annual blues festival (page 137).

SANTA BÁRBARA This is among the prettiest parishes of the island; in July/August the roadsides are flaming with orange-red montbretias and yellow gingers and there are photo opportunities every 200m. There is wonderful silence apart from the occasional crowing of a cockerel.

SÃO LOURENÇO On the northeast coast, the bay is well worth visiting for the spectacular descent by road down the cliff face. On the way down, three **viewpoints** give splendid bird's-eye views of the bay and its cliffside vineyards, but due to blind corners you're better off stopping on the way back uphill. The village has swimming facilities and good beaches.

SANTO ESPÍRITO A pretty village surrounded by pastures and green hills. The **Church of Nossa Senhora da Purificação** is well worth visiting and must rate population of roseate tern (*Sterna dougallii*), and, in most years, a pair of sooty terns (*Onychoprion fuscatus*) – the only breeding site in the western Palearctic. Small numbers of barolo shearwater (*Puffinus baroli*), Bulwer's petrel (*Bulweria bulwerii*) and Grant's petrel (*Oceanodroma granti*) also breed on Ilhéu da Vila.

Winter specialities on the plain include dotterel (*Charadrius morinellus*), skylark (*Alauda arvensis*) and snow bunting (*Plectrophenax nivalis*), while other northern species like fieldfare (*Turdus pilaris*), redwing (*Turdus iliacus*) and song thrush (*Turdus philomelos*) occur in hard winters.

The majority of Santa Maria's 240-plus recorded species are rare or occasional visitors from mainland Europe, North America, the Arctic and northwest Africa. Several desert species, not recorded before in the Azores, have appeared following Saharan storms, finding the island's southern arid plain a suitable temporary habitat. Amazingly, 15 migratory species of birds of prey have reached the island, including no less than five immature Barbary falcons (*Falco pelegrinoides*), a species recorded nowhere else in Europe. North American shorebirds and ducks are regular visitors, mainly in autumn, and a pair of killdeers (*Charadrius vociferous*) stayed on to breed in three successive years from 2010 – a unique series of events in Europe.

Around the perimeter fence of the airport can be found numerous ponds and small wetland areas which can reward the patient birder. Walking or cycling would be the best way to reach them, given that the road is prone to rutting after wet weather. Another of the most interesting sites is the small islet of **Ilhéu da Vila** just off Vila do Porto, which can be viewed from the shore or preferably a boat. Other islets good for birds and observable from land include **Lagoinhas** near Tagerete Bay, part of the North Coast Protected Landscape Area.

Ponta do Costelo on the southeastern corner of the island and its designated area of 300ha combines a coastal strip of steep cliffs 200m high with the offshore area, a passage point for bottlenose dolphin and loggerhead turtle.

among the best kept of all Azorean parish churches. You'll be welcomed by the scent of wax-polished floors and pews and sunlight reflecting from a gilt chapel. Originally constructed in the 16th century and beautifully restored in 1966, it is 17th-century Baroque with stone ornamentation on the front façade. It is also noted as the church linked to the first Holy Ghost festivals (page 34) in the Azores. The **museum** (page 136) is hidden behind the church. For handicrafts, the local **Cooperativa da Artesanato Santa Maria** (08.00–16.00 Mon–Sat) sells delicious bread and *biscoitos* from its own bakery, and traditional woven items from several looms such as tableware. Weaving takes place in the morning, baking in the afternoon; the dexterity of the half-dozen women working here is admirable, as they endeavour to keep alive traditional island skills. Find it about 400m west of the church, almost opposite the school. There is also a snack bar in the village.

MAIA Nearly all the houses here are holiday homes, and it is said that only a dozen or so people live here permanently, but between June and September the descendants of emigrants return from North America to take their holidays here and the place comes alive. There is a small port from where fishing boats set sail. It is the stone terracing for grapevines that is truly amazing. Walls enclose areas just a few metres square and these reach up the cliffside almost until it becomes vertical.

At intervals very narrow stairways run in straight lines up the cliff face to provide access to the vine enclosures. In September, the harvest takes place, with the grapes carried down by hand and the wine (and the local 'firewater') made in several small buildings. The wine, purely for local consumption, is *vinho de cheiro*, plus a very pleasant sweet aperitivo. A book of photographs of the stones of Maia is for sale at the museum at **Santo Espírito** (page 136). There are swimming facilities, but be sure to go to the very far end of the village to where the road finishes, especially after rainy times, to see the spectacular waterfall, Portugal's highest at 110m. The access path is stubbornly guarded by a colony of Muscovy ducks.

PICO ALTO The side road up to the highest point of the island, at 590m, leaves the main road between Almagreira and Santo Espírito just west of where it forks to Santa Bárbara. Here the landscape is utterly different from anywhere else on Santa Maria, as you ascend through dense cryptomeria plantations and laurel forest to arrive at a tiny summit with fine views and some native plants as well as a subspecies of goldcrest that's endemic to Santa Maria. There is a memorial to the 144 people killed when an Italian passenger jet clipped the summit in 1989.

PRAIA FORMOSA In a wide bay at the foot of steep cliffs is a very clean, pale sandy beach with rock pools at the eastern end, and it is Santa Maria's best-known swimming beach. Commercial development is really quite limited and the road, with parking, runs along behind the beach. Vineyards tumble down the hillside to meet it. There is a small apartment hotel and a campsite (both page 134). In the nearby village there is a restaurant. At the western end are the remains of the 16th–17th-century **Fort of São João Baptista**, which the sea has almost demolished. In summer the cliffs here, normally dark with pittosporum and myrica trees, are marked with 4m-tall yellow flower spikes of agave. The road from Santo Espírito has recently been paved and is absolutely charming.

Part Three

CENTRAL GROUP

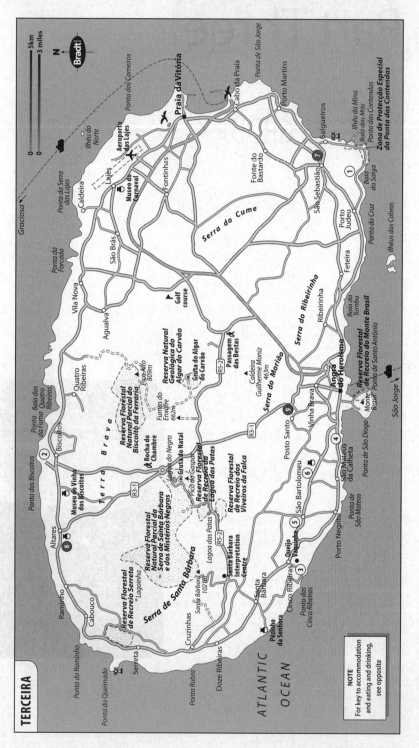

TERCEIRA

Bradt

N

0   5km
0   3 miles

Graciosa

ATLANTIC
OCEAN

NOTE
For key to accommodation
and eating and drinking,
see opposite

Ponta do Raminho
Ponta do Queimado
Ponta Rubra
Ponta dos Biscoitos
Ponta da Fuma
Baia dos Quatro Ribeiras
Ponta da Forcada
Ponta da Serra das Lajes
Ilhéu do Norte
Ponta da Vitória
Ponta dos Carneiros
Ponta de São Jorge

Raminho
Cabouco
Sereta
Altares
Biscoitos
Quatro Ribeiras
Vila Nova
Agualva
São Brás
Caldeira
Lajes
Aeroporto das Lajes
Museu do Carnaval
Praia da Vitória
Fontinhas
Porto Martins
Cabo da Praia
Salgueiros

Museu do Vinho dos Biscoitos
R3-1
Terra Brava
Reserva Florestal Natural Parcial do Biscoito da Ferraria
Pico Alto 809m
Furnas do Enxofre 662m
Reserva Natural Geológica do Algar do Carvão
Gruta do Algar do Carvão
R5-2
Golf course
Serra do Cume
Fonte do Bastardo

Reserva Florestal de Recreio Serreta
Lagoinha
Reserva Florestal Natural Parcial da Serra de Santa Bárbara e dos Misterios Negros
Rocha do Chambre
Pico do Negro
Lagoa do Negro
Gruta do Natal
Reserva Florestal de Recreio da Lagoa das Patas
Lagoa das Patas
Passagem das Bestas
Caldeira Guilherme Moniz 463m
Serra do Morião
R3-1
Vinha Brava

Serra de Santa Bárbara
Santa Bárbara 1021m
Reserva Florestal de Recreio dos Viveiros da Falca
Posto Santo
São Mateus da Calheta
Ponta de São Diago

Cruzinhas
Pézinho da Senhora
Santa Bárbara Interpretation Centre
Santa Bárbara
São Bartolomeu
Porto Negrito
Ponta de São Mateus

Doze Ribeiras
Cinco Ribeiras
Ponta dos Cinco Ribeiras
Queijo
Taquinha

Serra do Ribeirinha
Ribeirinha
Angra do Heroísmo
Reserva Florestal de Recreio do Monte Brasil
Monte Brasil
Ponta de Santo António
São Jorge
Baia da Tumba
Ponta da Cruz
Feteira
Porto Judeu
São Sebastião
Baia da Salga
Baia das Mós
Ponta das Contendas
Ilhéu da Mina
Zona de Protecção Especial da Ponta das Contendas
Ilhéus das Cabras

8
2
3
5
6
4
9
1
7

5

Terceira

Terceira is perhaps best known for two things: the international airport and American airbase at Lajes and the historic UNESCO World Heritage Site of Angra do Heroísmo. This is unfair because, like all the other islands, there is much else waiting to be discovered for those not in a hurry. Coming in to land at the wide airport, you will be struck by the endless walled-off pastures that decorate the landscape as it gently rises towards the island's centre. Beyond, there are lovely villages, really wild country in the centre, volcanic caverns, vineyards, comfortable places to stay, some good restaurants to be sought out, an increasing number of land- and sea-based activities and even a golf course. It is an ideal island on which to hire a car and explore at your own speed: big enough to occupy you, but small enough to let you get to know it in just a few days.

It is easy to spend a whole day seeing the historic buildings of Angra do Heroísmo together with the fort and maybe take a walk around the whole of Monte Brasil. The drive along the beautiful west coast looking in at villages and charming museums is another joy and, if you choose to linger, a whole day can disappear in pleasant fashion. The island's rugged centre is a must, too; more or less in the middle of the island is the region known as Terra Brava, the 'Wild Land', and aptly named because of the bewilderingly broken country and, in places, dense vegetation. The island's highest point is Santa Bárbara (1,021m) in the west, and almost every day the summit is hidden in cloud. Its upper 300m is covered with typical scrub vegetation of juniper, erica, ling and bramble. On the northwest side of Santa Bárbara is the Serreta Forest, a mix of planted cryptomeria and eucalyptus and large patches of remnant native vegetation with endemic Azorean species. It is a good area for birds, as is the Lagoa do Negro a little to the east. Praia da Vitória is another town to explore, smaller and very different, and, if there is time, do seek out the view from the top of the Serra do Cume across the whole of the eastern part of the island. Between May and September some 220 Azorean bullfights will take place on the island, as well as bull-runnings in the streets, so there is a fair chance you will experience one or the other or both – remember, the bull is not killed or even wounded. It is the young men who run the risk of damage, but as the giant bull sculpture outside Angra's bullring evidences, Terceira has a very deep bull-related tradition to maintain. Generally known as the 'Purple Island', some Azoreans prefer the slightly derogatory nickname 'Party Island'.

TERCEIRA
For listings, see from page 149

Where to stay
1. Parque de Campismo da Salga
2. Parque de Campismo dos Biscoitos
3. Parque de Campismo das Cinco Ribeiros
4. Quinta das Mercês
5. Quinta do Espírito Santo
6. Quinta do Martelo

Where to eat and drink
7. Os Moinhos
   Quinta do Martelo (see 6)
8. Restaurante Caneta
9. Taberna Roberto

BACKGROUND

GEOLOGY The oldest part of Terceira, composed of basalts from the last million years, is below sea level, plunging down more than 1,500m to the seabed; it comprises 90% of the island. The remaining tenth is much younger. Like São Miguel, Terceira is made from four volcanoes, the oldest being Cinco Picos which covers much of the southeast, a stratovolcano that was once a steep-sided cone made of layers of lava. Its collapsed caldera is the largest in the Azores, about 7km across, and was formed some 300,000 years ago but it is now considerably eroded. The Serra do Cume in the northeast is the largest remnant, and the Serra da Ribeirinha is all that is left of the opposite rim, and between the two is the largest flat area in the whole of the Azores, disturbed only by five younger cinder cones in the crater bottom, the 'Cinco Picos'.

Behind Angra do Heroísmo is Guilherme Moniz volcano, another stratovolcano with a collapsed caldera. The crater's southern edge is the Serra do Morião crescent which forms the hills seen looking north from Angra. In contrast, the north side of the crater has been completely destroyed by the neighbouring Pico Alto volcano whose lava flowed into the Guilherme Moniz crater, a rare occurrence of lava forming the floor of another volcano. The vertical cave called Algar do Carvão was formed around the same time, about 2,000 years ago. Pico Alto was also responsible for the grey, acidic rock and the more than 60 domes seen to its north behind Quatro Ribeiras and Lajes. Domes form when lava is very viscous and does not easily flow, and so accumulates in the vent.

Around 23,000 years ago, present-day Angra was covered by a Plinian eruption, a powerful explosion of gas, steam, ash and pumice followed by avalanches of hot gas, ash and rock debris. Associated with this were two later Surtseyan volcanoes, when seawater entered the vent to mix with the rising magma and the resulting steam caused the magma to shatter into fine fragments. These two formed Monte Brasil, creating the historically significant bay and associated anchorage and, just to the east, off the coast opposite Feteira village, the now much-eroded Ilhéus das Cabras.

In the west is the Santa Bárbara stratovolcano, about 12km in diameter at sea level, with a caldera that collapsed 25,000 years ago, and again some 18,000 years ago forming a smaller caldera inside. The older eruptions produced many lava flows with cinder cones and spatter, cinder-sized lava fragments that are still molten when they hit the ground and therefore flatten, forming 'cowpats'; these can meld together and make steep-sided mounds, mostly less than 10m high. The latest eruptions over the last few thousand years on the flanks of Santa Bárbara are associated with trachyte flows, a pale greyish acidic rock whose molten viscosity can form rugged lava flows and domes, in this case more than 85 of the latter.

Between Santa Bárbara and Pico Alto, activity along the Terceira Rift (page 5) created cinder cones and lava flows. About 4,500 years ago, flows from Pico Gordo, by the main road between Angra and Altares, reached the north coast to form the jagged black reefs of the Ponta dos Biscoitos, now occupied by the Biscoitos vineyards. Along the same road, by the crossroad to Doze Ribeiras, the cone of Bagacina typifies the cinder cones, and between the two, near Lagoa do Negro, is a spatter cone.

In historical times, two eruptions occurred in 1761. The first created the Mistérios Negros, near Pico do Gaspar, and the second, a few days later, a collection of cinder cones including Pico do Fogo, just east of Lagoa do Negro. The Angra–Altares road runs conveniently between the two. In 1998, there was a submarine eruption 10km west of Terceira in a small area known as the 'Serreta High'. Surface signs were plumes of smoke coming from floating lava debris as it cooled. The basalt magma is rich in gases that are trapped inside, creating 'balloons' which float upwards towards the ocean's surface. As they rise the gases inside expand and cause the 'balloons' to explode. The debris floats on the surface for about 15 minutes and sinks when seawater enters as it cools. When great volumes of gas rise to the surface the sea becomes pale green, and it is very dangerous for boats, which could easily sink. This surface evidence is not continuous, and its absence reflects quieter periods of submarine activity. The earliest eruptions detected were at 400m below sea level, and the magma has subsequently risen to 180m.

HISTORY Originally known as the Island of Jesus Christ, the island was later named Terceira or Third Island as it was the third island to be 'discovered'; it is also the third in size. The first settlers in about 1460 were led by a Fleming, Jácome de Bruges, with the first settlements around Porto Judeu and Praia da Vitória. Like the other islands, farming became of paramount importance with cereals and woad the prime crops. For centuries it was the most important island because of its sheltered harbour, protected by Monte Brasil. In 1534, Angra was the first settlement in all the Azores to be formally designated a city and in the same year Pope Paul III made it the seat of the bishopric. Terceira was a stronghold of resistance to the Spanish when they annexed Portugal in 1580, holding out for the Portuguese claimant, Dom Antonio, who was backed by the French. It was the last Portuguese territory to submit to Spanish rule, when the Spaniards defeated the French fleet at Terceira in 1582, overrunning the island the following year and inflicting a terrible retribution. As a consequence of the later 16th- and 17th-century Spanish exploitation of the New World, the island's harbour became even more important. Ships bringing back gold and silver at this time assembled off Terceira to form a convoy for escort to Cadiz, to reduce the danger of attack by pirates from the north African coast. Later in the 17th century, this practice ceased and the island's economy plummeted, followed by emigration to Brazil. After Portuguese liberation in 1640, the islands became a staging post for British trading ships, until the opening of the Suez Canal in 1863. Oranges also came to the rescue and their export led to renewed prosperity, but as in the other islands their demise led once more to further emigration.

Along with São Miguel, Terceira played an important role in the struggle of the Liberals and Absolutists; at one time Terceira was the only Liberal stronghold in all of Portugal. In 1829, the Absolutists attempted to land at what was then called Vila da Praia and their defeat by the locals was marked by the new name of Praia da Vitória. In 1832, it was from Terceira and São Miguel that the Liberal forces set out for northern Portugal in their fight against the Absolutists. In 1766, the government of the Azores had been unified and based in Angra, which remained the capital of the whole archipelago when it was divided into three districts in 1832. For a short time that year it was also the capital of Portugal when King Pedro IV was in residence – commemorated by the change of name to Angra do Heroísmo.

Lajes Airport was constructed by Britain's RAF and local labour in 1943, as an anti-submarine base and as a transit point for troops flying to Europe, and today contributes, albeit with less importance, to NATO's strategic role. The main runway is 3,600m long, and is used by both civil and military aircraft; it was also a designated emergency landing strip for the Space Shuttle. A few years ago, China showed interest in investing in the airport for 'scientific research' and warehousing, but this seems to have been blocked by the US, which is increasing its military presence.

On New Year's Day 1980, a severe earthquake inflicted substantial damage, affecting also Graciosa and São Jorge islands. Many of the important buildings in

Angra do Heroísmo were badly damaged and have taken years to painstakingly restore. Tremors, thankfully smaller, do still occur. In 1983, Angra was declared a UNESCO Historic World Heritage Site.

GETTING THERE AND AWAY

For travel to Terceira, see pages 42 and 49. Terceira's airport has a tourist information office (📞 295 513 140; ☉ 08.00–21.00 daily), plus half a dozen car-hire desks (see below), ATMs, post office, café and the ubiquitous free Wi-Fi. If you have time to kill, the souvenir shop upstairs often shows footage of the bull-runnings which take place at major festivals. A taxi will cost €20–25 to Angra or €6 to Praia. There is a regular, almost hourly bus service between around 06.00 and 19.00 to Praia, with connections to Angra; a through ticket from the airport to Angra at time of writing costs only €3.29. Take the escalators to the third floor; the stop is just outside the airport complex.

Azores Airlines (SATA) [158 C2] Rua Direita 76, Angra; 📞295 403 650; ☉ 09.00–18.00 Mon–Fri.

The airport office can be contacted on 📞295 540 047, around flight arrivals/departure times.

GETTING AROUND

If you are without a car, and especially if you are making a short visit, then Angra has the most accommodation and dining options and is probably the best place to base yourself. If you wish to be nearer the airport, then Praia da Vitória is the sensible alternative, with Angra then becoming a day trip by bus or taxi. Out of season, however, Praia is very quiet and Angra has more restaurant choices. From the airport down to Angra in your rental car will take you little more than 20 minutes on the smart dual carriageway.

By Azorean standards, bus services on Terceira are fairly comprehensive and regular with hourly weekday services between Angra and Praia, connecting to the airport. Details of all routes, timetables and fares – which are low – can be found on w evt.pt, which has an English-language option, or you can ask for a leaflet at a tourist office. Tickets are bought on the bus and are very reasonable (Angra–Praia is €2.80, taking 50mins). There are also regular, but much less frequent, routes to towns such as Biscoitos, Porto Judeu, São Mateus and other coastal villages along the way. In Angra, there's a new bus station [158 B2]; in Praia the stop is opposite the fire station on Rua Barcelos; to reach the town centre, walk back in the direction from which the bus came and you soon come to a big junction; turn left and soon you are on the Rua de Jesus, whose undulating cobbles lead you to the main square. The return bus is from the same stop. Charles Darwin, when the *Beagle* put in at Angra for a week on the journey home in September 1836, also made the excursion to Praia, but on horseback.

There are seven buses daily to and from Biscoitos; the route goes round the west coast and takes 1½ hours. Note that, for all island buses, service is reduced on Saturdays and even more so on Sundays.

To hire a taxi to ferry you around will cost about €20 per hour, but you might negotiate a better deal in low season. It is, however, an island more easily enjoyed if you have your own transport. Taxis may be picked up at the places marked on the map of Angra [158 C2/B2] (📞295 213 088, 295 212 404) or on the main square in Praia (📞295 512 092).

The following **car-hire** firms all have offices at the airport.

Angracar Às Pedreiras, Lajes (100m from the airport); 295 663 505 (🕐 08.30–18.00 Mon–Fri); m 912 535 449, 918 268 268 (🕐 06.00–midnight daily); e reservas@rent.angracar.com; w angracar.com

Autatlantis Lajes Airport; 295 515 800; e info@ autatlantis.com; w autatlantis.com

Auto Ramalhense Lajes Airport; m 912 000 937; e reservas@autoramalhense.com; w autoramalhense.com

RentAngra Lajes Airport; 295 543 999; m 917 255 953; e reservas@rentangra.com; w rentangra.com

TOURIST INFORMATION

Angra's tourist information office [158 C2] (295 213 393; 🕐 Apr–Sep 09.00–19.00 Mon–Fri, 09.00–16.00 Sat & hols, Oct–Mar 09.00–17.00 Mon–Fri) is at Rua Direita 74. Note there are also a number of private information kiosks around the island, earning their living from commissions on tour bookings. In Praia, one such kiosk is beside the marina, though the stated hours seem a bit hit-or-miss (295 543 251; 🕐 winter 09.00–12.30 & 14.00–18.00 Mon–Fri, 09.00–13.00 Sat, summer 09.00–13.00 & 14.00–18.30 Mon–Sat). The following company provides island tours:

Comunicair [158 C2] Rua Direita 69, Angra; m 919 052 869, 910 503 800; e info@comunicair.pt; w comunicair.com. Excellent guided island tours by jeep, guided & self-guided tours by bike, kayaking & on foot, with a deep insight into the island's geology & botanical endemic species. With groups that never exceed 6 people, a worthwhile experience. Walks include areas not covered by the official trails.

🏠 WHERE TO STAY

June festival times and some of August can see prices rise on Terceira. The main **hotels** are in Angra, with a couple of good ones in Praia da Vitória, just 5 minutes' drive from the airport. The choice in Angra spans the range from the five-star overlooking the marina, through a state-owned *pousada* (hotel) in an old fort, to a city-centre hotel right on the main square and a few smaller establishments in and around the centre. A couple of resort hotels are just west of Angra, about 20 minutes' walk or 5 minutes' drive along a busy main road. Praia's options are modern, medium-sized hotels on the seafront.

As elsewhere in the Azores, **camping** is very cheap, but a telephone call in advance is advisable. It should be noted that the contact person and number change frequently, so it is best to enquire at the tourist office for updated details. Some sites can fill up at festival times.

ANGRA DO HEROÍSMO AND AROUND

Hotel Terceira Mar [158 A1] (139 rooms) Portões de São Pedro, São Pedro; 295 402 288; e tmhl@bhc.pt; w bensaudehotels.com/en/terceiramarhotel. A resort-style hotel 20mins' walk west from the centre of Angra. Restaurant, bar, large gymnasium, & splendid saltwater outdoor pool next to the sea, tennis courts, jacuzzi, indoor pool, Turkish bath, sauna, massage, hairdressers. Very comfortable. €€€€€

Quinta das Mercês [map, page 144] (12 rooms, 1 suite, 1 s/c house) Caminho de Baixo, São Mateus da Calheta; 295 642 588; e reservas@quintadasmerces.com; w quintadasmerces.com. Between Angra & São Mateus, this farm goes back to the 16th century; the manor house & chapel are 17th century. Set between sea & woodland it has spacious common rooms, b/fast & dining room, library, games room & an inner courtyard. Outdoor saltwater pool & tennis court, Turkish bath, jacuzzi, gymnasium & woodland walks. Also a s/c house with 2 bedrooms, kitchen & living room. Dinner available on request (24hrs' notice). B/fast inc. Stately manor house, a little quirky. €€€€€

Pousada de Angra [158 E3] (28 rooms, 1 suite) Forte de São Sebastião, Angra; ✆295 403 560; e reservas.pousadasaosebastiao@pousadas.pt; w pousadas.pt/uk/hotel/pousada-angra. Formerly the Castelo de São Sebastião dating from 1555, it looks foreboding from the exterior but houses decent rooms, many with sea view. Seasonal outdoor pool, terrace restaurant. Sat TV. €€€€

The Shipyard [158 D2] (31 apartments) Avda Infante D Henrique; ✆295 101 520; e res@ theshipyardangra.com; w theshipyardangra.com. This new designer place on the less touristy side of town has a gym, bikes, underground car parking & spacious apartments, of which those on the upper floor have fine sea views. The stylish A Oficina restaurant specialises in meats from a charcoal grill. €€€€

Azoris Angra Garden-Plaza Hotel [158 C2] (120 rooms) Praça Velha, Angra; ✆295 206 600; e centraldereservas@azorishotels.com; w azorishotels.com/angragarden. On the main square, with restaurant, bar, lounge, health club, sauna, small indoor pool, gym, private parking. Sat TV. Perfectly sited for exploring Angra. Rooms to the rear are quiet, overlooking 1 of the best public gardens in the Azores. €€€

Hotel do Caracol [158 A1] (100 rooms) Estrada Regional 1, Silveira; ✆295 402 600; e dep. reservas@hoteldocaracol.com; w hoteldocaracol. com. About 30mins' walk west from central Angra, with views across the bay to Monte Brasil, a resort hotel with restaurant & bars, leisure facilities including spa, massage, therapy treatments, sauna, jacuzzi, gym, adults & children's outdoor pools, indoor heated pool. Sea bathing possible with access by ladder. €€€

Angra Marina Hotel [158 D3] (130 rooms) Rua do Faleiro, Angra; ✆295 204 700; e angramarinahotel@gruposolpuro.com. The Azores' first 5-star hotel overlooks the marina; all rooms have a sea view & are large with sat TV. Indoor & outdoor pools, full spa. Discos across the marina pump out noise till late on summer w/ends, which can be intrusive. €€€

Quinta do Espirito Santo [map, page 144] (4 rooms) Rua Dr Teotónio Machado Pires 36, São Bartolomeu; ✆295 332 373; m 962 922 938; e geral@verdes-fragmentos.pt; w quintadoespiritosanto.com. Just 15mins' drive west of Angra, a welcoming country house with rambling gardens. The charming owners are full to

the brim with information & take a 'living history' approach, with modern comforts set amid antique furniture & artefacts. Ecologically focused, excellent b/fast featuring homemade products. €€€

Quinta do Martelo [map, page 144] (10 rooms) Canada do Martelo 24, Cantinho, São Mateus da Calheta, 6km west of Angra; m 962 812 796; e quintadomartelo@quintadomartelo.com; w quintadomartelo.net. 'I don't want to be best, I want to be different,' says Gilberto, the owner. In this he succeeds. Once an orange farm, this quinta is set up as a series of workshops including blacksmith/farrier, tinsmith, carpenter, & even a barber's shop – a private museum full of artefacts. Gilberto's 'project' is to give guests a feel for the atmosphere of an old rural house on Terceira, while providing comfortable s/c accommodation. Less traditional are the swimming pool, tennis court, gym & sauna, but they do have traditional Azorean games. Luxury? No, but utterly different. Each room has a bathroom, there's AC/heating & TV. All are differently furnished. B/fast inc. Rates can include car hire, or airport pick-up – specify when booking. There's a private museum for guests & diners. €€€

Casadangra [158 B1] (3 rooms) Rua da Miragaia 9, Angra; ✆295 628 038; m 966 648 238; e casadangra@gmail.com; w casadangra. com. Excellent renovated house, a peaceful place offering modern rooms with private bath, communal kitchen with tea, coffee, etc, TV lounge area, roof terrace. Pleasant hostess, and 3 friendly cats. A couple of mins' walk uphill from town. 2-night min stay in high season. Good value, even with €5 pp extra for b/fast. €€–€€€

Hotel Beira Mar [158 C2] (23 rooms) Largo Miguel Corte Real, Angra; ✆295 215 188; e reservas@hotelbeiramar.com; w hotelbeiramar. com. A slightly old-fashioned feel to this waterfront hotel, which sports a good restaurant. Above the marina, with a bit of noise in summer & at festival times. Not luxury, but pleasant & very central. AC, sat TV. €€

My Angra Charming House [158 A1] (6 rooms, 1 apartment) Rua de São Pedro 168; ✆295 213 181; e bookings@myangra.com; w myangra. com. In a 19th-century family house, bright, light & beautifully renovated with a glass-walled extension. Full (shared) kitchen facilities, communal lounge, outdoor space with garden, honesty bar, computer for guest use, fans.

Rooms with private or shared bath & trpls too. A welcoming place, very smartly designed & decorated. Good b/fast inc. €€

PRAIA DA VITÓRIA Map, page 167
Hotel Apartamentos Praia Marina
(31 apartments) Av Álvaro Martins Homem; ☎295 540 055; e reservas@hotelpraiamarina.com; w hotelpraiamarina.com. Overlooking the beach, very close to the town centre. Allergy-free rooms & apartments with fully equipped kitchenettes. AC in public areas, private parking. Bikes for hire (extra cost). Some apartments can sleep 4. B/fast inc. €€€€

Hotel Atlântida Mar (28 rooms & apartments) Boavista 9; ☎295 545 800; e reservations@ atlantidamarhotel.pt; w atlantidamarhotel.pt. A very modern 4-star with view over the bay. High-quality fittings, outdoor pool (all year, but not heated), sauna, outdoor hot tub (all year), gym & children's playground. Balconied rooms have AC/ sat TV & good buffet b/fast inc. Also family suites/ apartments for 4 people. 15mins' walk from the town centre, 10mins from the beach. €€€€

Hotel Varandas do Atlântico (30 rooms) Rua da Alfândega 19; ☎295 540 050; e reservas@

hotelvarandas.com; w hotelvarandas.com. In front of the beach, 50m from the main square & the marina, 5 mins' drive from the airport. Some rooms balconied, some with connecting rooms for children. AC, cable TV. €€€

Royal Beach Hostel Suites (3 dorms, 6 suites) Rua Dr Francisco Rodrigues Silva 4; m 935 990 240; w royalbeachhostel.com. This modern building just metres from the beach combines stylish private suites & hostel dorms, with bunk beds (from €15); all rooms are AC & there's a kitchen & bike rental. €

CAMPING Map, page 144
Parque de Campismo dos Biscoitos Caminho de Santo Antonio, Biscoitos; ☎295 701 111; ⊕ all year. Good site with amenities, close to natural swimming pool. €

Parque de Campismo das Cinco Ribeiros Canada do Porto, Cinco Ribeiras; ☎295 540 200. All-year campsite on grass beneath tamarisk trees. Full amenities, including laundry, bathing nearby. €

Parque de Campismo da Salga Caminho da Salga, São Sebastião, near Porto Judeu; ☎295 905 451; m 968 907 349. Good facilities including electricity. Sea swimming. Closed in winter. Popular, necessary to book in high summer. €

✖ WHERE TO EAT AND DRINK

Angra in particular has some excellent restaurants in the centre, offering good traditional island fare or more inventive cuisine. Spices such as cinnamon, cloves and coriander are used more in Terceira than on the other islands. *Alcatra* is a tasty, oven-cooked beef dish, done in Verdelho wine and a Terceira favourite. Like many other islands, there are excellent desserts and baked items guaranteed to worry your waistline. The Queijada de Dona Amélia, originally known as Bolo das Índias but renamed in honour of the royal visit of 1901, has a delicious gingerbread-like filling of eggs, flour, honey, cinnamon, raisins and molasses. Some village restaurants are also mentioned under the car tours described later on in this chapter.

In general, Praia's restaurants are in keeping with its resort image (or perhaps influenced by the nearby airbase), with burgers, pizzas and even a Korean on the waterfront: a town crying out for a few more authentic options.

ANGRA DO HEROÍSMO
Taberna Roberto [map, page 144] EN3-1A 3, north of Angra; m 966 431 126, 969 264 926; ⊕ noon–15.30 & 18.30–23.00 Tue–Sat. An unassuming place, the creation of genial Roberto, a charismatic, hands-on enthusiast responsible for excellent food in a homely environment. Phone in advance to reserve & for the widest options: the menu choices reflect Roberto's hunting & fishing

background, with a rabbit starter, excellent spare ribs, grilled fish. Goat & duck are also on offer, or a group could even share a suckling pig! The wood-fired oven plays a big part, portions are huge & his wine selection is extensive. €€€

Tasca das Tias [158 C2] Rua de São João 117; ☎295 628 062; f; ⊕ noon–23.00 daily. Since 2014 this has added a bit of finesse to Angra's dining scene. Tuna is an excellent choice & the side salads are a bit more inventive than the Azorean norm. Soft music, stylish furnishings & some wonderful portrait photos on the wall. €€€

Birou Bar [158 C2] Rua de São João 25; ☎ 292 702 180; **f**; ⏰ noon–15.00 & 19.00–midnight Mon–Sat. Known locally as 'the craft beer place', this is actually a nice simple restaurant, with a great ambience, well-priced, tasty food, & a few imported bottles of beer. Their fresh fish is recommended, but the sirloin steak is also excellent. €€

Casa do Jardim [158 B1] Rua Ilha Terceira, inside the public garden; m 960 342 361; ⏰ year round 11.00–17.00 Mon–Sat, sometimes later in summer. An Azorean rarity: organic & virtually all vegetarian! Serves up salads, light meals, lentil burgers, soups, etc, in a modern building perched above the beautiful gardens. €€

Élio's [158 B2] Rua de São Pedro 47; ☎ 295 216 382; **f**; ⏰ noon–14.30 & 18.00–22.00 Wed–Sun. A good local restaurant on the west side of town, serving up well-loaded pizzas, pasta, omelettes, burgers & grilled meats. €€

Alto Sé Café [158 B2] Alto das Covas 1; ☎ 295 707 700; m 932 530 555; ⏰ 07.00–22.30 Mon–Sat. Very filling portions & a wide choice in this cafeteria-style establishment. Prices are low, guaranteeing a steady flow of locals. Burgers, sandwiches, salads, as well as daily dishes of a more Azorean nature. Excellent desserts, too, though service can be snail-paced – even though you order at the counter! €

PRAIA DA VITÓRIA *Map, page 167*

R3 Boa Vista 40, opposite the Atlântida Mar; ☎ 295 513 878; m 912 310 990; **f** r3restaurante; ⏰ noon–15.00 & 18.00–midnight Sun–Mon & Wed–Fri, 18.00–midnight Sat. An unusual name, in an unusual, space-age building, & for Terceira, an unusual restaurant. It's mainly a marisqueira, specialising in seafood, such as octopus, & fish, but meats & pasta are available, & for lunch a selection of main-course salads. €€€

Restaurante O Pescador Rua Constantino Jose Cardoso 11; ☎ 295 513 495; **f** O.Pescador.PV; e opescadorreservas@gmail.com; ⏰ noon–22.00 Mon–Sat. Reliable option, serving traditional fish & meat dishes, including octopus & shrimps. If you can't decide which fish, they'll let you meet it before you eat it. Lunch of the day posted on Facebook. €€€

La Barca Av Marginal; ☎ 295 542 808; ⏰ summer noon–23.00 Mon–Thu & Sun, noon–midnight Fri

& Sat, winter noon–15.00 & 18.00–23.00 Fri–Wed. On the beach just south of the Atlântida Mar hotel, a well-established pizza & pasta place, though meat & fish are also offered. Bright & light, with sea views, service is warm & welcoming. €€

SÃO MATEUS DA CALHETA

Quinta do Martelo (page 150) m 962 812 796; w restaurante.quintadomartelo.net; ⏰ noon–15.00 & 18.30–22.00 Thu–Tue. Good Azorean food in a typical farmhouse setting; reservations advisable. A bit pricey, but a splendid ambience, providing traditional & festive meals cooked on wood-burning stoves with home-baked bread. €€€

Beira Mar Canada Porto 46; ☎ 295 642 392; **f** Beira-Mar-São-Mateus-100064281626074; ⏰ noon–22.30 Tue–Sun. Take a turn-off from the main coast road towards the São Mateus fishing port to find this gem. Often full, thanks to its sparklingly fresh fish; don't expect fancy sauces or sophisticated garnish. The fish is landed in the harbour a few steps away & the cooking here is a reference point for the island. Meat dishes, too. Book in advance. €€

SERRETA

Ti Choa Grota de Margarida 1; ☎ 295 906 673; **f** facebook.com/ti.choa; ⏰ noon–14.00 Mon–Sat, 19.00–21.00 Mon, Wed, Fri & Sat. On the west coast, look for a small sign on your left as you head north through Serreta. Serving a variety of island favourites, a traditional place with good cuisine & bread baked on the premises. Some rate it as the island's best, it won't disappoint. Occasional live music on Fri. Booking advisable. €€€

ALTARES

Restaurante Caneta [map, page 144] As Presas 13, Altares. On the main road, on the corner of the Canada José Romeira; ☎ 295 989 162; w restaurantecaneta.com; ⏰ noon–15.00 Tue–Sun. A smart restaurant with a well-deserved reputation, the speciality is the Aberdeen Angus beef. Fish also available. You pay a tiny bit more than elsewhere, but it's worth the extra. The car park is down the side street. €€€

SÃO SEBASTIÃO

Os Moinhos [map, page 144] Rua Arrebalde, São Sebastião; ☎ 295 401 580; m 967 962 137; ⏰ 11.00–15.00 & 19.00–23.00 Wed–Mon. Restaurant with terrific ambience in a converted watermill east of the centre. Charcoal-grilled meat & fish, an excellent alcatra, & top-quality desserts including a chocolate mousse to travel for; finally an extensive wine list, with bottles from €9. In winter, wood-burning fires. Reservations recommended; it can be popular with tour groups. €€€

OTHER PRACTICALITIES

Hospital [158 B1] Hospital de Santo Espirito, Canada do Briado, Angra; ☎295 403 200. Large & modern, serves as a centre for other islands too.

Police [158 D2] Praça Dr Sousa Junior 1, Angra; ☎295 212 022 or 295 401 580
Post office [158 C2] Rua Palacio, Angra; ⊕ 09.00–18.00 Mon–Fri

WHAT TO SEE AND DO

MUSEUMS
Angra do Heroísmo
Museu de Angra do Heroísmo [158 D1] (Ladeira de São Francisco; ☎295 213 147; ⊕ Apr–Sep 10.00–17.30 Tue–Sun, Oct–Mar 09.30–17.00 Tue–Sun; €2/1/free adult/under 25s & seniors/under 14s, free Sun; audio guides covering only some of the exhibits are €2; wheelchair accessible) In the old Convent of São Francisco (once the headquarters of the Franciscan Order in the Azores, and well worth the visit in itself) there's a useful bilingual chronology of the islands in the context of Atlantic history, and furniture, military exhibits, and an impressive collection of horse-drawn carriages (not to mention a Willys hearse in the huge church, as well as the memorial to Vasco da Gama's brother Paulo) also feature in the permanent displays. The videos are in Portuguese with English subtitles and there are interesting temporary exhibitions. On summer Sundays, there is often free live music in the church inside the museum.

Museu de Angra do Heroísmo: Núcleo de História Militar [158 B3] (Rua da Boa Nova; ⊕ Oct–Mar 09.30–17.00 Tue–Sun, Apr–Sep 10.00–17.30 Tue–Sun; €2/1/free adult/under 25s & seniors/under 15s) Opened in 2016, this former hospital is now a well-presented military museum giving useful insight into the history of the island, including the importance of the Liberalist movement and the period under Spanish rule. There is also the charting of the development of weaponry and uniforms, together with a gallery of Azorean luminaries and others who have influenced the island's development. All information panels are helpfully translated into English.

Volcanic-Speleological Museum [158 C2] (Rua da Rocha 8; ☎295 212 992; m 961 362 215; w montanheiros.com; ⊕ 08.00–noon & 13.00–16.00 Mon–Fri; free) The museum of O Montanheiros (the Mountaineers, the club that also runs the Algar do Carvão and the Gruta do Natal) gives perhaps the best overview of Azorean geology, with videos and 3D models of the islands. They have a fine collection of different types of basalts and pyroclastics, as well as sedimentary rocks from Santa Maria, and in the second room minerals, fossils, shells and even butterflies from around the world.

Around the island
Museu do Vinho dos Biscoitos (Canada do Caldeiro, Biscoitos; ☎295 908 305; ⊕ 13.00–16.00 Tue–Sat; closed 3rd week of Sep during the grape harvest; admission free) Good small private museum showing most interesting details of the Flemish

5

Brum family business and wine production. Francisco Maria Brum (1860–1928) first began making wine over 100 years ago and was the first to graft grapes after the disastrous Phylloxera outbreak that decimated the vines. The years between 1910 and 1960 saw the maximum production. The family make white wines including a special small production of only 500 litres. There are small demonstration vineyards, and other fruit orchards, plus a tasting of a wine or aperitif – dry, medium or sweet – and an opportunity to buy. The museum is signposted just off the main coastal road in Biscoitos village (page 165).

Museo do Carnaval [map, page 144] (Rua Dr Adriano Paim, Lajes; ☏ 295 517 305; ⊕ 10.00–17.00 Tue–Sat; €1.50) Reopened in 2020, across a play area through a seemingly closed gate, this is not huge but well done, with videos, costumes and Portuguese/English information panels. The focus is on the dances and *bailinhos* of Terceira, with humorous or satirical performances freshly written every year, but there is coverage of the traditions elsewhere as well.

GARDEN
Duque da Terceira Garden [158 C1] (⊕ Nov–Mar 08.00–17.30 daily, Apr & Oct 08.00–20.00 daily, May–Sep 08.00–22.00 daily; free admission) A charming historical urban space with some interesting plants, in the centre of Angra (pages 67 and 161).

BIRDS AND FLOWERS A mix of bird hides and urban recreation is to be found at the Ponds of Praia, or Paúl Environmental Park, just north of the centre of Praia da Vitória. The coastline here was once the largest coastal wetland in the Azores, but when the town expanded most was destroyed. Now only a small area remains, but it has been cleverly improved and is certainly effective as an urban landscape enhanced by habitats for waders, several species of waterbirds, herons, egrets and terns (plus some very unwild ducks and geese).

The best-known site among dedicated birders is a rather grotty disused quarry at **Cabo da Praia** [map, page 144] that supplied the stone for the island's deep-water harbour in the 1980s. If you are visiting for the birds and not the scenery then it is regarded by many as the best place in Europe for spotting western Nearctic and Palearctic waders as well as ducks, egrets and seabirds; it is also an important breeding site of the Kentish plover. The special thing about this quarry is that it was dug to a depth where the sea seeps through fissures in the rock and enters from underground. The twice-daily sluicing by the tide has created a remarkable wetland habitat, protected from the wind. Species usually seen only in Africa and North America seem to be able to find this quarry so if you visit two to five weeks either side of mid-September and go during the 2- to 3-hour period either side of low tide you could be rewarded with very interesting sightings. To find it, initially follow the signs for Porto Oceânico and park at the oil tanks when the tarmac runs out. The quarry is along a wooden boardwalk 100m past the tanks, ending at the **Centro de Interpretação Ambiental** (🕐 09.30–noon & 13.30–16.00 Mon–Fri; admission free) where there should be someone to discuss the site and its avian visitors.

To salve your aesthetic sense, drop down to the Special Protected Area of **Ponta das Contendas** and the **Baía das Mós**, the southeast corner of Terceira. Originally there was a 500m-long peninsula created by lava flow, but through erosion and chemical change it is now discontinuous, the furthest point being **Ilhéu da Mina**. Many species of both resident and migratory birds may be seen, but it is botanically uninspiring. Around the **Lagoa do Negro** (page 166), over 150 bird species (both resident and migratory) have been recorded and botanists will be pleased that this small lake and the surrounding **Mistérios Negros** provide them with rich pickings. West of the island's centre, this remarkable volcanic area has formed a swamp and other special ecosystems rich in mosses and lichens; of special interest are the bog-lovers *Littorella uniflora* and *Isoetes azorica*. However, if birders continue on towards **Pico Alto**, 808m high with a collapsed caldera, woodcock and snipe might make a change from their usual observational menu.

RECREATIONAL FOREST RESERVES **Monte Brasil** (page 161), the volcanic peninsula overlooking Angra do Heroísmo, and **Serreta Forest** (page 165) are the highlights of the forest reserves.

SPORTS AND ACTIVITIES
Activity tours
Rope Adventures Clube Naval, Av Beira Mar, Praia da Vitória; m 961 804 496; e ropeadventures@ hotmail.com; w ropeadventures.pt. A variety of activities, including canyoning, coasteering, paddleboarding & sea-kayaking.

Diving
Octopus Diving Center Clube Naval, Av Beira Mar, Praia da Vitória; m 965 431 985, 912 513 906; e geral@octopusportugal.com; w octopusportugal.com. PADI courses, shore & boat dives, snorkelling & boat trips. Near the marina in Praia. Variety of courses, Open Water €230, single dive from €50, including equipment.

Golf

Club de Golf da Ilha Terceira Fajãs de Agualva, Praia da Vitória; ✆ 295 902 444/299; e reservas@ terceiragolf.com; w terceiragolf.com; ⊕ Tue–Sun, email for tee-off times; green fees for non-members: 18 holes, €60/70 low/high season on w/days. Large clubhouse with restaurant (⊕ May–Sep 08.00–19.00 Mon–Fri, 07.30–19.00 Sat, Sun & hols, Oct–Apr 08.00–17.00 Mon–Fri, 08.00–18.00 Sat, Sun & hols) Small pro shop. Designed by Cameron & Powell & opened in 1954 at 350m above sea level, just west of the Angra–Praia road, it is set in another beautiful Azorean landscape of tall trees, lakes, colourful azaleas & hydrangeas. With its wide fairways, reckoned to be the easiest of the 3 Azores courses. 18 holes, par 72. Handicap requirements: men 28, ladies 36, though production of handicap certificates not strictly enforced. There is also a driving range & golf lessons are available. Multi-day packages are offered.

Swimming *Map, page 144*

Around the coast there is a mix of semi-natural rock pools & artificial pools, many with toilets & changing rooms open in summer. The long sand beach at **Praia da Vitória** is popular, as is the smaller one on the other side of the marina. In **Angra** there is a small beach near the marina with facilities, a beach with a long history as it was used for careening ships.

Silveira By the Hotel do Caracol at the western end of Angra, with a public bathing area in the deep inlet protected by Monte Brasil.

Negrito With harbour swimming facilities, changing rooms & a small café/bar.

Ponta das Cinco Ribeiros Harbour swimming, changing rooms & a small café/bar. Campsite nearby.

Biscoitos Very popular natural rock pools amid interesting volcanic rock formations; changing facilities & café available.

Baía das Quatro Ribeiras Natural swimming pool, changing facilities & nearby campsite.

Porto Martins Near the harbour. A natural swimming pool, like a conventional pool but with a wave machine! There are changing rooms & a restaurant.

Salgueiros Sea swimming with changing facilities and picnic area.

Praia de Salga Near Porto Judeu. Sea swimming with changing facilities & bar-café. Campsite nearby.

Whale watching

Picos de Aventura Marina de Angra; m 918 377 926; w picosdeaventura.com. A branch of the São Miguel operator, offering whale watching & swimming with dolphins (€60–95).

WALKS ON TERCEIRA

There are now eight official trails on Terceira, with the Monte Brasil walk easily accessible for those staying in Angra without a car. The seven circular walks are summarised below; maps and detailed guides on all walks are available on the hiking section of the website: w visitazores.com.

On Terceira, walkers should keep a wary eye open for bulls; these are not typical farm animals, but those raised for the *tourada à corda* bull-running events. **Os Montanheiros** (The Mountaineers Association) offers guided walks between March and October from 09.00 to around 17.00, usually taking place on Sundays. Walks are announced at least a month in advance with details available online (see w montanheiros.com, in Portuguese only). There is no charge. You will need to be reasonably fit if you want to participate and have transport to the start of the walk. Comunicair (page 149) is a private enterprise which also offers guided walks, different from the official trails.

MISTÉRIOS NEGROS (Difficult, 5.8km, 2½hrs) A circular walk from the Gruta do Natal cave, beside Lagoa do Negro (page 166). You will see plenty of native plants before you get to a difficult stretch over some 'recent' lava deposits.

BAÍAS DA AGUALVA (Easy, 4km, 2hrs) With a bit of road walking at the end this can be a circular walk between Agualva and Quatro Ribeiras in the middle of the north coast, offering good birdwatching.

SERRETA–LAGOINHA (Medium difficulty, 7km, 2½hrs) A circular walk including the lake of Lagoinha, and plenty of native flora. Care is needed at some steep places.

MONTE BRASIL (Easy, 7.5km, 2½hrs) Beginning and ending at the Relvão Park, by the Spanish fort in Angra.

RELHEIRAS DE SÃO BRÁS (Easy, 5km, 2hrs) A circular route from the picnic area in São Brás, near Lajes Airport, revealing ancient oxcart tracks, very evocative of earlier times.

ROCHA DO CHAMBRE (Medium difficulty, 9.3km, 2½hrs) A comparatively recently created circular walk; alternatively you can continue to the coast at Biscoitos.

PASSAGEM DAS BESTAS (Medium difficulty, 4km, 2½hrs) This walk lets you see the tracks of oxcarts which, over centuries, came here to collect the abundant wood.

TOURING THE ISLAND

The programmes suggested below take a total of three days, but can certainly be done in less time. Alternatively, you can easily select your own itinerary from the notes. Angra do Heroísmo is a must and will take you a morning. You could then spend the afternoon and early evening on Monte Brasil. Travelling slowly around the west coast to Biscoitos will never fail to delight, passing through small villages and past many houses, their whitewashed exteriors sparkling in the sun, even when the hills of the interior are covered with cloud. Including the museums and a reasonable lunch this will comfortably occupy a day. If the skies are clear or the clouds are not too low then a day could be spent exploring the wild hinterland, with many old volcanic cones and extensive areas of broken and tumbled land covered in grasses, mosses or tree heathers. This gives the opportunity to judge which day to do what, according to the weather. Since almost every visitor goes to Angra, the two car tours detailed on pages 162 and 165 begin from the city.

ANGRA DO HEROÍSMO Given the setting and Renaissance urban planning, it is difficult not to slip back through time to the period when Angra was the centre of the Atlantic universe. Trading and treasure ships gathered and passed through here from both the East Indies and the New World, and the town grew ever more prosperous. It was central, too, to the Azores archipelago until usurped by Ponta Delgada. Ban the cars, change the shop windows, clamber into period costume, and all you need is a pirate ship to come sailing into the bay! Well, perhaps not quite, but it is fun to wander around at night when the streets are empty, and allow the imagination to fly.

The Earl of Cumberland's flotilla of English privateers sank the Spanish galleon *Nuestra-Señora de Guia* off Terceira in 1589, just one of almost 900 ships lost from various causes in the Azores in the past 500 years. In the Bay of Angra alone there are some 80 shipwrecks, the deepest lying in 60m of water, the oldest from 1543. Angra provided the safest haven but, when storms blew in from the southeast, it became a dangerous dead end and disastrous for those ships too slow or unable to

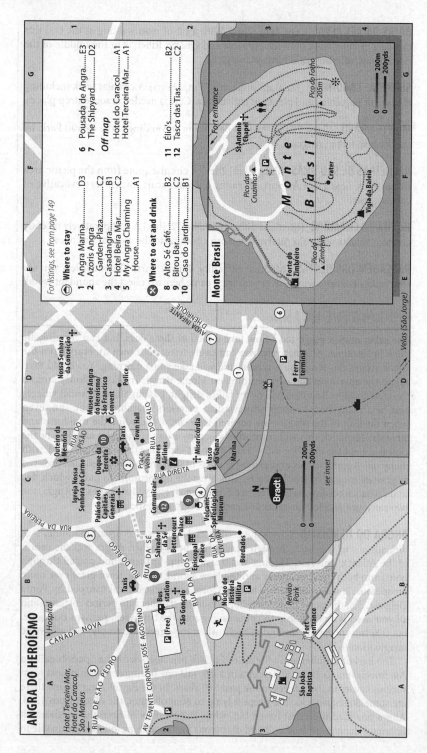

ANGRA DO HEROÍSMO

For listings, see from page 149

Where to stay

1	Angra Marina	D3
2	Azoris Angra Garden-Plaza	C2
3	Casadangra	B1
4	Hotel Beira Mar	C2
5	My Angra Charming House	A1
6	Pousada de Angra	E3
7	The Shipyard	D2

Off map
	Hotel do Caracol	A1
	Hotel Terceira Mar	A1

Where to eat and drink

8	Alto Sé Café	B2
9	Birou Bar	C2
10	Casa do Jardim	B1
11	Élio's	B2
12	Tasca das Tias	C2

Monte Brasil

leave in time. It seems there are few doubloons to be found because any treasure was recovered soon after the shipwreck, since such losses would severely impact upon the Portuguese and Spanish economies. These wrecks, however, represent the most marvellous sites of marine archaeology, time capsules because of the suddenness of their demise. There is also an 'anchor graveyard' near Angra, created by over 40 ships cutting their anchor lines in a hurry to avoid rough weather.

Although no-one wants to live in a theme park, what a stimulating centre Angra could become for the study and interpretation of a most exciting and vivid period of history. The exploration, exploitation and colonial expansion of new lands and the maritime consequences of politics and war on mainland Europe could become a major visitor site like the one at Faial's Capelinhos.

Angra city tour (This walk includes a bit of up & down & sections on the cobbled pavements. Suggested time: 1½hrs. At major sights, there are a number of 'paddle-shaped' panels, giving additional information in English.) In summer, several buildings are open to visitors and the tourist office has a helpful handout of which and when. They also have a leaflet with pictures, worth picking up before you start your tour. Begin at the centre of the city in the **Praça Velha** [158 C2], a most attractively paved square with a Renaissance influence. At the eastern end, the 19th-century **Paços de Concelho** (Town Hall) [158 C2] is open to visitors – except at weekends – and has one of the largest and finest great halls in the whole of Portugal. Admire the tiled floors, chandeliers and the occasional art exhibition inside. Leave the square to the south by the Rua Direita [158 C2] and almost immediately on your right at numbers 113–21 is the balconied house (no sign) of the **Count of Vilaflor**, later Duke of Terceira, commander of the Liberal armies and leader of the Liberal army at the Battle of Praia in 1829. The visual unity of the long front elevation is satisfying. The house is no longer open to visitors, but the downstairs space is shared between a pharmacy and a café. The Rua Direita is Angra's first main street and leads from the harbour directly to the main square and to the governor's house a little beyond. It serves also as a focus for shoppers.

At the lower end of the Rua Direita, on the left, is the dominating **Misericórdia church** [158 C2] (⊕ 10.00–13.00 & 14.00–17.00 Mon–Fri, 13.00–17.00 Sat, 16.00–18.00 Sun; donation of €1.50 expected, English-language information provided). The first hospital in the Azores was built on this site in 1492, supported by the Brotherhood of the Holy Spirit; one of the founders was João Vaz Corte-Real, Governor of Angra, who is thought to have been the first to 'discover' Newfoundland. The present church dates from 1728–46, built by an association of the earlier brotherhood and a charitable institution, the Misericórdia. It was badly damaged in the 1980 earthquake. Erected in front of the church in 2016 is a statue of **Vasco da Gama** [158 C2], the famous Portuguese explorer who stopped off here with his dying brother, Paulo, who is buried in the town's São Francisco monastery. The statue was a gift from an emigrant, but is not universally popular with locals. Down below, towards the sea, is a stylish, modern water feature. Further round the harbour wall to the west, the small sandy beach was once the site of the shipyards that supported the early trading ships. The yachting marina [158 C3] off to the east is seen by many as an ugly intrusion and violation of a historical patrimony, but brings activity and money to the waterfront, especially in summer.

Walk west along the front, away from the marina and past the Beira Mar Hotel, taking one of the sets of modern steps up to the parallel road. Walk a little bit further west and take the **Carreira dos Cavalos**, the Way of the Horses, so named because a festival devoted to the horse was held here.

If you are interested in picking up some embroidery as a souvenir, before you turn right into this road, go along the Rua da Rocha to number 50 to find a showroom called **Bordados** [158 B3] (☏295 214 239; ⊕ 09.00–noon & 13.00–18.00 Mon–Fri, 09.00–noon Sat; may open w/end afternoons in high season). All the product is made in houses across the island and finished here. After visiting, retrace your steps.

Halfway up Rua Carreira dos Cavalos on the left is the former **Episcopal Palace** [158 B2], now a government building with little remaining of the original dating from 1544. Richard Nixon and Georges Pompidou met here in 1971. On the next corner, on the right-hand side is the **Bettencourt Palace** [158 C2]. Built around the start of the 18th century, it has a fine portico above which is the Bettencourt family coat of arms. Until recently in use as a library, it is now sadly closed to the public.

At this same corner, turn left and follow the **Rua da Rosa** westwards and towards the end on your right are the bright walls of the massive **Convent of São Gonçalo** [158 B2] (⊕ 09.30–11.30 & 14.00–16.30 Mon–Fri, 09.30–11.30 Sat; €2/free adult/child), founded in 1545 for the nuns of the Order of St Clare. It is Angra's oldest and the largest in the Azores. The small side door should be unlocked, and it is well worth visiting. There are figured choir stalls, 18th-century Portuguese tiles, a 17th-century silver crucifix, paintings and an ornamental ceiling. Sometimes a nun will give you a guided tour, perhaps in English, pointing out the damage caused by earthquakes. A section of the wall will be revealed, showing the criss-cross wooden strengthening used in the 16th century to minimise the damage. You can also see the 'cages' which let the nuns receive visitors without any danger of physical contact taking place.

After visiting, continue in the same direction as before for one block and turn left into the Rua da Boa Nova to quickly find the **Hospital da Boa Nova**, built by the Spanish as a hospital for the soldiers stationed in the castle. It is now a military museum, the **Núcleo de História Militar** [158 B3], and is well worth visiting (page 153).

Now retrace your steps to the Bettencourt Palace. Across the road from its entrance is the rear of the cathedral of Angra, **Santíssimo Salvador da Sé** [158 C2] (⊕ 10.00–17.30 Mon–Sat, 17.00–19.00 Sun), founded in 1570. Of interest are the 16th-century painted panels, the small Indo-Portuguese-style lectern made in the Azores of Brazilian jacaranda wood and whale ivory, and the altar's early 18th-century silver antependium made on Terceira. The church was finished in 1618 while Angra was under Spanish rule, and its craftsmanship is influenced by Flemish, local and Spanish Baroque styles. There is also a museum of religious objects. An English-language leaflet is available, explaining the building's history; plaques inside, and a statue outside, mark the visit by Pope John Paul II in 1991.

From the front of the cathedral, continue down the road in the direction of the Praça Velha, taking the first turning left into Rua do Palacio to find the splendid **Palácio dos Capitães Generais** [158 C2]. Built in 1595–1652 as a Jesuit college, the islands' governors had it modified in the 1770s and made into a palace. Two kings have stayed here: King Pedro IV in 1832, and King Carlos I in 1901. Guided tours include the state rooms and the gardens, but otherwise you can only see some ground-floor displays (⊕ 10.00–17.00 Tue–Sun; guided tours with English-speaking guide €3/2/free, without guide €2/1/free adult/seniors & under 25s/under 15s). After visiting, proceed along the front on the Largo Prior do Prato, to the Jesuit church, the **Igreja Nossa Senhora do Carmo** [158 C2] (also known as Santo Inácio de Loiola), which contains a beautiful gallery on wooden columns and wonderful azulejos in the chapel of the Holy Sacrament. Continue to the public garden, the

Jardim Duque da Terceira [158 C1]. Initiated in 1862 as an experimental garden for agricultural development, it later became a public garden that was enlarged in 1888. This garden was developed by a Belgian, Francisco (François) Gabriel, who began his horticultural career in a Liège nursery before moving aged 18 to work on São Miguel. He managed the garden for 15 years, until his death in 1897. A wonderful urban period garden of the late 19th century, it was noted in its heyday for its many exotic ornamental species. In February/March the magnolias are at their best and, of course, never get damaged by spring frosts.

From the garden a steep flight of steps will take you up to the **Outeiro da Memória** [158 C1], the Memorial Hill. This was the site of the first fort built in the Azores around 1474; the obelisk was erected in 1846 in memory of King Pedro IV. The reward for making the climb is the fine view over Angra and across to Monte Brasil.

Go out of the garden and take the small road off on the right, the Rua do Pisão. Once there was a stream flowing in this area, and early in the town's development this was put into an open conduit and for some 500 years served the industries that sprang up alongside: watermills, tanneries and other enterprises. The narrow winding streets here are fun to explore and at the bottom you come to the **Convent of São Francisco** [158 D1], which now houses the **city museum** (page 153); the entrance is off the Ladeiro de São Francisco, the road running up from the main square beside the public garden. The building alone is well worth seeing, and the museum offers permanent displays about the Azores and temporary exhibits. Afterwards, you can simply walk down the hill to the square where this walk began, or go up the hill, the Rua da Guarita, to see the impressive exterior of the **Convent of Nossa Senhora da Conceição** [158 D1], built in the 16th century with 17th- and 18th-century alterations. According to a contemporary account by Edward Boid, when King Pedro gathered his supporters in Angra prior to his invasion of Portugal in 1832, the monasteries were converted to military barracks but officers left the convents untouched: conventual infamy was shocking and the Conceição convent became the most fashionable resort of faithless husbands and amorous celibates, with the nuns in amorous communication through the grated windows, and 'the grass was worn away under every window of this convent by the frequency of these communications'. Opposite the convent is the impressive **Palacete Silveira e Paulo**, built in 1899–1901 and refurbished in 2000–04 to house the Regional Secretariat of Culture; there's a good modern library behind it.

MONTE BRASIL During the Spanish occupation Sir Francis Drake unsuccessfully attacked Angra and eight years later, in 1597, the Earl of Essex with around 100 ships failed to seize a fleet of Spanish treasure galleons anchored in the bay. To defend the harbour against such attacks and at the same time secure control of Angra, King Filipe II constructed the Fort of São Filipe at the foot of Monte Brasil in 1592–94, given its more familiar name of **São João Baptista** [158 A3] once Spain's Philippine dynasty no longer ruled Portugal. The exterior wall is 4km long and some 400 artillery pieces defended it. Three other smaller forts along the coast, including that of São Sebastião, provided crossfire, so completing the defence. Inside the fortress is the **Igreja de São João Baptista**, commemorating the restoration of Portuguese sovereignty in 1640, and the governor's palace. You can walk up from the Relvão Park, through the gate and past a plaque to Gungunhana, the last emperor of Mozambique, who was brought here in 1896 when Portugal seized his country and died on Terceira in 1906. Ahead is a closed military area, but the road and hiking trails to the left are open in daylight hours.

If you are in a hurry, drive or take a taxi up to the 200m-high **Pico das Cruzinhas** [158 F3] to enjoy the view of Angra. The tall stone cross and the surrounding wall again incorporating the cross is a typical monument that the Portuguese built wherever they landed and claimed new lands; this one was erected in 1946 commemorating the five centuries of settlement in the Azores. There are peacocks and guinea fowl here, as well as a macaw in a cage, and beyond that four British anti-aircraft guns placed on the hilltop in 1940. From the statue of King Alfonso VI (who was exiled on Terceira in 1669–74) you can clearly see the old historical core; look for the obelisk erected in 1846 (page 161) on the first fort to be built, then below it the governor's palace, the Santíssimo Salvador da Sé cathedral, then down Rua Direita to the Misericórdia church and the harbour. To the right on higher ground is the conspicuous Convent of São Francisco; to the left is the Convent of São Gonçalo, close to the large modern indoor sports complex. Note also the 17th-century Castelo de São Sebastião that protected the eastern approaches, now a pousada. To the left, westwards, is an area known as Caminho de Baixo where the rich people of Angra once had their summer houses; now there's a surprising amount of suburban sprawl.

You can spend a very enjoyable full day exploring this old volcanic hill on foot, walking easily from the centre of Angra, or from Pico das Cruzinhas. You can also incorporate a free guided visit of the Fort of São João Baptista, booked through the military museum (\295 218 383; e museum.angra.agenda@azores.gov.pt). (In truth, there's not a lot to see inside, and your guide may be one of the soldiers, who may not speak a word of English. Still, he will take you round, duly unlocking the main entrance to the fort and letting you in to the church. If you're in a car, you can park inside beyond the barrier – just ask the guard on duty. The fort has been home to troops for over 500 years.)

Following the surfaced road, these are some of the walks you can do. The first signposted side road will take you to the little chapel of **St Antonio** [158 G3] at the end of the asphalt road. From here it takes about 45 minutes to walk to the end of the unsurfaced track and back; you will have good views of Angra and views eastwards of the south coast. Alternatively, from near the chapel, you can take the signposted trail as described in the Tourism Authority's trails booklet. This is a good place to see day-flying bats.

Return to the main road and continue until you reach the rim of the caldera. The caldera itself is used by the military as a rifle range and you are not allowed to go down. Look for the signpost to the **Vigia da Baleia** [158 F4]; it takes about an hour to walk there and back. It is a good walk, often in the shade of trees, and the reward is a commanding view seaward; if you have binoculars and the time, try your hand at whale watching. You can also walk in the other direction up to **Pico do Zimbreiro** [158 E4], Juniper Peak, on the west side of the caldera. The junipers have long gone, but endemic laurel and heather remain, and the *forte* (fort) can also be seen.

When you return to the main road, continue round the caldera until you come to another large track on your right. There is a children's play area, picnic tables and a lavatory. From here it is another very pleasant walk up to **Pico do Facho** [158 G4], Signal Peak, the highest point of Monte Brasil at 205m. For four centuries it was a semaphore station, using large and small flags to signal the number of vessels approaching and from which direction.

THE WEST-COAST TOUR: ANGRA DO HEROÍSMO TO BISCOITOS
São Mateus da Calheta Just 3km west of Angra is this pretty village, one of the most important fishing harbours in the Azores. Between 16.00 and 17.00 the

boats land their catches to sell on the quayside. The colourful little vessels create a cheerful scene and there is a small fort overlooking the harbour. Take time, too, to explore the nearby backstreets. This is a great place to eat fish (page 152) and to visit the boat shed (Casa das Botes), open daily, which has a few of the old whaleboats, some great vintage photos and usually a few octogenarian ex-whalers hanging around; if you speak Portuguese, or can find an interpreter, they are willing to share some tales of derring-do. Nearby, by the Beira Mar restaurant (page 152), their wives sell handicrafts at the **Associação Marítima de Pesca e Aquicultura da Ilha Terceira** (✆ 295 643 270; m 935 624 111; ⊕ 14.00–20.00 Mon, 13.00–16.00 & 18.30–22.30 Wed–Fri, 18.00–22.30 Sat), which also offers Pesca Turismo, ie: fishing tourism, in which you get to go out on a boat and then take some of the catch to a restaurant to be cooked for your dinner (€70 for 3–4hrs May–Oct).

Porto Negrito This is a small village with an old fort by the harbour, with swimming facilities and a small café/bar. An old small trying area has been preserved where in basalt are the fireplaces and pots for reducing the whale blubber. As you continue, you should be able to see São Jorge island on the horizon.

Cinco Ribeiras Soon on the right-hand side of the main road you will reach the small ceramics studio of Aurelia Rocha, **Azulart** (Estrada Dr Marcelino Moules 78; m 967 529 099; ⊕ 10.30–18.00 Mon–Thu). Her pots are all wheel-thrown and in stoneware are traditional Terceiran designs, and in earthenware traditional shapes and designs of the Azores. All are hand painted, and commissions are accepted. Reflecting the enterprise needed for life on an island in the mid-Atlantic, she has built her own kilns. Ceramics in the early days on Terceira used clay imported from England, shipped over in the empty sailing boats coming for the orange crop, and clay is still imported from the continent as the island clay from Santa Maria does not take glazing and can be used only for alcatra pots and similar that do not need a glaze.

Further on, in Cinco Ribeiras, take the **Canada do Pilar**, a narrow road between houses going down to the coast, to the left for 100m to reach the **Queijo Vaquinha** cheese factory (Canada do Pilar; ✆295 907 138; ⊕ 09.00–22.00 daily), which makes the *vaquinha* cheese. You can sample and buy the four cheeses made here, try some yoghurts and enjoy a coffee and a cake. *Queijo vaquinha* is the traditional cheese, made with salt only on the outside and sold in small blocks like butter. *O Ilha* cheese is offered in two varieties, matured for either one or two months and has the salt incorporated into the milk, and the spicy *queijo vaquinha picante* has red peppers added. The dairy does not make any butter, so all the milk, not separates, goes into the cheese. Cheese was first made on Terceira in 1912, and vaquinha translates as 'small cow'.

At the end of the road you get to **Ponta das Cinco Ribeiras**, a harbour with swimming facilities, also the remains of a small fort that the sea has almost washed away. Close by is a camping site under trees with electricity and amenities.

Rather than return to the main road, you can continue close to the coast always following the winding asphalt road. It is a very pretty drive through a landscape of stone-walled fields and pastures, and eventually you will come to Pézinho da Senhora, a leisure area with picnic tables and barbecue facilities, and an old-style oven for use by people who no longer have them in their modern houses. There is also a bullring, and the four red-and-white boards are the only means of defence from the bull. The arena is also used for music and folklore events.

From the picnic area, the road inland quickly comes to a little chapel with white tiles on the Largo Nossa Senhora da Ajuda. The name Pézinho da Senhora comes from a rock in the river that supposedly has the imprint of the Virgin's foot, and the chapel was built above a grotto where an image of the Virgin was found. The large house next to the chapel, originally a small priest's house but later enlarged, was for pilgrims to these miraculous places to stay, an equivalent to a Romeiro house on São Miguel; it's now a holiday let. There were no springs in this area, so water was at a premium. To the left of the house is a small cistern; you will see steps going up to a small door. Look inside and you can see where a bucket can be lowered into the water, stored from rainfall falling on to the roof.

Continue on the asphalt road to Santa Bárbara. If you missed all this, you can pick it up turning from the main road signposted to Largo Nossa Senhora da Ajuda, opposite the Mercado Bárbarense.

Santa Bárbara As you continue around the coast you come to the farming community of Santa Bárbara, with its white-painted houses so startlingly bright in the sunshine. The Spanish colonial influence in the architecture of the parish church suggests the 16th century. Inside there is a 17th-century organ from the Convent of Nossa Senhora da Conceição in Angra and the furniture in the vestry is made from jacaranda and other tropical hardwoods. You can find beautiful New-World woods used in often unexpected places, brought to the Azores as ballast. Near the church is a café and a 19th-century império.

Doze Ribeiras Some 200m before the church on the right-hand side of the road, look out for the oldest house, indicated by a sign that says 'Casa Etnografico'. In front of the stone building is a large tank for rainwater with a half-dome catchment roof. Behind, you'll see the windmill that would have ground *burra de milho* or donkey corn, used for feeding farm animals; note the sheets of zinc on the corn store to keep the rats away. In summer there are folk-dance performances here. Nearly all the adjacent small houses were built with the help of the Portuguese military for the elderly unable to afford to rebuild after the disastrous earthquake in 1980. Houses are painted annually for the Holy Ghost or summer festivities.

Serra de Santa Bárbara Beyond Doze Ribeiras, take the right-hand R5–2 turning inland, eastward, to the impressive volcanic area behind Santa Bárbara. Be sure to stop at the **Santa Bárbara Interpretation Centre** (Estrada Regional ER5 2a; \ 295 403 800; ⏱ Oct–May 10.00–17.00 Tue–Fri, Jun–Sep 10.00–18.00 daily), which is small, modern and with excellent bilingual information on the geology of this area, the most extensive natural park in the Azorean archipelago. Turn right and right again for the road up the Serra de Santa Bárbara (5km). From the car park at the top, new boardwalks lead to the highest point (beyond the radio masts) and down into the caldera – this is a strict nature reserve due to its sphagnum bogs and copses of *Juniper brevifolia*, so do not leave the boardwalk. From the top of the mountain, if the weather is clear, you may see the most beautiful views of Terceira island. Return to the main road and turn right to rejoin the main road along the coast.

Serreta This is a small village with its important Church of Our Lady of Miracles where promises are made by people from all over the island; up to 10,000 pilgrims walk overnight to be here for the feast of Nossa Senhora da Serreta on the second Sunday of September, continuing with afternoon bullfights on *Serreta Monday*. The current church was built in 1895–1907 to house the miraculous late-17th-century image of the Virgin, across the road from a brightly painted império on the site of the previous church. Beyond the village you will come to a sign to a *farol* or lighthouse which makes a nice walk, or you can continue to Raminho and take the trail back to the lighthouse. It's a couple of kilometres drive through good forest and fields to reach the picnic area and WCs by the modern red and white metal column that replaced the original lighthouse, built in 1908 and destroyed by the 1980 earthquake; the road continues a bit further to a slipway. It was off this stretch of coast that the undersea Serreta volcano was active as recently as 1999, and the volcanic bombs could be seen coming to the surface. Roughly midway between Serreta and Rominha lies the much-visited **Serreta Forest Recreational Reserve**; of some 15ha, it provides numerous trails to picnic areas. The village is home to a very good restaurant (page 152).

Raminho The signposted Miradouro do Raminho is a substantial viewpoint looking along the coast and is a good place for seabirds, with toilets, parking, and picnic tables beneath the trees. There is also a vigia, a simple lookout shelter for spying whales. In the distance on a clear day you can see São Jorge and Graciosa.

Altares The local **ethnographic museum** (⊕ 14.00–17.00 Tue–Sun; admission free) is right next to the blue-and-white church. It is small, with some agricultural equipment, old radios and a video showing the bullfights. Nearby, you will see a hill on the coast called Pico de Altares (signposted Pico Matias Simão) with a monument at its summit. This was once a vigia. If you have time, climb to the top (153m) for the view along the coast. The village is home to a very good restaurant (page 152).

Biscoitos This area was always intriguing because of its volcanic origins and black lava; *biscoito* means 'biscuit'. This came from the last eruption in 1761, when lava flowed down from the area around Pico do Gaspar. It was also known for its Verdelho wines, and is again becoming recognised in the Azores for its wine production and wine museum (page 153).

From the west end of the village, you can follow signs for 'Zona Balnear/Porto da Pesca' to reach the sea and find natural rock pools for swimming, with changing facilities, toilets and a small café. Turning east to continue parallel with the sea on a one-way road, you can view the remains of defensive structures used in World War II, then the vineyards, tiny walled enclosures called *curraletas* where the vines grow horizontally. The houses here, built from black volcanic rock with a white 'trim', are strangely attractive. This road will bring you back on to the main coastal road. Continuing east, this passes some dramatic cliffs, while if you take the inland road back to Angra (18km), in July and August this is made spectacular with all the flowering hydrangeas.

THE WILD HINTERLAND TOUR, WITH PRAIA DA VITÓRIA Setting out from Angra, take the R3-1 road heading across the interior of the island for Biscoitos. At the crossroads near Pico do Gaspar turn left to take the R5-2 leading to Doze Ribeiras; this road is called the Estrela dos Ribeiros. Continue until the road to São Bartolomeu is signposted off to your left; take this to reach a forestry park with picnic tables beside a lovely clear and sparkling stream beneath lofty cryptomeria trees. The Viveiro da Falca forest nursery is also here.

Returning to the Doze Ribeiras road, turn left and continue as before for a short distance to the turning off on your right to Lagoa do Negro; it goes across to the R3–1. This is a beautiful road, particularly in July and August when much of its length is lined with hydrangeas. You soon leave the pastures and enter wild country with native vegetation, especially the area called **Mistérios Negros**, an extensive area of black cinders and obsidian thrown out by the last major eruption on Terceira in 1761. The *mistérios* take their name from the locals being unable to understand why, on such a green island, vegetation refused to grow here; the answer lay in the acidity of the terrain. You will find the Lagoa do Negro on your left, and opposite is a stone house by the road. This is the entrance to a cave, the **Gruta do Natal** (⊕ mid-Oct–mid-Mar 14.30–17.15 Mon, Wed, Fri & Sat, mid-Mar–end May 14.30–17.15 daily, Jun–mid-Oct 14.30–18.00 daily; exact dates change from year to year, so check **w** montanheiros.com for updates; admission €10/free adult/under 12s, or €15/free combined ticket with Algar do Carvão), a 697m-long, branched horizontal lava tube with stalactite- and stalagmite-like structures. There is a small interpretation centre here, with volcanic materials and geological explanations, and information about the eruptions in 1761.

Continue on the same road until you come to a major junction. Turn right to go to Angra (left goes to Altares, opposite to Biscoitos). Just before you get to the crossroads you came to earlier, take a left turning to an area for car parking where there is a *tentadeiro*, an area where bulls are selected for the bullfight. On summer mornings you are likely to find plenty of activity here.

Now continue on the main road to the crossroads, and turn left towards Cabrito. If you would like a sharp reminder that you are on a volcanic island, then take the wide road you soon come to on your left signposted to **Furnas do Enxofre**; after 700m this ends in a turning area/car park. A narrow walkway (which can be slippery, so take care) takes you around this area, which has several small caves. Stay behind the wooden railings: the gases emitted are very dangerous. The ground is quite hot, and steam emissions have often turned the grass brown. The area is a geological protected zone. This was one of Charles Darwin's two excursions on Terceira when the *Beagle* put in to Angra on her homeward voyage.

Return to the main road and continue, taking a turning on your left, signposted to **Algar do Carvão**. The **caves** (⊕ times and prices as per Gruta do Natal; see above) are a huge 'empty volcano'. As you descend the 338 wet steps, above you is the mossy vegetation around the wide hole admitting daylight. The cavern is the remains of an eruption some 2,000 years ago; there are stalactites and stalagmites, formed by silica. The caves were opened to the public in 1968. Opposite is the Caldeira do Guilherme Moniz, a primary volcano with a crater perimeter of 15km that is among the largest in the archipelago.

As you return from the caves, look for the turning to Agualva, now off on your right. This is a really good drive passing a tumultuous volcanic landscape covered with native vegetation. Growing along the Ribeira Agualva are the most impressive tree ferns. From Agualva, follow the main road along to Vila Nova and Lajes, and to Praia da Vitória.

Praia da Vitória In contrast with other towns in the archipelago, Praia always feels open and bright. It has an attractive main square and a long pedestrianised shopping street. In winter, it wears the clothes of an out-of-season resort, with slow business at the hotels and restaurants. In summer, its large, artificial beach and sheltered bay attract holidaymakers and the town kicks into life: the major festivals take it to a whole different level again. Seasonal ferries land visitors from other islands here and Praia is also home to the island's commercial port. The extensive lowlands of this eastern half of the island produced large quantities of wheat, and the wealth created is reflected in many fine houses in the town. At first called simply Praia, it gained town status in 1640. In 1581, after bombarding Angra, a Spanish fleet of ten ships was reconnoitring the Terceira coast and anchored in Salga Bay, in the southeastern corner. They were seen and the alarm given but by the time the Portuguese arrived 1,000 Castillians had already landed, bent on destruction. After a morning's fierce but indecisive fighting an Augustinian friar had the idea to drive cattle at the enemy. Over 1,000 animals were stampeded at the Spaniards, who fell back in disarray and were either killed or drowned on the shore. Thus ended the Battle of Salga. Again battle came to Praia in 1829, when the town, supporting the Liberal cause, successfully resisted an attempted landing by an Absolutist fleet of 21 ships. In commemoration, the town was called Praia da Vitória in 1837. The nearby Lajes Airport now covers much of what were the great wheatfields of earlier days.

In the main square, the **Praça Francisco Ornelas da Câmara**, is the Liberty Statue, erected on the centenary of the 1829 battle won by the Liberals in homage to the heroes. Overlooking the square is the attractive town hall, and further along

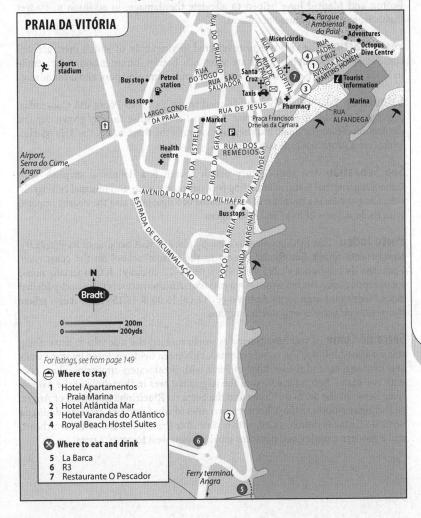

PRAIA DA VITÓRIA

Sports stadium

Parque Ambiental do Paúl

Rope Adventures

Misericórdia

Octopus Dive Centre

RUA DO CRUZEIRO

RUA DO HOSPITAL

RUA DE SÃO PAULO

RUA PADRE CRUZ

AVENIDA ALVARO MARTINS HOMEN

Bus stop

Petrol station

RUA DO JOGO

RUA SÃO SALVADOR

Santa Cruz

Taxis

Tourist information

Bus stop

LARGO CONDE DA PRAIA

RUA DE JESUS

Pharmacy

Marina

RUA ALFANDEGA

Market

Praça Francisco Ornelas da Camara

Health centre

RUA DA ESTRELA

RUA DA GRAÇA

RUA DOS REMÉDIOS

RUA ALFANDEGA

AVENIDA DO PAÇO DO MILHAFRE

Bus stops

POÇO DA AREIA

AVENIDA MARGINAL

ESTRADA DE CIRCUMVALAÇÃO

N

Bradt

0 ——— 200m
0 ——— 200yds

For listings, see from page 149

🏠 **Where to stay**
1 Hotel Apartamentos Praia Marina
2 Hotel Atlântida Mar
3 Hotel Varandas do Atlântico
4 Royal Beach Hostel Suites

❌ **Where to eat and drink**
5 La Barca
6 R3
7 Restaurante O Pescador

Ferry terminal, Angra

Airport, Serra do Cume, Angra

on the Rua de São Paulo is the parish church of **Santa Cruz**. This was founded by one of the first settlers and has a 15th-century Gothic doorway and a 16th-century Manueline side doorway. Inside there are fine carvings, rich gilt ornamentation and various works of art. Further along on the same road, on the left, is the house where the writer **Vitorino Nemésio** (1901–78) was born. He held several senior academic posts in Lisbon and was a novelist, poet and scholar and also a popular television personality; his novel of 19th-century life on Faial and Pico, *Stormy Isles*, is in English translation.

In the opposite direction, towards the far end of the main pedestrianised Rua de Jesus, is the town market, built in the final quarter of the 19th century. Alternatively, in the opposite direction, take the Rua da Alfândega which becomes Avenida Álvaro Martins Homem and leads down to the beach and along to the modern marina.

The reduced strategic importance of Lajes Airport hit the town's economy hard, with the number of US military personnel reduced in 2012 from 2,500 to fewer than 200, but numbers have now risen again to around 500. New direct flights from Boston and Madrid have helped to alleviate the damage, in addition to budget flights from the Portuguese mainland.

Porto Martins
The area was once covered in vineyards, of which there are still some small traces, but now there are many new houses, summer homes for people in Praia da Vitória. Near the harbour is a natural swimming pool and a restaurant.

Salgueiros
Take the minor road (signed to the Farol) to Ponta das Contendas, passing a field of *Strelitzia reginae*, the bird of paradise flower, grown for cut decoration. From the headland there are views of the three rocks, the Três Marias, which are a protected bird sanctuary.

São Sebastião
The 15th-century parish church is a delightful surprise, with interesting internal features including frescoes on the walls and unusual ceilings. In the facing square is a monument to the Battle of Salga; note also the nearby império with its depictions of food and hydrangeas.

Porto Judeu
This fishing village is a happy place to visit because of its simplicity. **Restaurante Snack-Bar Rocha** is next to the infants' school on the coast road, Caminho da Esperança (❧295 905 185; ☉ 08.30–22.00 daily). It is especially noted for octopus cooked in red wine (*polvo guisado*). An alternative is the wood-panelled **Boca Negra** on Largo Santo Antonio (☉ 12.15–15.00 & 18.15–22.00 daily) where the *alcatra da peixe* is well worth sampling.

Serra do Cume
If you have time, it is worth making the side trip to drive along this elongated hilltop. The view is of small, rich green fields enclosed by stone walls and hydrangeas, and the harbour of Praia with breakwaters appearing like a crab with two claws. Behind is a view of the largest flat area in the whole of the Azores, lying between the Serra do Cume and the Serra da Ribeirinha northeast of Angra. At the highest point (545m), between two rows of wind turbines, the Miradouro da Serra do Cume is double-sided, with a view over Praia and Lajes to the northeast, and a modern cantilevered platform looking southwest towards Angra.

6

Graciosa

The general opinion is that Graciosa, meaning 'gracious', is the most relaxed of all the islands. Certainly it would make for a great escape from the mainstream, a place to stay if ever strife and tribulation became too great to handle. Perhaps there has been little change, or at least slow change, in the past few decades. The least humid island of the archipelago, the roughly oval-shaped Graciosa's highest point is Pico Timão at only 402m. As a result, villages are distributed more or less equally across the countryside, and not only around the coast – very different from some of its fellow islands. The pace is slow, men can still occasionally be seen travelling in pony traps or riding donkeys along the roads, there are at last some good restaurants, the walking is easy and everyone recognises the visitor second time round. The scenery is picturesque, an idyll of pastures and neatly walled enclosures, little clusters of whitewashed houses – with their peculiarly shaped chimneys – around village churches, occasional windmills with their distinctive red, onion-shaped domes (there were once 36) and all surrounded by a glittering blue sea. Like rare wine, it is an island to be enjoyed slowly. It is also, perhaps, a window into what the world could be like with fewer inhabitants.

Of greatest interest is the Furna do Enxofre, the cavern at the bottom of the caldera, first seriously explored in 1879 by Prince Albert I of Monaco. The excellent, modern museum in Santa Cruz is worth your time. Otherwise, just relax and enjoy being on Graciosa, free from stress. The entire island is a UNESCO Biosphere Reserve.

BACKGROUND

GEOLOGY Graciosa consists of two main regions. The first is a mountainous zone comprising the Caldeira volcano, the Serra das Fontes and the Dormida and Branca *serras*. The second is the northwest plateau, generally flat and low; it is characterised by several cinder cones and associated lava flows now weathered enough for lava-walled vineyards, pastures and arable fields to thrive.

Starting from 1,500m below sea level, the oldest emerged rocks, at around 600,000 years old, are the stacks of horizontal flows forming the base of the Serra das Fontes. The Serra Dormida and Serra Branca date from around 350,000 and 270,000 years ago respectively. These uplands are steeply scarped, probably formed by faulting.

The Caldeira volcano started to build 50,000 years ago with violent eruptions caused by water mixing with magma and creating tuff deposits of ash and rock fragments, such as at Ponta da Restinga and Carapacho. During the course of several thousand years, many powerful explosions of gas, steam, ash and pumice took place, alternating with less explosive eruptions producing lava flows or highly dangerous avalanches of hot gas and rock fragments which together built the stratovolcano – a fairly steep-sided cone of layered lava fragments and flows

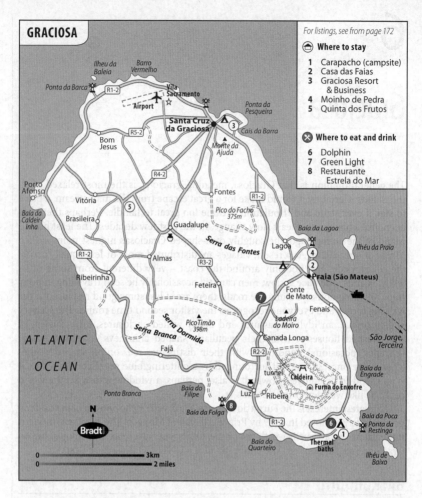

For listings, see from page 172

Where to stay
1 Carapacho (campsite)
2 Casa das Faias
3 Graciosa Resort & Business
4 Moinho de Pedra
5 Quinta dos Frutos

Where to eat and drink
6 Dolphin
7 Green Light
8 Restaurante Estrela do Mar

and other emissions. On its flanks other eruptions formed the cinder cone Ladeira do Moiro that dominates Praia and also, among others, what are now the eroded remnants of two offshore islets: the Ilhéu da Praia and Ilhéu de Baixo. The volcano's crater dates back 12,000 years and had a lava lake that might have overflowed from the shallow northwest flank and branched eastwards to the sea near Praia and west to Baía da Folga. The well-known Furna do Enxofre is a chimney or vertical vent left as the magma drained when still liquid. The associated cavern has two main fumaroles and an underground lake 22.5m below sea level.

The last eruption was 2,000 years ago, by Pico Timão at the end of the Serra Dormida. Its lava flow left a very rough broken surface known as *aa* lava (from the Hawaiian word), 4km long by 1km wide, reaching the sea and forming the Arrochela headland, just north of Praia. An earthquake damaged Praia and Luz in 1730, and the Terceira earthquake of 1980 devastated Carapacho and Luz.

HISTORY There has always been a strong relationship between Graciosa and Terceira, so it's assumed that it was sailors from Terceira who discovered the island and first encroached upon it. The leading settler, responsible for clearing tracts of vegetation, was one Vasco Gil Sodré who came originally from Montemor-o-Velho in Portugal along with his family and household retinue and established himself at Carapacho. He was not, however, given the governorship; this went to Christopher Columbus's brother-in-law. It is thought many of the first settlers came from the Beiras and Minho regions of Portugal and from Flanders.

Graciosa proved very suitable for the cultivation of cereals and vines, and well within a century of first settlement was already exporting wheat, barley, wine and brandy. These exports were first shipped to Terceira, the economic and administrative centre that also had a harbour useable by large ships. Needless to say, the wealth this generated attracted pirates, and some 13 forts were built to protect the island and its women. Grain had to be stored in hidden underground chambers. The farming of crops remained dominant for very many years, but now, apart from grapes, like the rest of the islands, beef and dairy products are the main farming outputs. Fishing has become difficult in recent years because of the decline in fish stocks, though some is still exported to Spain.

At one time the population numbered around 14,000, but emigration reduced this substantially and again there was a considerable exodus in the 1950s. At first only one member of a family was allowed to leave, but this was relaxed by 1959. Many ruined, abandoned properties can be seen in the island's interior. The population is now just under 4,400 and has stabilised somewhat. As with many of the smaller islands, there is no tertiary education, so some youngsters leave to study in São Miguel, Terceira or the Portuguese mainland and may choose to stay there to seek job opportunities.

Graciosa proudly claims visits from three historical figures. Firstly, Chateaubriand stopped over when fleeing to America from the French Revolution, afterwards to become known for his romantic novels and political writings. In 1814, the poet Almeida Garrett wrote some of his earliest poetry during his stay with an uncle on the island, and lastly the hydrographer Prince Albert I of Monaco visited in 1879, and descended the Furna do Enxofre cave at the bottom of the caldera.

GETTING THERE AND AWAY

For getting to Graciosa and away, see pages 42 and 49. Servicing a small population, Graciosa's airport dozes outside of flight arrival/departure times. The tourist information desk is only occasionally manned (⊕ 09.00–17.00 Mon–Fri, in theory), but a few leaflets are available outside. It's a 1-mile walk to Santa Cruz; a taxi will charge around €5, or €9 to Praia. Cars can be rented from **Graciosa Rent-a-Car** (☏ 295 712 274; e rent-a-cargraciosa@hotmail.com), or **Medinha & Filhos** (airport office, or Rua da Misericórdia 9, Santa Cruz; ☏ 295 712 094; m 969 996 644; e geral@ medinharent.net; w medinarent.net), who also rent scooters, motorbikes (if you have the correct licence) and off-road bicycles.

Airport information ☏ 295 730 170. Worth trying outside of Azores Airlines' office hours.

Azores Airlines ☏ 295 730 160; ⊕ 09.00–12.30 & 13.30–17.30 Mon–Fri. On a corner of the square in Santa Cruz.

GETTING AROUND

Having access to a car is the best option. Even though the island is small, the best restaurants are scattered, and shops are few and far between. If you really don't want to drive, then bus, taxi or bicycle provide the other options; if you are here simply

Graciosa   GETTING AROUND

6

to stay in one place and relax, take an island tour (see below) to familiarise yourself. Half-sized electric buses run to every village, on infrequent loop routes starting and finishing in Santa Cruz. A printed timetable is available from the tourist information office (see below), or the bus company in Rua Boa Vista, Santa Cruz (✆ 295 732 363; m 916 456 470; w pt.azoresguide.net/servicos/empresa-de-transportes-colectivos-da-ilha-graciosa), and fares are nominal. You could make the outward journey by bus from Santa Cruz to your chosen destination, and return by taxi. Taxis are available in Santa Cruz, Luz, and Praia, and any bar will telephone for one, though there is no central number. The distances are not great and therefore taking a taxi is hardly expensive. Taking you to the caldera, waiting for you to visit the Furna do Enxofre and bringing you back will cost around €20 in a taxi from Santa Cruz, and hiring a taxi for 3–4 hours should set you back €60. Some accommodations have bikes for rent, otherwise you can get hybrid bikes from car-hire firm Medinha & Filhos (page 171) or Calypso (page 177).

ISLAND TOURS Any taxi will take you around the island, or to the start point of the walks. **Taxis Quadros Ilha Graciosa** (m 963 817 766; e taxisquadros.grw@gmail.com) is a good family firm, and English-speaking **Marta Quadros** (m 967 677 445; e marta.quadros@yahoo.com) may be available for an island tour.

TOURIST INFORMATION

There is an information kiosk, staffed sporadically, tucked away with the car-hire companies inside the airport. In Santa Cruz, the official tourist office, with English speakers, is close to the main square (Rua D João IV 28; ✆ 295 712 430; ⊕ 08.00–19.00 Tue–Fri, 11.00–18.00 Sat), and in the square itself you will find an information kiosk (Largo Dr João Pereira; ⊕ Jul & Aug 09.00–noon daily), though the staff there may not speak English and the service is not as slick. They also sell a limited range of souvenirs.

 ## WHERE TO STAY *Map, page 170*

There is one large hotel, just out of Santa Cruz, plus a few smaller options in town and elsewhere around the island. A movement to renovate and convert old family properties has seen the out-of-town options increase in recent years, and if you've ever wanted to stay in a windmill, Graciosa can oblige.

Apart from the Carapacho campsite, listed opposite, there are other seasonal campsites at Pinheiro (up the hill behind Praia; ✆ 295 712 125; m 913 439 312) and at Santa Cruz (✆ 295 730 040), on the coast road between the town and the Graciosa Resort Hotel.

SANTA CRUZ

Graciosa Resort & Business Hotel (46 rooms, 6 villas with rooftop patios) Porta da Barra; ✆ 295 730 500; w hoteis.inatel.pt. Overlooking the pretty bay of Cais da Barra & surrounded by old vineyards, in part incorporated into the hotel grounds. Ask for a sea-view room. Restaurant, small gym, sauna, decent-sized pool (seasonal), sat TV & buffet b/fast. €€€

Hotel Santa Cruz (16 rooms) Largo Barão de Guadalupe; ✆ 295 712 345; w santacruzhotel.pt. The most central option, neat but old fashioned. All with private bath, some with AC/heating, b/fast inc. Also sgls & a trpl. Open all year. €€
Residencial Ilha Graciosa (15 rooms) Av Mouzinho de Albuquerque 49; ✆ 295 730 220; e gracitur@gmail.com. Just 5 mins' walk from town, a simple but well-restored town house with lounge & bar with a lovely old basalt wine press.

Also boasting wooden floors & shutters, this is not an option if you value modernity. A triumph of character over style, the pinnacle of quirk. There is a small garden courtyard. €€

✳ **Boa Nova Hostel** (4 dbls, male & female dorms) Largo da Calheta 16; ☎ 295 712 027; m 926 627 541; w boanovahostel.com. Excellent boutique hostel (with largely white décor offset by black basalt toilet roll holders & the like) just north of the town centre. Attractive common area & kitchen; b/fast & bikes available. €

PRAIA

Casa das Faias (6 rooms) Rua Infante D Henrique 10; ☎ 295 732 766; e casadasfaias@sapo.pt. A highly rated place, 100m from the marina, 200m from the beach. Rooms in beautiful modern style with TV. Roof conservatory, with views to the sea & Serra Branca. Pool table & table football to help pass the evenings. Convenient if you are arriving by boat. €€€

Moinho de Pedra (4 apartments) Rua Moinhos de Vento 28; ☎ 295 712 501; m 917 403 791; e azorianwindmill@gmail.com; w moinhodepedra.

pt. S/c, a typical island windmill, tastefully renovated, overlooking the sea, 200m from the beach. Can accommodate up to 4 people. €€€

ELSEWHERE AROUND THE ISLAND

Quinta dos Frutos (4 rooms) Carreira Aberta 10, near the village of Vitória, 500m from Guadalupe; ☎ 295 712 557; m 916 950 199; e quintadosfrutos@sapo.pt, w casasacorianas. com. Traditional basalt farm buildings set in a large orchard, charming owners. Bicycle available. Sometimes 2-night min stay in high season. S/c & BBQ. Laundry service available. €€

CAMPING

Carapacho ☎ 295 712 959; ⏲ Jun–Sep. A lovely, basic small site on 3 levels with sea views & sheltered by trees, overlooking the Ilhéu de Baixo. Showers, toilets, electricity, stone BBQs. If unattended, you'll have to go to the post office building in Luz village to make enquiries. Carapacho Spa, the sea swimming pool & the Dolphin restaurant are all nearby, but the nearest shop is in Luz. A pitch for a small tent is a paltry €3 per night! €

✕ WHERE TO EAT AND DRINK

The Graciosa Resort and Business Hotel on the edge of Santa Cruz has a restaurant; otherwise many of the better restaurants are out of town. However, a taxi to and from each is not expensive and takes only minutes. Fish is excellent although fresh, crisply cooked vegetables seem a rarity on this island. Residents like to get out at weekends in summer, so the restaurants can be busy. Many of the places here are open early for café service; the times given are kitchen hours.

SANTA CRUZ

Amunì Green Bar Praça Fontes Pereira de Melo; m 963 772 476; e amuni.graciosa@gmail.com; ⏲ 11.00–15.00 Tue–Sat, daily plus some eves in summer. Friendly Italian-run kiosk offering vegetarian & vegan food (quiches, pasta, burgers, salads), also to take away for later. €€

Jale Rua 25 da Abril 60; ☎ 295 712 344; ⏲ noon–15.00 & 19.00–22.00 daily. A basic place with old-fashioned dining room, bar & back room for playing pool. Food is average, prices reasonable. €€

Grafil Largo Conde de Simas 4; ⏲ early till late daily. Opposite the line of taxis, across the road from the câmara municipal (town hall), in the main square, this virtually unsigned café is thoroughly modern & a good place for that unhealthy b/fast pastry & excellent coffee. No meal service. €

Snack Bar Santa Cruz Rua da Boa Vista 3; ⏲ noon–15.00 & 19.00–22.00 Mon–Sat. Specialities are *frango no churrasco* (a kind of barbecued chicken) & *alcatra peixe e carne* (a very slow-cooked stew of fish and meat). A tiny place, with a few tables (and more outside) & good prices. €

BAÍA DA FOLGA

Restaurante Estrela do Mar [map, page 170] Folga; ☎ 295 712 560; m 960 123 251; f estreladomar.graciosa; ⏲ noon–15.00 & 19.00–22.00 daily. Very simple small restaurant near the harbour. A few outside tables, but you might prefer the interior on a windy day. Good fish selection, though you need to order in advance for the fish stew. On summer w/ends, booking advisable. A good place to watch the waves, with São Jorge & Faial visible on clear days. €€

FONTE DO MATO

Green Light [map, page 170] Canada dos Ramos, Fonte do Mato; m 967 112 655. Take the road from Praia towards Luz, then fork right when the road splits; it's then signposted after 100m. In a delightful rural setting, the chef barbecues up great fresh fish & generous meat dishes; the food is usually excellent & good value, if you take the dish of the day. €€

PRAIA

Café O Ilhéu Rua Fontes Pereira de Melo 138; ☎295 732 146; ⊕ 06.00–23.00 daily. With the same owner as the Queijadas de Graciosa factory, this is the best place to sample the island's own delicious pastries. For more substantial food, try the Vintage Snack Bar next door. €

CARAPACHO

Dolphin [map, page 170] Just above the campsite; ☎295 712 014; ⊕ 10.00–22.00 Tue–Sun. Modern, simple & good, both the restaurant & an open terrace enjoy a great sea view. Fish always very fresh, but plenty of steak & other meat choices, including hamburgers. Very busy on summer w/ends. Lunchtime specials are excellent value here. Island wine is €2/litre! €€

NIGHTLIFE

There is very little nightlife, especially outside Santa Cruz. On summer evenings many islanders gather in the spacious centre of town to stroll and talk until after midnight. There are several bars, some of which have small discos – identified by their music. Near the airport is a discotheque-pub, the **Vila Sacramento,** open on Saturday nights (€5); the real action starts at midnight, and it stays open until 06.00. At the other end of the scale, a constant pleasure comes from just sitting on a wall above the harbour and listening to the sea, especially if there is moonlight.

SHOPPING

A fairly recent initiative has introduced several kiosks into Santa Cruz's main square, selling Graciosa wines, lacework made by local women and other items. The best time to catch them open is on weekday mornings. The tourist office kiosk itself sells some good leaflets – on whaling, for example – plus other souvenirs of a tasteful nature. Graciosa cheese is another island speciality, quite strong for some tastes. *Queijadas da Graciosa*, small cakes, are rather like a treacle tart mix in a crisp, thin pastry cup and are delicious with an espresso coffee. Made of flour, sugar, eggs, milk, butter and *canela e sal* (cinnamon and salt), they make a fantastic energy source when descending calderas. The little factory making them is in Praia and visitors are welcome, though there is no factory tour. The best place to sample *queijadas da Graciosa* is at the Café O Ilhéu in Praia (see above), which is under the same ownership, but you will stumble across them in other cafés and shops.

OTHER PRACTICALITIES

Free municipal **Wi-Fi** is available in Santa Cruz's main square and by the beach toilets in Praia. Some cafés, including the Grafil (page 173), also provide free Wi-Fi.

Health centre (Centro de Saúde) Rua Dr Vasco Rodrigues; ☎295 730 070. 24hr A&E, but serious cases are helicoptered to Terceira or São Miguel.

Police Rua Boa Vista, Santa Cruz; ☎295 730 200
Post office Av Mouzinha Albuquerque, Santa Cruz; Rua Rodrigues Sampaia, Praia

THE CALDERA AND FURNA DO ENXOFRE VISITOR CENTRE (☏ 295 714 009;
w parquesnaturais.azores.gov.pt/en/parques/8/areasprotegidas/89; ⊕ Nov–Mar 09.00–17.00 Tue–Sat & hols, Apr–Oct 09.00–17.00 daily; €5/2/free adults/under 15s & seniors/under 7s; family tickets €10; guided tours available Oct–Apr 14.30 & 15.30, May–Sep 11.30, 15.00 & 16.30; may be closed in poor weather) The visitor centre provides information about the volcanology of Graciosa, especially the caldera and cavern, and generally about the Biosphere Reserve classification. The centre staff also survey the interior through CCTV cameras.

As you enter the caldera through a road tunnel, built in 1953, a dramatic landscape confronts you. Small meadows are grazed by cows and all around cryptomeria forest climbs the steeply enclosing slopes towards the sky. The road soon forks, to the left down to a picnic site, to the right down to the visitor centre and the Furna do Enxofre. Please note the gas emissions are closely monitored and sometimes it may be too dangerous for visits; this is more likely in summer when the air may circulate less well. Unfortunately, there is no way of knowing this until you get there.

In summer, it is said by some that the best time to visit is between 11.00 and 14.00 when sunlight enters. Descend a concrete spiral staircase of 184 steps to the cave floor, stopping perhaps at one or two of the six 'windows' to admire the view. Opened in 1939, the staircase was a great improvement over the rope ladder used on the first descent by Prince Albert I of Monaco 60 years earlier. It seems that it was built to enable farmers to get water for their animals. The narrow opening allows a few ferns and mosses to grow. A short way into the cave is a small gently bubbling mud pool, sounding rather sinister in the darkness. The ropes preventing further descent into the cavern result from the deaths, some years ago, of two visiting sailors who were overcome by an unexpected emission of sulphurous fumes deeper inside the cave. There is a lake, and at one time a rowing boat enabled further exploration when the lake was 130m across and 15m deep. In recent years the lake has gone down to a depth of 11m, though it varies with rainfall, and there is speculation there may be an underground connection with the thermal area of Carapacho. The floor of the lake is below sea level.

After leaving the cavern, a day can be spent very happily exploring and enjoying the peace of the caldera, or taking the walk described on page 179.

MUSEUMS
Museu da Graciosa (Largo Conde de Simas 17, Santa Cruz; ☏ 295 712 429; **w** museu-graciosa.azores.gov.pt; ⊕ Apr–Sep 10.00–17.30 Tue–Sun & hols, Oct–Mar 09.30–17.00 Tue–Sun; €1/0.50 adult/under 14s, students & over 65s) Established in 1977 in a late 19th-century barn used for storing corn and making wine, a modern extension was added in 2010. Here you will find a furnished family room, various antiques and paintings, the tools of several important trades and all the gear to make wine in the old way, plus information on geology and agriculture. Information panels carry translations into English. Perhaps most impressive is the section devoted to carnivals, with bright costumes and some videos of the dancing that takes place during the island's big party. You can also see some examples of the island's renowned guitars, with distinctive heart-shaped holes in the body. In an annexe on the seafront signed *Barracão das canoas* there is a whaling boat and exhibits to do with whaling. This is often closed in winter, due to the weather: ask at the main museum reception. Because this is so simply done and in a shed

by the harbour you get the feeling that if a rocket were to be fired a crew would come rushing down to launch the boat. If you want to visit the restored windmill at Fontes, a short drive from Santa Cruz and standing resplendent in the landscape with its white base and bright-red cupola, access is also by request at the main museum. Windmills appeared here in the 17th century, but most were of the larger Nordic type introduced in the 19th century.

Museu da Vida Rural da Ilha Graciosa (Caminho de Cima 97, Luz; ✆ 295 732 787; ◷ 10.00–noon & 14.00–16.00 Mon–Fri; €1. It's better to ring in advance to ensure it's open; enquiries can also be made through the main museum, ✆ 295 712 429) A restored house opened in 2015, with original furniture left in situ, plus a separate building with old photos. In an outbuilding, there is an old oxcart. There is no English-language information, as yet.

Reservatorio do Atalho (Town water tank) (Rua da Boa Vista, Santa Cruz; ◷ May–Sep 10.00–12.00 daily, or call ✆ 295 730 040; admission free) Full of water until around 20 years ago, this 1,800m² capacity water tank is now drained – and open to visitors! It is over 150 years old; with amazing acoustics, it is tempting the municipality to make it available as a venue for concerts. A guided tour is available, and is surprisingly interesting, given that you are standing in an empty tank. There is no archive material documenting the history of the tank, so the information for the guided tour has been constructed from word-of-mouth testimony passed down by locals.

Loja Museu João Tomaz Bettencourt (Caminho da Igreja 3, Guadalupe; m 916 522 483; ◷ 08.00–noon & 13.00–16.00 Mon–Fri; it may be possible to arrange a w/ end visit; admission free) A small and fairly new museum, this is set out as the village shop, a few kilometres from Santa Cruz. Very genuine looking, it is tempting to want to buy one of the period hats or coats behind the counter. A sign claims there's a sale on – but the museum curator will earnestly inform you that it ended in 1960!

BIRDS AND FLOWERS With little high ground and almost everywhere farmed, not many naturalists have studied the island thus far. The avian jewel in the crown is the Monteiro's storm petrel (*Oceanodroma monteiroi*), which is endemic to Graciosa and of which there are only 200 specimens on Graciosa's two islets.

The basalt islet of **Ilhéu da Praia**, little more than 1km out from Praia, is a Special Protected Area of 11ha and is said to have one of the richest and most diverse concentrations of seabirds in the Azores with many migratory species. Breeding colonies have declined through human disturbance so while it is nice to know they are there, it is best they are left in peace. However, from the harbour quay or nearby coast it is easy to observe the action with a good telescope. Another possibility, in the far southeast, is the Special Protected Area of the **Ilhéu de Baixo** and adjacent rocky shoreline.

Disappointed wildflower enthusiasts will just have to resort to 'applied botany' – the study of the grape vine and its products.

SPORTS AND ACTIVITIES Built in the early 20th century, the *Estefânia Gorreia* played a key part in Graciosa's economy during the whaling period (until 1974) when it supported the small boats, towing the whales back to shore. At Porto, by the Clube Naval and yacht harbour, you can usually see this boat on the slipway in winter, and next to it the trying area. The large buildings nearby are all to do with whaling.

The boat also played an important role in emergencies, taking people to the hospital in Terceira before the time of the air services. Beautifully restored, it nowadays takes the island's rowing team to other islands to compete, towing their vessel behind. Very occasionally, it makes trips round the island; check at the Clube Naval or the tourist office for further details.

More regular opportunities for boat trips, kayaking, dolphin watching, fishing and diving are provided by the companies listed here.

Adventure trips

Nautigraciosa – DivinGraciosa Rua Corpo Santo 11, Cais da Calheta, Santa Cruz; ✆295 732 811; m 962 513 41; e geral@divingraciosa.com; w divingraciosa.com; ⏲ May–Oct 08.00–19.00 daily. Based in the Santa Cruz harbour but with a 2nd, bigger boat in Praia. Diving & diving with sharks. Also boat trips, kayak rental, big-game fishing & sea-based birdwatching trips. Some English spoken.

Biking

No-one as yet is doing guided bike excursions, but you can rent bikes from Medinha & Filhos (page 171) or Calypso (see below) if you want to devise your own circuit.

Fishing

Calypso Rua Rodrigues Sampaio 10, Praia; ✆295 732 892; m 919 103 414; e info@calypsoazores. com; w calypsoazores.com; ⏲ winter 09.00–12.30 & 13.30–17.00 Mon–Fri, 09.00–noon & 13.00–17.00 Sat, summer 09.00–18.00 Mon–Fri, 09.00–17.00 Sat. Based in Praia, organises sport fishing, as well as birdwatching, snorkelling, kayak hire & boat trips, including inter-island cruises. English spoken.

Spa

Carapacho Spa (Termas do Carapacho) Rua Dr Manuel de Menezes; ✆295 714 212;

⏲ 10.30–19.00 Tue–Sun, all year; €3/6/40 indoor pool/hydromassage bath/full massage. At the island's southeastern tip, this dates back to 1750. It has recently been renovated & as well as its modestly sized indoor hot swimming pool, it now once more offers massage, Vichy shower, whirlpool bath & medical consulting. Nearby is the natural rock pool & it is altogether a very popular place to relax in summer.

Swimming

Santa Cruz There's a tiny pool in front of the harbour & another just west on Rua Pedro Roberto da Silva, plus the seasonal municipal open-air pool beside the Rua Corpo Santo on the way to the airport.

Barro Vermelho There is a natural, partially enclosed rock pool at Barro Vermelho, less than 2km north of Santa Cruz, with showers & changing facilities (Jun–Oct, lifeguard 11.00–19.00 daily), as well as picnic tables & BBQs; the area is backed with tamarisk trees which makes it more attractive.

Praia Graciosa's only beach – small, with grey sand – & very popular, although the sand can sometimes disappear after a winter storm. There are changing rooms & showers, & a counter selling ice creams etc; across the road are a couple of café/bar/restaurants.

Carapacho Carapacho has good access to protected sea swimming, in a walled-off pool.

WALKS ON GRACIOSA

There are now five official trails on Graciosa, four of which are summarised on page 179. There's also a new Grande Rota da Graciosa (Great Route of Graciosa), which runs to 40km (easy, 15hrs) and should be attempted over two days. The trail guides and maps for all these routes are usually available, free of charge, at the tourist offices and also at some of the hotels. Route maps and narrative may also be printed off from the hiking/trails section of the Visit Azores website (w visitazores.com). Remember that the times and distances given for the three

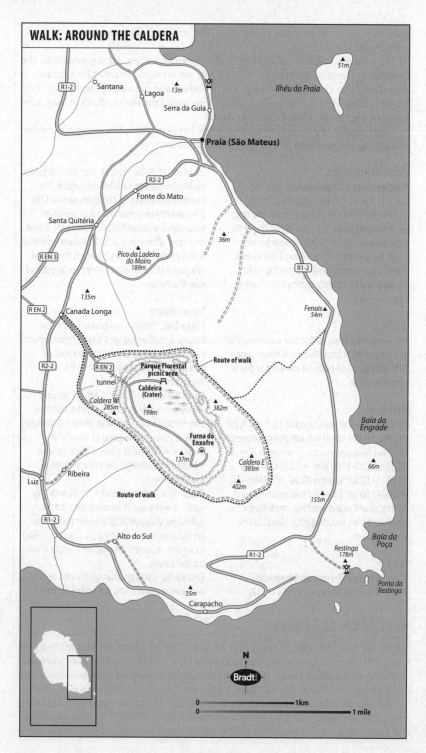

WALK: AROUND THE CALDERA

Santana

R1-2

Lagoa

▲ 13m

Serra da Guia

Praia (São Mateus)

Ilhéu da Praia

▲ 51m

R2-2

Fonte do Mato

Santa Quitéria

R EN 3

Pico da Ladeira do Moiro
189m

▲ 36m

R1-2

▲ 135m

R EN 2

Canada Longa

Fenais ▲
54m

R2-2

R EN 2

Parque Florestal picnic area

Route of walk

tunnel

Caldeira (Crater)
199m

Caldera W
285m

▲ 382m

Furna do Enxofre

Baía da Engrade

▲ 137m

Caldera E
393m

▲ 66m

Ribeira

Luz

▲ 402m

▲ 155m

Route of walk

R1-2

Baía da Poça

Alto do Sul

R1-2

Restinga
178m

Ponta da Restinga

▲ 35m

Carapacho

N

Bradt

0 ——————— 1km
0 ——————————— 1 mile

linear walks should be doubled if you are returning; otherwise, take a taxi to the trailhead or arrange a pick-up at the route's end.

VOLTA À CALDEIRA (AROUND THE CALDERA) AND FURNA DO ENXOFRE (Easy, 10.8km, 3hrs; see map, opposite) A torch is recommended. Take a picnic and you can happily spend most of the day exploring this route. If you have no car, a taxi from Santa Cruz into the caldera and down to the entrance to the cavern is the easiest way to start this walk. From the visitor centre (page 175), walk back up the road and through the tunnel, and down the road to take the first turning off on the left (with red-and-yellow waymarking, though the colours change at points along the route). This gives access to the intermittently tarmacked road that runs round the outside of the caldera. After a few hundred metres, take a very sharp left turn to follow the route in a clockwise direction. After 100m, take a diversion up some rough steps to your right, signposted Furna Maria Encantada; this is a lava tube some 60m long and was probably formed when the lava lake inside the caldera reached its highest point. After visiting it, descend the steps and continue clockwise as before.

If you are feeling lazy, you can simply drive the route round the exterior of the caldera. Whether walking or driving, be sure to stop to enjoy the views over the coast and later on, over to São Jorge and Terceira.

In addition to the Grande Rota (Great Route), the official routes are these:

SERRA BRANCA–PRAIA (Easy, 8.7km, 2¾hrs) A walk that descends gradually, crossing most of Graciosa from west to east, with good views across the island.

BAÍA DA FOLGA (Easy, 2km, 1hr) A linear walk starting in Luz village, following the regional road then descending to the coast at the Baía da Folga where a swim is possible in good weather. It also offers views over to Pico and Faial.

SUBIDA AO CUME (Hard, 9.7km, 3½hrs) A circular route from Luz, climbing to the rim of the caldera and down to the Furna do Enxofre visitor centre, then via the Reserva Florestal picnic site and up on a switchbacking path to reach the rim again. From here the path follows the rim all the way around the eastern and southern sides of the caldera (a little higher than the path used by the Grande Rota) before dropping down to Luz again.

DAS VINHAS AO MAR (Medium, 6.6km, 2½hrs) Starting from Bom Jesus, this route takes a loop through typical small vineyards before heading north to reach the coast at the Ponta da Barca lighthouse. From here it follows the coast east through the geosite to end at the Barro Vermelho picnic site, north of the airport.

TOURING THE ISLAND

FULL-DAY DRIVING TOUR Whether driving or in a taxi, a day tour should take in the caldera and Furna do Enxofre, the view of Santa Cruz from **Monte da Ajuda**, Praia with its windmills and beach, the lighthouse at **Ponta da Restinga**, Carapacho and the Serra Branca. In the northwest, you can then also take a short side trip down to Porta Afonso (the track is often too rutted for cars and you may have to walk). Here the sea churns and boils, and an offshore wind skims the tops of the waves in spectacular fashion, making for some great video footage. The lighthouse at Farol da Ponta da Barça, with its whale-like rock formation and a geosite, might be your final stop before returning to Santa Cruz. As an alternative, and if you like to swim, you could undertake an itinerary which includes a longer stop at Carapacho, taking a dip in the sea or the hot baths. As soon as you arrive there, book your lunch at the Dolphin restaurant (page 174), then have a swim and a shower before lunch. After your meal, continue the tour clockwise around the island, visiting the places listed on page 179, before returning to Santa Cruz in the early evening. If you don't want to swim, then take your midday break at Folga and enjoy exploring the tiny harbour and its surrounds and isolation, maybe incorporating the official trail, before returning to base.

If you are on the island for a few days, you might want to visit the Furna do Enxofre (page 175) as a separate trip, perhaps combining it with a walk (page 179), rather than trying to cram it into a day tour. After all, there is no rush on the island of Graciosa.

SANTA CRUZ DA GRACIOSA The town focuses on the spacious main square of cobbles laid beneath large *Metrosideros* trees, elms and araucarias, and two large water reservoirs, originally used for watering cattle, accessed by a sloping cobbled road. The water is brackish, and the level depends on the state of the tide. There are several understated small bars and cafés nearby, and some shops. The shops are rather scattered and are not always obvious, which is inconvenient if you need something in a hurry, but make a most charming and welcome contrast to the ubiquitous commercial units emblazoned with neon. The taxi rank is in the square, with telephones each housed in a little model windmill. Roads leading off are often lined with grand townhouses and domestic buildings with interesting wrought-iron balconies and other architectural detail. The larger of the two churches just south of the centre is the Matriz or **parish church**, built in the 16th century and enlarged in the 18th, with the addition of excellent azulejo panels on the side altars. The main altar is a masterpiece of 16th-century painting on wood.

The tiny harbour with its simple quay and a semi-natural swimming pool has some charm; above is a narrow, cobbled street and pairs of seats in the wall. It is on a small and intimate scale. Further north is the modern Cais or quay, built in the 1960s. In winter, the harbour will be devoid of boats: it doesn't take much of a swell for the water to spill over the quay, so caution is advised. On the hill above, the **Monte da Ajuda**, are three chapels: São João, São Salvador and Nossa Senhora da Ajuda, sometimes floodlit at night. The last can be likened to a castle; it is 16th century and has 18th-century azulejos. All three chapels are usually closed, but sometimes, if anyone is around to ask, a key may be found. (Your best bet is the priest, who lives to the right of the town's main church.) There is a surfaced road to the top where a splendid view can be had of the whole town. A little below the chapels, a tiny crater contains a small bullring, used during festivities in August; a stepped path leads down and continues into town.

From the town square, if you take the coastal road south to Praia, Rua Infante Dom Henrique, and walk for about 10 minutes, you will pass the island's dairy co-operative. On the same road is the **Associacão de Artesãos da Ilha Graciosa** (Artisans' Association of Graciosa Island); you will see a silver nameplate on the building, though they now have a sales kiosk in the town square. The entrance is towards the end of the side passage. Here you will find the women working, and a display of their completed work and items for sale. It is open weekdays during normal business hours.

Take the turning to the left down to the old harbour, the **Porto da Barra**, just near the **Graciosa Resort Hotel**. It is a pretty bay with a new yacht harbour, used mainly in summer. Here you will find the Clube Naval building and maybe refreshments. You will soon realise this is on the site of an old fort, **Forte de Santa Catarina**, which dates from the period before 1800, and there are old rusty cannons still threatening the ghosts of long-dead pirates. Peer over the wall and in the black lava you will discern an old ramp where whales were once hauled ashore. On the headland beyond (reached by the farm track along the coast) are the remains of a large building and defensive walls, which the sea is slowly undermining. This was once a Jewish settlement, the **Forte Deis Judeus**, and there is a tiny cemetery in black basalt engraved 'Cemitério Judaico' nearby. This coastal stroll makes for a good after-dinner perambulation for those staying at the Graciosa Resort Hotel. For those who are not, the stroll back along the asphalt road following the coast is a pleasant return walk into town.

PRAIA Also known as São Mateus, Praia is a fishing and ferry port with a high sea wall (necessary in the wilds of winter), and an arched gateway leading from the beach through the wall into a long, arcing street. The houses are small and pretty, some a bit weather-beaten. The usual cobbled square is in the road behind, at the **Church of São Mateus**, rebuilt in the 19th century; inside there are Flemish images of St Matthew and St Peter and a *pietà*, all 16th century. The beach itself is of grey sand and very popular, with two cafés and other amenities nearby. Immediately to the north is the modern **Negra Quay**, the island's main port and where the inter-island ferry comes in during the summer. A little further on and there is a trio of picturesque windmills, of which a couple are now converted into accommodation options.

ILHEU DA BALEIA If you walk out of Santa Cruz along the north coast you first pass what was once the main vine-growing area and a stretch of coastline that is a popular bathing area among the rocks near the few houses of **Barro Vermelho**.

FESTIVALS ON GRACIOSA

In August, the weekends start early and finish late, with an extended party to celebrate each of the saints' days which come thick and fast. In particular, the **Festival of Santo Cristo** is celebrated with boat races, *touradas* (bullfights) and cultural and musical happenings. Santa Cruz really decorates itself for the celebration, and becomes uncharacteristically busy (by its own standards) with visitors from the other islands as well as returning North American emigrants. One feature of the more raucous events is that various associations – musical, sporting or other – dance until they drop, then take photos of their 'survivors', namely the members who last the pace. The one with the most 'survivors' in their photo is the unofficial winner, and owner of the bragging rights!

When the **Espírito Santo** or **Holy Ghost** celebration takes place seven weeks after Easter, one can enjoy participating in the island's hospitality, taking the special bread and local wine. This occurs widely over the island, but especially in Santa Cruz, Luz, Guadalupe and Praia (São Mateus). **Carnaval** starts to build as early as January, reaching a crescendo, a riot of colour and costumes, in February or early March. On 24 May, there is a **procession** from Guadalupe to Monte da Ajuda and back, to pray for the prevention of future earthquakes.

Beyond this you come to **Ponta da Barca**, with its lighthouse, about 5km from town. Close to the shore is a rocky islet, Ilheu da Baleia, that looks, without much imagination, like a whale, hence its name; there may be some seabirds as well. Unless you have a car, you have to walk along the road to get there, but there is little traffic; in summer the best time to do this is in the cool of the evening.

VIEW OF THE OTHER ISLANDS

The west coast road is very quiet between Luz and Ribeirinha, with a big climb over the Serra Branca; there's a good miradouro at the top of the climb, which gives the best and most readily accessible view of the other Central Group islands. Pico, São Jorge, Faial and Terceira can all be seen on a clear day. Other great views can be had from the walk around the exterior of the caldera.

7

São Jorge

Town of Velas so beautiful
Leaning on the sea side
More beautiful I have yet to see
Not kissed by the moonlight

Oh, island of infinite grace
Far away from you, thinking with
    obsessive thoughts
My longing has no end

In my beating heart
The days: eternity
In the heart separation…
being more 'cold' in the friendship,

is more 'warm' the absence to
    be alone…
when the sweetest is the missing
the heart is more crucified.

Anselmo da Silveira, Angra, November 1949.
On an azulejo in the town garden, Velas.

An islander used to greet visitors with 'Welcome to São Jorge, my island with around 9,000 people and over 20,000 cattle'. Known widely beyond its shores for its delicious, strong, Cheddar-like cheese, the other attributes of this long, cigar-shaped island are far less recognised. To some, São Jorge is an island of mystery, sometimes disappearing into cloud or mist. Arriving at the Velas quay, the imposing sea gateway and walls dating from the time of pirates promise quiet pleasure. Velas town itself features narrow streets, small shops, an impressive church, some manor houses, a little square or two and the sound of voices drifting out from tiny bars.

Elsewhere, there is an intense pleasure to be derived from walking along little-used farm roads in utter silence with stone walls, hedgerows, cows and occasional trees giving depth to the stage. In sunshine and with a deep-blue sea beyond, the cliff paths are magnificent for scenery, combining landscape grandeur and intimate vignettes together with unexpected human interest, while steep descents to isolated fajãs on tiny tracks give a tender appreciation of the hardships of the islanders.

Although it is an island with good walks, graded unsurfaced roads have in recent years ramified throughout the island and in reasonable weather allow the motorist to explore many of the previously hidden beauties of the island. Many very happy days can be had exploring its back roads as well as the little-trafficked main roads from which side roads lead into small, often charming villages.

On a full moon the island comes into its own; the channel across to Pico island reflects and shimmers, while the great black unequal-sided triangle of Pico mountain massively provides the theatre setting. In Velas, drop down to the harbour, and on the tiny terrace, if you are lucky, thrill to the haunting mew of Cory's shearwaters as they fly just above your head in the dark.

By car, São Jorge is an island on which to spend slow days relaxing, stopping to explore the accessible little settlements along the coast – or walking to the more isolated ones – and pausing to enjoy the scenery. On the southern coast, it

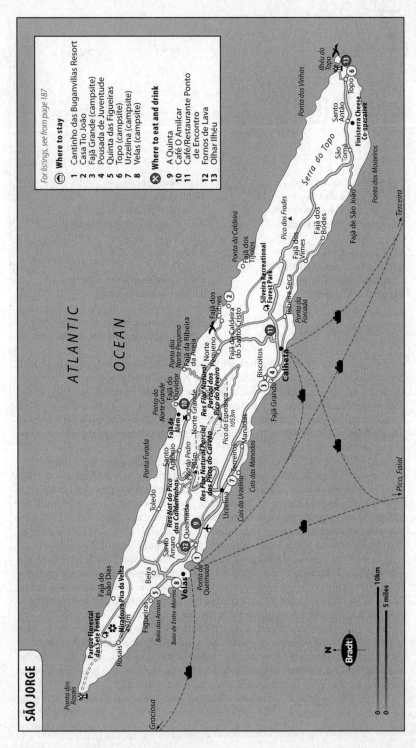

SÃO JORGE

ATLANTIC OCEAN

Ilhéu do Topo

Ponta dos Vinhas

Serra do Topo

Santo Antão

São Tomé

Topo 6

Finisterra Cheese Co-operative 13

Ponta da Caldeira

Pico dos Frades

Fajã de São João

Fajã dos Bodes

Fajã dos Vimes

Silveira Recreational Forest Park

Ponta da Forcada

Ribeira Seca

Fajã dos Cubres 2

Ponta dos Tijolos

Fajã da Caldeira do Santo Cristo

Fajã da Ribeira da Areja

Ponta do Norte Pequeno

Fajã do Ouvidor

Ponta do Norte Grande

Biscoitos

Calheta 4

Fajã Grande 3

11

Fajã de Além 10

Santo Antón'o

Norte Grande

Ricardo Pedro

Res Flor Natural Parcial dos Picos do Cavão

Res Flor Natural Parcial Pico do Areeiro

Norte Pequeno

Pico da Esperança 1053m

Terreiros

Manadas

Cais das Manadas

Urzelina 7

Cais da Urzelina

Res Nat do Pico das Caldeirinhas

Santo Amaro

9

Queimada

12

Ponta Furada

Toledo

Beira

Fajã do João Dias

Figueiras

Quinta das Figueiras 5

Rosais

Parque Florestal das Sete Fontes

Miradouro Pico da Velha 993m

Baía das Arraias

Velas 8

Ponta da Queimada 1

Baía de Entre-Morros

Ponta dos Rosais

Graciosa

Pico, Faial

Terceira

Ponta dos Mosteiros

N

Bradt

0   10km
0   5 miles

can be difficult to tear your eyes away from the imposing pinnacle of Pico. The fajãs, while not unique to São Jorge, are a very special feature of this island. Now classified as a UNESCO Biosphere Reserve, their microclimates and settlements are most rewarding to explore – some are only accessible on foot. There are numerous viewpoints, the two ports of Velas and Calheta, lovely sites for picnics, and opportunities to make easy short walks – there are plenty to take you to lovely places. One can also take the ferry and visit Pico and Faial islands, the other two islands that make up the so-called *triangulo*.

BACKGROUND

GEOLOGY Cigar-shaped São Jorge is 56km long but only 8km at its widest. A long ridge running its length characterises the island, arising abruptly from the sea and ascending to Pico da Esperança (1,053m) at about the centre. The average height of this central ridge is 700m. The coasts are very steep, in places over 400m and almost vertical, particularly on the north side. Much of the land surface is above 300m and villages are at much higher altitudes than anywhere else in the Azores.

Unlike all the other Azores islands, São Jorge originated from fissures, cracks or faults so deep in the earth's crust that magma rises to the surface. From these, lava usually erupts with little or no gaseous explosions and so mostly produces lava flows; however, they can also erupt explosively, forming cinder cones. There are no stratovolcanoes like on Pico or on Faial, nor are there any big calderas or craters. Initially, though, these fissural eruptions, some 1,000m down on the sea floor, would have been very explosive as the hot magma met the seawater, but as the island built up above the sea, the thermal shocks ceased.

The island has a northwest–southeast orientation, reflecting the regional plate tectonics and fault lines. Two areas make up the island, separated by the Ribeira Seca fault line cutting obliquely across the middle; wearing deeply into this fracture, largely covered with recent volcanic emissions, is the Ribeira Seca creek, just east of Calheta.

The Topo complex is the island's oldest, at least 600,000 years old, but the relief of this eastern side is more difficult to interpret and it is harder to identify the volcanic features and lava flows because it is so eroded. The younger areas to the west of the Ribeira Seca fault mirror the same eruption style of Topo: lava flows and explosive eruptions, leaving cinder cones. The wide spine of the central and western region comprises the Manadas and Rosais complexes, at around 24,000 and 30,000 years old respectively. From fissures lava welled out and piled up to thicknesses of over 500m, burying older cinder cones under newer flows. The glorious walk or drive along the island's spine passes the cones of the youngest eruptions from just a few thousand years ago.

The sheer cliffs of the coast are probably due to faulting. The island's fajãs are caused in two ways: detritus fajãs are gravity deposits produced by landslides caused by erosion of the base of the cliff such as Fajã dos Cubres, while lava fajãs are created by lava flowing over the cliffs into the sea making a platform, as with Fajã do Ouvidor. São Jorge has over 70 in total, the majority on the north coast, but many were abandoned following the 1980 earthquake and now only the larger and safer ones are inhabited. They are much valued for their microclimate and the cultivation of vegetables and fruit.

During historical times there have been several volcanic eruptions, the first in 1580, east of Velas, whose lava flows formed the Ponta da Queimada. It also emitted hot gas and ash that spread quickly close to the ground, burning those unfortunate enough to be caught, and killing many cattle. In 1808 came the infamous eruptions at Urzelina that continued for six weeks, with 13 large cinder cones exploding over several days together with lava flows. This was followed by avalanches of hot gas and stones that extended over Urzelina as a dense black cloud. Terrified villagers cowering in the church were protected, but endured the sound of falling debris on the roof. Not long after came a lava flow half-burying the church, whose tower can still be seen in the village today. The survivors said they had seen a vision of hell.

HISTORY Topo, at the island's eastern extremity, was settled from 1439, but there was little development until the arrival in 1470 of a Flemish nobleman, Willem van der Haegen (known in Portuguese as Guilherme da Silveira) – he had first been made Captain of Flores, but this was so remote no-one wanted to settle there and he asked the king if instead he could have São Jorge. Velas was founded around the middle of the 15th century and within 50 years developed sufficiently to be given its town charter, with an economy based on exporting wool and archil, a lichen used for dyeing, and growing wheat and grapes. Introduced in 1635, oranges became an important export crop, with schooners coming to Urzelina from England to load the boxes of fruit. As with some of the other islands, the lack of a good harbour meant isolation until the airport was built. The principal products are now cattle and, most importantly, three large co-operatives and one private factory making the cheese for which São Jorge is renowned. Like all the other islands, São Jorge suffered from the predations of pirates; its history has also been ravaged both by earthquakes and the two major volcanic eruptions of 1580 and 1808.

GETTING THERE AND AWAY

For travel to São Jorge, see pages 42 and 49. Ferries arrive and depart in Velas throughout the year from nearby Pico and Faial. The sleepy island airport, a few kilometres east of Velas, is equipped with a café, tourist information office, free Wi-Fi and an ATM outside. Taxis to Velas cost €8–10, plus €2.50 extra for your luggage. Car-rental companies (see opposite) are at both the ferry terminal and the airport.

Airport information (Azores Airlines airport office) ✆295 430 360

Azores Airlines [map, page 195] Rua Maestro Francisco Lacerda 40, Velas; ✆295 430 350; ⏱ 09.00–17.30 Mon–Fri

GETTING AROUND

BY BUS There is a limited weekday bus service (fewer on Saturdays and none on Sundays) which brings passengers into Velas from all the significant villages in the morning, returning in the evening. One early morning service from Velas runs to Calheta, returning in the afternoon. It is designed to take workers to the tuna factory, and they take priority over mere tourists. Other morning services run from Velas to Rosais in the west, and from Topo in the east to Velas. In the afternoon, you can get all the way from Velas back to Topo; this takes well over 2 hours and you'll have to stay overnight. The Velas tourist office (see opposite) has the full timetable. Buses leave Velas from opposite the Municipal Auditorium, on the waterfront and from next to the supermarket.

BY TAXI If you want to make a tour of the island by taxi, or to use taxis to access the walks, then taxi rates start at around €18 per hour, but drivers should be able to show you a set price list for island tours as well as specific destinations. You can contact **Taxi Ilha de São Jorge** on m 917 763 280 or 962 930 604 (also e saojorgetaxi@sapo. pt; w saojorgetaxi.pt).

In Velas, taxis can usually be found behind the main church. A full list of taxi drivers is displayed in the airport. Bars and restaurants in other villages will also summon a cab, if you need one.

BY CAR Rental cars should be pre-booked, as the companies' desks may only be staffed to receive pre-booked customers. In high season, the few cars available can get booked very quickly. São Jorge has half-a-dozen car-hire companies, including:

Ilha Verde Rent-a-Car Largo João Pereira 21, Velas; ☎295 432 141, 295 240 940; e rentivsaojorge@ilhaverde.com; w ilhaverde. com; ⊕ 08.00–19.00 daily; & at the airport (☎295 240 940; m 910 546 493; ⊕ 08.00–17.30 Mon– Fri, 08.00–17.00 Sat–Sun)
Autatlantis Velas ferry terminal; ☎295 412 800; ⊕ 09.00–19.00 Mon–Sat; also at the airport.

Parking Free of charge and outside of high season, parking is generally available in the centre of Velas. There is a large, free car park north of the Jardim da Republica.

TOURIST INFORMATION

The tourist office [map, page 195] (Largo Dr João Pereira, Velas; ☎295 412 440; e pt. sjo@azores.gov.pt; ⊕ winter 09.00–13.00 & 14.00–17.00 Mon, 09.00–17.00 Tue–Fri, 09.00–16.00 Sat–Sun, summer 09.00–19.00 daily) is efficient and well organised. At the airport, there is an office (☎295 432 395) which opens for flight arrivals.

 ## WHERE TO STAY   *Map, page 184, unless otherwise stated*

There's a reasonable variety of accommodation options on São Jorge. In addition to the hotels and hostels below there are a number of camping options. Out of season, it's essential to ring ahead, as the sites may be unmanned. In each case, pitching a tent will cost no more than a few euros per person. Hot showers are available at the campsites, except for Topo.

VELAS AND AROUND
Hotel São Jorge Garden [map, page 195] (58 rooms) Av dos Baleeiros, Velas; ☎295 430 100; e reservas@hotelsaojorge.pt; w ceanohoteis.com. A long low resort-style hotel looking over the sea to Pico, just a few mins' walk from the centre of town. Comfortable rooms have balconies & AC, cable TV. Swimming pool (seasonal), bar, b/fast but no other meals. Wi-Fi is available in public areas. €€€€
Quinta das Figueiras (5 apartments) Figueiras; ☎295 438 121; e quinta.das.figueiras@gmail.com; w casasacorianas.com. S/c apartments sleeping 2–8 people, a few km west of Velas on the road to Rosais. Seasonal pool. B/fast provisions inc. Off-season prices are good value. €€€€
Cantinho das Buganvilias Resort (19 apartments) Rua Padre Augusto Teixeira,

Queimada; m 918 201 535, 912 922 032; e cantinhodasbuganvilias@gmail.com; w cantinhodasbuganvilias.net. Beautiful coastal location 5km from Velas & 1.5km west of the airport. Spacious modern s/c apartments with lots of light. Outdoor pool, fitness centre, bar & restaurant. B/fast extra. €€€
Casa do António [map, page 195] (8 rooms) Rua Infante D Henrique 21, Velas; ☎295 432 006; e geral@casadoantonio.com; w casadoantonio. com. This is a wonderfully quirky & personal, well-designed, well-built new extension to an old building so there are quirky stairs & corners & the whole thing comes together in a mock Art Deco style. A really fun place sitting above the harbour with, in summer, Cory's shearwaters whipping by overhead to their nesting sites in the nearby cliff

face. The ceramicist owner has put considerable thought into making guests comfortable. There is a b/fast room (with excellent varied b/fast), AC & a small elevated garden. A good choice. €€

Hotel Soares Neto [map, page 195] (23 rooms) Rua Cons Dr José Pereira 14, Velas; ✆ 295 412 403; e reservas@hotelsoaresneto.com; w hotelsoaresneto.pt. In the very centre of town, close to the harbour. Simple rooms, few frills, though with TV, bar & small seawater swimming pool (seasonal). B/fast inc. €€

Quinta do Canavial [map, page 195] (4 rooms in main house, 20 rooms in annexe) Lugar do Canavial, Velas; ✆ 295 412 981; e quintacanavial@hotmail. com. High up above the football ground, overlooking the bay of Entre-Moros on the very western edge of Velas, this is an old manor house in a garden setting. Pool, restaurant serving evening meals on request, pick-ups from port or airport. Rooms are full of characterful antiques. B/fast inc. €€

CALHETA

Pousada de Juventude (Youth hostel) (6 dorms, 9 rooms, 9 family rooms) Canada da Vinha Nova, Fajã Grande; ✆ 295 460 000; e saojorge@ pousadasjuvacores.com; w pousadasjuvacores.com. A good modern building looking out over the town, with dorms & private rooms. Communal TV & bar. Airport transfers. €

FAJA DA CALDEIRA DO SANTO CRISTO

Casa Tio João (5 rooms) m 969 153 722; e casa.do.tio.joao@outlook.pt. A true wilderness experience; you need to walk here or get a quad-bike (page 198, owners can arrange, extra cost). Bunks, dbl rooms & trpls, fully s/c but you need

to bring your own food (cooking oil, salt, etc, provided). The setting is unique, a peaceful place for those genuinely seeking a retreat. Power is by generator, part-time; rooms are simple, no Wi-Fi, no TV, shared bathroom. Communal wood-burning stove, garden. Open year-round, subject to weather. €€

CAMPING

Fajã Grande Rua Cabo Vicente Dias, Fajã Grande, Calheta; ✆ 295 417 366; m 963 797 170; e camping.cht.siz.2014@gmail.com; ⊕ May–Sep. Just west of Calheta, close to the sea, there is a good natural rock pool with European Blue Flag status. The campsite has a children's playpark, kitchen & washing machine, & tents can be rented. It is very attractive with a pergola & belvedere, a great place to sit & watch the sunset. To find the campsite, take a steep cement road down to the sea. Shops are very limited; there is no bakery, but there is a kiosk & a snack bar (⊕ 09.00–23.00). €

Topo Just below the lighthouse & the Olhar Ilhéu restaurant, a simple campsite with basic facilities, including a barbecue, but great views. €

Urzelina ✆ 295 414 401. All amenities & resident warden. Swimming pool & natural rock pools. Clothes washing facilities. Close by are restaurants, grocery, bakery & coffee shop. €

Velas ✆ 295 421 721. Next to the football ground & swimming pool in the Baía de Entre os Morros, about 15mins' walk west of town. It has a freshwater swimming pool & tents, with sleeping bags for hire. Clothes washing facilities. €

✖ WHERE TO EAT AND DRINK *Map, page 184, unless otherwise stated*

São Jorge's pastry speciality is not a *queijada* tart, but the *espécie*, a sort of horseshoe-shaped biscuit with cinnamon and other spices. You can occasionally find them in cafés, though more often in family-sized bags in the supermarket.

Alas, the island has no really stand-out restaurants. Velas has enough places to eat around the centre, though with little variety and a standard that rarely exceeds average. There are some better options outside Velas, listed opposite.

VELAS

Açor [map, page 195] Largo da Matriz 41; ✆ 295 432 463; ⊕ 08.00–midnight Mon–Sat. A spacious bar and café that serves a good range of food including pizza (with a choice of crusts) &

other vegetarian options, as well as the usual set lunch. €€

Cervejaria São Jorge [map, page 195] Rua Francisco Lacerda 31; ✆ 295 412 861; ⊕ summer 08.00–15.00 & 18.00–22.00 Mon–Sat, winter

08.00–15.00 Mon–Sat. With friendly staff serving up soups, snacks & burgers, plus more traditional fare. Bargain lunches served noon–14.30. €

Clube Naval [map, page 195] Rua Conselheiro Dr José Pereira 9; ✆295 098 091; ⊕ 08.00–22.00 Mon–Fri, 09.00–22.30 Sat. Serves meat & fish dishes, plus sandwiches & snacks while the locals watch football on the TV. Dish of the day is a cheap option at w/day lunchtimes. €

SANTO AMARO

Fornos de Lava Travessa de São Tiago; ✆295 432 415; m 917 394 977; w fornosdelava.pt; ⊕ 19.00–23.00 Thu–Tue. Not far from Velas, this is a delightfully rural place, with luxuriant views over pastures; the owners are really trying hard &, a true novelty for the Azores, they grow their own vegetables & herbs for the restaurant. €€

QUEIMADA

A Quinta Fajã de Santo Amaro 93 (100m west of the airport, on the main road); ✆295 432 590; ⊕ 10.00–22.00 daily. In a characterful, stone building, part of a professional college, this is definitely one of the island's better options. Menu is fairly standard, but off-season it can draw a midweek crowd when other places are empty. €€

FAJÃ DO OUVIDOR

Café O Amilcar Close to the harbour; ✆295 417 448; m 912 259 501; ⊕ (meal service) noon–15.00 & 17.00–22.00 Wed–Mon. This simple café offers good fish – the owner is also a fisherman – plus standard meat dishes. Service can be patchy. €€

RIBEIRA SECA

Café/Restaurante Ponto de Encontro Canada dos Vales; ✆295 417 045; ⊕ 07.30–midnight Wed–Mon, food noon–15.00, 19.00–22.00. On the main road just before Ribeira Seca, this is an inviting restaurant with views across to Pico. They offer a buffet lunch & à la carte dinner – a good opportunity to try the island's famous clams – cheaper here than elsewhere. €€

TOPO

O Caseiro Rua Joaquim Homem da Silveira Noronha 165; m 964 740 504; ⊕ 09.00–midnight Tue–Sun. Buffet lunch, also snacks & drinks all day. €

Olhar Ilhéu Ponta do Topo; ⊕ 10.00 –23.00 Thu–Tue. New in 2023 in a modern wood-and-glass box at the viewpoint below the lighthouse; there's a good range of snacks, drinks & formal meals available. €

NIGHTLIFE

The plush **Municipal Auditorium** in Velas sometimes has events such as fado – ask at the tourist office for information of upcoming shows. In summer the Palco dos Pescadores, an open-air stage near the rock arch, is also used.

OTHER PRACTICALITIES

Free **Wi-Fi** access is available in the Jardim da Republica in Velas, at the Velas marina, in Calheta and at the airport. Many cafés and restaurants also provide it.

Health centre Velas; Rua do Corpo Santo; ✆295 412 122. Open 24hrs for emergencies. Calheta; on the regional road towards Topo; ✆295 460 120.

Police Velas; ✆295 412 339

WHAT TO SEE AND DO

MUSEUMS

Casa Museu Cunha da Silveira (Rua Guilherme da Silveira 36, Velas; ✆295 432 568; w cmvelas.pt/casa-museu-cunha-da-silveira-o-mar-e-a-terra-a-sustentabilidade-de-um-povo; ⊕ May–Sep 10.30–17.30 Tue–Sun, Oct–Apr 10.00–17.00 Tue–Sun; €3/1/free adult/senior & 7–14s/under 7s) In the townhouse

Velas is making quite a local name for itself with the Semana Cultural or week-long cultural festival held in early July to coincide with the annual Horta–Velas–Horta yacht race, when numerous events are staged including cultural conferences and exhibitions as well as more usual pop, rock and folk music, and bullfights. There is another festival in April. In July, in Calheta, is the biennial festival with various cultural and sports events. The dates of many festivals vary each year, so please check with the tourist information office (page 187). There has been some criticism of the way these festivals have developed, with too much imported rock music, but spectators can still enjoy some elements of traditional Azorean culture.

Festa de São Jorge Velas; 23–25 April.
Espírito Santo Island-wide; always eight weeks after Easter (so, May or June).
Semana Cultural Velas; first week of July.
Festa de São Tiago Ribeira Seca & Calheta; last w/end of July.
Festa do Sant'Ana Velas; last week of July.
Festival de Julho Calheta; second week of July.
Festa de N Sra das Neves Velas (Norte Grande); first w/end August.
Festa de N Sra Rosário Velas (Rosais) & Norte Pequeno; 15 August.
Festa da Caldeira do Sr Santo Cristo Calheta; first week of September.
Festa de N Sra Rosário Topo; second week of September.
Festa de N Sra das Dores Velas (Fajã do Ouvidor/Norte Grande); third week of September.
Festa de Santa Catarina Calheta; always falls on 25 November.

of the family which once owned the western half of the island, the museum does briefly touch on them, but is more concerned with ordinary people living from agriculture, fishing and weaving. The bilingual displays are very well put together, and there may be a temporary exhibition too.

Museu Francisco Lacerda (Rua das Alcaçarias, Calheta; ☏ 295 416 323; ⊕ Apr–Sep 10.00–17.30 Tue–Sun, Oct–Mar 09.30–17.00 Tue–Sun; €1/€0.50/free adult/senior & 14–24/under 14s) Recently installed in a former tuna factory by the harbour, this has three permanent exhibitions about the history and ethnography of the island, tuna fishing, and music, focusing on this Azorean composer (1869–1934) who worked and studied in Lisbon and Paris. New interactive displays should allow you to hear some of Lacerda's compositions.

Casa do Parque São Jorge (Norte Grande; on the left, just after taking the Fajã da Ouvidor turn-off from the northern coast road; ☏ 295 417 018; ⊕ 09.00–12.30 & 13.30–17.00 Mon–Fri; free) With English-language information on plant life and wildlife plus a short video with subtitles.

FINISTERRA CHEESE CO-OPERATIVE (☏ 295 415 216; ⊕ 09.00–noon & 13.30–16.00 Mon–Fri; €1.50 inc tour & tasting) There are three dairy co-ops on the island, but this one, on the main road just west of Santo Antão, is the only one making both the famous São Jorge cheese and the softer and smoother Topo cheese. The tour is in English, with a very entertaining guide, and the cost is merely to cover the hygiene-related clothing you have to wear. Around 50% of the product is exported, much to the USA.

BIRDS AND FLOWERS The most interesting areas for avian and floral action are undoubtedly the fajãs. Best known is **Fajã dos Cubres** on the north coast east of Norte Pequeno, formed largely by the 1757 earthquake and subsequent erosion and with a biologically rich, very indented lagoon. Groundwater enters the lagoon but causeways built across it have created two habitats, essentially marine to the west and fresh water in the east. It is among the most important wetland habitats in the Azores. Growing among the pain-inflicting sharp rush, *Juncus acutus*, is goldenrod, *Solidago sempervirens*, or cubres after which the fajã is named. Other plants include wild celery, wild carrot, orache and the submerged herb beaked tasselweed. Eurasian coot and greenshank, snipe, terns and a long list of rarities can make this a rewarding site for birds, especially coming as it does at the end of a beautiful cliff walk (page 193).

A little further east along the coast is the **Fajã da Caldeira do Santo Cristo**. Its lagoon is well known as the only place in the Azores where clams are found. Although remote, it is also one of the best places for surfing in the islands. This nature reserve has one of the largest populations of endemic scabious, with the potentially off-putting name *Scabiosa nitens*.

Ilhéu do Topo, off the far eastern end of São Jorge, is a Special Protected Area because of its birdlife. The islet has in excess of 2,000 Cory's shearwaters among its many breeding seabirds. It is also a renowned dive site, though with strong currents.

At the island's other, western, extremity, the high coastal cliffs at **Ponta dos Rosais** support an interesting vegetation that can only be glimpsed from a distance without difficulty and danger. It is an important site for migratory birds and is a passage point for whales, dolphins and turtles.

RECREATIONAL FOREST RESERVES
Parque Florestal das Sete Fontes (Seven Fountains Forest Park) Signposted from the Velas to Rosais road. The forestry department has laid out an attractive 12ha park with ornamental planting sheltered and shaded by trees. There are picnic tables, a barbecue area, and some animals such as Vietnamese pigs, parakeets and deer. The surrounding countryside is a mixture of pastures and forestry. Many of the roads are unsurfaced, and a relaxing day can be spent exploring the area on foot (see also page 194).

Parque Florestal da Silveira Off the EN–2 main road from Velas, 5km beyond Calheta. This 10ha forest, between 300m and 375m altitude on a steep south-facing hill, is picturesquely crossed by several streams, once used to power watermills. There are numerous paths and shady walks, picnic areas, a deer enclosure, and some amusing exercise equipment. It is quite charming.

SPORTS AND ACTIVITIES
Adventure activities
Aventour Rua Nova 91, Calheta; m 963 831 986; e info@aventour.pt; w aventour.pt. A huge range of active adventures are available, including canyoning, coasteering, guided walks & birdwatching. See website for full range & prices, which vary according to group size.

Diving
São Jorge Dive & Sail Centre Porto de Velas; m 915 106 268; e sjzdiveandsail@gmail.com; w urzelinatur.com; ⏰ 09.00–18.00 Mon–Sat, 09.00–12.30 Sun. Known until 2017 as Urzelinatur, they are now based in the Velas marina & offer everything from try-dives to week-long courses.

Fishing and boat tours

Azorean Dream Estrada Marginal dos Casteletes, 7, Urzelina; ☎ 912 553 039; e azorean@gmail. com; w azoreandream.com. Yacht charters, from sunset tapas to a half or full day or a week around the archipelago.

Velas Fishing Tur m 919 821 513; e jaimefbpereira@hotmail.com; w velasfishingtur.webnode.pt. Big-game fishing or bottom-fishing. Groups from 2 to 6 people, duration from 2 to 8 hrs, from €200. Boat tours around the coast from €180, depending on group size. Also climbs of the Pico volcano.

Swimming

The following are listed geographically, heading east and anticlockwise around the island. See the maps on pages 184 & 195 for locations. Always take advice on weather conditions.

Velas Natural pools at Poça dos Frades, just west of the auditorium, & at Preguiça, just west of the Hotel São Jorge Garden.

Urzelina Natural pools & harbour swimming with changing facilities.

Portinhos About 100m further on from Urzelina, there is another access to the sea at Portinhos with facilities & a grassy relaxation area.

Fajã Grande Natural rock pool with all facilities.

Fajã do Ouvidor The Simão Dias natural swimming pool is in a dramatic setting a few hundred metres west of the harbour (don't confuse it with the pool at the start of the trail through the lava flow). There's a pool with showers & a restaurant by the harbour.

WALKS ON SÃO JORGE

São Jorge has some memorable walks; several are long established and so fairly clear to follow. There are seven official trails suitable for day walks, summaries of which are given opposite. For hardcore hikers, there is now also the 'Grand Route'

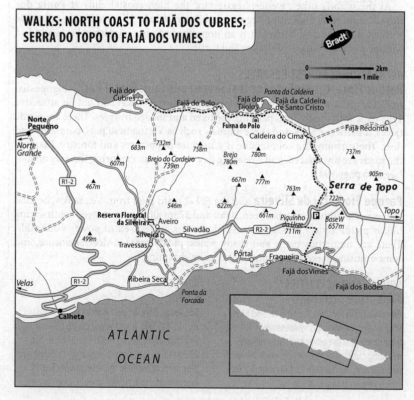

which covers the length of the island from Ponta dos Rosais and Velas to Fajã dos Cubres in the north and Topo in the east. This is best done over several days, using the information on w visitazores.com to plan food and accommodation needs. Although all routes are downloadable from that site, you should always check at the tourist office to ensure that your chosen route is open and safe before setting off as they are prone to weather erosion.

Aventour (page 191) offers **guided walks** of between 4 and 18km, so suitable for all levels of fitness. Their off-the-beaten-track routes give insights into island history, geology and culture; prices depend on group size.

SERRA DO TOPO–FAJÃ DA CALDEIRA DO SANTO CRISTO–FAJÃ DOS CUBRES [map, opposite] (Medium difficulty, 10km, 2½hrs) Down to and along the north coast, starting at a viewpoint (with shelter and car park) east of the wind farm. Steep downhill sections will not suit the weak-kneed. There are restaurants at both Fajã da Caldeira do Santo Cristo and Fajã dos Cubres.

SERRA DO TOPO–FAJÃ DOS VIMES [map, opposite] (Hard, 5½km, 2½hrs) Mostly downhill, on the south coast. Use the car park detailed above, a few hundred metres east of the trailhead.

FAJÃ DE SÃO JOÃO–LOURAIS–FAJÃ DOS VIMES (Hard – recently upgraded from medium difficulty, 10km, 3½hrs) Along the south-coast cliffs.

PICO DO PEDROPICO DA ESPERANÇA–FAJÃ DO OUVIDOR (Medium difficulty, 16.8km, 4hrs) Along the spine of the island and down to the north coast.

FAJÃ DE ALÉM (Hard – recently upgraded from medium difficulty, 5km, 3hrs) A shortish, circular walk down to the fajã from near the Santo António chapel, west of Norte Grande.

TRILHO DO NORTE PEQUENO (Medium difficulty, 11km, 3hrs) A circular walk from Norte Pequeno descending the cliff face to the fajã settlements.

FAJÃ DOS VIMES–FRAGUEIRA–PORTAL (Medium difficulty, 3km, 1½hrs) Short linear walk on the south coast.

TOURING THE ISLAND

São Jorge is skinny and elongated so, unlike in many of the islands, to travel places seems to take a disproportionate amount of time. Many visitors are based in Velas and content themselves with seeing Rosais in the far west, and then undertake a central circuit taking in both north and south coasts but not going further east than Calheta. There is a considerable amount of 'up and down' and roads are narrow and twisting; beware of injudiciously parked tractors and pick-up trucks.

VELAS Velas, the island's main town, remains very small, and the old part around the pretty harbour has been generally well cared for and retains its charm. Built upon a fajã, the harbour and old town are beautifully set against high cliffs, and the marina complements them. The narrow backstreets, some fine houses with their wrought-iron balconies, the little shops, and the inviting, intriguing and imposing 18th-century gateway, or **Portão do Mar**, all go to make a pleasing whole. You may even find a boat or two parked on the road along with the cars. Some of the little streets have been very prettily pedestrianised and paved in the traditional manner of small black setts with designs in white depicting activities of the island. One street, Rua Maestro Francisco Lacerda, is now an attractive pedestrianised area, replete with banks and souvenir shops, hanging baskets filled with flowers, a good cake shop at one end and the attractive town square at the other, with a fine replica bandstand. Above the car park just north of the square, a switchback path up the hill to a viewpoint has been branded both as a fitness trail and as a botanic garden, although there's little to see except some fruit trees. Down by the sea, the unmistakable postmodern community building declares Velas is really part of the 21st century; inside is the public library, meeting rooms and a splendid 220-seat auditorium/theatre, as well as a bar with a terrace on the old fortifications. There is an imposing parish church, the **Church of São Jorge** no less, which has been built and modified from the 17th century – of particular note is its carved wooden retable. The 17th-century **Church of Nossa Senhora da Conceição** was a former Franciscan monastery and is now cared for by nuns and well worth seeing.

ROSAIS Rosais itself is a very linear village running along the road, but this is also the name given to the whole of the end of the island west of Velas. After passing through the village you will come to the signposted Miradouro Pica da Velho, and at 493m this gives a commanding view over this part of the island. The viewpoint is generously planted with camellias, hydrangeas, azaleas and agapanthus so it is very pretty when they flower; it is part of the Parque Florestal das Sete Fontes (page 191).

FAROL DOS ROSAIS This lighthouse is at the far western end of the island, and is reached by a dirt road from the Parque Florestal das Sete Fontes which gets worse as you go on. The 1980 earthquake made the cliffs unstable, and the lighthouse is now unmanned, with a solar-powered light that only has a range of 8 miles. Be very careful if you walk near the lighthouse as there are deep holes in the ground; it's better to climb the steps to the Vigia da Baleia (whale-watching post) 250m east.

THE CENTRAL PART OF THE ISLAND BETWEEN VELAS AND CALHETA Leaving Velas, take the road to the north coast signposted to Norte Grande, and go first through **Beira**; continuing on the north road you pass through **Toledo**, now just a tiny village, which was probably first settled by Spanish immigrants soon after King Philip of Spain seized Portugal. Next along the road is the settlement of **Santo António**, destroyed in the earthquake of 1980, and rebuilt.

Norte Grande–Velas Norte Grande is the largest village in the north. Do visit its church, Nossa Senhora das Neves (Our Lady of the Snows), dating from 1762; it has a quiet and beautiful interior with splendid azulejos and modern stained-glass windows. Note the weathervane in the shape of a fish; this is peculiar to São Jorge and is the symbol adopted by early Christians. Just 50m past the church, take a left where signposted to **Fajã do Ouvidor**. Stop in at the Casa do Parque (page 190), then continue down to the miradouro (just off to the left from the road) for a fine view of the village below, and to your right, further along the coast, Fajã da Ribeira da Areia: you will appreciate how inaccessible these fajã settlements are. (On a clear day you can also see Graciosa and Terceira.) Now continue down to the fajã where there is a small harbour, a natural swimming pool and a restaurant (page 189). Even on a fairly calm day, the swell creates quite a spectacle as it crashes into a circle of rocks with rock-arches, a sort of semi-submarine Stonehenge. You can't help but

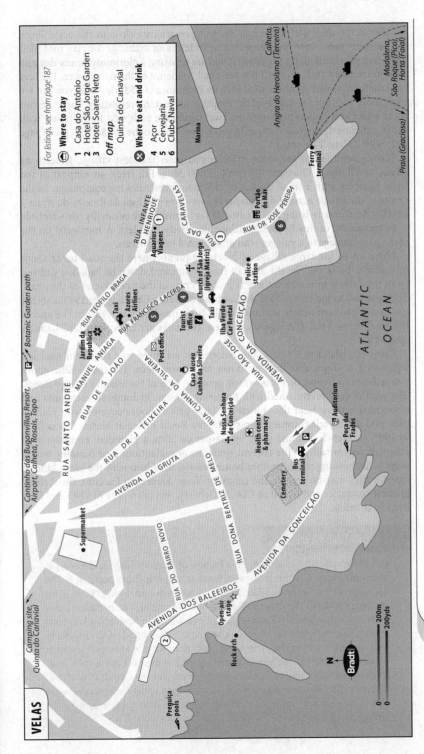

VELAS

For listings, see from page 187

Where to stay
1 Casa do António
2 Hotel São Jorge Garden
3 Hotel Soares Neto

Off map
Quinta do Canavial

Where to eat and drink
4 Açor
5 Cervejaria
6 Clube Naval

Camping site,
Quinta do Canavial

Cantinho das Buganvillas Resort,
Airport, Calheta, Rosais, Topo

Botanic Garden path

Prequiça pools

Supermarket

RUA SANTO ANDRÉ

MANUEL ANIAGA

Jardim da
Republica

RUA TEOFILO BRAGA

Taxi

Azores
Airlines

RUA FRANCISCO LACERDA

RUA DE S JOÃO

Post office

RUA DR J TEIXEIRA

RUA CUNHA DA SILVEIRA

Casa Museu
Cunha da Silveira

Nossa Senhora
de Conceição

AVENIDA DA GRUTA

RUA DONA BEATRIZ DE MELO

RUA DO BAIRRO NOVO

AVENIDA DA CONCEIÇÃO

Cemetery

Health centre
& pharmacy

Bus
terminal

Poça das
Frades

Auditorium

AVENIDA DOS BALEEIROS

Open-air
stage

Rock arch

RUA SÃO JOSE

AVENIDA DA CONCEIÇÃO

Aquarius
Viagens

RUA INFANTE D HENRIQUE

Church of São Jorge
(Igreja Matriz)

Tourist
office

Taxi

Ilha Verde
Car Rental

Police
station

RUA DAS CARAVELAS

Portão
do Mar

RUA DR JOSÉ PEREIRA

Marina

Ferry
terminal

Calheta,
Angra do Heroísmo (Terceira)

Madalena,
São Roque (Pico),
Horta (Faial)

Praia (Graciosa)

ATLANTIC

OCEAN

N

Bradt

0   200m
0   200yds

wonder at the shelf life of the houses built precariously close to the edge. From the harbour, yams were once exported to Graciosa in exchange for clay roof tiles. There are waterfalls along the coast; if you are enjoying a gloriously sunny day and a period without rain, you will not see much evidence of them, however. The lava here came from what is now called Pico da Esperança (1,053m), which you can see high above you, but the details of the eruption are lost in pre-history. There are two short walks you can do here over the lava, taking the path next to the house with the conspicuously upgraded stone driveway; one leads to the Simão Dias pool (page 192) with its basalt columns.

Having returned to the main road, as you enter the next village, **Ribeira da Areia**, you'll see A Queijaria (🕓 09.00–17.00 Mon–Fri; free), an outpost of the Velas museum with a small display of old-style cheese-making equipment. In the centre of the village a stone sign points the way down to Fajã da Ribeira da Areia – another dead end, twisting and turning its way down to the ocean. By the waterside is a community of tiny houses, inhabited by hardy islanders. A memorial on the rocks pays homage to a villager who disappeared in the ocean.

Move on to the large village of **Norte Pequeno** where the road turns south to Calheta. Look out for the asphalt road signposted down to Fajã dos Cubres; from the clifftop miradouro there is probably one of the finest views of the coast. The next fajã to the east is **Fajã da Caldeira de Santo Cristo** (page 198), another isolated settlement nearly an hour's walk (or a quad-bike ride) from the end of the road below you. The lagoons of these two fajãs are important bird habitats (page 191).

Cross the island to Calheta, but before you get there take the main road left signposted to Topo and then go down to **Ribeira Seca**. On the skyline above you will see five wind turbines which generate 15% of the island's energy needs. The road is very pretty, lined with flowering azaleas, hydrangeas, escallonia and tibouchina shrubs. Near the church is a large private house covered with painted tiles, and a 17m-tall chimney inspired by the Royal Palace at Sintra. It was built in 1905, in French colonial style, by Gaspar de Silva, a Hawaiian emigrant who returned very wealthy – the current epidemic of pretentious new building would seem to be nothing new! Another house belonging to him with the same kind of exterior tiles may be seen in the centre of Velas. Francesco Lacerdo, the Azores' greatest composer and friend of Claude Debussy, was born here in 1869 and later lived in Urzelina.

DECORATIVE PAVING

Decorative paving has long been a feature of Moorish Spain and Portugal, although today it is the latter and Brazil where it is most popular. It first appeared in the Azores in 1825, when the governor had it laid in front of his residence in Horta. The idea soon spread but most of the present paving dates from the 1940s. The black stones are, of course, basalt from abundant local sources but the white are limestone and have to be imported. On mainland Portugal the situation is reversed, and white dominates. A knapping hammer is used to shape the individual stones which are then laid on a thick layer of sand and dry cement, with the gaps filled with dry sand. It is always fascinating to watch the paviors at work as they apply their considerable skill in a seemingly most nonchalant manner to give great charm to the archipelago's streets.

Go along the lower road into **Calheta**, in size second only to Velas. Velas has the better harbour and so became the principal town, later reinforced by the construction of its nearby airport, but there remains a healthy rivalry. Calheta is on Fajã Grande, one of the flat coastal plains around the island. There is an extended busy harbour, with its small fishing fleet, near which may be seen an old tuna factory, now the museum (page 190). There are public toilets, a post office and a café/bar serving light meals. There is also the Santa Catarina tuna factory, the island's biggest private employer, at the west end of town, which can no longer be visited. This is on the lower road from Calheta, and you pass through **Fajã Grande** itself. Santa Catarina is held to be among the best brands and is exported to Europe, the USA and now China.

Following the main road back to Velas, you will come to **Manadas** (meaning 'herds of cows'), where you must stop to see the small **18th-century parish church** (⊕ Apr–Sep 10.30–18.00 Tue, 09.30–18.00 Wed–Sat, 13.00–18.00 Sun, Oct–Mar 10.00–noon & 13.00–17.00 Tue–Sat, noon–17.00 Sun; €1/0.50/free adult/senior & 15–25/under 15s, free Sun) dedicated to Santa Bárbara. It has a most beautiful setting by the sea, adjacent to the ruined remains of a fort that once defended the little harbour. This gem of Azorean Baroque is the finest in the archipelago, and the riotous interior has remained almost unchanged for many generations. There are splendid tiles telling the story of Santa Bárbara, a rich gilt carved altar and a cedarwood ceiling. Legend has it that in 1485, a sailor, Joaquim António da Silveira, found an image of Santa Bárbara in a wooden box off the coast nearby and thought a church should be built in her honour. Work started in 1510, but it was enlarged to its present form in about 1770, with a window and the font remaining of the original.

At **Terreiros** there is a small harbour with picnic tables and a snack bar. **Urzelina** suffered tremendously in the eruption of 1808 when the lava flowed down and buried everything except the church tower, which remains today as a monument to the buried village. Many of the villagers sheltered inside the church and were either buried or suffocated. It is on the right, close to the main road, surrounded by a pretty little garden. Overlooking the small harbour is a seating area with two commemorative stones. The first concerns a former harbour master. A British schooner, the *Tamar Queen*, anchored offshore and was boarded by the harbour master Amaro Soares, but bad weather quickly blew up and the ship set sail for England. Sadly, Senhor Soares was murdered, and the crew later punished. The second gives the names of early settlers. Immediately above the harbour are the remains of an old fort, now a summer café/bar. On the harbour's other side is a house with a large tile picture on its wall; this was once a temporary store for oranges before they were exported to England. There are some manor houses in the village that reflected the wealth of the orange farmers. A small ethnographic museum in an orange store was severely damaged by waves in 2016, but has been restored. To visit, call José Guilherme (**m** 919 921 272) in advance. Urzelina gets its name from the lichen that was such an important export in the early days after settlement.

Ribeira do Nabo is a small village beyond Urzelina which is home to the **Cooperativa Artesanato Senhora da Encarnação** (signposted off the main road, then just before the church; ☏ 295 414 296; **m** 962 296 734; **e** coopartesanato@sapo. pt; **w** senhoradaencarnacao.wixsite.com/senhoradaencarnacao; ⊕ 09.00–17.30 Mon–Fri; at w/ends, call & someone will open up). It offers a good range of nicely handmade goods including knitted pullovers, appliqué, macramé, ceramics, items in wood, jams and many other things. Only three local women still operate the weaving looms here, making a total of five in the whole island. In a few years, their

FAJÃ DA CALDEIRA DE SANTO CRISTO

Only a handful of people reside permanently in Santo Cristo, safely out of reach of the road network. Having been destroyed by earthquake and abandoned, it was then resettled, but following a further quake, social housing was built for the villagers on the south side of the island and many never returned.

Until now, perhaps. You have three options to get to the village, two of which involve walking and the other clinging on to the back of a quad bike as it negotiates the bumpy 4km along the side of the ocean, a couple of hundred metres below. Best not to look down.

No new-built properties are allowed in the village, but many of the abandoned houses are being renovated, all the building materials being brought on the snarling quads. Tranquillity attracts: the settlement now includes a couple of seasonal restaurants, and there are a couple of surfhouses and a guesthouse (page 188). You can learn about the environment and history of the fajãs at the **Environmental Interpretation Centre** (⌕ 295 403 860; ⊕ Oct–May 09.30–12.30 & 13.30–16.30 Fri & Sat, Jun–Sep 09.30–12.30 & 13.30–16.30 daily; free), opened in 2013. Part-time power to the village is by generator, and meals are taken by candlelight. With no shops, you need to bring your own provisions with you.

In the mixed salt-freshwater lagoon in front of the houses, a diver looks for the famous clams which adorn the menus across the island.

It's a beautiful place, free of vehicles, Wi-Fi and television. Electricity is on its way, however, though surely not a road. In summer, the snap and snarl of those quads disturbs the peace; in winter, the few hardy residents are joined by some intrepid outsiders, making it the ultimate retreat.

Will it change? To some extent, it already has, but the locals currently call the shots, determined to keep it as something special. An otherworldly place, a unique atmosphere. Just don't forget the tea bags: there are no shops, and it's a long way back.

---

skills may be lost forever. After you reach the airport at Queimada a road leads down to the sea and a very primitive landing place called **Porto da Queimada**. In summer there used to be a boat that ferried between here and Velas, long before construction of the new marina. The blackened stone tower that looks as if it might once have been a windmill is in fact an old lime kiln. The best thing though is the sea-level view of Velas, worth seeing if you travel by air and do not come or go by the ferry.

THE EASTERN PART OF THE ISLAND To reach **Fajã dos Vimes**, going down from the main road to Topo, is a most beautiful drive through luxuriant forests of largely acacia, the high humidity offering shelter for ferns and mosses. Stop at the Miradouro dos Vimes; 300m below is Fajã Fragueira and in the distance your immediate destination of Fajã dos Vimes. As you further descend note two old watermills and the overhead wires still used today for transporting forage and fuelwood to the houses way below. In the village, find the **Café Nunes** (⌕ 295 416 717; ⊕ 08.00–midnight daily); here they make arabica coffee from beans grown in the village, the only coffee grown in Europe. The beans are picked between May and September. Above the café, there is a small weaving centre where Senhora Nunes and her sister make *colchas de ponto alto*, woven woollen bedspreads. Made with natural colours and traditional designs and looms, and wool imported from Santa Maria and mainland Portugal, they are not only collectors' items, but also a great pleasure to use. Sadly, there are now only two people weaving here and it takes a week and a half to make a double bedspread. These cost around €600. Towards the cliff you will see many pollarded willows growing that are used for basket making; *vimes* means 'withy' or 'osier'. From the eastern end of the village there is an obvious footpath eastwards to make the short walk to **Fajã dos Bodes** and its waterfall and mill.

Return to the main road and continue eastwards; if you have time, drop down to **Fajã de São João** with its mixed orchards enjoying the microclimate, the watermills and dragon trees. Back on the main road, you will reach the **Finisterra Cheese Co-operative** (page 190), then pass extensive areas of pasture to come to **Santo Antão** and finally **Topo** with its lighthouse. Take the road to the right of the lighthouse to find a viewpoint over the **Ilhéu do Topo**, a strictly protected sanctuary for birds which they share with some hardy sheep, and to Terceira. The very first settlement on São Jorge was at Topo, but the Serra do Topo so separated the people from the rest of the island that it was easier to go by boat to Terceira for supplies rather than travel by land. Young oxen were also brought from Terceira for fattening here.

On the way back to Velas, above Fajã dos Vimes, you will see a surfaced road going off on your right by the side of the wind turbines. This ranks highly among the many beautiful roads of the Azores, as it winds along through a gentle landscape of small pastures surrounded by hedges, especially lovely in July and August when the hydrangeas are flowering. It is not a long drive, so do stop along the way and enjoy late-afternoon shadows and the tranquillity. You will come to a junction. Turn left to Silveira; if you turned right you would go to Norte Pequeno. Soon you will see signs for the **Parque Florestal da Silveira**, a beautifully green semi-gardened area to stroll around. Should you arrive earlier in the day, then it is a cool place to enjoy a picnic (page 191).

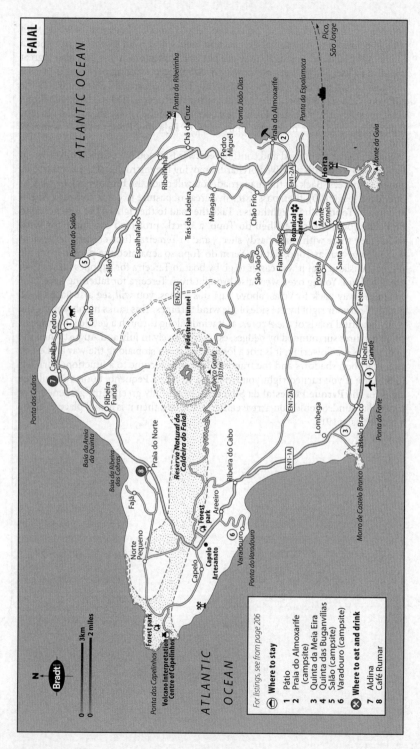

FAIAL

ATLANTIC OCEAN

Pico,
São Jorge

Ponta da Ribeirinha

Chã de Cruz

Ribeirinha

Pedro
Miguel

Ponta João Dias

Praia do Almoxarife

Ponta da Espalamaca

Trás da Ladeira

Espalhafatos

Miragaia

EN1-2A

Horta

Salão

Chão Frio

Ponta do Salão

São João

Flamengos

Botanical
garden

Monte
Carneiro

Monte da Guia

Canto

Cedros

Casealba

Portela

Santa Bárbara

EN2-2A

Pedestrian tunnel

Feteira

Ribeira
Funda

Reserva Natural da
Caldeira do Faial

Cabeço Gordo
1043m

Ponta dos Cedros

Praia do Norte

Ribeira
Grande

Ribeira do Cabo

Lombega

EN1-2A

Baía da Areia
da Quinta

EN1-1A

Baía da Ribeira
das Cabras

Fajã

Areeiro

Castelo Branco

Ponta do Forte

Norte
Pequeno

Forest
park

Capelo
Artesanato

Morro de Castelo Branco

Capelo

Varadouro

Ponta do Varadouro

Volcano Interpretation
Centre of Capelinhos

Forest park

Ponta dos Capelinhos

ATLANTIC
OCEAN

Bradt

N

0   3km
0   2 miles

For listings, see from page 206

Where to stay
1 Pátio
2 Praia do Almoxarife
   (campsite)
3 Quinta da Meia Eira
4 Quinta das Buganvilias
5 Salão (campsite)
6 Varadouro (campsite)

Where to eat and drink
7 Aldina
8 Café Rumar

200

8

Faial

Known as the Blue Island, Faial is quite spectacular when the hydrangeas are blooming from mid-July through August, as the acidic, aluminium-rich soil gives the flowers particularly intense shades of blue. One taxi driver said he had calculated that there are 56km of hydrangea hedges here. Some years ago a letter appeared in *The Times* newspaper bemoaning the abundant hydrangeas in the Azores and appealing for something else to be planted!

Much of the landscape here is pasture, although there is now some forest; at one time the tree cover was so depleted that wood for fuel was imported from Pico. At the time of settlement the island was luxuriously forested, including an abundance of what the Portuguese called *faya*, and so named the island Fayal. The plant was collected in 1777 by Kew Gardens' first paid plant hunter, Robert Masson, and was scientifically named *Myrica faya*.

Although the island is dominated by its central caldera and nearby highest point of 1,031m, the visitor is not really aware of this, travelling around the island past its pretty villages, lush pastures and vigorous hedgerows. For some, Faial is simply Horta – the two become almost interchangeable.

If you arrive from a tour of the smaller islands, approaching Horta from the airport can fool you into thinking you are at the entrance to a city: a smattering of industry and a spate of large villas line the way into town. Once inside, this impression soon disappears in the face of simple, elegant Portuguese architecture and cobbled streets and pavements. Picturesque Horta has long been a major port of the Azores; today its marina is a major tourist attraction and the harbour has the world's largest collection of paintings by departing yacht crews. Around 1,100 yachts put in each year for supplies and repairs as they make the Atlantic crossing and this influx of around 5,500 mostly young crew members certainly enlivens the evenings, especially between May and August.

History is everywhere among the streets and old buildings, and always across the channel is the great cone of Pico. Sometimes it is totally clear, seeming arrogantly to challenge the elements to renew their erosive attacks. More often, it is adorned with a fast-changing wardrobe of clouds, engulfing its summit, encircling its midriff, or clothing it from apex to base and obscuring it from our sight but not our consciousness; you never tire of glancing across the channel. In winter with its uppermost quarter dusted with snow and fronted with a travel-brochure blue sea, the mountain is breathtakingly beautiful.

Horta, the only town, will take at least a half day to explore, easily a full day with the museums. Seeing the highlights of the rest of the island can be done by taxi or hire car and could occupy a day. There are now a few more official walks too, to stretch the legs. The view into the caldera, green and a nature reserve, and the reverse view down to Horta, across the channel to Pico island and up to its volcano summit with São Jorge beyond, make it well worth a drive up. Then there is Capelinhos, the site of the major 1957–58 eruption which added another 2km² to Faial; the devastated lighthouse and half-buried village houses slowly becoming exposed from their smothering of ash by wind erosion, bear witness to the human drama. All of this is enhanced by the high-tech Volcano Interpretation Centre of Capelinhos spectacularly built below ground in the fallout from the eruption, for which you should allow 1½–2 hours. Recently there have been many new developments and Faial now offers a good range of interests and maritime and land-based activities. There's a museum and a small aquarium (currently closed) at Porto Pim, as well as a decent range of quality accommodation and a few restaurants offering some welcome sophistication.

BACKGROUND

GEOLOGY Faial is the nearest island to the Mid-Atlantic Ridge, some 100km to the west, and grew up on its flanks from a depth of 1,500m from the same northwest–southeast-aligned fissures that gave rise to Pico. It was formed by four volcanic complexes. First, the Ribeirinha complex in the northeast of the island, part of a shield volcano (one that is gently sloping, built of very fluid basaltic lava from many closely spaced vents) and forming the oldest rocks of Faial at around 700,000 years ago. Associated with this are two major fault lines, or scarps, to the north and to the south of Pedro Miguel village. Second, the Cedros complex in the north, linked to the development of the central Caldeira volcano; the Horta Formation, the third stage of Faial's construction, began around 11,000 years ago, with what at first were Surtseyan eruptions when seawater could enter the vent, mix with the rising magma, and create steam causing the magma to shatter into fine fragments. Once the vents were above water, eruptions changed to more moderate types. Monte Queimado and Monte da Guia, which protect Porto Pim, Horta's first harbour, date from this period. Monte da Guia, consisting of thin layers of yellowish ash, often compacted or welded into tuff, erupted in shallow water whereas the burnt cinders of adjacent Monte Queimado burst on to dry land. Finally, there is the Capelo Formation; the Capelo Peninsula grew westwards from a series of eruptions on land, remaining evidence being the alignment of domes starting from near the Caldeira volcano that are a continuum of the Pedro Miguel Fault. Only two eruptions at the very end of the peninsula occurred underwater: these were Costa da Nua and, the latest, Capelinhos. The Ilhéus dos Capelinhos were evidence of an earlier eruption, but they were destroyed by the 1957–58 eruption. In historical times, the Cabeço do Fogo (meaning 'head of fire') and Picarito erupted in 1672; they caused seven months of intermittent earthquakes, spreading ash over the island and lava flows which buried houses and farmland in and around Praia do Norte and formed the present Zona do Mistério. It is assumed some of the four systems may have been active simultaneously.

The Caldeira volcano that today dominates the island began as a stratovolcano, a steep-sided cone with a medium or low basaltic explosive activity forming bedded layers of lava fragments and flows. Some 16,000 years ago, this eruptive pattern changed to a mainly explosive acidic form, producing a pale viscous acidic rock which often formed rugged lava flows and domes. During this later period the Caldeira volcano erupted at least 14 times, one of them coinciding with the opening of the caldera 1,000 years ago. This was a Plinian eruption, a highly dramatic and powerful explosion of gas, steam, ash and pumice rising kilometres into the air, together with pyroclastic flows – avalanches of hot gas, ash and rock debris. The caldera is now 400m deep and 1,450m in diameter with almost vertical walls.

The highest point of the island is Cabeço Gordo at 1,031m, a basaltic cinder cone on the side of the Caldeira volcano, which can be accessed by tarmac road – from a turn-off on the R1-1 road, just north of the junction to Capelinhos, it's 10km to the top. The views on a clear day are spectacular, over to Pico, down into the caldera and over the entire west of the island.

Future volcanic events will most likely occur in connection with the Capelo Formation and the Caldeira volcano. At a second level, the Horta platform or the faults of Pedro Miguel might offer excitement.

HISTORY Early maps present the island as *Insule de Ventura*, and the Portuguese discovered it in the first half of the 15th century and began settlement. Led by Josse Van Huerter, a few Flemish settlers came to Faial in 1468, and just 20 years later their number had grown to 1,500. Establishing themselves first at Praia do Almoxarife, they soon moved inland to the Vale dos Flamengos ('Valley of the Flemish'), not far from Horta. The first two areas developed were at either end of what is now the main port and marina of Horta. The Azores have always played an important role in the history of the Atlantic. Laden Portuguese ships returning from the Indies would seek protection from the many pirates awaiting them off the African coast. As both the new English settlements in North America and the West Indies and the Portuguese empire grew, Horta, then the only really safe anchorage in the Azores, became a busy sea port. Horta was not only trading but also victualling, supplying good fresh water and vegetables, repairing ships and providing crews for East Indiamen, West Indiamen, codfishers, slavers, ships carrying wine, or sugar, or salt, or miscellaneous cargoes, and men-of-war. In addition, there has always been a great deal of inter-island trading, as well as between the islands and mainland Portugal.

Of course, it was not always peaceful; in 1583, the Spanish attacked and fought a battle for the Santa Cruz fortress. This still overlooks the harbour, but is now a pousada (state-owned hotel). During Spanish rule English privateers attacked several times; Sir Walter Raleigh razed Horta by fire, carried off the governor and either captured or destroyed all of a Spanish fleet home-bound from Mexico. A far more peaceful English visitor was Captain James Cook who, in 1775, merely checked his navigational instruments onshore before sailing off to explore the South Seas.

Early whaling fleets came to Horta for supplies, anchoring in Porto Pim to rest, offload whale oil and recruit crews. Later, entrepreneurs developed warehouses and other facilities to further attract ships to Horta. Among these was American John Dabney who arrived at the beginning of the 1800s, and whose family influenced commerce for 100 years. The family house, lookout, wine cellar and whaleboat house are all preserved today. Oranges and Pico wine were two important exports they handled, as well as whale products, ships' chandlery, and much else. Extremely successful, they lived life on a lavish scale, building several large houses, entertaining and exchanging latest news with ships' officers, and being generous benefactors to the islanders. The number of whalers increased, especially from New Bedford, which is now twinned with Horta. Work began in 1876 on the docks and sea wall to better protect the port so that steam ships could also call as well as sailing ships, and so bunkering services were added with much of the coal shipped out from Liverpool, England.

The world's first reliable **transatlantic telegraph cable** connection was laid in 1866, and more quickly followed during the next 50 years, linking many regions of the world. In 1893, the first cable linked Horta with Ponta Delgada and on to

Carcavelos south of Lisbon. This was operated by an English company, the Europe and Azores Telegraph Co, which in 1934 became part of Cable & Wireless.

These early telegraph cables had a relatively short operational range, and Horta's mid-Atlantic position was ideal for a relay station for transatlantic cables. It was also a good interchange location, and Deutsch-Atlantische Telegraphengesellschaft, founded in 1900, laid its first cable to link the USA and Germany via the Azores. Further cables followed, from Horta to Waterville in Ireland and Porthcurno in Cornwall, and to Mindelo in the Cape Verde Islands to connect with other cables to Africa and South America.

In the early 1900s there were some 300 employees – British, Germans, Americans and Portuguese. The last cable connecting Horta was laid in 1928, the latest technology allowing simultaneous transmission of five messages in each direction, a total of 500 words per minute. At this point Horta was one of the most important cable centres in the world. The cables linking the Azores with mainland Europe also meant the meteorological observations made in the Azores, so far out in the Atlantic, could be transmitted rapidly; this had a tremendous influence on the development of weather forecasting. It was in 1969 that the last cable company left, superseded by new technology. In 1901, construction of the Prince Albert of Monaco Observatory began on the summit of Cabeço das Moças, above what is now the Azoris Faial Garden Hotel, and it is still in use today, monitoring both weather and volcanoes. Colloquially, *moça* means 'mistress', and the hill was thus named because it was where visiting sailors courted the town's young women.

The first transatlantic crossing by seaplane was made in 1919 by Albert C Read of the US Navy, who called at Horta en route from Newfoundland to Lisbon; a line of naval ships was stationed every 50 miles to allow radio direction-finding. He was followed by many others, notably in 1933, Charles Lindbergh, who flew to Horta seeking an acceptable year-round stopover for Pan Am's seaplanes from America to Europe. Pan Am's clipper flights were soon calling regularly at Horta, along with Lufthansa, Air France and Imperial Airways, now British Airways. However, there were disadvantages: the harbour was not large enough for landings and take-offs and the big flying boats had to use the open ocean, taxiing in and out of the harbour. Ocean swells could delay flights and in December 1939, four clippers were stranded for three weeks. This romantic era of travel ended with improved land-based aircraft and a runway constructed on Santa Maria.

Now the summer maritime traffic crossing the Atlantic enhances the cosmopolitan life of Horta, the giant cruise ships berthed on one side of the harbour facing off with the sleek yachts on the other. Tourism generally is the new growth industry. Meanwhile, cattle and fishing continue in the background.

GETTING THERE AND AWAY

For travel to Faial, see pages 42 and 49. Compared with some of the smaller islands, Faial's airport (✆292 943 511), near Castelo Branco, is a step up, receiving as it does direct flights from Lisbon. It can offer an ATM, Azores Airlines (SATA) office, gift shop, cafeteria, and a few car-hire firms, **Autatlantis** (m 926 210 123; w autatlantis. com), **Ilha Verde** (✆292 943 945; w ilhaverde.com) and **Autoturistica Faialense** (✆292 292 308; w autoturisticafaialense.com). There's also a tourist office and free Wi-Fi. A taxi to Horta will cost around €10, or €13 with luggage. There's a 20% uplift between 21.00 and 06.00, and on Sundays or holidays. Airport buses to Horta are infrequent. There's a good modern ferry terminal north of the town centre, with a bar, Wi-Fi and more car-hire offices.

Azores Airlines (SATA) [216 E4] Largo do Infante Dom Henrique, Horta; ☏ 292 202 291; ⏰ 09.00– 17.30 Mon–Fri. The airport office (☏ 292 202 310) opens for flight departures & arrivals.

GETTING AROUND

Within Horta itself, buses tootle around on four routes, on weekdays only. For most visitors, these will be unnecessary, given the modest dimensions of the town, but all of them go to (or very near to) the ferry terminal, so could be useful if you have luggage. There are infrequent public buses around the island, but you will need to obtain the current timetable from the tourist office, or search online (w farias.pt). They are inexpensive, but not always of great help to the visitor. Most frustratingly, the Volcano Interpretation Centre at Capelinhos is not well served; currently you can only get out there at around 12.30 and return about 20 minutes later. If you get stuck, you will find local drivers amenable to hitchhikers.

The best way to see the island is to hire a car for a day or two, or to take a taxi tour. A taxi price list is available at the tourist office. A return taxi trip to the caldera costs €35 and hiring by the hour will set you back €20.

If you are pushed for time and literally just want to see the island, without stopping, you can take the 11.45 bus which goes westwards from the stop close to the tourist information office. This will take you clockwise around the coast to Ribeira Funda and onwards, back to Horta, taking 2 hours. When you board the bus, ask for a ticket to go right round the island. First, following the coast and a sparkling blue sea, you get to Capelinhos, and a good view of the 1957–58 eruption site and the half-buried lighthouse. Twenty-five years ago the area was pretty well deserted, with damaged or destroyed houses lying abandoned or buried in ash. Now people are returning, and either restoring the old houses or building new ones, and it is becoming very attractive. On to Praia do Norte and to Cedros, passing through some well-forested areas, it is then down to Ribeirinha before climbing up to Espalamaca, looking down to the dark-sand beach of Praia do Almoxarife on your left, to Pico, and opposite, the splendid view of Horta.

A couple of companies can hire you a bicycle. Try **AL Bike** (Rua das Angústias 64; m 961 335 165; e al.bike@hotmail.com; ▊ albike.horta; ⏰ 09.30–18.30 Mon–Fri, 09.30–12.30 Sat) or **Moto Rent C & R** (Rua Conselheiro Medeiros; ☏ 292 945 434; m 967 215 135; e crmotorent@gmail.com; ▊ MotoRentFaialCR; ⏰ 09.00–17.00 Mon–Fri, 09.00–noon Sat), who also hire scooters. **EcoMoov** (Avda 25 de abril; m 967 561 326; e ecomoov.info@gmail.com; w ecomoov.pt; ⏰ 09.30–18.00 Mon–Fri, 09.30–16.00 Sat) rents e-bikes and e-scooters.

EXCURSIONS TO OTHER ISLANDS Faial, Pico and São Jorge share close links and are known as the 'triangle islands', partly because of the ferry routes that link them all year round, some carrying cars as well as passengers. Operated by Atlântico Line (w atlanticoline.pt), the most frequent are the 30-minute crossings from Horta to Madalena (Pico); in winter, ferries sail four times daily (07.30, 10.45, 13.15 & 17.15), with two more crossings in summer (09.00 & 20.15). Return departures from Madalena are at 08.15, 11.30, 14.00 and 18.00 in winter, plus 09.45 and 21.00 in summer. A single fare costs €3.80. There is a less frequent service to Velas on São Jorge, usually calling in at least one direction at São Roque, on Pico's northern coast; a few boats also call at Calheta on São Jorge. There's also a summer service from Horta to Graciosa and Terceira; a very long round trip (page 50).

TOURIST INFORMATION

The main tourist information office [216 E4] (\292 292 167; e qit.horta@artazores. com; ⊕ 09.00–12.30 & 14.00–17.00 Mon–Fri) is on Largo Infante D Henrique in central Horta. An additional office serves the cruise-ship hordes and ferry passengers in the Maritime Terminal [216 F1] (\292 293 097; e pt.gm.fai@azores. gov.pt; w visitazores.travel; ⊕ 08.30–19.00 Mon–Fri, 08.30–12.30 & 14.00–17.00 Sat, Sun & hols) and an airport office (⊕ 09.00–17.00 daily) opens to meet incoming flights. There's information on sustainable tourism at w discoverfaial.com.

 # WHERE TO STAY

Horta has a decent range of large hotels, plus a few smaller, characterful options, plush apartments and budget choices. Out of town, you'll find some tasteful, relaxed places. The Tourism Association (w casasacorianas.com) lists half a dozen inviting rural tourism establishments around the island, offering from two to ten rooms. Note that some, though not all, of these may be only bookable by the week. All prices will rocket during Sea Week, in early August.

HORTA

Hotel do Canal [217 E5] (103 rooms) Largo Dr Manuel de Arriaga; \292 202 120; e hoteldocanal@bensaude.pt; w bensaudehotels.com/en/hoteldocanal. Friendly staff, in a large, international-class hotel by the busy harbour. Large rooms enjoy AC, & cable TV. Reasonable restaurant, bars, winter garden, games room, compact fitness centre, sauna, jacuzzi, Turkish bath, hairdresser, conference room, garage. Excellent buffet b/fast inc. €€€€€

Pousada Forte da Horta (formerly Pousada de Santa Cruz) [216 E4] (28 rooms) Rua Vasco da Gama; \210 407 670; e recepcao.stacruz@ pestana.com; w pousadas.pt/uk/hotel/pousada-horta; ⊕ Apr–Oct. A 16th-century fort declared a national monument in 1947. Renovated to the high standards of Pousadas de Portugal, only the balconied superior rooms have a sea view; the restaurant offers regional dishes at prices a little more than elsewhere, & there's also a bar with terrace & pool overlooking the harbour, with views across to Pico. €€€€€

Apartamentos Kósmos [216 E2] (12 apartments) Av 25 de Abril; m 927 517 518; e kosmosreservas@sapo.pt. Spacious, modern, fully equipped s/c apartments in an unnumbered blue building on the waterfront. Cable TV. Rooms are land or sea view. €€€€

Azoris Faial Garden Hotel [216 D4] (131 rooms) Rua Cônsul Dabney; \292 207 400;

e reservas.faial@azorishotels.com; w azorishotels. com/faialgarden. Established in 1973, occupying what was the Western Union telegraph company's residential compound plus new wings. Bar, games room, spa, conference rooms, indoor & outdoor pools, fitness room. Restaurant with good vegetarian options & sharing plates & copious buffet b/fast. €€€€

✱ **Estrela do Atlântico** [216 D1] (5 rooms) Calçada de Santo António 25; \292 943 003; m 918 197 755; e info@edatlantico.com; w edatlantico.com. Individualistic, stylish rooms in a traditional house built in 2006, in rich gardens with seasonal outdoor pool & less than 10mins' walk from town. Soft colours & tasteful furnishings enhance the relaxed ambience. Large living room with myriad books & an honesty bar. Duplex rooms can accommodate families. Excellent, inventive b/fast inc. €€€

Faial Marina Apartments [216 E4] (6 apartments) Rua Conselheiro Medeiros 8; \292 391 313; m 962 822 441; e torrinhasazuis@gmail. com. Spacious modern apartments, some of which can accommodate up to 10 people. Fully s/c, with AC, cable TV & private parking. Very central & good value. €€€

Casa da Baia [217 E5] (8 rooms) Rua Vasco da Gama 20; \292 293 105; m 969 656 355; e geral@casadabaia.com; w casadabaia.com. Bright, light, sealife-themed rooms with private bath, shared kitchen with full s/c facilities & lounge area. Roof terrace. Bright & modern, this is central

& good value, especially off-season. 1 suite & a trpl, too, some with sea view. €–€€

Casa do Lado [216 E2] (14 rooms) Rua D Pedro IV 23; ☎292 700 351; m 961 964 414; e reservas@ acasadolado.com; w acasadolado.com. Decent budget option; go for a standard room but specify a balcony. Cable TV, private bath. B/fast inc in mid & high season. Low-season rates are excellent. €

ELSEWHERE ON FAIAL *Map, page 200*

Pátio (8 rooms & apartments) Quinta do Moinho, Rua da Igreja, Cedros; ☎292 946 805; m 964 803 777; e cristina@patio.pt; w patio.pt. Linked to the horseriding centre on the north coast (page 213), you can stay here in these modern rooms & apartments, without jumping on a gee-gee. Pleasant outdoor space, BBQ area & a relaxed ambience. €€€€

Quinta das Buganvílias (8 rooms) Castelo Branco, by a bus stop on the EN1–1A, just east of the airport & 6 miles from Horta; ☎292 943 255; e info.quintadasbuganvilias@gmail.com; w quintadasbuganvilias.com. An old family property, now a long-established guesthouse with a lounge & bar – which doubles up as a museum – all in a pleasant garden & orchard setting of 2ha. AC. €€€

Quinta da Meia Eira (6 rooms, 2 apartments) Rua dos Inocentes, Castelo Branco; ☎292 943 037; m 965 435 925; e info@meiaeira.com; w meiaeira.com. Set well off the main road, west of Horta, with views down to the sea. A pleasant rural retreat with lovely rooms, swimming pool (Apr–Nov) & lovely spacious gardens. Cable TV, AC, plus b/fast inc. Restaurant & shop nearby, excellent café-bakery in Lombega. Excellent reputation, good value. €€€

CAMPING *Map, page 200*

Praia do Almoxarife ☎292 949 855; e parques. campismo@urbhorta.pt; ⊕ Jun–Sep. Near the small beach, a wooded site with a lovely view across to Pico. A 15min taxi drive from Horta, or reachable by local bus. €

Salão ☎292 946 042; ⊕ Jun–Sep. On the north coast. A nice isolated site down the road east of the modern church of Salão (where there's a café & restaurant). It's a long way down steps to the bathing place. €

Varadouro ☎292 945 339; e campismo. hortaludus@mail.telepac.pt; ⊕ Jun–Sep. In the west of the island, close to tidal swimming pools, up the unmarked road behind the Princesa Alice restaurant. €

✕ WHERE TO EAT AND DRINK

In Horta, you will generally pay a little more than on some of the other islands, but you can eat well here with great fish and a few sophisticated choices. Things are definitely improving, and if you're on a budget you can hunt down places offering a cheap lunchtime feed. Some recommended places are listed below.

HORTA

Clipper Restaurant (Hotel do Canal) [217 E5] (see opposite) ☎292 202 120; w bensaudehotels. com/en/hoteldocanal/clipper-restaurant-bar; ⊕ 12.30–15.00 & 19.30–22.00 daily. In a swish, modern setting, good fresh fish & other dishes at prices a bit above the norm. A set dinner is also on offer, changing daily. €€€€

Genuino [217 E6] Areinha Velha 9; ☎292 701 542; w genuino.pt; ⊕ noon–15.00 & 18.30–22.00 Thu–Tue. Overlooking Porto Pim, a place top-rated for its fish, & while you pay a bit more, you can contemplate the achievements of the owner, Portugal's first solo round-the-world sailor (in fact he's done it twice – w genuinomadruga.

com). Even better, talk to him – this fine gentleman may greet you at the door. Serves everything from fish stew to lobster – you could spend a lot of money in here, but you don't have to. Save some appetite for dessert, as the *perdição do Genuino* (chocolate cake with passion-fruit ice cream) is a must. Children's menu & vegetarian choices. Accommodation available. €€€€

Canto da Doca [217 E5] Rua Nova; ☎292 292 444; e reservas@cantodadoca.com; CantodaDoca; ⊕ noon–14.30 & 18.30–23.00 daily. At the corner of the harbour, this offers a very different meal where you cook your own dinner of seafood or meat on a very hot lump of basalt. It is great fun, albeit noisy & rather expensive for the experience, but at least there can be no complaints about the chef! Vegetarian option available. Best enjoyed in a group. €€€

Principe Gastro-bar [217 D5] Estrada Principe Alberto do Monaco; **m** 967 173 184; **f** gastronomicprincipe; ⏰ 18.30–22.00 Mon–Sat. A high degree of sophistication in the cooking, the setting is the least impressive part of this establishment. Well-balanced dishes, demonstrating innovation which can be lacking in some islands. Well worth the visit, the service is slick & professional, too. €€€

Cantinho das Provas [216 E3] Rua Conselheiro Medeiros 38; **m** 911 816 139; **e** cantinhodasprovas@gmail.com; **w** cantinhodasprovas.com; ⏰ 18.30–21.30 Mon–Sat. Literally 'the tasting corner', this stylish wine bar & shop is the perfect setting for getting to know Azorean wines (mainly from Pico). Soups, tasty small dishes & dish of the day available. €€

Oceanic Café [216 E4] Rua Vasco da Gama 46; **m** 966 151 762; **w** azores-oceanic.com; ⏰ summer noon–midnight Wed–Mon, winter 18.00–late Thu–Sat. A relaxed café in a former Dabney warehouse with elegant tables hewn from black poplar & a large patio; the short, tapas-style menu might feature octopus salad, crab burgers or grilled sandwiches. Good selection of draught beers. Live rock & reggae 22.00 Fri & Sat. €€

Peter Café Sport [217 E5] Rua José Azevedo (Rua do Peter) 9; ☎ 292 292 327; **w** petercafesport.com; ⏰ 09.00–midnight Mon–Sat, 10.00–midnight Sun. Definitely an island institution, beloved meeting-point of yachties & telegraph staff since 1918. Come armed with a tale of maritime derring-do (or 2) & you'll fit right in. A pubby place with lots of signed flags, terrace across the street, pretty standard menu & their own Gin do Mar with maracujá. Now the street has been named after 'Peter', perhaps the town is next? €€

Restaurante Atlético [217 D5] Rua Filipe de Carvalho; ☎ 292 292 492; **e** atletico@nngromov. com; **f**; ⏰ noon–15.00 & 19.00–23.00 Tue–Sun. First, finding it: don't confuse it with the Atletico Bar, 50m away. Recently expanded, they cook up

excellent fish & meat over a wood-fire. Prices have gone up, but standards are good & even with 200 covers it can be packed in summer. €€

Taberna de Pim [217 E6] Rua Nova 3, by Porto Pim; ☎ 292 392 239; **e** tabernapim@gmail.com; **f** tabernadepim; ⏰ 11.00–01.00 daily. Small, nice atmosphere, food cooked to order. A few vegetarian options are available. €€

A Padaria [216 E3] Rua Walter Bensaúde 17; ☎ 292 391 357; ⏰ 07.00–20.30 Sun–Fri, 07.00–14.30 Sat. Also with an outlook on the harbourfront Rua Conselheiro Miguel da Silveira, this is a posh bakery-café offering pastries & coffee but also bread, a lunch of the day, vegetarian dishes & beers. Also at Travessa do Porto Pim [216 D6] (☎ 292 293 092; same hours). €

Café Porto Pim [217 E6] Rua Areinha Velha 5; ☎ 292 292 979; **e** cafeportopim@gmail. com; **f** cafeportopim; ⏰ 07.00–21.00 daily. Overlooking the sea in Porto Pim, great for its location (pedestrianised in 2023), outdoor tables & proximity to the beach. Excellent for a snack lunch, offering good soup & a welcome range of sandwiches. Vegetarian options. €

PRAIA DO NORTE

Café Rumar [map, page 200] On the main road, just west of the village church; ☎ 292 945 170; ⏰ 07.30–midnight Mon–Wed, Fri & Sat, 08.30–17.00 Sun. A simple place serving excellent traditional Azorean dishes, from land & sea. Much of what you eat is made or grown on site: homemade sausages, black pudding. You can see the yams growing from the window. Fish dishes are also on offer, desserts are cheap & generally prices are low. Book in high season, ask for a window seat. Service can be a bit slow. €€

CEDROS

Aldina [map, page 200] Estrada Regional 71; ☎ 292 946 155; **m** 961 280 377; **e** supermercado. aldina@gmail.com; **f** aldinacedros; ⏰ 07.30–15.00 daily. Behind a supermarket & café on the main road, a bright & modern dining room with daily dishes at attractive prices. €€

ENTERTAINMENT AND NIGHTLIFE

In sailing season, there's always lively chatter among the crews taking downtime in **Peter Café Sport** and weekends can feature live music there, and at **Oceanic Café** (for both, see above). Horta's tastefully renovated **cinema** [216 E2], near the main square, has a bar and with its ornate music-hall-style rows of boxes and Art Deco ceiling, offers a mix of Hollywood and art cinema, together with occasional orchestral and jazz music.

SHOPPING

Near Capelo, on the way to Capelinhos, you'll find the **Capelo Centro do Artesanato** (handicrafts) (Alto dos Cavacos, Capelo; ☎292 945 027; w artesanatocapelo.com; ⊕ Jun–Sep 09.30–18.30 Tue–Sat, Oct–May 09.30–17.30 Tue–Sat; opening times are a bit random, so at other times a notice invites you to call & someone will open up: m 969 996 509, 912 552 765), an obvious chapel-like centre, promoting local artisans' products, traditional to the island: incredibly intricate fig pith and fish-scale sculpture, lace, embroidery, corn dollies, basketry and much else. There is also a fascinating book of black-and-white photos of the various stages of the Capelinhos eruption: the photos are for sale, but you can browse for free. Not everything on display is Faial-made, so do ask if you want a genuine local souvenir. Small quantities of wine are also made in Capelo and Praia do Norte, though at present this is not sold commercially.

OTHER PRACTICALITIES

Hospital [216 B4] Estrada Príncipe Alberto do Mónaco, Horta; ☎292 201 000
Police [216 B5] Largo Duque d'Avila e Bolama, Horta; ☎292 208 510

Post office [216 E2] Largo Duque d'Avila e Bolama, Horta; ⊕ 08.30–18.30 Mon–Fri

WHAT TO SEE AND DO

Wandering through the streets of Horta, enjoying the present and past harbours, and making a tour to see the caldera and the scene of the last eruption is what most visitors do. One thing you should not miss is the Capelinhos Interpretative Centre, an outstanding design concept packed with information about volcanoes. If you have a car, then there are little villages to explore, tempting places to stop from which to make your own short walks, and whale watching from the clifftops.

For diving, whale-watching and fun fishing trips, see page 213 for some ideas. The tourist office carries a full list of the many operators.

MUSEUMS
Horta These are listed from north to south, finishing with the three clustered together on the shore beneath the Monte da Guia.

Museo de Arte Sacra da Horta (MASH) [216 D2] (Igreja do Carmo; m 963 369 090; e museuartesacrahorta@gmail.com; f mashorta; ⊕ 11.00–13.00 & 14.00–18.00 Mon–Fri; €2.50) In the Carmelite church (built 1649–1751), which was a busy staging post for missionaries heading to Brazil, there's a limited range of paintings and statues (almost all Baroque) plus vestments and silverwork, including crowns of the lay Ordem Terceira do Carmo. Information is only in Portuguese. The church was reopened for worship in 2018, but is pretty bare.

Museu da Horta [216 E3] (Largo Duque d'Avila e Bolama; ☎292 392 784; w museu-horta.azores.gov.pt; ⊕ Oct–Mar 09.30–17.30 Tue–Sun & hols, Apr–Sep

10.00–18.00 Tue–Sun; €2/1/free adult/under 25s & seniors/under 15s) Housed in a former Jesuit college, it is noted for its collection of incredibly detailed fig-tree pith sculptures, one of the island's traditional handicrafts, but also has excellent displays dedicated to the transatlantic seaplane crossings and the submarine cables that once made Faial so important in intercontinental communications, and the construction of Horta's modern port from 1876. Other rooms focus on paper-cut and religious art, while the main corridor exhibits antique furniture and paintings. Some of the information panels are bilingual.

Casa Manuel de Arriaga [216 D3] (Rua Jose de Freitas Fortuna; ✆ 292 293 361; ⊕ Apr–Sep 09.00–18.00 Tue–Sun, Oct–Mar 09.30–17.30 Tue–Sun; €2/1/free adult/ under 25s & seniors/under 15s) Opened in 2011, this well-laid-out museum is in the home of the Faial-born first President of the Republic of Portugal, in office from 1911 to 1915. A humanist and political intellectual, the museum celebrates his life, private ideals and Republican values. There are permanent and temporary exhibitions, a library and other resources, but the information is only in Portuguese, save for a couple of videos.

Museum of Parliament (Museu do Parlamento dos Açores) [216 D3] (Rua Marcelino Lima; ✆ 292 207 811; e museu@alra.pt; w alra.pt/index.php/ artigossite/1510; ⊕ 10.00–17.00 Mon–Fri, 14.00–17.00 Sat–Sun; free) Opened in 2023 near the modern parliament building, this has interesting coverage of the move towards autonomy, with a timeline that for some reason focuses on the telegraph companies. QR codes give detailed English texts.

German Colony exhibition [216 D4] (Edificio do Relógio, Rua Colónia Alemã; ⊕ 09.00–17.00 Mon–Fri; free) In the main building (recognisable by its clock tower) of the German telegraph company DAT, a small exhibition (in Portuguese, German and English) tells the story of the most tight-knit of the expat communities here (the British and Americans, with their sport and cultural clubs, were much more integrated into local life). The distinctive buildings were erected just before World War I, but unfortunately the German cables were cut on the outbreak of that war and again in 1939, and German nationals interned then expelled. The prize exhibit is some fine stained glass depicting German Imperial heraldry, created in 1912 but not installed until the mid-1920s (although the empire had ended in 1918).

Just down the hill on Rua Cônsul Dabney, **Trinity House** (now a school) was built in 1902 as a joint technical centre for the three companies; the Azorean government promised in 2021 to create a museum here, but there's no sign of progress as yet. Incidentally, the playwright Sir Christopher Hampton was born in Horta in 1946, as his father was a telegraph engineer here.

Museu Scrimshaw [216 E5] (Rua José Azevedo (Rua do Peter); ⊕ 10.00–13.00 & 14.00–17.30 Mon–Sat; €2.50/free adult/under 12s) A private collection of over 300 scrimshaw items, upstairs in the famous Peter Café Sport (page 208). It is illegal to use bone from dead whales to make scrimshaw, so the artists who still produce these pieces use material from days gone by; an ever-decreasing stock, of course, so prices stay high.

Fabrica da Baleia (Whale factory)/Observatório do Mar dos Açores [217 E7] (Monte da Guia; ✆ 292 292 140; w oma.pt; ⊕ Oct–Mar 10.00– 17.00 Mon–Fri, Apr–Sep 10.00–18.00 Mon–Fri, noon–18.00 Sat, Sun & hols;

By far the busiest celebration is Sea Week at the beginning of August. Primarily a yachting regatta with whaling-boat, kayak and even jet-ski races, the channel between Faial and Pico is a mass of fluttering sails and buzzing craft. Different musical groups perform each evening, including bands from mainland Europe, local bands and folklore groups; everything from brass bands to reggae. There are exhibitions too, and the road along the seafront is closed, allowing thousands of people to promenade. On the first Sunday of Sea Week the Festival of Nossa Senhor da Guia, Protector of the Fishermen, takes place with a procession from Porto Pim. The dates of many festivals vary each year, so please check with the tourist information office.

Sports and Cultural Week Horta; end of April.
Festa de N Sra das Angústias Horta; sixth Sunday after Easter.
Festas do Espírito Santo From the seventh Sunday after Easter until September, intermittently.
Festa de São João da Caldeira Horta; 24 June.
Horta City Anniversary 4 July.
Sea Week Horta; the week between the first and second Sunday in August. Horta's big annual party.
Festa de N Sra de Lourdes Feteira; last week in August.
Festa de N Sra da Saúde Varadouro; first week September.
December festival Horta; exact date varies.

€5/2.50/free adults/under 14s & seniors/under 7s; family tickets €10) This recently renovated museum focuses on the story of whaling in the Azores. In addition to all the machinery in situ, there is now a new room dedicated to the hunted species, complete with the 10m skeleton of a sperm whale. Visitors can watch videos with English subtitles and inform themselves further via the enthusiastic staff. Begun in 1943 with German- and Norwegian-made equipment, the former whaling station processed sperm whale oil, bonemeal, and meatmeal for cattle feed and remained operational for 30 years. In addition, concerts, theatre performances, art exhibitions, conferences and ecology/marine workshops are held in a separate space, there's a children's programme on environmental subjects, and a museum shop. To get here, either follow the road to Monte da Guia at the southern end of the harbour or simply walk across the beach from Porto Pim.

Casas Dabney (Antiga Adega/Antiga Casa Veraneio/Antiga Casa das Botes das Dabney) (Dabney Museum)

[217 E7] (Monte da Guia; ✆ 292 240 685; e pnfaial.casadosdabney@azores.gov.pt; w parquesnaturais.azores.gov.pt/parques/3/centro/27; ⊕ Apr–Oct 09.00–12.30 & 13.30–17.00 daily, Nov–Mar 09.00–12.30 & 13.30–17.00 Mon–Fri; free) The former wine cellar, summer house and boathouse of the Dabneys contain bilingual information about this family whose influence was important in the island's history. Three generations of the family were US consuls in Horta from 1806; they were successful merchants and bought this house in 1855. Immediately to the west, the Porto Pim aquarium is a small privately run collection that closed after storm damage in 2018 and has not reopened – see w parquesnaturais.azores.gov.pt/pt/parques/3/centro/14 for any updates.

Faial WHAT TO SEE AND DO

8

Around the island

Centro de Interpretacão do Vulcão dos Capelinhos (Volcano Interpretative Centre of Capelinhos) ⊙ 292 200 470; w parquesnaturais. azores.gov.pt/pt/parques/3/centro/12; ⊕ Apr–Oct 09.00–18.00 daily, Nov–Mar 10.00–17.00 Tue–Sat; €10/5/free adult/under 15s & seniors/under 7s, family ticket €20; guided tours Apr–Oct 10.00, 11.30, 14.30 & 16.30 daily, Nov–Mar 11.00 & 15.00 daily) Your visit begins with a 15-minute film in English which uses heaters and fans to dramatise different climatic phases. The 13-month story of the destructive 1957–58 Capelinhos eruption is then explained using an 8-minute holographic projection dramatically showing the stages of eruption. A series of galleries follow, illustrating the Azores microplate and how the islands began to form, highlighting some of the key elements of volcanology on each island, explaining the different sorts of eruption, and covering some of the most active volcanoes around the world as well as the volcanic peculiarities of each Azorean island. There's also a video on emigration, which accelerated after the eruption, and rocks from here and elsewhere, including ropy lava, quartz, granite and desert rose. The centre is built underground, in the ash and debris that buried the nearby villages and half the nearby Capelinhos lighthouse; all that appears in the bare landscape is a very low raised circle that allows natural light to the main chamber below. The internal design creates a great feeling of space and swirling lines and is aesthetically both stimulating and pleasing. The building was opened in 2008 to coincide with the 50th anniversary of the eruption, and has deservedly gained many national and international awards for its design and content. You should allow 2 hours to do it justice, finishing with the lighthouse itself; a modern spiral staircase (with 140 steps, rather steep and narrow) leads to the top for views of the site. There is a shop and a café (free access).

BIRDS AND FLOWERS The Caldeira do Faial Nature Reserve is good for the smaller endemic or rarer plants, and in the grassland by the footpaths and around the viewing area through the tunnel *Lactuca watsoniana*, *Daboecia azorica*, *Thymus caespititius*, *Centaurium scilloides*, *Hypericum foliosum*, yellow pimpernel and more can be found. The two most common birds are chaffinch and blackcap. The new volcano at **Capelinhos** regularly has nesting common terns and the roseate tern has also been recorded. Waders and ducks put into the beach at **Porto Pim**, and sea daffodils (*Pancratium maritimum*) grow in a small area of dunes (the only ones in the Azores) at the back of the beach. The protected area of **Monte da Guia** supports several native and endemic plant species.

RECREATIONAL FOREST RESERVES

Capelo An 80ha area of woodland with numerous trails, including much of the walking trail from Capelo to Capelinhos Interpretative Centre. In the early days after settlement, woad was cultivated here, but the good land was lost when the 1672 eruption of Pico do Fogo covered all with lava and it became another area of mistério. It is now a protected area, and in the woodlands on higher ground Azores endemics can be found. Picnic tables, etc, make this a very popular place on summer weekends. You can look in to the Casa Tipica, with an *atafona* or animal mill on the ground floor and external stairs to the nicely furnished rooms above.

SPORTS AND ACTIVITIES Faial's underwater heritage, ie: the thousand-odd ships wrecked nearby, is increasingly recognised not just as exciting venues for divers but as important sites in terms of history and biodiversity. A subaquatic archaeological park was created in 2015, covering 35 separate sites, of which the best-known include the *Main* (a Dabney ship that sank in Porto Pim in 1892 and is only 5m down), the *Caroline* (which sank in the channel off Madalena in 1901, carrying guano from Chile to France), and the 18th- and 19th-century cannons 18m down in the bay of Entre Os Montes, alongside 1920s telegraph cables.

Quayside cabins down in front of the Peter Café Sport in **Horta** are home to operators of all sea-based activities, including those listed below. Around the island, various old vigias (**whale lookouts**) are signposted – look out for them, especially near Cedros. This is a splendid initiative, for they are the perfect places for a picnic and using your binoculars; it is amazing how many waves turn into dolphins by the end of a bottle of wine.

Diving

Dive Azores [216 E4] Marina da Horta; **m** 967 882 214; **e** info@diveazores.net; **w** diveazores.net. PADI scuba courses & a range of diving experiences, including with sharks; scientific research tourism is also an option. Also offers whale watching (see right).

Haliotis [216 E4] Marina da Horta; **m** 911 913 624; **e** faial@haliotis.pt; **w** haliotis.pt. A range of dives here & on Santa Maria & Madeira, visiting wrecks & sea mounts such as Princess Alice Banks, 70km from Horta.

Norberto Diving [216 E4] Marina da Horta; ✆292 293 891; **m** 969 197 077; **e** info@ norbertodiver.pt; **w** norbertodiver.pt. With dives from €45 & with a 'menu' of over 20 dive spots around the islands, plus longer trips to the offshore Princess Alice sea bank.

Fishing

Oceanic Fishing **m** 966 783 101; **e** les@ oceanic-fishing.com; **w** oceanic-fishing.com. Tuna fishing May–Jun & blue marlin Jul–Sep. Coastal fishing Apr–Oct. Essential to reserve well in advance – even though it costs €2,500/day they are fully booked in season.

Horseriding

Pátio ✆292 946 805; **m** 964 803 777; **e** anja@ patio.pt, booking@patio.pt; **w** patio.pt. Beginner rides, day rides & riding holidays which could include a week-long circuit of the island. Good, solid reputation, 15 well-looked-after Lusitano horses. Accommodation on site if required (page 207). English, French & German are all spoken.

Island tours by jeep, by bike or on foot

Azores Experiences [216 E4] Marina da Horta; **m** 965 650 452; **e** booking@azoresexperiences.

com; **w** azoresexperiences.com. A full range of land- & sea-based tours, full & half day.

Naturalist [217 E5] Largo Dr Manuel de Arriaga; **m** 916 746 917; **e** contact@naturalist.pt; **w** naturalist.pt. Relatively new to Faial island, this company offers jeep & bike tours, birdwatching & whale watching.

Our Island [216 E2] Rua Serpa Pinta 32; **m** 967 172 754; **e** info@ourisland-azores.com; **w** ourisland-azores.com. In addition to jeep tours & hiking, the company also offers guided mountain bike and trail-running adventures.

Swimming

Varadouro On the southwest coast, on the way to Capelinhos. Natural rock pools, changing facilities & occasional lifeguard. Swimming only advised in very calm conditions – follow local advice. There was once a thermal bath here, but the spring stopped flowing after the 1988 earthquake. A lovely bay, with a jetty & campsite.

Porto Pim The relatively long sandy beach in the bay with almost sand-coloured plants, was once the original harbour. Shallow water, often calm, for some way out, so the water is warmer. Very popular, & on the edge of Horta town; there are facilities at the far end of the beach, towards the Observatório do Mar, & cafés nearby.

Praia do Almoxarife Small sandy beach, near the campsite. Some 15mins by taxi from Horta, with facilities, campsite & restaurants nearby.

Whale watching

Azores Experiences See left for contact details. With 1 boat, a small but reputable whale- & dolphin-watching operation run by enthusiastic owners. Also offer trips that combine sea- & land-based activities, such as jeep tours. Whale-watching trips (3–4hrs) from €67.

Dive Azores See page 213 for contact details. Whale watching & snorkelling with dolphins.
Naturalist See page 213 for contact details. Whale watching from €55–75. A 98% success rate due to their land-based spotters.
Peter Whale Watching \292 292 327; w petercafesport.com. Half day from €70 (children €50), full day from €120 (children €90).

Whalewatch Azores \292 293 891; e info@ whalewatchazores.com; w whalewatchazores. com. For the serious or avid whale watcher, 5/9-night holidays (€1,280/2,155) between Apr & Jun focusing on whale & dolphin observation. The *Physeter*, their 12m catamaran, has just 2 cabins but can take 12 passengers, so there's usually space for day trippers.

WALKS ON FAIAL

There are now ten official walks, including a coast-to-coast walk of 37km, two other longish linear hikes, one easy linear hike and six shorter circular ones. Full details of all walks, with maps and narrative guides, are on the 'Trails' section of w visitazores.com; leaflets for them are also available from tourist offices. Note that the caldera itself is a nature reserve and descent into it is not permitted unless you are with a specially licensed guide. Climbing up into the Capelinhos volcanic area is subject to the same restriction and the tourist office has a full list of guides with licences. Brief summaries of the six circular routes are given below.

CALDEIRA (Easy, 7km, 2½hrs) A circuit of the crater starting at the caldera viewpoint. Only to be attempted in settled weather with good visibility.

ROCHA DA FAJÃ (Easy, 5km, 2½hrs) A circular walk out of Praia do Norte, reaching the coast before returning.

CABEÇO DO CANTO (Medium difficulty, 2.6km, 2hrs) A circular walk; the bus will take you close to the start.

ENTRE MONTES (Easy, 3.5km, 1½hrs) A walk within easy distance of Horta town centre, so no need to get transport to/from the start/finish.

RIBEIRINHA (Easy, 8.3km, 2½hrs) A longer circuit, in the island's northeast.

RUMO AO MORRO DE CASTELO BRANCO (Easy, 4km, 1½hours) A circular walk from Lombega village, in the island's southwest, to view Morro de Castelo Branco, a headland noted for its birds and flora. Be aware that ascent of the headland itself is dangerous, and should not be attempted.

TOURING THE ISLAND

CAR TOUR Faial is small, and this itinerary provides a fascinating half-day tour. If you can, take a picnic to enjoy in the forest park at Capelinhos. See the map on page 200 for locations.

Horta–Espalamaca–Ribeira Funda–Praia do Norte–Capelinhos–Castelo Branco–Horta
Leave **Horta** and begin by driving up to the ridge that overlooks the town from the north and stop at the belvedere at **Espalamaca**. Here you have a fine view over Horta, the harbour, and of fields nudging their way up to the houses, so quickly does town end and countryside begin. Along the ridge of Espalamaca are

several windmills and, neatly nestling in its valley, **Flamengos** village. Turn around and look down upon a pretty valley and **Praia do Almoxarife**.

Take the EN1–2a on your way to the caldera, and the little **Chapel of São João** is your next stop, after a cool drive beneath cryptomeria trees. São João is at the junction, where you have a view down over meadows to Horta and across the channel to Pico. In early summer the hedgerows here are bedecked with tiny double red roses, coinciding with the Festa do São João in June (page 211).

Turn right in front of the chapel (EN2–2a), and follow signs up to the **caldera** along a narrowing road lined with tall hydrangeas. You will pass a road off to your right leading to Quebrada and Ribeira Funda on the north coast. There are wonderful views across to Pico and São Jorge.

The road ends by a pedestrian **tunnel**, at an altitude of 900m. The tunnel is very short, and sometimes windy and cold. Walk through and view the caldera, which is now a nature reserve, with access restricted to properly licensed guides and their small groups. The large crater is 400m deep and 1,450m in diameter. Common native shrubs here include juniper and erica. Above the tunnel on the caldera's rim is the Oratory of São João. On a clear day Pico, São Jorge and Graciosa can be seen. To the east you can make out the impressive Pedro Miguel Graben, where the earth's crust has been displaced downwards between faults on either side of it. From the German *graben*, meaning 'trench', and orientated west northwest–east southeast, it is a major volcanic feature of the island. An alternative opportunity to look down into the caldera is to drive up from the west to **Cabeco Gordo** – see map, page 200. Almost due west from the summit is a line of cinder cones marking the fracture along which eruptions have occurred in recent geological time.

Drive back down to the turn-off previously mentioned, and turn left to **Ribeira Funda**. For flowers, this is one of the prettiest roads, and during July and August the hydrangeas are at their best. There are good views from two viewpoints along this road, and between trees and hydrangeas there are glimpses of villages and the sea beyond. Stop and enjoy, too, the glorious view over the Ribeira das Cabras, and note the extensive lava beds before coming to **Praia do Norte**.

From here a road cuts west through thick, low forest to Norte Pequeno and **Capelinhos,** one of the most interesting volcanic sites in Europe, as captured in its state-of-the-art museum (page 212).

Turn southeastwards more or less parallel with the coast on the EN1–1a to **Castelo Branco**, where there is a fine view of the coastline, before proceeding to **Feteira**. You will often see this place mentioned in brochures. Lying between the airport and Horta, it is a length of coast with contorted lava rocks and rock arches of some curiosity.

HORTA The island's only town is made up from two adjacent bays: one small and rounded, Baía do Porto Pim; the other larger and more open. They are separated by an isthmus leading to the remains of a volcano crater, known as Monte da Guia, and splendid views of the Central Group islands can be had from the top. The smaller bay is intimate, seemingly almost separate from the town, and was an American whaling centre from the end of the 18th century and during the 19th century, with as many as 400 ships recorded at one time. Even by the beginning of the 20th century, two-thirds of all sperm whales harpooned were caught off the Azores. The old whale factory and the slipway where whales were landed and hauled up for processing after being caught by the Azorean open boats is now an excellent museum (page 210). In the town itself there are some fine buildings, and there is a walk northwards along the esplanade out to a little park. The €35 million northern

HORTA

For listings, see from page 206

Where to stay

1	Apartamentos Kósmos.........E2
2	Azoris Faial Garden.............D4
3	Casa da Baía......................E5
4	Casa do Lado.....................E2
5	Estrela do Atlântico............D1
6	Faial Marina Apartments.....E4
7	Hotel do Canal...................E5
8	Pousada Forte da Horta......E4

Where to eat and drink

9	A Padaria.....................D6, E3
10	Café Porto Pim..................E6
11	Cantinho das Provas..........E3
12	Canto da Doca..................E5
	Clipper.........................(see 7)
13	Genuíno..........................E6
14	Oceanic Café....................E4
15	Peter Café Sport...............E5
16	Príncipe Gastro-bar...........D5
17	Restaurante Atlético..........D5
18	Taberna de Pim................E6

Espalamaca, Praia do Almoxarife, campsite

Madalena (Pico), São Roque (Pico), Velas (São Jorge)

Ferry terminal

Cruise/ship terminal

Petrol station

Nossa Senhora da Conceição

RUA DA CONCEIÇÃO

R MAESTRO A A GARBETT

R ALMEIDA GARRETT

AVENIDA MIGUEL DA SILVA

AVENIDA 25 DE ABRIL

R SERPA PINTO

R CONSELHEIRO MIGUEL DA SILVA

Praça da República

Market

Our Island

Torre do Relógio

RUA DA VISTA ALEGRE

University of the Azores

CALÇADA DE SANTO ANTÓNIO

RUA A GRAÇA

RUA DE SÃO PAULO

RUA DE SÃO JOÃO

RUA E REBELO

São Salvador

Museu da Horta

R E SULCÃO

R DE JESUS

R WALTER BENSAÚDE

R CONSELHEIRO MEDEIROS

AVENIDA 25 DE ABRIL

Café Internacional

Marina da Horta

Largo Infante Henrique

Pousada Forte da Horta

Azores Airlines

DA GAMA

Museu de Arte Sacra da Horta (MASH)

RUA MINISTRO AVILA

RUA DR NEVES

RUA DO PAIOL

RUA MANUEL JOAQUIM DIAS

Flamengos

Monte Carneiro

CANADA DOS DUTRAS

RUA ILHA DO PICO

Regional Legislative Assembly

Museum of Parliament

German Colony exhibition

RUA MARCELINO LIMA

Casa Manuel de Arriaga

Convent of St Francis

Trinity House

RUA CONSUL DABNEY

Botanical Garden, Flamengos, Caldeira

Espalamaca, Praia do Almoxarife

RUA CONSELHEIRO TERRA PINHEIRO

RUA PRI

Hospital

Flamengos & Caldeira

216

ATLANTIC OCEAN

Whale-watching & diving operators
Museu Scrimshaw
Naturalist

3
15
7

Nossa Senhora das Angústias

16
R F CARVALHO

RUA PRINCIPE ALBERTO DO MÓNACO

Prince Albert of Monaco Observatory

Modelo Hypermarket

ALBERTO DO MÓNACO

R ILHA AZUL

ALBERTO DO MÓNACO

RUA ILHA DE SÃO LUIS

R ILHA DA VENTURA

RUA DO PASTELEIRO

Airport,
Quinta das Buganvílias,
Quinta da Meia Eira

Police station

AVENIDA GAGO COUTINHO E SACADURA CABRAL

RUA DO PASTELEIRO

São Sebastião Fort

9

17

RUA C IVENS

C D'AVILA

13
10
18

12

R NOVA

R DA ROSA

Largo Manuel de Arriaga

Monte Queimado 86m

TRAVESSA DO PORTO PIM

Baía do Porto Pim

Fabrica da Baleia/
Centro do Mar

Dabney Museum

Aquarium
(temporarily closed)

National Park
Information Centre

P

P

Senhora da Guia 105m

Caldeira do Inferno

Monte da Guia 145m

F

ATLANTIC OCEAN

KEY
Town tour
Direction of tour

N
Bradt

0   400m
0   400yds

Faial TOURING THE ISLAND

8

217

quay complements the one built in 1876 on the south side of the bay and now takes medium-sized cruise ships. As in Ponta Delgada, cruise-ship passengers are able to walk from their ship straight into town.

Town trail This conveniently divides into two walks, and we begin with the central and northern parts of town. Do keep an eye out for the information panels on many of the town's bus stops, which provide detailed, bilingual information on the various points of interest: rather unexpected, they are useful – and unfortunately almost unnoticeable!

Central and northern Horta Start at the entrance to the **Pousada Forte da Horta** [216 E4], the *castelo* (castle) built in 1567 to defend the harbour. It's now a hotel. With your back to the castle entrance, go right, passing the little garden on your right overlooking the marina and then take the left fork along the Rua Conselheiro Medeiros at the side of the pastel-green wedding cake of a building, charming with its wrought-iron balconies. First, however, check out the inside of the 'cake', which is the **Café Internacional**, with its impressive Art-Deco interior.

Soon you will see above you on your left the former **convent of St Francis**, built at the end of the 17th century; the original convent was destroyed by Essex and Raleigh in 1597. To its right is the towering, charming St Francis church, built in 1696; still (theoretically!) scheduled for restoration, it has been closed to the public for some years. At the junction with the narrow Rua do Telegrapho, you will see the **Casa Manuel de Arriaga** [216 D3] set back a hundred metres or so.

From the church continue northward and you soon come to the old Jesuit college, up to your left, founded in 1719 for the training of missionaries to serve in the Portuguese colonies. It is now the **Museu de Horta** [216 E3], plus government offices. Although a small museum, it is well worth visiting. Among its exhibits is statuary of several centuries, some originating from Flanders but many carved from cedarwood in the Azores. The Friends of Heart School in Angra made figures which were taken to the other islands and the figures come not only from churches and chapels no longer extant, but also private homes. Next door is the **Church of São Salvador** [216 E2], the principal or Mother (*Matriz*) Church of Horta, begun in 1680 and completed in 1760.

From the museum and church, descend down the cobbled slope and pass in front of the *Correios* (post office) to turn left into the Rua Serpa Pinto. After a few blocks you reach the covered **market**, recently refurbished but still not very lively. Next to this is a little garden square, the **Praça da República** [216 E2]; on the diagonally opposite corner is another wedding cake of a building, this time pink and slightly weather-beaten, with splendid white balustrades. In earlier times houses painted pink were owned only by the aristocracy. Almost equally smart is the fire and ambulance station to its right. Take the narrow road (Rua Dr Arriaga Nunes) that leads uphill next to the pink building, then take the first right, and you will see a clock tower at the top. This is the **Torre do Relógio** [216 E1], built in the early 18th century; it is a symbol of Azorean perseverance in the face of seismic forces which destroyed the 16th-century Mother Church. The adjacent public garden dating from 1857, the **Jardim de Florêncio Terra**, has a fine dragon tree, while the massive building behind is the former **Hospital da Misericórdia**, now usefully housing the oceanography and fisheries faculty of the **University of the Azores** [216 D1]. Leave this area by the road below the clock, taking you steeply down towards cobbles. At the bottom go left and at the end cross a small stream, the Ribeira da Conceição, near which Faial's first settlement was begun in the 15th century. You will see the small,

In 1875, a house burned down and the governor was so angry that no-one came in time to extinguish it that he offered a reward to the first eight men to come with a pump to the next fire and a lesser sum to the first 12 men with buckets. This was how a rudimentary fire service began, continuing until 1912, when Horta's water supply was improved and the Associaçao Faialense de Bombeiros Voluntarios could be established. Church bells would sound the alarm and each district in Horta had its own signal; four bells for Angusuas, six for Matriz, eight for Conceição, until they were replaced by a siren in 1966.

Extinguishing shipboard fires was and still is their responsibility. Their payment for dealing with a fire on a World War I Italian troopship enabled the volunteers to purchase in 1930 their first two motorised fire engines. Shipboard fires were frequent between 1958 and 1968 because of the number of ships transporting fishmeal, which had a tendency to self-combust. Today's very professional association of *bombeiros* is one of more than 450 departments nationwide (including the other Azores islands) supervised by the Portuguese National Fire Authority, the SNB.

The firemen (and women) are still volunteers who give their time and risk their lives, thus continuing a long tradition. Horta has 60, all with understanding employers. Volunteering tends to run in families, sometimes three generations serving at the same time. They can join the association from age 14 and remain until 60. Training is done on the island, often with imported specialists. The department is also involved in civil rescue service, and disaster simulations from fires to earthquakes and volcanic eruptions are undertaken twice a year. Volunteers also visit each school on the island at least once a year to teach the children how to respond in emergencies. The service is funded by a combination of private, municipal and central government sources, supplemented by demonstrations and firefighting courses around the island to raise money. The fire department is also responsible for the ambulance service, whose crews are the only permanently paid members of staff.

pretty white church, the **Igreja de Nossa Senhora da Conceição**, inscribed with the dates 1527, 1597, 1749, 1926 and 1933. This church has suffered a traumatic history. Originally built by the early settlers, it was destroyed during the first sacking of the town in 1597. A church built much later was destroyed in 1926. Its replacement was built in the Art Deco style of the time and this in turn was damaged in 1941 by an explosion in a nearby army barracks. Following a major restoration, it is now pristine and most elegant. From here, either return along the roads through the town, or go east to the sea and return along the esplanade.

Southern Horta To explore the second, southern sector, again leave from the **Pousada Forte da Horta** [216 E4]. This time turn left and walk down the road to pass the **Peter Café Sport** (page 208) on your right. Many years ago this was a small bar known to all sailors who called in at Horta, and a visitors' book was maintained which had many amusing entries. Now there is a shop and other enterprises including a museum of scrimshaw (page 210), yacht services, whale-watching tours and restaurant, and the guest book with all its early entries is posted on the internet;

with good self-publicity the café is now known to a much wider circle around the world – almost a global brand!

Move up to the higher road behind the café and you will soon come, on your left, to the **Igreja de Nossa Senhora das Angústias** [217 E5], the attractively restored Church of Our Lady of Anguish. Continue straight on to **Porto Pim**, the original harbour of Horta. Note the defensive walls and the remains of the **Fort of São Sebastião** [217 D6], constructed during the 17th century as protection against pirates and other attackers. You should try to visit at night when the gateway is floodlit and very pretty.

Take the road running behind the sea wall left of the gateway to access the beach. You will see the small houses of one of the oldest remaining parts of Horta, all nestling at the foot of **Monte Queimado** [217 E6]; *queimado* means 'burned', referring to the cinders. Walk along the beach – tide permitting – to the far end to visit the old whale factory [217 E7]. This was built only about 50 years ago and there is an earlier factory dating from 1836 that was built originally for drying cod. It is now a **whaling museum** (page 210), renovated in 2018, with machinery intact and a cultural centre with occasional events and exhibits to do with the sea. This small area is full of history, for you can find near the museum the point where the submarine cables came out to connect to relay stations. This area is indelibly linked to the influential Dabney family. Their summer house is now a museum devoted to the family and their role in the development of the island (page 211).

From the whale factory, take the road that climbs to the summit of **Monte da Guia** [217 F8]. On the way you will pass a little chapel, dedicated to the Senhora da Guia, also once used as a lookout for whales. The actual summit of Monte da Guia (145m) is closed to visitors. Return down the road, enjoying the splendid views of Porto Pim and Horta. Look also across Porto Pim bay and to the hill behind, **Monte das Moças**, where you will see an observatory. The building dates from around 1901, and has been in use as a meteorological observatory since 1915. It was named **Prince Albert of Monaco Observatory** [217 D5] in 1923, a year after the prince's death. Just below this are the buildings and tennis courts of what is now the Azoris Faial Garden Hotel; previously this was the residential compound of the American Western Union Telegraph Co, built in the 1920s with reinforced concrete to withstand earth tremors. As you return to town and pass the harbour (built from 1876), pause to view the drawings and cartoons on the walls left by visiting yacht crews. This free outdoor art gallery exists because it is said to be bad luck to sail away without leaving your mark. Sadly, however, one or two have become memorials. Considerable care and time have clearly been taken by some artists, others are rushed scrawls, but all show a record of the many crews that have put in at Horta on their travels across the oceans.

PRAIA DO ALMOXARIFE Just the other side of the ridge immediately to the north of Horta is one of the prettiest valleys on the island, and one of its earliest settlements. The large houses have charming gardens and there are a few restaurants, at least one of which will be open year-round. There is a small, black-sandy beach with changing facilities, and the camping site is nearby. It is a relaxing place from which to enjoy a fine view of Pico. A bus runs (three or four times Mon–Fri, one on Sat) to Praia do Almoxarife along the Horta waterfront past the marina and ferry terminal.

FLAMENGOS
Jardim Botânico do Faial (Rua de São Lourenço 23, Flamengos; ☎292 948 140; w parquesnaturais.azores.gov.pt/en/parques/3/centro/13; ⊕ Nov–Mar 10.00–17.00

Tue–Fri, 14.00–17.30 Sat & hols, Apr–Oct 10.00–18.00 daily; €5/2/free adult/ under 15s & seniors/under 7s; family tickets also available) Established in 1986 at the Quinta de São Lourenço, near Horta, Faial's small but excellent botanic garden is devoted to the endemic and indigenous plants of the archipelago, and is most attractively designed with gentle hills and a ravine filled with ferns. Sheltered by magnificent hedges to protect it from the salt-laden winds, the garden is able to grow species that are found at both sea level and at various altitudes in the mountains, and four altitudinal zones are represented. Here some of the more showy species such as *Thymus caespititius*, the native thyme, *Azorina vidalii*, the native campanula, dramatic *Euphorbia stygiana* and the most desirable shrub of all, the endemic bilberry *Vaccinium cylindraceum*, can be enjoyed in season. In addition, if you (understandably) have been struggling to identify all the different evergreen shrubs native to the islands, here is an excellent opportunity to study them close at hand and compare them: they have labels. Start at the new visitor centre (with gift shop) to see a short film with English subtitles, documenting the sterling work being done to save rare species from extinction. You'll finish at the new orchidarium, built to house a stunning collection donated by a Finnish couple and including the five very unshowy species found in the Azores.

CAPELINHOS This is the site of the 1957–58 eruption and it is fascinating to see how it is, years later, with a few hardy pioneering plants trying to establish

THE CAPELINHOS ERUPTION

Earthquakes started on 16 September 1957 and on 27 September, the sea began to boil near the Capelinhos rocks. On 29 September, explosions began and cinders were thrown into the air. By 1 October, cinders were being projected some 600m high, the eruption cloud rose to 6,000m and an islet began to form round the crater. Six days later, there was a cone-shaped island 60m high and 640m across, but already the sea was starting to destroy it. Two days more and it was 100m tall and over 700m across in the shape of a horseshoe, opening to the south. The sea entered this break so that the vent of the volcano was underwater, causing very violent explosions and fragmenting the new lava into ash and cinders. By 30 October, the sea had washed away the entire island.

In early November, eruptions began again and by the middle of the month a new island was linked to Faial by a narrow bar of black ash. Eruptions continued through the winter and by March 1958 more than 2km² of land had been added. During the following months lava flowed into the ocean, and, with the vent protected from the sea, incandescent lava was thrown up most spectacularly more than 500m, continuing intermittently until 24 October. In one period of 36 hours over 300 earth tremors were registered, shaking the whole island. In total some 300 houses were destroyed and almost every house on the west side of Faial was damaged; 2,000 people were rehoused. Crops were destroyed and a 5m layer of ash and rocks buried houses and many of the fields around the villages of Capelo and Norte Pequeno. Wind erosion is now slowly exposing these once more. The eruption changed the lives of many islanders, with hundreds subsequently emigrating to the US and Canada. Now, some have returned and houses have been renovated for holiday letting.

themselves, and the effects of wind erosion. Come here on a blustery day and you see the fine particles blowing on the wind and indeed feel them stinging your face. The stunning visitor centre explains it all (page 212). It is worth walking or driving down to see the small cove and whalers' settlement below Capelinhos. Also near the village is the forest park (page 212), which is a pleasant place to walk.

9

Pico

To most visitors, Pico is defined by the lofty volcanic cone of Pico itself: remarkable, steep-sided, dormant and rising to 2,351m, this is Portugal's highest mountain. Certainly this peak and the numerous black lava flows in different parts of the island make Pico the most distinctive of all in the archipelago. The finest views are to be had looking across the channel head-on from Faial, or the long side view from São Jorge; on the island itself, there's also a superb view of the summit to be had from Lajes. In the western end of the island you are always aware of Pico's overshadowing presence, whether dense clouds hang just above Madalena's rooftops obscuring everything above 40m, or the sky is at its bluest and all is revealed. As late as April, it can wear a snowy covering. The mountain always looks over your shoulder.

Of all the islands this is the most obviously volcanic, especially around Madalena and along the coast by the airport where the black stones have been gathered and made into tiny walled enclosures, square ones for vines, round ones for figs. Long ago, red and pink scrambling roses, the dark purple-blue trumpet flowers of the climbing ipomoea and carpets of nasturtium escaped from cultivation, and now add wild colour for many weeks if not months of the year. Houses are of black stone, dressed around the windows, whitewash on the walls. Pico, with nearby Faial, was the centre for land-based open-boat whale hunting; some seven years after the last whale was killed, boats again went to sea looking for whales, only this time just to watch, and Pico has become one of the main centres.

The southern slopes of the island are more sheltered and less windy and so protective enclosures go high above the coastal villages. In contrast, the northern slopes are far more forested. Pittosporum and native myrica have invaded the lower slopes where there were once extensive vineyards among the stones, adding further large areas of tree cover. On the uplands most of the native vegetation has been cleared for cattle pasture, helped by subsidies from a then embryonic European community – a dubious investment, since the resultant grass is very poor. However, there are pockets of native and endemic plants and hopefully current measures will be sufficient to save them; 1,500ha above the 1,200m contour is a designated protected zone. These remnants provide Pico with the most easily accessible areas of indigenous vegetation where you can begin to imagine just how the islands might have appeared to the very first settlers.

To explore the island's uplands by car, to find the lakes and other beautiful areas, just to stop and enjoy the grand scenery and the ever-changing cloud patterns around the mountain, is reason enough to come to Pico. But added to this are the cultural and historical interests and, for the experienced walker, the extraordinary experience of being on the summit of Pico where on a clear day the stupendous views embrace the sister islands of Faial, São Jorge, Graciosa and Terceira. Much closer, below, daughter cones and craters pockmark the plateau giving a tiny hint of what an extraordinary scene this must have been when it was most active. The

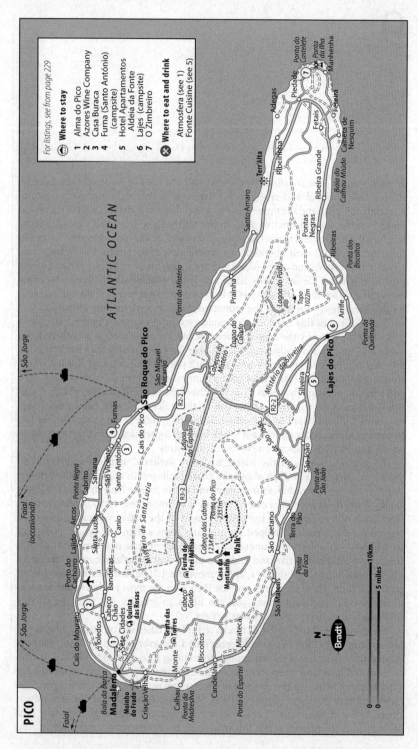

PICO

ATLANTIC OCEAN

São Jorge

Faial (occasional)

São Jorge

Faial

Baía da Barca **Madalena**
Cais do Mourato
Porto do Cachorro
Moinho do Frade
Criação Velha
Calhau
Monte
Toledos
Sete Cidades
Cabeço Chão
Quinta das Rosas
Lajido
Arcos
Santa Luzia
Bandeiras
Canito
Ponta Negra
Gabrito
Santana
São Vicente
Santo António
Cais do Pico
Furnas
São Miguel Arcanjo
São Roque do Pico
Ponta da Madrisilva
Ponta do Espartel
Candelária
Biscoitos
Gruta das Torres
Cabeço Gordo
Mirateca
São Mateus
Terra do Pão
Ponta da Foca
São Caetano
Furna de Frei Matias
Casa da Montanha
Cabeço das Cabras 1234m
Ponta do Pico 2351m
Walk
Mistério de Santa Luzia
Mistério de São João
São João
Ponta de São João
Silveira
Mistério do Silveira
Arrife
Ponta da Queimada
Lajes do Pico
Prainha
Lagoa do Capitão
Cabeços do Mistério
Lagoa do Caiado
Lagoa do Pau
Topo 1022m
R2-2
R3-2
R2-2
Santo Amaro
Ter'Alta
Ribeirinha
Adegas
Piedade
Ponta do Castelete
Ponta da Ilha
Manhenha
Feteira
Fetais
Calheta de Nesquim
Baía do Calhau Miúdo
Ribeira Grande
Ribeiras
Pontas Negras
Ponta dos Biscoitos

7
4
3
2
1
5
6

Ponta do Mistério

N
Bradt

0   5 miles
0   10km

224

mountain only is dormant; on Piquinho, also called Pico Pequeno, the little peak that is a small cone in the summit crater, there are fumaroles, rocks are very warm to the touch and there is a smell of sulphur. Escaping gases and flowing hot magma when the surface lava was cooling have created caves and tube-like tunnels; several are known and named, but others are buried beneath vegetation or a thin tumble of rocks so great care is needed and it is essential not to wander away from paths.

An island tour by car or taxi is a must, driving as high as the road reaches on Pico mountain and down to sheltered areas by the sea, enjoying impressive landscapes and exploring villages and country life, while the coast has numerous headlands, some of which provide spectacular miradouros. The central mountain road running the length of the island offers endless interest (although the eastern half is badly pot-holed), with side excursions off to small lakes and viewpoints. Museums in Lajes and São Roque tell the fascinating story of whaling in the Azores. The more adventurous can go whale watching or attempt the ascent of Pico. The island was once famous for its fortified Verdelho wine and, in the last several years, more modern methods of cultivation and production are once again making saleable table wine. Originally the vines were grown in very small stone-wall enclosures to protect the plants from salt winds and to gain extra heat, and they are an extraordinary memorial to the tenacity and hard work of the earlier settlers. Extensive areas stretching along the western coast from just outside Madalena are so impressive that in 2002, UNESCO designated them a World Heritage Site. Just follow the 'Património Mundial' road signs to get a close-up at these compact vineyards. A visit to the winery followed by a tasting completes the picture.

BACKGROUND

GEOLOGY Given that the channel between Pico and Faial is only 100m deep it is quite likely the two islands are part of the same volcanic complex. Pico mountain may be 2,351m above sea level, but it rises 3,500m above the surrounding ocean floor.

The island can be viewed as three sections: the stratovolcano of Pico mountain that dominates its western part; Topo volcano, a shield-like structure above the town of Lajes do Pico on the southern part of the island; and the 29km-long westnorthwest–eastsoutheast-orientated plateau, the Planalto da Achada, between the centre and eastern end of the island and characterised by scoria and spatter cones and associated lava flows.

Pico mountain began as a shield volcano, a broad and gently sloping volcano formed by repeated eruptions from a cluster of vents eventually creating a large plinth some 16km wide at sea level and about 1,100m altitude. Extensive lava flows have completely covered the base of the volcano, thought to be around 240,000 years old. Most of the conspicuous cinder cones of the lower slopes originate on this shield, and are relatively recent.

The magnificent summit cone was created by eruptions from vents clustered closely together, forming a stratovolcano, a steeply sided cone of lava fragments and flows. Its development can be divided into three phases. The first terminated with the formation of the older summit of the collapsed crater at 2,050m, presently 550m across and 25m deep. The second phase was the creation of Piquinho, the small lava cone 125m high in the larger crater, some 17,000 years ago. This, too, has a very small collapsed crater, which gives off occasional fumes from between warm rocks. The third phase included eruptions from Piquinho 1,300 years ago, and from an eruptive fissure on the top of the stratovolcano. The larger crater was once much deeper, but has filled with *pahoehoe* lava discharged from Piquinho, a smooth lava usually formed from molten basalts. Wherever plants have failed to gain a foothold on the steep slopes, basaltic cinders, ash, small stones and scree dominate the landscape.

Topo volcano rises 1,022m above sea level and 2,500m above the ocean bottom, and its oldest formation not under the sea has been dated at 250,000 years old. Topo is a basaltic shield volcano with two subsidiary structures: Terra Chãs and Santa Bárbara, which some authors have interpreted as volcanic calderas. While the Santa Bárbara area does correspond to the remains of an old collapsed crater, or caldera, it has been suggested the Terra Chãs depression could be due to lateral movement of the flank driven by gravity and tectonic instability.

The **Planalto da Achada** is an elongated plateau occupying the central part of the island from Pico mountain in the west to its eastern termination; as one very apt description has it, stretching out eastwards like a comet's tail. Numerous volcanic cones lie along the axis of the plateau and are mostly made of cinders, with a wide range of size and shape. The largest cone has a diameter of 900m at its base and a height of 190m, while the smallest represent fissure eruptions building small spatter ramparts, ie: lava fragments spewed upwards as a fountain that are still molten when they hit the ground and thus form 'cowpats' which often weld together building ramparts or cones. Lavas issuing from sources along the plateau are mostly *aa* flows, with a very rough broken surface, and have cascaded down the steep slopes of the plateau towards the coast and then spread, sometimes into the sea such as to form the Ponta dos Biscoitos near Santa Bárbara, between Lajes and Ribeiras.

The plateau's oldest above-sea-level formation is 230,000 years old, which means the oldest sections of Pico island are the Topo volcano, followed by Pico mountain; this is by far the youngest of the Azores islands.

Data shows 14 eruptions have occurred on Pico island in the last 1,000 years and more than 35 in the last 2,000 years, with longer quiet periods on the Planalto da Achada than on Pico mountain. Historic volcanism and carbon dating of lavas suggest that eruptions are not evenly distributed through time, but are separated by alternating short and long periods, and that peace reigns on average for 130 years. Since settlement, eruptions occurred in 1562, 1718 and 1720.

Visitors arriving on Pico soon hear about the **Mistérios**, extensive areas of sharp, broken and often forbidding black lava. These puzzled the first settlers arriving from 1466, who had yet to witness an eruption and experienced almost 100 years of volcanic tranquillity before they saw their first eruption in 1562. This created the Cabeços do Mistério cinder cones and sent a basaltic lava flow into the sea to form the Ponta do Mistério, east of São Roque on the north coast. It must have been terrifying as the surrounding forests caught fire and sometimes as many as 40 glowing hot streams of lava illuminated the night, continuing for two years. The 1718 eruption left an inheritance of several cinder cones and a lava flow that created Cachorro, near the present airport, a dramatic formation as though inspired by a punk hairstyle. At the same time, on the opposite south coast, a lava flow destroyed the then village of São João and formed the headland of Ponta de São João. The 1720 eruption occurred just northeast of São João and created the Mistério da Silveira.

HISTORY The first houses are thought to have been built in Ribeiras, but real settlement began in the area of what is today Lajes, in about 1460, and this for many years was the principal port and town. Later it was to develop as the centre of the whaling industry in the Azores. São Roque was settled in 1542, probably by people from Graciosa. Later, it too was a whaling base with a large processing factory.

Until the latter half of the 19th century, wine production was a very important economic activity and the island's Pico Madeira wine was exported in substantial volume, to England, the US, and famously Russia. The vineyards, especially those along the west coast south of Madalena, were owned by some half a dozen families from Horta who came over for the summer to oversee the grape and wine production. Their large summer houses may still be seen today. The port of Horta on Faial was the export centre for Pico's wine. This brought greater prosperity to Faial and boosted the development of Horta, which in turn influenced the development of Madalena. Facing each other across the channel, the two towns have always been closely linked. In 1852, the mildew fungus *Oidium tuckeri* nearly wiped out the vines and 20 years later the Phylloxera insect destroyed the remaining vines. This was the final blow to a very valuable export, for already the market had been declining. In the US the fashion for fortified wine was losing out to American-made whiskey, and the belief that wine was good for one's health was under question, with increasing movements for total abstinence. Sadly, with the loss of the vines, exactly what constituted and characterised the Pico wine so extolled by the tsars is now a mystery. (The Madeiran wine trade did, however, slowly recover, although minus the American market.) This collapse of the wine trade brought terrific hardship, causing a mass emigration of many of Pico's then population of 32,000 to Brazil and California. Those who could afford to paid their way on to passing ships, while the less fortunate embarked illegally on whaling ships serving a minimum contracted term of two years. With the vines gone, the large land holdings were sold and so people were able to acquire small plots of their own. Later, returning islanders brought with them the American Isabela grape, which thrived, and so the smallholdings began producing low-alcohol, partly fermented wine for local consumption, known as Vinho de Cheiro. Around this time, with skills gained from working on the American whalers, land-based whale hunting began from Pico, using small open boats. This soon spread to other islands, and whaling made a substantial contribution to the economy until world demand for whale oil fell: cheaper synthetics replaced it for use in lamps and machinery. Many factories closed, while hunting continued on an ever-decreasing scale until the final whale was killed in 1984.

Today, like all the other islands, cattle and dairy produce drive the economy, despite the relatively poor quality of the land. In Madalena there is still a small tuna-fishing fleet, though the closure of the island's processing plant means that the boats go to sea less and less. Wine makes a contribution, and tourism is increasing, with many houses converted to holiday lodgings.

GETTING THERE AND AWAY

For travel to and from Pico, see pages 42 and 49. Pico's sleepy, modern airport, 7.5km east of Madalena, is only occasionally disturbed by a flight arrival, and rarely in low season. The ferry terminal hosts a few car-rental companies, including **Autatlantis** (𝗇 292 692 800; w autatlantis.com) and **Ilha Verde** (𝗇 292 622 002; m 925 508 877; w ilhaverde.com), and a tourist office; they also have airport offices, open only to meet incoming flights. A café, free Wi-Fi and an ATM are also available at the airport. A taxi will take you to Madalena for around €15, or to either Lajes or Piedade for €35.

Azores Airlines/SATA Rua D Maria da Glória Duarte, Madalena; 𝗇 292 628 391; ⊕ 09.00–18.00 Mon–Fri. Also at the airport; 𝗇 292 628 380; usually open 09.00–18.30, but certainly during flight arrivals & departures.

GETTING AROUND

Bus services follow two routes: the north-coast Madalena–São Roque–Ribeirinha–Piedade, and the south-coast Madalena–Lajes–Piedade–Ribeirinha, but they run only twice daily in each direction and only once on Sunday. Nevertheless, they do allow budget travellers to make an island circuit. Take the south-coast bus going to Ribeirinha at 10.00, arriving at 11.45, and after lunch, return via the north-coast route to Madalena, leaving Ribeirinha at 13.30 to arrive back at 15.15. From Lajes to Madalena departures are 06.45 arriving 08.00, and 14.00 arriving 15.15, with returns from Madalena to Lajes at 10.00, arriving 11.00, or 17.45, arriving 18.55. The tourist office will provide an up-to-date timetable; the bus stop is at the side of the ferry terminal.

The island divides quite easily into a half-day car tour – Madalena–Santa Luzia–São Roque–Lagoa do Caiado–Lajes/Madalena or variations – and a full-day tour taking in most of the above plus going down to the little-visited far eastern end of the island. The price for a taxi carrying up to four passengers is around €110 for a day, €80 for a half-day tour, and the tourist office has a helpful list of taxi drivers, their linguistic abilities and set prices. One English-speaking driver whose vehicle can carry up to eight passengers is Carlos Costa (m 962 525 517; e carloscostapicotaxi@gmail.com). António Garcia (m 962 408 419; e antoniofmgarcia@sapo.pt) and José Vieira (m 962 526 011) also speak English. In Lajes call m 964 863 778 for a taxi, and in São Roque, m 918 113 100. Car hire is available from the airport, in Madalena town or in its ferry terminal, and you can arrange to pick up or return a car at the São Roque ferry terminal too.

Bikes and motor-scooters can be rented from Pico 447, opposite the ferry terminal (page 238). There's an excellent cycleway along the coast east from Madalena to Cachorro, near the airport, and a coastal route is also being built south from Madalena. See w bikotels.com/destinos/ilha-pico for other routes – basically all the paved roads.

EXCURSIONS TO OTHER ISLANDS There are regular ferry connections from Madalena to Horta on Faial throughout the year, a 30-minute journey, operated by Atlântico Line (w atlanticoline.pt). In winter they sail four times daily, with two or three more crossings added in summer. Exact times vary from year to year, but generally the service operates between around 07.30 and 21.00. A single fare costs €3.80. You can also visit Velas on São Jorge, with a boat or two departing from Madalena or São Roque each day (1hr 30mins, €10.50). Less frequently, there is also a service to Horta from São Roque, on Pico's northern coast (1hr 10mins, €12), continuing to Velas or Calheta on São Jorge, a 45-minute journey (€10.50). Careful study of the Atlântico Line website is advisable, as there are certain exceptions to the schedules. After a ferry was wrecked in 2018, the previous service to Terceira has been terminated, at least temporarily.

TOURIST INFORMATION

In Madalena (✆ 292 623 524; e pt.pic@azores.gov.pt; ⊕ 08.00–noon & 14.00–17.00 daily), this is based inside the ferry terminal. There are also municipal tourist information offices in Madalena (Rua Pimentel 4; ✆ 292 623 345; e postoturismo@cm-madalena.pt; ⊕ 08.30–12.30 & 13.30–16.30 Mon–Fri); Lajes (Praça do Museu dos Baleeiros; ✆ 292 672 486; e postoturismo@cm-lajesdopico.pt; w cm-lajesdopico.pt; ⊕ 09.00–12.30 & 13.30–17.00 Mon–Fri), and São Roque (Rua dos

Cais 25; ☎ 292 642 280; e cpcj.saoroquepico@cnpdpcj.pt; ⊕ Apr–Sep 09.00–12.30 & 13.00–16.00 Mon–Fri, Oct–Mar 09.00–16.00 Mon–Fri); however, the national office in Madalena is preferred.

🏠 WHERE TO STAY

There is one hotel in Madalena, two in Lajes, and one in nearby Silveira. There are various excellent guesthouses scattered around the island, especially in and around Madalena. In the east, Piedade has one excellent accommodation option. Many of the private homes offering lodging will pick up guests from the ferry. Check with the tourist office for details of all rural tourism accommodation and guesthouses.

MADALENA AND AROUND *Map, page 241, unless otherwise stated*

Alma do Pico [map, page 224] (15 cabins) Rua dos Biscoitos 34; m 914 231 436; e booking@almadopico.com; w almadopico.com. Cabins set in delightful wooded surroundings, either alone or in pairs; 1 is adapted for those with limited mobility, & all have kitchenettes. The reception/restaurant block has great views to Faial & Pico volcano plus outdoor pool & yoga room (classes twice weekly). Run by an enthusiastic Italian couple, who are keen to share their knowledge about island activities & attractions. Restaurant Atmosfera on site (page 231); advanced booking required. €€€€

Azores Wine Company [map, page 224] (6 rooms) Rua do Poço Velho 34, Bandeiras; ☎ 292 241 840; m 918 266 989; e reservas@azoreswinecompany.com; w antoniomacanita.com/en/wineries/azores-wine-company/pico-accommodation. A beautifully minimalist intervention in the World Heritage vineyards just east of Madalena, this actually plays the role of a traditional Pico *adega*, where wine is made but people can also eat, drink & stay the night, although not usually in this much comfort. They've worked to recover the almost lost Terrantez do Pico grape varietal & to create the first Azores sparkling wine; the restaurant offers a tasting menu & à la carte dishes. €€€€

Jeirões do Mar (10 apartments) Rua Alexandre Herculano; ☎ 292 628 310; e info@jeiroesapartamentos.com; w jeiroesapartamentos.com. On the southern side of the harbour, spacious & fully equipped apartments, each named after a grape varietal, close to the ocean & the public sea swimming pool. Cable TVs in lounge & bedroom, 1 apartment suitable for those with limited mobility. No b/fast. Can sleep up to 4 per apartment. Restaurant across the road. €€€€

Hotel Caravelas (137 rooms) Rua Conselheiro Terra Pinheiro 3; ☎ 292 628 550; e geral@hotelcaravelas.net; w oceanohoteis.com. The island's only truly large hotel sits right opposite the harbour. A bit dated in places, so ask for one of the newer (slightly larger) rooms & a balcony. AC, cable TV. B/fast inc. Seasonal outdoor pool. €€€

Calma do Mar (5 rooms) Av Padre Nunes da Rosa; m 914 443 408; e info@calmadomar.com; w calmadomar.com. In a quiet location by the coastal path, a few mins' walk from central Madalena. Spacious rooms with tiled floors, communal kitchen & TV lounge with wood-burning stove. Guests can use the garden, with BBQ, or hire bikes (extra cost) & use the trails provided by the young owners, who also have strong connections to activity companies & can further advise on suitable walks from the doorstep. Buffet b/fast inc. €€

Joe's Place (5 rooms) Rua Secretário Teles Bettencourt 54; ☎ 292 623 586; m 910 033 357; e info@joesplaceazores.com; w joesplaceazores.com. Charming guesthouse in a 200-year-old building a short stroll from the town centre. Relaxing terraces with views to Faial. Spacious rooms retain original features. Private parking. Delicious, creative vegan/vegetarian b/fast using tasty, homemade products. Dinner available with advance notice, also yoga classes. €€

Villa da Madalena (11 rooms) Rua 8 de Março 15; ☎ 292 622 249; m 961 090 174; e info@villadamadalena.com; w villadamadalena.com. Very smart dbls, family rooms & trpls in a new, villa-style building just southeast of Madalena centre. Plenty of space & light, some rooms have balconies, all with TV (international channels). Buffet b/fast inc. €€

Porto Velho Hostel (6 rooms, 6 dorms) Rua Doutor Freitas Pimentel 5; ☏ 292 623 777; m 925 550 909; e geral@hostelportovelho.com; w hostelportovelho.com. This lovely boutique hostel, overlooking the cove of Porto Velho in the town centre, has stunning penthouse rooms plus en-suite dorms with 2, 4 or 6 beds. No kitchen or meals. €

LAJES AND AROUND
Hotel/Alojamento Bela Vista (16 rooms & apartments) Rua do Saco, Lajes do Pico; m 962 413 409; e camilocosta@sapo.pt; w lajesbelavista.com. Nestled in the town centre, with apartments close to the sea near the whalers' museum, & remodelled in 2007, providing rooms or s/c apartments. TV with international channels. Some rooms have balconies with sunloungers. Apartments have washing machine, cooker, fridge, microwave. B/fast inc for both hotel & apartments. Whale watching available with Espaço Talassa (page 239). €€€–€€€€
Hotel Apartamentos Aldeia da Fonte [map, page 224] (16 rooms, 8 suites, 16 studios) Silveira; ☏ 292 679 500; e info@aldeiadafonte.com; w aldeiadafonte.com. A series of basalt-built s/c cottages & bedrooms 5mins by car west of Lajes (down a lane by the petrol station), with a central restaurant & lounge bar in a charming garden/ woodland setting on cliffs a few metres above the sea. A great effort has been made to integrate the buildings with the landscape. Offers a very wide range of leisure activities, including whale watching & climbing Pico, & a series of self-guided walks from the hotel. Fitness, sauna, seasonal outdoor pool. Cable TV & b/fast inc. The suites are s/c. Excellent restaurant (see opposite). €€€
Residencial Whale'come ao Pico (17 rooms, 2 houses) Rua dos Baleeiros, Lajes do Pico; ☏ 292 672 010; m 917 405 630; e viallelle@espacotalassa. com; w espacotalassa.com. Next to & run by the Espaço Talassa whale-watching company, right on the harbour front. With TV & buffet b/fast inc. Ideal base for whale-watching enthusiasts. Great off-season rates. €€

PIEDADE
❋ **O Zimbreiro** [map, page 224] (5 rooms) Caminho do Cruzeiro 83, Ponta da Ilha; ☏ 292 666 709; m 910 778 903; e lebonj@zimbreiro.com; w zimbreiro.com. Almost at the extreme eastern tip of the island, a Belgian/French-run guesthouse in a lush rural paradise, overlooking the channel between Pico & São Jorge. Rooms, which can be made to accommodate families on request, are spacious & stylish. B/fast is different every day, with produce from the garden. Evening meals on request, verging on the gourmet. Swimming pool. Delightful owners can advise on nearby walks, or you can simply enjoy the active birdlife or try to spot a passing whale. €€€

SÃO ROQUE AREA
Pico Dreams – Sportfish Rua do Laranjal 9, São Roque; m 914 201 564; e info@picodreams. com; w picodreams.com. A fairly spacious site at the top of town offers a variety of modern s/c accommodation, including villas & apartments. Similar rooms are available in the village of São Miguel Arcangelo, about 1km away. €€€
Casa Buraca [map, page 224] (7 rooms) Estrada Regional 35, Santo António; ☏ 292 642 119; m 917 398 083; e pico@adgeaburaca.com; ◼ adegaaburaca. Allied to the museum/wine-tasting establishment, a very cheap option to stay in the area. No b/fast served & a 2-night min stay, but rooms have TV, most with private bath. A great budget option. €
Pousada da Juventude (Youth Hostel) São Roque; ☏ 296 629 431; w azoresyouthhostels.com. In the former monastery of San Pedro Alcântara, set on a terrace looking out over the sea to São Jorge, this has small dorms & private rooms. Most unusually, reception is open from 08.00 until midnight! B/fast inc. The church, with its fine azulejos, is opened for mass at 19.00 on Sat; the cloister can be seen at any time. €

CAMPING
Furna (Santo António) [map, page 224] São Roque; ☏ 292 644 409; m 966 271 579. Excellent 24hr supervised sheltered site amid pine trees with all amenities, BBQ, tennis court, children's playpark, deer enclosure. Within 200m are restaurants, a disco & the sea. Close by are the Furnas pools. €
Lajes [map, page 224] ☏ 292 679 700, 292 623 496. At the far southern end of town within easy walking distance of all amenities. €
Madalena [map, page 241] ☏ 292 628 700; e geral@cm-madalena.pt. On the edge of town, next to a café-bar, this has showers & lavatories, though a bit exposed to all & sundry. €

Pico now lists more than 40 restaurants, with around half of them in Madalena. Many serve up buffet-style feasts at lunchtime, good value but of variable quality. Listed below are a few which offer something a bit different and of a better standard, though not always Azorean cuisine. The further east you go, the fewer options there are.

MADALENA AND AROUND

Atmosfera [map, page 224] Rua dos Biscoitos 34 (inside the Alma do Pico; page 229); m 914 231 436; ⏰ May–Sep 19.30–21.30 Wed–Mon. About 10 mins' drive from town, with just 24 seats. Rated by many as the island's best, so book early if you want some truly excellent Italian/international dishes in a rural setting. In any case you need to choose your menu in advance, as part of their no-waste policy. Specials are the homemade pasta & ham shank. Vegetarians & gluten-free catered for. €€€

A Tasca O Petisca Av Padre Nunes da Rosa; ✆292 622 357; f tascapetisca; ⏰ 10.30–midnight Mon–Sat. Full meals noon–15.00 & 19.00–22.00. Styled as a 'tidbit house', very popular with locals, serving snacks & tapas, plus grilled fish, meat & lobster. Going for the buffet (details posted daily on Facebook) works out slightly cheaper. €€

Cella Bar Barca, just north of Madalena, signposted off the coast road; ✆292 623 654; f cellabar; ⏰ summer noon–midnight daily, winter 15.00–midnight Thu–Mon. A strange, pod-like space, winner of architectural awards, & great ocean views make this a decidedly 'cool' place. Food choices feature a short selection of tapas-style dishes, plus favourites such as oven-cooked octopus, steaks with a choice of sauces, BBQ ribs & other dishes. Occasional live music. Good for a drink & snack, mixed reviews on the meals & service: you are paying slightly more for location & the architecture, not for the food. Always busy on Sundays. €€

Mercado Bio Rua Carlos Dabney 6; ✆292 623 778; f MercadoBioPico; ⏰ noon–15.00 & 18.30–22.00 Wed–Mon. Despite the name ('Organic Shop') this is a welcoming restaurant, serving a fusion of Asian & Atlantic cuisine, with beef, chicken & vegetarian options. They do sell local wines & Gorreana tea. €€

Restaurante Marisqueira Ancoradouro Rua João de Lima Whitton, Areia Larga, 400m beyond the wine co-operative, heading out of town; ✆292 623 490; ⏰ noon–15.00 & 19.00–22.00 Tue–Sun.

Rated as one of the island's best. Offers seafood & traditional dishes such as black pudding with pineapple, along with a view of the lights of Horta across the channel. €€

Caffe 5 (O Cinco) Rua Carlos Dabney 5; ✆292 623 970; w mybedinpico.com/caffe-5; ⏰ 09.00–23.00 Mon–Fri, noon–midnight Sat. A popular, unassuming little central café, with freshly squeezed orange juice, pastries, snacks & full meals. Even kebabs can be found here! Vegetarian options including a burger, falafel, salad or omelette. A pleasant, friendly place to browse the web, or people watch from the few outdoor tables. Small & busy, so arrive early at mealtimes. €

LAJES AND SURROUNDING AREA

Fonte Cuisine [map, page 224] (Hotel Apartamentos Aldeia da Fonte; see opposite); ✆292 679 505; ⏰ May–Sep noon–15.00 & 19.00–22.00, Oct–Apr noon–15.00 & 18.30–21.30. Belongs to the Hotel Apartamentos Aldeia da Fonte Hotel & offers a traditional menu, & also international specialities. Nice ambience, good surroundings; definitely trying to do things differently & deserving of its good reputation. €€€

Bistrot Whale'come ao Pico (see opposite) Rua dos Baleeiros; w espacotalassa.com/en/bistrot-whalecome-ao-pico; ⏰ Apr–Oct restaurant noon–16.00 & 18.30–21.00, bar 08.00–midnight. Everything from soup to fish, with baguettes, pasta & snacks in between. Vegetarian & children's options, too. If you've been craving a decent, main-course salad since you left home, you'll find it here. Subscribes to the 'slow food' movement, with no plastic bottles or aluminium cans in use. Great variety, decent prices. €€

Fonte Tavern Rua Capitão-Mor Garcia Gonçalves Madruga 13; ✆292 241 225; e info@fontetavern.com; w fontetavern.com; ⏰ noon–16.00 & 18.30–22.00 Tue–Sun. Owned by the hotel in Silveira (see opposite), this is a stylish venue for petiscos & light meals; the outdoor decking is particularly attractive. €€

Pico **WHERE TO EAT AND DRINK**

9

Aromas e Sabores Rua Capitão-Mor-Garcia Gonçalves Madruga, Lajes; 📞292 672 877; 🄵 PastelariaAromasSabores; ⊙ meals at lunchtime only, bakery 08.00–19.00 Mon–Fri, 08.30–18.00 Sat. Famed mainly for its delicious sweet pastries, but also serves a well-priced dish of the day, sandwiches, sausage rolls, soup & snacks. €

PRAINHA DE BAIXO

Magma Travessa do Outeiro das Eiras 2A, Santo Amaro; 📞292 241 200; e contact@lavahomes. com; 🄵 Magma.Restaurant.Bar. In the clifftop Lava Homes hotel, this very stylish place offers inventive cooking, with fried lapas (limpets) or sausage with blood pudding as starters and roast tuna, fish soup, shrimp linguine or tender steaks as main courses. The north-facing floor-to-ceiling windows give stunning views across the channel to São Jorge. €€

Tasca Rua do Ramal 4; 📞292 242 336; 🄵 tasca. pico; ⊙ 19.00–22.00 Wed–Sat, 12.30–15.00 & 19.00–21.30 Sun. Just up from the church, this new restaurant is already regarded as one of the best places to enjoy *comida tradicional*, authentically Azorean meat & fish dishes, but with modern standards of comfort, service & of course wine. €€

Adega Açoriana Tapas & Wine House Rua da Poça Branca; 📞292 655 211; w adegaacoriana. com; ⊙ 11.30–23.30 Mon & Wed–Sat, 11.00– 20.30 Sun. With outdoor tables overlooking the rock pools at Poca da Branca, at the north end of Prainha, this is a lovely spot for fresh, well-made snacks & drinks, with an excellent wine list, of course. €

SÃO ROQUE

Casa Ancora Rua do Cais 29; 📞292 644 496; ⊙ Apr–Sep noon–15.00 & 19.00–22.00 daily, closed Oct–Mar. Between the pharmacy & post office, this is a popular new place with daily-changing menus. You'll pay a couple of euros extra for the sophistication on offer here. Watermelon gazpacho with crab is an example starter. €€€

Clube Naval On the harbour, by the museum; 📞292 642 105; ⊙ 08.30–23.00 Sun–Thu, 08.30– midnight Fri, 08.00–01.30 Sat. Snacks are served all day, meals at regular times. Very much the locals' hangout, with cheap eats, predominantly a male clientele at lunchtime. No great finesse. €

FETEIRA/CALHETA DE NESQUIM

Restaurante Faia Rua da Feteira de Baixo, Feteira, Calheta de Nesquim; 📞292 701 066; ⊙ 18.00–22.00 Thu–Fri, noon–14.00 & 18.00–22.00 Sat–Sun. Signposted off the main road, good to see a newcomer in the culinarily impoverished east of the island. This lovely place justifiably receives praise, with its great location high up & overlooking the churning ocean. Vegetarian options, homemade ice cream. Excellent food & service. €€

SHOPPING

All Azores Avda Machado Serpa 2, Madalena; 📞292 623 450; e allazores@titos.pt; ⊙ 10.00– 13.30 & 15.00–18.00 Mon–Fri, 10.00–14.30 Sat. Owned by Tito's Vineyard, this sells their A Cerca Dos Frades wines & other island products.

Artesanato Picoartes Rua da Mãe de Deus, São Mateus. On the main Madalena/Lajes road; 📞292 699 400; w picoartes.com; ⊙ May–Sep 09.00–20.00 Mon–Sat, Oct–Apr 09.00–18.00 Mon–Sat. 3 industrious family members produce genuine Pico handicrafts, including embroidery, woodwork & artwork from fish scales, cowbone & whalebone.

Barro & Barro Rua Dr José Vieira Alvernaz 43, Ribeirinha; m 911 828 270. Pottery pieces & souvenirs with Azorean themes, creating ideal souvenirs, hand-crafted by a Dutch woman. Also organises pottery workshops.

O Oleiro Ponta da Ilha, Piedade; 📞292 666 020. Although from Belgium, this potter takes his inspiration from Pico & its surrounding waters, having resided here for 18 years.

OTHER PRACTICALITIES

Health centres Largo Edmundo Machado Ávila, Lajes: 📞292 679 400; Rua da Misericórdia, Madalena: 📞292 242 210, 292 240 570; Avda António Simas Costa, Santo Antonio, São Roque: 📞292 648 070

Police Town hall, Estrada Regional, Lajes: ↖292 672 410; Rua Secretário Teles Bettencourt, Madalena: ↖292 622 860; São Roque: ↖292 642 115

Post offices Rua Gen Lacerda Machado, Lajes; Rua Visconde Leite Perry, Madalena; Rua do Cais, São Roque

WHAT TO SEE AND DO

Essential to Pico's past, and very much to the present because of the tourism that is keeping the island's history in the forefront of consciousness, are wine and whales. Their history and significance are presented through the extensive vineyards around the coast near Madalena, the wine museum and three very different whale museums. Then there is the landscape itself, with plenty of visitors coming to climb the mighty peak, and of course all the little villages that can be visited on a car tour (page 240).

MUSEUMS The Museo do Pico has three branches, in the island's three towns (and may add a fourth; page 245).

Madalena

Museu do Pico: Polo do Museu do Vinho (Wine Museum) (Rua do Carmo, Madalena; ↖292 672 276, 292 622 147; ⊕ Oct–Mar 09.30–17.00 Tue–Sun & hols, Apr–Sep 10.00–17.30 Tue–Sun & hols; €2/1/free adult/senior & under 25s/under 15s, free Sun) Take the coastal road north past the stadium, then turn right (signposted 'Museu') and find this museum beneath some tall araucaria and *Metrosideros* trees at the next junction. It's part-housed in an old Carmelite convent enclosed by a high stone wall. There are fascinating old photographs and English-language information on laminated sheets and some translated wall panels. A walkway and gazebo take you out amid the vineyards, and you'll also see a pair of big wine presses and some stills. A real bonus in the garden is a small grove of dragon trees and their seedlings, totalling around 70 stems. The largest individual tree is over 850 years old and has a canopy spread of about 16m and a stem diameter of 1m.

Esposição Permanente do Espólio de Cachalotes e Lulas (Exhibition of Sperm Whales and Squid) (Rua Pimentel 4; ⊕ 08.30–noon & 13.30–16.00 Mon–Fri; €2/free adult/under 12s) Formerly in the home of the collector Malcolm Clarke, this is now housed above the municipal tourist office. It concentrates on the anatomy of the whale itself, rather than the whaling industry and whalers. There are two short films in English, with Portuguese subtitles, and bilingual wall panels. You can find out the crucial role that squid beaks play in the world's finest perfumes.

Cooperativa Vitivinícola Pico Wines (Wine Co-operative) (Av Padre Nunes da Rosa 29, a short walk southwest of the harbour; ↖292 622 262; m 912 533 243; e enoturismo@picowines.com; w picowines.com; shop ⊕ Nov–Mar 10.00–17.00 Mon–Fri, Apr–Oct 10.00–19.00 Mon–Fri, 14.00–19.00 Sat; tours (45mins) Nov–Mar 11.00, noon, 14.00, 15.00, 16.00 Mon–Fri, Apr–Oct also 17.30 Mon–Fri & 14.00, 15.00, 16.00, 17.30 Sat. Tastings must be booked in advance – 3 wines €14, 6 wines €20, 9 wines €50) Pico's wine co-operative has over 230 active member-producers, growing around 500 tonnes of grapes annually. Here you can see the production and bottling plants, with tastings of their products included. Aperitifs and a brandy are also available, a dozen or so products in total.

Moinho do Frade (windmill) (Take the coast road south of Madalena, and look inland for the windmill; ⊕ Jun–Sep 09.00–17.00 Tue–Sun, Apr, May & Oct 16.00–17.00 Sat, 09.00–10.30 Sun, Nov–Mar 09.00–10.00 & 14.00–15.00 Sun; when not open, you can still climb the steps to get a good view & take a photo) The historically important UNESCO World Heritage wine-growing area just south of Madalena that starts at Criação Velha captures an important economic and social period of the Azores. This restored windmill provides a splendid elevated view over an extraordinary landscape. It is claimed in the Museo do Vinho that if all the stone walls of Pico island were joined end-to-end, they would go twice around the globe. Hard to prove, but the effort that must have gone in to clearing the ground and creating the walls is quite astounding. The track past the windmill is part of the Mistérios do Sol do Pico trail.

Lajes

Museu do Pico: Polo dos Baleeiros (Whalers' Museum) (Rua dos Baleeiros 13, Lajes; ☏ 292 679 340; ⊕ Oct–Mar 09.30–17.00 Tue–Sun & hols, Apr–Sep 10.00–18.00 Tue–Sun & hols; €2/1/free adult/under 25s & seniors/under 15s, free Sun; optional audio guide is €2 extra) In front of Lajes harbour, this is a fascinating exhibition about whaling as it was in the Azores until 1987. In 1893–94 the Azorean whaleboat was developed here in Lajes, longer and thinner than the American ones and perhaps one of the most perfectly evolved vessels on the seas. The exhibits are appropriately displayed in three original 19th-century boathouses plus ancillary areas. They include full-size boats, tools and other artefacts, photographs, many good examples of scrimshaw, a blacksmith's workshop and much else. Displays are constantly being improved. There is English-language information on laminates and some wall panels, a 20-minute English-language film of a 1960s hunt and temporary exhibitions from time to time.

Centre for the Arts and Marine Sciences (Rua do Castelo, on the western outskirts of Lajes – beside the tall chimney; ☏ 292 679 330; w siaram.azores.gov.pt/centros-interpretacao/CA-e-Ciencias-do-Mar/texto-en.html; ⊕ 09.00–17.00 Mon–Fri; €2.50/1.25/free adult/senior & under 18s/under 12s) In the restored whale-processing factory, much of the original processing machinery can be seen, with a shortened version of the historic film of the hunt, as well as multimedia presentations about cetaceans (some in English) and a good book/gift shop; they also hold various exhibitions and events.

São Roque

Museu do Pico: Polo do Museu da Indústria Baleeira (Rua do Poço; ☏ 292 679 349; ⊕ Oct–Mar 09.30–17.30 Tue–Sun & hols, Apr–Sep 10.00–18.00 Tue–Sun & hols; €2/1/free adult/under 25s & seniors/under 15s; free Sun) The most important Azorean whale factory, which was built in 1946 and closed in 1984, became a museum ten years later. Over 5,000 whales were processed here, yielding almost 20,000 tonnes of oil; in addition, this was the only factory to produce vitamin-rich whale liver oil. The US-manufactured machinery is well oiled, as though it had only just finished working. A black-and-white film shows what it was like when a huge sperm whale was brought in for processing; definitely missing is the smell, not even a lingering whiff, which would really have brought it to life. Of all the many Azorean whaling museums, it probably wins the prize for having the most gruesome photos of whale dismemberment on display – and set in such an elegant building, too, down in the harbour by the Clube Naval. Just to the east at Rua do Poço 10 is a small scrimshaw museum (Casa dos Sofias; ⊕ 09.00–17.00 Mon–Fri; free). Continuing eastwards along the coast, the multimedia room at the rear of the Turismo (Rua do Cais 25; ✆ 292 642 507; e posto.turismo@cm-saoroquedopico.pt) displays a whaling boat fitted with an engine, a few radios and portraits of whalers.

GARDENS
Quinta das Rosas (Rua Francisco Ignacio de Medeiros, Areia Funda, east of Madalena; hard to find, ask at the tourist office; ⊕ Jun–Aug 08.00–20.00 Mon–Fri, 10.00–20.00 Sat, Sun & hols, Oct–Dec 08.00–18.00 Mon–Fri, May & Sep 08.00–19.00 Mon–Fri, 10.00–19.00 Sat, Sun & hols; admission free) This was a private garden, bequeathed by its owner to the government. It is filled with plants, especially roses (hence the name) and some interesting exotics from Africa, Australasia and South America; the garden has been well tended and is popular for picnics. A visit will pass an hour or so if you have time to fill; it is about 10 minutes by taxi from Madalena. There's also a pretty chapel in the grounds, some frog-filled ponds and a children's play area.

BIRDS AND FLOWERS Pico offers the easiest access to remnant laurisilva forest and, provided there is no thick fog, the road passing **Lagoa do Capitão** will reveal a good number of the typical Azorean species including superb specimens of the handsome and critically endangered shrub, *Euphorbia stygiana*. The various lakes in this highland area can attract migratory ducks and waders, as well as the Azorean chaffinch. Further east, peatbogs are dominant, with the Caveiro Nature Reserve protecting rare beetles. The harbours offer good opportunities for birding, especially Madalena; the recommended place is **Ponta do Arieiro**, just to the south. **Lajes** has a number of habitats beyond the harbour, thanks to a large eroded lava flow that offers intertidal pools and marshland. Vitally, it helps protect the town from winter storms, but has suffered badly in recent years. It is rated one of Pico's best sites for shorebirds, herons, terns and avian rarities.

RECREATIONAL FOREST RESERVES
Mistério de São João Along the south coast EN-1 just west of São João, this small area is a narrow lava flow stretching down almost to the sea. Originally mainly heather, it was planted in the 1960s with various conifers and is now dominated by the Mediterranean maritime pine, *Pinus pinaster*. Now adapted for leisure use, it has trails, barbecues and picnic tables, exercise facilities, deer in an enclosure, an observation tower for birdwatching and an interpretation centre for volcanism.

Prainha Along the northern EN-1 from São Roque to Piedade, Prainha offers extensive recreation facilities beneath the pines including children's play area, a multi-sports facility with showers, deer enclosure, footpaths and some restored typical rural buildings. Plenty of endemic plants.

GRUTA DAS TORRES (Caminho das Grutas das Torres, Criação Velha; m 924 403 921; w parquesnaturais.azores.gov.pt/bilheteira/grutadastorres/?lang=en; ⊕ Nov–Apr 10.00–17.00 Tue–Fri, 14.00–17.30 Sat & hols, May–Oct 10.00–18.00 daily; advanced booking strongly advised; guided tours (compulsory) Nov–Apr 09.30, 11.00, 14.00 & 15.30 daily, May–Oct 09.30, 11.00, 14.00, 15.00 & 16.30 daily; €8/4/free adult/under 15s & senior/under 6s; family ticket €16) A 10-minute drive south from Madalena, the cave is signposted near Criação Velha. This lava cave is

a fascinating volcanic phenomenon arising from lava flowing from the eruptions of Cabeço Brava and appears as a tunnel running through and emerging from an old lava flow. The principal tunnel is 4,480m long and mostly around 15m high. There are much smaller lateral secondary tunnels that show greater geological diversity. There is good public access and explanation and the entrance has been built of basalt rocks, cleverly designed to blend into the landscape. The maximum tour group size is 12; after a briefing and a video, there's a 450m walk, which all takes about an hour to 90 minutes. Hard hats and lamps are provided, and you will need strong shoes, as some scrambling is required. Guides are generally informative and speak English.

The surfaces of basaltic lava flows develop into two types which have been given the Hawaiian names of *aa* and *pahoehoe*. The *aa* is formed from the more viscous lava which soon congeals and does not travel far and the surface is a jumbled mass of angular and rugged rocks. A *pahoehoe* surface is formed from more fluid lava and frequently resembles huge coils of rope; as the lava cools it often produces a skin-like surface beneath which the lava is still liquid and as this continues to flow the smooth skin gets wrinkled and ropey. The image comes to mind of a dollop of hot jam on a plate to test the setting point from the wrinkles when pushed by a finger. Occasionally this skin-like solidified crust gets attached to the sides of the channel and when the molten lava beneath drains away the crust is left suspended, thus forming an empty tunnel. Liquid lava dripping from the roof congeals into stalactites and other curious shapes and the tunnel may present numerous different manifestations of the lava flow. They can also develop secondary features such as stalagmites and stalactites of limonite, an iron mineral, or silica. This tunnel shows good examples of both lava types and is rich in geological forms. The temperature

FESTIVALS ON PICO

On 22 July and around, Madalena celebrates its patron saint, Santa Maria Madalena, with several days of cultural and musical events. Coinciding with the Festival of Our Lady of Lourdes is the week-long Semana dos Baleeiros or Week of the Whalers. This is celebrated every August in Lajes by a whaling boat regatta and with fado and other traditional music as well as modern concerts, an arts and crafts fair and other cultural events. São Roque celebrates Cais de Agosto at the end of July with music and guest bands, guided excursions on Pico mountain, other guided walks, and exhibitions. Especially popular are the boat trips in restored whaleboats belonging to the São Roque Yacht Club.

Espírito Santo Lajes; seven weeks after Easter.
Domingo do Espírito Santo São Mateus, Candelária & other villages; seven weeks after Easter Sunday.
Terça-Feira do Espírito Santo Madalena; Tuesday following the seventh Sunday after Easter.
Festa de Santa Maria Madalena Madalena; towards the end of July (inc 22 Jul).
Cais de Agosto São Roque do Pico; last week of July/start of August.
Festa do Sr Bom Jesus Milagroso São Mateus; first week of August, with 6 August being the high point.
Festa de São João Pequenino São João; middle of August.
Semana dos Baleeiros Lajes; fourth week of August.

inside the tunnel is a constant 15°C throughout the year, and a high humidity is maintained by water filtering through the roof.

SPORTS AND ACTIVITIES
Climbing Pico mountain
Ascending Pico mountain is a serious business and the first thing to do is to decide whether to 'go solo' or book an authorised guide through one of the outdoor activity companies (page 238). The registration process thereafter is handled at the **Casa da Montanha**, signposted 'Reserva Natural Montanha do Pico' off the R3–2 road (m 967 303 519; w montanhapico.azores.gov.pt; ⊕ Nov–Mar 08.00–18.00 daily, Apr & Oct 08.00–20.00 daily, May–Sep open 24hrs daily; €5 to climb 30–45mins to the Furna Abrigo shelter, €15 to climb to the volcano crater, €25 to climb to the top of the 'little Pico', the final 100m rock scramble to the summit. An overnight stay is €10 extra. Numbers are limited to 160 people on the mountain at any one time.) You will be issued with a compulsory GPS, at no extra charge, but which you can optionally insure against loss for €30, which is refundable (a replacement will otherwise cost you €300!). When the Casa da Montanha is closed, you will have to return the GPS at the fire station on the Estrada Regional to São Roque, about 20 minutes' walk from Madalena harbour (✆ 292 628 300). It is also compulsory to bring crampons if there is snow present. Visiting the website (see above), which has an English-language option, is recommended preparation.

The ascent and descent of Pico mountain, a round trip of about 9km, can take over 7 hours, depending upon how fit you are and the weather conditions, with the descent usually taking more time than the ascent. You can go on your own, without a guide, but it is strongly recommended to go with one of the official guides, who since 2016 can be contracted only through the outdoor activity companies licensed by the government. If choosing the latter option, expect to pay around €60 per person, which should include transport to and from the Casa da Montanha, park entrance/climbing fee and insurance against accident. Night-time and overnight ascents cost more. Guides are trained in mountain rescue and first aid. Taking a guide means you are their responsibility; without a guide you are responsible for yourself and if you get into trouble and need rescuing, as a result of straying off the path or other deemed negligence, there is a very substantial fee to pay (around €1,500 to get you off the mountain; with a proper guide, such an eventuality should be covered by their insurance, but do ask). In bad weather, the staff at the Casa da Montanha will advise you not to go and in extreme conditions the mountain will be closed.

Beginning at Cabeço das Cabras, a small cone near the Casa de Montanha at 1,231m, it is an ascent of over 1,100m, in part over loose stones and scoriae. There are marker posts, each visible from the previous one in good conditions. It is a steep, not technically difficult climb but you need to be a strong walker and capable of coping with fast-changing weather conditions. You will need boots or substantial shoes with a good gripping sole and layers of clothing including gloves, a windproof jacket and waterproofs.

At the Casa da Montanha, there is a briefing room with two videos, one on safety and another more general one. There are also photographs with explanations about Pico and its ecology, also a small bar with coffee and a few emergency-type snacks, though you should bring your own supplies, including water. There are also lavatories. The GPS, which you will be loaned, is monitored by the rescue service, which will call you if you go badly off-trail. The above precautions are imposed because climbing Pico has become very popular and walkers do get into trouble. Over 15,000 people now climb each year and some people have been killed as the ground can be dangerous off the small footpath and the weather changes very quickly. Incautious visitors have had to be rescued by the Civil Protection Service and a cavalier attitude to the mountain is irresponsible. The best – and busiest – time is in June, July and August; later it can get very cold, with snow on the summit as late as April.

To watch the sunrise from the summit, start out at 02.00, or to see both sunset *and* sunrise, go up the evening before, between 17.00 and 19.00, and bivouac, enjoying the warm rocks (a maximum of one night on the mountain is permissible).

However many mountains you might have climbed, to be on the top of Pico is to be 2,351m high in mid-Atlantic, something which will stay with you for life. To the south is Antarctica, 9,000 miles away and with nothing in between. In other directions and given luck with the clouds you should be able to see Faial, São Jorge, Graciosa and Terceira. In June and July the two native species of thyme and heath, *Thymus caespititius* and *Daboecia azorica*, are in full flower and the higher slopes are a spectacular pink and white, a veritable rock garden of massed colour.

Before setting off it is wise to see what the day's weather is likely to be, for to make the ascent without the views would be terribly disappointing. Therefore make your decision by 08.00. Alternatively be bold and arrange to reach the start of the climb by 02.00 so you can be high on the mountain, if not at the summit, for sunrise. The early morning light has a special quality and as the sun catches the lower daughter volcanic cones and slowly spreads up the mountainside to strike you, banishing the cold of dawn, it vindicates the decision to make the effort. The ultimate, of course, is to watch the sunset, then bivouac and wait for the sunrise. As with all mountains, it is a mixture of luck and timing as to what rewards you reap.

A full list of **licensed guides** (many female) is available at w servicos-sraa.azores. gov.pt/grastore/DSCN/Guias_Montanha_Pico.pdf. The three companies listed here come recommended.

atiPICO m 915 340 487; e atipicoazores@gmail. com; w atipicoazores.com. A small specialist company with a growing reputation for its small-group trips to climb Pico. Day & night climbs are available, costing €60/80 respectively. They limit their groups to 9 climbers per guide, fewer than other companies & the personable guides speak perfect English.

Caminhando m 962 408 417; e caminhandoazores@gmail.com; w caminhandoazores.com. A well-known company run by João Xavier, an English-speaking guide who is often recommended by locals & visitors.
Up2Pico m 964 414 181; e go@up2pico.pt; w up2pico.pt. Overnight experiences also possible.

Other activities
Cycling
Pico 447 Rua da Gare Maritima, Unit 1 (opposite the ferry terminal), Madalena; m 961 101 404; e infopico447@gmail.com; w pico447. com. Mountain & road bikes, €18/21 per day respectively, helmet & lock included. Can provide a variety of suggested trails/routes & organise guided bike tours from €30 pp (min 4 persons). Scooters also available from €25/day, including helmet.

Whale'come ao Pico (See page 230 for contact details) Although mainly intended for the residents of their guesthouse, this Lajes-based shop has mountain bikes available for €25/day.

Diving
Brizaçores Rua D João Paulino de Azevedo e Castron 5, Lajes; m 917 778 823; e brizacores@gmail.com; w brizacores.wixsite.com/brizazores. Diving, sailing & a liveaboard combo on their 14m yacht.
CW Azores (Cetacean Watching Lda) Cais da Madalena; \292 622 622; m 926 919 645; e info@cwazores.com; w cwazores.com. PADI centre based on the harbourfront in Madalena, with everything from beginners' dives up to Divemaster courses. Trips to dive with sharks & to Princess Alice Seamount (45 miles from Pico) available, to see mobula rays. Dives from €45, snorkelling from €40.

DBM Azores Rua do Navalhão, Santo António; m 960 018 362, 916 635 932; e info@dbmazores. com; w dbmazores.com. Diving, fishing & spearfishing.

Twin Peaks Rua do Furna 5, Santo Antonio; m 910 634 403; e info@twinpeaksdivingcentre. com. Sustainable scuba specialists.

Horseriding

Quinta do Cavalo/Turispico Caminho de Cima 17, Piedade; m 919 890 485; e info@turispico. pt; w turispico.pt. Offering trips of varying length, lessons & carriage rides, from a rural base in the island's east. A 2hr ride costs from €50, lessons from €25.

Swimming

In **Madalena**, right in town, south of the harbour at Areia Funda, there is a swimming area with views of Faial across the channel. There's a good natural rock pool, where even with a swell the surface is usually stable. There are changing facilities, showers, etc, & all for no charge, & there are bars & restaurants nearby. Just west, by the Jeirões apartments, is the municipal pool, only operational in summer. On the other side of town, by the Cella bar, is the Barca bathing place & picnic area. There are numerous sea bathing areas (signposted Piscinas naturais) around the island; in the **São Roque** area the best

are at Furna & Cais do Pico. The Canto da Areia beach, just east of Prainha, is the island's only sandy beach.

Whale watching

At the harbours of both Madalena & Lajes, many companies vie for your business with offers of trips to observe cetaceans. Pico is a major whale-watching centre; Lajes is where it all began. Approved boat operators are listed on noticeboards by the quay. The boats are generally smaller here than some across the channel in Horta.

CW Azores Madalena; see opposite. Well established with 2 RIBs, theoretically open all year, but with Mar–Oct being the main season. Swimming with sharks & dolphins also offered, plus land-based trips. Whale-watching trips start from €65/48 adult/child.

✳ **Espaço Talassa** Rua dos Baleeiros 15, Lajes; ☏ 292 672 010; e espacotalassa@espacotalassa. com; w espacotalassa.com. Back in 1989, Frenchman Serge was a pioneer in Azorean whale watching. His enthusiasm undimmed, his business has also grown, but the personal touch remains. Evening talks on subjects such as island geology, sea turtles & whales (of course) are executed professionally. Half-day whale-watching trips are €63/48 high/low season, & week-long packages can be booked, too.

WALKS ON PICO

Pico so far has 14 official trails, all detailed on the Azores Tourist Board website (w visitazores.com), but the daddy of them all is of course the ascent of Pico mountain (page 237). There is some glorious countryside with a lot of hidden history and of course landscapes unique to Pico, especially among the forested land, vineyards and on higher ground. You do have to be on guard for quickly descending cloud and mist, not forgetting there are 81 known cavities in the lava and many holes well concealed beneath the moss, ferns and other vegetation, so keep to obvious paths. The official trails' waymarking is usually well maintained, but a quick check with the tourist office is always advisable. The three walks summarised below are all circular.

LADEIRA DOS MOINHOS (Easy, 3.4km, 1¼hrs) A circular walk beginning and ending in São Roque, passing on the way several old watermills, some rebuilt, some in ruins, and an old threshing floor.

PRAINHA DO NORTE (Easy, 8km, 3hrs) A circular route beginning and ending in the public garden of the village of Prainha (also known as Prainha do Norte). It passes old houses and beautiful stone bridges and heads down to Pico's only sandy beach (the Praia da Areia) and the Caso do Fio, a building used for the early transatlantic communications cable. It then follows the coastline, reaches a natural swimming pool in the rocks, and returns to the village.

CALHETA DO NESQUIM (Medium difficulty, 9km, 3hrs) A circular walk from the church in Calheta do Nesquim, a village with a long history of whaling. The route goes along the coast, with an option to extend it to Feteira where there are swimming opportunities, before climbing up through pastures and woodland to high points giving good views, and past a whale lookout. It then returns to the church.

TOURING THE ISLAND

MADALENA–SÃO ROQUE–LAJES–MADALENA Madalena years ago was a little sleepy sort of place and because it had not been touched for ages had a pleasing air. With the modern harbour, large hotel, increase in activity companies and the opening of a couple of stylish restaurants, it has stirred from its slumber and can be a hive of high-season activity. Viewed from the sea at a distance, with mighty Pico mountain in the background, it still looks very picturesque. Just south of the centre is the cove of Areia Funda, where the caique *Adamastor* is preserved, perhaps the island's last traditional trading vessel, in use from 1927 to 2007.

From **Madalena**, first take the main road east to the airport at Bandeiras and then follow the road signs to **Porto do Cachorro** on the northern coast. The tiny harbour, no more than just a slipway, is set among a tumble of black lava – a rather unique landscape, even by Azorean standards. An explanatory signboard maps out the points of interest, helping you to find the *rolas pipas*, the ramps made in the lava for rolling wine barrels to the sea. Lava here is contorted into many weird shapes (look for the dog's head!) and rock arches where the ocean rushes in; in fact the sea has obviously at times rushed in rather too effectively: notice how the original cement pathway that once led the visitor safely through has been destroyed, precariously resting on a crumbling natural stone arch and with its days surely numbered. Thankfully, a replacement path has been constructed, letting you get close to the foaming ocean below. A distinctive whooshing noise emanates from seawater being sucked in and spat out by the flat concrete building at the edge of the sea, used for experiments in harnessing wave power for generation of electricity. The black lava buildings are mostly adegas, places where village wine, the *vinho de cheiro*, is made and stored. (In some of the villages along this section of coast, these have been converted into small bars.) Down by the ocean, there's a working distillery, and between October and December you may be able to pop your head in and watch the process. The distillery is unmarked, and not an official tourist attraction. Smile at the distiller and he may offer you a sip of the aguardente – 58° proof, after its second distillation. Here and in nearby Santa Luzia and Bandeiras you will find a series of wells, known as tidal wells, which were dug near the sea so that seawater entering them would be filtered and at least made brackish for general use and, in times of severe drought, drinking. Note also the typical stone and cement cisterns with their roofs sloping down to the centre to catch and store rainwater.

Continue parallel with the coast, coming first to **Lajido** where there is another communal well, this time in the middle of the road. Lajido is surprisingly attractive in a heavy black-basalt way, and a couple of old warehouses have been converted into museums. At the wordily named **Centro de Interpretação da Paisagem da Cultura da Vinha da Ilha do Pico** or Pico Vineyards Interpretation Centre (**m** 965 896 313; **w** siaram.azores.gov.pt/centros-interpretacao/ci-paisagem-protegida-

MADALENA

ATLANTIC OCEAN

Velas (São Jorge)

Horta (Faial)

Airport, Cachorro, São Roque

Barca (swimming), Cella Bar

Wine museum

RUA DO CARMO

Quinta das Rosas, airport, São Roque

N
Bradt!

0 — 200m
0 — 200yds

AVENIDA MACHADO SERPA

RUA CARLOS DABNEY

Football stadium

Pico 447

Autatlantis

Pharmacy

CW Azores

Azores Airlines

Bus stop

Ferry terminal

Post office

Exhibition of Sperm Whales & Squid

Church

RUA VISCONDE LEITE PERRY

RUA 8 DE MARÇO

RUA SECRETÁRIO TELES BETTENCOURT

RUA 8 DE MARÇO

Medical centre

Pico mountain, Lajes (inland route)

ESTRADA LONGITUDINAL

RUA D JAIME GARCIA GOULART

Swimming pool

RUA ALEXANDRE HERCULANO

Cooperativa Vitivinicola (Wine Co-operative)

RUA JOSÉ GARCIA MARTINS

AVENIDA PADRE NUNES DA ROSA

Ponta da Areiro

Moinho do Frade, Restaurante Marisqueira Ancoradouro

Gruta das Torres, Lajes (coastal route)

For listings, see from page 229

Where to stay
1 Calma do Mar
2 Hotel Caravelas
3 Jeirōes do Mar
4 Joe's Place
5 Madalena (campsite)
6 Porto Velho Hostel
7 Villa da Madalena

Where to eat and drink
8 A Tasca O Petisca
9 Caffe 5
10 Mercado Bio

Off map
Cella Bar
Restaurante Marisqueira
Ancoradouro

cultura-vinho-pico/texto.html; ⏰ Nov–Mar 09.00–12.30 & 13.30–17.00 Tue–Sat, Apr–Oct 09.00–12.30 & 13.30–18.00 daily; free. Guided tours, which need advance booking, are €5 per person) you can find out more about the wine culture, the tidal wells and the natural environment. An adega nearby has been converted into the Bar do Lajido which serves bar snacks at lunch and dinner. Next door, the **Casa dos Volcões** is a new interpretation centre dedicated to volcanoes (📞 292 644 328; **w** parquesnaturais.azores.gov.pt/pt/parques/5/centro/10; Apr–Oct 09.00–12.30 & 13.30–18.00 daily, Nov–Mar 09.00–12.30 & 13.30–17.00 Tue–Sat; €5/2/free adult/seniors & under 15s/under 7s). The compulsory tour (20mins) is actually an immersive video (without commentary) on volcanoes followed by a virtual reality simulation (on a shaking platform) of the 1980 and 1998 earthquakes, which does actually give a pretty good idea of the experience. You have been passing through an area of mistério, a tumble of lava from the 1718 eruption emanating some 900m up the side of Pico. The lava took two years to cool and prevented travel between São Roque and Madalena so that people were obliged to go by sea. A modern road continues eastwards across very flat lava to Arcos and Cabrito; right by the roadside just before you get to **Arcos** you should be able to make out the *relheiras*, or wheel tracks, of oxcarts in the lava flow. After Cabrito the road cuts inland to reach **Santana**. Some of the large, and totally out-of-scale modern houses intruding upon the landscape are summer holiday homes, with some of their owners still working in North America. As you enter the village of **Santo António**, look out on your right for **Adega 'A Buraca'** (📞 292 642 119; **w** adegaaburaca.com; 🇫; ⏰ winter 09.30–17.30 Mon–Fri, summer 10.00–20.00 Mon–Fri; €2.50–12.50, depending on tasting package chosen), a restored wine cellar, which offers tastings and the chance to see around a small, family-run, wine-orientated museum. For groups of four or more, they will cook meals of a traditional nature, given a day's notice. They also now have rooms at their Casa Buraca (page 230).

Just past **Santo António** you come to an area called **Furnas**. Here the lava solidified as it flowed down and met the sea, and the smooth swirls of rock resemble congealed chocolate sauce. Continue to **São Roque do Pico** where there are restaurants in the centre of the village (page 232). If you want to visit the impressive whale factory, turn left down to the sea just before the centre of São Roque to reach the harbour where you will find the museum.

From **São Roque** take the R2–2 signposted to Lajes and head for the mountains. There are glorious views behind you back to the coast as you climb. When the road stops climbing at around 700m the landscape is of rounded hills, pastures and remnants of the original forest that once covered much of the island. You will come to a junction with the EN–3 (also called the R3–2 on some maps) heading back to Madalena. Turn right, taking the EN–3 for about 2.5km to come to an asphalt road off on your right leading to **Lagoa do Capitão**. This is just a small lake with a few isolated endemic junipers still withstanding the winds; walk anticlockwise round and follow the path leading off right uphill. Go behind the hill to be rewarded with a magnificent view of the whole length of São Jorge and, below, the coast of Pico around São Roque, something most visitors miss.

Retrace your route to the R2–2, and turn right in the direction of Lajes. Soon you come to a narrow side road off to your left, signposted to **Lagoa do Caiado**. Drive down this road for a few hundred metres and here you will see some of the important native plant species, many of which are endemic to the Azores. While botanically fascinating, do be very careful if you wander from the road because there are many deep hollows between the rocks under the covering of mosses for the unwary to fall into and possibly disappear!

Return (again) to the R2–2 road and descend to **Lajes do Pico**. It is a pretty drive; do allow time to take it slowly. Images that come to mind are of tall, stately cryptomeria trees, green meadows, hills, rounded hills, conical hills and glimpses through trees of hills going on higher up. Sunshine and shadow on the road; shining bright leaves; leaves of large-leaved gingers give a subtropical effect; and occasional camellia trees 5m tall are in full red bloom in January. Arriving in Lajes, on your right is the SIBIL former whale-processing factory, now the Centre for the Arts and Marine Sciences (page 234).

Lajes was the first settlement on the island and is well worth an hour's exploration. The 17th- and 18th-century houses offer interesting architectural details and the little chapel of São Pedro at the far end is a delight inside, built around 1460 by the first settlers. Regrettably it has been rendered with cement so that it could easily be mistaken for somebody's outbuilding; for centuries it had a thatched roof. Next to the Church of Our Lady of the Conception is the town hall, formerly a Franciscan convent. From the harbour there are fine views of Pico mountain; the whalers' museum is also just by the harbour (page 234). At the west end of the harbour, the Whalers' Boathouse was renovated in 2023 and is now the centre for a new whaleboat racing scene – 23 boats, owned by the regional government and allocated to clubs, have been restored, and the summer regattas are followed closely.

As you drive back to Madalena following the coast, you will see in the woodlands around **Mistério de São João** inviting picnic areas built by the forest service (page 235). Then, before you reach Madalena, turn off the main road towards the coast to the village of **Criação Velha**. (If you have time, turn off before this and explore some of the coast and its settlements.) Criação Velha begins the wine-producing area along to the small port of **Areia Larga**, formerly used whenever bad weather closed nearby Madalena. This UNESCO-recognised heritage area captures something of former times when Pico wine was in full production and would have been swarming with hundreds of workers. You will see clearly above all the stone walls the **Moinho do Frade**, a restored windmill which provided an elevated view over the vineyards (page 234). Entering Madalena from Areia Larga, you'll pass the wine co-operative (page 233).

AROUND THE COAST OF THE EASTERN PART With a whole day stretching ahead of you, a tour of the eastern sector is really a journey of gentle exploration following the main road that encircles the island and dropping down to explore little places on the coast that appeal as and when you get to them. Coming from Lajes along the southern coast, drop down from the main road to Calheta de Nesquim following the steep winding road and stop at the Church of São Sebastião. This is a typical village church, dated 1856, immediately overlooking the harbour. In front, note the statue to the man who led the first whale hunt on Pico. There is also a whaleboat house nearby, with six refurbished whaleboats, as well as a *gasolina* motor launch usually on the slipway. You'll also find a decent restaurant in nearby Feteira (page 232). Return to the main road by the road you came down and follow signs to Manhenha and along the coast to **Ponta da Ilha** and the immaculately kept lighthouse at the eastern tip of Pico. From here there is a fine view of the eastern sector of São Jorge and, in the distance, Terceira looking almost circular with a central plateau. There's another good walk on a lava flow here. Return to the main road and immediately follow the tourist sign to **Parque Matos Souto** and the **Desenvolvimento Agrario**. Awaiting you at the end of the winding road is a delightful garden with shade trees and ornamental flowers, lily pond and picnic tables maintained by the forestry service. Even if you are not ready for your picnic, it is charming to visit.

THE DRAGON TREE

Not surprisingly, the extraordinary appearance of this tree has ensured it a place in parks and large gardens wherever there is a suitable Mediterranean climate. However, in its native state it is classified as endangered. The tree is endemic to the Canary and Cape Verde islands, where it is already extinct on some individual islands, and there are just two surviving wild trees on Madeira, where it was once widespread in the arid lowland areas, especially on adjacent Porto Santo where it is incorporated into the town's coat of arms. So abundant was it on Porto Santo it seems that when the first settlers arrived they felled trees in large numbers without learning how to propagate them, and flooded the market with resin until the price dropped so low they ceased harvesting, thus inadvertently saving whatever trees remained. The fruits became famous for fattening pigs, but here, too, the tree is now extinct.

Bound to mythology, it would seem Hercules might have been the first plant hunter associated with the dragon tree. His 11th and last Labour was to seek and bring back three golden apples from the Garden of the Hespérides, and after searching all the known world he is thought to have located the garden on an island beyond the Atlas Mountains. The garden was guarded by Landon, the hundred-headed dragon, and when Landon was killed his blood flowed out across the land and from it trees sprung up which we now know as dragon trees.

With the scientific name of *Dracaena draco*, this very slow-growing umbrella-shaped tree grows to a height of 15m or more, develops a hugely wide crown, and produces numerous branched inflorescences of small greenish-white sweetly scented flowers followed by 1cm-wide fleshy orange fruits. After each flowering, the tree then branches. Their trunks do not have annular rings like most other trees so to determine their age one has to know roughly how often they flower – once every ten to 15 years (maybe more frequently in the Azores) – and count the number of branches. Once thought to live for very many hundreds of years, this has been revised downwards to 600 or so. It would be fun to determine the oldest specimen in the Azores, since they have been cultivated here for at least 500 years, and used for nail varnish as well as medicinally.

From the dragon tree comes dragon's blood, the sap of the tree that upon drying becomes a reddish resin, and in the Canary Islands this was used by the aboriginal Guanche to embalm their dead. Dragon's blood was widely known in ancient times, used as a dye and medicine, but this probably came from *Dracaena cinnabarini* on the island of Socotra, and from Somalia. Other plants produce resins also known as dragon's blood and *Daemonorops*, a palm from Sumatra, is the main source of the dragon's blood varnish for violins.

That *Dracaena draco* is now an endangered species is probably due to habitat loss and other human influences, but before the Spanish invaded and colonised the Canary Islands, we are told a flightless bird related to the pigeon and about the size of a turkey used to feed upon the fruits of the dragon tree. It soon became extinct, and one theory is that the dragon trees there declined because the seeds had to pass through the bird's digestive system before they would germinate. If this is true, it would be interesting to know if anything eats the seeds in the Azores, because they certainly seem to germinate well in the garden of Pico's wine museum!

Once more return to the main road and shortly you will come to **Piedade** where there is a bank and some shops. Along the very straight stretch of road that bypasses Ribeirinha look out for the viewing point of **Terr'Alta**, a narrow concrete belvedere 330m atop the steep sea cliff; it provides a fine view across the channel of São Jorge while directly below you is a forest of pittosporum and a few native laurels trying to compete with the invader.

Take the turning down to **Santo Amaro** and stop in the square by the Church of Nossa Senhora do Carmo. About 100m east, following the sea wall, is the **Escola Regional de Artesanato** (✆292 655 418; m 914 084 522; ⊕ Oct–Apr 09.00–17.00 Mon–Fri, May–Sep 09.00–18.00 Mon–Fri; donation expected), a most charming crafts museum and school, set in a traditional house and dedicated to keeping traditional crafts alive. Very original corn dollies, straw hats, embroidery, fish-scale flower pictures, weaving and other crafts are displayed, together with three rooms furnished in traditional manner. Another room is a craft workshop while a third is a small shop selling many crafts plus Angelica liqueur and delicious fig jam. Near the slipway, just to the west, is the boatyard, the main centre for the whole of the Azores. Access to the sea at this point is very gentle, something so rare in the islands that this may be the reason boatbuilding began here. The house by the slipway at Rua António Maria Teixeira 23 houses a **private museum** explaining the art of wooden boatbuilding and aspects of Azorean maritime history, but the owner has emigrated to the US. In mid-2023 politicians talked of it becoming part of the Museo do Pico, but nothing has happened yet. For the time being you can ask about access at the shop at Rua Sarmento 31 (m 911 121 720).

Stay on the lower road and continue to **Prainha** and the square with its little garden and a café at the side of the church. From the main door of the church is a good view of São Jorge. Take the road that continues behind the church, which quickly turns steeply uphill to rejoin the main road and continue to São Roque. You will soon pass by the **Parque Florestal de Prainha** (page 235), a splendidly manicured and laid-out picnic and recreation area beneath the trees, featuring a restored windmill.

Part Four

WESTERN GROUP

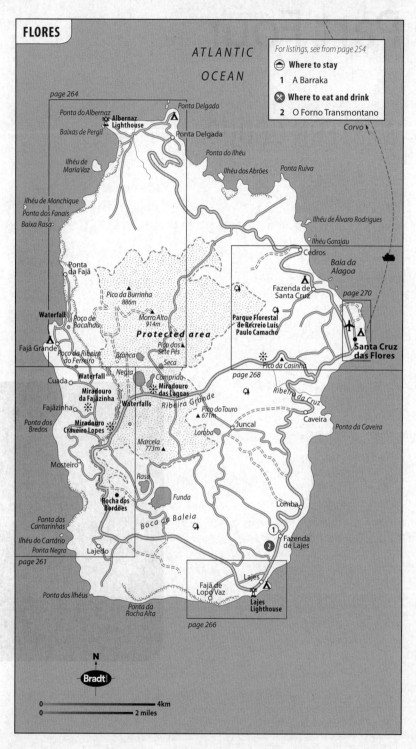

ATLANTIC

OCEAN

page 264

Ponta do Albernaz

Ponta Delgada

Albernaz Lighthouse

Ponta Delgada

Baixas de Pergil

Ponta do Ilhéu

Ilhéu de Maria Vaz

Ilhéu dos Abrões

Ponta Ruiva

Ilhéu de Monchique

Ponta dos Fanais

Baixa Rasa

Ilhéu de Álvaro Rodrigues

Ilhéu Garajau

Cedros

Baía da Alagoa

Ponta da Fajã

page 270

Pico da Burrinha 886m

Fazenda de Santa Cruz

Waterfall

Poço de Bacalhau

Morro Alto 914m

Parque Florestal de Recreio Luís Paulo Camacho

Protected area

Fajã Grande

Poço da Ribeira do Ferreiro

Pico das Sete Pés

Branca

Seca

Santa Cruz das Flores

Pico da Casinha

Waterfall

Negra

Comprida

page 268

Cuada

Miradouro da Fajãzinha

Miradouro das Lagoas

Ribeira da Cruz

Fajãzinha

Waterfalls

Ribeira Grande

Ponta dos Bredos

Miradouro Craveiro Lopes

Pico do Touro 671m

Caveira

Juncal

Ponta da Caveira

Lomba

Marcela 773m

Mosteiro

Rasa

Rocha dos Bordões

Funda

Lomba

Ponta das Cantarinhas

Boca da Baleia

Ilhéu do Cartário

Ponta Negra

Lajedo

①

②

Fazenda de Lajes

page 261

Lajes

Ponta dos Ilhéus

Fajã de Lopo Vaz

Lajes Lighthouse

Ponta da Rocha Alta

page 266

Corvo

N

Bradt

0 ——————— 4km

0 ——————— 2 miles

For listings, see from page 254

Where to stay

1 A Barraka

Where to eat and drink

2 O Forno Transmontano

10

Flores

> At night, in the silence of this small sanctuary, you can almost hear the sound of the sun falling against the horizon…afterwards, everything seems even more serene, but at the same time more intense, fragrant, inexplicably captivating, as if part of a poem.
>
> Quoted from the Aldeia da Cuada's brochure.

For many visitors, certainly for those seeking nature and tranquillity, Flores will be their favourite island. Not only have you now reached the westernmost island of the archipelago, you are also at the western extremity of Europe. Europe ends at Flores, the Isle of Flowers, on longitude 31° 15' W, and 2,220km from Lisbon. Given the island's small area, only 17km long and 12.5km wide, it is probably the most intensively rugged of the archipelago, with peaks, valleys, crater lakes, waterfalls and precipitous cliffs. Small pastures and arable fields all surrounded with hydrangea hedges or lichen-encrusted stone walls tie these together. Like Graciosa and Corvo, Flores is a UNESCO Biosphere Reserve.

Although it is a long way from almost anywhere, Flores is an island of quite spectacular natural beauty and well worth the effort to reach. July and August are the peak times, June and September are busy, then tourism fades away. Come in winter, see no other tourists, enjoy cloud effects, rainbows, storms, waterfalls, brilliant sunshine, wonderful conditions for photography – for in winter there is tremendous clarity – and simply escape from the madding crowds. Today, however, all too often the tourist is in a hurry to see everything and move on. Having invested travel time and fares to reach Flores, do stay at least three nights, even if you are not a walker; if you are, then think of five nights. If you want to visit nearby Corvo, you should allow an extra day. Ideally, you would spend a whole week. In winter, be tempted to rent an old restored comfortable cottage with a wood-burning stove, bring books and music, and retreat for a month or three.

Whatever you do, make sure you have spare days in your itinerary to allow for cancelled flights due to bad weather. It is bad luck when this occurs, but it can happen at any time of the year, especially in winter when Flores bears the brunt of the Atlantic gales. There is a lovely story about a consul in Flores who had never left the island and, in the mid 1800s, boarded a ship that had called to take on fresh provisions. The weather became too rough for the ship to remain at the anchorage and stood out to sea for safety; the wind became stronger and it was impossible for a small boat to go ashore. Being short of provisions, the ship sailed away with the consul to its intended destination, arriving a week or two later in England!

The main highlights are the landscape and geological features: the peaks of Sete Pés, Burrinha, Marcela and Flores's highest point at 914m, Morro Alto, all best seen from the viewpoint overlooking the Fazenda da Santa Cruz Valley; the Rocha dos Bordões basalt pipes; the seven different lakes in the centre of the island; several waterfalls, spectacular after rain; sea cliffs 600m high; and, for navigators, the islet of Monchique, used as one of the main reference points to check navigational aids when sailors relied upon astronomy. Everywhere the countryside is beautiful, and there is constant temptation to stop the car and quietly take in the atmosphere. For walkers, there is the ultimate in conversation stoppers: walking almost the entire length of Europe's westernmost coastline (unless you count Greenland). In the calmer weather of summer, one of the finest ways to appreciate the island is to take a boat trip around the coast, part of which you will see anyway if you go to Corvo by sea. For manmade attractions, the two museums in Santa Cruz are the treasures.

This rugged island defiantly stands proud of the ocean, with many lengths of precipitous cliff challenging the sea to do its worst. In a few places the land descends less abruptly to meet the ocean, resulting in ravines and narrow river mouths, and just occasionally the descent could almost be described as sharply gradual, for example in the northeast and the odd point of flat land in the east, providing just enough space for the airport and main town of Santa Cruz. All the villages lie around the island's circumference, either by the sea or perched upon the clifftops. Flores is unique among the Azores for being without a large caldera or dominated by long fissures. The chance of history made Flores the frontier post of Europe rather than of the US. Fewer than 3,800 people live here, with about the same number of visitors each year. It deserves more, though savvy locals are fearful of their beautiful mid-Atlantic nugget being tarnished by uncontrolled mass tourism. And another threat, not directly related to tourism: there are plans to upgrade the island's hydro-electric plant with a reservoir to extend its hours of operation and increase the island's renewable energy share from 52% to 89%. However there are fears over the effect of this scheme on the island's waterfalls and opposition is gathering.

BACKGROUND

GEOLOGY Flores is the westernmost island of the Azores and together with Corvo rests upon the North American Plate. Both islands are on a 9- to 10-million-year-old oceanic crust. Flores's volcanic build-up occurred in two phases: first a complex that formed the embryonic island mostly below sea level with the oldest rocks around 2.5 million years old and the youngest some 650,000 years old, which were partly emergent and influenced by sea-level changes. The second complex, all above sea level, was active between 670,000 and 3,000 years ago, and created a diverse geological landscape. It consisted of thick, sometimes very thick, lava flows which alternated with lesser pyroclastic (rock and ash) deposits, with a final eruptive stage of considerable lava flows from two or three volcanic centres.

One of the special features of Flores is the 'Lake District', consisting of lagoas Lomba, Funda, Rasa, Negra, Comprida, Seca and Branca. These are *maars*, shallow, flat-floored craters caused by multiple explosive steam eruptions when rising magma comes into contact and interacts with groundwater or surface-derived water below the original ground surface. No cone is formed, and ejected material can form a low rim around the crater and the resulting depression often fills with rainwater. In all the tourist brochures are photographs of the Rocha dos Bordões, a fine example of columnar jointing above the road between Mosteiro and Lajedo. These arise in the inner part of very thick lava flows when the hardening process proceeds slowly relative to the outer surface and sets up tensional stresses during contraction. Hardening along numerous parallel axes, usually perpendicular to the flow's surface, breaks the lava down into pentagonal or hexagonal prisms. Later weathering exposes them as 'basaltic organ pipes', 'elephant roadways', and other suggestive forms. More familiar examples are Scotland's Fingal's Cave and Ireland's Giant's Causeway.

There have been no eruptions during historic times and geological evidence suggests the island's volcanoes are now extinct.

HISTORY The name Flores, pronounced 'Florsh' and meaning 'flowers', is thought to derive from the many yellow *cubre* flowers that adorned the sea cliffs at the time of Portuguese discovery. This is the local name for *Solidago sempervirens*, a North American species of goldenrod that might have been introduced, but has certainly been in the Azores for a very long time.

Diogo de Teive and his son João discovered the island around 1452, much later than the other two island groups. The first settlement was attempted by a Flemish nobleman, Willem Van der Hagen (known locally as Guilherme da Silveira), at the bottom of the Ribeira da Cruz, a deep and dramatic valley with a small rocky beach giving access from the sea. The settlers tried to grow woad for export but because of the island's isolation and lack of a good natural harbour this failed after a few years, and they retired to Topo on São Jorge. **Permanent settlement** began only in around 1504 with people mainly from Portugal, Terceira and Madeira together with slaves from Cape Verde, and supplemented by Spanish, German, English, Jewish and Moorish families. Possibly by 1515, Lajes was already a small town, and 30 years later so was Santa Cruz, and by the end of that century the parish of Ponta Delgada on the north coast was also well established. Many places in Flores owe their names to towns in other Azorean islands. Contemporary accounts tell us the population of Flores was around 1,300, and conditions primitive. The houses were straw-thatched huts, the paths were muddy and so bad they could not be used by wheeled carts. Seldom did they get a boat visit from Terceira, and then only between March and September because of the winds.

However, the Azores were good hunting grounds for **pirates and corsairs**, especially when they were under Spanish rule. In June 1587, five English vessels destroyed Lajes, but soon they were paying for supplies, and even intermarrying. Each year the Spanish organised two major convoys called the *Flota* and the *Galeones* to protect ships bringing back bullion from South America. In 1591, a British squadron waited to intercept the *Flota* on its way back from Mexico. The British crews had suffered greatly from illness and were largely ashore when a Spanish fleet sent to protect the *Flota* hove into sight. The British rapidly embarked but one ship, the *Revenge*, was slow to escape and was cut off. Single-handedly the ship, under the command of Sir Richard Grenville, a wealthy landowner and cousin of Sir Walter Raleigh, fought the entire Spanish fleet for 15 hours, sinking two enemy ships before surrendering; an action immortalised by Tennyson's poem, *The Revenge*, beginning 'At Flores in the Azores Sir Richard Grenville lay…'. Sir Richard was mortally wounded and buried ashore but, being Protestant, not in consecrated ground. Around the end of World War II, a storm exposed near the shore the buried remains of a man much taller than the islanders, together with a big sword. Could this have been the long-lost grave of Sir Richard? If it was, the remains are again lost.

By 1770, the island was no more peaceful, for in that year two American privateers badly bombarded Lajes, but were eventually fought off with a cannon firing broken crockery, bottles and stones and finally a cannonball. However, by the end of the century the relationship changed, and the islanders ended by trading with the pirates to mutual advantage.

The early economic activity was survival; yams were the mainstay, plus potatoes and other vegetables together with fish and wheat, with the export of woad and minor products such as archil (lichen) and dragon's blood, while sheep produced wool. There was also casual trade and repairs with passing ships, and by the middle of the 18th century supplying whalers and other shipping provided the island with a good income. Its economy peaked around the middle of the 19th century with meat, fruit and vegetables being exchanged or sold for export to the other islands, Madeira and beyond. Reflecting this, the population also peaked at this time, and since then has gradually declined, largely through emigration, from over 10,000 down to its present total. Open-boat land-based **whaling** began in 1860 and reached its peak in the late 1930s; there followed construction early in the next decade of the whale factory in Santa Cruz and a second one in Lajes, but these were always handicapped by the lack of a good harbour. Whales killed by Corvo men were towed to Flores for processing, and the last whale killed in the Western Group was off Corvo in 1981.

Roads within the island were bad or non-existent for a very long time, and only in the 1950s did this begin to change. What really ended the isolation of the island was the building of an airport, port improvements and the opening of a French **missile-tracking station** in the 1960s. The French have gone, made redundant through new technology, and the economy depends upon meat and tourism. Fishing is small and enough for the island; tourism is very slow in winter but in the peak of summer the infrastructure struggles to meet demand.

GETTING THERE AND AWAY

For getting to Flores, see pages 42 and 49. Certainly one of the smaller airports in the Azores, here you'll nevertheless find a couple of car-hire companies, **Autatlantis** (☎ 292 542 278; m 961 393 996) and **Ilha Verde** (☎ 292 542 372; m 910 546 619), a tourist office which is sometimes manned to meet incoming flights (though not always in winter), a cafeteria, free Wi-Fi, ATM, gift shop and not too much else. There's a solitary urinal in the gents' toilet.

To get to town, or to any of Santa Cruz's accommodation establishments, it's less than a 10-minute walk, or 2 minutes in a taxi.

Azores Airlines Rua Senador André Freitas 5, Santa Cruz das Flores; ☎ 292 590 340, 292 590 350; ⊕ 09.00–18.00 Mon–Fri

RIAC (Ferry ticket office) Praça Marquês de Pombal; ⊕ 09.00–noon & 13.30–17.00 Mon–Fri. Sells tickets for the public ferry only.

GETTING AROUND

BY CAR A rental car (see above) lets you stop for photos whenever you want, and gives maximum flexibility. Flores is not over-blessed with petrol stations, and while you'll have to work hard to use a full tank in a week's visit, don't get caught out. Santa Cruz has two petrol stations, one on each of the roads that flanks the airport runway. There's another one in Lajes.

BY BUS There are public buses connecting most of the towns for a few euros, but they are infrequent and do not always operate every weekday, and certainly not at weekends. A printed timetable is available from the tourist office (see opposite) and you are advised to pick one up on arrival, as schedules change according to season. Alternatively, you can navigate around the operator's website w utc.pt (in Portuguese only, look for the UTC Açores tab and click on *Horários*). The most useful buses are likely to be Line 4, running five times a day down the east coast from Santa Cruz to Lajes. Only one continues to Fajã Grande, departing at 17.00

and arriving at 17.45. Walkers could then spend two nights in Fajã Grande, allowing them to do Stage 1 of the west-coast walk (page 260) from Lajedo the next day and Stage 2 to Ponta Delgada the day after that (page 263). From Fajã Grande, the 07.45 departure on Line 3 will drop you 25 minutes later at Lajedo to start Stage 1 of the walk. Arriving in Ponta Delgada at the end of Stage 2, an evening bus (Line 1; departs 17.45, arrives 18.35) can return you to Santa Cruz. Alternatively, you could take the 07.00 bus from Santa Cruz to Ponta Delgada and walk from there to Fajã Grande. Otherwise, the logistics can be mind-blowing: if you're not on a tight budget, a taxi to any trailhead is between €15 and €25 to/from most places.

BY TAXI Taxi hire for a day's sightseeing tour costs around €18 per hour from Santa Cruz. Most likely your driver will follow the tour (Car Tour 1) described on page 269, which takes about 4 hours. The tour to Ponta Delgada on the north coast (Car Tour 2, page 273) takes around 2 hours. Book ahead if possible.

John Coelho ✆965 261 663
Luis Freitas ✆917 479 341

ISLAND TOURS

Experience OC Rua da Esperança 14, opposite Santa Cruz airport; m 965 444 505; e experienceoc@gmail.com; w experienceoc. pt; ⏱ 09.00–noon & 13.00–19.00 Mon–Sat, 14.00–19.00 Sun & hols (summer only). An agency offering island tours, hikes, canyoning & trips to Corvo. As an agency, some of these are outsourced. They also sell equipment from their shop, useful if you've forgotten something from home. Island tours €45/85 half/full day.

Noya Tours Santa Cruz airport; m 917 479 341, 917 477 850; e noya-tour@sapo.pt; w noya-tours.pt. A range of tours & transfers with multilingual drivers.

Passeios Turisticos Ilhas das Flores m 918 804 210, 926 532 014; e toursofflores@gmail.com;

w toursofflores.com. English-speaking drivers who will drop off/pick up at trailheads, & also do tours of the island in car or minibus (max 8 people), depending on group size. €80/120 half-/full-day tours for up to 4 passengers. Will also do shorter, customised tours on request.

WestCanyon Turismo Aventura m 968 266 206; e info@westcanyon.pt; w westcanyon.pt. Local company offering jeep tours, canyoning, guided walks & trips to nearby Corvo. Great enthusiasm for the island & its natural delights. Jeep tour €55/75 half/full day pp, guided hiking from €40 pp (both based on group of 2). Prices for Corvo trips, including lunch & a trip up to its caldera, depend on numbers (€75 pp based on group of 4).

TOURIST INFORMATION

The tourist office (Rua Dr Armas da Silveira, Santa Cruz; ✆ 292 592 369; ⏱ 09.00–18.00 Mon–Fri; also at the airport (✆292 542 429) when flights arrive) has up-to-date opening times for restaurants, museums, etc. English is spoken by helpful and informative staff. In Lajes, the tourist *quiosque* only opens for cruise ship arrivals, which are rare.

Flores TOURIST INFORMATION

10

253

⌂ WHERE TO STAY

In Santa Cruz das Flores there are three conventional hotels, but few other options. There is good-quality rural accommodation in Fajã Grande, which is the island's tourist hotspot. In the peak summer months, especially July and August, demand is such that you will have to book well in advance. The Santa Cruz tourist office (page 253) carries a full list of places to stay.

There are five sites set aside for camping and theoretically they are open all year. As with everything, your ability to camp is subject to weather and in winter you might wake to find that your tent has taken off in the direction of Lisbon. **Fajã Grande**, **Santa Cruz**, **Lajes** and **Ponta Delgada** are the best ones, with barbecue grills, toilets and hot water for showers. **Alagoa** only has very basic toilet facilities. It is advisable to contact the tourist office in Santa Cruz to get further details. At most, there will be a nominal charge, but often they are free.

SANTA CRUZ DAS FLORES
Map, page 270

Inatel Flores Hotel (26 rooms) Zona do Boqueirão; ☎292 590 420; e inatel.flores@ inatel.pt; w hoteis.inatel.pt; ⏰ May–Nov. Offers gymnasium, games room, outdoor pool & restaurant. On a headland with views of Corvo island. The closest you'll get to a luxury hotel on Flores, rooms are smart & spacious, advance reservation essential. 15mins' walk into town. B/fast inc, sea-view rooms are slightly more expensive. **€€€**

Acquamarina (6 rooms, 2 houses) Rua Senador André Freitas 22; ☎292 592 960; m 963 929 613; e acquamarinasintra@mail.telepac.pt; w acquamarina.com.pt/flores. Very central, good quality & spacious rooms, each with private bath & TV with international channels. Fans are provided & there's outside space for sunbathing. B/fast is included at a nearby café. The houses are fully s/c, 1 sleeping 4, the other 6; these need a 3-night min stay. **€€**

Hotel Ocidental (36 rooms) Av dos Baleeiros; ☎292 590 100; e info@hotelocidental.pt; w hotelocidental.pt. Good location, next to the sea. Many rooms have balconies & a splendid sea view. TV with international channels. The hotel is tiled throughout & although spotlessly clean, it looks cheerless & b/fast is uninspiring. Has a small pool & gym, & organises boat tours. **€€**

Hotel Servi-Flor (32 rooms) Bairro dos Franceses; ☎292 592 453; e hotelservi-flor@ mail.telepac.pt; w servi-flor.com. Also known as the 'French Hotel', this occupies the old accommodation & restaurant building of the French missile tracking station. Rooms have AC, TV with international channels & fridge. Rather dark & gloomy, but well heated in winter. Bar, outdoor pool (seasonal), children's play area & mini-golf. B/fast inc. **€€**

Malheiros Serpa (5 rooms) Rua do Hospital 8; ☎292 592 201; m 963 165 190; e malheirosserpa@hotmail.com; w malheiros. net. Modest guesthouse on the edge of town, 4 rooms with private bath, 1 without, & TV. Washing machine & kitchen available to guests. 2-night min stay. **€€**

FAZENDA DAS LAJES
A Barraka [map, page 248] (4 rooms) Rua Erinha Velha; m 925 926 808, 961 724 290; w abarraka. com. French-owned, English-spoken, international clientele. Somewhere between a youth hostel & a guesthouse, with shared kitchen, washing machine, garden, 2 shared bathrooms. Owner is a masseuse & teaches yoga – there's a small studio upstairs. Good value, b/fast not inc. **€**

FAJÃ GRANDE AND AROUND
Sítio da Assumada [map, page 264] (5 chalets) Estrada Regional da Fajã Grande; m 924 195 407; e sitiodaassumada@hotmail.com; w sitiodaassumada.com. Just outside Fãja Grande, these ultra-modern chalets are an ecotourism award winner. The site is solar powered, the garden plants all endemic. AC, kitchen (fridge, cooker, microwave), TV with international channels. Chalets are either 2- or 3-person, extra bed may be possible. No b/fast available; closed in winter. **€€€€€**

Aldeia da Cuada [map, page 261] (16 cottages) Cuada, Fajã Grande; ☎292 552 127; e info@

254

aldeiadacuada.com; w aldeiadacuada.com. Through emigration, Cuada village, 2km from Fajã Grande, became deserted. Now, 16 of the abandoned houses have been tastefully refurbished to a high standard, with TV, kitchen (cooker, fridge, microwave) & wood-burning stoves, offering 1-, 2- & 6-bedroomed accommodation. Excellent b/fast & dinner available. Each cottage has a small simple garden, BBQ, & access is by narrow paths between walls. It is charming, in a delightful pastoral setting near the sea. €€€€

Residência Argonauta (5 rooms) Rua Senador André de Freitas, Fajã Grande; ✆292 552 219; e info@argonauta-flores.com; w argonauta-flores.com. This charmingly refurbished traditional & characterful house, over 300 years old, has retained many early features, while providing a high standard. There are 5 en-suite rooms in the main house with b/fast room & bar. 1 unit is s/c. TV lounge & a great selection of books to browse. If the budget stretches to it, the top-floor suites are recommended. The owner is an Italian photographer & photography courses are available, too. Airport pick-ups & transfer service to trailheads can be organised. B/fast inc. €€€

Casas da Cascata [map, page 264] m 926 582 177, 926 582 032; e info@casasdacascata.com; w casasdacascata.com. A range of houses in Fajã Grande, but the star is the Moinho de Cascata (3 rooms), sitting high above the village close to the Poço de Bacalhau. €€

Palheiro da Assomada & O Palheiro (1 cottage, 1 studio) Fajã Grande; m 964 257 731; e neilking84@hotmail.com; w fajagrande. jimdo.com. These consist of 2 beautifully renovated properties, a compact studio & a cottage on the peaceful west coast, with full s/c facilities including oven, plus a private garden to enjoy the sun. English-speaking owners. To rent by the night, week, or any period in between. Attractive off-season rates. Closed Dec & Jan. €€

� WHERE TO EAT AND DRINK

The options for sophisticated dining on Flores remain fairly limited, more so in winter when some close due to lack of business. Most offer the basic Azorean fare without much variation in presentation. There are many 'snack bars' and insufficient restaurants. While Santa Cruz has the biggest choice of places to eat, the best options are in Fajã Grande and elsewhere.

SANTA CRUZ DAS FLORES
Map, page 270

Lanchonete Orquídea Rua Alm. Gago Coutinho; ✆292 592 096; ⊕ 08.00–19.00 Mon–Fri, 09.00–15.00 Sat. A simple, friendly place that offers burgers, build-your-own salads & pastries. €€

Restaurante O Moreão Rua Dr Armas da Silveira 21; ✆964 619 142; ⊕ 11.30–16.00 & 19.00–midnight Mon–Sat. Known for its fish & (very specifically) limpets, as well as standard Portuguese fare, this is a friendly local restaurant that's busy at lunchtime. €€

Big Love by Monica's ⊕ noon–19.00 Mon–Thu, 10.00–14.00 Sun. Despite Monica's odd opening hours & awkward location at the rear of the Centro Cultural, it's the town's best café. Clifftop views are matched by the coffee, cakes, sandwiches & pancakes. €

BuenaVista Caffe Av das Baleeiros 1; ✆292 542 248; ⊕ 10.30–22.30 Mon & Wed–Thu, 10.30–02.00 Fri–Sat, 11.00–23.00 Sun; shorter hours in winter. In a glass box near Santa Cruz's natural pools, this offers coffee, salads & snacks until 20.00. Outdoor tables too – on a good day, you can line up Corvo island as you sip your beer, watch the surf or surf the internet. €

Lucino's Bar Praça 25 de Abril; ✆292 592 633; ⊕ 07.00–22.00 daily. Serving good coffee, this usually has the most early-morning buzz of anywhere in town; later, you can pick up a bowl of the soup of the day for next to nothing. Cheap eats. €

LAJES *Map, page 266, unless otherwise stated*

Casa do Rei Rua Pixote Pimentel 3 (on the road towards Fäja Grande); ✆292 593 262; m 912 776 732; e steiner-flores@web.de; w restaurantcasadorei.com; ⊕ Apr–Sep 18.00–21.30 Wed–Mon, closed Oct–Mar. 'House of the King' is how the name translates & this German-run establishment probably wears the crown as the island's best. A Teutonic touch can be detected in the cuisine, but the food is nearly all sourced on the island, some from their organic farm. English spoken. Fish, meat & vegetarian options, too. A good evening choice. €€€

O Forno Transmontano [map page 248] Fazenda das Lajes; ✆ 292 593 137; e ofornotransmontano@gmail.com; ⏰ daily, but only on advance reservation – it's essential to book ahead. Traditional island cuisine, with a choice of fresh fish or meat dishes. Menu may be limited, but not the quality or friendly service. €€€

O Arruda Rua dos Baleeiros 40; ✆ 292 593 079; ⏰ (restaurant) noon–14.00 & 18.00–21.00 Tue–Sun, (café) 07.00–22.00 Tue–Sun. A simple stopover for a drink, pastry or the dish of the day. €€

FAJÃZINHA *Map, page 261*
Pôr do Sol Rua dos Rolos; ✆ 292 552 075, 919 342 214; ⏰ May–Sep noon–14.00 & 19.00–21.00 Tue–Sun, Oct–Apr noon–14.00 & 19.00–20.30 Sat, noon–14.00 Sun. Generally recognised as the best traditional restaurant on the island & with friendly service, too. €€€

FAJÃ GRANDE *Map, page 264*
✳ **Restaurante Maresia** Rua do Porto (by the bathing area); m 965 665 649; ⏰ (restaurant) Apr–Oct 13.00–16.00 & 19.00–22.00, (bar) noon– 02.00 daily, closed Nov–Mar. With a great location down by the sea, a limited but quality menu is served in an alternative atmosphere. Expect some world music & relaxed service. Steaks are good here. Tables out front catch the best views of the mesmerising waves. Book ahead. €€€

Restaurante Papadiamandis Rua do Porto (by the bathing area); m 917 947 118; ⏰ (restaurant) noon–15.00 & 19.00–21.00 Tue–Sun, (bar) 11.00–22.00 Tue–Sun. Named after a cargo ship that sank off this coast in 1965. Outdoor seating & paddling pool, a good place to watch the waves or the waterfalls. Casual bar area & smarter dining room, serving everything from pizza, pasta & hamburgers to fish & meat mains, plus a few vegetarian options. €€

Barraca Q'abana Avda Marginal; ✆ 969 317 901; ⏰ 08.30–23.30 daily. A glass-box café by the campsite & a natural swimming pool, this serves drinks, snacks & burgers plus a dish of the day. €

PONTA DELGADA *Map, page 264*
O Meireles Rua da Terra Chã; ✆ 292 592 692; ⏰ noon–22.00 daily. A small restaurant serving well-priced though mainly unexceptional food in a basic dining room. Formerly known as O Pescador, which didn't make much sense when the lamb is the dish to choose. Limpets, beef & goat also feature; the house wine is a bit rough so trade up to the inexpensive bottled stuff. €€

OTHER PRACTICALITIES

There are two **banks with ATMs** in Santa Cruz, and an airport ATM. Lajes has two banks with ATMs, and Ponta Delgada and Fajã Grande also now have their own ATMs. You'll find open-access **Wi-Fi** at various spots in the centre of Santa Cruz, in the airport, the port at Lajes and even along the cobbled main street of sleepy Fajã Grande.

Health Centre Someone is always in attendance at the health centre in Santa Cruz; ✆ 292 590 270. The pharmacy (⏰ 09.00–18.00 Mon–Fri, 09.00– noon Sat) next door has an emergency number (m 962 537 839). There is no hospital on Flores & emergency cases are flown to Terceira.

Police Santa Cruz das Flores; ✆ 292 592 115
Post office Rua Senador André Freitas 13A, Santa Cruz das Flores; ⏰ 09.00–12.30 & 14.00–17.30 Mon–Fri

WHAT TO SEE AND DO

Santa Cruz das Flores (page 269) is the principal town, though Fajã Grande is the biggest draw for visitors, being a useful base for walking, with better-quality accommodation and restaurants. There are three good reasons to spend at least half a day in Santa Cruz: two excellent museums and the environmental centre.

MUSEUMS As well as the flagship whaling museum and the renovated Museu das Flores in Santa Cruz, there are also tiny museums in Lomba, Lajes, Ponta Ruiva and Fajã Grande, but the opening hours are sporadic and the exhibits of fairly limited interest. Look for the *museu* signs as you tour the island and poke your head in. The **Santa Cruz whaling museum** and the main **Museu das Flores** are must-sees, however, testament to what can be achieved with a determined will and some funds. The striking modern **Centro Cultural** (Av Principe de Monaco), at the southern exit from Santa Cruz, puts on occasional exhibitions, films and concerts, but more importantly is home to Big Love by Monica's, the best café on the island (page 255). When it opened it was named the Museu e Auditório Municipal, but the story is that the 'museum' tag was simply added to obtain EU funding!

Museu da Fábrica da Baleia do Boqueirão (Whaling Museum) (Rua do Boqueirão 2, Santa Cruz; ☏ 292 542 932; w museu-flores.azores.gov.pt; ⊕ Apr–Sep 10.00–18.00 Tue–Sun, Oct–Mar 09.30–17.30 Tue–Sat; guided tours (in English) available at 10.00, 11.30, 14.30 & 16.00; €1/0.50/free adult/under 17s & seniors/under 12s) Even without the guided tour, a truly excellent and fairly recent museum, with a chronology of whaling, a superb French-made video (with English subtitles) showing an actual whale hunt, a full-sized whaleboat, 'talking heads' of old whalers spinning their tales, and bilingual informative wall panels outlining the relationship between American whalers and their recruitment of Azorean crew. It's all housed in the town's former whale-processing factory, with the original but renovated Babcock and Wilcox machinery eerily left in situ, accompanied by an explanation of the gruesome process. Possibly the best whaling museum in the archipelago. Recommended.

Centro de Interpretação Ambiental do Boqueirão (Environmental Interpretation Centre) (Rua do Boqueirão, Santa Cruz; ☏ 292 542 447; ⊕ Nov–Mar 09.00–12.30 & 13.30–17.00 Tue–Fri, 14.00–17.30 Sat & hols, Apr–Oct 09.00–12.30 & 13.30–17.00 daily; €3/1/free adult/under 15s & seniors/under 7s; guided tours 4 person min, by appointment) Right next door to the whaling museum in the former whale oil tanks, this is another excellent installation with plenty of English-language information, this time concentrating on Azorean environment and nature. Here, you can find out about the birdlife on Flores, the unique island plants – including the forget-me-not – and of course the whales and other sea life. There are excellent video presentations showing turtles, whale sharks, manta rays and all sorts.

Museu das Flores (Edifício do Convento de São Boaventura, Largo Misericordia, Santa Cruz; ☏ 292 592 159; w museu-flores.azores.gov.pt; ⊕ Apr–Sep 10.00–18.00 Tue–Sun, Oct–Mar 09.30–17.30 Tue–Sat; €1) After four years of painstaking renovation, this reopened in 2016, with much of the ethnographic collection shunted off into storage and new multimedia exhibits installed in their place. Built in 1641–50 as a Franciscan convent, in 1734 the building became a hospital and then later a school, before finding its present purpose in 1993 documenting in user-friendly fashion the building's history, before moving on to the island history. Wall panels are translated into near-perfect English, telling the stories of legal and illegal emigration, the battles between the co-operative movement and

industrialists, stories of pirates and privateers, as well as the recent history of the French military on the island (the Hotel Servi-Flor (page 254) is a remnant of those times). There is a room dedicated to shipwrecks, a highlight being the film made by an Italian interviewing some islanders about the booty salvaged from the stricken Cunard liner *Slavonia* by their ancestors and now adorning their houses. Some are understandably a bit coy, even 100 years after the event – fascinating footage! The exhibition rooms are set around an internal cloister, from which you can also visit the **Church of São Boaventura**. Look for the Hispanic–Mexican influence in the chancel, the plant motifs and allegorical figures painted on the magnificent cedarwood ceiling, and a 16th-century Portuguese School *Annunciation*.

BIRDS AND FLOWERS There are three protected zones: the extensive central area of lakes; the south coast from Lajes and along the west coast up as far as near Mosteiro; and the northeast coast from Santa Cruz to the Albernaz lighthouse and down to include the Ilhéu de Maria Vaz. These include the islets where the largest European colonies of roseate tern nest. It is thought that with their potential for Nearctic land birds and storm-tossed American vagrants, the westernmost islands offer the greatest birding excitement. A noted area for the land birds, with its small fields and woodlands, is around **Fajã Grande**. The central area has considerable and complicated geological interest while its humid Atlantic climate of fogs, strong winds and high rainfall has created boggy habitats dominated by juniper and sphagnum moss and other parts good for laurisilva species. Resident birds include canary, goldcrest, chaffinch, blackcap and grey wagtail, and the whole wetland complex is regarded as an important area for regular migratory birds and also for the common tern.

RECREATIONAL FOREST RESERVES
Parque Florestal de Recreio Luís Paulo Camacho (Signposted left off the main Santa Cruz to Ponta Delgada road, in Fazenda de Santa Cruz, 10mins' drive from Santa Cruz; ⊕ May, Sep & Oct 09.00–17.00 Mon–Fri, 11.00–18.00 Sat–Sun, Jun 09.00–19.00 Mon–Fri, 10.00–19.00 Sat–Sun, Jul–Aug 09.00–20.00 Mon–Fri, 10.00–20.00 Sat–Sun; admission free) This is a charming park set in a valley surrounded by evergreen forest, dating from when the then extensive common lands were cleared and converted to more productive pastures and timber in the early 1960s. In addition to a small formal garden with azaleas, there are picnic tables, a barbecue area, children's play area and toilets. There are also strutting, barking peacocks, some handsome chickens, caged birds and a deer enclosure. There is a building with a modest exhibition about the birds, but no café or shop. A short walk leads up to a viewpoint overlooking a small dam. You could also go slightly further on to reach the dam ('*barragem*'). This is a peaceful spot with picturesque views, good for a picnic, and you can easily walk back to the park. If you cross the dam you will see a cobbled path leading steeply uphill beneath the trees. This goes between stone walls and hydrangeas and comes out after about 30 minutes into pastures where you get a fine view of the Ribeira da Badanela. Return the way you came. A longer linear walk from the park, returning to Santa Cruz, is detailed on page 265.

SPORTS AND ACTIVITIES On a small and remote island what is available is inevitably going to vary each year, but boat trips in summer around the Flores coastline make a fascinating excursion to see the rock formations and seabirds; you can also see islets and various caves, including the intriguing Gruta dos Incharéus below Caveira, 50m long and 25m wide. In winter, when the public ferry schedule is limited, the operators listed opposite are worth contacting. If they have enough people interested, they will run a boat over to Corvo, and you can hop on board for a €35–40 adventure. All boats leave from Santa Cruz and price depends on passenger numbers.

In summer there is a **public ferry service to Corvo** from Santa Cruz on Tuesday, Thursday and Saturday as a minimum, and in winter on Tuesday and Saturday. In high summer (July and August), the schedule increases to almost every day and even twice daily on festival days. The single/round trip costs €10/20 and one way takes 40 minutes to cover the 21km journey. See w atlanticoline.pt for the detailed timetable as there may well be more sailings. All crossings are subject to weather conditions on the day. Tickets should be bought in advance from the RIAC office (page 252). Note that the ferry terminal is the Porto das Poças, a simple quay at the end of Rua Dr Armas da Silva; don't wait at any of the other, former quays – the ferry will not arrive!

Boat trips

Elisário Serpa m 964 220 645; e elisariomalheiros@hotmail.com; w viagemailhadocorvo.blogspot.com. Worth contacting as an alternative to the public ferry. **Extremocidente** Hotel Ocidental; ☏ 292 590 100; e extremocidente@yahoo.com; w extremocidente.pt. Worth contacting as an alternative to the public ferry; diving also available.
Zagaia Rua da Esperança 14, opposite the airport; m 911 015 805; e zagaiaflores@gmail.com; w zagaiaflores.pt. More fishing-oriented, but they also offer trips to Corvo & the caves.

Canyoning

WestCanyon Turismo Aventura m 968 266 206; e info@westcanyon.pt; w westcanyon.pt. Focusing on canyoning, also with a few bikes for rental. Most activities go with a min 2 people. Canyoning (half day) from €60 pp.

Diving

Longitude 31 Rua dos Baleeiros 10, Lajes; ☏ 918 838 414; e longitude31@gmail.com; f longitude031; ☉ Jun–Sep. A summer-only activity, based out of Lajes. Boat & shore dives, min 2 people required. 2-dive package from €70. Prices reduce with bigger packages.

FESTIVALS ON FLORES

In July, the Festa do Emigrante (Emigrant's Festival) is Flores's biggest celebration, with music and folklore groups coming from other islands as well as Flores; there are exhibitions and various cultural events and a Carnival Ball. Other lesser festivals occur, mainly in late summer.

Festa de N Sra de Lourdes Santa Cruz; second week of February.
Festa do Espírito Santo Throughout the island; end of May.
Festa de São Pedro Santa Cruz; end of June.
Festa do Emigrante Lajes; middle/late July.
Cais das Poças Santa Cruz; first week of August, now the second most important after the Emigrante festival.
Festa de Santo Cristo dos Milagres Fazenda dos Lajes; first/second week of August.
Festa de N Sra dos Remédios Fajãzinha; third week of August.
Festa de N Sra da Saúde Fajã Grande; first or second week of September.
Festa do Bom Jesus Caveira (Santa Cruz); third week of September.
Festa de N Sra do Rosário Lajes; fourth week of September/first week of October.
Festa de N Sra da Conceição Santa Cruz; first/second week of December.

Swimming

Fajã Grande Black-pebble beach & a quay for access, with facilities & restaurants open, though mainly in summer. You can also take a dip in the freshwater Poço do Bacalhau, north of town.

Lajes Black-pebble beach (Praia da Calheta) reached by a footbridge at the bottom of the village, with picnic tables & WCs.

Santa Cruz das Flores There is a great natural rock pool halfway between the Ocidental & Servi-Flor hotels with showers & toilets. The BuenaVista Caffe is up above.

WALKS ON FLORES

There are now five official waymarked trails, and three of these are described in full later in this chapter, as is an 'unofficial walk' from the Parque Florestal back to Santa Cruz (page 265). The fourth of the official walks is graded hard and spans the 7.5km between Miradouro das Lagoas and Poço do Bacalhau. Clear weather is needed for this 3-hour walk, as low cloud can make way-finding difficult. The fifth walk, which incorporates the whole of the west-coast walk detailed below, runs from Santa Cruz all the way to Lajedo and thus goes via Ponta Delgada and Fajã Grande along the way. To complete it requires around 18 hours of walking, so it is at least a two-day affair. Details of all walks are on the w visitazores.com website.

Eventually, there may be a circular walk around the entire island. As it is, any stroll into the countryside within sight of the sea carries the added frisson of excitement on account of the distance from anywhere else (Corvo excepted) – half the Atlantic before major landfall. Always check beforehand with the local tourist office if the trails are open and safe, as landslides can make them impassable, especially in winter.

WAYMARKED TRAILS For the popular west-coast walk (see below), starting at Ponta Delgada in the north would mean descending to Fajã Grande, but many prefer the other direction, ascending from Fajã Grande, since the path can be wet and slippery, thus difficult on the downslope. To cover the entire west coast, you could start from Lajedo and end in Ponta Delgada as described below; this can be done either as a tough single hike, or over two days, overnighting in Fajã Grande.

Flores west coast walk
[maps, opposite and page 264] (Time (both stages together): approx 7½hrs; total distance: about 24km) The walking is not too strenuous, but there are steep ascents and, more importantly, steep descents which can be slippery in wet conditions or when smooth cobbles are hidden by soft juicy foliage. There is also some boulder-hopping to do and a few streams to cross. After rain it will be muddy in places, and sometimes the path may be running with water. You should avoid this walk on very windy days, especially in winter. Otherwise it is straightforward and you will be rewarded by wonderful ever-changing views of coast and countryside, and experience walking a route that has been in use for 500 years. Should your schedule only allow time to do one of the stages detailed here, then the second one is definitely the more beautiful, though slightly harder. For walkers who are scared of heights, the first stage is the one to choose.

Stage 1: Lajedo–Mosteiro–Fajãzinha–Fajã Grande
(Time: approx 3½hrs; distance: 13.5km; see map, opposite. For a shorter walk, simply arrange to meet a taxi in either of the villages en route. This first stage crosses a series of hills & river valleys & passes within sight of the Rocha dos Bordões, the famous basalt rock formation, as well as giving some excellent coastal views. It includes a long & steep descent into Fajãzinha.) To start, take a taxi to the church in the centre of Lajedo,

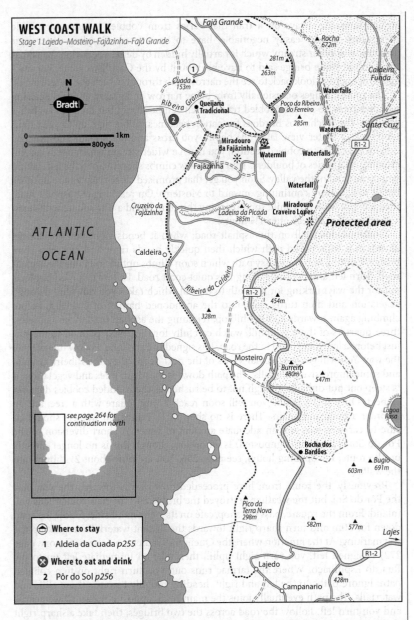

N

Bradt!

0   1km
0   800yds

Fajã Grande

Rocha
672m

281m

263m

Caldeira
Funda

Cuada
153m

Ribeira Grande

Queijaria
Tradicional

Poço da Ribeira
do Ferreiro

Waterfalls

285m

Waterfalls

Santa Cruz

R1-2

Miradouro
da Fajãzinha

Watermill

Waterfalls

Fajãzinha

Waterfall

ATLANTIC
OCEAN

Cruzeiro da
Fajãzinha

Ladeira da Picada
385m

Miradouro
Craveiro Lopes

Protected area

Caldeira

Ribeira da Caldeira

R1-2

454m

328m

Mosteiro

Burreiro
480m

547m

Lagoa
Rasa

Rocha dos
Bardões

603m

Bugio
691m

see page 264 for
continuation north

Pico da
Terra Nova
298m

582m

577m

Lajes

R1-2

Lajedo

428m

Campanario

🏠 **Where to stay**
1 Aldeia da Cuada *p255*

❌ **Where to eat and drink**
2 Pôr do Sol *p256*

or park your car at the village post office, near the church. If you're staying in Fajã Grande, a third option is to take the early-morning school bus and get dropped off in Lajedo. Opposite the church is an império with brown-painted doors. Follow the road that rises steeply to the right of this building, and then go left. The road levels off and you continue to where it ends. Continue straight on and you are on the footpath. There is a signboard marking the official start of the walk.

Follow the cobbled trail, keeping left at the junction you come to in a couple of minutes. From here, clear red-and-yellow waymarking makes route finding straightforward, always on a trail that varies from cobbles to grass. A couple of streams, usually easily negotiable, have to be crossed. Gurgling water later announces another stream, which is partially hidden by dense vegetation. You cross it on an old stone bridge said to have been built by the Castilians some 500 years ago. Once across, look back to see the narrow arch through which the water rushes.

The route changes occasionally from being narrow and grassy, at times entering wooded areas, to a wide cobbled track which can be slippy, but the path is always obvious. The Rocha dos Bordões formation becomes visible high up to your right (you'll get a better view later on) before you cross another stream and proceed downwards. After a cobbled section, you reach a wider stream which needs careful crossing on a series of boulders. Your path now climbs sharply up to the left, taking you up and out of the valley. Soon you get that promised closer view of the Bordões basalt rock, before continuing onward to Mosteiro. On reaching the asphalt road, turn left and walk downhill, soon reaching the church and a tiny square with seats, a good spot for a break after 1½ hours.

Continue downhill on the asphalt road; when it bends right you go straight ahead on a wide paved path which then quickly bends right and crosses a river bridge. Continue on the grassy path which soon climbs uphill and joins the asphalt road. Turn left and continue along this quiet coast road. Follow this road but look out for the waymarking for the path to the left which takes you downhill through vegetation and then turns right into the abandoned hamlet of Caldeira, before climbing again towards another hilltop, rejoining the asphalt road. Approximately three-quarters of the way uphill, watch carefully for the grassy path off to the left, just before a left-hand bend in the road. It is signed to Fajãzinha. Follow this path all the way. You will get spectacular views of the next deep valley, the Ribeira Grande and some impressive waterfalls. The path down is mostly in trees and vegetation; it is steep but not difficult, though not to be rushed as the rounded cobbles demand respect. Once in Fajãzinha you will soon reach a tiny square with a tree, and in summer a table and chairs. There is no shop in Fajãzinha, so walkers should be sure to carry snacks and an adequate amount of water. A short diversion to the Pôr do Sol restaurant (signposted) is an option, though this is no longer directly on the route; for opening hours, see page 256. You are now about 2½ hours into the walk.

Previously, the route from here proceeded downwards towards the sea, past the Pôr do Sol, but the weather destroyed the bridge and the new route turns you inland. From the square, pass the shop/café on its right-hand side, follow the road down for 50m and turn sharp right towards the distant waterfalls to pick up the waymarking. At the junction where the Queijaria Tradicional (cheese factory, page 272) is signed left, you turn right uphill then take an immediate left on to the Rua do Espinhaço. Where the tarmac runs out, you turn right on to a cobbled path. Ignore paths to the left and right, heading roughly towards those cliffs and waterfalls. The path eventually joins the main road, opposite the small watermill, and you turn left. Follow the road across the two bridges, then take a sharp right uphill (waymarked) on to another road. (If you are fed up of hills by this point, an alternative finish to the walk is to simply continue along the main road all the way down to Fajã Grande.) Continue upwards for around 1km to the end of this dead-end road, then take the waymarked grassy path to the right, by the side of a stone wall. The walk is now around 40 minutes to Fajã Grande, mainly downhill and flanked by stone walls. At times it takes you very close to the foot of the cliff face, allowing you to fully appreciate the density of the vegetation. After a few minutes, ensure you keep right at a Y-junction. Less than 15 minutes from leaving the dead-end road, the path reaches another road, but instead of joining it, look out for the waymarking which ushers you down to the right again, between two more stone walls. Soon, the first buildings of Fajã Grande village will become visible to your left. Again, the path reaches a tarmac road: this time, you simply cross over it and continue between yet two more stone walls. Keep a look out for a sharp turn to your left (waymarked) and take it to proceed on a narrow path between two more stone walls. Away to your right, you can now see the distant church of Ponta da Fajã village, which you will visit on Stage 2 of the walk, if you choose to do it. The grass path soon brings you out next to a large modern house. Fifty metres beyond it, you turn left on to a tarmac road which after 400m deposits you on to the cobbles of Fajã Grande's main street. Turn right to find a café, shop or to continue on to Stage 2 of the walk.

Stage 2: Fajã Grande–Ponta da Fajã–Ponta Delgada (Time: approx 4hrs; distance: 13km; see map, page 264. There are ways of shortening the distance, which can make sense as the middle section is the most interesting. To do so, either take a cab to Ponta da Fajã (or park your car behind its church), or else phone a taxi when you reach the concrete road 3km from the end of the walk, rather than walking into Ponta Delgada – or do both! The description below is for the full walk from Fajã Grande to Ponta Delgada centre.) From the north end of Fajã Grande, simply follow the tarmac road to Ponta da Fajã, with its church always visible in the distance. You soon pass the turn-off for Poço de Bacalhau (Codfish Pool), but it's maybe too early for a swim. On reaching the church at Ponta da Fajã, take the path to its left and pick up the waymarking. You set off down a wide grass and dirt track, cross a stream bed and continue across grass. After going through a gap in the stone wall, the path turns slightly right up towards the cliffs. Be sure to look back for the first of many excellent views of Fajã Grande. Ahead and offshore is the lonely pinnacle of **Baixa Rasa**, stranded mid ocean.

After a gradual climb of a few hundred metres, the waymarking takes you sharp right on a couple of stone steps, then left on a grassy track and zig-zags up towards a small waterfall (except in really dry times). Go left along a grassy ridge, still climbing. The path climbs more steeply as you enter the first of a series of low forests. You exit this on rough stone steps. You enter another wooded area, zig-zagging upwards. Watch carefully for the waymarking as it steers you off to the left. You enter a narrow grassy track lined with trees. Reach and climb some rough wooden steps with a handrail, with cliffs towering above. The path levels out briefly, skirting along the front of the rockface, before turning inland and climbing on rough stone steps in another wooded area. On exiting the trees, turn round again for more stunning coastal views. Up to your right, you will soon see a handrail and some stone steps leading to a wooden stairway. This leads you to a small grassy plateau, an ideal resting place after your climb. You now head across the grassy clearing, but halfway head left through bushes. Continue to climb on rough steps. This section can be muddy in places. Reach a stream and a gate, cross another stream bed and go through another gate. The path now levels across moorland and soon you will catch your first sight of Corvo (assuming the weather is being friendly).

Waymarking takes you sharply left towards the sea, then right again to continue your descent through bushland. Follow the waymarking through this moorland, peppered with bushes. Soon the whole of Corvo island should be visible. Briefly you head back towards the sea, then right again opposite the rocky islet of Baixa Rasa. Descend to a stream, usually easily passable, then climb up again alongside a stone wall. Go through a gate and up through more bushland. A further muddy

ATLANTIC OCEAN

For listings, see from page 254

Where to stay
1 Casas da Cascata
2 Sítio da Assumada

Where to eat and drink
3 Barraca Q'abana
4 O Meireles
5 Restaurante Maresia
6 Restaurante Papadiamandis

Ilhéu Francisco

Ponta do Albernaz
Farol de Albernaz
88m

Ponta Ruiva

Ponta Delgada
60m

36m

Terra da Costa
99m

Castelhanas

Ponta Delgada 4

117m

Ilhéu de MariaVaz

Pedra Alta
363m

N

Bradt

449m

0 ——— 1km
0 ——— ½ mile

Ilhéu de Monchique

Quebrada Nova

Ladeiras

593m

623m

Casteletes

Ponta dos Fanais

Baixa Rasa

448m

Vigia da Rocha Negra
685m

715m

768m

Ponta da Fajã

752m

Protected area

73m

836m

863m

Pico da Burrinha
886m

762m

5
6

Poço de Bacalhau

686m

Fajã Grande

1

187m

see page 261 for continuation south

3

131m 2

165m

244m

654m

564m

Branca

Rocha
672m

Lajes

Funda

264

section comes next; continue in the same direction between two stone walls. Reach a grassy clearing, from which on a clear day you will have a truly breathtaking view of the **Ilhéu de Maria Vaz**, the various other islets, the Atlantic waves, the **Albernaz lighthouse** and Corvo as a backdrop.

Continue through more bushland. You now cross moorland, crossing the occasional stream – in spring, these streams play host to some vociferous frogs! With the giant heather, this could be Scotland on steroids. The path now descends over rough stones – very slippy when wet – and the gap between the two stone walls becomes wider, levelling then descending to a narrower, stony path. Down to your left, you will see ahead the concrete road which you will eventually join. When the path emerges on to this road, you will have about 4km to (mainly) descend to the end of the walk. (If you have had enough, taxi drivers know this spot and will pick you up: a return from here to Fajã Grande will cost around €35.) Turn left on to the concrete and follow this cement road. Continue straight on and soon the cement road reaches a T-junction. (If you divert left here, it is a 500m walk to the Albernaz lighthouse, where you get a good close view of the large Ilhéu de Maria Vaz just offshore, and, beyond, Ilhéu de Monchique. If you take the diversion, you will have to return to the junction.)

Turn right and simply follow the asphalt road, contouring past pastures and hedgerows with Corvo getting ever closer, and keep descending gently to the road end, ignoring any tracks coming in from the right. Reach a T-junction. Turn left here, and in 100m you have a view of the tiny harbour below you and the village of Ponta Delgada to your right. Return to the junction and continue straight uphill. Continue up until you come to the império building on your right and the O Meireles restaurant on your left.

Down to Fajã de Lopo Vaz (Time: 45mins each way from the clifftop picnic park, total 4km; 1½hrs each way from Lajes, 8km; map, page 266) This linear, waymarked walk descends from a small attractive picnic park to the largest beach on Flores (pebbles and sand) some 300m below. It claims to be the hottest area with a 'microclimate tropical' and bananas are grown here.

You can take a taxi or drive the short distance from Lajes up to the picnic site (Parque das Merendas) above the fajã, where the road ends. This is a pleasing spot, with lovely views over the countryside and out to sea, with picnic tables, barbecues and toilets beneath *Myricaria* trees. Stand in front of the stone cross and look down to get a preview of your walk.

The walk down the cliff to the beach takes approximately 45 minutes each way as the descent needs care. The path down has more than 300 uneven stone steps; there are also well-formed sections of path on grass or earth. At times the drop off to the left is sheer but it is mostly well protected by vegetation, though not recommended after rain. There is no onward path from the beach, no road access and no facilities, so bring your own water. There is an occasional house and parts of the beach may be suitable for swimming when very calm – there is a strong undertow. It was one of the sites adopted by the early settlers, and gives a good feel of how hard life must have been in such an isolated place. The path is one of the oldest manmade constructions on Flores: some 500 years old.

If you started in Lajes, simply follow the path parallel to the road above back to town.

Parque Florestal de Recreio Luís Paulo Camacho to Santa Cruz das Flores walk (Time: approx 2½hrs; distance: about 7km; map, page 268) This is a glorious,

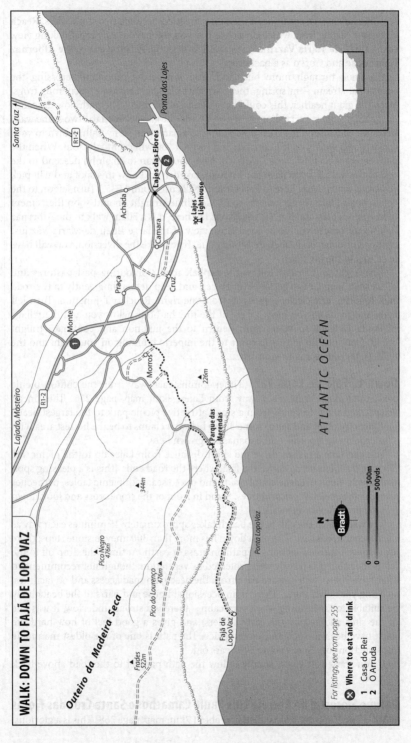

WALK: DOWN TO FAJÃ DE LOPO VAZ

Santa Cruz

R1-2

Lajado, Mosteiro

R1-2

Monte **1**

Praça

Achada

Camara

Cruz

Morros

Lajes das Flores **2**

Lajes Lighthouse

Ponta das Lajes

226m

344m

Parque das Merendas

Pico Negro 476m

Pico do Lourenço 476m

Frades 522m

Outeiro da Madeira Seca

Fajã de Lopo Vaz

Ponta Lopo Vaz

ATLANTIC OCEAN

N
Bradt

0   500m
0   500yds

For listings, see from page 255

✕ Where to eat and drink
1   Casa do Rei
2   O Arruda

easy walk through magnificent pastoral country surrounded by high valley sides and largely sheltered from wind. Magnificent on a sunny day if you want to be idle and take a long time over an easy walk, splendid on a windy or cloudy day, and absolutely perfect in winter. Although much is on the road, you are unlikely to meet a vehicle until the end. Although the distance can be covered in a couple of hours, try to allow longer because it is so tranquil. You could extend the walk by combining it first by visiting the Parque Florestal (page 258) and then walking back to the road fork to the start of the walk.

At the Parque Florestal, instead of descending where the carved wooden signpost points down to the park, continue to walk up the road to the next Y-junction and take the left fork, which is a cinder road, going uphill between trees. You slowly climb up the valley of the Ribeira da Fazenda. This road is used by dairy farmers, but not by many others. Look back from time to time and you will glimpse the ocean and Fazenda church. Towards the head of the valley the road turns briefly to tarmac, and you have glorious pastoral views all around you, except eastwards where lies the sea. At a double green gate on your left you see a *levada*, or water conduit, contouring off up a small side valley. Look up and slightly to your right and you will see the Pico da Sé, the highest point. You soon reach the highest point of the road, the tarmac runs out again and you descend for a short distance on a rough, grassy track to where it finally ends by some trees. By now, you'll have heard the gurgling of the stream, so follow the tiny path down and you'll reach the

THREE SHORT WALKS FOR MOTORISTS

Each of these can be incorporated into a day's car tour, as they are very short.

SHORT WALK 1: ALAGOA (Time: approx 20mins) From Santa Cruz take the road to the north towards Ponta Delgada and at Alagoa, before you reach Cedros, leave your car by the main road where you see a large rock-crushing depot, and walk down the unsurfaced road starting by the notice declaring that the area has special protection for wild birds. This leads you between the scattered houses and down to the beach. There are five islets in the bay and for centuries this was the island's only accessible natural harbour when a strong southwest wind was blowing. There is a very basic campsite here.

SHORT WALK 2: POÇO DE BACALHAU (THE CODFISH POOL) (Time: approx 10mins) After you turn right to take the cul-de-sac to the village of Ponta da Fajã (page 263), you immediately come to a small bridge over the pretty little Ribeira das Casas and its gurgling stream. A signposted, paved footpath follows the stream past three old watermills. You'll soon reach the pool and its waterfall, where swimming is permitted – ideal on a hot day.

SHORT WALK 3: POÇO DA RIBEIRA DO FERREIRO (Time: approx 20mins) Signposted from a car park on the main road (page 272), a short but steep walk on a red, yellow and white waymarked stone track – slippery when wet – through forest takes you to a stunning vista, especially after rain. A whole series of waterfalls, perhaps up to 70m, plummet down the rockface. A small lake completes this essential photo opportunity. Indeed, it's so picturesque that it has featured in a couple of minor movies. There is usually some water, though in dry periods it may be a trickle.

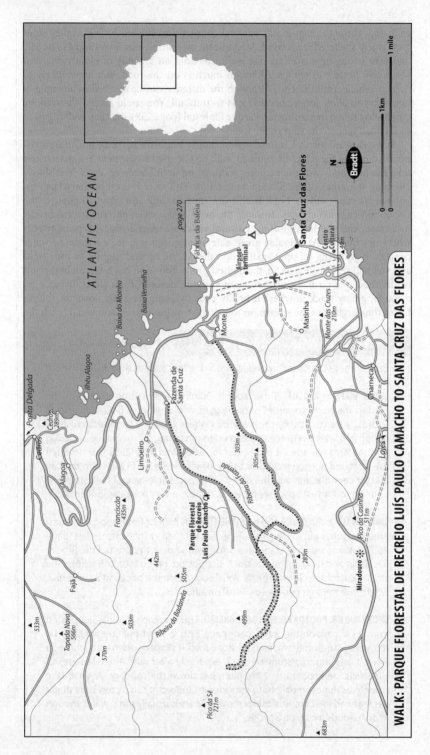

WALK: PARQUE FLORESTAL DE RECREIO LUÍS PAULO CAMACHO TO SANTA CRUZ DAS FLORES

waters. There is a pool deep enough for a refreshing splash (if you're brave enough) and to leave a bottle of wine to cool in time for your picnic. Endemic plant species you can find around here include *juniperus*, *rhamnus*, *faya*, tree heath, *vaccinium* and *viburnum*.

To return to Santa Cruz should take you no more than 1½ hours. When you are ready to continue, walk back down the road for about 1.5km. Turn 90° right on to what is now a waymarked asphalt road (though it sees virtually no traffic), first weaving right, left, then right again until it reaches a concrete bridge crossing a stream. The road climbs steeply then wends its way along the valley side. Santa Cruz will eventually become visible down to your right after a couple of kilometres. The road descends seawards to the village of Monte and reaching a T-junction you turn right, then left soon after. After 100m, at a square stone tower with a noticeboard, take a right turn to descend steeply to another T-junction where you turn right down another steep road which you follow to join the main road. Cross this carefully to immediately find a path to the left of a house. This very soon becomes stone steps which you take back to Santa Cruz, to the end of the airport runway.

TOURING THE ISLAND

SANTA CRUZ DAS FLORES This is the island's principal town [map, page 270] and includes the airport, whose landing strip runs the town's entire length. It's an enjoyable enough place to potter for an hour or two. The most striking building is certainly the 19th-century **Nossa Senhora da Conceição church**, of substantial, solid architecture made more imposing by two towers framing the front elevation. Equally substantial is the charming Baroque **Convento de São Boaventura**, now the **Flores Museum**. Two British visitors, Joseph and Henry Bullar, described Santa Cruz in 1839:

> The streets are long and narrow, and fields intervene between the houses. There are no large private dwellings, the great majority being cottages of the poor. Above them all rises the church, which is one of the largest in the Azores…

Traditionally, visiting strangers were accommodated in the convents in rooms set aside for guests. Nearby is Pimental Mesquita's house, built in the 17th century for the then governor of Flores and Corvo, and now a public library. This is thought to be the oldest home on Flores and the first to have a tiled roof and glazed windows.

CAR TOURS One suggestion is to do the lakes area in the high country and the south and west coast in one day; in fact this is about a 4-hour tour. On another day, drive up to the northeast corner, to Ponta Delgada, about a 2-hour tour. If you have enough days on Flores, then time your journey to the lakes and high country when there is no fog. If the day is not clear but very windy this could be a good time, for often low clouds will be travelling quickly and you will get windows of clarity, often in spectacular light. The beautiful tarmac road from near Lagoa Comprida, which connects to the east coast between Cedros and Ponta Delgada in the far north, has cut journey times considerably. You should also include one of the shorter walks on your touring schedule (page 267).

Car tour 1: Touring the high country together with the south and west
Leave Santa Cruz by the Lajes road and take the first major turning off to your right, signposted to **Fajãzinha** and **Fajã Grande**. You will soon get marvellous

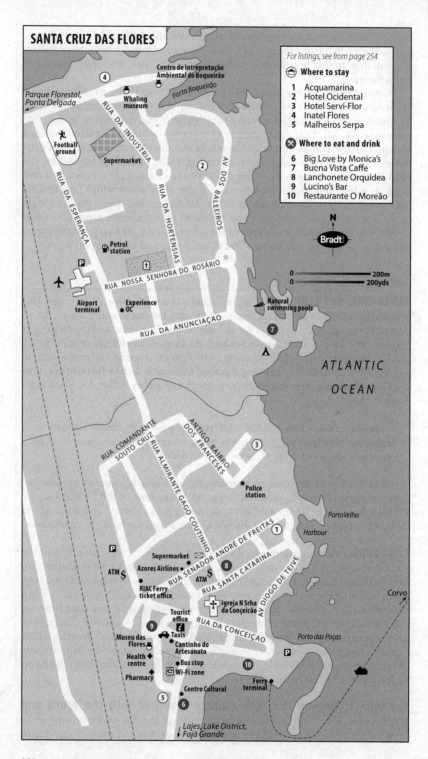

SANTA CRUZ DAS FLORES

For listings, see from page 254

Where to stay
1 Acquamarina
2 Hotel Ocidental
3 Hotel Servi-Flor
4 Inatel Flores
5 Malheiros Serpa

Where to eat and drink
6 Big Love by Monica's
7 Buena Vista Caffe
8 Lanchonete Orquídea
9 Lucino's Bar
10 Restaurante O Moreão

Bradt

N

0   200m
0   200yds

Parque Florestal,
Ponta Delgada

Centro de Intrepetação
Ambiental do Boqueirão

Porto Boqueirão

Whaling
museum

RUA DA INDUSTRIA

Football
ground

Supermarket

AV DOS BALEEIROS

RUA DA HORTENSIAS

RUA DA ESPERANÇA

Petrol
station

RUA NOSSA SENHORA DO ROSÁRIO

Airport
terminal

Experience
OC

RUA DA ANUNCIAÇÃO

Natural
swimming pools

ATLANTIC

OCEAN

RUA COMANDANTE
SOUTO CRUZ

ANTIGO BAIRRO
DOS FRANCESES

RUA ALMIRANTE GAGO COUTINHO

Police
station

Porto Velho

Harbour

RUA SENADOR ANDRÉ DE FREITAS

Supermarket

Azores Airlines

ATM

RIAC Ferry
ticket office

RUA SANTA CATARINA

AV DIOGO DE TEIVE

Corvo

Tourist
office

Taxis

Museu das
Flores

Cantinho do
Artesanato

Health
centre

Bus stop

Pharmacy

Wi-Fi zone

Centro Cultural

Igreja N Srha
da Conçeição

RUA DA CONCEIÇÃO

Porto das Poças

Ferry
terminal

Lajes, Lake District,
Fajã Grande

views on your left of the Ribeira da Cruz as you ascend, followed by a view to your right of Fazenda Valley. Look out for the **Miradouro Pico da Casinha**; here you might notice steep grassy slopes with narrow terraces running along the contours; these were made by hand 50 or more years ago to make the pasture accessible for cows. There is soon a further viewpoint with a car park, with views down both sides. The landscape soon becomes open wet grassland and trees and you pass through an area called Castanheiro. Continue, and after passing a pretty little chapel (Our Lady of Flores) on your left, soon you turn left at the intersection on to a road signposted for Lagoa da Lomba. At the next junction turn right, following the sign to Lagoa da Lomba which you soon reach on your right. This is the first of the seven lakes, nestled in its caldera and surrounded by a large landscape of rounded, weathered cones looking like a series of headless shoulders. In winter the boggy tufted grasses and mosses reflect an emerald shimmer in the low light, darkened in places by the almost black-green of the rushes. This lake is 15m deep. From the lake you can look across hydrangea hedges to the south coast.

Follow the road on, with views of the sea to the left. Note behind you the wind turbines; 85% of the island's power is still generated by diesel, but there surely must be potential to change this. Ignore a left turning down to Fazenda, and come to a junction. Ahead is a grand view of the **Boca da Baleia** – 'mouth of the whale'. Soon, you turn right, and as the road climbs you will see two lakes, one above the other. The top one is **Lagoa Rasa**, meaning 'flat', because, as you will see, the lake is almost level with the road; it is 16m deep. The lower lake is **Lagoa Funda** of Lajes, which means 'behind', named because it is at the back of Lajes. At the next road junction, turn left and drive up to get a closer view of the two lakes. You will see Funda on your left and then Rasa on your right. At Lake Rasa you will find a turning place and an information board.

Turn round and retrace your route; pass the intersection you came from and continue straight on. You will cross a cement bridge and a sign identifying the **Ribeira Grande**, and come to the main road. Cross this main road and take the road opposite to reach – after barely a kilometre – **Lagoa Seca** on your right, often dry as its name suggests. Away to your left you will see **Lagoa Comprida**, but a better view can be had from the opposite side. For now, continue on up the hill and shortly you'll come to **Lagoa da Água Branca**, a mere 2m deep. You then come to a turning place and retrace your route to the junction. At the junction turn right, signposted to Lajes. Very soon you come to a turn-off to the right, signposted to Lagoa Comprida and Lagoa Negra. Take this and now you will get a better view of **Lagoa Comprida**, 17m deep. (Caldeira and Lagoa are used interchangeably sometimes, but currently the signposts favour 'lagoa'.)

Continue on to the top of the road where there is a turning place. Here you see **Lagoa Negra** (confusingly, also previously called Lagoa Funda), at 108m the island's deepest lake. Often the water appears black, and it certainly earns its name, though in a certain light it also often appears in various shades of green and there is opposition to the name change! The highest mountain ahead of you, with a radio/TV mast, is **Morro Alto**, at 914m. Return to the junction at the bottom and turn right. Continue down and cross another bridge over the Ribeira Grande, then look out for a layby and a very narrow opening in the 'walls' with a cobbled pathway and miradouro; this is the **Miradouro Craveiro Lopes**, giving the most spectacular view over Fajãzinha and Ribeira Grande. Facing west, it is also a wonderful place to view the setting sun. Be careful of the sheer drop!

Take the next turning right to go down to **Fajãzinha** and **Fajã Grande**. Ignore the turning for Mosteiro on your left up to the radio masts; it is better to see this view on your way back up. In rainy times, you will become distracted by the incredible array of waterfalls cascading down the cliff face to your right. Continue down, ignoring the road off to your left to Fajãzinha; reaching a bridge you will see on your right a white-painted watermill, the **Moinho da Alagoa**, dating from 1869. It's now a branch of the Flores museum (⊕ 13.30–18.00 Sun–Fri; free admission). You can also take a short walk here.

A few hundred metres further, watch out for the sign to the **Poço da Ribeira do Ferreiro** (previously called Alagoinha), a must-do short walk if you like waterfalls (page 267). The road then descends. Now look out for a road off to your right, signposted Moinho da Cascata/Casas da Cascata. Take this; it is an upper road around Fajã Grande. The road descends through dense pittosporum and acacia trees, and then past many white stone walls enclosing small fields. These have now gone to pasture, but presumably in earlier times they grew vegetables and other crops. Continue down until you find a road going off to the right. Take this turning and at the bottom reach a junction where you will find a small bridge. (Starting at the bridge, you can also make a short walk to the so-called **Codfish Pool**; page 267. It is also near the start of the second stage of the west-coast walk to Ponta Delgada.) Turn right to go to the hamlet of **Ponta da Fajã**, but it is a cul-de-sac so you will have to return the same way when the road runs out beyond the church. Returning to the bridge, this time keep straight on to reach the natural pools of **Fajã Grande** and then the main cobbled street which courses up through the village itself. There are restaurants both by the pools and in the village.

Looking north along the coast there is a good view back to Ponta da Fajã, with its high cliff backdrop, and to more incredible waterfalls and, out to sea, the **Ilhéu de Monchique**, which really is Europe's westernmost point.

Retrace your route and, if you have time, divert and go down to **Fajãzinha**, a very charming village where time seems to have stood still. Signposted by the village shop is the road to the **Queijaria Tradicional** [map, page 261] (Pico do Redondo 6; ☏ 292 552 231; ⊕ 09.00–noon & 14.30–16.30 Mon–Fri, 09.00–noon Sat–Sun), the tiny village cheese factory. You will find it at the end of a very narrow road, passing many small houses and their productive gardens. Cheese is made here all year round: a soft cheese every day and a dry cheese when there is sufficient milk. Both are delicious. You can buy, but there are no free tastings, and no English is spoken by Ilda Henriques, the cheesemaker. They also have a cottage to rent. Below the village you will also find the traditional restaurant, Pôr do Sol (page 256), and it's worth going down to the end of this road to feel the force of the Atlantic waves.

To leave, head back up towards the main road you came by and climb the hill, this time taking the turn-off to the right, and stop at the viewpoint **Miradouro da Fajãzinha** beneath the radio/TV mast to enjoy the superb aerial view of Fajãzinha and Fajã Grande. Continue on this road, descending parallel with the coast, and you will soon see the deserted village of **Caldeira**. Shortly afterwards you come to the village of **Mosteiro**, the white-painted houses and church running down the side of a ridge with its background of 'organ pipes', the Rocha dos Bordões. It is a charming scene, with the village surrounded by small fields enclosed by stone walls. The population numbers about 70.

Beyond the village you'll come to a T-junction where you turn right on to the main Lajes road. Soon you get a good close view of the **Rocha dos Bordões**, and you can stop the car to better study the formation. The road continues on, curving round beneath the rocks and soon the hillside above the tarmac is covered in dense vegetation. There were once fields and pastures, all hedged with hydrangeas, and you can still make out these boundary hedges in among all the aggressive invading growth of pittosporum, tree heather and myrica. The next village to come into view on your right is **Lajedo**; the road then curves away and you follow a straight stretch into **Lajes**.

Lajes has no real focus but you will see the church on your right surrounded by a cluster of buildings, so turn right at the roundabout and park near the church. From the front of the church is a good view down to the harbour, where wooden boats are repaired, but now no longer built. There are also public toilets. To explore the harbour either walk down, or drive back to the main road and turn left and left again, signposted to the port. Park opposite the O Arruda café and take the narrow road in front of the café, forking left near the bottom. In a minute or two you will be at the beach, where there are picnic tables and WCs. There are a few seasonal snack bars. Above the main road is a modern museum and library, by the same architect as the Centro Cultural in Santa Cruz, but as yet there are no exhibits.

Tackling the last, short sector of this island tour, you pass the villages of **Lomba** and **Caveira**, then come into the **Ribeira das Cruz**, with a view to Santa Cruz. This ribeira you are crossing is dramatic with its broken topography and dense evergreen vegetation. Look down to the coast and see the small and sheltered **Fajã do Conde**, the site of the very first settlement on Flores and a fertile place where oranges and strawberries are grown. Minutes later you pass the first houses of **Santa Cruz**.

Car tour 2: Touring Ponta Delgada and the northeast

Leave Santa Cruz from the northwest corner of the airstrip and quickly climb, getting views of the rugged coastline. Soon you are crossing ravines filled with evergreen pittosporum and myrica trees, and all is cool and humid. The pretty little village of **Fazenda de Santa Cruz** is unmistakable thanks to its conspicuously sited church. On the clifftop high above you will see the rooftops of Cedros village. Below, in the bay, are many rocks including the largest, Ilhéu Alagoa. Drive round the **Ribeira do Cascalho**, passing the tiny settlement of **Alagoa**, and ascend to **Cedros**; just before the top of the climb there is a viewpoint marked by a low stone wall giving a fine view to Alagoa and Santa Cruz. As you continue you will get constant views of Corvo to your right – on clear days, anyway. Leaving Cedros the road travels inland, but gives you a fine view of Ponta Ruiva way below on its exposed fajã. After about 8km you will see **Ponta Delgada** village below you; this is the largest village on Flores. From above, the land looks flat but this is deceptive for when you descend to explore the village you will find there are plenty of steep hills. The road forks towards the bottom of the descent and by following the left fork you will get a good view of the tiny harbour.

Head back on the same road: turn right (it is signposted) to go to the **Farol do Albernaz**. Follow the narrow asphalt track going to the lighthouse, which was built in 1911 and is the most westerly navigational aid in Europe. From the field to the left there is a good view of the precipitous coast, and the large rock just off the boulder-strewn beach is the **Ilhéu de Maria Vaz**, while out to sea is the **Ilhéu de Monchique**, which can also be seen from Fajã Grande. Come back on the same road and this time continue into Ponta Delgada village until you reach the **Casa do Povo (village hall)** on your right. You can park here, since the streets below are very narrow, and exploration is better on foot. Don't forget the O Meireles restaurant (page 256). Return to Santa Cruz by the same main road, or, if you have plenty of time and light, you could take the road off on your right, just over midway between Ponta Delgada and Cedros, and go south through the centre of the island via the 'Lake District'.

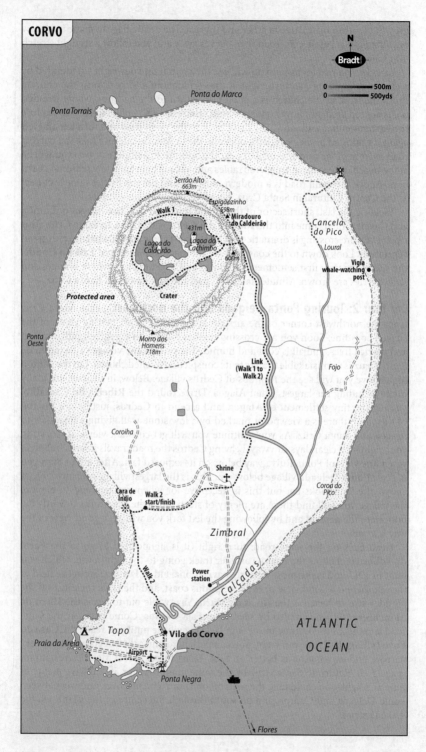

CORVO

N

Bradt

0   500m
0   500yds

Ponta do Marco

Ponta Torrais

Serrão Alto
663m

Espigãozinho
698m
Miradouro
do Caldeirão

Walk 1

Cancela
do Pico

Loural

431m

Lagoa do
Cachimbo

Lagoa do
Caldeirão

Vigia
whale-watching
post

600m

Protected area

Crater

Ponta
Oeste

Morro dos
Homens
718m

Link
(Walk 1 to
Walk 2)

Fojo

Coroiha

Shrine

Coroa do
Pico

Cara de
Índio

Walk 2
start/finish

Zimbral

Walk 2

Power
station

Calçadas

Topo

ATLANTIC

Praia da Areia

Vila do Corvo

OCEAN

Airport

Ponta Negra

Flores

11

Corvo

Corvo is by far the remotest island of the archipelago and must surely rate as one of the most isolated places in all Europe. This ancient volcanic remnant is surrounded by an often cruel and savage ocean, and remained inaccessible for months at a time, even from its nearest island neighbour, until the advent of the aeroplane. It is the tiny elusive gem at the apex of the Azores crown. Day visitors from Flores making the boat crossing in settled summer weather account for most of the visitors, but for the true traveller intent upon getting a feel for this island (and for ardent birders who arrive in October looking for American 'vagrants'), there are a slowly increasing number of accommodation options giving opportunities for longer stays.

Whether you arrive by plane or boat, you land in the island's only settlement, Vila do Corvo. It is the only suitable place to host a town, a lava delta left by the last eruption. Little has changed in the eastern segment of the town, the narrow cobbled streets between dark basalt walls of the houses all huddle tightly together in mutual protection against winter storms and to save valuable arable land much as they have always done. The only road snakes steeply up the hill to the cow pastures, and continues ever upwards to the caldera, a distance of some 6km.

On a day visit there should be time enough to walk to the road's end to enjoy the view down into the crater which, at 300m deep and 2km across, is among the largest in the Azores. However, be warned: it is often shrouded in cloud. For those with more time, there are two official walks to do, and the island is a high point for autumn birdwatching. But the greatest delight must surely come from simply being on Corvo and freeing your senses to absorb its atmosphere of truly splendid isolation.

As well as being the remotest island in the Azores, Corvo is also by far the smallest, at just 17.13km². It is also the smallest parish in Portugal: 460 people, 1,200 cows, and if you stayed for a week then you'd probably meet them all. The island consists of a volcano summit in the northern half with a caldera, in the bottom of which are small lakes. Given its size and isolation it is perhaps just as well that today there is no noticeable seismic activity and it is considered to be inactive. Since the western islands are the first obstacle that the Atlantic Ocean meets for over 1,000 miles, Corvo has been substantially eroded, so that the island now confronts the ocean with precipitous cliffs 700m tall, especially in the north and northwest. These are the highest in the Azores.

In 2009, UNESCO declared the island a Biosphere Reserve, encompassing all the land area above sea level and a surrounding marine zone totalling 25,853ha. The landscapes and biological value are considered to be of regional, national and international importance, and take in the previously protected sites.

BACKGROUND

GEOLOGY Like Flores, Corvo can be divided into two complexes, the older comprising submarine eruptions 1 to 1.5 million years old, and a superior complex of above-sea-level volcanism dating from around 700,000 years ago. The island appears to have a much simpler structure than Flores, and is the emerged summit of a basaltic stratovolcano (one that is a steeply sided cone of alternate layers of lava and other basaltic fragments). It would have been about 1,000m high before the caldera collapsed, and the highest point is now 718m.

The caldera's smooth and gently sloping sides suggest it could be one of the oldest in the Azores. The cinder cones within it, some up to 30m tall, are the result of later eruptions.

The last eruption occurred 100,000 years ago in the area of Pão de Açúcar ('Sugar Loaf') and it created the lava delta where Vila do Corvo and the airstrip are now located.

HISTORY Corvo means 'crow' or 'raven', but the name probably refers to cormorants, once known to the Portuguese as 'marine crows'; it was previously known as Marco or Landmark Island. Along with Flores, it was the last of the islands to be discovered by the navigators, sometime around 1450. Initial attempts at colonisation failed and it was not until 1548, when its donatory captain, Gonçalo de Sousa, imported enslaved workers from Cape Verde that permanent settlement was achieved. Thankfully they were sent home after de Sousa's death. Because of its size, isolation and lack of safe harbour, it has remained an agricultural society, and livestock farming and fisheries, both subsidised, together with subsistence agriculture and tourism, are the mainstays.

Early communication with Flores was by lighting fires, the number lit being code for a doctor, priest or other urgent need. Pirate attacks were a problem until 1820, and the island was overtaxed until 1853; given its extreme poverty, it seems an unofficial relationship was established with the pirates to mutual advantage. In exchange for water, food supplies and ship repairs, the islanders gained protection and luxury items.

The advent of the American whalers in the 18th and 19th centuries attracted able men to help crew the ships, and later land-based open-boat whaling generated some cash income. The first boys' school opened in 1845, followed by one for girls in 1874, thanks to a bylaw passed in Lisbon. Cows and hides were exported, but it was also a time of yet more emigration, to the other islands and Brazil, but mostly to North America. In 1864, the population was 883; it fell to just under 400 in 1981 (just one page in the Azores telephone directory) but is now growing again. In the 19th century there were between 5,000 and 7,000 sheep grazing on the common land around the caldera; this land was seized by the government in 1969 and the sheep industry was wiped out. When democracy returned and Portugal joined the EU, subsidies were paid for cattle but not sheep. Nowadays beef cattle graze on the mountain and are then winched from the quay into a boat during the summer months for transfer to Flores, where a larger ship takes them onwards to Lisbon. With an excellent school, easily identified by its windows and doors most attractively framed in traditional blue and yellow, the new generation maintains contact with the outside world via the very latest technology, and has far better internet access than is available in parts of rural England. Inhabitants of other islands comment on how the Corvo islanders are adept and adroit at getting their share of government spending. Previously, at 14 children had to go to Terceira or São Miguel to complete their schooling, but they can now complete it on their home island thanks to new facilities. Cast an eye across the townscape of white houses and your gaze may be halted by a dark, square building. This is Corvo's multi-purpose community hall; even bigger is a beautiful new sports centre; there's very little land left for growing crops.

GETTING THERE AND AWAY

Travel to and from Corvo is not always a straightforward process, whether by plane or boat. Weather conditions are all-important, crosswinds and waves being the enemies, and the visitor should always allow for delays when planning an itinerary. However, just because it is too windy for a plane to fly or the sea is too rough for a ship to come into port does not imply bad conditions on land. Azores Airlines (☏ 292 590 310) flies up to three times a week in winter, daily in summer, connecting Corvo with Flores, São Miguel, Faial and Terceira. General information on inter-island travel is given on pages 42 and 49. It's worth booking ahead for the lifeboat-style ferry to Flores, especially the busy morning crossing; do this at the RIAC offices (🕐 09.00–17.00 Mon–Fri) opposite the post office or in Flores (page 252). Other private boat companies are based here (page 280) and on Flores (page 259).

GETTING AROUND

There is no car hire, so…walk! If this really does not appeal, drivers (see below) meet boats or can be contacted direct to take you to the start of one of the two walks, or simply to peer down into the caldera (about €10 there and back). After that…well, where else would you go on tiny Corvo?

Ana Fonseca m 936 330 500;
e corvoturismo@gmail.com
Carlos Reis m 918 231 492, 964 577 765
Corvo Tours m 912 635 318;
e corvotours@gmail.com

Corvo Travel m 912 012 404;
e corvotravel@hotmail.com
João Mendonça m 969 568 941, 917 763 029

TOURIST INFORMATION

There are not too many attractions to point out on the island, but the **Caso do Bote** (Caminho dos Moinhos; ☎ 292 596 227; **w** cm-corvo.pt, in Portuguese only; ⊕ 09.00–17.00 Mon–Fri) facing the airport terminal usually has English-speaking staff available to help.

WHERE TO STAY

Accommodation is very limited, but there is a good reason for that: there are few visitors, even in high season. Nevertheless, advance booking is advisable: the arrival of one moderately sized group of birdwatchers could take up the island's capacity and leave nothing left for others! Addresses are superfluous for the listings below, as they will all pick up from port or airport; otherwise, in a place this size, everyone knows everyone and everything.

If you want to camp, head to the **Parque de Campismo** located near to the northwestern corner of the airport. Here you'll find a good, flat, grass field at the end of the airstrip, a stone's throw from Corvo's tiny boulder-and-sand beach. Facilities including a modern washblock (with solar hot water) and a barbecue are available, all free of charge.

Hotel Comodoro (13 rooms) Caminho de Várzea; ☎ 292 596 128; **m** 914 198 806; **e** corvoazores@yahoo.com; **w** comodoroazores. com. Everyone can tell you the way, but there's a free transfer for pre-booked guests from either airport or ferry, 5–10mins' walk away. Rooms come with private bathroom, AC & cable TV; some have terraces. There's a lounge area with myriad books on the island & welcome coffee- & tea-making facilities. Quiet, well established: Manuel – a former town mayor – is a delightful host. B/fast inc. €€€

Casa Dias (2 rooms) Caminho de Várzea; **m** 917 763 012; **e** paula_cvu@hotmail.com. A pink house just beyond the Comodoro, 2 twin rooms with shared bath. TV. B/fast inc. €€

Joe and Vera's Place (2 rooms) Caminho de Várzea; **m** 914 112 097; **e** vera.camara@sapo. pt; **w** joeveraplace.pt. In a new yellow house just beyond the Comodoro, 2 twin-bedded rooms with private bath, cable TV & b/fast inc. They also have separate chalets to rent. €€

Joe and Vera's Vintage Place (4 rooms) Rua da Matriz; **m** 914 112 097; **e** vera.camara@sapo. pt; **w** joeveraplace.pt. Vintage by name, but brand new by nature. Next to the church, a clean, cosy, comfortable & welcoming addition to Corvo's limited accommodation options. Cable TV. €€

✗ WHERE TO EAT AND DRINK

BBC Caffé & Lounge Av Nova; ☎ 292 596 030; 🄵 bbccorvo; ⊕ 08.00–23.00 Mon–Thu, 08.00–01.00 Fri, 19.00–01.00 Sat, 09.00–23.00 Sun. No connection to any broadcasting organisations, rather this is the domain of the volunteer fire service (Bar Bombeiros Corvo). A friendly place, the food is centred around toasties, burgers, etc, & choice is a bit limited. Social club upstairs. €€

Restaurante O Caldeirão Caminho dos Moinhos; ⊕ restaurant: noon–14.00 & 19.00–21.00; bar: 07.30–21.00 Wed–Mon. Facing the sea just beyond the airport terminal, this serves a lunchtime buffet (€17) & à la carte dinner, including fairly standard meat dishes, plus slightly more expensive fish & basic vegetarian options. The owner is an ex-fire-eater. €€

OTHER PRACTICALITIES

Everything is within spitting distance of each other, and a map is unnecessary to find the **Health Centre** (Centre de Saúde), **post office** and the two banks with

ATMs, all in the centre of the new town. Free **Wi-Fi** can be had at the airport or in the central area around the post office. The **police** can be contacted on ✆ 292 596 261.

WHAT TO SEE AND DO

WILD BIRDS INTERPRETATION CENTRE (Centro de Interpretação de Aves Selvagens do Corvo, Canada do Graciosa; ✆ 292 596 051; e parque.natural.corvo@azores.gov.pt; w parquesnaturais.azores.gov.pt/en/parques/1/centro/4; ⏰ 09.00–12.30 & 13.30–17.00 Mon–Fri; €3/1/free adult/senior & under 15s/under 7s) Birdwatching has become a key part of tourism on Corvo, especially the rush to spot rare vagrants during the October migration, and the exhibits and custodians here explain the environmental context. Downstairs, a 5-minute virtual reality film shows you the island, and bilingual wall posters give information on the bird and marine life. The recently restored building shows the traditional architecture, and is appropriately located in the town's compact historic core.

ECO MUSEO (Casa do Tempo, Rua das Pedras; ✆ 292 596 063; w ecomuseu-corvo. cultura.azores.gov.pt; ⏰ Apr–Sep 10.00–12.30 & 13.30–17.30 Tue–Sat, Oct–Mar 09.30–12.30 & 13.30–17.30 Tue–Sat; free) The new Eco Museo is growing fast, with a carpentry display opening in 2024 next to the Wild Birds Interpretation Centre, and a weaving display plus temporary exhibitions in the Multipurpose Hall at the top of the new town. You can also look in on the last remaining atafona (animal mill, worked by a cow). But its heart is here in the old town, by a promenade above the port; staff are keen to explain the items on display and let the conversations go where they may. Be sure to ask about the wooden locks.

VILA DO CORVO There is only one town, Vila do Corvo, and no villages or other settlements. If you have come just for the day, as do most visitors, then Vila do Corvo certainly justifies an hour or two. Wander around the old part of town enjoying the details: from the harbour, the narrow streets called *canadas*, the play of sun and shadow on the cobbles, and the Church of Nossa Senhora dos Milagres – Our Lady of Miracles – with origins dating back to the 16th century. The name remembers the defeat in 1632 of ten shiploads of Algerian pirates, when an image of the Virgin led to the pirates' cannon balls supposedly being turned back against them. The present church was built between 1789 and 1795, and paid for by the Corvo population together with remittances from emigrants; in 1796 the first priest arrived from São Jorge. Corvo was the first island to introduce a strategic development plan, in 1984, and all the old part of Vila do Corvo is a conservation area. The new half is not without interest, and reflects the enterprise of the islanders. If you explore the south coast below the airport you will notice the old slipway by the windmills, where whales were brought up before the factory was built on Flores, and the blubber was reduced on the shore in the open. If the clouds are high, then the main attraction is to visit and preferably to walk around the caldera, the crater with its lake and small islands. See below for details.

BIRDS In October every year, a faithful band of European birders arrive in Corvo, on the hunt for vagrant birds blown on to the island on their way from the US to South America. For some, it seems, the Atlantic storms can indeed be good news, while for ducks and waders the lakes in the caldera provide a welcome place to recuperate after the Atlantic squalls have blown them off course. British birder Peter Alfrey, who first identified Corvo's potential in 2005, has written detailed descriptions of his visits (page 302). In the autumn of 2023, 53 American species were spotted on Corvo, and some species are still being recorded in Europe for the first time.

BOAT TOURS Most boat tours come from Flores, but there are a couple based on Corvo.

Paralelo 39 m 919 696 822; **e** paralelo39corvo@gmail.com, lourenco79@gmail.com

Passeios de Barco Rota Azul m 918 933 635, 919 024 879; **e** rotaazulcvo@hotmail.com

WALKS ON CORVO

The best way to explore the tiny island is to walk. The two official walks, both easy, satisfying and well waymarked, are described in this section.

Most visitors will want to go to the highest accessible point and see the caldera. A taxi to the caldera edge then a circular walk around the inside is the best recommendation. The summit is frequently in clouds, but do not be put off as these often clear for short moments, enough to give you a window to see down into the caldera. The second walk is also easy, and is both picturesque with all the pastures and at the same time dramatic because of the rugged coastline and views down over town and airport. You can marvel at being in such a glorious place and yet in the middle of the Atlantic Ocean.

The road to the caldera turns off the original road above the east coast, now almost traffic-free, which leads past the Fojo woods, one of the island's popular birding sites, to a whalers' lookout.

WALK 1: AROUND THE INSIDE OF THE CALDERA (Time: 2½hrs; distance: 4.7km. Easy/medium, with descent at the beginning, ascent at the end. This walk assumes you get a taxi to the crater & that you get picked up again. However, you could choose to walk back down to town on the tarmac, which will take another 1½hrs. Winds around the crater can be bitter, so a windproof jacket is usually a good idea.) Corvo attracts so few visitors that you may have the caldera entirely to yourself, apart from numerous cows, blackbirds and the occasional seabird. From the official start of the walk at the crater edge, simply descend down a well-marked path following the red-and-yellow waymarking, usually visible on short wooden posts at intervals of 50–100m. You'll notice that the crater is valuable grazing land for cattle, some of which stay here even in winter. Many of them spend the winter in the numerous stone buildings you will have passed along the road up from town. The road itself was built in the 1950s and paved in 1995. On reaching the foot of the crater, these instructions take you clockwise, though anticlockwise is equally possible. Follow the waymarked posts towards a large grassy mound. The undulations in the caldera floor quickly make you realise that it is not as flat as it seemed from the top! From the top of a mound, descend to a rough stone bridge next to a small pond. Continue straight ahead towards the caldera wall. The path veers round to the right, taking you to the western end of the Lagoa do Caldeirão, boggy at times, then close enough to the shore to hear the croaking of frogs in spring. You cross the neck of a wide peninsula, and pick up the waymarking on a large, isolated boulder, before continuing down and resuming close to the edge of the eastern lake, the Lagoa do Cachimbo. You will have noted how few trees grow inside the crater, though there is a rich variety of moss and grass for the cows. Follow the path along the shore, then around the right-hand side of a rocky hill. By now you can see the lowest point of the eastern rim, where you started your walk. Be sure to keep to the waymarked path; trekking uphill on spongy moss will tire your legs considerably!

From the rim of the caldera a walk is waymarked all the way back to Vila do Corvo; we assume you will arrange transport to start Walk 2 as described below, but if you fancy a much longer walk, you can follow these instructions to link the two walks.

From the start/finish of walk 1, simply walk down the tarmac for around 30 minutes until you reach (on your left) a once-white barn just before a cattle grid. Without crossing the cattle grid, turn right down a grassy slope in the direction of a minor road which you can see before you. At the foot of the grassy path, turn right on the concrete road, which runs between two stone walls, and after 10 minutes you reach a junction with a shrine to St Anthony on your right. Turn right uphill on a wide dirt road which swings right back towards the volcano. Take the first road sharply back to your left and follow this until you see the signboard on your left, 10 minutes from the shrine, marking the start of walk 2. The waymarked route actually continues up the dirt road towards the volcano to loop behind the hill, passing two small reservoirs that are good birdwatching sites, before dropping down to the signboard.

WALK 2: CARA DE ÍNDIO ('THE INDIAN'S FACE') TO VILA DO CORVO (Time: 2½hrs; distance: 4km to Vila do Corvo, 4.5km to the west end of the runway. You could do this as an 'out-&-back' walk, but it is better to take a taxi to the start & walk downhill, thus avoiding a long uphill trudge & seeing the same scenery twice: these instructions assume that you start at the top. Starting from the top also ensures you see the spectacular views of the west coast, the town, & across to Flores.) From the signboard, go through a wooden gate and down a narrow grassy/cobbled path between stone walls. After 200m, turn sharp left down a narrow path beside an electric fence. A bit of wall climbing may be required, as farmers sometimes block gaps with electric fences or even stones to prevent cattle from wandering. After a further few hundred metres, you go sharp right through a gate, climbing slightly

11

along a wall, then swinging left and dropping slightly to reach a wooden fence on the edge of the cliff.

You will see the sea and the airport far below, and to the right the eponymous Indian's face silhouetted in the cliff (although it reminds me more of an Easter Island statue). Caution: keep well clear of the edge at this point, especially in high winds!

Follow the waymarking to the left towards the distant end of the runway, and go through a wooden gate and then another. Cross the very rough grassland, away from the cliff edge, before heading slightly inland to pick up the waymarking on a series of rocks which occupy the grassy pasture. Soon, the markings take you again inland, before you head briefly right to reach the end of a wall and fence. Hop over the wall to find the waymarking. Cross a second wall, by two new wooden posts, and continue in the same direction, with the town of Vila do Corvo now spread out before you.

You now cross a tiny wooden bridge, perhaps having to step over some more electric fencing, before continuing in the same direction, following the waymarked wooden posts. You now descend, fairly steeply and often between stone walls. The path, narrow and very churned up, eventually joins the main road, 35–40 minutes from the Indian's Head viewpoint. Turn briefly right on the road, then very quickly leave it again to your left to descend on a wide grassy short-cut path with the tiny harbour ahead of you. You also get excellent views of the town's cramped old quarter. This path takes you on to tarmac again, before veering left (waymarked) on to another descending grass track.

Soon, you reach cobbles at the top of the town. You can follow the cobbled road to the new town with its cafés and guesthouses, or follow the waymarks down steps to the left into the old town. The waymarking continues past the eastern end of the runway, then along the airport road before turning left a few hundred metres after the windmills to take you down to the sea, along the shore and eventually to the runway's western end and the town's two black-sand beaches, where the walk officially ends.

Appendix 1

LANGUAGE

Portuguese, and especially Azorean, pronunciation is notoriously difficult and takes much practice, and ought to be mastered before trying to use any vocabulary. Fortunately, you will meet plenty of friendly Azoreans happy to coach you to say a phrase to the point where they can recognise it!

Many words can be guessed from English or Spanish and some Spanish speakers get along quite well with a mixture of *português* and *espanhol*. Examples include many words ending with -ion or -on in English and Spanish respectively which are similar in Portuguese but end in -ão (plural usually -ões) – *televisão, associação*.

Take care, though, for some similar Spanish and Portuguese words have completely different meaning eg: *niño* (Spanish = child) versus *ninho* (Portuguese = nest); and it is best not to describe an ordinary man as *ordinário* as this implies he is common or vulgar.

PRONUNCIATION

ã + a followed by m	nasal (similar to 'ang')
c	ss before i or e; k elsewhere
ç	ss
cc	ks
ch	sh
g	soft j before i or e; hard g elsewhere
j	soft j (as in French)
lh	y (as in 'yacht')
nh	ny (as Spanish ñ)
o or ô	oo when unstressed
o or ó	o when stressed (as in hot)
ou	o sound (as in both or window)
õ + o followed by m	nasal (similar to 'ong')
qu	k before i or e; kw elsewhere
s	z or sh (at end of word)
x	sh or s
z	soft j

ESSENTIALS

Hello	*Olá*	Yes	*Sim*
Good morning	*Bom dia*	Yes please	*Sim, por favor*
Good afternoon	*Boa tarde*	No	*Não*
Good evening/		No thank you	*Não obrigado*
Goodnight	*Boa noite*	(masculine)	
Goodbye	*Adeus*	I am sorry	*Desculpe*

That is all right	*Está bem*
Good	*Bom*
Excellent	*Óptimo*
Excuse me (to pass someone)	*Com licença*
What is your name?	*Como se chama?*
My name is…	*Chamo-me*
I am	*Sou*
Do you have…?	*Tem…?*
You're welcome	*De nada* (ie: 'it's nothing' – reply to thank you)
Please	*Por favor*
Thank you (masculine)	*Obrigado*
Thank you (feminine)	*Obrigada*
Thank you very much (masculine)	*Muito obrigado*
Thank you very much (feminine)	*Muito obrigada*
It is very kind of you	*É muito amável*

QUESTIONS

How?	*Como?*	How much (cost)?	*Quanto custa/é isso?*
How much?	*Quanto?*	What?	*O quê?*

NUMBERS

0	*zero*	16	*dezasseis*
1	*um*	17	*dezassete*
2	*dois*	18	*dezoito*
3	*três*	19	*dezanove*
4	*quatro*	20	*vinte*
5	*cinco*	21	*vinte e um*
6	*seis*	30	*trinta*
7	*sete*	40	*quarenta*
8	*oito*	50	*cinquenta*
9	*nove*	60	*sessenta*
10	*dez*	70	*setenta*
11	*onze*	80	*oitenta*
12	*doze*	90	*noventa*
13	*treze*	100	*cem*
14	*quatorze*	1,000	*mil*
15	*quinze*		

DAYS, MONTHS AND TIME

Sunday	*Domingo*	Thursday	*Quinta-feira*
Monday	*Segunda-feira*	Friday	*Sexta-feira*
Tuesday	*Terça-feira*	Saturday	*Sábado*
Wednesday	*Quarta-feira*		

January	*Janeiro*	July	*Julho*
February	*Fevereiro*	August	*Agosto*
March	*Março*	September	*Setembro*
April	*Abril*	October	*Outubro*
May	*Maio*	November	*Novembro*
June	*Junho*	December	*Dezembro*

after	*depois (de)*	now	*agora*
before	*antes (de)*	today	*hoje*
day	*dia*	tomorrow	*amanhã*
never	*nunca*	yesterday	*ontem*

GETTING AROUND

aeroplane	*avião*	right	*à direita*
bus	*autocarro*	road	*estrada*
car	*carro*	Stop here, please	*Pare aqui, por favor*
closed	*fechado*	straight on	*em frente*
here	*aqui*	street, road, highway	*rua*
left	*à esquerda*	there	*ali*
lorry, truck	*camião*	Where is it?	*Onde é Cadê?*
open	*aberto*	Which way?	*Para onde?*

ACCOMMODATION

Is breakfast included?	*O pequeno-almoço incluído?*	guesthouse	*residencial*
		cold/hot water	*água fria/quente*
bathroom, toilet	*casa de banho*	hotel	*hotel*
bed	*cama*	toilet paper	*papel higiénico*
bedroom	*quarto*		

EATING AND DRINKING This includes sufficient restaurant Portuguese to help you through the usual menu.

In a bar/café

I would like…	*Queria…*
a beer, please	*uma cerveja, por favor* (for types of beer, see *Drinks*, below)
a sandwich, please	*uma sande, por favor* (these almost always come as rolls filled with ham, cheese or mixed: *fiambre, queijo* or *mixta*)
mineral water, please	*uma água mineral, por favor* (*com gás* = carbonated; *sem gás* = still)
two coffees, please	*dois cafés, por favor*
some more coffee, please	*mais café, por favor*
the bill, please	*a conta, por favor*

In a restaurant

For two, please	*Para dois, por favor*	dinner	*jantar*
The menu, please	*Ementa, por favor*	dish of the day	*prato do dia*
Enough, thank you	*Chega, obrigado*	the wine list	*lista de vinhos*
lunch	*almoço*		

Drinks Coffee comes in many forms: *café com leite* = white coffee; *café bica* = small strong black coffee; *café galão* = white coffee served in a long glass; for more details, see page 58.

tea	*chá* (*chá preto* = black tea; *chá verde* = green tea; *chá da Índia* = Indian tea; *chá de camomile* = chamomile tea)
fruit drink	*um sumo de frutas*
iced	*fresco*

house wine	vinho da casa (tinto, red; branco, white)
bottled beer	cerveja de garrafa
draught beer	cerveja de pressão or fino or imperial

Fish (*peixe*) See also pages 56 and 298.

clams	ameijoas	salmon	salmão
common sea bream	pargo	salted cod	bacalhau
forkbeard	abrotea	sardine	sardinha
octopus	polvo	shellfish	mariscos
horse mackerel	chicharro	shrimps	camarão
lobster	lagosta	squid	lula
mussels	mexilhões	swordfish	espadarte
prawns	gambas	tuna	atum
red fish	boca negra	wreck fish	cherne
red mullet	salmonete		

Meat (*carne*)

beef	carne de vaca	rabbit	coelho
chicken	frango	sausage	salsicha
chop	costeleta	smoked pork	
kid	carne de cabrito	sausage	linguiça
liver	fígado	spiced sausage	chouriço
loin	lombo	tongue	lingua
pork	carne de porco	veal	carne de vitela

Cooking methods

baked/roasted	no forno	smoked	fumado
boiled or *pot-au-feu*	cozido	steamed	suada
fried	frito	stewed	estufado
grilled	grelhado	tinned	conserva
roast/roasted	assado	with a sauce	com molho

Azorean/Portuguese foods

apple	maça	honey	mel
beans	feijão	ice cream	gelado
beans with mixed		lemon	limão
meats	feijoada	lettuce salad	salada de alface
beef	bife	lupin seeds (usually	tremoços
biscuits	biscoitos	in a saucer on the	
bread	pão	bar counter)	
bread soup	açorda	mixed salad	salada mista
butter	manteiga	olive oil	azeite
cabbage soup	caldo verde	olives	azeitonas
cake	bolo	omelette	omelete
caramel custard	flan	orange	laranja
chicken	galinha	peanuts	amendoins
egg	ovo	potatoes	batatas
fruit	frutas	rice	arroz
fruit salad	salada de frutas	sauce	molho
garlic	alho	soup	sopa

286

sugar	*açúcar*	yoghurt	*iogurte*
tomato salad	*salada de tomate*		

HEALTH

casualty department	*banco de socorros*	diarrhoea	*diarréia*
	(SAU – Serviço de	to hurt (or ache)	*doer*
	Atendimento	doctor	*médico*
	Urgente)	ill	*doente*
hospital	*hospital*	fever	*febre*

OTHER USEFUL WORDS

bank/credit card	*cartão do*	market	*mercado*
	banco/crédito	money	*dinheiro*
battery	*pilha*	mountain	*montanha*
book	*livro*	night	*noite*
change	*troco*	nothing	*nada*
child	*criança*	on the beach	*na praia*
church	*igreja*	rain	*chuva*
currency	*devisas*	sea	*mar*
enough	*bastante*	shop	*loja*
exchange	*câmbio*	small	*pequenho/a*
hill	*colina*	to swim	*nadar*
house	*casa*	too	*demais/demasiado/a*
lake	*lago*	town	*cidade*
large	*grande*	village	*aldeia*
a little (not much)	*pouco/a*	you	*você* (polite, formal),
a lot (very much)	*muito/a*		*tu* (familiar)

LANGUAGE COURSES The University of the Azores (Rua da Mãe de Deus, 9500 Ponta Delgada; ☏ +351 296 650 000; e cursoverao@alf.uac.pt; w uac.pt) offers summer Portuguese-language courses at beginner, intermediate and advanced levels on São Miguel. There are also courses in Azorean culture, society and art on São Miguel, Terceira, Faial and Pico. Courses run for two to five weeks in June and July. Accommodation is provided in university hostels and fees include costs of field trips and social events.

Appendix 1 LANGUAGE

A1

Appendix 2

FLORA

Given that there are some 850 flowering plants and ferns in the Azores, the following 60 have been selected as those most likely to strike the eye of the visitor. Books that describe European flowers will identify most of the Azorean flora apart from the endemics, and the well-illustrated *Mediterranean Wild Flowers* by Marjorie Blamey and Christopher Grey Wilson, published by Collins, London, is helpful. The most difficult plants to identify confidently are the evergreen trees and shrubs. As always, the one plant you really would like to name will not be included!

The Latin name is given in italics, followed in brackets by the Portuguese vernacular where known, and by the common English name if there is one, and then the family.

EVERGREEN TREES AND SHRUBS

Myrica faya **(faia); Myricaceae** Evergreen shrub or small tree up to 8m. Leaves lanceolate, leathery, dark green, margins often toothed towards the apex and frequently rolled backwards. Flowers are unisexual and borne on axillary catkin-like spikes, male and female on the same plant; overall colour olive-green, withering to brown. Fruit small, rounded and very hard. All Azores islands, Madeira, the Canaries and Portugal. Often a coastal shrub, but found up to 700m. At higher altitudes a member of the laurisilva association. Can form pure stands, but is often out-competed by alien *Pittosporum undulatum* and you can frequently see the two species fighting for dominance. Makes a good shelter hedge and was once used around orange orchards. Isolated trees make good garden specimens.

Ilex perado **ssp.** *azorica* **(azevinho; Azorean holly); Aquifoliaceae** Tree up to 5m, with a smooth grey bark. Leaves dark and glossy, stiff, elliptic-oblong, sometimes with a few spines. Madeira and the Canaries also have their own subspecies. Usually found above 500m, and an important member of the laurisilva forest; can be seen as isolated specimens or in hedgerows. Formerly encouraged by farmers for winter cattle feed. On all the islands apart from Graciosa.

Laurus azorica **(louro; Canary laurel); Lauraceae** Dark, glossy green, evergreen tree up to 10m, sometimes taller, with a dense crown. Young shoots clothed in dense brown downy hairs. Leaves alternate, varying between five and 15, 3–7cm, broadly lanceolate-elliptic, hairless above, softly hairy beneath at least when young, strongly aromatic when crushed; in the axils of the midrib and main veins are tiny, gland-like projections. Flowers creamy yellow, fruit ovoid, 1–2cm, broadly ellipsoid, green turning to black when ripe. Usually grows above 500m and a key member of the laurisilva forest.

Picconia azorica (pau-branco); Oleaceae Evergreen tree or shrub, leaves opposite, leathery, without hairs, two to three times as long as broad, with small white flowers on inflorescences from the leaf axils. Found mostly between 300m and 600m, once widespread and used for house building, its presence now rather scattered. Endemic to the Azores, but not found on Graciosa.

Frangula azorica (sanguinho); Rhamnaceae Large deciduous shrub or small tree with a wide spreading crown; branches little divided and leafy only towards the end. Leaves broadly elliptic, up to 15cm long with distinct parallel lateral veins. Flowers small, yellowish, in clusters from the leaf axils. Generally around 500m and up to about 1,000m altitude it is a member of the laurisilva forest, and also remnant hedgerows. On all islands except Graciosa and Corvo, now extinct on Madeira.

Prunus lusitanica ssp. azorica (ginja; Azores cherry laurel); Rosaceae Evergreen small tree to 4m, leaves somewhat leathery, to 10cm, oval and tapering at each end, dark green and shiny above, paler beneath, possibly finely toothed, leaf stalks red when young, the whole plant without hairs. Flowers rounded, white, in racemes of up to 20–30 from the leaf axils. Fruit cherry-like, oval to almost round, turning red at first, finally ripening purplish black. Above 500m in deep ravines or in dense laurisilva forest. Endemic and rare.

Myrsine africana (tamujo; African boxwood); Myrsinaceae Dense, low evergreen shrub to 1.5m, leaves 0.6–2cm, roughly egg-shaped with small teeth on margins. Flowers small, pale brown in clusters of three to six, followed by bluish-lilac 6mm-diameter fruits. Generally above 400m, it favours the shelter afforded by dense laurisilva forest where it can be abundant, but it also occurs in more open vegetation. Occurs in East and South Africa, and from the Himalayas to China.

Persea indica (vinhático); Lauraceae Evergreen tree up to 15–20m tall, with a broad, rounded crown. Shoots finely hairy when young. Leaves without glands, 10–20 × 3–8cm, elliptic, leaf stalks up to 3cm, reddish; whole leaf becomes reddish when old. Inflorescence on stalks shorter than the leaves, flowers small, whitish. Fruit about 2cm. Ellipsoid, bluish-black when ripe. Found above 200m, introduced long ago (from the Canaries?), now naturalised. *Persea americana* is the avocado.

Clethra arborea (lily of the valley tree); Ericaceae Evergreen shrub or small tree to 8m with a bushy crown, twigs have obvious leaf-scars, and young twigs, leaf stalks and flower stems all densely covered in rusty hairs. Leaves about 12 × 5cm, somewhat crowded towards the shoot tips, leaf margins with forward pointed small teeth, with fine hairs on veins on underside, leafstalk often reddish. Flowers in simple or branched racemes up to 15cm long, erect, the flowers to

8mm, nodding, white, cup-shaped, scented. Endemic to Macaronesia (Madeira), probably introduced into São Miguel, where it has rapidly naturalised on the hills above Furnas.

Pittosporum undulatum (*incenso;* Victorian box, orange berry); Pittosporaceae
Vigorous tree to 14m, leaves 10 × 3cm, narrowing to a point, shiny dark green above, pale beneath, young leaves yellow-green, margins wavy. Flowers bell-shaped, about 1cm diameter, creamy-white in clusters, sweetly scented, February. Fruit orange when ripe, the pale brown seeds very sticky. Native of southeast Australia, it was introduced as an ornamental and used as a hedging plant to shelter the orange orchards but is now widely naturalised throughout the archipelago and is a major and aggressive component of the tree cover, especially on Santa Maria and Pico.

Hedera helix ssp. *canariensis* (Canary ivy); Araliaceae
The familiar plant with climbing or creeping woody stems and evergreen leaves with three to five short, triangular lobes. Yellow-green flowers in many flowered umbels, fruit rounded, ripening black. Widespread between 100m and 1,100m, most common at mid altitude, and most luxurious in laurisilva forest. Also found in Madeira, Canaries, Portugal and northwest Africa.

Viburnum treleasei (*folhado;* Azorean laurustinus); Adoxaceae
Evergreen shrub with oval leaves and small white to pink flowers in large terminal convex clusters, spring. Fruits are at first a vivid deep metallic blue, turning black as they mature. Associates with laurisilva forest, but can be seen in remnant hedgerows on Pico; generally above 400m and up to 900m. *V. treleasei*, endemic to the Azores, is closely related to the Canary Islands endemic *V. rugosum*, and to *V. tinus*, native to southern Europe and long cultivated.

Vaccinium cylindraceaum (*uva da serra*); Ericaceae
Deciduous shrub generally less than 2m tall, with 20–50mm-long finely toothed, narrowly oblong leaves; when young these are attractively red-tinged. Flowers borne in clusters, yellow-green tinged red; just how red the flowers are varies, partly due to age, and the combination of young red leaves and good red flowers in June puts this among the most attractive of the Azorean endemic plants. Grows generally above 400m and is conspicuous among the laurisilva forest, and often may be seen in old hedgerows. Occurs on all the islands. Fruits locally harvested for preserves.

Euphorbia stygiana; Euphorbiaceae
Many-stemmed soft wooded shrub up to 2m tall with conspicuous narrow leaves 10–15cm long, apple-green and waxy with prominent pale midrib. Flowers terminal, yellow-green. Most easily seen in association with laurisilva, where it is moist and the surrounding vegetation provides shelter. A very noticeable plant of attractive form. Endemic.

Daboecia azorica; Ericaceae
Dwarf, heath-like evergreen shrub less than 15cm tall with alternate leaves to 8mm long. Flowers in terminal loose racemes,

nodding, bell-shaped, ruby-red. Mostly above 500m, can be found in grassland but is most spectacular on the upper slopes of Pico, where it forms magnificent carpets with *Thymus caespititius* in midsummer. Endemic.

Erica scoparia ssp. *azorica* (urze; besom heath); Ericaceae
Stout, evergreen shrub or small tree with narrow 4–7mm-long leaves in whorls. Insignificant reddish-brown flowers in interrupted terminal groups. Grows from sea level up to about 2,000m on Pico, at its best above 500m when part of the humid laurel forest. Long used for fuelwood, fencing poles, and woven shelter screens and brooms. Endemic, on all the islands, but large old specimens now rare.

Juniperus brevifolia (cedro-do-mato); Cupressaceae
This endemic conifer was once a major tree in the laurisilva forests, producing a superb timber from trunks 40–60cm in diameter; these may still be seen as roof beams in old buildings. Today they are small trees or mostly shrubs with crooked stems affected by exposure and are to be found in remnant cut-over forest associated with other laurisilva species or sometimes surviving in hedgerows or as forlornly isolated specimens. The branches are short and numerous, densely foliate with needle-like leaves in whorls of three with two white stomatal (breathing pore) bands on the upper surface. Found usually above 500m, but also lower and on Pico they reach up to 1,500m. On all the islands except Santa Maria and Graciosa.

Arceuthobium azoricum (espigos-de-cedro; dwarf mistletoe); Viscaceae
A genus of partly parasitic mistletoe found on conifers. The whole plant is yellowish-green with scale-like leaves and grows upon *Juniperus brevifolia*. At first difficult to find, the rather sickly colour of the small bunches of tangled stems becomes apparent from among the dense green leaves of its host. Above 600m altitude, it is found scattered in large laurisilva stands and is most easily discovered on Pico. An intriguing curiosity, it can be cultivated by taking cuttings of infected juniper when, after three years or so, the parasite will develop from the host tissue.

Lantana camara (cambará; shrub verbena); Verbenaceae
Evergreen shrub to 2m, leaves oval, shortly pointed at apex, up to 6cm long, margins toothed, surface wrinkled, rough to the feel with a strong, pungent, lemony smell. Flower in hemispherical heads to 3cm across, yellow to orange or red, often with a brighter 'eye'. Native to tropical America, this attractive flowering shrub has escaped from gardens and is naturalising and becoming a pest, as it has in so many other places worldwide; poisonous to cattle.

Solanum mauritianum; Solanaceae
Large shrub or small tree up to 4m tall, with foetid, softly hairy leaves ovate-elliptical, pointed at apex, up to 30cm long. Flowers up to 2cm across, violet-blue with yellow anthers, in many-flowered heads. Fruits round, 1.5cm across, deep yellow. Native of Central America, it is frequently found near habitation and on waste ground.

HERBACEOUS PLANTS
Rocky coastal areas, formed by variously aged lava flows or volcanic ash

Crithmum maritimum (perreexil-do-mar; rock samphire);
Umbelliferae A short, bushy plant with fleshy, hairless, once- to twice-divided greyish leaves. Flowers yellowish-green in umbels 3–6cm across. Usually seen growing alone or with few other species in lava close to the sea and tolerant of sea spray. Britain and western Europe.

Gnaphalium luteo-album (perpétua-silvestre;
Jersey cudweed); Compositae Shortish, white woolly annual. Clustered yellow-reddish flowers. In sandy soils and lava cliffs. Rare in Britain, occasional in Europe, and in warm temperate regions worldwide.

Solidago sempervirens (cubres); Compositae Fleshy,
with leaves ending in small broad points at the tip. Flowers yellow in a closely branched panicle. Found as a coastal plant and occasionally elsewhere, particularly noted on the sea cliffs of Flores. Native of northeast America, and spread to the Azores in prehistory times.

Tolpis succulenta (visgo); Compositae
Perennial herb with a woody base and becoming shrubby with age. Up to 30cm but can be as much as 100cm. Leaves narrow to broadly elliptic, often toothed, somewhat succulent. Flowers yellow, late summer/autumn. Grows near the coast on sea cliffs and gravelly places, as scattered individuals. To be found on all the islands, but in few localities, and on Madeira.

Azorina vidalii (vidalia; azorina); Campanulaceae Soft-wooded
shrubby perennial with a main stem and branches to 50cm. Young plants form ground-hugging rosettes. Leaves dark green, often shiny, narrow, edged with forward-pointing rounded teeth, the whole plant somewhat sticky. Flowers nodding, bell-shaped, waxy, greenish-white to white to pink in an elongated raceme. Coastal plant in rock crevices and sandy places – even grit on the edge of asphalt roads. Most abundant among the rocks and sand below the airstrip on Corvo where it gets frequent sea spray. On all islands except Graciosa and Faial, but is often difficult to find. One of the loveliest endemic Azorean species, it is becoming increasingly popular in Britain as a tender garden plant.

Silene uniflora (bermin; sea campion); Caryophyllaceae
Hairless, prostrate, much-branched perennial herb up to 30cm. Leaves without a stalk and often covered with a waxy bloom. Flowers with a bladder-like calyx, petals white, from March to late summer. Widespread coastal plant, also on Madeira, and in west and northwest Europe. Also found around the summit of Pico.

Plantago coronopus (dia-belha; buck's-horn plantain); Plantaginaceae
Small herbaceous annual, biennial or perennial plant with rosettes pressed closely to the ground. Leaves somewhat fleshy, usually 2–6cm, linear-oblong, not lobed or with a few teeth or often twice-lobed. Flowers yellowish-brown, 3mm, borne in long, dense spikes on

curved stems that are longer than the leaves. Very common in coastal habitats, and an early coloniser. Can also be found inland on dry, waste ground.

***Juncus acutus* (sharp rush); Juncaceae** Tall, up to 150cm, robust grassy perennial making dense prickly tussocks with stiffly pointed stems and reddish-brown flowers in a compact inflorescence. Although a widespread species – Madeira, Mediterranean, Britain, North America – it is included here because it is a typical plant of the coast.

***Festuca petraea* (*bracel-da-rocha*); Graminae** Grass with narrow, stiff leaves 30–50cm tall, flowers in whitish-green panicles. Coastal plant on cliffs, on lava and in sandy places often exposed to sea spray. Forms pure colonies but these are now rare because of human interference along the coast and this species is found commonly mixed with other species. Endemic to the Azores and found on all the islands.

In laurisilva forest and at habitats generally above 400m

***Leontodonfilii* (*petalugo-menor*); Compositae** Perennial herb with up to five 20cm conspicuous, more-or-less elliptical leaves, toothed and hairy, bearing one to five yellow flowers on a branched stalk. Associated with the laurel forest, it likes wet, open places, often in grassland, usually above 600m, lower on Flores. Endemic, but not found on Santa Maria or Graciosa.

***Senecio malvifoliius* (*cabaceira, figueira-brava*); Compositae** Perennial herb up to 120cm with rounded, lobed leaves 10–15cm, often found growing among shrubs which provide support. Flower colour varies from pale purple, bluish to white all on the same inflorescence, summer. An attractive plant usually growing in wet shady places, but I have seen it in a sunny hedgerow on São Miguel. Endemic, but not on Graciosa or Flores and Corvo.

***Tolpis azorica*; Compositae** Perennial herb up to 70cm, leaves crisp-looking, hairless, oblong, up to 15cm, margins deeply toothed. Flowers yellow on a branched inflorescence. Seen in laurel forest and on constantly moist grassy slopes where it is conspicuous, generally above 600m. Endemic, but not on Graciosa.

***Erigeron karvinskianus*; Compositae** Perennial, stems slender, flat on the ground with erect tips. Leaves to 3cm, flowers varying from white through pink to red-purple. A pretty little daisy from Mexico that has escaped from gardens in numerous temperate places worldwide; in the Azores it is adaptable to different habitats.

***Cardamine caldeirarum*; Cruciferae** Included here because it is endemic and widespread in the Azores above 400m (but not on Graciosa). In northern Europe it has bittercress relatives that are the weeds and curse of garden centres. Herb up to 50cm tall, basal leaves with five to six pairs of leaflets, flowers white. Likes wet places.

***Centaurium scilloides* (perennial centaury); Gentianaceae** Low, spreading perennial with non-flowering decumbent (flat, tips turning up) shoots, found usually above 400m. Upper leaves lanceolate, about 1cm long. Flowers white, solitary or just a few together in summer. Likes moist habitat, often with grasses. Could once easily be seen at several viewpoints, but seems to be disappearing, maybe due to visitor trampling. *C. scilloides* occurs in western Europe, generally with pink flowers, but some authorities classify the Azores plants as subspecies *massonii*, in which case they would be endemic. Francis Masson, Kew Gardens' first professional plant hunter, collected in the Azores in 1776 and this became one of the first plants from the Azores cultivated in England.

Hypericum foliosum; Guttiferae Deciduous shrub to 50cm with crowded, narrowly ovate leaves and conspicuous yellow flowers 2–5cm diameter in terminal inflorescences. Normally above 400m, a member of the laurisilva forest but survives where this has been destroyed, and can also be found on steep grassy slopes. Endemic, on all the islands.

Thymus caespititius (erva-úrsula); Labiatae Dwarf, mat-forming plant with woody growth and upright flowering shoots to 5cm. Leaves to 6mm, narrow, spoon-shaped. Flowers in lax, small heads varying in colour from white through rose to almost lilac. Grows from low altitude to high on Pico, often in crevices on lava flows and on sandy banks. On the upper slopes of Pico it makes a spectacular summer display with *Daboecia azorica*.

Anagallis tenella (bog pimpernel); Primulaceae If you are looking at this in detail you will either be bored or very keen. Mat-forming, slender perennial with mostly opposite rounded to elliptical leaves. Flowers pink to whitish pink, somewhat bell-like on slender stalks, opening fully only in sunshine. Around 500m in wet or moist places, often near lakes. Western Europe.

Lysimachia nemorum ssp. azorica (palinha; yellow pimpernel); Primulaceae Evergreen herb with procumbent stems, quickly creeping and rooting at the leaf joints. Leaves opposite, more or less egg-shaped. Flowers solitary on slender stalks. A pretty, modest plant most often found in moist grassland and happiest above and around 500m. *L. nemorum* is found from Britain through to the Caucasus, the endemic subspecies *azorica* is found throughout the archipelago.

Ranunculus cortusifolius (bafo-de-boi); Ranunculaceae A handsome buttercup being an erect, up to 1m-tall herbaceous perennial, with slightly leathery basal leaves, lobed, rounded and heart-shaped up to 21 × 30cm. Flowers shining yellow up to 50mm diameter in a branched inflorescence. Usually above 500m but lower on Flores in permanently moist areas, especially in the shelter of laurisilva forest in ravines, and occasionally in roadside gullies. Also found on Madeira and the Canaries.

Polygonum capitatum; Polygonaceae Prostrate perennial with rooting stems, often forming large ground-covering carpets. Leaves 2–5cm oval, green with purple V-shaped band, often covered with glandular hairs. Flowers pink in dense, stalked, more or less globular heads. Native to the Himalayas, it was introduced and has escaped on many of the islands, happily colonising young lava flows, stone walls and waste places.

Rubia peregrina (rapa-língua; wild madder); Rubiaceae

Distinctive, trailing or scrambling, hairless, rampant evergreen perennial. Stems square and rough with downturned prickles, leaves in whorls of four to six. Flowers yellowish-green, 4–5mm, forming a leafy inflorescence. Fruit rounded, ripening black and fleshy. Widespread, also in west and south Europe and North Africa.

Luzula purpureo-splendens; Juncaceae This charming woodrush is a perennial, leaves grass-like, wide and up to 60cm long with fine hairs along the margins; flowers brown-purplish in clusters. Found usually between 500m and 1,100m altitude, preferring a moist grassland habitat, often on slopes, and among moss carpets around remnants of laurisilva forest, but also can withstand drought. Endemic, on all islands except Santa Maria and Graciosa.

Platanthera micrantha (Azores butterfly orchid); Orchidaceae Two

basal leaves, about 10 × 4cm, erect to spreading. Two to six stem leaves, much smaller. Flowers in a rather dense narrowly cylindrical inflorescence, 8–13cm high and about 1cm across. Individual flowers numerous, small, yellow-green. Found between 200m and 1,000m but mostly above 600m in moist places in full sun to semi-shade; most often seen in grass on roadside verges. The plant's characteristics are variable and some authorities recognise a second, similar species *Platanthera azorica* that is more stocky with larger leaves and a more lax inflorescence of whitish-green flowers. Of the orchids recorded for the Azores, *P. micrantha* is the species most likely to be encountered; the other is a Tongue orchid.

Trachelium caeruleum (throatwort); Campanulceae

Perennial herbs up to about 50cm tall with numerous small slender blue or lilac flowers in much-branched, leafless, broad flat inflorescences. Found in walls, roadside verges, etc, São Miguel, Terceira and Faial, west and central Mediterranean.

Arundo donax (cana; giant reed); Graminae A tall (to 5m) perennial rhizomatous grass, leaves 60 × 6cm, grey-green. Flowers in large terminal, feathery inflorescences, autumn. Introduced long ago, it thrives in volcanic sands around the coast and is used widely for shelter hedging. Strongly invasive, it quickly spreads if not strictly controlled. When grown in ideal conditions in the south of France the canes are supplied to make the reeds for musical wind instruments.

FERNS
Asplenium marinum (feto maritime; sea spleenwort); Aspleniaceae A coastal, tufted plant with a short, thick rhizome with dense blackish-brown scales, the whole growing tightly in among the rocks. Leaves 20–30cm long, pinnate, mid green and glossy above, dull and paler below, thickened and rather stiff; tolerant of salt spray. Madeira, Britain to western Mediterranean.

Blechnum spicant (hard fern); Blechnaceae Evergreen fern forming attractive crowns of long, sterile, pinnate leaves with a herring-bone appearance lying close to the ground; the young leaves are flushed red. The fertile fronds have a longer stalk, are much narrower, and are erect.

Widespread in northern temperate lands, it is one of the commonest and most distinctive ferns in the Azores, usually above 300m.

Woodwardia radicans (chain fern); Blechnaceae
Found from the Azores to Java, this fern is one of the most attractive of the archipelago's fern flora. The fronds are 1–2m long and up to 50cm wide and often hang down over gullies and banks. The fronds produce bulbils towards the apex and these form new plants, hence the common English name. Usually found above 400m in moist places.

Culcita macrocarpa (*feto-do-cabelinho*); Dicksoniaceae
Conspicuous large fern with strong erect stems up to 1m tall. The frond is triangular in outline, often shiny and frequently of a yellow-green colour. Found mostly above 500m but also down to 150m. It is associated with laurel forest and can be readily seen between the tree stems on the lava flows of Pico, but it also survives the loss of forest cover and can be found beyond the laurisilva. It has a prostrate rhizome covered with hairs, which were once collected and used for stuffing cushions, etc. Found on all the islands except Santa Maria and Graciosa, it is native to Macaronesia and the Iberian Peninsula.

Lycopodium cernuum (clubmoss); Lycopodiaceae
A distinctive curiosity of a plant and a fern ally, its long creeping, looping stems rooting at intervals often spread over several square metres. Overall colour is yellowish-green and the tiny leaves are spirally arranged along the stems. The fertile leaves (sporphylls) are arranged in terminal cones (strobili). Generally found above 400m, frequently associated with laurel forest, but often also on steeply sloping banks where it can be a pioneer species on recently exposed surfaces. Also occurs by hot-water springs. On all islands, except Santa Maria and Graciosa. In central Europe the strobili of clubmosses used to be collected and dried, and the fine yellow spores kept for use as a medicated talcum powder; sensitive to pollution, they are now rare and strictly protected there.

Osmunda regalis (*feto-real*; royal fern); Osmundaceae
Large tufted fern with upright fronds up to 1m tall and 30cm broad, pinnate. Sporangia produced on some of the terminal pinnae of the fertile fronds. It has a distinctive, short, massive, erect rhizome and a tangle of wiry roots, once popular in mainland Europe until mid last century as compost for growing orchids. Growing in wet places, often in water, and found on all islands except Graciosa.

CULTIVATED PLANTS

Agapanthus praecox; Liliaceae
Perennial herb forming dense clumps from strong fleshy rootstocks with long strap-like leaves and large heads of blue flowers on leafless unbranched stems up to 60cm tall. Seeds black when ripe, borne in pendulous capsules. Native to South Africa, widely planted in towns and along roads, often naturalising.

Amaryllis belladonna (*beladona*; belladonna lily); Amaryllidaceae
South African bulbous perennial with strap-shaped leaves in two ranks. Large funnel-shaped pink flowers produced in late summer before the leaves appear, six or more together on stout 60m stems. Frequently planted in public gardens and along roadsides, also naturalised.

Abelia x grandiflora; Caprifoliaceae Attractive semi-evergreen shrub to 2m with long arching branches, the young leaves at first markedly bronze-pink; flowers tubular, five-lobed, in clusters, pink to white, flowering over an extended period from summer. Frequently planted on road verges.

Aloe arborescens; Liliaceae Perennial succulent from South and East Africa with 60mm long grey-green leaves having sharp forward-pointing teeth. Inflorescence unbranched to 80cm, flowers tubular, 4cm, scarlet tipped greenish-white. A good ornamental thriving in hot dry places in private gardens and public places.

***Acacia melanoxylon* (blackwood); Mimosoideae** Fast-growing Australian tree with leaves modified to reduced simple, flattened leaf stalks up to 14 × 2.5cm. Flowers in nearly spherical heads in branched racemes, very pale yellow, late winter. A much-desired timber tree for high-value products. Seedlings are abundant on disturbed land, mature trees in gardens and woodland.

Metrosideros excelsa; Myrtaceae Dense evergreen tree that in maturity develops massively heavy branches and trunk with many aerial roots swinging from its branches. The dark leathery leaves are silvery on their undersides, and in summer terminal flowers burst into a spectacular show of scarlet-stamened pin cushions, seldom all over the tree but in large patches. Called *pohutukawa* by the Maoris, in its native New Zealand it often begins life as an epiphyte and is commonly found on sea cliffs. Very tolerant of salt spray, this tree is often to be seen in public gardens and squares on most of the islands.

***Melia azedarach* (Persian lilac); Meliaceae** This tree has many local common names around the world where it has been widely planted, but originally it came from northern India and China. Deciduous, spreading tree with an open crown and handsome twice-pinnate leaves to 80cm somewhat like the European ash. Flowers violet-blue in loose sprays 10–20cm long, often with the new foliage, followed by 1–5cm-diameter round fruits ripening yellow, wrinkling and turning brown with age remaining on the tree long after the leaves have fallen. Planted as a street tree and in public gardens.

***Araucaria heterophylla* (Norfolk Island pine); Araucariaceae** A stately conifer endemic to Norfolk Island attaining 20m or more, with spreading branches in whorls. Leaves scale-like to 1cm, somewhat triangular, overlapping like roof tiles. Planted widely throughout the islands, they are all protected and special permission is necessary before they can be felled. Captain Cook on his second round-the-world voyage in the 1770s discovered them and enthused about their potential use for ships' masts but sadly the wood proved too spongy and heavy. In their natural state they grow to 60m with a trunk circumference of over 8m on dry but fertile shallow volcanic soils. This drought tolerance the Victorians soon realised made it an ideal house plant when young, and it is again coming back into fashion. Dating back to the Jurassic period 225 million years ago, they were browsed by dinosaurs, but in the Azores they are vulnerable to lightning strikes.

Appendix 3

FISH ON THE MENU

There are some 50 species of fish found in the waters around the Azores that can be eaten. Those more likely to be found in the islands' restaurants are detailed below in alphabetical order according to their Azorean common name. Resilience is an indication of how much exploitation a species can tolerate and how long a minimum population takes to double in time. Very low = more than 14 years; low = 4.5–14 years; medium = 1.4–4.4 years.

ABROTE Greater forkbeard *Phycis blennoides*. Commonly up to 45cm, max size 110cm long, max weight 3.5kg. Found over sand and mud bottoms, a deep-water fish 10–800m, usually seen in caves, very shy, gentle fish; young more coastal. Feeds on crustaceans and fish. Eastern Atlantic, Iceland down to West Africa, and the Mediterranean. Resilience medium. Served as transverse steaks or filleted.

ATUM Tuna or tunny. Three different ones are commonly eaten in the Azores: *Thunnus obesus* is mostly squeezed into tins, while albacora, yellowfin tuna, *Thunnus albacares*, and Bonito, skipjack tuna, *Katsuwonus pelamis*, are served under *atum* in restaurants. The yellowfin tuna reaches a max size of around 230cm and weight of about 180kg, and the skipjack 90cm and 23kg.

BADEJO Island grouper *Mycteroperca fusca*. Max size 80cm, max weight 3kg. Subtropical, found above rocky areas, depth down to 200m. Azores, Madeira, the Canaries and Cape Verde islands. Resilience low. Served stewed, maybe grilled or baked in the oven.

BICUDA Yellowmouth barracuda *Sphyraena viridensis*. Max size 128cm, max weight 8.2kg. Depth 0–100m. Tropical, eastern central Atlantic. Feeds on fish, cephalopods and crustaceans. Resilence low. Eaten best as a transverse steak, also baked whole in the oven.

BOCA NEGRA Blackbelly rosefish *Helicolenus dactylopterus*. Max size 47cm, max weight 1.5kg, reportedly living for around 40 years. Depth 50–1,100m. Deep-water fish found in soft-bottomed areas of continental shelf and upper slope, feeds on crustaceans, fish, cephalopods. Venomous. Eastern Atlantic Iceland to South Africa, western Atlantic. Resilience very low. Served whole, good grilled or fried.

BODIÃO VERMELHO Ballan wrasse *Labrus bergylta*. Max size 65cm, max weight just over 4kg. Found around rocks and offshore reefs to a depth of 50m. Feeds on crustaceans and molluscs. Eastern Atlantic. Born first as female, then changes sex after four-plus years. Resilience low. Served grilled.

CHERNE Wreckfish *Polyprion americanus*. Max size 210cm, max weight 100kg. Deep water (40–600m), solitary, likes caves and shipwrecks. Feeds on large crustaceans, cephalopods and fish. Wide distribution, eastern and western Atlantic, southwest Pacific. Resilience low. Best served as transverse steaks; when thick and simply grilled a gastronomic highlight.

CHICHARRO Blue jack mackerel *Trachurus picturatus*. Max size 60cm. Depth to 270m, a schooling species favouring shallow coastal waters of islands, banks and sea mounts, feeds on crustaceans. Eastern Atlantic, Bay of Biscay down to Tristan da Cunha. Resilience medium. Eaten small, about 10cm; fried really crispy they are quite yummy.

ESPADA Silver scabbardfish *Lepidopus caudatus*. Max size 2m, max weight 8kg. Depth 100–600m. A deep-water school-forming fish found usually over muddy or sandy

bottoms and migrates into midwater at night, when it is most often caught. Eastern Atlantic France to South Africa, southern Indian Ocean, southwest and southeast Pacific. Feeds on crustaceans, squid and fish. Resilience medium. Eaten as fillets.

ESPADARTE Swordfish *Xiphias gladius*. Max size 4.5m, max weight 650kg. Depth 0–800m. Oceanic, occasionally in coastal waters. Migrates to temperate or cold waters in summer, returns to warmer waters in autumn. Feeds on fish, also crustaceans and squid, using their sword to kill prey. Atlantic, Indian and Pacific oceans. Resilience low. Usually served as a transverse steak, too often cut measly thin; like a good beefsteak, it should be thick.

GAROUPA Blacktail comber *Serranus atricauda*. Max size 43cm. Depth 1–90m, found over hard bottom; carnivorous, distributed eastern Atlantic. Resilience low. Served whole, usually grilled.

GORAZ Garapau or Peixão blackspot seabream *Pagellus bogaraveo*. Max size 70cm, max weight 4kg. Inshore waters to a depth of 700m, feeds on crustaceans, molluscs, worms and fish. Eastern Atlantic. Resilience low. Served grilled or baked in the oven. Locally regarded by some as 'horrible'.

MERO Dusky grouper *Epinephelus marginatus*. Max size 150cm, max weight 60kg. Depth 8–300m, subtropical, likes reefs and rocky bottoms, solitary and territorial, feeds on crabs, octopus and fish. Eastern Atlantic and western Indian Ocean, and western Atlantic. Resilience low, endangered. Served as fillets rather than steaks but also good poached or cooked in the oven.

PARGO Common seabream *Pagrus pagrus*. Max size 91cm, max weight 7.7kg. Depth down to 250m. Subtropical, found over rock or sandy bottoms, feeds on crustaceans, fish and molluscs. Eastern Atlantic north to the British Isles, western Atlantic, down to Argentina. Resilience medium, endangered. Served whole or as transverse steaks. Excellent covered with sea salt and oven baked.

ROCAZ Large-scaled scorpion fish *Scorpaena scrofa*. Max size 50cm, max weight 2.9kg. Depth 20–500m. Subtropical, solitary, sedentary over rocky, sandy or muddy bottoms, feeds on fish, crustaceans and molluscs. Venomous. Eastern Atlantic. Resilience low. Very expensive but very nice! Served whole, grilled or poached.

SALMONETE Striped red mullet *Mullus surmuletus*. Max size 40cm, max weight 1kg. Depth less than 100m. Found over rocky places and also sand and soft bottoms, feeds on shrimps, molluscs and fish. Eastern Atlantic. Resilience medium. Eaten whole.

SERRA Atlantic bonito *Sarda sarda*. Max size 90cm, max weight 11kg. Depth range 80–200m, subtropical schooling species, cannibalistic, feeds on squid, shrimps and fish. Widespread Atlantic. Resilience medium. Served as fillets or transverse steaks.

Appendix 4

FURTHER INFORMATION

MAPS *Azores* published by Freytag and Berndt in their regional series. Folded map, scale 1:50,000. A topographical map of the islands with tourist information, lots of detail and easily readable; £10.99. Reise Know-How also publish a slightly smaller scale (1:70,000) Azores map, which is satisfactory for most visitors at £11.50. Hikers might wish to invest in the *Azores Tour & Trail Super Durable Map* by Jan Kostura (1:60,000) at £14.95. Individual island maps are available free from tourist offices.

BOOKS There are numerous publications on technical topics about the Azores, but they are almost all in Portuguese. In English there is virtually nothing readily available that is specific to the Azores, but there are several coffee-table books for sale in the local shops, mainly in Ponta Delgada, together with outline guides with lots of pretty pictures. One exception is the guide to Flores:

Bragaglia, Pierluigi *Flores–Azores–Walking Through History* Author's publication, 2009; w argonauta-flores.com

Nemésio, Vitorino *Mau tempo no Canal* (1944), translated as *Stormy Isles: An Azorean Tale* (1998). Nemésio's novel provides an intriguing window into early 20th-century Azorean life and society, with coastal whaling at times a prominent feature. It is a story of unrequited love and two warring families in locations on Pico, Faial and São Jorge, and the intervening channels, and was republished in 2019. Available online, or perhaps in Ponta Delgada bookshops.

Nature

Bento, Rita and Sá, Nuno *Diving Guide Azores* Ver Açor, Ponta Delgada, 2007. May be available on the island of Pico, but becoming hard to find. A 192-page guide with photography by Sá (265 photos). A total of 53 diving sites are described.

Cas, R and Wright, J *Volcanic Successions* Springer, 1987. One for specialists, available but now rare and expensive.

Clarke, Tony *Birds of the Atlantic Islands* Christopher Helm, 2006. The first comprehensive field guide to the birds of the Macaronesian islands – Canaries, Madeira, Azores and Cape Verde. Illustrated by Chris Orgill and Tony Disley.

Moore, Colm, Elias, Gonçalo and Costa, Helder *Where to Watch Birds in Portugal, the Azores and Madeira Archipelagos* Pelagic Publishing, 2020

Rodrigues, P and Michielsen, G *Birdwatching in the Azores*, 2010. Detailing habitats and distribution with many excellent colour photos and illustrations. Pbk, published by Azores Tourism but currently out of print.

Scarth, Alwyn, Jerram, Dougal and Tanguy, J-C *Volcanoes of Europe* (2nd edition) Dunedin, 2016

Schäfer, Hanno *Flora of the Azores* (3rd edition) Margraf Verlag, Weikersheim, 2021. In English, with 380 colour photographs and brief descriptions of 650 native and introduced plant species.

Soares de Albergaria, Isabel *Gardens and Woodlands of the Azores Islands*. Pbk, published by Azores Tourism (2012) but currently not for sale. In the format of a travel guide the 692 descriptions are liberally illustrated by excellent small photographs, old postcards and engravings, together with location maps and opening times. Most interesting and informative is the introduction in which the historical and social background sets the scene for the intriguing snippets appearing in the individual garden descriptions.

General reading

Abdo, Joseph C *On the Edge of History* Tenth Island Editions, 2006. The story of the Dabney family, merchants and American consuls to the Azores during the 19th century.

Ashe, Thomas *History of the Azores or Western Islands: Containing an Account of the Government, Laws and Religion, the Manners, Ceremonies and Characters of the Islands* Kessinger, 2009. Although republished in 2009, would-be buyers should be aware that the text is from 1813, and so is of historical interest only.

Birmingham, David *A Concise History of Portugal* (3rd edition) Cambridge University Press, 2018

Gordon, J S *A Thread Across the Ocean* Simon & Schuster, 2002. A fascinating account of entrepreneurial determination to lay the first Atlantic cable.

Robertson, Ian *A Traveller's History of Portugal* Cassell, 2002

ARTICLE

Alfrey, P 'American vagrants on the island of Corvo, Azores', 2005, *Birding World* 18 (11): 465–74

WEBSITES
Tourism

w atlanticoline.pt Inter-island ferry services, information and bookings.

w azores.com User-friendly site run by Portugal Online Corp, a company promoting Portugal on the internet. Information on packages, travel, hotels, tours, etc.

w azores.gov.pt Official website of the government of the Azores, which gives up-to-date information about the Azores and government activities.

w azoresairlines.pt For direct flights from the UK, mainland Europe and inter-island flight schedules.

w azoresyouthhostels.com Azores youth hostels.

w casasacorianas.com Owners of rural accommodation website, giving property details and booking online. Slightly cumbersome.

w destinazores.com Simple 'guidebook' in English, German and Portuguese giving very limited background information, plus some accommodation and eating places.

w flytap.com For flights throughout the year via Lisbon to the Azores.

w hostels.com/pt.az.html Azores youth hostels.

w ipma.pt/en A fascinating site from the Portuguese Institute of Sea and Atmosphere giving information about the Azorean weather, seismology, marine meteorology and atmosphere.

w noonsite.com/Countries/Azores Yachting information.

w visitazores.com Official Azores Tourism Authority site in six languages, including English, giving travel agents, accommodation, activities, walking trails, etc.

w weather2travel.com Excellent site giving detailed weather information for worldwide destinations, including the Azores.

Activities

w **angrajazz.com** For details of the jazz festival on Terceira.

w **azoresweb.com/diving_azores.html** Details of diving companies.

w **montanheiros.com** Website of the Sociedade de Exploração Espeleológica, whose headquarters are on Terceira.

w **teatromicaelense.pt** For programme details of the theatre in Ponta Delgada.

Natural history and conservation

w **azoresbioportal.uac.pt** An important and wonderful working tool providing a database for about 5,000 species, often accompanied by images. Groups include lichens and fungi, bryophytes, flowering plants, marine invertebrates, arthropods, and vertebrates.

w **azoresbs.weebly.com** Records bird sightings and disseminates interesting bird news from the Azores. Has not been updated for some years, but may still be relevant to enthusiasts.

w **okeanos.uac.pt** Okeanos is a research unit continuing the work previously undertaken by the University of the Azores, Department of Oceanography and Fisheries.

w **ospar.org** For nearly 50 years OSPAR has been identifying threats to the marine environment and has organised programmes and measures to combat them. Their Biological and Ecosystems strategy aims to restore, where practicable, marine areas adversely affected, and to create marine protected areas.

w **parquesnaturais.azores.gov.pt** Gives details of all the nature parks, including up-to-date opening times. A very useful site.

w **spea.pt** SPEA: the society for the study and conservation of birds in Portugal.

w **uk.whales.org** Whale and Dolphin Conservation, the world's most active charity dedicated to the conservation and welfare of all whales, dolphins and porpoises.

NOTES

NOTES

Index

Key to index: Co – Corvo; Fa – Faial; Fl – Flores; Gr – Graciosa; Pi – Pico; SJ – São Jorge;
SMa – Santa Maria; SMg – São Miguel; Te – Terceira

Page numbers in **bold** indicate main entries; those in *italics* indicate maps.

INDEX OF ADVERTISERS

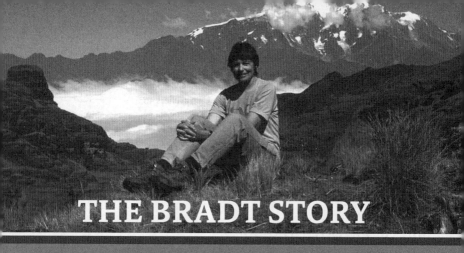

THE BRADT STORY

In the beginning

It all began in 1974 on an Amazon river barge. During an 18-month trip through South America, two adventurous young backpackers – Hilary Bradt and her then husband, George – decided to write about the hiking trails they had discovered through the Andes. *Backpacking Along Ancient Ways in Peru and Bolivia* included the very first descriptions of the Inca Trail. It was the start of a colourful journey to becoming one of the best-loved travel publishers in the world; you can read the full story on our website (**bradtguides. com/ourstory**).

Getting there first

Hilary quickly gained a reputation for being a true travel pioneer, and in the 1980s she started to focus on guides to places overlooked by other publishers. The Bradt Guides list became a roll call of guidebook 'firsts'. We published the first guide to Madagascar, followed by Mauritius, Czechoslovakia and Vietnam. The 1990s saw the beginning of our extensive coverage of Africa: Tanzania, Uganda, South Africa, and Eritrea. Later, post-conflict guides became a feature: Rwanda, Mozambique, Angola, and Sierra Leone, as well as the first standalone guides to the Baltic States following the fall of the Iron Curtain, and the first post-war guides to Bosnia, Kosovo and Albania.

Comprehensive – and with a conscience

Today, we are the world's largest independently owned travel publisher, with more than 200 titles. However, our ethos remains unchanged. Hilary is still keenly involved, and **we still get there first**: two-thirds of Bradt guides have no direct competition.

But we don't just get there first. Our guides are also known for being **more comprehensive** than any other series. We avoid templates and tick-lists. Each guide is a one-of-a-kind expression of an expert author's interests, knowledge and enthusiasm for telling it how it really is.

And a commitment to wildlife, conservation and respect for local communities has always been at the heart of our books. Bradt Guides was **championing sustainable travel** before any other guidebook publisher. We even have a series dedicated to Slow Travel in the UK, award-winning books that explore the country with a passion and depth you'll find nowhere else.

Thank you!

We can only do what we do because of the support of readers like you – people who value less-obvious experiences, less-visited places and a more thoughtful approach to travel. Those who, like us, take travel seriously.

Bradt GUIDES

TRAVEL TAKEN SERIOUSLY